To Live and Die in Dixie

To Live and Die in Dixie

Native Northerners Who Fought for the Confederacy

David Ross Zimring

The University of Tennessee Press • Knoxville

Copyright © 2014 by The University of Tennessee Press / Knoxville.
All Rights Reserved. Manufactured in the United States of America.
First Edition.

The paper in this book meets the requirements of American National Standards Institute / National Information Standards Organization specification Z39.48–1992 (Permanence of Paper). It contains 30 percent post-consumer waste and is certified by the Forest Stewardship Council.

Library of Congress Cataloging-in-Publication Data

Zimring, David Ross.

To live and die in Dixie : native northerners who fought for the Confederacy / David Ross Zimring. — First edition.

pages cm

Includes bibliographical references and index.

ISBN 978-1-62190-106-8 (hardcover)

1. Soldiers—Confederate States of America—Attitudes. 2. United States—History—Civil War, 1861-1865—Social aspects. 3. Soldiers—Confederate States of America—Social conditions. 4. Migration, Internal—United States—History—19th century. 5. Confederate States of America—History. I. Title.

E607.Z56 2015

973.7'42—dc23

2014024543

Contents

Acknowledgments	ix
Introduction	1
1. Native Northerners Move South	15
2. From Northerner to Southerner	45
3. Adoptive Southerners React to Slavery	67
4. Adoptive Southerners Choose Sides	99
5. Adoptive Southern Unionists	135
6. Northern Confederates in War	153
7. Emergence of a Confederate Identity and Nationalism	171
8. Northern Confederate Prisoners of War	201
9. Native Southern Reactions toward Northern Confederates	227
10. The End of an Era: Northern Confederates in Reconstruction and Beyond	267
Conclusion	305
Appendices	311
Notes	345
Bibliography	439
Index	463

Illustrations

FIGURES

Culp's Hill	3
General Johnson Kelly Duncan	23
Jedidiah Hotchkiss and His Family	34
Julia Gardiner Tyler, Wife of John Tyler	85
General Franklin Gardner	91
General John C. Pemberton	104
Albert Pike	113
John Slidell	124
Margaret Junkin Preston	141
Battle of New Orleans	156
Generals Pemberton and Grant at Vicksburg	181
General Mansfield Lovell	243
General Roswell Ripley	255

Tables

1. Distribution of Native States among Adoptive Southerners — 313
2. Distribution of Decade of Migration among Adoptive Southerners — 313
3. Distribution of Age of Migration among Adoptive Southerners — 314
4. Distribution of First Adopted State among Adoptive Southerners — 314
5. Distribution of Slave-owners among Adoptive Southerners — 315
6. Status of Slave-owners among Adoptive Southerners — 315
7. Residences of Adoptive Southerners in the South in 1860 — 315
8. Distribution of Confederate versus Union Supporters among Adoptive Southerners — 316
9. Postwar Residences of Adoptive Southerners — 316
10. Native State, Migration Decade, and Age at Migration of Individuals — 317
11. First Adopted State and Slaveholder Status of Individuals — 326
12. Location of Individuals during Secession, Civil War, and Postwar — 335

Acknowledgments

This project represents a decade of research and writing that could never have been realized without tremendous help from so many people. I would first like to thank my dissertation advisor at the University of Virginia, Gary Gallagher. His insights and guidance helped bring this manuscript to fruition from its earliest days as a short paper for a graduate class on the Civil War. Through countless meetings, discussions, phone calls, and emails, he provided crucial support and encouragement as well as helpful critiques for refining my arguments and honing my writing. I am forever grateful for my inspiration and knowledge he provided me in sharpening my skills as a historian.

Throughout the project's evolution, numerous historians offered further suggestions and critiques. Michael Holt, Joseph Kett, and Krishan Kumar provided detailed comments and suggestions for transforming my dissertation into a book-length manuscript. Michael T. Bernath, Jessica A. Cannon, Jason K. Phillips, Anne Sarah Rubin, Jonathan Daniel Wells, and many others shared conference panels with me, gave fresh perspectives on my work, and suggested other sources to broaden my approach. Wallace Hettle and Bob Kenzer read the first draft of the book manuscript and provided excellent comments to further highlight key themes in my work. I thank all of them for their generosity and assistance in making crucial improvements to the final manuscript.

I would also like to thank my colleagues at Virginia Tech, Lynchburg College, University of Maryland Baltimore County, and Montgomery College. Their support and encouragement, along with stimulating conversations, allowed me to complete my manuscript and prepare it for publication. Having the opportunity teach so many eager undergraduate students at these institutions also helped me refocus my understanding of the complexities of nationalism and identity formation that form the core of this project.

I am grateful to the librarians at various libraries and archives for their exceptional skill in locating source material I would not have found otherwise. I especially wish to express my gratitude to the wonderful staffs at the Marlene and Nathan Addlestone Library at the College of Charleston, the William R. Perkins Library at Duke University, the Library of Virginia, the Southern Historical Collection at the University of North Carolina, the South Caroliniana Library at the University of South Carolina, the Dolph Briscoe Center for American History at the University of Texas at Austin, and the Virginia Historical Society. I also received immeasurable assistance from the archivists at the Albert and Shirley Small Special Collections Library at the University of Virginia, with whom I had the privilege to work with for two years. Without all of their patience, skill, and dedication, this project would never have been completed.

Finally, I would like to thank my family for their constant support, assistance, and sparking my interest in history. Above all, I want to thank my wife, Emily, and my daughter, Hannah, for their love, understanding, and patience to see this project through to completion. I dedicate this manuscript to them.

Introduction

His journey unfolded like so many others of his generation. His name was Wesley Culp and he was born in Gettysburg, Pennsylvania, in 1839. His upbringing on a small farm did not differ markedly from the vast majority of all Americans in the first half of the nineteenth century. When he reached his teenage years, he began working as an apprentice for a carriage and harness maker. Yet Culp, like so many other young Americans of his generation, decided that his hometown offered too few opportunities for his ambitious nature. When his employer decided to relocate out of Pennsylvania for greater opportunity elsewhere, Culp eagerly followed in his footsteps. The young emigrant arrived at his new home in 1858 at the age of nineteen and quickly established himself in his new community. For three years he continued to work as a carriage maker, hoping to set up his own business one day, and wondering if he would ever return to his family and childhood home in Pennsylvania.

Culp got his chance with the outbreak of the Civil War. Eager to do his part for his community and his country, he enlisted in a local regiment and marched with his comrades to the battlefields in Virginia. For the first two years of the conflict, Culp fought in such famous battles as First Manassas, Fredericksburg, and Chancellorsville. Captured by the enemy in 1862, he spent several months in a prison camp before receiving his parole and rejoining his regiment. Finally, in the summer of 1863, Culp found himself back in his native state when Union general George Gordon Meade led the Army of the Potomac in pursuit of Confederate general Robert E. Lee's Army of Northern Virginia. Incredibly, the two armies clashed at Culp's childhood home in Gettysburg, with his uncle's farm on Culp's Hill a major sector of the battlefield. On the second day of the battle, Culp fought with his regiment on the slopes of his namesake hill. After a furious firefight, Culp died only a few hundred yards from his boyhood farm at the tender age of twenty-four. The Civil War brought the young soldier to a most unexpected homecoming and, like thousands of his comrades before him, he gave his life for the preservation of the nation. His relatives could at least take solace in knowing that their son died close to home, with his life coming full circle on the blood-soaked fields of Gettysburg.[1]

In all likelihood, however, Culp's family did not glorify their son's endeavors; in fact, they probably considered him a traitor. On the surface, he looked like any other young native Pennsylvanian who joined the Union armies to preserve the Union. Yet Culp did not follow that pattern because he did not die defending his childhood home; he attempted to seize Culp's Hill in pursuit of a Confederate victory. For Culp did not fight in General Meade's Army of the Potomac; he served in General Lee's Army of Northern Virginia. When he followed his employer out of Pennsylvania five years earlier, they did not embark west for Ohio or Illinois, as so many other northern settlers had done for decades, but instead headed south to Shepardstown, Virginia. Over the next few years, this native Pennsylvanian created a new home, both physically and metaphorically, in the Old Dominion.

The experience of living in both sections of the country gave Culp the opportunity not only to pursue his career but to also thoroughly transform his identity. At the beginning of the war, Culp sided with his adopted state and enlisted as a private in the Second Virginia Regiment, which became part of the famous Stonewall Brigade under General Thomas J. "Stonewall" Jackson. The adopted Virginian, before he mounted his fatal charge against his uncle's farm on Culp's Hill, even fought at the Second Battle of Winchester against one of his brothers, a member of the Eighty-Seventh Pennsylvania. In the process, Culp became part of a unique group of native northerners who took up arms for the Confederacy against their native section and their families.[2]

Incredibly, few historians have addressed the subject of northern settlers in the South, seeing them as a largely insignificant group. Perhaps one of the reasons for this omission is that, with few exceptions, northerners in the South rarely acted as a group.[3] A contemporary observer, Maine native Seargent Prentiss, admitted as much when he told his mother of his life in Mississippi, "But I frequently meet with Yankees, who are much more numerous here than I had supposed . . . but associate little with each other, except in

Culp's Hill on the Gettysburg Battlefield. Wesley Culp grew up in Gettysburg and died charging up his namesake hill as a member of the Second Virginia Regiment in the Army of Northern Virginia. Library of Congress.

the way of business. Self here is the sole object."[4] Rather than seeking out other northerners to find like-minded compatriots in a new setting, northern emigrants mainly relied on themselves in adapting to their new environment. If northerners did not act in unison when they came to the South, their relatively small numbers when compared to the rest of the southern population might logically indicate they had little impact on their surroundings. For this reason, while dozens of books deal with native southerners who remained loyal to the Union during the Civil War,[5] northern emigrants usually receive the briefest mentions buried in scattered paragraphs.[6]

The presence of northern emigrants in the South, however, reflected the complex dynamics of identity formation in the nineteenth century. A switch in region, as well as state, had enormous consequences for those who embarked on such journeys. Northerners who moved to the South did not have an automatic decision on where to place their loyalties. They still had families and memories of past experiences in the North; at the same time, they created new families and attachments in the South. On top of all this, identification with the Union loomed large in the minds of all Americans up to and during the Civil War. For these reasons, unlike many other Americans, northern emigrants had connections to the national union, both sections, and even multiple states at times. What circumstances brought them to the South in the first place and what kept them there? Why, when faced with the choice, did they often, like Wesley Culp, choose to fight for their adopted home and against their native section? Most importantly, what do their experiences tell us about the nature of sectional identity and Confederate nationalism?

American citizens in the nineteenth century espoused a multitude of attachments and priorities. These attachments ranged from family, local community, and state to the larger realms of region, section, and Union. Few Americans described themselves with only one criterion in mind. Southern nationalist William Gilmore Simms viewed himself in 1842 as "an ultra-American, a born Southron." Conversely, Philip Hone wrote in his diary, "I am a Northern man, and a New Yorker."[7] The fragile relationship between region and nation, however, meant that sectionalism could overpower national loyalty if local priorities appeared out of touch with the Union. Town or country, Pennsylvania or Virginia, North or South, even attachment to the Union fluctuated depending on the time and place.[8]

Northern emigrants in the South placed this paradigm on prominent display. Although these men and women may have started out as northerners in their birth and upbringing, they had the option of identifying with their adopted section when they moved to a southern state. A number of different factors influenced that decision, including families, communities, occupation, ideology, economics, etc. However it happened, by the time of the Civil War, these adoptive southerners joined native southerners in standing up for southern rights and eventually in supporting the Confederacy. Enlistment in the Confederate armies helped to clarify their self-identification. Those who served did not see themselves as northern at all but rather as genuine southerners, doing what any white southerner would do to protect his home, family, and nation.

Native northerners in both the South and the Confederacy thus revealed the malleability of sectional identities, challenging the assumption that these identities remained static during the antebellum era. Before the Civil War, native northerners had little trouble blending into southern society and, if it suited them, transforming their identities. Not everyone chose this transformation, but the option always remained. The Civil War ended that choice by solidifying sectional awareness through the rise of Confederate nationalism. As a result, in addition to all of the other ways that the Civil War represented a turning point in American history (most notably the abrupt and total end of slavery), this massive conflict also marked a major shift for the malleability of sectional identity in the United States. Although American nationalism appeared to have strengthened with the reunification of North and South, sectional identities also hardened to the point where few people could easily transition from northern to southern as they had in the past. Antebellum emigrants thus represented the last generation exhibiting malleable sectional identity in the nineteenth century. Those who supported the Confederacy did not fight as northerners dragged into the Confederate ranks against their will; they viewed themselves as both southerners and Confederates in thought and action, by adoption rather than by blood.

Analyzing the lives of northern emigrants in the South, therefore, improves our understanding of the nature of sectional identity, as well as the strength of Confederate nationalism. Rather than view sectional identity as permanent, we can instead see the options Americans possessed in the antebellum era when it came to identity formation. The idea of northern emigrants moving to the South to remake the region in their own image is shattered by observing these individuals adapting to their surroundings and absorbing the culture and identity of the South. These individuals also provide more evidence that Confederates created a viable nationalism that bred loyalty and devotion among its citizens, since even native northerners with no previous ties to the South could still feel connected with the Confederacy.

In addition, the experience of native northerners in the South offers a reevaluation of the effects of the Civil War on nationalism and sectional identity in the postwar era. Many historians argue that, before the Civil War, the Union existed more as an experiment than a solid entity. Only after the war, as historian James McPherson has argued, did the United States finally become a nation, where Americans changed their description from "the United States *are* a country" to "the United States *is* a country."[9] In this scenario, while the South kept its sectional distinction, southerners ultimately subscribed to an American nationalism that created a stronger bond between the sections by the end of the century.

While the broad outlines of this argument have merit, the tight bond between North and South actually contained a number of weak links that few appeals to greater nationalism could heal. The former Confederate states had a shared history of their struggle for independence that they believed northerners could never understand. Because of this shared mentality, Confederate veterans formed a shield against perceived penetrations by outsiders. Before the war, northerners who moved to the South had the possibility of transforming into southerners. Once Reconstruction began, that option no longer existed, as former Confederates looked upon native northerners as Yankee invaders, no less hostile than the Union armies who burned their houses, freed their slaves, and destroyed the white southern way of life. The Civil War redrew the line for identity formation and erected a wall of separation between the sections as solid as the Berlin Wall that separated the East from the West in the Cold War. Because of that barrier, American nationalism, as strong as it became, still carried with it a sectional underpinning.

Before the psychological divide between the postwar North and South solidified, prewar northern emigrants slipped through a narrow time frame to blur the sectional boundaries. By moving out of their native section, they broke a major unwritten rule of nineteenth century internal emigration in the United States. Whenever Americans of that era decided to uproot, they usually moved in only one direction: west. In the vast majority of cases, northerners moved into the northwestern territories, while southerners moved into the southwestern regions. In 1854, the *New York Times* ran an article based on the 1850 census that documented this trend: "From these facts we deduce a certain and almost universal law of *internal emigration*. It is, that emigration moves west, *on the same parallel of latitude* . . . Men seldom change their climate—because, to do so, they must change their habits, conditions and institutions; and this they are unwilling to do."[10] The pattern thus seemed obvious: northerners stayed among fellow northerners, while southerners lived with fellow southerners, changing their states but not their region. When they arrived at their destinations, settlers more often than not found not only familiar surroundings but also that their neighbors came from similar regions and backgrounds.[11]

Nevertheless, despite the assertions of the *New York Times* editor, thousands of native northerners proved that this supposed "universal law of internal emigration" was definitively not universal. According to the 1860 census, nearly three hundred and fifty thousand native northerners resided in a southern state by the time of the Civil War. This does not take into account untold thousands of other native northerners who moved to the South and died before the census workers recorded their movements. Over two hundred and eighty-nine thousand of these emigrants, four-fifths of the total recorded, came from the Mid-Atlantic and Lower North states of Pennsylvania, Ohio, Indiana, Illinois, and New York. The most popular destinations included the Border and Upper South states of Missouri, Kentucky, and Virginia, where nearly two hundred and thirty thousand northern emigrants set up new homes and careers. This pattern made sense, considering that these states shared common borders with each other, especially between the Lower North and the Border South. Nevertheless, many other native northerners embarked on much longer journeys. Northerners from as far away as Maine and Massachusetts settled in the cotton regions of South Carolina, Alabama, and Mississippi or the sugar country of Louisiana. Nearly forty-six hundred natives of Maine and twelve thousand natives of Massachusetts lived in a southern state at the time of secession. South Carolina listed over two thousand native northerners within its borders, with Alabama having nearly six thousand, Mississippi over five thousand, and Louisiana over fourteen thousand. No state in either the North or the South escaped this break in the trend of internal western emigration.[12]

Nor did northern emigrants remain invisible in their adopted states. In fact, they made their presence felt far more than one might assume. Far out of proportion to their numbers, they attained high ranks in southern political, financial, educational, and social circles. Numerous southern governors, legislators, college presidents and professors, ministers, even prominent slaveholders all traced their roots to the North. Observing life in both major sections of the country, northern emigrants challenged assumptions and generalizations made by both native northerners and native southerners who only saw one side of the country.

Acknowledging this exception reveals significant insights about what these men and women can tell us about sectional identity and nationalism. Some authors frame questions of the formulation of identity among nineteenth-century Americans purely in terms of national versus sectional attachments. In this interpretation, from the time of the War for Independence, Americans thought of themselves in a sectional manner, with American nationalism emerging as a sectional construction. While sectional differences did not always produce hostile relations, by the 1850s northerners and southerners developed ideologies that cast each other as a world apart. Basically, Americans only identified with the Union as long as their sectional interests remained secure and unencumbered; once white southerners believed that American nationalism had changed beyond what they desired, they retreated into their own sectional identity.[13] American nationalism thus split apart into regional nationalisms and the southern states ultimately seceded because the North had taken the Union and molded it into its own image at the expense of the South.[14]

Other historians stress the national character of Americans that overrode differences between states, sub-regions, and sections. They accept the influence of regions and states on American identity but insist that sectional similarities and differences reinforced, rather than eroded, American nationalism. These historians do not identify nationalism and regionalism as separate phenomena with clear delineations; they link the two as part of the matrix of American identity. Home, state, section, and Union all blended together into a complex mixture, with nationalism and regionalism constantly in flux. And although the majority of northerners, southerners, and westerners each had different views on slavery and its proper place in the Union, they also shared a common heritage and history. All Americans looked to the War for Independence for their collective heroes, shared the same Constitution, mainly practiced Protestant forms of Christianity (including Episcopalian, Presbyterian, Methodist, Baptist, etc.), and embraced principles of independence and self-government. Until the 1850s, white southerners also participated in the same political parties, which helped to keep the Union together by focusing on issues other than slavery and championing the benefits of Union.[15]

In addition, songs and literature linked Americans together. Daniel Decatur Emmet, an Ohioan who lived in New York City, wrote the popular song "Dixie," which became a kind of unofficial anthem for the Confederacy in later years. Another Ohioan wrote a book called *Cotton is King*, which spurred the myth of cotton driving the world economy and placing white southerners and their slaves as the beating heart of that economy. Native Pennsylvanian Stephen Foster wrote such classic songs as "My Old Kentucky Home" and "Oh Suzanna." Even Harriet Beecher Stowe, whom southerners hated for her portrayal of slavery, made her main villain, Simon Legree, a New Englander to showcase slavery as a national, rather than regional, problem.[16] For these reasons, according to this interpretation, most Americans felt akin to one another throughout the antebellum period.[17]

This synthesis did not mean that a strong American nationalism would inevitably take hold. If anything, the complex dynamic of union, section, subsection, state, and local community working together threatened to unravel if anything upset the balance among them.[18] Therefore, rather than have nationalism arise spontaneously, the American people had to undergo constant nation building in the late eighteenth and early nineteenth centuries. Along the way, American nationalism, because it coexisted with sectional identity, had several avenues open to its development. Synthesizing all of these various interpretations, the general historiographical trend on nationalism seems to focus on the fragile nature of American nationalism before the Civil War.[19]

Because of that fragility, Americans themselves had the ultimate say in how strong or weak they wanted their new American nation and had wide latitude in formulating their own identities. Author Peter Parish argues that "an American was someone who chose to be an American," and each new generation reenacted the nation-making experience.[20] While the Founding Fathers created the nation through the War for Independence and the Constitution, and the second generation achieved their national moment in the War of 1812, the third generation of Americans continued to search for its own defining moment amid the sectional tensions of the 1850s. Nationalism was a constantly evolving process that had to incorporate local and sectional identity throughout the antebellum period.

The debate over the strengths and/or weaknesses of nationalism does not end with the antebellum era. Another school of historians takes these arguments into the secession crisis and Civil War era. Rather than focus solely on the growth of American nationalism, however, these historians also analyze the question of Confederate nationalism. The major debate in this area focuses on whether the Confederacy actually created its own national ideology or failed to do so. That question addresses the bigger issue of the ultimate fall of the Confederacy, which is either viewed as a strong nation fighting to the bitter end or a weak one crumbling from within.[21] Regardless of their disagreements, these historians share one common perspective: Confederate nationalism, if it existed, did not appear out of thin air. As historian Drew Faust writes, "The formation of this new national ideology was thus inescapably a political and social act, incorporated both the powerful and the comparatively powerless into a negotiation of the terms under which all might work together for the Confederate cause." In other words, Confederate nationalism represented a compromise between many different factions of southerners, all with their own visible and/or hidden agendas. Confederate nation-builders needed such give and take to nurture a nationalism that had begun to develop before the war but had not yet reached its zenith. At its core, budding Confederate nationalism had to explain the Confederacy to itself.[22]

Within these studies, historians tend to analyze sectional identities with the assumption that individuals born in one section maintained their sectional identities for their entire lives. When they describe someone as "northern" or "southern," they generally cite certain characteristics with little room for flexibility.[23] Even some contemporaries made such observations. Alexis de Tocqueville, a French observer who toured the United States in the 1830s, told his fellow countrymen, "The Southerner of pure race is frank, hearty, open, cordial in his manners, noble in his sentiments, elevated in his notions; he is a worthy descendant of the English gentleman . . . The Yankee, on the contrary, is reserved, cautious, distrustful; his manners are without grace, cold, and often unprepossessing; he is narrow in his ideas, but practical." Diaries and letters of both white northerners and white southerners in the 1850s included such phrases as "a southern complexion," "Yankee heartlessness," "Yankee propensity to ask questions," and "Yankee love of bread & molasses."[24] According to this interpretation, internal emigrants carried their entire backgrounds and perceptions with them with little possibility of change or acceptance by their adopted communities. Northerners remained northerners and southerners remained southerners regardless of where they ended up. Or, as one South Carolinian commented, geography followed a man wherever he went "like a shadow."[25] Sectional identity thus remained static for all Americans before, during, and after the Civil War.[26]

Such observations did not reflect individual variations. In reality, sectional as well as national identity encompassed a matrix of characteristics and situations that often varied between different groups and individuals. Throughout the eighteenth and nineteenth centuries, white northerners and southerners often had the option of leaving their homes in search of new horizons. The 1860 census listed over five and a half million Americans, close to 25 percent of the total population, living outside of their native state.[27] Since attachments to home, state, region, and country all contributed to a collective feeling of belonging, changing any one of them potentially altered a person's outlook. To some, their core identity was tied to their native state. For others, it arose from where they found success in occupation or politics or marriage or ideology.[28] For still others, it represented what they lacked rather than what they had.[29] Within this matrix of sectional and national identity formation, people's identities could shift dramatically from the ones they had forged in their native homes.[30]

Still, not all antebellum northern emigrants were created equal. In order to provide a clear analysis of the experiences of northern emigrants and their sectional identity transformation, this study utilizes a group of individuals with specific parameters. Although the 1860 census listed hundreds of thousands of native northerners living in the South at the time of the Civil War, not all of them had the opportunity to undergo a meaningful shift in sectional identity. Specifically, the census includes those who emigrated to the South as adults and those who did so as infants or young children. Individuals in the latter group effectively grew up surrounded by southern culture and therefore did not face the same kinds of life-changing choices as those in the former group. Anyone born in the North but moved to the South as a young child, therefore, did not qualify for this study. In addition, because the main time frame for this study covers the Civil War, any northern emigrants who died before 1861 also did not qualify. In order to have undergone a meaningful change in sectional identity, northern emigrants needed to have been born in a northern (i.e., free) state, spent their early childhood and/or teenage years north of the Mason-Dixon Line, and moved to a southern (i.e., slave) state when they reached young adulthood.[31] European immigrants who first settled in the North and stayed there for years before moving to a southern state qualify as well. These criteria allowed the qualified individuals to experience both sections for an extended period of time.

Such standards understandably limit the number of individuals included, in this case a total of three hundred and three men and women. Out of a pool of nearly three hundred and fifty thousand possible candidates, using only a few hundred admittedly appears too small for adequate representation. Nevertheless, these individuals will prove satisfactory because they provide a large diversity of backgrounds, experiences, and outcomes. They came from all over the North, emigrated to all different parts of the South, worked in a wide variety of occupations, arrived in the South in different decades, joined both the Confederacy and the Union in the Civil War, and much more. Their motives, trials, and experiences covered nearly every conceivable scenario that a native northerner encountered in his or her move to the South, along with later experiences in the Confederacy and beyond.³² In a way, these men and women experienced the same situation as German and Japanese immigrants who fought for the United States armies in World War II. Although they had roots and families in their native countries, they became absorbed into American society and considered themselves Americans above all else. Even Japanese immigrants placed in internment camps still saluted the American flag and volunteered to serve in the American armed forces. Ultimately, when forced to choose between their native and adopted homes, German and Japanese immigrants largely chose the latter. Northern emigrants faced the same choice and followed the same path.

Thanks to their adopted identities, the individuals in this study differed substantially from another group of native northerners who tried to undermine the Union war effort: Copperheads. Unlike northern emigrants to the South, Copperheads were conservative northerners, mainly Democrats, who lived in the North and opposed President Lincoln and the Republicans for their war policies. They initially supported the war effort but began to turn against it when Lincoln made emancipation a war goal alongside preservation of the Union. Despite their increasingly anti-war stance, Copperheads still supported the Union as long as it meant very little would change as a result of the war. As historian James McPherson points out, the rallying cry for Copperheads after President Lincoln issued the Emancipation Proclamation became "the Constitution as it is, the Union as it was, and the Niggers where they are."³³ Encouraged by their leaders, including Clement Vallandigham and George Pendleton of Ohio, Copperhead Democrats protested not only Lincoln's emancipation policies but also what they viewed as unconstitutional expansions of federal power, including the suspension of the writ of habeas corpus. While Republicans considered them at best a nuisance and at worst traitors, Copperheads believed they represented the true embodiment of the Union and its preservation. By 1864, they even took control of the Democratic Party and inserted a plank in the party platform declaring the war a failure and advocated a negotiated settlement to bring the southern states back into the Union.³⁴

As a result, although Copperheads hindered the Union war effort in various ways, they still considered themselves northerners and wanted to reestablish the Union as it existed before 1860. Northern emigrants, on the other hand, largely did not identify as northerners any longer, had no intention of rejoining the Union, and worked hard to achieve the independence of the Confederacy. Therefore, in spite of their similar backgrounds, Copperheads did not qualify for this study.

Admittedly, because of these criteria and the records available, the northern emigrants in this analysis differ somewhat from those seen in the 1860 census. For example, they tended to emigrate more often to the Deep South and Upper South rather than the Border South. Whereas northern emigrants in the census mainly settled in Missouri, Kentucky, and Virginia, the most popular states for individuals in this study were Virginia, Louisiana, and Georgia. Also, those in the census more often came from the Mid-Atlantic and the Midwest, while those in this group had more representation from Massachusetts and Connecticut, as well as the Mid-Atlantic states of New York and Pennsylvania.[35] As a result, these individuals do not speak for all northern emigrants in the South and do not provide a definitive picture of all of their experiences. Future studies will determine if the patterns found in this analysis apply to all other native northerners who found new lives in the South, especially those in the Border States. Nevertheless, because they encountered such vastly different environments and communities, especially those who moved from New England to the Deep South, they provide valuable insight into cross-sectional experiences and their effects on identity formation and subsequent Confederate nationalism.[36]

As a further point of reference, the individuals in this study are mainly identified by two labels: "adoptive southerners" and "Northern Confederates." "Adoptive southerners" include anyone born and raised in a state north of the Mason-Dixon Line who subsequently moved to a state south of that line but did not necessarily join the Confederacy. "Northern Confederates," on the other hand, were adoptive southerners who then sided with the Confederacy during the Civil War. Therefore, all individuals in this study became adoptive southerners, but not all of them became Northern Confederates.

Each chapter will cover a particular part of the journeys of adoptive southerners. Chapter One sets the stage by analyzing statistical data on states of origin, age, education, decade of migration, and, most importantly, why these individuals embarked for the South in the first place. Chapter Two analyzes their prewar lives and the flexibility of sectional identity in the antebellum period. Chapter Three analyzes the adaptations adoptive southerners made in regards to slavery, which was arguably the largest adjustment native northerners endured when settling in the South. Chapter Four discusses adoptive southerners in the secession crisis, those who joined the Confederacy versus the Union, and the factors that influenced their decision. Chapter Five covers the minority of adoptive southerners who decided to remain with the Union and why they ultimately chose to return to their native section at the expense of their adopted section. Chapter Six outlines the contributions made by Northern Confederates to the Confederate military and home front. Chapter Seven covers the emergence of a Confederate identity and nationalism among Northern Confederates and how the experiences of the war hardened their devotion to their adopted nation. Chapter Eight extends the previous chapter by analyzing how Northern Confederates reacted when they were held as prisoners in the North. Chapter Nine covers the reactions of native southerners toward Northern Confederates. Finally, Chapter Ten analyzes the postwar period and the end of the fluidity of sectional identity.

Throughout their journeys from native northerners to Confederate veterans, adoptive southerners revealed so much, not only about their own complex transformations but also about the flexibility of sectional and national identity before the war and the loss of that flexibility in its aftermath. Native southerners who came into contact with these men and women had to reevaluate their assumptions and stereotypes toward the North. Analyzing adoptive southerners and Northern Confederates provides a novel perspective on the revolutionary changes the Civil War unleashed on American society.

1

Native Northerners Move South

The first step for northern emigrants on their journey to a transformed identity involved actually crossing the Mason-Dixon Line. That line, invisible on the landscape and etched only on maps, still had a significant impact on the behavior of restless Americans determined to spread across the continent. Most internal emigrants generally stayed along the same lines of latitude to maintain some familiarity in a new environment.[1] Northern emigrants who moved to the South broke that pattern, but the reasons for doing so varied considerably. Leaving behind not only their native homes but also their native sections represented probably the greatest break with the past they could have accomplished, other than leaving the country entirely.

So the major question remains: why did they choose to break that pattern? No one forced them to do so; every one of them made a conscious decision to abandon the North in favor of the South. Some settled in the South at the turn of the century while others did not arrive until 1860. They normally traveled individually, rather than in groups, and so had to forge their own destinies alone.[2] Many intended to spend only a few years in the South before ultimately returning to the North. Few came with the intention of adopting a southern identity. As a result, the transformation from native northerners into adoptive southerners occurred gradually and with many different variations.

Despite these variations, a general pattern emerged that became the personification of future adoptive southerners. Born in northern states, they grew up surrounded by the emerging ideologies of free labor and a rapidly expanding technological and territorial Union. After completing their formative years, including extensive education, they sought to create their own lives and fortunes away from their childhood homes as a mark of independence. Unlike most of their contemporaries in the North, these men and women looked to the South because they believed many more opportunities for careers, advancement, and success existed there. Although they always had the option of moving back to the North, most of them chose to remain because the North came to represent the past, while the South represented their future.

If northern emigrants had to choose one word to explain their unusual turn toward the South, "opportunity" gave all the justification necessary. These unique settlers symbolized American potential: young and ambitious individuals eager to assert their own independence through whatever environment offered them the greatest chance for success. At the same time, the journeys taken by northern emigrants revealed the fluidity of sectional identity in the antebellum era. Similar to early twentieth-century immigrants traveling to Ellis Island, native northerners proved that one's nativity did not always determine one's future. If anything, the South had much more of an effect on northern emigrants than the other way around. They may have arrived in the region eager for short-term gain, but eventually they found unexpected long-term roots within their adopted communities.

The start of this journey for any future adoptive southerner occurred in the North. If an unbiased observer wanted to make predictions about which northerners might emigrate in a southern direction, his task would have been nearly impossible. No northern state contributed all or even most of the emigrants in this study to the South; every northern state except for California, Iowa, Michigan, Oregon, and Wisconsin sent sons and/or daughters below the Mason-Dixon Line. Nearly two-thirds came from four states in the Mid-Atlantic and New England. New York contributed the most with fifty-five, followed closely by Massachusetts with fifty-one, Pennsylvania with forty-six, and Connecticut with forty-two. Out of the remaining states, Ohio sent twenty-five, Maine sent sixteen, New Hampshire and New Jersey each sent fourteen, and the rest sent fewer than ten apiece. In addition, twenty individuals in this study were born outside of the North, in locales including Indian Territory, Canada, England, France, and other parts of Europe. Emigrants to the South thus represented a broad swath of territory across the northern half of the Union.

Nor did these men and women have a distinguishing characteristic like southern ancestry or southern parents. Although data on this subject is sketchy and incomplete, only seven individuals had a confirmed southern parent, while the vast majority had northern parents and ancestors. Several of them even boasted a heritage stretching back to the founding of the British colonies. For example, Frederick A. P. Barnard, a native of Massachusetts who moved to Alabama and then Mississippi, traced his ancestry back to the Mayflower. His family stayed in Massachusetts for the next two centuries, with some of his ancestors serving in the War for Independence as generals and his father serving as a prominent state senator. Henry Handerson, an Ohio native who emigrated to Louisiana, had ancestors who landed in Hartford, Connecticut, in 1694. His great-grandfather fought as a corporal from Massachusetts in the War for Independence. Gail Borden, a native New Yorker who moved to Texas, counted as one of his direct ancestors Roger Williams, the founder of Rhode Island. Jedediah Hotchkiss, another native New Yorker who made his adopted home in Virginia, traced his ancestry to a prominent seventeenth-century New England family. Native Pennsylvanian John Clifford Pemberton had Quaker great-grandparents who settled in Pennsylvania as early as 1682. Another native Pennsylvanian, Johnson Kelly Duncan, had a family who resided in Pennsylvania for more than a century before he moved to New Orleans.[3] While many prominent southerners, such as the first families of Virginia, boasted of their extensive bloodlines, these native northerners possessed their own rich heritage in their native states. Ancestry alone, therefore, had little chance of pushing these individuals away from the North.[4]

At the same time, heritage did not guarantee a lifelong attachment to the North either. After all, those same ancestors reflected the fundamental American characteristic of forging new lives in a new land, whether in the established English colonies or farther west across the continent. The yearning for a fresh start only grew stronger by the early nineteenth century, when thousands of acres of new lands became available for settlement. Still, in order to undergo a full-fledged transformation, native northerners first had to have a northern-based upbringing. Most qualifying individuals spent between fifteen and thirty years in a northern state before emigrating to the South. Their formative years took place largely at the height of the antebellum era. Out of the three hundred and three individuals documented, only thirty-four were born before 1800. One hundred and fifty-seven, or slightly over half, were born in the 1810s and 1820s and thus grew up during the beginnings of the Market Revolution and the Jacksonian Era. Another fifty-seven were born in the 1830s and witnessed the expansion of the United States from the Atlantic to the Pacific amid increasing rancor between North and South over the future of slavery.[5]

They spent their childhoods in a wide variety of surroundings, including traditional New England villages, major Mid-Atlantic cities like New York and Philadelphia, small farms in the Old Northwest, army posts in the western territories, and many others. Their parents engaged in a wide range of professions, including soldier, sailor, farmer, blacksmith, miller, businessman, shoemaker, manufacturer, lawyer, judge, scholar, etc. Some of them stayed on the family farm, while others followed their families in constant migration. Basically, those who eventually became adoptive southerners did not all have the same background or come from the same town or city. Most of the time, they remained as distant from each other early in life as they were later on in the South. These individuals were not destined to settle in the South; any native northerner could have followed the same path.[6]

Still, future adoptive southerners did share some common patterns in their childhoods. First of all, they nearly all grew up as third- and fourth-generation Americans after the country's independence and therefore witnessed immense changes from the early days of the Union. The northern states became the powerhouse of the country in terms of manufacturing, industry, internal improvements, and technology. Factories spread across New England, the Erie Canal brought the East and West together, railroads began to link the countryside with the cities, cities themselves grew by leaps and bounds with new immigrants, the northern merchant marine became one of the largest in the world, and new northern states joined the Union at a rapid rate as the northern population itself grew astronomically.[7] The southern states experienced many of these changes as well, but not to nearly the same degree. Significantly, northern emigrants also lived in a region that had largely eradicated slavery, providing a dividing line between North and South. Both sections still had many similarities, including the percentage of people living in rural areas, engaging in the same party system, and settling across the continent, but sectional boundaries began to harden by the middle of the antebellum era.[8]

Northern emigrants also shared an exposure to a set of values that eventually coalesced into free labor ideology. By the early nineteenth century, the Puritan emphasis on community, godliness, and strict obedience, prevalent in the earlier colonial period, had largely given way to a desire for individual enterprise, freedom from dependence, hard work, and reaping the fruits of one's own labor.[9] Although free labor ideology did not fully coalesce until the 1840s, several of its planks guided social and economic life across the North throughout the early nineteenth century. New Englanders especially shed much of their Puritan past by embracing trade, commerce, and migration as virtues rather than vices. As historian Joseph Rainer commented, "After the Revolution . . . complaints of insubordinate children and servants became more common. More and more young adult men left their fathers' farms to live out their early adulthood in a state of semi-independence in the marketplace."[10]

Much of the Midwest became populated with these new generations of New Englanders, who brought their values with them to the new territories. Over time, New England and the Mid-Atlantic saw the area as an extension of themselves and the symbol of their future.[11] In many cases, they also learned to view southern life with contempt, especially since northern propaganda largely described the South as despotic and backward compared to the superior North, thanks largely to the differences between free labor and slavery.[12] Northern emigrants grew up surrounded by these values and eventually carried them across the country.

Equally important, northern emigrants also generally brought with them a strong background in education. Antebellum northerners took great pride in their level of education, especially when compared to the South. Institutions of higher education certainly existed in the southern states, including Transylvania University in Kentucky, the University of Alabama, University of Mississippi, University of Virginia, and several others. The North, however, not only had more colleges, including the future Ivy League, but also had traditions of sending their children to at least some form of primary schooling. Little wonder, then, that the North built a reputation of having a highly educated population.

Families of future adoptive southerners followed this tradition by providing extensive education for their children. At least two hundred and twenty-nine of the individuals documented, three-quarters of the total, attended local schools, received private tutoring, and/or attended colleges or universities. The universities in the North and West that provided advanced education for northern emigrants included such esteemed centers of learning as Amherst, Bowdoin College, Brown, Columbia, Dartmouth, New York University, Ohio University, Princeton, University of Pennsylvania, and many others. Fifty-seven attended Yale, while another nineteen passed through Harvard Yard. Eight more attended institutions abroad, including universities in Paris and Berlin.[13] The United States Military Academy at West Point, the premier military school in the United States, graduated at least thirty-nine native northerners who eventually joined the Confederacy. These graduates included such later luminaries as Josiah Gorgas, Samuel Cooper, John C. Pemberton, Franklin Gardner, and Roswell Ripley, all of whom later led Confederate armies, divisions, or departments. They all shared a bond through their ties to the northern educational system.[14]

Such an extensive educational background indicated that these adoptive southerners were largely among the ranks of the elite and middle classes. Their station in life provided them the means to advance their careers in a region desperate for their skills, as well as to promote the values and ethics dear to the nineteenth-century middle class. Historian Mary Ryan argues that the middle class in the nineteenth century molded its identity around domestic values and family practices. Such values were necessary because the second generation of young Americans constantly sought opportunities in new lands farther to the west. As a consequence, mothers used personal and moral persuasion on their children to shore up old values before they left on their own. Instead of passing on a farm or artisan tools, parents passed on moral capital, in the form of temperance and purity, to sons who left home.[15] Similarly, Stuart Blumin argues that the formation of classes in antebellum American society was a process rather than a sudden event. In his view, the middle class, which Americans previously associated more with the bottom of society, eventually became associated with the upper levels of society. Members of the middle class believed they had the duty to shape American society through moral capital, temperance, purity, and self-restraint.[16] Adoptive southerners grew up in this type of environment and utilized its cultural norms when they embarked for greater opportunities in the South.

When they arrived in the South, they discovered an environment amenable to the values they had absorbed in their childhoods and teenage years. Historian Jonathan Wells argues that, despite the seemingly insurmountable gulfs between northern and southern society, southern social relations did not simply involve a struggle between slave-owners and non-slave-owners. Instead, the South had a burgeoning middle class, like doctors and lawyers and merchants and teachers, who helped to bridge the divide between South and North. The middle class of the South adopted ideas from the North to promote gender issues and modernization but still held onto southern defenses of slavery. Northern emigrants could thrive in this environment because those who achieved success, including lawyers, politicians, teachers, and doctors, usually did so in professional careers first. With the exception of those who married into wealthy southern families, northern emigrants rarely arrived in the South with the resources, or even the desire, to become slave-owners. Instead, these men and women wished to exploit the opportunities available to well-educated northerners and become successful in their own right.[17] Native northerners thus helped fill the ranks of the emerging southern professional middle class. In the process, they revealed how smooth a transition a native northerner could make from the environment of the free labor North to that of the slaveholding South.

Northern emigrants' connection to the middle class, along with the infusion of free labor values, gave them an opportunity to attempt a reform of the South in the northern image. Northern intellectuals especially viewed the South as a place in need of restructuring. Always mindful of their weakening political power through the expansion of American territory, New Englanders sought to counterbalance that loss by spreading New England emigrants across the west and bringing northern institutions with them to ensure their survival. Northern emigrants, along with foreign immigrants, did help build places like New Orleans into the premier shipping ports and financial bases of the Deep South.[18] In addition, both New England pastors and educators felt a higher calling in their work when they settled in areas outside New England. As historian Richard Power elaborates, these intellectuals felt "a persistent consciousness of the need of preventing New England's achievements from being submerged and lost in the disordered process which was giving birth to national institutions and culture."[19] Although not always so blatant, emigrants from other parts of the North appeared set to maintain their own values whenever they ventured into the South. Some New England reformers also believed that cross-sectional migration rarely happened the other way around, since white southerners did not subscribe to the ethic of hard work. This theme of superior northerners having a mission to convert inferior southerners to northern values provided a backdrop for northern emigrants thinking of moving out of their native section.[20]

Native northerners who eventually settled in the South, however, rarely moved to the region with such lofty goals in mind. They did not form a grand experiment to remake the region in New England's image. Instead, each of them found their way to the South with little thought about how others viewed their journey. Northern intellectuals who expected northern emigrants to transform the South, as they had in the Midwest, did not see their cherished plans realized. Those who made the transition did so for their own benefit rather than for the benefit of northern society in general.

Nor was that transition inevitable. Many future adoptive southerners initially followed the same migration patterns as so many other northern settlers. Gail Borden, who grew up in New York, moved with his family as a teenager to Ohio, Kentucky, and Indiana Territory for constant life on the frontier. Franklin and Phoebe Farmer both grew up in Massachusetts and moved to Ohio, where they eventually married and started a family in Illinois and Indiana. Thomas Wharton initially moved from Ohio to New York to help start a school and serve as a professor. George Kendall came to New York from New Hampshire to work on various newspapers. Jedediah Hotchkiss originally moved to Pennsylvania from New York to begin his own teaching career. West Point graduates moved all over the country following the orders of their superiors, while young professionals often traveled to other parts of the North for a fresh start.[21]

So why exactly did these northerners break the pattern of internal emigration by moving beyond northern latitudes? Some biographers imply that at least part of the reason stemmed from the favorable impressions of the South made by their subject's personal contact with native southerners. In general, the northerners most likely to have some contact with southerners or the region itself either went to a school with a cross-sectional student body or served in the armed forces. Biographer Charles Cummings points out that, regardless of their origins, West Point graduates, including his subject Bushrod Rust Johnson, formed close bonds with their fellow officers, regardless of their origins, while serving alongside them in the Mexican War and at military posts around the country.[22] York County Academy in Pennsylvania, the hometown school of future Confederate general Johnson Kelly Duncan, attracted students from Maryland and Virginia, giving a cross-sectional element to the student body.[23] Another future Northern Confederate general, Edward Perry, attended Yale and made a lifelong friend of Alabama student Billy Maples. After graduation, Perry and Maples eventually taught together at an Alabama academy. Frederick Barnard witnessed the southern code of honor first-hand when he sat on a disciplinary committee at Yale for a South Carolina student accused of thrashing a fellow student for a public slight.

General Johnson Kelly Duncan. A native Pennsylvanian and West Point graduate, Duncan moved to New Orleans and became chief engineer of the Louisiana Board of Public Works. He commanded Forts Jackson and St. Phillip during the Battle of New Orleans in 1862. Library of Congress.

Alone among the committee members, Barnard voted against disciplinary measures because he felt the student's career should not be sidelined because of contrary values.[24]

A few others developed their first impressions of the South by taking short trips to the region itself. A year before moving to Virginia, Jedediah Hotchkiss went on an extensive trip through the west-central portion of the state, marveling at the beauty of the Shenandoah Valley. John Pratt left New Hampshire for Savannah for a year to earn money to pay off a mortgage for his employer before returning to New England. Massachusetts native Caroline Gilman spent four winters vacationing in Georgia with her brothers. Edward Drummond's family in New England had trading connections with Georgia, and he visited the state several times as a teenager.[25] Thanks to their observations of the South while still living in the North, and mingling with native southern students or serving with them in the army, these northerners may not have found moving to the South as shocking or strange as did other native northerners.

Nevertheless, this type of contact likely had a negligible impact on either perceptions of the South or decisions to move there. With the exception of the thirty-nine West Point graduates, only a few of the individuals in this study had confirmed personal relations with southerners and/or the South prior to their emigration. More often, like the majority of their fellow northerners in the antebellum period, they generally received much of their information about the region from newspapers, political speeches, pamphlets, or books, without ever actually seeing the South or the people living there. The average northerner formed opinions based on second-hand information, which only became more biased as the narrative of the "Slave Power" emerged in the 1840s and 1850s in the northern political arena. In addition, service in the prewar army itself did not necessarily make one a lover of the South. After all, most northerners in the prewar army stayed in the North and later joined the Union armies.[26] Finally, many native northerners had no connections with the South whatsoever yet still ended up moving there. As a result, pre-emigration contact with the South among northern emigrants did not largely dictate why they left the North or how they would view the South when they arrived.[27]

Not all of them left behind their thoughts on the subject, but for those who did, a pattern emerged for the greatest motivators behind emigration to the South. Chief among these motivations was the decision that the South offered them the greatest potential to improve their lives and carve out their own niche in the world. Although not all northern emigrants voluntarily came to the region, they all shared the same choice about whether or not to remain. Those who stayed believed that the South offered them advantages the North lacked. Northern emigrants did not follow a prearranged plan but, rather, responded as restless young Americans searching for their own place in the land of opportunity, whatever form it took, even if it meant crossing into the unknowns of the southern states.

Some of that opportunity stemmed from the adventure offered by frontier territories in the Southwest. In this case, abandoning their native section did not come with as much of a shock, because on the frontier every settler, regardless of origin, started from scratch. For example, Albert Pike left his native state of Massachusetts in 1831 to find adventure on the Santa Fe Trail. He and a friend traveled through New York, Ohio, Tennessee, Illinois, and

Missouri, eventually joining a hunting expedition to New Mexico. His traveling companions included northerners, southerners, and Comanche. Upon his return, he ended up in Arkansas almost by accident. Originally intending to travel to South America, Pike took a wrong turn at a crossroads and found himself at Fort Smith, where he decided to stay. The adventure itself served as the main motivation for his relocation, even though pure chance brought him to his eventual adopted state.[28]

Other northern emigrants found similar adventures in the Southwest. Elisha Pease and Walter Lane traveled to Texas to experience frontier life and fight for Texas against Mexico, seeking both opportunity and adventure.[29] Once they arrived, they never wanted to leave. As Pease wrote to his family, "'If we succeed in maintaining . . . [our independence], of which I have no doubt, I would not leave Texas for any country on earth . . . If my life is spared, I know I can acquire an independence for myself and such of my Father's family as choose to share it. . . . '"[30] Similarly, Lane did not care about the causes involved in the Texas war; he simply wanted to fight for liberty and the excitement of combat. He ended up serving in a scouting unit and even delivered messages personally to General Sam Houston. Lane did not consider returning to his family in Ohio because he found everything he needed in the wilds of Texas.[31]

Along with adventure, a few emigrants found inspiration in connection with the southern climate. Regardless of what Americans thought about each other, most agreed that southern warmth provided a pleasant contrast with the cold winters of New England and the Midwest, especially for those who wanted to improve their health. Gail Borden, for example, did not like how the cold winters of Indiana affected his health and sought a better climate farther down the Ohio River. William Pierce wrote to his sister about moving from Ohio to Mississippi after hearing from a southern traveler about both business opportunities and the prospect of warmer weather. Henry Watson decided to move to Alabama solely to improve his health; he had no idea how he would set up his living situation once he arrived. George Kendall sought to leave New York to escape a cholera outbreak in the city. Ironically, considering the regular outbreaks of yellow fever in the swamps of Louisiana, he believed New Orleans offered better health prospects. Eventually, he moved to Texas for the same reason, telling a colleague, "Who knows but what you might become so much enchanted with our country and climate as to break up in the North, and set up your lares and penates [*sic*] hereabouts." Kendall continued to emphasize the theme of weather to entice his friend to join him in Texas right up until the Civil War.[32]

The majority of northern emigrants in this study, however, moved to the South because they saw it as the best place to pursue their careers. Sixty-seven percent first came to the South in their twenties, with an additional twenty-five percent arriving in their teens or thirties.[33] They had not yet had time to establish themselves in their chosen occupations or to start their own families in the North. Just as thousands of citizens across the country looked to the West as the place for a fresh start, so too did these emigrants view the South as the place to secure their own independence. From the Chesapeake Bay to the border of Mexico, native northerners set out to establish themselves in a new land.

The South thus became an extension of the mythical West for these emigrants, where settlers since the seventeenth century moved beyond their past and reoriented their life's trajectory. Especially in the Southwest, which included Arkansas, Louisiana, Mississippi, and Texas, the land seemed like a blank slate where anyone could make a name for themselves and increase their social mobility. Mississippi, for example, long after its transition from territory to state, remained a place of woodland and swamp, filled with risk but also with potentially the best cotton growing land on the continent for anyone who wished to exploit it, regardless of ancestry.[34] The city of Natchez even gained a reputation as a haven for Virginia and New England emigrants in the state, a symbolic meeting of North and South in the wilderness.[35] As a result, native northerners did not have to limit themselves to the Old Northwest to acquire their own fortunes and escape from what seemed like an economic and social leash in their home states. As one author argued about why many New Englanders ultimately made their way to Texas, "The western lands offered economic betterment; while the Democratic spirit of the New West gave promise of relief from political ills. . . ."[36]

For those not inclined to take their chances in the wilderness, southern cities offered opportunity as well, especially when it came to commerce. Charleston and New Orleans attracted northern businessmen and traders eager to tap into southern wealth.[37] These cities even had organizations made up of native northerners, indicating the size of their northern-born populations. As both an untapped wilderness and business venture, the southwest and urban sectors of the South brought in thousands of northern emigrants in the antebellum period.[38]

Contemporaries confirmed this opinion of the South as an area ripe with possibilities for northern-born emigrants. Juliet Coleman, a native of Connecticut, informed her family that Alabama in the 1830s still resembled mostly wilderness, with Tuscaloosa as one of the only sizeable towns to compete with her hometown of Hartford. Henry Watson wrote to his uncle in 1834 describing his new surroundings in the same state as a constant rotation of fortune seekers, with people constantly passing through for the next opportunity over the horizon. Alabama graduated from territory to statehood years earlier, but the environment, especially in the northern half of the state, provided a nearly untouched landscape for anyone to exploit. Farther east, northern emigrants in northern Florida marveled at the mild climate and production potential. William Chase, originally from Massachusetts, claimed that the climate in Florida meant that four years in Pensacola equaled six years in the North, because the South had a longer growing season. Native Pennsylvanian George Catlin agreed when he wrote about Pensacola, "I would unhesitatingly recommend this to the enterprising capitalist of the North, as a place where they can live, and where (if nature has been kind, as experience has taught us) they will flourish." Sarah Williams, writing to her family from North Carolina, told her parents how sparsely populated the region was compared to New England.[39] Anywhere they looked, native northerners in the South found significant opportunities for a new life.

Ironically, some northern emigrants only discovered the opportunities available to them in the South by chance or because someone sent them there. Pennsylvanian Charles Dahlgren had no thought of leaving Philadelphia until he came under the wing of Nicholas Biddle, president of the Second Bank of the United States. In 1835, Biddle sent his employee to Louisiana to work as a teller in the bank's New Orleans branch. Within a year, Dahlgren resigned to take up a more lucrative position at the Commercial Bank of Natchez in Mississippi. From that time on, Dahlgren began to acquire plantations in Mississippi and Louisiana through financial transactions and marriage. Dahlgren thus became a resident of the South by a quirk of fate rather than a prearranged plan.[40]

Other native northerners experienced the same situation. Edward Drummond, though he came from a family of devoted abolitionists in Maine, ultimately decided to move to Georgia to work in a commission house on the advice of friends he made on his family's trips to the state. Anson Jones, a native of Massachusetts, originally hoped to start his career as a physician or merchant somewhere in the North. However, after his initial businesses failed in New York, Pennsylvania, and Venezuela, and with mounting debt, he accepted an offer from a Philadelphia merchant to work as a partner in a new merchant house in New Orleans. As Jones remembered, "never having as yet met with any satisfactory success in my profession, and, consequently a good deal disgusted with it, too readily acceded to this proposal and . . . sailed from New York in the ship *Alabama* for New Orleans." Jones left the North more out of frustration than anything else, but the decision ultimately brought him wealth and fame as one of Texas's original freedom fighters.[41]

Still, some who planned to move to the South for financial gain intended to do so only as a short-term leave of absence. They knew about the opportunities available in the region but did not initially consider it a permanent place to settle. Instead, their original plans involved building up a nest egg before returning to the North. For instance, William Hora wrote to his sister back in New Jersey that he had moved to South Carolina because he could make more money there. However, once he saved up enough, he wanted to return to New Jersey to buy a small farm. South Carolina represented just a brief stopover in his long range plans.[42] Similarly, a young student named Seargent Prentiss in Maine viewed the South as a brief intermission in his otherwise typical New England life. His first law tutor recalled, "When he [Prentiss] left Maine for the West, he hoped to better his fortunes, and acquire fame in his profession . . . He had confidence in his own success and thought, that in a few years, he should return to New England . . ."[43] As it turned out, the brief intermission ended up as a permanent residence. Prentiss became so successful he found a new home where he had never planned. Prentiss's biographer Joseph Shields quipped, "How often has that dream of ambition been realized but in part! how often has the young sapling transplanted to other soil, after its roots are deeply struck as an exotic, found it impossible to tear itself from its adopted home!"[44]

On the other side of the country, Connecticut native Daniel Pratt experienced the same type of situation in Georgia. Pratt first went to the South only to help clear up a debt for his carpentry master. After a year, he made enough to pay off the debt and returned to New England, but he then went back to Georgia because he believed his carpentry skills were in demand in the state. He ended up with nearly two hundred and fifty acres of land given to him as payment for some of his early jobs. After several more years, his lands grew, his businesses prospered, and he even acquired a few slaves. Any thoughts of returning to New England seemed more like an afterthought than actual fact. As his biographer wrote, "he proposed to Mrs. Pratt that, if she preferred, they would return North and settle themselves among their relations . . . Mrs. Pratt very wisely decided to remain in the South and share with him his fortunes."[45] What began as just one step on a lifelong journey ended up as the focus of the journey itself.[46]

It took more than simple economics, however, to draw native northerners away from their native section permanently. After all, they could find similar financial opportunities for land and profit in the Old Northwest, California, Iowa, and the western territories. In order to understand why they chose the South over these more typical areas for northern emigrants, we have to look at the advantages available to aspiring young northern professionals in the South that they could not find in the North or West.

One factor that enticed northern emigrants into the South was the realization that the region offered them more money for the same amount of work. John Quitman of New York explained to his friend his decision to leave his aspiring career as a lawyer in Ohio for the wilderness of Mississippi: "In this section [the Northwest] it is easy to make any kind of property but money . . . I think, therefore, of Alabama or Mississippi. Money is there more plenty; trade is brisk; their cotton commands cash . . . It is bad policy for a young man to move about, but much depends on the location we make when we first set out in life."[47] Similarly, Arthur McArthur of Maine wrote to his friend about the great prospects waiting in Missouri. He predicted St. Louis would soon reach the heights of New York City thanks to its location along the Mississippi River. "I like this country you see yet my stay here has been only about six months, but as far my observation has informed me, this is the very place for a young man to start."[48] William Pierce told his sister he heard from southern students and travelers that aspiring professionals could make four to six times as much in fees in places like Virginia and Mississippi than in the North.[49] Ashbel Smith also heard from southern acquaintances about the fortunes to be made in the Southwest. Smith claimed that in New Orleans or Alabama he might make four thousand dollars in profit in a single year. As he told one of his friends, "The extreme southern country is extremely flourishing in Al. Miss. & Lou and therefore they have my decided preference."[50]

Along with better money-making potential, native northerners also faced less competition in the South for their services. Wealthy southerners offered higher fees for northern professionals because they knew northerners generally received better educations and, with so many southern children only wanting to become plantation owners, many of the professional classes lacked native southern members. One observer argued, "Young men who come to this country, to make money soon catch the mania, and nothing less than a broad plantation . . . can fill their mental vision . . ."[51] At the same time, professions in the North often had too many qualified members, which made it more difficult to start a new practice. Young northern professionals thus saw both a need for their services and a way to escape competition by emigrating to the South. As one author described the situation in Maine, "The professions were crowded to excess. Large numbers, therefore, of the young men, who had received a liberal education, emigrated to other parts of the country, especially to the West and Southwest."[52] The rest of New England and many other parts of the North had similar conditions, which helped to propel otherwise disinterested northerners out of their native section.

These northerners enjoyed another advantage: multiple options for settlement. One might assume that northern emigrants would naturally drift toward the Border South and Southwest, as indicated in the 1860 census, because of shorter travel distances, greater access to land, and the fact that the Southeast had more established communities. Instead, native northerners found opportunities all across the South. The Deep South became the initial destination for one hundred and sixteen northern emigrants in this study, the Upper South eighty-nine, and the Border South thirty-six. Broken down between east and west, one hundred and fifty-four settled east of the Appalachians, while one hundred and thirty-seven settled west of that mountain range. Virginia had the most number of northern emigrants with fifty, followed by Georgia with forty-three and Louisiana with thirty-seven. On the other end of the scale, only one emigrant settled in Delaware, seven in Maryland, and eight each in Missouri and Arkansas.[53] Instead of only one southern state or sub-region welcoming native northerners, and the rest shunning them as unwanted aliens, the entire South opened its doors for those who wished to remake their lives outside of the North.

White southerners especially wanted northerners to contribute to the South's educational system. Since southern states lacked the support for public school systems, families who could afford it relied on private tutors to educate their children. Colleges in the region also needed trained faculty for their student bodies. Though they likely would have preferred southern college graduates, wealthy southerners understood that the best tutors and professors came from the North, thanks to the prevalence of colleges and academies. The situation worked out well for both sides. "Gentlemen planters preferred college graduates to instruct their children, and southerners with a high education were of an economic and social class which had neither the necessity nor the inclination to teach," historian Elizabeth Pryor argues. For northern students, on the other hand, "To repay debts incurred at college or to defray expenses while studying law or theology many graduates took up teaching, both in New England and elsewhere."[54]

Both native northerners who moved to the South and those who witnessed a friend or colleague do so confirmed the opportunities available for an educated northerner in a southern state. Seargent Prentiss wrote to his mother in 1827, "In Ohio it is much the same with regard to schools as in New England; but it is quite different in Mississippi, and the other Southern States. There they have no system of common schools; and the rich planters, living at a distance from each other, are obliged to have, each of them, a teacher in his own family."[55] Reverend Newcomb of Iowa, reflecting on the life of Lewis Parsons, noted that, "Following the example of many other Northern college graduates of those days, he [Parsons] decided to go to the South and teach school for a time the compensation being much better that section [sic] than in the North."[56] William Pierce excitedly told his sister that he saw an opening for a male and female teacher in Oakland, Tennessee, offering to pay two hundred dollars for five months work.[57] Caroline Gilman, after moving to South Carolina with her husband, recorded a fictional story about a Connecticut farmer's son who engaged in a conversation with a local resident in Charleston: "I calculate it's pretty difficult to git edication down at Charleston.' 'Dreadful difficult, said the captin; I reckon they aint much better than niggers.' 'An't you agreeable, captain . . . to my going down to Charleston and trying what I can do to help them a trifle at schooling?'"[58] Gilman's story might have been fiction but it still reflected how both northerners and southerners viewed education and how northerners contributed to the profession in South Carolina. In probably the most intriguing case, Amanda Trulock, a native northerner who originally worked as a plantation tutor before marrying and starting her own family in the South, wanted to hire a northern tutor for her own children's education.[59]

Even those who did not consider teaching their principal career, the lucrative benefits of the profession available in the South intrigued many northern emigrants. Seargent Prentiss followed that route after graduating from Bowdoin College in Maine. Originally intending to practice law, Prentiss did not have the resources to finish his studies and so looked for teaching positions to supplement his income. At first, he intended to stay in the North by moving to Cincinnati but quickly found that teaching would barely cover his expenses, because of the overcrowding of the profession in the city. One of his friends provided his saving grace by introducing him to two wealthy Mississippi travelers (one of whom was a native northerner himself), who told him about much better prospects for teachers in Mississippi. Prentiss immediately moved to Mississippi based on their advice. Though his hasty decision likely caught his parents by surprise, he believed it provided him a way to save up for his later career in the law. The educational field thus allowed northerners like Prentiss either to establish their careers as educators or to earn a living while pursuing other careers.[60]

In their eagerness for financial and personal independence, these men and women pursued opportunity whenever and wherever it led them. Much of the time they received their appointments thanks to invitations extended from southerners eager for their services. President Jeremiah Day of Yale more than once steered one of his graduates toward the lucrative southern tutoring market through his contacts with prominent planters. Ashbel Smith got his first taste of the South after Day recommended him to Colonel Charles Fisher of North Carolina, who hired him as a tutor for his family in Salisbury. Even though he only stayed with the family for a year, the town's residents came to respect him as a schoolmaster. Frederick Barnard also utilized his connections with Day to meet Basil Manly, president of the University of Alabama, who offered him a position as a professor of English, which he then utilized as a springboard for a lucrative career as a southern educator in both Alabama and Mississippi.[61]

A graduate of West Point, native Ohioan and future Union general William Tecumseh Sherman, also made his way to the South thanks to the recommendations of his native southern commanders. After fighting in the Mexican War, Sherman served at army posts in California, Missouri, and

Louisiana. Along with his military duties, Sherman also found time to work in business ventures, including a new bank branch in California and a law firm in Kansas. Unfortunately, his dealings in business mainly ended in failure, and so he relied on the army to make a living for his family. His contacts in the army ultimately brought him an opportunity to work as an education administrator in the Deep South. While inquiring about possible jobs for army paymasters in 1858, he heard about a new war college opening in Louisiana. As it turned out, his old commanding officer in the Mexican War, a native Louisianan, was the half brother of General G. Mason Graham, one of the members of the search committee. Thanks to his contacts with Graham, Sherman received an appointment as the new superintendant of the war college and moved to Louisiana in the summer of 1859. Like so many other native northerners of his generation, Sherman followed opportunity wherever it led and ended up in the South as a consequence.[62]

None other than one of the most famous and effective Confederate generals, Thomas Jonathan "Stonewall" Jackson, bore witness to the prevalence of northern-born middle class professionals. After serving in the military, Jackson accepted a position as a professor at the newly opened Virginia Military Institute (VMI) in Lexington, Virginia. After several years working as a teacher, Jackson turned himself into a successful businessman. He only had savings from his time in the army when he arrived in Lexington, but by 1854 he had learned to make investments and joined the Board of Directors at Lexington Savings Institution. By the time the Civil War erupted, Jackson had solidified his position as a respected member of the southern professional middle class.[63] In the process, Jackson became friends and acquaintances with several native northerners. His bunkmate at VMI, native Indianan William Gilham, had also attended West Point and served in the Mexican War before joining VMI as a professor. He became close friends with Jackson and even partnered with him in several business ventures. Another northern emigrant, native New Yorker Jedediah Hotchkiss, who would later serve as Jackson's mapmaker in the Civil War, met Jackson through their mutual connection to the president of nearby Washington College, native Pennsylvanian George Junkin. In fact, Jackson ended up marrying one of Junkin's daughters, Ellie, and honeymooned in Pennsylvania before returning to Lexington. Much of Jackson's professional life thus involved close cooperation with native northerners seeking the same dreams of success as Jackson. In the heart of Virginia, and throughout the rest of the South, well-educated northern emigrants smoothly entered and thrived in the southern middle class through educational opportunities.[64]

Even without such connections, aspiring educators still managed to find positions as tutors for southern families. Jackson's friend Jedediah Hotchkiss, before establishing his school at Mossey Creek in Virginia, began his educational career as a tutor to a southern family in the town. Theodore Clapp, upon finishing his theological studies at Andover Theological Seminary in Massachusetts, accepted an offer to serve as a tutor for a Kentucky family. Henry Handerson received an invitation from Washington Compton of Louisiana to tutor on his plantation and, as he recalled, that offer alone "induced me to settle in that state."[65]

Education was even more critical for northern women as a reason to leave their native section. Other than factory work, teaching represented one of the few professions where single women could earn an independent living in the

Jedidiah Hotchkiss and his family. A native New Yorker, Hotchkiss ran several schools in Virginia before serving as General Stonewall Jackson's chief mapmaker. Courtesy of Virginia Historical Society.

antebellum period. And in a lucrative twist, tutoring on a southern plantation or in a southern school represented one of the few places in the country where women earned as much as men for the same work.[66] Joseph Ingraham, a New Englander who spent over three decades in the Southwest, recorded that some women from New England came to the South to "repair their broken fortunes" as governesses on plantations or teachers in seminaries.[67] Little surprise, then, that the prospect of earning a sizeable salary as a teacher could induce a single northern woman to venture south. Not many women actually opted for that choice, but those who did relied on education to get them there. Massachusetts-born Tryphena Anne Holder moved out of New England to accept a position as a plantation tutor for George Messenger, a Mississippi planter. Caroline Seabury also traveled from Massachusetts to Mississippi to teach French at Columbus Female Institute. Caroline Hentz combined education with constant migration by teaching at girls' schools all across the South over the course of her thirty year career.[68]

In all, ninety-five individuals in this study served as either private tutors or teachers, with an additional fifty-two eventually accepting positions as school headmasters or professors at southern universities. Nearly half of the people documented thus either originally came to or stayed in the South thanks to the opportunities given to them by teaching white southerners. Because of the relative importance of higher education in different parts of the country, young and aspiring white northerners possessed a ready-made skill that white southerners desperately needed, providing the perfect situation for a mini-exodus across the Mason-Dixon Line. Under the right circumstances, the iron law of latitudinal migration broke down under the clarion call of educational opportunities summoning northerners to follow a longitudinal path instead.

Other occupations also provided white northerners with greater opportunities for advancement in the South. The law profession was especially lucrative because, as with education, northerners believed they faced less competition in the South than in the North. Because northerners who graduated law school tended to emigrate to places like the Midwest, the South offered a less competitive alternative. John Quitman recognized this fact when he decided to move from Ohio to Mississippi in the early 1820s. As he informed one of his friends, "The bar is not overcrowded with well-read lawyers, and fees are high."[69] Seargent Prentiss initially wanted to go back to Maine after finishing his short time as a tutor, but he quickly discovered he could get a law license more easily in Mississippi. Plus, after he passed the bar, a local lawyer in Natchez offered him a stake in a lucrative partnership.[70] Even so, Prentiss could have easily returned to the North after a few years of building up his practice, but by then he had acquired too much of a stake in his adopted state. One of his acquaintances understood the dilemma when he wrote to Prentiss's mother that her son had established himself as a first class lawyer and orator in Mississippi within only two years, whereas in the West it was difficult to find a job.[71]

Seventy-seven law graduates in this study ultimately established law practices in southern states, making it the second most lucrative profession among northern emigrants behind education. Of those seventy-seven, twenty-two eventually accepted appointments as judges in southern courts, further cementing their reputations as respected legal minds in the South.[72]

Along with education and the law, medicine also provided aspiring young northerners with lucrative opportunities and lighter competition. Twenty-two moved to the South to build their medical practices amidst populations in need of their services. Anson Jones, one of the future leaders of the Texas revolution against Mexico, ultimately found his way to the Rio Grande thanks to his medical degree. He originally hoped to make a fortune as a merchant and traveled to New Orleans for that purpose. When that venture failed, he took advantage of the opening of Tulane College and yellow fever outbreaks in the city by starting a medical office. Still facing debt, Jones finally decided to practice medicine in Texas because few doctors lived in the territory and Texas settlers desperately needed trained medical professionals.[73] Ashbel Smith followed a similar path when he received his medical degree from Yale. After working at a mental institution in Connecticut and receiving more training in France, Smith decided to establish his practice in North Carolina at the urging of his former mentor. Within a few years, his practice flourished, and members of the local militia even nominated him as their surgeon.[74]

Beyond the professional elite, other northern emigrants embarked for the South to take advantage of business opportunities. At least fifty-eight individuals in this study pursued business or merchant endeavors in their transition to a southern state, making this the third most popular profession for northern emigrants. Connecticut native Joseph Claghorn took over his father's grocery and chandelier firm upon his father's death and moved to Georgia to expand the firm's operations. Massachusetts native William

Drake began his career as a teacher in Chicago but then moved to Tennessee in 1858 to work in a lumber business. Daniel Shearer, also from Massachusetts, settled in New Orleans to create his own furniture company. George Franklin Drew, a future governor of Florida, originally moved from New Hampshire to Georgia as a machinist and, later, mill owner. George French Senior, who worked as a child in shoe factories in his native Massachusetts, relocated to North Carolina at the age of twenty to start his own shoe store and general merchandise business. Samuel B. Myers moved from his native Pennsylvania to Virginia in 1852 to run the Columbia Iron Furnace. William Weaver, although already a successful businessman in Philadelphia, decided to move to Virginia to buy and oversee iron manufacturing plants. In each case, lucrative business ventures helped these fortune-seekers to make the South their permanent adopted home.[75]

Newspaper work proved to be another popular profession. In a touch of irony for later southern nationalist propagandists, at least some of the rhetoric defending the South against northern criticism came from northern-born editors. Often taking the skills they acquired working for northern newspapers, at least twenty-nine northern emigrants fulfilled their dreams for economic and social advancement by working for or owning southern newspapers. Arunah Abell, a Rhode Island native who had earlier established newspapers in Rhode Island and Pennsylvania, founded the *Baltimore American* in Maryland and advocated for the development of commercial ventures in the South. In Virginia, Kenton Harper of Pennsylvania founded and edited the *Staunton Spectator,* a leading newspaper in the Shenandoah Valley. Dennis Heartt, a native of Connecticut, moved to North Carolina and established the *Hillsborough Recorder,* which became one of the most popular newspapers in the state and helped train future editors, including future governor William Holden. Farther south, New York native Ezra Bauder edited the *Port Royal Times* in South Carolina, while Aaron Willington of Massachusetts co-founded the *Charleston Courier*. In Alabama, native New Yorker Willis Clark edited the *Mobile Daily Advertiser,* and in Texas, New Englander Francis Moore edited the *Telegraph and Texas Register* for seventeen years. These and several other northern emigrants contributed significantly to the voices of their adopted states.[76]

Even northern emigrants who did not come to the South voluntarily often liked the region so much they decided to stay. As mentioned earlier, nearly forty future northern-born Confederate generals went to West Point, and at least fifty-eight northern emigrants served in the United States army before the Civil War. Under orders to serve wherever their superiors demanded, many of these soldiers ended up on assignment in one or several southern states. They often had mixed reactions to the region yet never failed to come away with some kind of connection. For example, after native Pennsylvanian John Clifford Pemberton graduated from West Point, he served at forts in states all over the country, including Florida, Maine, New York, and Virginia, over the course of twenty years. Pemberton's time in Virginia especially affected him because, when his father thought about buying some land in the state, Pemberton told him, "I should like to become a Virginian by adoption." Similarly, William Henry Chase of Massachusetts served at forts all over the South, and upon retirement declined an invitation to teach at West Point because he decided to operate a business in Pensacola. Charles Dimmock, also from Massachusetts, served at Fortress Monroe and liked Virginia so much that he moved there as an engineer when he resigned from the army.[77]

A few northern emigrants without military careers made their way south thanks to family connections. Stephen Duncan, a Philadelphian who eventually made his fortune through Mississippi plantations, first received introductions in the state through his maternal aunt and uncle. In the 1850s, George Cary Eggleston, born and raised in Indiana, joined his extended family in Virginia, where they had lived on a plantation for years. New Yorker Gail Borden first decided to go to Texas after hearing about the area from his brother.[78]

Thanks to all of these motivations, a relatively small but steady stream of native northerners embarked for the South in pursuit of opportunity and the chance for a better life. In the process, native northerners had a remarkably easy transition into southern life. In fact, northern emigrants became overrepresented, in relation to their percentage of the population, in various professions in the southern states. By 1850, New Orleans had three of its five major banks run by northern-born presidents (two from New York and one from Connecticut), five of eight private banking houses with northern chief executives (from Pennsylvania, New York, and Massachusetts), and eleven of twenty-one bankers, as well as many educators, churchmen, merchants, and newspaper owners, all from the North.[79] Major southern cities, including Baltimore, Charleston, Mobile, and New Orleans, either had northern editors or owners of major newspapers. Some southern cities gained a reputation as havens for northern emigrants, who ended up as high ranking officials. In the 1820s, northerners ran most of the businesses in Mobile, while Augusta became known as a "Yankee town."[80] In the city of Natchez, out of twenty-four mayors who served before the Civil War, a majority came from New England, Pennsylvania, New York, and Ohio. As historian Hershel Gower summarizes, "Recent historians agree that Natchez was early marked with a stratum of ambitious, wealth-pursuing young men from the North who would influence its social and political life."[81]

These men and women either began or improved their careers in the South and thus regarded the region as their adopted home. As time passed, they often branched out into other endeavors and cemented themselves even further into their adopted communities. Their accomplishments included such varied positions as author, architect, blacksmith, carpenter, engineer, grocer, clerk, machinist, manufacturer, railroad worker, rancher, salesman, and surveyor. At least twenty-eight ran small farms and, in probably the most potent symbol of their success and assimilation into southern society, over one hundred of these individuals owned slaves by the time of the Civil War.[82] Not everyone became rich or famous, but they did find what they sought when they first embarked for the South: opportunities not available in their native section and a chance for a fresh start.

Once they settled in an adopted community, many native northerners quickly learned how to rise even further in the ranks of southern society. Certainly not all of them succeeded, but the ones who did became minor celebrities among their neighbors. Frederick Barnard, after accepting a position as a professor at the University of Alabama, quickly gained a reputation as a speaker after a well-received speech on the Masons, which led to further speaking engagements across the state. He also edited several newspapers before moving to Mississippi to take over the main university there.[83] Another New Englander, Charles Dimmock, used his army training to work as a civil engineer in Virginia, participating in such projects as surveying routes for a canal in Princess Anne County and building various railroads. Within seven years, he became president of the Portsmouth and Roanoke Railroad. For the next two decades, he also started up an iron business, helped develop a new type of screw propeller steam boat for use in canals, ran the Virginia Public Guard and Armory, and, to the delight of native Virginians, oversaw the raising of a statue of George Washington in Richmond's public square.[84] Johnson Kelly Duncan of Pennsylvania settled in New Orleans after resigning from the army. Within only a few years Duncan's skills as an engineer elevated him to chief engineer of the Louisiana Board of Public Works.[85] Albert Pike, after a brief tenure as a teacher in Arkansas, quickly became a newspaper editor and lawyer. Widely regarded as one of the most respected lawyers in the state, he argued cases before both the Arkansas State Supreme Court and the United States Supreme Court.[86] John Pratt went even further by not only establishing his own cotton gin business but even founding a new town in Alabama, eventually called Prattville, after a long career in Georgia.[87]

One of the best and quickest ways to climb the social ladder involved marrying into a prominent southern family, since the union often brought both prestige and wealth at the same time. Though many northerners originally came to the South as single men, marriage represented an excellent way to solidify both their financial and social ties to their new states. Charles Dahlgren, a native Pennsylvanian who moved to Mississippi as a banker, married his first wife in 1839. She happened to be the widow of a man who left her hundreds of acres and slaves, which then passed to Dahlgren. Fellow native Pennsylvanian and adopted Mississippian Stephen Duncan also rose from humble origins into the planter ranks through strategic marriages. His first wife came from one of the first families to settle in Natchez, and after she died, he married the daughter of another wealthy Natchez family. New Jersey native Samuel French married into a Mississippi family and took over a plantation with over a hundred slaves, which represented a much greater income than his previous salary as an army officer.[88] Without these marriages, acquiring the same kind of wealth in either the North or the South would have been much more difficult.[89]

Not all northern emigrants found such wealthy spouses, but marrying into any southern family did help secure their connection to the South. At least one hundred and fifty-three of the men and women in this study had southern spouses before the war, with an additional nine acquiring such spouses during the war, and twenty-three during Reconstruction.[90] For instance, native Pennsylvanian Josiah Gorgas remained a career army officer in the antebellum era, maintaining a mobile lifestyle through various army assignments around the country, but still maintained some connection to Alabama thanks to his marriage to the daughter of an Alabama governor. John C.

Pemberton also did not abandon his army career yet strengthened his ties to Virginia after marrying the daughter of a prominent Norfolk family. Adopted Missourian Abiel Leonard cemented his ties to his adopted state by marrying the daughter of a popular state politician.[91]

Nor did native northerners necessarily have to marry southern spouses to show their commitment. An act as simple as joining the local militia regiment presented an intention to assimilate into and defend an adopted community. Many a northern emigrant proudly served in volunteer regiments for their adopted states in the militia or in the United States Army. For example, adopted Texan Walter Lane joined a volunteer Texas company in the Hays Texas Rangers that saw action with General Zachary Taylor during the Mexican War, eventually getting elected lieutenant by his comrades. He later organized his own company in San Antonio and ended the war as a major. Over in Arkansas, Albert Pike helped organize both a militia company of artillery and then a cavalry company that fought at Buena Vista, with himself as captain. Charles Dimmock accepted a commission as captain of the Richmond Grays in Virginia thanks to his reputation as an accomplished engineer and veteran soldier among his peers.[92]

One of the greatest symbols of the assimilation of native northerners into southern society, however, occurred when they received appointments to high office in their adopted states. Gail Borden, before moving to Texas, settled in Amite County, Mississippi, as a teacher. Within two years, the community recommended him for County Surveyor. John Quitman underwent a similarly rapid rise in the same state; only a few years after his arrival from New York, he received a high rank in the state militia, as well as an appointment as state chancellor of Mississippi for several terms. The legislatures of both Alabama and Florida requested Frederick Barnard to serve as state astronomer and to determine the boundary between the two states. Eugene Hilgard accepted an appointment from the Mississippi legislature in 1858 as state geologist. In Georgia, New Englander William Wadley, thanks to his reputation as an experienced railroad operator and blacksmith, was appointed by the governor as superintendent of government works on Cockspur Island only a year after he arrived in the state. Seventeen years later, Governor Howell Cobb selected him as superintendent of the Western and Atlantic Railroad. None of these men sought these appointments, but their adopted communities chose them nonetheless. Any thoughts of leaving the states that had become their homes quickly vanished with the acceptance of these appointments.[93]

A few native northerners even received the greatest endorsement from their communities by winning statewide elections. In terms of local government, fourteen served as aldermen or city councilmen, seven as district attorneys, and another seven as mayors. The cities of Augusta and Greensboro in Georgia, Thibodaux in Louisiana, Brazoria and Houston in Texas, and Charlestown and Staunton in Virginia all had northern-born mayors. At least thirty-six native northerners served in the legislatures of their adopted states, with an additional sixteen elected to other state offices.

Several native northerners included in this study managed to reach even higher in the quest for elected office. In Virginia, native New Yorker Joseph Johnson achieved the distinction as the first popularly elected governor of the state in 1852. Voters in Texas sent New England native and adopted Texan Elisha Pease to the governor's mansion for two terms in the 1850s.[94] Before Pease took office, two other northern emigrants, Anson Jones and Ashbel Smith, held significant elected positions in the independent country of Texas prior to its annexation to the United States. Jones won election to the Texas Congress, served as Texas's representative to the United States, won election to the Texas Senate, served as secretary of state, and finally served as the last president of an independent Texas.[95] Smith replaced Jones as secretary of state and served under him in preparation for annexation, which he ironically opposed until the last minute because he believed Texas would function much better as an independent country.[96] Finally, southern communities also elected eleven native northerners to represent them in Congress. Native Ohioan Robert Hatton served his adopted state of Tennessee as a congressman, first as a Whig and then as a Know-Nothing in the 1850s, while John Slidell of New York served for several terms as a senator from Louisiana.[97]

Starting out like millions of other Americans born in the northern states, these men and women opted for a different path by willingly crossing the sectional barrier into a land few knew anything about from personal experience. They came for opportunity and for their own independence, which they felt they could not obtain in the North. As time passed, their connection to the South manifested itself through marriage, landholdings, professional contacts, community organizations, even elected offices. They arrived as strangers but emerged as full-fledged members of their communities. In every way possible, northern emigrants worked hard to adjust and assimilate into the surroundings and communities that became their homes. In the process, attachment to the South had the potential to override their previous attachments to the North. By the time of the secession crisis and Civil War, these native northerners not only lived and acted as southerners; they often made a full transition in their personal identities by identifying completely as southerners in body, mind, and soul.

2

From Northerner to Southerner

After native northerners arrived and established new lives in the South, they experienced a major culture shock, along with questions about their identity. These men and women encountered different environments, including social and cultural characteristics not usually seen by emigrants who remained in northern latitudes. These included, but were not limited to, warmer climates, greater disparities of wealth, fewer immigrants, a less educated population, and slavery. Life in the North did not prepare them for these conditions, and each emigrant had to adjust in his or her own way.[1]

Because of those adjustments, the foundations for their identities had to adjust as well. They now had homes, families, and livelihoods in the South but also still had families in and ties to their native states. Northern emigrants almost lived in two worlds: their past in the North and their present in the South, with the future in the balance. Few other Americans at the time had such dual connections in the Union, which made sectional conflict that much more potentially destructive.[2] A northern upbringing combined with adulthood spent in the South presented options not even considered by other antebellum Americans. Did these native northerners remain "Yankees" in terms of social and cultural constructs and only regard the South as a place of residence? Did they shed their past entirely to become southern in all but birth? Or did a middle ground emerge where they thought of themselves as both northern and southern at the same time? Finally, what did it mean for them to be "northern" or "southern" in the first place? The opinions and reflections of adoptive southerners in this study showed that many had no doubt of their sectional identity transition, while others were more uncertain, and still others did not transition at all. Regardless of the end result, the process alone provides an insight into the nature of state, sectional, and national identity in the antebellum period. Rather than remain locked in place, these types of identity remained flexible enough for Americans to reestablish themselves not only geographically but also socially, culturally, and even mentally.

The fact that northern emigrants to the South even had such a choice pointed to the fluid nature of sectional identity in the Union. Instead of regarding all northern emigrants as coming to the South with an unchangeable sectional identity in place, historians need to consider a complete shift from a northern to a southern identity. In such cases, individuals did not just live in the South, but thought of themselves as southerners and expressed that change both privately and publicly. This shift did not happen to everyone, nor was it ever guaranteed to happen, but those who went through it demonstrated the extent of the flexibility of antebellum sectional identity. The lives they created for themselves turned them into southerners as effectively as if they had been born there. Even those who did not make that shift still had the option to do so; choice mattered more than anything else. A native northerner could choose to keep his or her sectional identity, modify it, or transform it completely. Sectional identity did not come from birth; it came from experience and personal preference. Northern emigrants did not change the South; the South changed them.

To the detriment of the Union, this flexibility later extended to the national level as well, with the Confederacy born out of those adaptations. State identity competed with sectional identity, and both competed with ties to the Union. Americans had to decide for themselves which ones they valued as more precious, especially when the interests of one conflicted with the interests of another. Neither native northerners nor native southerners presented a united front, as the Northwest clashed with New England and the Southwest clashed with the Old South on various occasions. That situation only started to change around the time of the Missouri Compromise, and even then it happened slowly. By 1860, people across the country, especially in the South, still argued about their ultimate loyalties. Hundreds of thousands of white southerners would give their lives for the newly created Confederacy, while tens of thousands of others placed their loyalty to the Union above their love for their state. The Mason-Dixon Line thus did not represent an impenetrable barrier between North and South. It acted much more like a sieve, through which anyone could pass and remake themselves in the American tradition.

In terms of northern emigrants to the South, trying to find a predictive characteristic for transition versus no transition remains elusive. Native states, adopted states, occupation, education, spouses, religion, ownership of slaves, and political leanings did not matter on their own. It did not turn out that everyone who came from New England retained their sectional identity, while those who came from the Midwest changed theirs. Plus, northern emigrants sometimes changed their minds or made contradictory statements, making it difficult to tell if a complete transition had taken place. The very fluidity of sectional identity in the antebellum era allowed for unexpected twists and turns, even uncertainty.

The best answer encompasses individual choice, circumstances, and the effects of time and place. In the end, the answers northern emigrants came up with mirrored their own experiences, actions, and declarations. Despite their backgrounds, if a native northerner regarded himself as a southerner, adapted to a southern lifestyle, and defended his adopted state and section, then for all intents and purposes he had switched his sectional identity. In addition, the longer they lived in the South, the more likely that such a transition would happen. Finally, northern emigrants did not always migrate into established states but, rather, into territories or parts of states still considered wilderness.[3] As a result, they had a potentially easier transition because everyone else adapted alongside them. Out of that adaptation came a renewed sense of self, oftentimes with a transformed sectional identity.

Among historians who analyze sectional and national identity in the antebellum period, few dispute the idea that antebellum Americans viewed their sectional identities as set in stone from the moment of birth. Whatever their opinions about sectional similarities and/or differences, these scholars argue that a person born in the North remained a northerner and a person born in the South remained a southerner, regardless of where they lived. In one example, historian Richard Power cites New England reformers wishing to bestow "Yankee culture" on the South, both to lift the region out of barbarism and save New England's influence in the nation.[4] Indeed, some contemporary white southerners feared the consequences of such a project and made the counter-argument that North and South not only existed as two separate regions but as two separate races. One wealthy planter in Georgia insisted that northerners and southerners were "'two races which, although claiming a common parentage, have become so entirely separated by climate, by morals. . . . that they cannot longer coexist under the same government.'"[5] Based on this type of rhetoric, historians like Susan-Mary Grant insist that such sectional thinking emerged as early as the eighteenth century, with calls for nationalism itself taking on a sectional construct. This construct reached its apex in the 1850s with the emergence, as many contemporaries saw it, of a fully unified North against a fully unified South. That perception gained such strength, Grant claims, that some northerners believed no one from their region could safely stay in the South.[6]

If the two sections had solidified as much as these historians argue, then northern emigrants to the South had no other choice but to retain their northern upbringing as the basis for their sectional identity. Though they lived in the South, they did so as northerners living in what amounted to a foreign land. Even though they might participate actively in public life and become members of the local communities, they nevertheless maintained their regional attachments and remained separated from the rest of the population.[7] Northern emigrants thus never truly left their backgrounds behind and either maintained their status as northerners, in which case they lived as transplanted Yankees, or became confused about their identities.[8]

This interpretation of life-long sectional constructs, especially when applied to northern emigrants to the South, suffers from several flaws. First of all, those who portray these emigrants as temporary squatters overlook the hundreds of others who made new lives in the region, and sometimes even became leaders of their adopted communities and states. Admittedly, few went to the South expecting to stay, but once they arrived their plans went through adjustments as they took advantage of the many opportunities available to them. The image of a Yankee peddler, or tutor, or businessman distancing themselves from their neighbors, or forming organizations for native northerners to intermingle, does not reflect the level of adaptation that occurred on a regular basis. Cities like New Orleans and Charleston did have clubs formed by native northerners, but these men and women just as often spoke out in favor of southern interests, married into southern families, and built relationships with their southern neighbors. Personal interactions, developed over many years, eventually eliminated the initial feelings of alienation and isolation.

Permanent residencies point to a second flaw of life-long sectional constructs: an assumption of inflexible sectional identity. Historians who mention northern emigrants generally refer to them as Yankee transplants who never fully adapted to life in the South. Yet an extended stay, sometimes lasting decades before secession, allowed northern emigrants to adjust to environments far different from those of their upbringing. Northern intellectuals may have boasted of the superiority of northern culture, yet they knew a New England childhood did not always translate into a New England adulthood. Northern emigrants may not have grown up with southern culture, but they could adapt to it when needed. If anything, much like foreign immigrants had to do throughout American history, northern emigrants went to great lengths to conform to the social and cultural norms around them.[9]

This flexibility manifested itself within both the North and the South. Especially before the 1850s, neither section ever spoke with one voice, as each sub-section guarded its own local interests. These divisions sometimes caused settlers to abandon previous attachments in favor of their new homes. For example, the great orator and 1860 presidential candidate Stephen Douglas tried to distance himself from his Vermont roots once he settled in Illinois. Douglas acknowledged he was not born in Illinois but rather in "Yankee land," as he referred to New England. Nevertheless, when he reached the western prairies, he considered himself forever after as a part of the Old Northwest.[10] Such a fluid environment allowed newcomers who settled into different communities to support those communities as their own. The alienation many northerners might have expected to feel in the South turned into familiarity and camaraderie.[11]

For those who made the full transition toward an adopted identity, it did not happen automatically but rather over many years of adjustment and adaptation. Generally, the longer native northerners lived in the South before the Civil War, the stronger the prospects of adopting a new sectional identity. Those who emigrated from the 1820s through the 1840s especially had an easier time because sectional animosity did not reach nearly the same levels as in the 1850s. The fact that over half of the individuals in this study first came to the South during those years indicates that northern emigrants generally had plenty of time to adapt and transform into adoptive southerners. The Mason-Dixon Line may have reigned as inviolate in the popular imagination, but in reality Americans could transform their identity at will if they made the effort and if circumstances permitted.

In fact, native northerners who settled in southern territories often found an easy path toward an adopted identity. Prior to statehood, all settlers in a territory had the same status because few of them actually came from the area. Northerners and southerners mingled together in both the Northwest and the Southwest, creating a melting pot where talent and ambition overshadowed sectional background. And since all settlers in a given territory became the first citizens of that state when it reached statehood, they all felt the same attachment to both the state and one another. As Albert Pike, who settled in Arkansas territory only by chance, wrote in an article on the eve of Arkansas statehood in 1836, "We are a citizen of Arkansas for life. Our heart and our hand are with its people, and we commence a new editorial year, with the warm hope that our present connexion [sic] may not soon be dissolved."[12] Since nearly two-thirds of the emigrants in this study settled in the Southwest, frontier, or wilderness areas, their accomplishments could easily overshadow their origins in their adopted states and territories.

Texas especially offered a vivid demonstration of this phenomenon. New Yorker Gail Borden and a few of his siblings fought in the armies of Sam Houston during the Texas War for Independence, and their families took shelter on Galveston Island as refugees. Massachusetts-born Anson Jones, who eventually served as the last president of an independent Texas, joined as a volunteer surgeon after the Alamo, and eventually received a promotion to assistant surgeon general and medical purveyor of the Texas army. New Englander Ashbel Smith directed the medical screening board for the Texas army on behalf of the Texas Congress. Several others joined as regular soldiers simply out of a sense of adventure or commitment to Texas independence. Locked in a bitter and uneven struggle with Mexico, Texans deeply appreciated the assistance given by these native northerners. Sectional animosity found no place in the greater pursuit of Texas independence. And thanks to their participation in the conflict, native northerners in the Texas armies sealed their connection to their adopted state through blood.[13] The fact that such veterans as Anson Jones, Ashbel Smith, and Elisha Pease all held high office in the Texas Republic and in the early years of Texas statehood only reinforced their standing as adopted Texans. As Pease wrote to his wife just before taking office as one of Texas's first governors in the Union, "the sun has browned my face and hands so much that I fear I should hardly pass for a white man in New England—." He went on to say that he had lived in Texas for so long he could not imagine feeling at home anywhere else.[14]

Whether in territories or established states, adoptive southerners expressed their transition in various ways. One method involved acceptance of local customs and other symbolic rites of passage to demonstrate adaptation. In just one example, northern emigrants sometimes committed themselves to a southern lifestyle by upholding their honor through dueling. Charles Dahlgren participated in several duels and other fights in Natchez after moving from Philadelphia. Dahlgren carried the scars from these duels, including knife wounds in his hands and skull and a bullet wound in his chest, for the rest of his life as a mark of his connection to his adopted home. Over in Missouri, Abiel Leonard, a native New Englander, understood that his new community consisted mostly of native southerners and so made a conscious effort to adapt to their customs, even fighting a duel to preserve his honor. Albert Pike fought a duel as late as 1848 for the same purpose. After Pike wrote an article in a local newspaper expressing his disapproval of the conduct of an Arkansas regiment in the Mexican War, the lieutenant colonel of that regiment, John Roane, took offense and challenged Pike to a duel. Pike accepted and met Roane at the appointed time, though neither participant was harmed. Nevertheless, after over a decade in his adopted state, Pike understood the importance of the southern code of honor and showed no hesitation in defending it when necessary. Although northern emigrants did not grow up with such customs, that did not preclude them from adopting those customs as their own.[15]

Of course, adoptive southerners did not need to engage in violent activities to demonstrate their adaptation. Simply residing in an adopted community for an extended period reflected the changes they experienced since leaving the North. Henry McClellan of Pennsylvania needed very little time to feel acclimated to his adopted home in Virginia. After only two years of teaching in a local school, McClellan reported back to his alma mater in Pennsylvania, "I am in Virginia . . . where I have learned to eat bacon and greens, corn-field peas, shoat, and many other delicacies you fellows who have never been south of Mason and Dixon's line don't know anything about. . . . I am comfortably situated in every respect, and only hope that all my classmates have had as pleasant times as I have had."[16] Without any overt declarations, McClellan revealed how much had changed since his emigration to the South. His adopted home felt closer to him than his native one, which in turn pushed him toward a southern identity. Joseph Ingraham, who spent much of his life touring the South before his death in 1860, likely said it best when he described a Mississippi planter originally from New Jersey, "a state which has contributed many valuable citizens to Mississippi. But he had been too long in the south to preserve his identity as a Jersey man."[17]

In addition, since they now considered themselves a part of the South, adoptive southerners wanted to contribute to the development of their adopted section. Rather than scold the South for not operating like the North, they wanted to build the South into a self-sufficient unit capable of withstanding northern encroachments. Author and journalist William Tappan Thompson, a native Ohioan, expressed such frustration in regards to the South's lack of literary circles. Directing his ire not only at his adopted state of Georgia but at the whole South, Thompson accused his fellow southerners of a humiliating dependence on the North for mere survival. As he wrote in one of his pamphlets, "We have been accustomed so long to receive our dry-goods and groceries from the 'BIG NORTH' that it seems but right that we should receive our literature—our mental aliment—from the same source. We receive our axes, and hoes, and ploughs, for the cultivation of our soil, from the North, and we must receive our books magazines, and papers, for the cultivation of our intellects, from the same market."[18] Though his critiques may have sounded harsh, Thompson actually loved his adopted region and wanted to see it prosper in the face of perceived threats from the North. Many native southerners, such as James De Bow in his publication *De Bow's Review*, gave similar critiques for the same purpose. Only states of birth separated the two.[19]

Similarly, throughout his long career as a professor in southern colleges, Frederick Barnard constantly emphasized the need to train native southern teachers to properly educate southern youth. While at the University of Mississippi, he deplored the fact that parents sent their children out of the state for higher education. Barnard asked in one of his pamphlets how Mississippi's population tolerated the trend, when the state's interests depended on home-grown education. "Few Southern parents can be found, who are not ready to admit the truth of all this," he wrote, "And yet a great many Southern parents are found, who still send their children away, not merely to other Southern States, but to New Jersey, to New York, and to New England. . . . Is there any describable benefit which these parents expect to secure, by a measure so in conflict with public sentiment all about them?"[20] Incredibly, Barnard seemed either not to notice or to care that he himself grew up in New England and attended Yale. Instead of highlighting his experiences in that school system, he adopted the tone of a native Mississippian worried about corrupting southern youth in northern school halls.

The years Barnard spent in his adopted region pushed him to identify with its shortcomings, as well as its benefits. Barnard did not wish to recreate the South in a northern image; he only wanted to create a better South with its existing institutions and culture intact. An 1857 public address he gave on the subject not only revealed his passion for education, but also his identification with the South. Asking whether Mississippians should send their children to schools outside the state, or accept teachers who might disagree with the state's values, Barnard declared, "it seems to me that there can be little doubt as to what should be the decision. But you will say, let us do neither. That, unquestionably, would be best of all; but what is the alternative? *Either Mississippi must have no teachers, or we must prepare teachers for ourselves.*"[21]

The last sentence in Barnard's pamphlet indicated a much more fundamental way for adoptive southerners to express their altered identities. Had they still felt like outsiders, these northern-born men and women would have referred to the South with a tone of distance, curiosity, awe, and/or contempt. Such references might have included phrases like "these people," "this State," "this country," "they," "Southern ladies," "Southerners," and perhaps to themselves as "northern," "Yankee," "stranger," etc. As their time in their adopted states lengthened, however, such phrasing often gave way to more familiarity, connection, and belonging. Adoptive southerners used such words as "our," "we," and "us" in connection to the South, while referring to the North as the alien "them." The switch happened without any sense of irony or shame, since they now considered themselves a part of the South.

The language of transitioned identity pervaded the writings of adoptive southerners across the South. Barnard himself declared in an 1856 Thanksgiving speech that, while he still considered himself a solid member of the Union, he did so now as a southerner. He constantly referred to Mississippi using such phrases as "our own fellow citizens," "our own people," "We love it," etc. A fellow Massachusetts native, T. Butler King, expressed his own change when he addressed a crowd in 1850 and described himself "as a Georgian and a southern citizen." Caroline Gilman told one of her friends in 1832, "—the South is all to me now and if I can benefit the children here it is all I will ask." Henry Watson was even more direct when he declared in 1848, "I am now a Southerner." The use of such language demonstrates the importance of choice in developing sectional identities. The journey they had undertaken, and the choices they had made, enabled northern emigrants to reconsider their own loyalties and attachments. Having established careers, families, and homes in the region, as well as absorbing southern cultural values, they believed they had the same right to call themselves southerners as anyone born in the region.[22]

More commonly, adoptive southerners declared their identification with the South through their ties to their adopted states. As many other Americans of the time acknowledged, states counted as much as, if not more than, the Union in regard to loyalty and identity. Between their native states and adopted states, the latter had much more significance than the former for these adoptive southerners. They still loved their families and wanted to stay in contact with them, but that did not mean a continued connection to their native states. Elisha Pease made such comments in describing his attachment to Texas. He wrote to his family that, while he missed them, he never considered moving back to his home state of Connecticut. "My feelings, interest, all are identified with Texas," he told them in 1836. Pease followed up that declaration early the next year by saying, "I feel that Texas is my home, and that here I shall spend the balance of my life." Almost fifteen years later, Pease reminded his wife during a trip to New England, "You must not become so attached to Poquonock, as to forget that Texas is our home, and the birth place of our children."[23]

Other adoptive southerners echoed Pease's love for an adopted state. Amanda Trulock wrote to her family on how "we Georgians" enjoyed the pleasures of life.[24] Ashbel Smith, in a speech delivered to the Phi Beta Kappa Society, told the audience, "Standing in my own state of Texas, surrounded by descendants of the pilgrims of Plymouth and of the settlers of Jamestown, I mused on what would be the effect of that warm and genial climate on the descendants in future generations of my fellow citizens then around me."[25] More simply, John H. B. Latrobe, originally from Pennsylvania, signed his letters, "John H. B. Latrobe of *Md*," highlighting his adopted state to forestall any confusion.[26]

The transition from their former sectional identity caused many of these individuals to speak out on behalf of their adopted states against any and all challenges. These declarations covered a range of topics, but the common theme remained a defense of the South they now considered their own. For instance, adopted Arkansan Albert Pike made several speeches in favor of a transcontinental railroad, but he insisted that the North should not monopolize such a railroad. In 1847, he even suggested the southern states pool their funds to finance a southern route to prevent northern domination.[27] Meanwhile, North Carolina representative Henry Shaw, a native of Rhode Island, launched his own passionate defense of his adopted state's interests by not only condemning Republican attacks on the South, but also other North Carolina representatives who voted against the Lecompton Bill for the Kansas Territory. In one of his speeches in Congress, Shaw laid out his attachment to North Carolina as such: "Mr. Chairman, I feel as anxious a desire as my colleague to see the State of North Carolina, in which every earthly interest I possess is centered, and which has honored me with a seat on this floor, prosperous and happy. I would go as far, according to my humble abilities, as any one of her sons, in all proper efforts to promote her prosperity and happiness . . ."[28] He knew he did not belong as a native son, but that did not stop him from defending the South as passionately as one. Shaw's previous ties to New England seem not to have entered his mind at all.

These types of declarations extended beyond the political realm, with defenses of an adopted state as an extension of personal honor. As Caroline Gilman recorded in her trip to Washington in 1836, "The secret is all in state feeling. I am sorry for this, sorry for the clanship which prevails, for it seems to me that at Washington the Union only, and its great interests, should fill our thoughts; but thus it is; and I am carried away by the stream, and a word against Carolina, is a personal offense to me!"[29] Despite her roots in Massachusetts, Gilman's reaction could have easily come from any native South Carolinian.

Along with these statements, adoptive southerners provided contrasts between the sections, usually assigning more positive attributes to the South in the process. Albert Pike provided a vivid example of this trend in a series of pamphlets he wrote in the 1850s highlighting southern interests in the lead-up to secession. Referring to the Missouri Compromise in relation to the Kansas/Nebraska Act, Pike argued that the boundary gave "You, in the North" at least six to eight new states, while "If the country which we had, had been continued to us, we could have had but *three* more States." Addressing northern leaders, Pike continued, "We are as humane as you, and as intelligent as you . . . Let all of us live in peace, and do our duty at home, in our own portion of the country, minding each our own business . . ." Each time he used "we," he referred to southerners; "you" referred to northerners. Though Pike may have once counted himself among the latter in his youth, he now identified fully with the former as an adult.[30] In fact, his prose made it appear as though he never had any previous attachments to the North at all. Such feelings of alienation were now directed toward his native section. This reversal caused many adoptive southerners to discount their pasts in their efforts to defend the present.

Some adoptive southerners even came to regard the South as superior to the North. John Quitman expressed his own sense of alienation upon returning to New York for a visit after a decade spent in Mississippi. Convinced that the North did not resemble anything he remembered from his youth, he remarked, "I am heartily tired of the North, and except parting from my relations, shall feel happy when I set my face homeward."[31] Even more bluntly, Amanda Trulock wrote to her family in early 1838, "'the only thing I have to regret is that you are not all here to participate in my enjoyments, but I trust and hope that . . . you shall come and spend at least one season with me and then you will see what superior advantages, we Southerns have over you Northerns in that cold and dreary region.'"[32] Trulock's family likely would have disagreed with her on the relative advantages between the sections, but for her there was no question. The South now reigned supreme in her own imagination.

Combined with their efforts to promote the advantages of the South, adoptive southerners often tried to subordinate, and eventually eliminate, their status as northerners. By the outbreak of secession, many of these former northerners looked back on their years outside the North as a time of growth into a rare but proud element of the southern narrative. Frederick Barnard reflected on his transition to a southern identity and how origin meant nothing to him. "'I am a yankee; that is—good heavens! what am I saying?—I am *not* a yankee, not I; don't know a wooden clock from a wooden nutmeg—I am a Southron now . . . I *was* a yankee—born—and deemed it no sin to have been so. . . .'"[33] To his chagrin, Barnard had to repeat those thoughts on the eve of secession, when members of the University of Mississippi accused him of harboring secret abolitionist views because of his roots in New England. Barnard told his accusers, "I was born at the North. That I cannot help. I was not consulted in the matter."[34] For Barnard, having roots in the North represented a mere inconvenience, with no effect on what he actually felt about his place in the Union. He may not have grown up with a southern identity, but he claimed it as his own.

Native New Englanders Theodore Clapp and Caroline Gilman reflected on their own transitions in a similar manner. Gilman wrote to one of her friends in the midst of the Nullification Crisis in 1832, "I used to feel a strong desire to stay in Massachusetts and that made me uneasy . . . but now Charleston is my dear home, the home of my choice . . . It took ten years for me to get weaned [from Massachusetts]."[35] Clapp went into much more detail while recalling his four decades in the South. "I went there fresh from the Theological Seminary at Andover, Massachusetts, a firm believer in the superiority of the north, in every respect, over all the rest of the Union. . . . I was sorry that the prejudices of education and northern society had led me, even in thought, to undervalue and disparage a large class of fellow-citizens entitled to my sincerest respect and admiration."[36] Clapp, like so many others, discovered that his rearing in the North did not prepare him for how his life would eventually unfold. Northern upbringing did not bear down on them like an iron weight, or as a vehicle for social change, but rather provided guidelines to be modified if needed. In many cases, northern emigrants modified those guidelines out of all proportion as they took on the persona of adoptive southerners. As Joseph Ingraham told his readers, "One important fact ought not to be overlooked, which, that ninety-nine out of every hundred of the governesses, tutors, professional men, and others, who flock to the South, 'ten thousand a year,' for the improvement of their fortunes, remain . . . and identify themselves fully with the Southern Institution."[37]

Still, the transition toward an adopted identity did not always reach full fruition. In fact, some northern emigrants did not make the transition at all. In those cases, they really did function as, biblically speaking, "strangers in a strange land." Sectional identity, while fluid, still remained a choice. If a northerner did not wish to become a southerner, then his or her sectional identity remained unchanged, regardless of his or her experiences.

Understandably, nearly all native northerners who emigrated to the South felt like outsiders when they first arrived and began to settle into their new communities. For example, Ohioan Henry Handerson described his first trip through the Louisiana bayous as one of disorientation and fear. "All the sights and sounds around me were so different from those to which I had been accustomed that a feeling of isolation and sadness crept over me, and the prospect of spending a day or two in this mournful place seemed almost intolerable."[38] Caroline Seabury used similar descriptions in a lengthy diary entry in October 1854 regarding her travels to Mississippi to work as a tutor. She kept referring to herself as a "Yankee" and "stranger." The end of the entry summarized her impressions: "O, the loneliness of that great half furnished place, it overpowered us both. Miss S. who had just left school & for the first time tried a life among strangers—far from home—I who had no home felt—both of us utterly heartsick—& took the usual woman's way of making things better—sat down & cried . . ."[39] Sally Baxter Hampton revealed her own homesickness and longing for the North to her sister five months after her marriage into the Hampton family of South Carolina. "Thank Heaven Sarah that . . . you will be spared a separation from home & friends & above all from your Mother . . . There isn't a stick or a stone of New York that I don't love, not a person however indifferent that I don't think of kindly."[40] The South may have offered greater opportunity but that did not mean the region felt like home immediately. Northerners still had much to overcome to feel included in their adopted communities. Henry Watson likely said it best when he wrote to his uncle, "I am now at a distance, in a land of strangers; Though many about me salute me with the endearing affiliation of friend, my northern habits & feelings do not permit me to acknowledge their claims upon so short an acquaintance."[41]

Echoing these sentiments, several northern emigrants came to the South determined to stay for as short a time as possible without altering their sectional identities. That decision had crucial ramifications because it often took several years or more to adapt to the new surroundings. These emigrants instead carried out their original plans to relocate to the Northwest once they completed their work in the South. As a result, they had no need to develop any kinds of permanent attachments to the region. In fact, they often looked down on the people around them as alien from their own upbringing. For example, Julius Reed, a Yale graduate from Connecticut who spent several years tutoring on a plantation in Mississippi before moving to Illinois in the early 1830s, personified this particular trend. He described southerners as lazy, selfish, frivolous, and beneath hard-working New Englanders like himself. Living in Mississippi did absolutely nothing to change his mind. As he wrote to a friend, "You think the south better than the north—The more I see of the south the more I love the home of my childhood . . ."[42] Reed's initial assumptions about southern society held firm even after witnessing it first-hand.

New Yorker William Pierce also felt alienated from southerners even after four years in the South. Pierce opened a medical practice in Mississippi in 1852 but eventually resettled in southern Illinois in 1856. He actually thought about moving out of Mississippi only a year after arriving, but he held back because many of his patients had not settled their bills. Once he closed those accounts, Pierce felt he had nothing left to keep him there. Incredibly, he even broke off an engagement with a Mississippi woman he loved because she refused to go with him to Illinois.[43] Pierce had no qualms about his decision because he still saw himself as a northerner temporarily domiciled in the South. He made his intentions clear in one of his final letters before leaving Mississippi: "When others manifest so complete an aversion to that kind of society—that kind of life which has made of me whatever I am either mentable or consumable can it be expected to have any influence upon me other than to deepen and intensify my affection for the dear old land of my birth?"[44]

Even though Reed and Pierce stand out because of their limited time away from the North, others who stayed in the South for longer periods still appeared to favor their native section over their adopted one. Some, like Thomas Clemson and William Bostwick, actually moved out several decades after establishing themselves in their adopted states.[45] Others, even though they stayed, still refused to think of themselves as genuine southerners. Joseph Ingraham, who spent over thirty years in the Southwest and wrote books defending southern institutions, still regarded his observations as "the experiences of a stranger from the North."[46] Ezekiel Birdseye spent over two decades in eastern Tennessee, yet he always gave his permanent address as his old home back in Connecticut.[47] Phoebe Farmer and her husband settled in Florida yet still thought of themselves as a northern family living in a southern state.[48] In addition, according to his biographer, Daniel Pratt never really considered himself a southerner, despite his many contributions to Alabama, including founding a town called Prattville. The author cited as evidence that Pratt married a Connecticut woman, modeled his town on New England towns, worked mainly with northerners in the cotton gin business, and only acquired a plantation for business purposes.[49]

Some northern emigrants even used phrasing on several occasions that revealed their continued isolation from their surroundings. Tryphena Fox wrote to her mother several times explaining how she made breakfast for her husband "Yankee style,"(meaning in a hurry) describing a shrimp as "the *prawn* of the North, only smaller," and that fifty-five dollars for a cow was "An enormous price to New England ears . . . ."[50] On a trip to Cuba five years after moving to South Carolina, Sally Baxter Hampton remarked on the local cuisine, "I don't think my Yankee love of bread & molasses will survive this."[51] Caroline Seabury continued to refer to herself as a "Yankee teacher" two years after settling in Mississippi and considered Massachusetts her real home.[52] Henry Watson used the same reference to home despite the fact that he felt more comfortable in his surroundings than when he first arrived. As Watson told his mother, "Here have I been now for three years. . . . and yet I never for a moment have felt myself at home, I have always felt as if away from home in a measure a stranger in a strange land."[53] These statements reveal how much influence individual circumstances and lengths of time spent in the South had on decisions concerning identity. Those who only saw the South as a place to temporarily occupy out of necessity before moving on had a harder time identifying with the region.[54]

Nevertheless, some evidence indicates that, without the intervention of war, over time at least some of these recent emigrants had the chance to transition toward a southern identity. Tryphena Holder Fox, though initially uncomfortable in the Southwest, married a Louisiana physician and planter after three years as a tutor to increase her financial security. Fox then wrote to her mother that she was learning how to act like a good southern wife. She did not actually consider herself a full southerner yet, but a few more years as a southern spouse had the potential to push her in that direction. Caroline Seabury's connection came in the form of a grave for her sister, who died from consumption. As she recorded in her diary, "The only spot on earth I can call my own, that in which lies her precious body—is given me—by those almost strangers—by this deed." Like Fox, Seabury did not consider herself a southerner, but the presence of part of her family, and the friendliness of her community, gave her reasons to at least consider a change. Even Henry Watson, who did not feel at home after three years, declared himself a southerner over a decade later. Regardless of their ultimate decision, the option still remained for any northern emigrant to adopt a new sectional identity. The flexibility of antebellum sectional identity did not guarantee a change but still provided the possibility for those who wished to take advantage of it.[55]

When native northerners did utilize the possibility of a shift in sectional identity, they did so by choice rather than necessity or compulsion. Northern-born soldiers, especially those who moved constantly from one base to another, did not have the chance to develop lasting ties to the region. Yet after they resigned and moved to their eventual adopted states, they still managed to formulate a southern identity if they so chose. For example, William Chase spent all but four years of his army service stationed at forts along the Gulf Coast, even gaining a reputation as the largest slave renter in the area. By the time he retired, Pensacola had replaced his native state as the place where he belonged. Similarly, Charles Dimmock spent the majority of his army career in Virginia and felt it natural to remain after he resigned.[56] Without such connections, northern soldiers gave the matter little thought. Josiah Gorgas, despite his marriage to the daughter of an Alabama governor, still felt uncomfortable in the South. He actually spent most of his tour of duty in the 1850s in Maine and Pennsylvania, at his own request.[57]

Adoptive southerners who leaned one way or the other sometimes gave more nuanced or even contradictory hints about what they thought about themselves. For example, Thomas Clemson appeared to have everything he wanted after marrying into the Calhoun family, but after almost ten years in South Carolina he began to have second thoughts. Saddled by debt and failed business ventures, and increasingly upset with his in-laws, Clemson considered abandoning the South altogether. As he wrote to his father-in-law in 1849, "If there ever was a person that should be sick of a country I am the person that should be sick of the south, and if it pleases the Almighty to grant me a safe deliverance I promise never again to place my foot on its soil." As it turned out, Clemson did move out of South Carolina, but then, after a year in New York, moved his family to Maryland, where they remained until the Civil War. He claimed he had outgrown the South, yet something still drew him there, if only to a different part of the region. Rather than settle into a permanent transition, his sectional identity remained in a state of flux based on his perceived needs at the time.[58]

Others felt the same way, especially when it came to what actually counted as their home. Tryphena Blanche Holder Fox wrote to her mother shortly after her wedding to a Mississippi planter asking whether she was upset or happy "that your daughter has found a protector, who will shield her with his love and a haven which promises fair to be a 'home' when she may rest secure from the hardships and trials of the world and its selfishness."[59] The fact that Fox put "home" in quotation marks indicated that she was not sure what her residence in Mississippi meant. She still missed her family back in Massachusetts, but at the same time she now had a new home that offered the same love and protection. Her sectional identity remained fluid until she figured out which "home" truly felt like home.

Every northern emigrant in the South faced the same situation. William Pierce, who vowed to remain in the South only temporarily, admitted that circumstances could change. After two years in the South, while he had no plans to do so, he knew that he might still marry a southern woman, which would in turn keep him in his adopted state. Reflecting on his uncertainty, he wrote to his sister, "Unquestioned, if it is *decreed* that I make my future residence in the south I shall do so. Otherwise, I may not."[60] Lucadia Pease, a Connecticut native who moved with her northern-born husband to Texas in the 1850s, ended up not making a full transition to a southern identity, but she did not know for certain that such a transition would not take place eventually. On her way to Texas, Lucadia admitted to her sister that, while scared to leave Connecticut, she was open to the idea of a new life in the Southwest, "for I cannot yet call but one place home . . ."[61] Like all emigrants of the time, northerners who ventured south embarked on a new beginning, with no certainties of how their destinies would unfold. They knew that the concept of "home" might change. In their situation, that change included a possible, but not guaranteed, shift in sectional identity.

Uncertainties remained a factor both for newly relocated northern-born residents and for those who had resided for decades in the southern states. Jedediah Hotchkiss seemed to waver when describing his adopted state of Virginia to his family two years after moving there. On the one hand, he remarked how "the people here" were awakening to the opportunities brought by railroads for the benefit of the whole country, and how "they" needed good transportation for markets. In the same paragraph, however, he mentioned how "we" had a dry season in the early summer. The phrasing Hotchkiss utilized showed that he did not consider himself either as a total outsider or total insider, almost unsure of where exactly he stood. Eventually, he leaned more toward Virginia, but that was not guaranteed at the time.[62] Even those with a longer residency in the South had their moments of uncertainty. Frederick Barnard had such an episode when members of the University of Mississippi accused him of disloyalty on the slavery question and even of acting as a Yankee spy. In his defense, Barnard brought up his contributions to southern education and his many southern friends who could vouch for him. What he did not do, however, was emphatically call himself a southerner or a Mississippian. The very accusation seems to have shaken him, especially since not even decades of living in the South could dispel such suspicions among some of his native southern colleagues.[63]

Amanda Trulock made perhaps the most poignant statement about such uncertainties among adoptive southerners. Originally from Connecticut, she ended up living in Georgia and Arkansas after marrying into the Trulock family. She quickly adapted to her role as a plantation wife, but still wrote to her family saying she would likely move back to New England as soon as her husband paid off his debts. That did not happen, however, because her husband died in 1849, and she insisted on remaining in Arkansas to take care of the plantation.[64] Her family begged her to reconsider, but Trulock refused to back down. She wrote to her father explaining why: "It would be impossible for me to write you, so that you could have any idea of my feelings, as you know nothing about a Plantation, and slaves, even if you were to come here and stay for years, it would be impossible for you to have the same feeling I have or the same ties that I have to bind me here; it may seem strange to you, but this is my home, and it is to my interest to remain here for the present at least." Trulock had not expected to become a permanent resident of the South, but circumstances had changed. The plantation in Arkansas now represented her home, and she would not abandon it, not even for the family she loved back in New England. Nevertheless, she added the caveat "for the present at least" to indicate that the situation might shift yet again.[65]

One major factor causing such uncertainty, as Trulock indicated, involved continued contact with families and friends in the North. Correspondence with northern families remained prevalent among northern emigrants, especially during their early years in the South. To emigrants faced with an uncertain future and new surroundings, northern families represented a measure of familiarity. Even those who eventually embraced their status as adoptive southerners still liked to visit the North, or urged their relatives to visit them as a way to reach back to their roots. Unlike native southerners, these individuals needed to take into account ties to the North, because those relations did not disappear. Unless they cut themselves off completely from their northern families, a rare occurrence, adoptive southerners did not completely lose touch with their pasts.[66]

Some of these individuals used such correspondence as a way to cope with homesickness. William Pierce once wrote to his sister complaining that no one had written to him from New York for five or six weeks, making him feel isolated.[67] Upon leaving for Texas, Lucadia Pease lamented to her sister, "—for truly life would seem a desert to me were I not to hear often from home—."[68] Tryphena Fox, during the first year of her marriage, wrote to her mother, "The day seems rather long and it would make me so happy to step in and see you & talk & tell you all about my Southern life & hear about your affairs since I left you." Ashbel Smith told his cousin he wanted to hear all about her recent marriage and to receive updates on everyone back in New England. He even wanted to hear about relatives he had never seen before. Such exchanges benefited both sides: families got to hear about southern life, and emigrants got to stay informed on family developments.[69]

Nevertheless, the longer they stayed away from the North, the less emigrants seemed to recognize it. Juliet Coleman, a native New Englander who married a widower and moved to Alabama, reflected this trend. Like many other northern emigrants, Coleman referred to "Yankees" when trying to explain the differences between northern and southern life, claiming "Yankees" who had not visited the South before never fully understood its customs. Toward the end of her life, she wanted desperately to visit her family but knew where her destiny lay because of her years spent in the South. As she wrote to her sister, "I am glad to hear of the improvements in Old Suffield but I know nothing of it. It is a 'dream that is past' with me & Ala is my home for life. I never expect to move again."[70] Similarly, in 1858, John S. Ryan wrote nostalgically to his friend A. F. Girard from South Carolina about his past in New York and how he missed his friends there. He congratulated Girard on his daughter's upcoming wedding and told him to tell any friends from Hyde Park to call on him if they ever came to the South. Ryan had no intention of moving back North, but he wanted to extend a hand to those from his past.[71]

Northern emigrants, as Coleman indicated, partly distanced themselves from their native region because they believed the North they had known as children had changed beyond recognition. Those who emigrated in the 1820s did so at a time when the slavery question appeared settled with the Missouri Compromise. By the 1830s, abolitionist societies had formed and started to make their voices heard. By the 1850s, disputes over territories, the collapse of the Second Party System, and the thrusting of the slavery issue into national debate, highlighted by the rise of the Republican Party, widened the gap between North and South. Faced with these divisions between native and adopted sections, adoptive southerners increasingly leaned more toward the latter. Having acclimated themselves to southern society and culture, they hated to hear criticism of either from those who had never traveled beyond the North. Tryphena Fox, commenting on the 1856 election, lamented that Fremont and the "fanatics" that made up his party might win the election. She appreciated that her mother sent her a newspaper with a more moderate stance, "for it is like a gleam of sunshine from my native land, now so wrapped in the *blackness* of Abolitionism."[72] Connecticut native Stephen Olin considered it a personal affront when his friends asked how he could possibly support slavery while working as a teacher in the Deep South. "I am much reconciled to Southern life," he replied. "The little invectives in which my Northern friends sometimes indulge wound me almost as if I had been born in Carolina."[73]

One clear test case of the importance of choice and adaptation in sectional identity involved Elisha Pease and his wife, Lucadia. Both came from Connecticut, grew up there, and received an education in New England. Both emigrated to their adopted state of Texas while in their twenties, and both received the same type of warm welcome in that state. Yet Elisha came to identify with his adopted state, while Lucadia consistently felt herself an outsider with continued attachment to New England.

Their different responses arose from their own views of Texas, along with the timing and conditions of their arrival. Elisha first arrived in 1835, eager to start a new life away from the failures he endured back in Connecticut. Viewing Texas as his new home and the place for a fresh start, he actively established himself as an adopted Texan. That decision led to his participation in Texas's War for Independence, election as governor, and residence of more than twenty-five years in the state before the Civil War. In contrast, his wife Lucadia came to Texas for a very different reason. Elisha courted her on one of his trips back to New England, and after their marriage, she went with him to Texas in 1851. Unlike her husband, Lucadia had no compelling reason for relocating other than following her husband back to his home. As a result, she never felt the same kind of connection to her adopted state as Elisha did. Over the first few years of her marriage, she wrote constantly to her family and friends revealing her continued identity as a New Englander living in a southern state. She described Texas as a foreign place and did not feel the need to adapt beyond learning the local customs. As she told her sister after three years in Texas, "I think although I am very partial to my native state, that in 'culture, intelligence hospitality &c' equal at least to northerners—I wish you would follow Watts example and see for yourself, and not depend upon other persons opinions."[74] While her husband made the full transition to a southern identity, Lucadia did not.[75]

The different paths experienced by the Peases highlight the fundamental flexibility and fluidity of sectional identity in the antebellum era. Native northerners who ventured south had no desire to recreate the region on a New England model. Instead, they viewed the lands and people around them as steps toward greater opportunities and a better life for themselves. In the process, they consciously adapted themselves to their new surroundings by making new homes, families, careers, even worldviews. Over time, many of these northerners came to identify with their adopted section, professing themselves as southerners in everything but birth. They did not exist as northerners living in the South, but rather as individuals able to alter their sectional identity if they so chose.

3

Adoptive Southerners React to Slavery

Along with new families, new homes, new careers, and new shifts in their identity, northern emigrants also confronted the greatest difference between their native and adopted sections: slavery. More than any other institution, slavery lay at the heart of sectional differences and animosity. From the Second Continental Congress eliminating a passage against slavery in the final draft of the Declaration of Independence to the three-fifths clause in the Constitution to the numerous compromises over the future of the institution in the nineteenth century, slavery represented one of the greatest challenges to forging a common bond among all Americans. Whether actively opposed, reluctantly tolerated, or enthusiastically promoted, slavery brought the entire Union to the brink of collapse on more than one occasion. Whereas all the North American colonies under Great Britain participated in African slavery in some way, anti-slavery laws passed in New England and the Mid-Atlantic in the early decades of the republic gradually forced the institution farther and farther south, forming a symbolic divide between the free labor North and the slave labor South.

Because of that divide, not many white northerners found common ground on the issue with white southerners, and vice versa. In fact, by the eve of the secession crisis, most white northerners rarely witnessed slavery themselves, relying either on second-hand reports or stereotypes from newspapers, political speeches, or novels. As a result, white northerners and southerners often talked past each other while discussing the future of slavery. Abolitionists, using testimony from escaped slaves as well as biblical arguments, called slavery a sin against God that needed to disappear as quickly as possible. Other anti-slavery white northerners, in a less humanitarian mode, called for preventing the expansion of slavery into the territories to secure white northern settlement and the gradual, voluntary elimination of slavery where it already existed. Conversely, pro-slavery white southerners argued that slavery brought civilization to otherwise "barbarous" Africans, promoted equality among all white Americans, and had biblical foundations. Southern politicians also claimed that white northern opposition to the expansion of slavery represented a direct threat to southern interests and survival. By the 1850s, white northerners and southerners thus seemed unable to agree on the proper future of the institution.[1]

Into this environment stepped adoptive southerners, a potential wildcard in the debates over slavery. With few exceptions, most of these men and women grew up in areas that had either eliminated slavery or never allowed it. They consequently absorbed the values of the developing free-labor ideology that pervaded the antebellum North, especially the idea of keeping the fruits of one's own labor.[2] They also attended northern churches, which usually either took a neutral stance on slavery or actively opposed it. Much like the rest of the northern population in the nineteenth century, few if any northern emigrants witnessed slavery themselves or met ex-slaves in their formative years. Only a small minority ever came to the South with plans to become slave-owners or run plantations. Slavery thus remained either an unimportant or unsavory element in the minds of native northerners as they embarked for the South.

Based on their backgrounds and experience, these emigrants should have either ignored slavery or actively opposed it, especially those who subscribed to abolitionism. Edwin Upson, a native of Connecticut, was forced to leave Mobile in 1856 because he sold abolitionist literature. Ezekiel Birdseye, another Connecticut-born abolitionist, actively wrote and distributed abolitionist literature while living in East Tennessee.[3] Historian Elizabeth Pryor insists that most native northerners in the South "felt a general abhorrence of the 'peculiar institution' and believed it brought untold horrors upon both master and slave."[4] Going even further, author Dennis Rousey claims that northern emigrants and foreign immigrants to the South did not invest in slavery as much as native southerners, were generally less prosperous, did not hold slaves as long even when they did have them, and in general were more likely to harbor antislavery views.[5]

According to this interpretation, even adoptive southerners who participated in slavery only did so reluctantly or for practical reasons, without actually adopting pro-slavery views. For example, several biographers of Samuel and Caroline Gilman, natives of Massachusetts who lived in South Carolina, argue that the couple owned slaves as domestic servants but only did so in order to give them an education in anticipation of freedom. They remained silent in deference to their neighbors but still believed slavery was wrong and immoral.[6] Biographers of Stephen Duncan and Abiel Leonard, a Pennsylvania-born Mississippi slave-owner and a Vermont-born Missouri slave-owner respectively, point out that they treated slavery purely as a practical matter without any deep attachment to it. Duncan served as an active member of the American Colonization Society, and Leonard represented slaves in freedom suits in Missouri courts.[7] Summing up their position, one of Duncan's biographers writes "Duncan's affinity for plantation slavery was not so much as a way of life but as a way of making a living," and Leonard's biographer describes Leonard "not as a crusader for or against slavery, but as a working lawyer representing a client."[8]

While such arguments certainly have merit, they only offer a partial revelation of northern emigrant reactions to slavery. Much as adoptive southerners experienced changes to their identity while living in the South, their opinions about slavery changed as well. Even if they opposed slavery when they first came to the South, oftentimes they emerged as pro-slavery advocates.[9] As new residents of the South eager to improve their own lives and obtain acceptance from their neighbors, the majority of adoptive southerners modified their views to conform to their adopted homes. Few events in the antebellum period had the potential for a greater transformational effect on native northerners as coming face to face with the institution of slavery. Defying the predictions of free labor northern intellectuals, the South had much more of an influence on its adopted residents than the other way around.

Studying adoptive southerners' attitudes toward slavery also addresses the question of southern distinctiveness in nineteenth-century American society. Historians have argued extensively over whether the North and South had greater similarities or differences between them. One of the more extensive debates on this issue has occurred between James Oakes and Eugene Genovese. Genovese argues that master/slave relations always depended on paternalism and a specific southern worldview. In this interpretation, the South was ruled by a monolithic aristocracy of slave-owners who created a paternalist society antithetical to freedom. In contrast, Ira Berlin challenges

Genovese by pointing out the differences of slave systems in different regions of the country. He especially stresses the differences between "societies with slaves" and "slave societies" and how regions could switch between the two.[10] James Oakes also challenges Genovese by showing how slave-owners were in fact not monolithic but, rather, a diverse group willing to abandon paternalism to seek acceptance of liberal democracy and capitalism. Whereas Genovese mainly concentrates on the worldview of large slave-owners, Oakes points out that most slave-owners only owned a few slaves and occupied a middle-class status. As Oakes writes, "But the goal of many southern doctors and lawyers was to own a plantation worked by slaves, and in the sickly and litigious atmosphere of the antebellum South that goal was not unreasonable."[11] As a result, southern society had a lot of similarities with northern society because non-slaveholders could move into and out of the slave-owning class, much like free labor in the North. Plus, slave-owning professionals were influential in southern society as newspaper owners and politicians, who represented the embodiment of the traditional American dream of bettering oneself through hard work and luck.[12]

Adoptive southerners who owned slaves largely conformed to the arguments of Oakes and Berlin, rather than Genovese. Thanks to the fluidity of the slave-owning ranks, northern emigrants had little trouble acquiring slaves when the opportunity arose. Some inherited slaves from their wives, while others, after building up successful careers, bought slaves as a status symbol. Adoptive southerners thus cemented their position as full members of their communities by subscribing to the white southern version of the American dream. Because anyone could join the ranks of slave-owners, northern emigrants simply transformed their original ambitions of wealth and prestige to include slaves and plantations, along with successful businesses and practices. These men and women did not attempt to keep apart from southern society because of their background but, rather, embraced it in any way they could.

Even before moving to the South, northern emigrants often lived in conditions that eased the path toward eventual acceptance of, or at least indifference to, slavery. Although all northern states had passed emancipation laws by the nineteenth century, slavery did not immediately disappear. In fact, most of the original colonies passed gradual emancipation bills designed to slowly phase out slavery rather than eliminate it immediately. The details of the laws varied, but they each authorized freedom for the children of slaves after reaching a certain age, and freedom for all other slaves far in the future, if at all. While states like Massachusetts and New Hampshire eliminated slavery within their borders relatively quickly, others, especially New York and New Jersey, required decades to complete the process. The census of 1860 famously listed eighteen elderly slaves still living in New Jersey at the start of the Civil War precisely because the state's gradual emancipation laws did not originally stipulate freedom for slaves born before the law took effect. Even in states that made a concerted effort to eliminate slavery quickly, the delays and vague wording in the laws often allowed slave-owners to simply sell their slaves further south or reclassify slaves as "indentured servants."[13]

As a result, the first and second generations of white northerners in the Union, including future emigrants to the South, occasionally lived in areas that still had slaves within their borders. For example, Stephen Duncan grew up in Carlisle, Pennsylvania, in the 1790s, when slavery and black "indentured servitude" still existed. John Quitman, a future governor of Mississippi, was born and raised in Rhinebeck in southern New York, which also continued to have slavery during his childhood.[14] Although few native northerners witnessed slavery first-hand after the early decades of the nineteenth century, the institution was by no means a part of the distant past.

More importantly, the vast majority of antebellum white northerners expressed as much, if not more, racism as white southerners. Antislavery did not mean pro-black; if anything, white northerners wanted to eliminate slavery to prevent an increase in the black population in the Union, preserve white supremacy, and prevent a possible future race war. In fact, most northern states passed laws limiting the rights of free blacks within their borders. Rhode Island and Indiana prohibited interracial marriage, Ohio and Connecticut forbade black suffrage, Vermont and New Hampshire kept blacks out of militias, and Indiana did not allow black jurors.[15] The abolitionist movement, long a staple of white southern fears, did not appear until 1831 and only represented a tiny minority of the white northern population. Until the Civil War, white northerners were much more likely to attack abolitionists than support them, as happened to Elijah Lovejoy in Illinois when a white mob burned down his house to stop the printing of his abolitionist newspaper. Even individuals who promoted antislavery often had white supremacist goals in mind. Pennsylvania congressman David Wilmot, who called for preventing the spread of slavery into any new territory acquired from Mexico in 1846, partly justified his stance as a way to make the territories the exclusive province of white men, without any influence from either slaves or free blacks.[16]

Among emigrants conditioned by white northern society to regard blacks as at best inferiors and at worst savages, exposure to slavery actually solidified that image. Tryphena Blanche Holder Fox, a Massachusetts-born tutor who became a Mississippi plantation mistress, wrote to her mother constantly about the inferiority of both slaves and free blacks in her midst. Contrasting the work ethic of northern whites to that of blacks, Fox remarked in one letter, "Negroes are so slow that they put me out of patience, not doing in all day what a good white man would do in an hour." A week later she told her mother that free blacks, and Creoles especially, were largely ignorant, devoid of principle, and earned meager livings. Incredibly, in the same letter, she admitted that some Creoles had great wealth but still dismissed these exceptions by saying, "On the whole I consider them as a class only one grade higher than the negroes and that owing to the little European blood in them."[17]

Many other adoptive southerners, both supporters and opponents of slavery, expressed similar thoughts. Sally Baxter Hampton, who married into the prominent Hampton family of South Carolina, commented that her husband, looking for a suitable summer house, wanted one with enough room for "'man and beast' under which latter denomination I include *servants*."[18] Abiel Leonard, a Vermont-born justice on the Missouri Supreme Court, insisted that blacks had no civil rights whites needed to respect. Commenting on the inadmissibility of slave testimony against whites, Leonard argued that "the degraded condition of this class of persons, and the interest they may have to fabricate falsehoods and conceal the truth" prevented blacks from ever giving proper testimony.[19] Even Caroline Seabury and Calvin Robinson, two New Englanders who abhorred slavery in their adopted states, still looked upon blacks with contempt. Seabury remarked that they looked like "a happy, careless thoughtless race," while Robinson insisted ignorant slaves would not work unless forced to do so under white supervision.[20] Despite the fears by many white southerners about stereotypical northerners coming south to agitate slaves, those who actually moved to the South rarely brought abolitionist principles with them. If anything, northern emigrants usually arrived with their minds firmly set against any hint of racial equality, a reality that helped close the gap between native southerners and adoptive southerners on the slavery issue.

With such views already in place, native northerners had the possibility of adopting a pro-slavery stance under the right circumstances. Rarely did such a transition happen within the North, since the overwhelming majority of white northerners did not have any contact with slavery, did not require slaves to earn their living, and focused their racial animosities largely on free blacks. But when northern emigrants arrived in the South and observed slavery personally, everything changed. Slavery all of a sudden became real, a part of life, even a necessity for the economic, social, and cultural survival of their adopted homes. As these individuals became more and more a part of the antebellum South, so did their views on slavery conform to the majority opinion in that section. Joseph Ingraham, a native northerner who toured extensively across the antebellum South, observed this transformation repeatedly in his travels. As he wrote poetically in one of his pieces explaining the acclimation, "A monster of such horrid mien; That to be hated heeds but to be seen; But seen too oft, familiar with her face; They soon endure—and in the end embrace."[21]

Adoptive southerners largely conformed to Ingraham's observations. Regardless of their previous views of slavery, whether positive or negative, native northerners who witnessed slavery firsthand quickly realized the South's entire economic, social, and cultural well-being depended on slave labor for its survival. In just one example, a native Pennsylvanian who originally detested slavery changed his mind when he arrived in Texas because he believed admitting more slaves into the territory would boost economic production.[22] Caroline Seabury, a Massachusetts native who moved to Mississippi to work as a tutor in 1854, recorded a conversation she had with a southern preacher on a train traveling through her adopted state. The preacher told her southerners bought land to make cotton, bought slaves to produce the cotton, sold the cotton to buy more land and slaves, all in a never-ending cycle.[23] Juliet Coleman, visiting her brother in Alabama, wrote back to her parents in Connecticut about her astonishment at the wealth generated by cotton and slaves for plantation owners. "A man will pay 120 dollars a year for a negro man, cloathe him—pay his taxes—& c. to work in the field—& make 4 or 500 dollars from him clean gain!"[24] Albert Pike, another Massachusetts native whose friends included the likes of abolitionist William Lloyd Garrison, nevertheless came out in favor of slavery for his adopted state of Arkansas because he believed the future welfare of the state required it and any attempt to outlaw the institution would cause massive upheaval for its citizens. Defending his stance at the Arkansas constitutional convention, Pike remarked, "Surrounded, as it would be, by Missouri, Tennessee, Mississippi, Louisiana,

Texas and the Indian tribes—all of them slave countries—our state would become the land of refuge for runaways and vagabonds." He then pointed out the economic necessity of the institution by reminding his critics, "Besides this, our revenue is to be raised from and our rich lands settled by the slaveholders."[25]

Still, favoring white supremacy and favoring slavery represented two very different phenomena. Just because northern whites did not want blacks to have the same political and social rights as whites did not mean they would automatically favor slavery over free labor. Especially from the 1830s onward, with the spread of not only abolitionism but also free labor ideology, northern whites took great pride in the concepts of free labor, and northern leaders promoted it as the greatest social system in the world. In addition, by the 1850s, northern whites received a steady influx of descriptions concerning either the horrors of slavery or the manipulative character of southern slave-owners pushing for the expansion of slavery at the expense of white settlers. Nothing guaranteed that northern emigrants would change their views of slavery when they reached the South.

Indeed, some evidence suggests that seeing slavery firsthand would only increase their disgust with the institution and how it operated. Several northern emigrants wrote back to their families about how everything they had heard about slavery was either just as bad or worse in real life. For example, Caroline Seabury, though she viewed blacks with contempt, did not hesitate to record her severely negative impression of slavery itself. When she arrived in Mississippi, her first experiences with slavery included hearing a maid whipped for stealing money she did not take and a slave-catcher bringing back a caught runaway. As she recorded in her diary, "It is my first experience in the workings of slavery—I hope it will have no second."[26] Of course, living in Mississippi meant she would have many more eyewitness accounts of slavery. A year later, describing a gathering of southerners who wanted to hire out slaves for the season, she compared the experience to the worst parts of a slave auction. "It was new strange talk to me—indescribably revolting," she wrote. "How from my inmost soul I detested those creatures in the form of men who could thus calmly in a perfect matter-of-fact way discuss subjects which to me seemed only fit converse for fiends . . . and yet it is done at the beginning of every year all over the 'Sunny South.'"[27] By 1859, despite having spent more than five years in the South, Seabury still could not reconcile herself to the realities of slavery. Commenting on what she perceived as the paradox of southern thinking, "All of the ministers are loudly denouncing the sin of bringing them [slaves] from their native land into slavery. Yet—no one says that constant buying & selling here is wrong in the least."[28]

And Seabury was not alone. William Pierce, a doctor and native New Yorker, lived in Mississippi at the same time as Seabury and held similar views. He told his sister that the North was generally superior to the South in terms of education precisely because of southern slave-owners. Unwilling to pay for public education, these slave-owners hired private tutors for themselves and left poorer whites in a state of ignorance and much worse off than in the North.[29] Over in Texas, Lucadia Pease wrote to her family back in Con-necticut about her inability to sometimes tell slaves apart from whites. "'[The] niggers are not so black' as could be wished, for I have been puzzled almost every day to tell black from white," she wrote to her mother. "One of the servants in the house here is whiter than any of the ladies, with light sandy hair, and yet she is a slave & must associate with real black negroes, an awful feature in slavery."[30] Similarly, a northern tutor expressed his shame at witnessing the corrupt nature of slavery and agreed with what he read in *Uncle Tom's Cabin*.[31] Thinking in more economical terms, Sarah Williams, a native New Yorker, wrote to her family after living for two years in the South, "I am very glad that he [Mr. Williams] is disposed so to invest his money, instead of purchasing negroes, which I do believe is the most unprofitable property a person can possess . . ."[32] Even Stephen Duncan, a large slave-owner himself, on several occasions promoted the gradual emancipation of slaves across the South. In addition to leading the Mississippi Colonization Society and later serving as vice president of the American Colonization Society, Duncan helped free blacks petition to remain in the state and once interceded on behalf of slaves whose owner, though granting his slaves freedom on condition they emigrate to Liberia, had children who sought to block the will.[33]

In a few cases, adoptive southerners actively opposed traditional southern attitudes toward slavery. New Englander Calvin Robinson set up schools and orphanages for black children after moving to Florida in the 1850s. Lucadia Pease referred to slaves by their names rather than calling them "servants" and routinely bought eggs and chickens for them. Franklin and Phoebe Farmer, Massachusetts natives who moved to Louisiana, made no secret of their antislavery views and endured the enmity of their neighbors because of their stand. Julian Reed, who moved to Mississippi to work as a plantation tutor, left after a few years because he hated slavery and believed he endured discrimination from his southern neighbors because of his views.[34]

Nevertheless, when native northerners witnessed slavery, much more often they became its defenders rather than detractors. Unlike the impressions made by Seabury, Robinson, and others, many other adoptive southerners commented that, despite what they had heard from second-hand reports in the North, slavery actually functioned as a benign or even helpful influence on both slaves and whites. As would happen with the secession crisis, these individuals believed they had the best platform for judging slavery because they had seen both the free labor North and the slaveholding South firsthand. Instead of confirming the horrors of slavery that abolitionists expected, adoptive southerners generally chose to report the positive or neutral sides of slavery. In the process, they took one more step on their transformation toward an adopted southern identity. By the time of the Civil War, these individuals acted as slavery's most ardent defenders and advocates.

The transition toward a greater acceptance of slavery happened fairly quickly once northern emigrants reached the South. Whatever their previous convictions about slavery growing up in the North, adjusting themselves to southern culture also meant adjusting their attitudes toward slavery. For instance, within a week of settling in Georgia, Connecticut native Amanda Trulock wrote to her parents about first coming into contact with slaves on her new husband's plantation. "I must say I have a different opinion with regard to the Negroes than I had when in B Port . . . for certainly they are the happiest people in the world."[35] Similarly, Sarah Williams, after moving to North Carolina, told her parents that the slaves she saw each had three suits of clothes and a few even had their own money.[36] Emily Sinkler, a Pennsylvania native who moved to South Carolina with her new husband, described slavery as a benign institution where the slaves seemed happy and even amusing.[37] Arthur McArthur, a Maine native who settled in Missouri and then Louisiana, told his sister that slaves had a better life than laborers in the North and heard that few escape attempts occurred even though the free state of Illinois lay right across the river from Missouri. Considering himself a newfound expert on the subject, McArthur proclaimed, "I find that people of the North have a very erroneous opinion of treatment of slaves."[38] Native New Yorker John Quitman concurred when he wrote to one of his acquaintances, "So far from being fed on 'salted cotton-seed,' as we used to believe in Ohio, they are oily, sleek bountifully fed, well clothed, well taken care of . . . ."[39]

Out of these initial observations, northern emigrants often came to the conclusion that slaves did not suffer as much as native northerners thought. As Quitman noted above, rather than describe whippings, splitting up families, or other detrimental effects of slavery, many adoptive southerners pointed out that slaves lived comfortable and happy lives. A typical example came from Juliet Bestor Coleman, who described to her parents the conditions of slaves on her brother's plantation in Alabama. Using language that would make white southern apologists for slavery proud, Coleman insisted that "He [her brother] indulges his servants too much—does not whip them when they deserve it. –they do not wish to be free—they look to their master as a protector not a tyrant. –I often tell Nancy I shall take her to Connecticut & then she will be free—this is a terrible idea to her."[40] Though Coleman herself hinted she wanted to set her brothers' slaves free, she was not sure she could do it since his slaves apparently wanted to stay with their master. Her description showed that native northerners would not automatically condemn slavery when they saw it for themselves.[41]

If anything, opinions of slavery among northern emigrants tended to skew in the direction of paternalism. The paternalist interpretation of slavery, prevalent in the antebellum South in the decades leading up to the Civil War, stipulated that white southern masters functioned as the heads of large families, with their wives as trusty partners and their children and slaves as dependents. Everyone had their own unique responsibilities: masters provided for all the needs of the family, wives managed the household, and children and slaves willingly granted masters their full obedience and trust. In this worldview, everyone in the slave-owning family lived happily, and any rare punishments that occurred justifiably maintained the structural order. Certainly paternalism masked the inhumanity of slavery, but it also allowed white southerners, and slave-owners especially, to portray their society as holy and just.[42]

Northern whites did not grow up under such a system and had a better opportunity to judge the system from an outsider's perspective. The fact that the majority of northern emigrants did not challenge the concept of paternalism, but instead defended it as accurate, reveals the dramatic influence southern society had on its adopted citizens. Especially when adoptive southerners realized their success and stability in their adopted homes depended on the continuation of slavery, they rushed to its defense as quickly as any native white southerner. To do otherwise meant the loss of everything they held dear, including their position, livelihood, and acceptance by their communities. As Daniel Pratt said to his father, who worried about his son's connection to slavery, "Did you know my situation and the situation of the country I live in you would think differently. I will ashure [sic] you that to live in anny [sic] country it is necessary to conform to the customs of the country in part. I have brought no man in to bondage and I am in hopes I have rendered no mans situation more disagreeable than it was before. . . ."[43] As a result, casual readers would have a hard time distinguishing between native southern pro-slavery apologists and their adoptive southern brethren.[44]

Following paternalist logic, several pro-slavery arguments from the pens of adoptive southerners concentrated on the lack of harsh treatment supposedly meted out by cruel masters. Adopted South Carolinian Caroline Gilman insisted that, though masters disciplined their slaves, the latter were never locked in prison or chains and never received punishment without a good reason. Caroline Lee Hentz, a native of Massachusetts who traveled across the Deep South with her husband for twenty years, argued that in all of her travels she never witnessed any cruel punishments inflicted on slaves. Julia Gardner Tyler, wife of President John Tyler, noted with pride that her husband, unlike other masters she heard about, did not whip his slaves, break up slave families, or sell his slaves indiscriminately. Tryphena Blanche Holder Fox added in her observations that, "I think it is wrong for people to talk about the horrors and evils of slavery, for in nine cases out of ten the slaves would be in a worse condition if they were free than they now are." Within their own plantations at least, slavery appeared just as paternalists conceived: noble, just, and beneficial to both slave-owner and slave alike. Mosley Curtis, a Massachusetts native, even admitted that cruel masters who separated families existed but insisted that southerners would gradually eliminate the practice themselves on their own terms.[45]

Another type of argument utilized by adoptive southerners echoing paternalist defenders involved contrasting the workloads of slaves with those of northern whites. Refusing to acknowledge the back-breaking labor slaves endured, and possibly reflecting the work ethic of antebellum white northerners with whom they had grown up, adoptive southerners insisted that slaves worked less than northern whites. For instance, Amanda Trulock wrote to her family in the 1830s about how she felt slaves were better off than free blacks and even poor whites in the North. "They have no cares, and are not either aspiring after wealth nor fame," she claimed. "Each family has a hous [sic] which they call their own, they do not work half as hard, as some of the farmers at the north. their victuals is all prepared [sic] for them by Cook expressly for the purpose, evening they sing and sometimes dance."[46] In her view, slaves led a good life because their masters took care of all of their needs, something northern white workers did not enjoy from their own employers. Caroline Lee Hentz went further by describing slaves who dressed as well as their masters, while northern factory owners overworked and underpaid their workers with no protection for illness. Ignoring the fact that slaves had no control over their own lives, Hentz believed slaves led much better lives because they had all of their needs taken care of, while the northern white factory workers used up all of their wages simply to survive.[47]

Building on this line of reasoning, O. T. Hammond, a northern reverend who taught at the Leon Academy in Tallahassee in the late 1830s, wrote to one of his former students about the easier work slaves had versus white northerners. In his mind, white northerners who complained about the detriments of slavery had no basis for their accusations. He insisted, "The slaves are much better off than most people north of the Potomac imagine [sic]—true, they are slaves! deprived of freedom—but they are generally happy—they do not work hard, the tasks are light—I could do as much as two are required to do." Hammond also cited the medical care slaves received, the food and clothes their masters provided, the nice clothes they wore for Sunday services, etc. Only half in jest, he told his student, "the negro has more of the delicacies of life than many of your canal Irish, nay, they are better fed than many of the N. E. girls connected with the manufacturing establishments." And responding to accusations of cruel treatment, Hammond admitted, "There are some cruel masters! nor can it be wondered at—Have you not cruel fathers in N. Y.? A cruel master is soon put down by public opinion." Between the structured and pampered life perceived among her slaves and the cutthroat conditions of northern factory workers, Hammond believed white northerners had more cause for complaint than any slave.[48]

The most potent argument in favor of slavery from an adoptive southern perspective, however, did not depend as much on defending slaves' conditions as protecting southern society from outside influence. The idea that northerners who had never even visited the South could call for the end of an institution that formed the core of adoptive southerners' new homes, without any regard for consequences, created a unifying base from which most northern emigrants could support slavery. In this regard, they had the same views as their native southern brethren. Although only a small percentage of white southerners owned slaves, the vast majority of non-slaveholders still looked to slavery as the basis of their society and defended it to the death. Adoptive southerners, reflecting their absorption into white southern society, largely expressed a similar attitude. Regardless of how they felt about slavery as an institution, these men and women insisted on handling the issue in their own way. Especially now that they had seen slavery for themselves and formed their own opinions, they believed anyone who did not have a personal investment or firsthand knowledge of slavery did not deserve to pass judgment on the practice or dictate its future. Adoptive southerners, in a very real sense, had stepped into the shoes of southern whites and agreed with their perspective.

Such sentiments only increased in the decades after the formation of the abolitionist movement. Even though abolitionists only formed a tiny minority of the population, and even though most northerners shunned them, their radical ideas terrified white southerners with images of race wars. Incidents such as Nat Turner's rebellion only added to the fears in southern society that unchecked criticism of slavery by outsiders could put white southern families and communities at risk of slaughter in future slave revolts.[49] Northern emigrants felt just as threatened as their native southern neighbors.[50] One such example emerged from the pen of John Quitman, the native New Yorker who twice became governor of Mississippi. In 1836, Quitman urged the Mississippi legislature to counter the dangerous rhetoric of the emerging abolitionist press. Quitman thundered that "the morality, the expediency, and the duration of the institution of slavery, are questions which belong exclusively to ourselves." And since Mississippi's citizens, himself included, chose to continue slavery, no one, least of all abolitionists, should challenge the will of its people. Such arguments provided yet another means for adoptive southerners to display their adopted identities and distance themselves from their origins. As would happen in the secession crisis and beyond, when forced to choose between defense of native or adopted homes, adoptive southerners invariably chose the latter.[51]

Ministers Theodore Clapp and George Armstrong offered their own defiant tones against their native sections as the rhetorical wars over slavery persisted. Clapp, despite a strict Puritan upbringing in Massachusetts and education at Andover Theological Seminary, tempered his views of slavery after living in Kentucky and New Orleans in the 1820s and 1830s. If anything, by the late 1830s Clapp sounded like a native southern preacher in his defense of slavery for the safety of both whites and blacks. "I now feel certain, that by emancipating our slaves we should be guilty of the greatest injustice.... We dare not manumit our slaves. It would be an act of unmixed oppression, wrong, cruelty, robbery, and murder," he preached in one of his sermons. "Christian love, forebearance and equity, require us to hold the Africans in bondage. We are perfectly persuaded that emancipation would be the destruction of the poor, dependent, helpless slave."[52] Ending slavery, in Clapp's view, risked condemning slaves to misery by prematurely sending them into a world for which they were ill-prepared. Incredibly, he made slavery sound like the just and humane option required by good Christian white southerners.

Similarly, George Armstrong, a New Jersey native who oversaw a church in Norfolk, also cited Christian ethics and white supremacy to defend his adopted state's institutions. Blaming northern antislavery men for provoking the issue, Armstrong told his flock that the South had a dependant race that, for its own safety, had to be controlled by the dominant race. He also claimed northerners had no right to condemn the South because when the northern states ended slavery, northern slaveholders simply shipped slaves farther south rather than emancipate them.[53] Later on, when a pro-emancipationist urged Virginians to rid themselves of the curse of slavery, Armstrong wrote a pamphlet answering each of his points with a counter-argument. A key part of his pamphlet contrasted the supposed cheerfulness and industriousness of southern slaves versus what he termed "the most idle and worthless class" of fugitive slaves who settled in the North and Canada. Just like Clapp, Armstrong believed releasing slaves into immediate freedom represented cruelty and oppression among blacks worse than slavery itself. "If then the slave race among us," he wrote, "do not possess the ability 'to exercise beneficially the rights' of freemen—and I know that you will agree with me that such is the fact at the present time—it follows that their present slavery involves no violation of any right of theirs to freedom, for they have no such right."[54] Both Armstrong and Clapp thus show that a native northerner in the pulpit could advocate proslavery as well as antislavery arguments, when placed in the right environment.

Beyond the church, other northern emigrants added to the proslavery rhetoric of the antebellum South in the language of self-determination and defense against abolitionists for the preservation of the white race. One such diatribe emerged from Felix de Fontaine, a Massachusetts native with French ancestry who worked as a reporter for New York newspapers before moving to South Carolina in 1860. In spite of his limited time in the South, de Fontaine, no fan of abolitionists, wrote pieces excoriating antislavery organizations for pressing the slavery question and threatening the Union. In one pamphlet, de Fontaine sketched a brief history of slavery in the United States, including slavery in the North in the 1780s, the Missouri Compromise, early manumission societies in Tennessee and Virginia, etc. In his view, North and South had dealt with slavery disagreements peacefully, but abolitionists upset everything, including northern communities angered by the abolitionists' aggressive tactics. Summing up his argument, de Fontaine laid out a few general conclusions: abolitionism ended ideas of gradual emancipation, put wild ideas in slaves' minds about freedoms they did not have the capacity to exercise, endangered the cotton trade, weakened the foundation of the Union, and spawned sectional parties.[55]

De Fontaine also highlighted two areas especially relevant to northern emigrants such as himself. They prided themselves on having balanced views of sectional discord, because of their experiences in both sections, and considered anything that threatened their standing in the South a menace to themselves and the Union. De Fontaine was no exception, blasting New England abolitionists for living in isolated communities and only hearing about slavery through second-hand sources. "It is worthy of notice in this connection," he wrote with contempt, "that most abolitionists know little or nothing of slavery and slaveholders beyond what they have learned from excited, caressed and tempted fugitives, or from a superficial, accidental or prejudiced observation. . . . Their information is acquired from discharged seamen, runaway slaves, agents who have been tarred and feathered, factious politicians, and scurrilous tourists . . . ."[56] Considering that de Fontaine grew up in Massachusetts, his comments indicated that he hated antislavery men, not just because of their rhetoric, but also because they did not see what he saw. Instead of basing their opinions on facts, abolitionists used rumor and lies to advance their agenda, when they only had to come to the South and see for themselves the reality of slavery, as de Fontaine had done.

As a result, in de Fontaine's view, these pretend experts on slavery threatened not only the Union but also the futures of all cross-border emigrants. As he stated at the end of his pamphlet, "Northern men can no longer travel in the South without being regarded as objects of suspicion and confounded with the abolitionists of their section. In short, all the kind relations that have ever existed between the North and the South have been interrupted, and a barrier erected, which, socially, commercially and politically, has separated the heretofore united interests of the two sections . . ."[57] For de Fontaine, as for other adoptive southerners, silencing abolitionists meant not only saving the Union but also saving himself and his position as an adopted son of the South.

Echoing de Fontaine's tactics, Thomas Clapp, writing from New Orleans, claimed that if "our northern brethren" could visit the city, they would see that slave-owners lived like Christian gentlemen, regardless of the charges levied by abolitionists. He still appreciated the sympathies given by northerners, "notwithstanding the people of the free states are so widely separated from us, in opinion and feeling, with respect to the subject of slavery."[58] Charles Dimmock in Virginia likewise defended slavery against abolitionists in his native state of Massachusetts. After hearing about a Norfolk slave illegally set free in Boston, Dimmock wrote an article denouncing the state's violation of the Constitution, predicting such violations would only lead to disunion if northerners did not respect the South's institutions. The fact that Dimmock grew up in the very state he criticized did not faze him. The growth of abolitionism had forever altered his childhood home, and thus his entire future lay with his new home in Virginia.[59]

A few adoptive southerners went further by attacking what they perceived as the centerpiece of the abolitionist assault: Harriet Beecher Stowe's *Uncle Tom's Cabin*. One of the best-selling novels of all time, with hundreds of thousands of copies sold in its first year of publication alone, Stowe's work highlighted the detrimental effects of slavery on everyone involved, whites and blacks, northerners and southerners. Unlike most antislavery works at the time, Stowe's book did not condemn white southerners as inherently evil for having slavery; they still had a chance to make a morally righteous decision once they understood that slavery hurt themselves as much as it did their slaves. And northerners could not wash their hands of the problem either, because their ancestors had owned slaves and continued to permit slavery to exist in a supposedly free country, which made everyone responsible for its elimination. In order to further her theme of cross-sectional responsibility for the sin of slavery, Stowe made the arch-villain of her novel, the infamous Simon Legree, a Vermont-born slave-owner in Louisiana who beat to death the protagonist Uncle Tom in a Christ-like fashion. Stowe intended to show that slavery by its very nature corrupted whoever came into contact with it, regardless of origin.[60]

Yet despite her attempts to portray slavery as a national problem requiring a national solution, white northerners and southerners alike viewed the novel in a sectional manner. White northerners, especially antislavery men, praised the novel as legitimizing their positions on slavery and the need to reign in the "Slave Power," which would extend its evil across the continent if given half the chance. White southerners, on the other hand, condemned Stowe's work as at best exaggeration and at worst a lethal assault on southern culture and honor. Some southern towns and cities banned the novel, just as they had burned abolitionist literature that reached their shores two decades earlier.[61]

The views of Julia Tyler and Caroline Lee Hentz, natives of New York and Massachusetts respectively, symbolized the adoptive southern perspective on this controversy. One of the key arguments these individuals made for weighing in on slavery, as so many others before them had done, was that they had experienced life in both sections and had actually seen slavery firsthand. That knowledge, in their minds, gave them the best platform for a balanced view on the matter. In the context of *Uncle Tom's Cabin,* Tyler and Hentz emphasized that Stowe had neither visited the South nor witnessed slavery, and so her work could not stand up to scrutiny against native northerners who had done both. Tyler responded publicly to Stowe's publication through an article she published in 1853 in both the *Southern Literary Messenger* and the *New York Herald,* symbolizing her own efforts to reach a bi-sectional audience. Basing her argument on her own observations of her husband's plantation in Virginia, Tyler presented standard white southern arguments in defense of slavery, including the kindly treatment of slaves by masters, how slavery helped spread Christianity, and the fact that slaves lived more secure and comfortable lives than northern factory workers. She did not describe slavery as one of the greatest labor systems in human history, as some southern apologists claimed, but argued against the idea perpetuated by Stowe that slavery was inherently brutal. She hoped to counter the Stowe

Julia Gardiner Tyler, wife of John Tyler. A descendant of one of the most prominent families in New York, Tyler not only served as First Lady but also served as a link between the New York and Virginia social circles. Library of Congress.

narrative by bringing up a personal and firsthand account, rather than speculation and bias.[62]

Challenging Stowe on her own level, Caroline Lee Hentz not only drew on twenty years of her personal experiences with slavery across the Deep South but also presented them in the form of a novel. Hentz's book *Marcus Warland: Or a Tale of the South* came out in 1852 and represented the first major literary challenge to Stowe's novel. A follow-up novel, *The Planter's Northern Bride,* was a not so subtle allusion to her own situation as a New England native in the South. Citing her unique experiences, Hentz reminded her readers of her northern heritage as the perfect reason why her retellings counted more than others. As she wrote in the preface of her second novel, "during our residence in the South, we have never *witnessed* one scene of cruelty or oppression, nor beheld a chain or manacle, or the infliction of a punishment more severe than parental authority would be justified in applying to filial disobedience or transgression. This is not owing to our being placed in a limited sphere of observation, for we have studied domestic, social, and plantation life, in Carolina, Alabama, Georgia, and Florida."[63] Hentz thus attempted to defend southern slavery by pointing to her status as an observer from both her native and adopted regions. Few other authors on the subject, either northern or southern, had such personal knowledge of both sides of the debate.[64]

Ironically, Hentz had similar goals to her rival Stowe. In a situation that would repeat itself in the secession crisis several years later, Stowe and Hentz, both native northerners, ended up taking diametrically different sides in the slavery debate for the same reason: to reduce sectional tension through their literature. While Stowe wanted to portray slavery as a national problem that both North and South had to solve together to prevent civil conflict, Hentz took the opposite approach by showing how both sections could continue to live with slavery peacefully as long as agitators did not upset the status quo. This theme became interspersed with Hentz's pro-slavery rhetoric and personal experiences throughout her work. For example, in *The Planter's Northern Bride,* one of the characters, a northern-born minister named Mr. Brainard, said he came to the South to preach to unconverted blacks and whites. His friend, a white southerner named Mr. Mooreland, replied that he would prefer southern preachers because he feared northern influence and prejudice, especially from "fanatics."[65] Taking Stowe's religious references in a different direction, Hentz showed that, rather than advance the cause of evangelical Christianity, northern "fanatics," by which she meant abolitionists, limited the abilities of preachers to expand the Christian message. By the end of the novel, she reiterated that theme by telling her readers she loved both the North and the South and warned them that only extremists could disrupt them. "The North and the South are branches of the same parent tree," she wrote, "and the lightning bolt that shivers the one, must scorch and wither the other."[66] Without abolitionists, she implied, white northerners and southerners could live in peace and harmony. Thinking of her own situation, Hentz implored her readers to listen to those with personal experience rather than those who claimed to have a cure-all solution based on insufficient evidence.

Some of Hentz's fellow adoptive southern women expressed similar anxieties outside of the public realm. Tryphena Holder Fox, for example, wrote to her mother in 1857 defending her conduct after one of her slaves ran away with his wife. She complained that she treated her slaves well and could not understand why they would want to leave. Nevertheless, she knew that others, including her mother, would judge her for using slaves at all. "You will doubtless be astonished & think Dr Raymond & myself the most cruel & hard of *wretches*," she cautioned, knowing of the antislavery sentiments brewing in the North. She then outlined what she and her husband had done for their slaves' well being, blaming the incident on the wiles of her slave's wife, who lived on another plantation. Having made her case, Fox believed she could convince her mother of her righteousness but not those who had never seen slavery personally. She thus warned her mother, "But I know what those ranting abolitionists will think that *Triphen Holder,* has turned out to be a Southern monster, so you must keep my troubles to yourself." Fox could justify slavery to herself and her family but believed abolitionists would view her as a villain regardless of what she said. The North she had left behind did not seem the same now that abolitionists freely condemned white southerners, including Fox herself.[67]

Even adoptive southerners who took a neutral or antislavery stance still hated the presumption that white northerners could dictate if and when slavery should end in the South without thinking of the consequences. Such a momentous step needed guidance from those whom it would impact the most, i.e., white southerners. Reverend O. T. Hammond told a former student that, while slavery certainly had its evils, attempting to carry out the abolitionist plans could only lead to destructions and annihilation. If anything, Hammond believed abolitionists were the worst enemies of slaves, rather than their friends. "What have the anti-slavery societies done for the black man?," he asked. "How many have they freed? They have bound the chains closer—they have made the southern people very jealous—they have stopt [*sic*] all manumissions which were very common before. They have put a stop to the black schools in Charleston & Savannah—they have sown the seeds, I fear, of a civil war . . . I am thoroughly convinced that the abolitionists are the indirect means of cruel treatment."[68]

By the 1850s, such opinions had only hardened among adoptive southerners, even among those who maintained anti-slavery views. Elisha Pease, a Connecticut native and one-time governor of Texas, considered himself a solid unionist in the 1850s but warned his northern colleagues he would support anything, possibly even secession, to protect slavery against Republican encroachment.[69] Sally Baxter Hampton, a harsh critic of slavery despite her marriage to the Hampton family of South Carolina, disagreed strongly with abolitionists because she believed slaves would only exist as a "superior animal" if the North forced emancipation on the South.[70] Similarly, Amelia Lines, another ardent antislavery adoptive southerner, commented that though she believed that slavery was a horrible system, at the same time, "Negroes seem to be a necessary evil. If abolitionists knew them surely they would not wish to abolish slavery, & give them liberty to roam at large through the country."[71] Timothy Flint personally hated slavery but also did not like the tactics of abolitionists, warning northerners that the South just started to respect Yankees again and agitation against slavery would do much harm to future of the Union.[72] Joseph Ingraham also favored eventual emancipation but insisted it needed to unfold slowly and with forethought, lest it destroy the Union. He believed most white northerners had not seen enough of slavery to really make a solid opinion, implying that white southerners had to have more control of the process.[73]

Utilizing similar rhetoric, William Pierce and Moses Curtis argued that abolitionist tactics actually hurt the chances for granting blacks greater freedoms and privileges. Pierce wrote to his sister about the harm abolitionists caused to both the Union and slaves themselves. Contrasting slavery in the Upper South versus the Deep South, Pierce wrote, "Here [Mississippi] they are comparatively far from such influencers northern fanatics [*sic*] and abolition colporteurs can not reach them consequently they can safely be allowed much greater liberties and the further you go South the more markedly is this the case." Completely ignoring the fact that the Deep South had equally strict, if not stricter, laws against slaves' well-being as the rest of the South, Pierce contended that the Deep South allowed greater flexibility for slaves precisely because abolitionists could not penetrate the region as easily. Yet he could not speak for future safety because "the fluid zeal of northern sympathizers has done much to oppress and degrade them even here."[74] In addition, Curtis, who readily acknowledged the horrific nature of slavery, nevertheless insisted that white southerners needed to correct its flaws themselves. The situation remained complex and delicate, so abolitionist calls to end slavery immediately only exacerbated the problem. In fact, Curtis believed that, without abolitionist meddling, slavery would have already disappeared in Virginia, Kentucky, and Maryland through peaceful means.[75] Curtis may have misread white southern determination to defend slavery in those states, but his criticism indicated that he placed the blame for slavery's continuation much more on northern abolitionists than southern slave-owners.[76]

Moving beyond simple rhetoric, many adoptive southerners not only became absorbed into slave-holding society but even became slave-owners themselves. Joining the ranks of slave-owners cemented their status as middle-class or upper-class white southerners, depending on the size of their plantations. Out of the three hundred and three individuals surveyed in this study, at least one hundred and nine owned slaves in 1860.[77] Therefore, at least 35 percent of the individuals documented, more than a third, owned slaves. Compared to the regional average of 20 percent slave ownership across the entire South, adoptive southerners, at least among this limited segment, achieved the white southern dream at an even greater rate than native southerners themselves. A small majority of these northern-born slave-owners had fewer than ten slaves and thus did not qualify as planters. Forty-one of them had fewer than five slaves, seventeen owned between six and ten slaves, and twenty-seven owned between eleven and twenty-five slaves. Nevertheless, at least twenty-four reached planter status with more than twenty-five slaves. In fact, two adoptive southerners, Stephen Duncan and Zebulon York, natives of Pennsylvania and Maine respectively, achieved every native southerner's dream by acquiring thousands of slaves on plantations across Mississippi and Louisiana.[78] Few other achievements symbolized the success and acceptance of native northerners into their adopted homeland than acquiring the property that came to define the South.

And unlike so many other members of the white southern elite, who came from long-established slave-owning families, northern emigrants often acquired slave property only after establishing their careers. Charles W. Adams, a Massachusetts native, originally moved to Arkansas to study law. After solidifying his legal career, Adams expanded his wealth through cotton plantations and a total of thirty-four slaves. Another Massachusetts native, Daniel Whitaker, originally moved to Georgia as a minister before relocating to South Carolina as a planter. Vermont native Porter Ingram also started his career in law and politics before becoming a planter with thirty-nine slaves. Benjamin Dunkin, a native Pennsylvanian who eventually acquired two hundred and thirty-seven slaves in South Carolina, originally moved to the South for his legal career. Amos Akerman, a native of New Hampshire, started as a teacher when he moved to South Carolina but then became a lawyer and moved to Georgia, where he bought a farm and rented slaves to work it. Another New Hampshire native, Daniel Pratt, moved to Georgia as a carpenter, received land as payment for some of his projects, and eventually invested in gin and cotton factories after founding a new town in Alabama. As his landholdings increased, he purchased one hundred and seven slaves by 1860 to improve his investments. These men, ironically, used the Puritan ethic of hard work to achieve the white southern dream of planter status.[79]

Other adoptive southerners, however, became planters through marriage. Former northern army officers, following extensive tours across southern forts and territories, especially utilized this method to obtain wealth and privilege after leaving the army. New Jersey natives Samuel Cooper and Samuel French married into prominent Virginia and Mississippi families respectively, gaining plantations as part of their wives' dowries. Similarly, New Yorker Franklin Gardner and Pennsylvanian Robert Maclay, both junior officers, left the army after marrying into Louisiana families and taking over the management of their wives' plantations.[80] In addition, northern-born women sometimes became plantation mistresses after marrying southern husbands. Massachusetts native Tryphena Blanche Holder Fox, who originally moved to Mississippi as a tutor, ended up marrying a local planter and became a plantation mistress in the 1850s. Amanda Trulock, born in Connecticut, moved to Georgia with her new husband and helped manage the sixty-two slaves he owned on his plantation. Emily Sinkler and Sally Baxter Hampton each had an even larger task when they married South Carolinians and ended up as plantation mistresses for hundreds of slaves. And Julia Gardner, a member of a prominent New York family, not only became a plantation mistress after marrying into a prominent Virginia family, but eventually became first lady of the United States as Mrs. John Tyler.[81]

Regardless of how they acquired their slaves, each of these individuals proved that a northern upbringing, even one in the heart of abolitionist strongholds, did not prevent them from living the life of a slave-owner. Out of the one hundred and nine known adoptive southern slave-owners in this survey, fifty-five, a majority, came from New England. Connecticut produced twenty-two, Massachusetts close behind with twenty-one, New Hampshire five, Maine four, Vermont two, and Rhode Island one. Therefore, the area that many southern whites imagined as the center of abolitionist sentiment also sent sons and daughters who ultimately participated and benefitted from the South's most important institution. Not to be left out, the Mid-Atlantic states produced most of the rest of the slave-owners in this survey, a total of forty-three. Twenty of them came from New York, nineteen from Pennsylva-

General Franklin Gardner. A native of New York City, Gardner attended the same West Point class as Ulysses S. Grant. He married into the Mouton family of Louisiana in the 1850s and gained notoriety in 1863 as the commander of Port Hudson, the last surviving Confederate stronghold on the Mississippi River. Library of Congress.

nia, and four from New Jersey.[82] They all collectively held thousands of slaves from Virginia to Florida and South Carolina to Texas.

Sadly for their slaves, slave-owners who did not grow up around slavery oftentimes became its most vocal defendants, as well as its harshest practitioners. The image of Vermont-born slave-owner Simon Legree, the arch-villain of Harriet Beecher Stowe's *Uncle Tom's Cabin,* as a heartless man who treated his slaves ruthlessly conformed far more closely to reality than Stowe or any other abolitionist may have imagined. Joseph Ingraham even commented in his travel accounts that, if anything, native northerners defended slavery more urgently and treated slaves with greater harshness than native southerners, precisely because the former had not grown up with slavery. One northern preacher named Andrew Peabody said, "adopted citizens of the South are for the most part, among the strongest and least tolerant advocates of slavery," fueling the cliché that the worst slave-owners were actually native northerners.[83]

Native white southerners agreed with this assessment as well. Either speaking from experience or attempting to soften attitudes about slavery, white southerners sometimes commented on the unusually harsh nature of northern-born slave-owners. Anthony Keiley, a southerner with northern relatives, argued that white southerners were less racist than northerners because the former actually interacted with blacks, while the latter rarely saw blacks before coming to the South and therefore did not know how to properly treat them. "The Northern people, and I speak from long acquaintance with them," he claimed, "care infinitely less for negroes than we." Similarly, Mary Boyken Chesnut, one of the more prolific Civil War diarists, touched on the issue in her own writings. After rereading through *Uncle Tom's Cabin* in 1862, she chastised Stowe for assuming that all white southerners acted like Simon Legree. If anything, according to Chesnut, the Legrees among the slave-owners were primarily New Englanders. "The Northern men and women who came here were always hardest, for they expected an African to work and behave as a white man. We do not." Over in Mississippi, Kate Cummings, a young woman who worked as a nurse during the Civil War, expressed disgust at the cruelty of northern-born slave-owners. "As for Mr. Legree," she wrote, "few southerners deny having such among us . . . Two are New Englanders and one a Dutchman. They beat their negroes, but they are despised by all who know them."[84]

Trying to understand the differences, Cummings gave her own theory on why northerners and foreigners treated slaves more cruelly than southerners. She believed these outsiders were so used to white servants working all day that they expected the same amount of labor from slaves. "These people," she reasoned, "not understanding the character of the negro, lose patience with him, and try by whipping to get the same amount of work from them as they have been in the habit of getting from white servants." If only northerners and foreigners could understand slavery through the eyes of white southerners, Cummings implied, they would not treat slaves so harshly. Until that revelation occurred, slaves would continue to suffer under the hands of non-southerners. In terms of actual native northerners living in the antebellum South, the imaginations of Stowe often conformed to reality.[85]

Interestingly enough, the opinions about slavery and blacks among adoptive southerners seemed to decline in significance after the secession crisis. The establishment of Confederate independence ranked much higher in importance and flooded the diaries, journals, and letters of adoptive southerners who joined the Confederate cause. Though slavery represented the dominant issue that led to the Civil War, few adoptive southerners made more than token mention of either slavery or blacks during the conflict. Rarely if ever did these men and women make full-throated defenses or apologies for slavery once the guns started firing and the armies took to the field. By that point, slavery seemed an accepted part of life and did not require any more justification for its own sake.

On the rare occasions when adoptive southerners did take time to mention the topic, their comments usually concerned something about the war effort, especially the use of black soldiers. The enlistment of free blacks and slaves by the Union army symbolized both a significant escalation of the Union war effort and their willingness to make emancipation a major war aim alongside the preservation of the Union. For several adoptive southerners in the Confederacy, however, black soldiers simply represented one more part of the Union army's depredations against their adopted homeland. For example, Confederate general and New Jersey native Samuel French brought up the subject when black soldiers in Mississippi raided his house in November 1863. Rather than focus exclusively on black soldiers, however, French recorded the damage done by both black and white soldiers as part of the overall Union campaign to attack Mississippi families. Black soldiers simply became another part of the evils of Union invasion of what French saw as his new nation and adopted state.[86]

Other northern-born Confederate soldiers expressed similar disinterest when it came to blacks in the context of the Civil War. Rather than take every opportunity to condemn the Union for enforcing emancipation and recruiting black soldiers, they more often kept silent on the issue or expressed an almost indifferent tone. In March 1862, Edward Drummond, a Maine native serving in a Georgia regiment, briefly mentioned a black man who came to Savannah to deliver letters to the soldiers at Fort Pulaski. A month later he wrote about a "Negro Cook named David" who went missing and assumed he got caught by Union soldiers (never contemplating the possibility that the man had escaped). Silas Grisamore, an adopted Louisianan, recorded the execution of a black man condemned to die for attempting to run away to Union lines. The very next line he talked about skirmishing that happened that day. Henry Handerson, a native Ohioan who became a Confederate prisoner during the Wilderness Campaign in 1864, wrote about his experience marching to the Union rear with his fellow captives and passing a column of black Union soldiers. Despite threats by their guards that the black troops would massacre the prisoners, Handerson wrote, "I cannot say, however, that we felt greatly alarmed, and the Negroes in fact offered us little, if any, more insult than their white companions had done before. For the most part we simply eyed each other with mutual curiosity and dislike."[87]

Still, black soldiers could elicit a sharper response from northern-born Confederate soldiers when disputes over the legitimacy of black soldiers prevented prisoner exchanges. In those cases, condemning black soldiers added to an existing narrative of upholding white southern honor or wishing to leave prison. Edmund Dewitt Patterson, a native Ohioan serving in an Alabama regiment, never talked too much about blacks until he ended up in prison in the summer of 1863. At that point, he insisted the Confederacy should never negotiate with the Union about exchanges of black soldiers. "Some Northern journals," he wrote, "state that there will not be any more exchanges until our government consents to treat captured negroes as prisoners of war. If this be the case, then I hope that there may never be another exchange . . . If we lose everything else, let us preserve our honor."[88] Another adoptive southerner, John F. O'Brien, claimed he did not care about blacks one way or the other but only hated them because he believed they prevented prisoner exchanges. While imprisoned on Johnson's Island in 1863, O'Brien wrote with frustration, "Something about the everlasting nigger busted up the whole thing. Then we'd curse the whole nigger race from Ham down." At the same time, however, O'Brien also condemned and ridiculed northern whites for the problem and remarked, "we would cheerfully give all full harems of nigger winches if they would consent to keep the question from preventing the exchange of thousands of white men."[89] As a result, even in this heated context, mentioning black soldiers simply fed an existing perception of frustration and honor related to the larger war effort.[90]

In each of these cases, northern-born Confederate soldiers only brought up slavery or blacks when it related to the Confederate war effort or their own well-being. Like their native southern comrades, by the time of the Civil War, slavery was such an accepted and critical institution for southern society that few thought to question it or even bring up the subject. What had seemed exotic when they first emigrated to the South now seemed natural and commonplace. The issue of slavery thus rarely merited more than a brief mention in journals and letters, and even then more from a practical standpoint.

When adoptive southerners did record their thoughts on slavery in the midst of war, the opinions formed in the antebellum period rarely changed as a result of wartime experiences. They continued to have a paternalistic view of slaves as ignorant and in need of white supervision. For instance, when Edward Drummond learned that Union authorities planned to emancipate the slaves of captured Confederate soldiers and send them to New York, he thought the Union men had done a disservice to the slaves. He wrote in his journal, "All the Boys [blacks] are in trouble, some crying and some begging to be let stay with us. . . . They have no where to go and nothing to do. Unaccustomed to such treatment they had almost rather starve." Like so many other Confederates, Drummond believed slaves could not function on their own, and so emancipation actually hurt slaves, rather than helping them.[91] Silas Grisamore expressed similar contempt for the hypocrisy of Union soldiers treating slaves worse than their masters. In 1863, after passing over a battlefield in Louisiana, Grisamore commented that the slaves left behind were in the worst condition he had ever seen from Union treatment. "The roads from Franklin to Tigerville," he observed, "were lined with Negroes half starved, almost destitute of clothing, sick and unable to help themselves; the only question of the poor wretches, who had been two months experiencing Federal sympathy and charity, was the inquiry if their master was coming after them." Ignoring the harshness of slave conditions in Louisiana, Grisamore instead focused on Union mistreatment of slaves and a paternalistic interpretation of slavery. Little had changed from the antebellum period.[92]

If anything, both during and after the Civil War, adoptive southerners who recorded their thoughts on emancipation sometimes expressed rage at the lengths the Union went to destroy southern society. The old hatred of abolitionists and expressions of white supremacy only intensified in the context of war. In Georgia, Amelia Lines wrote to her parents back in New York about the misery she suffered thanks to Union meddling in slavery. "We have eaten our share of negro filth," she complained. "Anna I do *despise* the race. I wish the abolitionists had to eat sleep and live with them. until they had enough of their 'colored brothers and sisters.' *'Poor oppressed, down trodden colored individuals'* Dont you pity them? I think it is a pity, they cant [*sic*] be made to feel a little of the care which oppress white people these hard times."[93] Farther north, while languishing in a Union prison camp, Edmund

DeWitt Patterson hated Union emancipation policies because he believed it would lead to miscegenation. He wrote in his journal, "Never before has any man or woman been found so degraded, so lost to all sense of shame, so devoid of every enobling principle which makes a man, as to breathe such foul slander against the noble women of the South."[94] And in Mississippi, Confederate general Samuel French excoriated the Union for unjustly stealing southern property without adequate compensation. He called the Confiscation Acts and Emancipation Proclamation unconstitutional and sanctioning theft. In his mind, "It was the largest steal ever committed by a nation; and, furthermore, they stole from the South slaves that they had sold the South. Call it by what name you will, it was robbery."[95] The views of native southerners and adoptive southerners had merged to the point where they were indistinguishable in terms of race and slavery.

From the antebellum period all the way through the end of the Civil War, adoptive southern reactions to slavery reflected the significant influence southern society and culture exerted on northern emigrants to the region. Instead of reacting to slavery with abhorrence or disgust, these emigrants generally looked upon slavery with curiosity or even acceptance. Their eagerness to succeed in their new homes and gain acceptance from their adopted communities almost required them to adapt to white southern views of slavery, or at the very least to keep negative opinions of the institution to themselves. As time passed, and slavery became more familiar, adoptive southerners often became slavery's most ardent defenders. Probably one of the most revealing stories of this transformation came from the experience of Amanda Trulock. Barely a month after she moved to Georgia with her new husband in 1838, Trulock told her family back in Connecticut she could not imagine going back to live in New England again after she had witnessed southern life. She depended on slaves for duties she used to perform herself, and moving back to Connecticut would have meant doing all her chores alone. Trulock even hinted that staying with her family in the winter would cause too great a burden because of her dependence on slavery.[96]

The growing acceptance and defense of slavery among the adoptive southern population set the stage for the secession crisis. While the Union drifted toward a breakdown thanks to the seemingly irreconcilable differences between North and South, adoptive southerners occupied a unique position that grew out of their experiences of living in the slaveholding South. As sons and daughters of one region and successful adopted citizens of another, these individuals would utilize their experiences in responding to secession. Just as many northern emigrants believed they had the best qualification for judging slavery, so a similar argument emerged in trying to find a solution to the secession crisis. The choices that adoptive southerners needed to make mirrored those they had already made in terms of their sectional identities. The main test for sectional loyalty came with the secession crisis. Until then, adoptive southerners always had the option of readjusting to a northern identity or even moving back to the North if they so chose. Once the southern states started seceding, however, they faced a critical choice: would they side with their native section or their adopted section? Adoptive southerners were about to prove how much more "southern" they felt with or without their northern heritage.

4

Adoptive Southerners Choose Sides

Few events in American history forced Americans to face a more difficult choice than the secession crisis. A man who as a child saw George Washington sworn in as the first president also witnessed the breakup of the Union by his eightieth birthday. With their beloved Union falling apart around them, all Americans had to decide between two options: stay with the Union or join the Confederacy. Even after seven states seceded in the wake of Abraham Lincoln's election as president, that decision did not always come automatically. Some people made their choices immediately while others waited on the sidelines, hoping for some kind of peaceful resolution. Only after the firing on Fort Sumter and President Lincoln's call for troops did the middle ground disappear, forcing nearly all Americans to decide what formed the foundations for their ultimate loyalties and identities.

For a majority of Americans, the secession crisis presented obvious choices. When family, community, state, and region all pointed in one direction, the path seemed self-evident. It comes as no surprise, therefore, that nearly all native northerners ultimately sided with the Union. No northern states seceded, nor did any northern state other than New Jersey still have slaves. In addition, all northern states had voted for Lincoln in 1860, and so they naturally looked to their elected president for guidance. When Lincoln issued the call for volunteers to put down the rebellion, northern communities responded with enthusiasm. Even places like New York City, where some Democrats had sympathized with secession and even contemplated setting up an independent city, abandoned such plans after the war began. A person who lived in the North his or her whole life had little reason for abandoning the Union in favor of the uncertain fate of secession that offered little benefit to them.

Likewise, the vast majority of white southerners did not hesitate to join the Confederacy. In the Deep South especially, decades of conflict with the North over slavery's expansion made them feel increasingly hemmed in, as though they were losing the power they had previously enjoyed. The Upper South sat on the sidelines for a longer time, hoping for some kind of resolution, but ultimately the majority of their populations switched their allegiance from the Union to the Confederacy. Regardless of the misgivings they may have had about going to war or their lingering love for the Union, the prospect of invasion united the Deep South and Upper South in a way not possible in the previous decades of the nineteenth century. Almost by default, native northerners in the North and native white southerners in much of the South sided with their states and regions; no other option seemed relevant.[1]

A potentially more difficult decision awaited those who looked at the secession crisis in shades of gray, rather than in black and white. These individuals fell into two general groups: native southerners who sided with the Union and native northerners who sided with the Confederacy. On many occasions, they severed their ties to their birthplaces, their homes, even their families. In the process, they brought to light not only the continued flexibility of sectional identity, but also the varying strengths of Union and Confederate nationalism. If both sides could command support from individuals in direct conflict with their native homes, then both nations had stronger foundations beyond state and sectional loyalties.

Between these two groups, native southerners who fought for the Union have received much more attention from historians. These southern unionists prove beyond a doubt that the Civil War did not represent simply a fight between North and South. Mainly motivated by an enduring commitment to the Union and believing secession counterproductive or treasonous, these native southerners abandoned ties to community and family to support the Union cause. The ranks of southern unionists included General George H. Thomas, a Virginian who commanded Union armies in Tennessee; Admiral David G. Farragut, a Tennessean who commanded Union naval fleets and played a leading role in the capture of New Orleans and Mobile; Colonel Montgomery C. Meigs, a Georgian who directed Union supply efforts; and General Winfield Scott of Virginia, the highest ranked general in the prewar United States Army.

For the most part, these men had more obvious and logical reasons for staying with the Union even though their native states seceded. Southern unionists saw themselves as Americans first and southerners second and thus refused to take the ultimate step into secession. They had often served as officers in the United States military for years and developed strong attachments to their respective branches, and to the country they had sworn to defend (though admittedly thousands of others resigned their commissions to join the Confederacy). Moreover, several southern states, including Maryland, Delaware, Missouri, and Kentucky, stayed in the Union during the Civil War. All in all, even though the decision was often gut-wrenching, southern unionists did not lack reasons to fight in the Union armies, even if their own states and families sided with the Confederacy.[2]

Native northerners who fought for the Confederacy, on the other hand, present more of an enigma. Few of the conditions that enabled white southerners to embrace national patriotism over state loyalty applied to native northerners who fought for the Confederacy. No Confederate army existed before the war, no northern states seceded, and Confederate agitators were few and far between in the North. Their family members tended to support the Union and often considered these sons and brothers as traitors. In light of these circumstances, what motivated these men to turn their backs on their heritage and take up arms for a Confederacy that did not even exist before 1861? More importantly, how did these soldiers justify their decisions to fight against native home and hearth and what did these justifications mean for sectional identity and Confederate nationalism?

The motivations of these men and women generally fell into two categories: necessity and conviction. Discussions of perceptions of necessity—caused by such factors as marriage, economics, and peer pressure from southern friends and communities—generally imply that adoptive southerners still viewed themselves as northerners and unionists and only fought for the Confederacy by force. In contrast, reasons stemming from conviction, including ideology and identification with the South and the Confederacy, meant that adoptive southerners supported the Confederacy voluntarily and with passion, rather than under compulsion.

Two very different images of these individuals emerge depending on which of these factors held greater sway. If motivations from necessity largely guided them, then for the most part adoptive southerners were merely northerners who abandoned their native section because of opportunity or peer pressure, which implies that they did not have the same kind of stake in the Confederacy as native southerners. On the other hand, if they relied on ideology and identity to guide their decisions, then they held as much, if not more, of a stake in the survival of the Confederacy as native southerners. For the vast majority of adoptive southerners in this study, conviction outweighed necessity and thus ensured their entry into the Confederacy with the full intention of making it their new nation. The transformations that had begun in the antebellum era reached their fruition in the ultimate decision over secession.

As in the antebellum era, the situation of adoptive southerners during the secession crisis challenges assumptions about sectional identity. These assumptions predict that sectional identity will originate from the state and section where a person was born and bred. In this interpretation, such links through ancestry, culture, and values taught through family, school, and community solidified an individual's consciousness and personality, regardless of where they ended up in life. Therefore, when the crash of cannons signaled the call to arms, the choice would be difficult but clear. Weston Rhea, a southern unionist newspaper editor who ultimately sided with the Confederacy, summed up the case for this idea in January 1861: "However much we might regret the necessity that impels the Southern states to dissolve their connections with those of the North, yet 'being native here and to the manor born' we are with them forever."[3]

The typical stories reflecting this theory included white southerners basing their decisions on what happened in their native states and sections. One of the most famous of these episodes involved Colonel Robert Edward Lee, one of the most well-respected prewar U.S. Army officers and a rising star thanks to his exploits in the Mexican War and his leadership in the capture of John Brown at Harper's Ferry. After the firing on Fort Sumter, the Union government offered Lee a promotion to general and command of the new Union army to put down the rebellion. Lee, knowing that this army would eventually have to march through his home state of Virginia, turned down the offer and resigned his commission to avoid fighting against his native state. When Virginia officially seceded, Lee offered his services to the state militia and ultimately to the embryonic Confederate army. Less prominently, native southern students at several northern colleges publicly and defiantly dropped out of school to return home to fight for the Confederacy. While the "born and bred" argument was not universal, it certainly suggested the power of nativity and upbringing in the formulation of sectional identity and national loyalty.

Despite the convenience of this argument, the decisions of adoptive southerners expose a major flaw in such thinking. As native northerners, they should have ultimately sided with the Union because of their ancestry and ties to the North. One author even argues that most northerners living in the South openly or secretly backed the Union.[4] Yet out of the three hundred and three individuals in this study, only forty-seven, or 15 percent, supported the Union. Two hundred and forty eight, over 80 percent, either enthusiastically or reluctantly sided with the Confederacy.[5] Regardless of which side they ultimately supported, sectional identity, and the path through secession and war, involved a lot more choice than destiny.

The decisions faced by adoptive southerners, and their eventual acceptance of secession, have rarely surfaced in historical studies on the subject. When historians do mention adoptive southerners at the start of the war, they often cite only one major reason why a native northerner would fight against his native section: southern wives. James M. McPherson provides a typical example of this conclusion. "Scores of southern officers . . . remained loyal to nation rather than section," McPherson writes. "At the same time, a few northern-born officers who had married southern women chose to go with their wives' section rather than with their own, and rose to high positions in the Confederacy."[6] Author Christian Keller adds that "protecting their wives and families became ideological motives. Similar to many other Confederates, defense of hearth and home proved the decisive factor in convincing them to fight."[7] Following this logic, native northerners would never have fought for the Confederacy had they married northern spouses, indicating that their identification with the Confederacy remained superficial at best.[8]

Some contemporaries of adoptive southerners also believed these individuals fought for the Confederacy because of the southern spouses in their lives. The editor of the *Charleston Mercury,* commenting on the preparations to protect Charleston from Union attack, praised the efforts of Roswell Ripley, an Ohio native who had lived in Charleston for several years. Explaining to his readers why Ripley joined the Confederate cause, the editor declared, "Having no sympathies for Abolitionism, and having married a Carolina woman, with interest here, his place was naturally and appropriately among us."[9] Because a majority of northerners hated abolitionists as much as southerners, the editor here argued that having a wife from South Carolina provided the necessary motivation for Ripley to stake his future with the Confederacy. Another revealing statement came from Confederate general Stephen D. Lee, who served with General John C. Pemberton in both the prewar U.S. Army and the Confederate army. Lee speculated after the war on why Pemberton joined the Confederacy: "He was a Northern man, who had married one of the Southern ladies, and from conviction and from his wife, he liked the South and her causes and knew she had the Constitution and right on her side . . . ."[10] Although Lee hinted that other considerations came into play, having a southern wife came first.

A closer look at northern-born Confederates, however, reveals that marriage to southern women alone cannot explain why they decided to support the Confederacy. At least 12 percent of the individuals in this study, and possibly as high as 30 percent, either never married or only married after the war began. Ohioan Edmund DeWitt Patterson, for example, moved to Alabama in 1859 and remained single when he enlisted as a private in the Ninth Ala-

General John C. Pemberton. A native Pennsylvanian, Pemberton gained his notoriety by unsuccessfully defending Vicksburg against Ulysses S. Grant, ultimately surrendering the city and his army in 1863. He resigned his generalship the next year but reenlisted as a private as a symbol of his loyalty to the Confederacy. Library of Congress.

bama Infantry. Pennsylvanian Henry B. McClellan, nephew to Union general George B. McClellan, enlisted in the Confederate army after living in Virginia barely three years as an unmarried man. In 1865, his alma mater reported that he did marry a Virginia woman but not until the last day of 1863. Even for those who did have southern wives, the latter often had little to no influence on the decisions of their northern-born husbands. Author Norman Johnson aptly points out that the Union's highest-ranked general, Ulysses S. Grant, married a southern colonel's daughter who was also related to Confederate general James Longstreet.[11] In another instance, Confederate general Albert Pike married a local Arkansas woman in 1835, but by 1855 Pike's marriage completely dissolved and he moved to New Orleans for a couple of years before eventually returning to Arkansas as a single man.[12] Whatever Pike's reasons for joining the Confederacy, they certainly did not involve his estranged wife.

Even for the soldiers most often quoted as fighting because of their wives, doubts remain as to whether they actually did so. Josiah Gorgas seems to provide the perfect example, because he married the daughter of an Alabama governor and served at army posts in the North before the war. A closer inspection, however, reveals some flaws in this line of thinking. Christian Keller, who argues that consideration for Gorgas's wife's home state guided him into the Confederacy, cites the March 31, 1861, entry in Gorgas's diary, which includes the phrase "I thought I might as well make a move of it & go where I should ultimately have to go."[13] In the same entry, however, Gorgas also said, "An Army being organized at the South a commission was offered to me in it. I declined then, but being much urged by my own sympathies & likings, & importuned by my Southern friends, I sent in my resignation on the 27th." Gorgas's own words reveal his personal sympathies with the Confederate cause and his southern friends as his reasons for resigning from the United States Army.[14] Clearly, other considerations besides the wishes of his wife guided Gorgas away from his native state.[15]

The person most often cited by historians in favor of the marriage argument is John C. Pemberton. A West Point graduate, this native Pennsylvanian married the daughter of a prominent Norfolk family in 1845, while serving in the army, and kept close ties with the rest of his family in the North. His brothers sided with the Union at the start of the war and told him that both his family and his state would consider him a traitor if he did not follow suit. At the same time, his wife urged him to come to Virginia and fight for her native state. Since he ended up siding with the Confederacy, most historians conclude that his wife's pleas overpowered those of his family back in Pennsylvania. Historian Allan Nevins goes so far as to claim that Pemberton "took the Southern side although every consideration of personal interest counseled him to stay with the Union."[16]

Such a simple conclusion, however, obscures the complicated choice Pemberton faced. First of all, Pemberton's connections with the South extended beyond his wife's Norfolk roots. During his army career, he served in bases all over the South, including locations in Virginia, Texas, and Florida. In 1838, seven years before he met his wife, his father proposed buying some land in Virginia, and Pemberton liked the idea immensely. As he wrote to his father, "I should like to become a Virginian by adoption." His subsequent marriage thus continued, rather than started, his affection for the South.[17]

Pemberton also thought long and hard about his decision before joining the Confederacy. After Fort Sumter, when his wife returned to Norfolk, Pemberton stayed at his post in Washington, D.C., contemplating his next move. He even followed orders from his superiors and detained steamers around the capital to prevent them from sailing farther south. During that time, Pemberton received pleas from both his family and his wife, the former urging him to stay loyal to the Union and his native state, while the latter asked him why he did not follow her immediately back to Norfolk, especially since by then President Jefferson Davis had offered him a commission in the Confederate forces. Although he left no record of his thoughts at this time, his mother seemed to understand the wrenching decision he faced and even predicted he would ultimately side with the Confederacy, but not solely because of his marriage. In a letter she wrote to her daughter-in-law, Pemberton's mother confessed that, although he loved his family in Pennsylvania, Pemberton felt duty- and honor-bound to the Confederacy, "for his heart and views are that the South is right and we are wrong" in terms of justice and preserving southern rights.[18] Finally, ten days after Fort Sumter, Pemberton resigned his commission and traveled to Richmond. It took far more than a simple plea from his southern wife to prompt that fateful leap into the Confederacy's arms.

If marriage alone cannot explain the decisions made by adoptive southerners, other factors must fill in the gaps. Continuing to follow the theory that these men and women could only abandon their native section out of necessity, several historians state that economic considerations compelled these men to fight for the Confederacy to protect their financial well-being. This idea appears to make sense because, as shown previously, many native northerners who ventured south did so because of greater opportunities to make money and advance careers. According to this interpretation, despite the risks and unknowns in abandoning the Union, some native northerners held too much of a financial stake in the Confederacy to consider returning to their native states.[19]

By the time of the Civil War, many of these men had indeed acquired substantial fortunes in money and property. For instance, the 1860 census listed Charles Dahlgren as the owner of around seventy-one hundred acres and more than two hundred slaves, either individually or through partnership. When war broke out, he had a huge investment, not only in southern property, but also in the hard-won social position he had cultivated over decades. As his biographer Hershel Gower writes, "He would not forsake the South when his domain in Louisiana had produced one thousand bales of cotton in 1860."[20] Since Louisiana and Mississippi held his fortunes and his livelihood, according to this reasoning, Dahlgren sided with the Confederacy out of necessity, to protect his fortune, without truly committing to its cause. Similarly, Maine native Zebulon York established himself in Louisiana as a prominent lawyer and cotton planter. By the time of the Civil War, his assets included six plantations in Louisiana and Mississippi, worked by over fifteen hundred slaves and producing thousands of bales of cotton every year."[21] Even though he hailed from a state situated near the heart of abolitionist strongholds in the North, York made his fortune through slavery and would defend his interests accordingly.

Other adoptive southerners had significant financial stakes in land and slaves as well. Samuel French resigned from the army in 1856 to manage a plantation in Mississippi he obtained through marriage. In the same state, Ohioan Charles Clark acquired thousands of acres and over one hundred and forty slaves by 1860. Native Pennsylvanian Stephen Duncan, one of the wealthiest men in Mississippi, owned vast amounts of property and slaves across Mississippi and Louisiana. Duncan's assets in 1861 included thirteen thousand acres valued at over a million dollars, with an additional hundred thousand dollars' worth of equipment and livestock and a workforce of over two thousand slaves. In Louisiana, Robert MacClay, a West Point graduate from Pennsylvania, only gained ownership of his plantation in 1860, but that proved more than enough to get him to wear Confederate gray. For all these men, returning to the North would have meant giving up substantial wealth in both land and slaves. Rather than risk losing everything they had acquired financially, they seemed to have no choice but to support the Confederacy, regardless of personal preferences.[22]

Nor did native northerners have to own slaves to have an economic tie to a southern state. The biographer of Rufus Bullock, a native New Yorker living in Georgia, argues that Bullock opposed secession but stayed in the South because of his financial interests in the state, especially railroads.[23] Similarly, Bushrod Rust Johnson, born into a Quaker family in Ohio, worked as a teacher in military colleges in Kentucky and Tennessee. By 1860, Johnson had secured a respected position as a teacher, five thousand dollars in real estate in Nashville and twelve thousand dollars in personal property. As his biographer observes, "Johnson had almost three times as much property in the South as he held in the North—a potent economic motive for choosing the side he did . . . He had no sentimental or romantic ties to his adopted state; his wife was dead, his son was in the protective hands of northern kin; his school was suspended indefinitely; his faculty colleagues and his 'boys' were gone."[24] Nothing seemed to hold this native Ohioan from his home state except the financial investments he held in Tennessee.

Nevertheless, few if any of the individuals mentioned above ever directly declared that joining the Confederacy meant saving their property above all else. The biographers merely imply that, since these men had built up fortunes in their adopted states, they did not want to risk the loss of such fortunes by abandoning the Confederacy.[25] Moreover, slave-owners especially took a huge risk to their property by supporting secession. If slave-owners stayed in the Union, they would have continued to receive the protection of the fugitive slave laws enforced by the Union government and army. If they joined the Confederacy, on the other hand, nothing would have prevented their slaves from running away to seek asylum in the Union, since the fugitive slave laws did not apply outside the Union. For this reason, prominent slaveholders often took positions as conditional unionists before the war; they felt their slave property was better protected inside the Union than out of it.[26] In addition, the majority of adoptive southerners had little or no heavy financial stake in the South yet still enlisted in the Confederate armies. Nearly two-thirds of the individuals documented did not own slaves or have significant landholdings. These numbers do not to point to economics as the critical tipping point for most adoptive southerners when it came time to decide on secession.²⁷

Beyond a desire to protect their marriages and property, another potential influence came from southern families and communities. For example, in the fall of 1860, a local Nashville militia company called the "Rock City Guard" elected Charles Quintard, a native of Connecticut, its chaplain, even though he did not consider himself a military man and remained a steadfast unionist during the secession crisis. Once hostilities commenced, the company became part of the First Tennessee Regiment and was ordered to Virginia for active duty. At that point, Quintard recalled, "being very urgently pressed by members of the Rock City Guard and their friends in Nashville to accompany the regiment as chaplain, I resolved to do so." Not wanting to let his friends and neighbors down, Quintard threw aside his earlier hesitations and followed them into the defense of the Confederacy. Likewise, Henry Handerson, an Ohioan who moved to Louisiana in the late 1850s, explained one of his motivations when he wrote to his uncle in the summer of 1861, "I thought that if the war was speedily ended I should soon return to my usual pursuits. And if not, my services would certainly be required, and I might be drafted into a company of total strangers. Capt. Stafford himself is a war friend of mine . . . and nearly all my most intimate friends are with me." Having their close friends around them made them feel a part of the Confederate armies even though they did not have the same native link to the South. Similar to the situation of all Civil War soldiers, peer pressure from neighbors and comrades could override hesitations in volunteering for the war.²⁸

Such a perception reiterates the notion that adoptive southerners were still just northerners facing a wrenching pull between their northern and southern interests. Rather than having the same commitment as native southerners, native northerners simply gave in to peer pressure from their southern friends and neighbors. Following this logic, adoptive southerners might just as easily have tilted their allegiance back to the North, if only their northern families and friends had made better pleas or if they had simply visited the North at the right moment.²⁹

In a few instances, adoptive southerners themselves expressed such feelings. Josiah Gorgas, for example, had a strong relationship with his in-laws. As he wrote to his wife in the late 1850s, "It is strange what an attraction he [his father in law] exercises toward even me.—a stranger to his blood—But I owe him. 'Heaven's last best gift.'—my darling wife—and he is associated with all the happiest period of my life."[30] Even more directly, Henry Handerson seemed to indicate he went into secession reluctantly and almost wished he could take it back. Nevertheless, though he still considered himself a northerner, Handerson decided to side with the Confederacy mainly because of his interests in the South and his southern friends. "All my interests, present and future, apparently lay in the South and with Southerners," he wrote in his memoirs. "When I add to this that I was 24 years of age, and naturally affected largely by the ideas, the enthusiasm and the excitement of my surroundings, it is easy to understand to what conclusions I was led."[31]

Just like marriage and economic considerations, however, ties to southern communities raise as many questions as they answer. Gorgas did not even live in the South during the secession crisis; he and his family resided in Philadelphia, after transferring from Charleston in June 1860, which meant his surroundings should have compelled him to stay in the North.[32] In regards to Quintard's assertions that the insistence of his neighbors compelled him to join the local militia, the story he shared with a Memphis newspaper editor tells a far different tale. Interviewing Quintard at the end of 1865 about his recollections of the secession crisis, the editor quoted the Confederate veteran as saying, "I never believed in secession; I never taught secession; I never voted secession. But the crisis came; my path of duty was plain before me. The State, in her sovereign capacity, had dissolved her connection with the Government. The Church . . . must of necessity recognize the *de facto* government elsewhere, and submit to it."[33]

Even Handerson's insistence on thinking of himself as a northerner overwhelmed by his surroundings only partly explained his actions. Handerson actually wrote the above statement thirty years after the war, when he had returned to the North after leaving the Confederate army. With such a distance in time and space, he very likely felt far different about his motivations in the 1890s than he did on the eve of secession. He also seemed to forget that, at the time the war broke out, he was staying with a staunchly unionist family in Louisiana who tried to talk him out of joining the local regiment. In fact, Handerson recorded that his hostess cried when he told them his intentions.[34] Clearly, though they made some contribution, neither southern families nor southern communities held enough clout to get native northerners to abandon their native communities en masse.[35]

While all of these different motivations tell part of the story of adoptive southerners' transition into the Confederacy, they all suffer from one crucial flaw: authors who cite such reasons tend to assume that these native northerners continued to think of themselves as northerners who ended up joining the Confederacy out of necessity or peer pressure. These authors contend that these men never abandoned their upbringing, whether they had southern wives, held an economic stake in the South, or were influenced by their southern friends and communities. Their commitment, according to this interpretation, remained contingent on Confederate success and therefore did not rank on the same level as that of native southerners, who fought for their very survival against Union invasions.

In reality, this view ignores the fact that these adoptive southerners represented more than simply native northerners in the South. In order to fully understand why over 80 percent of the adoptive southerners in this study supported secession over the Union, we must understand that, because of the fluidity of sectional identity in the prewar years, these individuals had far more than money and community to guide their actions. Adoptive southerners found a new way to express their adopted identities by proclaiming their allegiance to a southern nation. Throughout the secession crisis, northern emigrants, even those who did not consider themselves fully southern, still expressed their identification with the Confederacy and defended its rights with the same fervor as native southerners. Ideological arguments, as well as identification with the Confederacy and the South, reveal that adoptive southerners considered themselves as much a part of the new nation as anyone else from the beginning. No one needed to force them into the ranks; they felt they belonged there.

Before the guns started blazing, however, some adoptive southerners tried to use their unique position to promote a peaceful solution. Thanks to their heritage, these men and women, if they so chose, had the opportunity to act as a kind of ambassador corps, or at least neutral observers, between the North and the South. The vast majority of Americans in the early nineteenth century either did not travel more than twenty miles away from their homes or migrated along the same latitudes as their birthplaces. The most they ever learned about their counterparts from other sections came from newspapers, pamphlets, or travel journals. Stereotypes often took hold in the minds of the populace about different sections of the country. Most white northerners did not understand the South and wanted southerners to adopt a free labor ideology. A similar pattern held for white southerners, who did not understand why northerners believed they could interfere in southern affairs with impunity. Through all of their conflict, neither side seemed able to bridge the gap.[36]

Adoptive southerners, however, believed they represented the perfect messengers to provide that bridge because of their experiences living in both places. Reared in northern states and immersed in the culture of southern states as adults, they managed to bring firsthand accounts of life on both sides of the Mason-Dixon Line. As a result, northern emigrants often considered themselves the best judge of sectional harmony or discord, because of their associations with both sections. Thanks to their experiences, they could challenge the propaganda of extremists and theoretically provide a more balanced view of how northern and southern worldviews intersected.

Building on their personal knowledge, some adoptive southerners took the opportunity to dispel myths and give an accurate impression of both sections from their own personal observations. Such an experience could not help but force them to evaluate what others said and confront misconceptions or outright lies. Sometimes they witnessed stereotypes play out exactly as envisioned, but other times they recognized that distance and miscommunication had obscured the facts. For example, Joseph Ingraham wrote in the preface to his book *The Sunny South* that he had written it because, "when hitherto so much in relation by our people and institutions is misunderstood and misinterpreted by those who have no personal knowledge either of Southerners or of Southern life . . . The object of this work is to do justice to the Southern planter, and, at the same time, afford information in an agreeable form to the Northerner."[37] Since few others had made the same journey, northern emigrants like Ingraham felt no one else possessed the same unbiased perspective.[38]

A few of these individuals readily embraced their role as go-betweens for white northerners and southerners, especially if they believed it might help forestall war. Albert Pike tried to foster some understanding between the sections by highlighting his northern roots and southern adulthood. He outlined his arguments in a series of anonymous letters written for both the Arkansas populace and a northern audience. Specifically, Pike told his readers, "let me simply say that I was born and bred up until after manhood in New England, and educated in Massachusetts. I have lived just one half of my life in the extreme Southwest; and with Southern soil has mingled the dust of four of my children. I have owned such slaves only as I needed for household servants, and have never in my life held, or desired to hold, public office."[39] In Pike's opinion, his upbringing in New England combined with his experiences in the South gave him the perfect perspective for an unbiased view of both slavery and secession.

Once he established his credentials, Pike pleaded with his native North to see the wisdom of allowing the South to work out its own problems. While admitting that slavery had its evil characteristics, he reminded northerners that wage laborers suffered as well. He remembered seeing a female apprentice in Boston as cruelly treated as any slave he had ever seen in the South. He went on to say that "Pauperism, in your cities, separates more families than slavery does on our plantations." Pike jokingly concluded that Americans might as well abolish commerce and capitalism itself if they wanted to

Albert Pike. A native New Englander and prominent Mason, Pike served as the Confederate ambassador to Indian Territory, even leading a Native American regiment at the Battle of Pea Ridge. From the Paul Dolle Civil War Collection, courtesy of the Butler Center for Arkansas Studies, Central Arkansas Library System.

right all the wrongs of society. Unlike most conditional unionists, Pike had the benefit of seeing both sides of the equation and argued that each needed to see the other's perspective. As he summarized in another of his letters, "Let all of us live in peace, and do our duty at home, in our own portion of the country, minding each our own business . . . If we keep on wrangling and quarreling, we shall go to pieces. . . ."[40]

When he brought up the secession crisis, Pike again turned to his status as a go-between. He described to his readers how his wife and children called the South home, while he himself still loved the New England of his childhood, and how his ties to the Union stemmed from both sections. Just as he could not conceive of himself as anything except a product of the North and South together, so he claimed the rest of the country felt the same way. "Owing all that I am, and all that I and my children ever shall be, to the institutions and influences of the Union . . . and my heart clinging alike to the North and the South," he pleaded with his readers, "how can I look upon the strife, the antipathies, the bitterness, and the hatred, ominous of disaster, of the North and the South, with out the profounded [sic] sorrow and the gloomiest apprehension."[41]

Sally Baxter Hampton, a New Yorker who married into the powerful South Carolina family, also utilized her status as a go-between. Unlike Pike, Sally still thought of herself as a northerner living in the South, rather than as an adoptive southerner, because she only lived in South Carolina for a few years before secession. Indeed, she often referred to southerners in a scornful manner and felt that northerners were their superiors in character.[42] And unlike Pike, she believed that little chance existed for true camaraderie between the two sections because of the vast differences she had seen. Five years before secession engulfed the country, she made a prediction to her father: "The more I see of the South and Southerners the more am I convinced of the utter impossibility that a northerner can ever properly judge the institutions of this part of the country . . . Anybody who stops to investigate can't but see how utterly unpracticable to the southern mind is any idea of compromise, and how northern fanaticism on this subject is ever to be moderated Heaven alone knows. . . ."[43]

Nevertheless, by 1860 she came to believe her residence in South Carolina gave her the perfect platform for formulating a well-rounded view of secession. More than anything else, Sally felt that a failure to engage with each other created the biggest obstacle to peace and moderation. She understood, based on her observations, that the agitation stirred up by abolitionists and Republicans in the North provided the South with a justification for resistance based on self-preservation.[44] She claimed that if everyone saw the South as she did, with her own eyes rather than through northern propaganda, most northerners would agree with the South's fears.[45] Significantly, when she spoke about her opinions, she specifically said her combination of upbringing in the North and residence in the South provided her with the proper perspective. She wrote to a friend, "These matters have been quite sufficiently discussed by far wiser heads, but it may not be useless that I—a northern born & bred woman, living on a plantation in the midst of three hundred Negroes . . . seeing constantly the Southern people of every age, condition & grade—mixing with them freely & intimately on all occasions, it may not be in vain that I speak when I speak to a man like you."[46] Drawing on her personal experiences as a transplanted plantation mistress, Sally told her family that the secession fervor in the South was very real and stemmed from principle rather than self-interest. If the North did not heed her warnings, then the blood shed by the Founding Fathers in the War for Independence to create the country would amount to nothing.[47]

She then outlined her own solution to the problem, which involved the Middle Atlantic states leading the way to compromise and putting down the abolitionists of New England and the secessionists of the Deep South. Everything depended on keeping everyone's interests at heart. "The whole fifteen Southern states would gladly follow their Northern *friends,* who can render powerless their fanatical disturbers," she insisted, "but they will resist to the death, engulphing themselves & the whole country in one common destruction if their enemies attempt to restrain them or force them to a Union abhorrent to their interests." Once again, she warned her friends and family of the real dangers of civil war should the radical elements prevail. As she wrote in her final words to her friends and family, " In God's name I conjure you, place the matter clearly before them & endeavor to have it left to the voice of the people . . . whether they will leave that sect of fanatics who have been so far such 'blind guides' & assume the place which will be gladly conceded to them in a fraternity with their Southern sister states."[48]

Building on the themes expressed by Hampton, other adoptive southerners who wished to lessen sectional animosity tried to use their knowledge to call for a more nationalist view of the country rather than a sectional one. Aware that many northerners believed people from their section could never live safely in the South, adoptive southerners pointed to their own life stories as a refutation of that concern. Soon after arriving in Missouri, Arthur McArthur told his sister about how all regions of the country melded together in the state that personified the border between North and South. He wrote that people in the West had a noble spirit, "a scarce article with our sharp, shrewd, cunning Yankees," while the families from Virginia had the "noble traits" of hospitality, generosity, and honor.[49]

Theodore Clapp and Seargent Prentiss went further by directly refuting the fears expressed by other northerners about the roughness of the Southwest and the dangers awaiting northern travelers. Clapp admitted that most people in New England thought a place like Mississippi was barbarous and lawless, but he countered that impression by saying that such fears arose from only a few isolated incidents blown out of proportion by newspapers. In his view, "it is not inferior even to Massachusetts or Connecticut in the manifestations of moral excellence, truth, honor, justice; a patriotism willing to die for the land it loves . . ."[50] Seargent Prentiss highlighted this idea in a speech he gave in 1845: "We love the land of our adoption, so do we that of our birth. Let us be ever true to both; and always exert ourselves in maintaining our country, the integrity of the Republic."[51] In a situation similar to that of the Border States, adoptive southerners knew that a break-up of the Union would hit them the hardest, forcing them to make a difficult choice between their native and adopted lands and likely cutting them off completely from their families. They wanted to remind people of what had brought all Americans together rather than what might tear them apart.

Ashbel Smith expanded on this theme as well. In his mind, the North and the South complemented each other through the combination of their special traits. In a speech he gave to the Phi Beta Kappa Society in Texas, Smith brought up his childhood home in Connecticut, which he called the remotest state in the Union and very different in climate and landscape from Texas. Yet that did not matter because he considered the populations of the North and the South as homogeneous, with pioneers from across the Atlantic States. Smith himself counted as one of those pioneers because he had left his home in New England for greater opportunities in the frontiers of Texas, where North and South mixed to further the Manifest Destiny of the Union.[52] As Smith explained further in a separate speech, "From the frozen loins of the North comes a population of untiring energy and indomitable courage; the ardent South send forth in her generous sons a people of more fiery and furious valor. . . . But broad as is our land, wide spread as are our people, we are one in language, one in institutions, homogeneous in race."[53]

Several other adoptive southerners, in a more pessimistic tone, tried to warn their northern and southern friends and families alike about the potential for disaster should no compromise arise. Henry Watson wrote that people in Alabama did not hate Lincoln but abhorred the meddling by free states into the slavery affairs of the South, as well as personal liberty laws directed against the Fugitive Slave Act. "The two sections each sadly misunderstand the feelings, opinions & intentions of the other," he told his cousin, "and cannot be made to know better & each is obstinate to a sin in the cause they have adopted. . . . We regret the present state of things, but the majority against us is so overwhelming that we cannot stay the tide . . ."[54] A few months later he wrote to a friend that any hint of coercion by the North would end any hopes of a peaceful reconstruction. Conditional unionists like himself still held out hope for such a solution but "Force would *unite* the whole southern states and make *unanimous* the people of each state & the feeling would be so bitter that a future reconstruction would be impossible."[55]

Similarly, Henry Richardson, a Maine native living in Louisiana, told his parents he doubted they received an accurate account of the situation in the South from northern newspapers. He warned them about white southerners' eagerness to resist coercion and that the best solution involved the North repealing their "unconstitutional laws," meaning the personal liberty laws that directly violated the Fugitive Slave Act. John S. Ryan followed this logic by saying that both sides were misrepresented but also that the South suffered more because the North "slandered" her institutions and because she faced possible invasion by northern armies.[56] In a similar manner, Julia Tyler wrote to her mother in January 1861, "The South asks no other than *just* treatment, and this she must have to be induced to remain in the Union." Amelia Lines, a New England native living in Georgia, despite her own unionist leanings, railed against abolitionists and predicted that by nominating Lincoln, "the abolitionists set up a candidate which no honest & *honorable* southern man can vote for or hold an office under. . . . the South will not submit to be ruled by the north, and a dissolution of the union will be inevitable . . . ."[57]

Of all the adoptive southerners trying to act as go-betweens, Frederick Barnard gave one of the most detailed and impassioned analyses of the misunderstandings between North and South. Although he ultimately left the South in the second year of the war because of his support for the Union, that did not mean he forgot his experiences there. In a personal letter to President Lincoln, Barnard tried to make the nation's chief executive understand the intricacies of white southerners in the midst of secession. He claimed secession fever swept across the South thanks to demagogues fanning anti-northern propaganda without the slightest basis in fact. He firmly believed, as did Lincoln, that secessionists brainwashed white southerners who supported the Union into thinking of the northern people as their enemies. As he summarized for Lincoln, "It is probably that, since time began, there has never been an example of the hatred of one people for another so measureless in degree, so unfathomable in depth, so utterly groundless in fact, and so intensely absurd in its alleged causes, as the hatred of the people of the South, and especially of South Carolina, for the people of the North, and especially of New England . . . ."[58] In his opinion, the fire-eaters of the South prevented any logical discourse of the true feelings between northerners and southerners. As someone who lived in the South and absorbed its culture, Barnard felt his own assessment represented an accurate picture of the misperceptions that helped spark civil war.

Nevertheless, despite their good intentions, adoptive southerners revealed their own biases at the same time that they claimed to speak as unbiased observers. In each of these warnings, they created a version of the crisis most favorable to southerners. It seemed that the North needed to make every concession, including repealing personal liberty laws and leaving the South alone. As Albert Pike had said to his northern audience, "Let us, and our slaves, alone. Let the whole matter of slavery alone. We are as humane as you, and as intelligent as you, and will do the very best we can with that which is with us to be dealt with."[59] Although they claimed to speak for both sides, much of the time adoptive southerners defended their adopted section much more than their native section. Abolitionists remained a much greater danger in their minds than rabid secessionists.[60]

When forced to choose, even adoptive southerners who regarded themselves as conditional or unconditional unionists mostly supported their adopted section. Pike ultimately sided with the Confederacy once Arkansas seceded, while still priding himself on at least attempting to use his status as a go-between to prevent war. Sally Baxter Hampton, though saddened by her separation from her family, opted to stay with her husband and in-laws in South Carolina. Henry Watson fled for Europe rather than choose sides. Even Julia Tyler and Frederick Barnard, who ended up returning to the

North, did so not as northerners against the South but rather as southern unionists saddened at the prospect of imminent destruction for their beloved adopted homeland. While they may have considered themselves the perfect go-betweens, in the end their adopted identities prevented any truly unbiased observations. And once war appeared inevitable, adoptive southerners showed the extent of their transformation by embracing arguments that highlighted ideology and identity as the cornerstones for supporting the emerging Confederacy.

In terms of ideology, adoptive southerners believed fervently in the righteousness of the Confederacy's actions. Secessionists declared repeatedly that the South had to secede because they needed to protect slavery, uphold states' rights, protect their families and homes, and prevent the South from getting overshadowed by an increasingly powerful North. Upbringing in the North did not keep adoptive southerners from adopting these arguments as their own. As historian James McPherson remarks, "Every schoolboy and schoolgirl knew how they had fought against the odds to forge a new republic conceived in liberty. Northerners and Southerners alike believed themselves custodians of the legacy of 1776." Northerners uprooted from their native states might see nothing wrong in calls to defend their adopted states in the name of liberty and self-government. In a sense, the values and traditions held by all Americans could provide a relatively smooth transition to a Confederate allegiance.[61]

Many of these men and women felt no hypocrisy because in their minds the North they left behind did not exist at the time of secession. Adoptive southerners still felt close to their northern families and rarely blamed them for the troubles confronting the Union. If anything, one of the only reasons they would want to return to the Union was to see their families. Nevertheless, adoptive southerners also came to believe their native section had betrayed everything they loved as Americans. Native southerners who joined the Confederacy certainly felt that way about the North. As one author wrote, "The South, Confederates insisted, was the legitimate heir of American revolutionary tradition. Betrayed by Yankees who had perverted the true meaning of the Constitution, the revolutionary heritage could be preserved only by secession."[62] Yet even native northerners could agree with this perception. For instance, adopted Texan Ashbel Smith received a letter from one of his neighbors who wrote to him from Germany, saying, "Our sympathies are entirely for the South in this struggle. I am a northerner by birth, but I think the Southern States had a prefect right to secede and that the attempt to coerce them back is exceedingly unjust." Though she readily acknowledged her northern roots, Smith's neighbor still believed secessionists deserved her support.[63] Such thinking gained credibility in several places in the North, especially New York City, New Jersey, and the counties of southern Ohio, Indiana, and Illinois. Although they did not actually join the Confederacy, these northerners still pushed for peaceful secession rather than allow the federal government to exert dictatorial power over the states.[64]

Adoptive southerners took such rhetoric to a whole new level as they blended their own experiences in the South with traditional states' rights arguments, distancing themselves from their native section. They generally blamed the North for the problems facing the Union while defending the South's right to resist. Despite their background, a lot of these native northerners could not stand what their former section had become and therefore felt they had no connection to it whatsoever. Specifically, the rise of the Republican Party, which took place years after many northerners left the South, alarmed them as they looked upon the dangers of such a party through the eyes of the South. As Ashbel Smith told his nephew in Connecticut in February 1861, "The madness of Black Republicanism has destroyed the best government ever devised by man. . . . God grant that the mortification may never fall on me of hearing that you have affiliated in the smallest iota with Black Republicanism."[65] Even though a majority of the North supported the Republicans by 1860, adoptive southerners like Smith viewed them and their platform as the greatest threats to sectional harmony and the preservation of the country's ideals.

Rather than see themselves as northerners forced to choose between competing sections, these men made a conscious effort to place themselves in the secessionist mold. Maine native Arthur McArthur provides a vivid image of the transformation of a native northerner into an avowed and immediate secessionist. McArthur found himself in the heart of Louisiana after Lincoln's election and immediately got caught up in the excitement of potential secessionist movements. This product of New England at times sounded like a man coming out of Charleston. As early as December 1860, when only South Carolina had actually seceded, McArthur told his parents back in Maine that he predicted that all the Gulf states would soon follow suit and that he intended to serve in the forefront. Through it all, McArthur placed all the blame, not on white northerners in general, and least of all on his own family, but on "Black Republican Fanatics," whom he hated for meddling with slavery. McArthur declared, "You may tell them all that I wear the blue cockade & am Captain of a Company of 'minute men'—and that I go with the South."[66] A few months later, McArthur reiterated his political philosophies and stated proudly his views on secession. "I was a Breckenridge man, a secessionist, immediate, no compromise—never go back fire eater, as you at the North would call us & from principle I am this knowing as I do political believe [sic] & policies of both sections and all parties."[67] William Lowndes Yancey and Robert Barnwell Rhett, who helped lead the South into secession, could not have stated the immediate secessionist views any clearer. A native son of New England managed to take on the mantle of a Deep South secessionist.

Edward Wells, a native of Massachusetts, echoed the sentiments of McArthur when he found himself in Charleston during the firing on Fort Sumter, after moving there for health reasons in 1860. Despite the fact that he had only spent a year in the South before the war erupted, Wells firmly backed the secessionist cause thanks to his states' rights views nurtured by his parents during his childhood. He hailed the coming of secession and believed every "right thinking & honourable man" needed to back the South Carolina secessionists. In fact, even before South Carolina officially seceded, Wells declared the Union already broken up "because of the Yankee States having vilified it" with acts like the personal liberty laws.[68] Several months later, in one of the most revealing statements expressed by a northern emigrant towards his former section, Edward Wells told his father, "I believe that [the North] with its present folly, fanaticism & wickedness it is a doomed Nation, & that the South is to become 'America'. I therefore think the sooner I get a toehold here, the better." [69] Like many native southerners, Wells defended secession as the only honorable way to save the Union from the perceived perversions of northern fanatics. One did not have to possess southern heritage to hold such views. At the end of April 1861, Wells reiterated his sentiments one more time to his family when he wrote, "Their [the North's] purpose, in that case, will be to enslave . . . a free & noble people so will oppose them, deo volente, in the bitter end. They will call me at the North a rebel, & traitor. If contending for the rights of free men is treason, than every honorable man is a traitor. I rejoice in the name."[70]

Expressions of southern righteousness occurred among other young men who spent little time in the South before the war as well. Felix de Fontaine, a native Frenchman who spent many years in the North before moving to the South just before secession, wrote about the 1860 election, " . . . for the first time in the history of our confederacy, we look upon the spectacle of a sectional party, defiant, unyielding and uncompromising, whose principles aim a blow direct at the annihilation of one of the institutions of the South . . ."[71] Similarly, native Pennsylvanian Joseph Garey only moved to Cockrum, Mississippi, in 1860. Despite his brief sojourn in the state, he enlisted in a Mississippi regiment early in the war. Joseph's wartime diary offers few clues as to his motivation, but at times he revealed traces of ideological determination. On May 10, 1862, while discussing the Confederate conscription act, Garey took offense at any attempts to curtail individual rights. He hoped his comrades would stay, "but we cannot blame them for resisting any encroachments on their rights. . . . We are fighting for our unalienable rights & for them we inaugurated the war."[72] Again, the notion of "southern rights" entered into the thinking of a native northerner fighting for the South.[73]

George G. Junkin followed the same course, in spite of personal pleas from his family. A native Pennsylvanian who grew up in the North, Junkin moved to the Shenandoah Valley at the age of eighteen. Graduating from Washington College in Lexington, Junkin began his career as a teacher at the Montgomery Male Academy in Christiansburg in 1859. In 1861, after only five years in the South, Junkin had to decide whether to support his adopted community or follow the wishes of his staunchly unionist relatives. Junkin's uncle, George Junkin, Sr., who served as president of Washington College before returning to Pennsylvania in 1860, even traveled to Harpers Ferry in May 1861 to meet with his nephew and his son-in-law, Professor Thomas Jonathan Jackson at the Virginia Military Institute. The elder Junkin hoped to persuade both of them to side with the Union, reminding his nephew that his entire family back in Pennsylvania supported the Union as well. Instead, both Jackson and the younger Junkin promptly refused his entreaties and stayed in Virginia. For the younger Junkin, such a move meant betraying his family, but he accepted that course of action because he deeply believed in the Confederate cause. One of his comrades, James Langhorne, explained Junkin's decision: "He is fighting against the S[t]ate that gave him birth, Father, Mother, Bro. & Sister, and for what [?] because he thinks our cause is just . . . he was not to be persuaded, he could not give up the loyal principles of his noble heart & made the sacrifice of all family connection. . . ."[74] While he still loved his family, his ideological convictions and love for the South dispelled any doubts for this young man.[75]

If Wells, Garey, and Junkin could support the Confederacy after living only a few years in the South, it is no surprise that similar rhetoric prevailed in the declarations of other adoptive southern secessionists who spent far more years under the southern sun. Caroline Gilman, who lived in South Carolina for three decades, wrote to her children that "our citizens" and "our state" were standing up to the law-breaking northerners who harbored runaways and kept slavery out of the territories. She also claimed that, despite the propaganda spreading in the North, she slept in her home without any fear of slave uprisings and challenged white northern women to feel just as secure in their own homes.[76] Another Massachusetts native in South Carolina, Moses Curtis, excoriated northern radicals without any indication that he had ties to any of them. He left no doubt of his stance when he wrote to his colleagues in the North, "let me say to you, our Union is in serious danger, & unless the Northern states *recede* from their hostile position, & repeal their 'personal liberty' Laws, the Southern States will *secede* inevitably. . . . We believe we are, in the main, right; & we *know* that in some things the North is wrong, has insulted & injured us, & we shall of course, act upon our own sense of the matter, whatever be the consequences."[77]

Down in Louisiana, native New Yorker John Slidell, who would later serve as Confederate ambassador to France, felt nothing but relief after Lincoln's election because it forced all white southerners, including himself, to face the prospect of separation. He wrote to one of his business partners, "The most skeptical will now be convinced that the South is in earnest and you may consider the Union as already dissolved for I have no hope of the North retracing its steps. We have many true friends there from whom it will be painful to separate but self preservation is the supreme law . . ."[78] A few months later, another adopted Louisianan, Thomas K. Wharton, wrote in his diary after hearing about the firing on Fort Sumter, "It is hoped that one or two other victories on our part will convince the madmen of the North that their system of aggression must be abandoned."[79]

Even adoptive southerners who considered themselves conditional unionists, and did everything in their power to prevent secession, insisted their unionism depended on the North acting in good faith. If forced to choose, they warned, preserving southern rights meant more to them than preserving the Union, with little regard for their native section. For instance, Robert

John Slidell. A native New Yorker, Slidell served as a lawyer and senator from Louisiana. Jefferson Davis selected him as the Confederate ambassador to France, where he unsuccessfully tried to bring the French into the war on the side of the Confederacy. Library of Congress.

Hatton, an Ohio-born Tennessee congressman and devout unionist, told his friend Lawrence Lindsley, "If it cannot be preserved—if the North will not yield to us what are our rights—will not guarantee to us those rights—destroy the Union, by the destruction of what it was intended to secure and establish—*then,* we will have no alternative but to look to ourselves—rely upon our own strength for security."[80] Ashbel Smith echoed Hatton's sentiments in a speech he gave in the late 1850s, saying the Union would lose its purpose if the northern states infringed on southern rights. At that point, according to Smith, secession would then be "our solemn duty." Nathaniel Pratt, a long-time resident of Alabama, supported John Bell in the 1860 election and urged moderation, yet still believed "that the South ought to maintain her rights at all hazards." George Kendall, an adoptive southerner in Texas, put it more bluntly when he wrote to one of his northern friends, "I am not a Secession man myself—I am still for attempting to hold our Union together . . . But I am all the time doubtful whether there is good faith enough left in the North to do justice to the South. If you in the North openly nullify by setting aside a plain and palpable provision of the Constitution, any State in the South has an undoubted right to secede or nullify."[81] Akin to most southern unionists, each of these men placed the rights and safety of the South as more important than the preservation of the Union. Adoptive southerners thus believed in the righteousness of secession as passionately as any of their white southern neighbors.

Still, amid all this rhetoric on southern rights, identification with the South lay at the heart of adoptive southern adherence to secessionist ideology. After all, some white northerners at the time, especially Democrats, had similar fears of Republicans, abolitionists, and an active federal government, yet did not opt for secession. What separated adoptive southerners from all other northerners was their sectional identity transformation before the war, along with their loyalties to their adopted states. Those loyalties guided their thinking on secession, much like the issue of slavery guided white southern views on the theory of states' rights. Whether they advocated immediate secession or unconditional unionism, these men and women made clear that they did not feel the same attachments to the North as they had in the past. As Christian Keller rightly comments, "Loyalty to one's respective section or state . . . was not necessarily a foregone conclusion. New ties outweighed devotion to older ones, and place of birth did not always predetermine national identity." Adoptive southerners epitomized the accuracy of Keller's statement. Moving from one region to another even a couple years before the war often meant the difference between a man becoming a Union soldier or a Confederate one. The fluidity and flexibility of sectional identity ultimately added native northerners to the ranks of an otherwise all-southern Confederacy.[82]

Like so many other Americans of that era, adoptive southerners identified themselves by their state and region as much as their nation. People referred to themselves as a "New Yorker," "Mississippian," "northerner," "southerner," or wherever they placed the most value for their existence. For that reason, the whole philosophy of states' rights took hold in both the North and the South at different times before the Civil War, with New England threatening secession during the War of 1812 and South Carolina attempting nullification in the 1830s. In each case, proponents of secession or nullification cited state sovereignty as the most important liberty for a free people. Adoptive southerners, because of their identity transformation, would more often than not follow the course of their adopted state over their native state, which meant a greater likelihood for supporting the Confederacy.[83]

Professions of connections to the South appear profusely in their writings. For example, Edmund DeWitt Patterson, an Ohio native who moved to Alabama, recorded in his wartime journal: "I intended to spend one year there. I liked the South, I found nothing existing as I had heard it represented, and I concluded to make my home there. Soon the dark clouds of war arose . . . I saw that there was no alternative but war or disgrace and everlasting dishonor for the South, and embraced the first opportunity of becoming a soldier in the confederate army . . ." Though he only intended to make his stay in the South temporary, Patterson ultimately considered the South his home and would do anything to protect it. As a result, if the South left the Union, Patterson would not stay with the Union either.[84] In a similar manner, Jedediah Hotchkiss, a native New Yorker living in Virginia, explained to his wife that he would have preferred to stay home, "but then I owe a duty to my country that I must discharge that she may be enabled to put the shield of her protection over my family . . ."[85] Another adoptive southerner in Virginia, Joseph Johnson, gave his full support to the Confederacy because his adopted state needed protection.[86]

John C. Pemberton, a native Pennsylvanian who eventually became a top-ranking Confederate general, went through his own struggle and came out in favor of his adopted state. Taking everything into consideration, Pemberton decided to make Virginia's destiny his own. As he explained to a Mississippi newspaper after the war, nothing prevented him from enlisting in the Confederate armies except "the remoteness of my station and the deliberation evinced by my adopted State Virginia."[87] Of course, such a declaration may not have meant anything, since he wrote that statement in 1874 and might have simply wanted to reaffirm his credentials as a Confederate in the wake of his military defeats. In this instance, however, his mother backed him up. Rebecca Pemberton was heartbroken when her son turned his back on his family but she understood the reason why. She knew he loved his family, but he would not do anything to jeopardize Virginia. As she told her daughter, "As long as he remains, he will do he says, anything he is ordered to, excepting going to attack & fire upon Norfolk—if he is ordered to do *that*, he would resign at once. . . . Israel says John is most dreadfully distressed & worried, *on our account*—for his heart & views are that the South is right & we are wrong."[88] Just like Robert E. Lee, Pemberton drew the line at attacking his state, except this time it was not his native state of Pennsylvania but his adopted state of Virginia.

An even more cautious adoptive southerner, native Ohioan Robert Hatton, ultimately gave up his unionist position thanks to his love of an adopted state, in his case Tennessee. Throughout the secession crisis, Hatton remained one of the most committed unionists in Congress. A fierce advocate of moderation, Hatton hated both Republicans and secessionists alike as the greatest threats to both the Union and peace. He gave numerous speeches urging compromise as the best medicine for the ills of the nation. Nevertheless, even this committed unionist admitted that, if forced to choose, he would ultimately side with his adopted state. On several occasions, he wrote to his wife about his work on behalf of "our southerners" and "our Tennesseans."[89] Such statements merely laid the foundation for his speech to the House in early 1861. He started off by saying that Tennessee would allow neither the North nor the South to force her into a decision but instead would decide her own fate. If Tennessee was called upon by her sister states to join together for a common cause of self-defense, he would sacrifice his love for the Union to protect the interests of his adopted state. "I shall not follow the example of gentlemen in making protestations of my devotion to the South or to my State," he said plainly to his colleagues. "No, sir, but if, at this time, with my convictions of duty, I should bend before the angry storm that is sweeping over my State, I would despise myself, and bring dishonor upon my children . . . in no event, I repeat, can I be robbed of that richest of earthly blessings—the consciousness of having done what my carefully informed judgment told me was right."[90]

Loyalty to an adopted state manifested itself in many other places outside of Virginia and Tennessee. As far south as Florida and as far west as Arkansas, adoptive southerners vowed to follow their adopted states into secession. Albert Pike addressed his colleagues in Arkansas as someone who had as much stake in the success of Arkansas as any of its citizens. When Arkansas seceded, he willingly went along with his state's decision despite his own previous attempts at moderation. Samuel French immediately offered his services to his adopted state of Mississippi once the state convention took the state out of the Union. In addition, Henry Handerson credited his Louisiana citizenship as a major factor in his decision. As Handerson wrote to his uncle, "When the war broke out I was a citizen of one of the Southern States. The citizens of that state, by their representatives in convention assembled, withdrew from the U.S. government and united themselves with their sister states of the South. Whether they had the right to 'secede' is a question of little moment. . . . To that government I swore allegiance; not only to obey its orders, but to support it against all its enemies." Each of these men felt a natural inclination to side with the Confederacy because their adopted states led the way.[91] Any study of adoptive southerners simply cannot ignore the fact that these individuals, though formerly northerners, simply did not think of themselves as such anymore. The main reason they ended up siding with the Confederacy was because of new identities formed and nurtured in the South.

Because of these transformations, every time they discussed the lingering crisis these individuals spoke with northerners as though talking to strangers. In the process, they continued a trend that began in the antebellum era and would survive through the Civil War of using phrases like "we" for the South and Confederacy and "you" for the North and Union. For instance, Robert Hatton, while attempting to salvage a compromise in Congress, consistently asked northern representatives to make concessions to save the Union. "I answer you, gentlemen of the North, we demand nothing that it is unfair to ask, that would be dishonorable to grant." He did not appeal to northern patriotism or his own childhood in Ohio at any point. Hatton did not need to because in his mind, as he suggested in his speeches in Congress, the South formed the basis for his love of the Union.[92] Albert Pike also expressed such feelings by asking his northern colleagues to make more concessions while urging his southern colleagues to speak with one voice. Pike pointed out that the North had vast stretches of territory to choose from, while "we had none," and that the North had nineteen states, while "we" had only fifteen. "They outnumber us, in white population, nearly two to one. They increase principally by foreign emigration, in a much larger ratio than we do." Throughout all his speeches, Pike never indicated that he acted as an ambassador for his former state of Massachusetts. Instead, Pike was an Arkansan speaking for his adopted state of Arkansas.[93]

Those who advocated immediate secession adopted a more militant tone in regards to their identity transition. For instance, John S. Ryan wrote to a friend in New York about the excitement of secession down in South Carolina in early December 1860. After mentioning that he had already joined a militia company, Ryan said, "I am rejoiced to employ a moment of leisure, to drop a line, to inform you how we are in So. Carolina. We are all for Secession, in fact we, as a State, are out of the Union. Tomorrow is the Election for Electors to declare the fact to the world."[94] A few weeks later, after

South Carolina officially seceded, Ryan told his friend, "We feel, we have done right, and prepared to defend our rights."[95] Similarly, Moses Curtis, another adoptive southerner in South Carolina, informed his own friend back in the North, "We all, to a man, look upon the election of Lincoln . . . as an *insult* and an outrage. . . . This is an unusual sort of discourse from me, but it may serve a purpose in showing you that we are in dead earnest here now, even the most conservative of us."[96] In Georgia, Ohio-born William Tappan Thompson declared in his Georgia newspaper, "The Rubicon is passed—a new nation is born! The only question now is what line on the map will be the Northern boundary of our glorious Southern Confederacy."[97] As Ryan and Curtis and Thompson demonstrated, adoptive southerners deliberately used "we" to refer to southerners and "they" or "you" to refer to northerners to separate themselves from their pasts.

Even when they acknowledged their northern roots, they brushed off such facts as an accident of birth that did not preclude a southern identity. As president of the University of Mississippi, Frederick Barnard told the university board, "I was born in the North. That I cannot help. I was not consulted in the matter."[98] Basically, he implored his fellow southerners to overlook his background and judge him on his actions at the present time. Several others acknowledged in one way or another that, though they spent their formative years in the North, they continued their development after they migrated to their adopted states. Hatton readily admitted that he did not achieve his work ethic until he arrived in Tennessee. As he told his wife, "Whatever faults I may have, of one thing I can boast; that is, that since I was fourteen years old, I have never spent a month in idleness. In the Hollow, I learned to work—to stand the sun, and the Winter's wind—to do what was exceedingly painful to me, at the time—I learned to endure hardship."[99] Since he spent his early childhood in Ohio, Hatton actually credited his years in Tennessee as having a greater impact on his life than his earlier life in the Midwest.

In an effort to have the country reflect their own situation, a few adoptive southerners advocated one of the more novel ideas arising from the secession crisis: setting up an entirely new Confederacy of conservative northern and southern states to break the hold of radicals. This idea especially appealed to these individuals because it would allow them to hang onto both their past and their future. For example, John S. Ryan suggested that his former state of New York divide down the middle, with the northern half going with New England and the southern half with the Confederacy. Once that occurred, "then the Southern United States from N.Y. to Texas will be what God ordered them to be a great, free and glorious people." In a way, Ryan almost wished to be back with his native state, but only if it aligned with the South.[100] Similarly, Julia Tyler, wife of former president John Tyler, told her parents back in New York that the best solution, proposed by her husband, involved setting up a new Union of southern, border, and a couple of northern states to counter New England Republicans.[101] Adopted Marylander John H. B. Latrobe wanted a central confederacy made up of the Border South, Pacific Coast, and Northwest full of reasonable men far away from the extremists in New England and the Deep South. He believed states like Virginia and Pennsylvania could come to terms much more easily than more radical states like Massachusetts and South Carolina.[102] Considering that he originally came from Pennsylvania and lived in Maryland, Latrobe subconsciously wished for the Union to live with two separate sections as he himself had learned to do.

At the same time, in an effort to completely detach themselves from their pasts, several adoptive southerners went so far as to openly disown their former attachments to the North to make their transformation official. Aaron Willington, a native of Massachusetts, wrote to his friend from South Carolina, "This is my last visit North, for I am thoroughly disgusted with abolitionism."[103] Though he died shortly thereafter, Willington made clear that his destiny now laid with his adopted state of South Carolina and, by extension, the cause of the Confederacy. He never expected to see his native state again.

Even more explicitly, Edward Wells informed his family on numerous occasions of his own efforts to divorce himself from his native section. He took offense at the assumption that just because he grew up in the North he needed to return to defend its policies. Speaking for many other adoptive southerners, Wells told his family in mid-April 1861, "People ignorantly think they are bound by patriotism to rally to the aid of Lincoln, whether right or wrong, merely because they are Northerners. They seem to imagine that the contest . . . is to be purely sectional. If it is to become purely sectional all my feelings are with the South."[104] Wells focused on that theme in hopes of making all of his family and acquaintances understand the fallacy of their assumptions of sectional loyalty. While Wells wished he could return to stay with his family, he did not consider that reason good enough to abandon everything else he held dear. "If it were not for my family, I declare I would never desire to see the North again," he wrote in the same letter. "I blush for such a country & I disown it as mine."[105] By the end of April, in a final break with his past, Wells declared, "The whole tone of feelings at the North is entirely repugnant to my sentiments & I can not desire to resume my citizenship there. . . . The invading army of the North is already on the march to Washington & must be opposed."[106] Forced to choose between his native and adopted section, Wells did not hesitate to abandon the former to pursue what he saw as the just cause of a people he now considered part of himself.

As Wells demonstrated, despite their acknowledgement of a northern past, these men viewed the emerging Confederacy as the nation that required their services and symbolized their destiny. Wells himself declared triumphantly, "Calmly & dispassionately then, I would rather make any sacrifice & undergo any privation, rather than help to sustain the would-be tyrants. . . . I should think it our honor to be hung, as a traitor by the Northern Government."[107] John S. Ryan described South Carolina as the place "in which I live, and where I hope to die."[108] Ashbel Smith told his cousin a few years after moving to Texas, "The settlement which I am about to make will be my home . . . here I hope to see my friends, and here to live with Mrs. S. if I ever marry!—"[109] As long as their adopted state stayed in the Union, they could defend it to the death. If the relationship ever changed, however, then their own feelings about the Union would change as well. Caroline Gilman said as much when she wrote that if secession ever loomed, she and her husband would send their children back to Massachusetts but stay in South Carolina themselves. "The truth is, the South is dearer to us for its troubles, and I as a woman feel proud that my husband is more highly appreciated, where he is best known."[110]

No other person, however, summed up the position of adoptive southerners more than Edmund Dewitt Patterson. Writing in his diary after a couple of years in the Confederate army, Patterson looked back on his decision not to return to Ohio and did not regret anything:

> . . . and then it was that I saw that there was no alternative but war or disgrace and everlasting dishonor for the South, and embraced the first opportunity of becoming a soldier in the confederate army, and can truly say that I have never for a moment regretted the course I have pursued, although had I returned North at the commencement

of the hostilities, I would have had the benefit of a thorough education, which I fear that I now never will have. The time that has been devoted to my country might have been spent in acquiring knowledge which would have been more advantageous to me individually than anything I have learned or will learn in the army, but then, I have the consciousness within my bosom of having done right which amply repays me for all I have lost.[111]

As much as they loved their families in the North and the memories of their childhoods, the South still represented the land where men like Patterson made their fortunes, their homes, their families, and often their identities.

Those who might have questioned the sincerity of secessionists to make the Confederacy a reality need only have turned to adoptive southerners for confirmation. The fact that native northerners, with no ties of blood or heritage to drive them on, eagerly participated in this task of nation building helped symbolize its validity. The Union may have boasted both northern and southern supporters, but so did the nascent Confederacy. Although it appeared as though the Confederacy was a homogenous country, like any other young nation its people had to create it from scratch, which allowed for flexibility. Adoptive southerners, utilizing the same types of adaptation that allowed them to transform their sectional identities in the first place, made the Confederate nation their own from its inception. Though northern by birth, these men and women, backed by identity, ideology, and to a lesser degree by family and economics and community, prepared to suffer, fight, and die for their new country's survival.

At least twelve adoptive southerners followed in the footsteps of the Founding Fathers by participating in their states' secession conventions. Just as the members of the Second Continental Congress made their own final breaks with England when they signed the Declaration of Independence, so did these men have the opportunity to cast a vote to take their adopted states out of the Union and wage a war against their former section. One of these men, native Pennsylvanian Benjamin Faneuil Dunkin, represented Prince George Parish in South Carolina and became one of the original signers of the South Carolina Ordinance of Secession. A month later, John P. Sanderson, a Vermont native, forcefully defended John C. Calhoun's compact theory of Union as he cast his vote to withdraw Florida from the Union. Massachusetts native Hiram Warner initially voted against secession but signed the secession ordinance when his adopted state of Georgia passed it. Farther west in Louisiana, Edward Sparrow, who grew up in Ohio, served in the Louisiana secession convention as an immediate secessionist before accepting a position as a Confederate senator. Over in Arkansas, a native of Massachusetts named Charles W. Adams (in a twist that might have horrified the famed Adams dynasty of that state) voted to take his adopted state out of the Union that John Adams had worked so hard to help create. New Jersey native Harris Flanagin, originally a unionist, followed Adams's example and changed his vote after Fort Sumter.[112]

Scores of adoptive southerners from outside of the secession halls took to the field by signing up for military service. Without waiting for actual hostilities, many of them followed their friends and neighbors in setting up new state governments, drilling new troops, or seizing federal forts. Once General Pierre G. T. Beauregard fired on Fort Sumter and Lincoln issued his call for militia to put down the rebellion, even more adoptive southerners joined their adopted states' regiments, eventually getting incorporated into the Confederate armies. The Civil War from its inception became a truly inter-sectional war, with not only white southerners fighting on behalf of the Union, but also native northerners fighting on behalf of the Confederacy.[113]

At that point, regardless of their motivation, all of the adoptive southerners who sided with the Confederacy underwent another significant transformation. No longer would they have to see themselves solely as adoptive southerners. Now, in their contributions toward crafting a new nation, they transformed themselves once again, this time into Northern Confederates. They never officially gave themselves that title (indeed, many likely would have felt insulted if anyone ever called them that), but the term seems appropriate. Whether they acknowledged it or not, they still had northern families whom they now vowed to destroy, if necessary. Instead of a kind of ambassador between sections, Northern Confederates now stood as either the ultimate patriot or the ultimate traitor, depending on the observer. In their own minds, they served as the ultimate patriots, because they vowed to preserve a nation for which they had no native claim but had adopted voluntarily through their own ideology and identity.

5

Adoptive Southern Unionists

Despite the overwhelming response by adoptive southerners in favor of secession, and their eventual transformation into Northern Confederates, a visible minority ended up fulfilling the wishes and expectations of their northern families by coming out in support of the Union and even returning to their native states. Although they only represented approximately 20 percent of the individuals in this study, they deserve mention because they appear to contradict the notion that native northerners adopted a southern identity before the Civil War. The combination of their northern background and unionist support made their situation potentially even more difficult, since Confederates who lived near them were doubly incensed because they not only opposed the Confederacy but also came from the hated North. Therefore, the presence of these particular northern emigrants brought up an important question: did they support the Union because of their northern background or because they wanted their adopted section to remain in the Union?

As it turns out, while they did not join the Confederacy, they were more akin to southern unionists than native northerners. In fact, out of thirty five Union generals who originally came from the South, nine of them grew up in the North. Like their southern unionist counterparts, they considered themselves Americans first and wanted to be recognized above all else as Union supporters, regardless of their backgrounds.[1] As a result, adoptive southern unionists still considered themselves southerners, even though they either remained neutral or supported the Union. Rather than contradict the pattern of northern emigrants adopting southern identities, these individuals actually reinforced that pattern.

Admittedly, a few northern emigrants never gave up their northern identities, regardless of how long they resided in the South. In their minds, their northern heritage forever barred them from feeling at home in the South, especially when they espoused unionist principles. Several historians even use the example of northern-born unionists as a way to connect northern roots with unionist sympathies in the Confederacy. For example, author Gerald Capers, describing unionists in New Orleans, argues that most of the unionists in the city either came from Europe or the North. He cites individuals like state treasurer James Belden, superintendant of education John McNair, and auditor A. P. Dostie, all native New Yorkers who lived in New Orleans and ended up supporting the Union. Capers admits that native northerners initially supported the Confederacy before the fall of New Orleans but contends that did not matter because "these groups had already changed their citizenship or their residence once in their lifetime, and their attachment to their adopted community was simply not as deep as that of most natives."[2] According to this interpretation, native northerners in the South only reluctantly supported the Confederacy because they still thought of themselves as northerners. Once the Union army arrived, they quickly reverted to unionist loyalties.

A few native northerners in this study did still think of themselves as northerners, as well as unionists. For instance, Franklin and Phoebe Farmer, a couple from Massachusetts who resided in Louisiana, considered themselves outsiders because of their northern heritage as well as their staunch unionism. They even supported Abraham Lincoln and the Republicans in the 1860 election, something unheard of in the Deep South, especially since Lincoln did not even appear on the ballot in Louisiana.[3] As a further indication of their alienation from their surroundings, a couple of months before the election Phoebe wrote to one of her friends about conditions in New Iberia. "Either the Southern mind has experienced a change, or had a preponderance of northern energy imparted to it," she said. "[I] find them now generally at home, spending their money on improvements which were much needed."[4] The tone of her letter reflected the observations of someone distant from her community, rather than a part of it. Despite having lived in Louisiana for several years, she did not feel much connection to the state. As a result, the Farmers experienced harassment for their unionist views and fled their own home and those of their friends several times before finding refuge in New Orleans. Franklin Farmer ended up separated from his wife and daughter, who served as nurses in the Union hospitals in the city.[5]

Calvin Robinson, a Vermont native living in Florida, went even further by describing the discrimination heaped on native northerners in the midst of secession. Robinson especially came under the ire of secessionists because of his outspoken unionism. He ascribed the discrimination directed toward him not just to his unionist views but also to his northern heritage. When Florida passed its secession ordinance, Robinson likened it to the dark times of the French Revolution. Robinson recalled that "the reign of terror gained full sway, and the time came when for a northern man to utter openly his love for the Union would be almost suicide. Men who were born and reared in the South could speak against secession long after it was unsafe for northern men to do it." Not surprisingly, during the early years of the conflict, Robinson claimed that secessionists in Jacksonville threatened all unionists, whom he equated with northerners, with death and the destruction of their property. He even wrote that another northern-born couple had their hotel burned to the ground for their unionist opinions.[6]

In response to such threats, Robinson and his fellow unionists needed to proclaim their secessionist sympathies simply to save their lives, but they continued to meet in secret to plot defenses. At the same time, they sought out fellow northerners and dreamed of the day when the Union army would arrive and save them from southern secessionists. As he wrote about the formation of the unionist militia, "A little later on there was a movement made to organize a military company of younger men. A number of these individuals were northern men and Unionists, and some few were Germans who had no sympathy with secession. Believing the majority of this group to be loyal at heart, I joined the company. I had the advantage of considerable military training at a military school in Vermont, and so I drilled a squad of these fellows a few times."[7] Their saving grace came a year later when Union gunboats ascended the river and gave the unionist population protection. At that point, "northern citizens" helped prevent secessionists from burning Jacksonville. At all times, Robinson never separated unionism from native northerners.[8]

One of the most outspoken native northerners to reject a southern identity during the secession crisis was Sally Baxter Hampton, a native New Yorker who married into one of the premier families in the heart of South

Carolina. Throughout the secession crisis, Sally wrote her opinions in the tone of an outsider giving a firsthand account of a national tragedy. Unlike other northern emigrants, Sally constantly referred to South Carolinians as "them" and "they," rather than "we." As she wrote to her family back in the North, "I am no Southerner heaven knows & at heart if not abolition at least anti-slavery . . . ." Since she continued to think of herself as a northerner, Sally lamented the inevitable breakup of the Union. She had no illusions about the secessionist fervor spreading across the South and felt the country she loved did not stand much chance of survival.[9] And although she opted to remain in the South to stay with her husband, she never gave any indication that she adopted a southern identity. As she wrote to one of her friends, "And what does it do for me? Do you care to know? Apart from home and friends, alone among strangers, the husband for whom I left all, in arms against the country where are still all I love . . ."[10] Only loyalty to her husband kept her from rejoining the family and Union she loved back in New York.[11]

While Sally Hampton endured her trials in the Confederacy itself, William Tecumseh Sherman decided to abandon the South altogether and return to the North. In the first half of 1860, in the midst of the secession crisis, Sherman worked as the superintendant of a war college in Louisiana. He had only accepted the position the year before and had spent very little time in the South. Unlike other native northern emigrants who lived in the South a short time and still adopted a southern identity, Sherman never felt a close association with his adopted state and did not give up his northern identity. While he respected the people in his community and claimed they treated him with "the greatest courtesy and kindness," Sherman never truly felt at home in Louisiana. In fact, when his brother, John Sherman, an antislavery Republican representative from Ohio, ran for Speaker of the House in 1860, Sherman faced guilt by association from parts of the community. As he wrote in his memoirs, "many people of Louisiana looked at me with suspicion, as the brother of the abolitionist, John Sherman, and doubted the propriety of having me at the head of an important State institution."[12] Even though the faculty and staff at the war college admired and trusted him, those who did not know him well simply assumed he held the same views as his brother and therefore could not be trusted.

Even if Sherman did not face suspicion for his northern roots, he still would have had a hard time identifying with Louisiana because he remained a die-hard unionist. During the first six months that he ran the school,

Sherman took frequent trips to Ohio and New York City, maintaining his family and friends in the North. He still thought of himself as a northerner living in the South merely for convenience. Once the secession crisis reached Louisiana, Sherman made his position perfectly clear. He wrote to Governor Moore in January 1861 that he only accepted the position on the assumption that Louisiana would remain loyal to the Union. When that assumption came under assault, he did not hesitate to abandon Louisiana in favor of the Union. As he told the governor, "'If Louisiana withdraws from the Federal Union, I prefer to maintain my allegiance to the Constitution as long as a fragment of it survives. . . . I beg you to take immediate steps to relieve me as superintendant, the moment the State determines to secede, for on no earthly account will I do any act or think any thought hostile to or in defiance of the old government of the United States."[13] Despite the fact that his acquaintances at the war college and even Governor Moore expressed deep regret at Sherman's decision and did everything they could to persuade him otherwise, Sherman simply did not belong in the South. He even admitted that he liked his work and would miss everyone at the college. "I entertain the kindest feelings toward all," he wrote to the governor, "and would leave the State with much regret; only in great events we must choose, one way or the other."[14] In Sherman's case, that choice meant preventing a breakup of the Union. As it turned out, though he admired southerners, as a Union general he carried out war policies designed to crush their morale and force their return to the Union he loved and admired.

Yet another native northerner who ended up abandoning his adopted section because of his unionist sympathies was George Junkin, Sr. A native Pennsylvanian, Junkin had moved to the South to serve as president of Washington College in Lexington. He brought his family with him and at least two of his children, daughters Ellie and Margaret, married into prominent southern families. Ellie married future Confederate general Thomas J. "Stonewall" Jackson and died in childbirth, while Margaret married into the Preston family and became one of the most well-known poets in Virginia. Junkin thus had plenty of familial and professional connections in Virginia, but his heart always belonged to the Union. At the height of secession in 1861, he made his unionist views well known, to the point where his students at Washington College started calling him "Lincoln Junkin." He angered both the faculty and student body further by demanding that a rebel flag be taken down from one of the college buildings, a demand that the faculty refused to honor.

Rather than witness his students use his beloved college for the purpose of destroying the Union, and after failing to convince his son-in-law Thomas Jonathan Jackson to remain loyal to the Union, Junkin angrily resigned and returned to Pennsylvania, proclaiming upon his departure, "I will not stay where the students dishonor their country's flag!"[15] His decision tore his family apart, because his daughter Margaret, three of his sons, and one nephew all stayed in Virginia and supported the Confederacy. Nevertheless, although he loved his time in Lexington, Junkin ultimately remained a Pennsylvanian and unionist above all else. As author James Robertson described his return to the North, "After the carriage crossed the Potomac River, Junkin reined in his horses on the northern side and wiped the mud from the wheels. 'Thus purified,' he 'journeyed north, never to return.'"[16] The Farmers, Robinsons, Sally Hamptons, William Shermans, and George Junkins among the northern emigrant population represented those who continued to identify with their native section more than their adopted home.

Despite their refusal to abandon their northern identity, however, these men and women represented only a small minority of the individuals in this study. Like-minded northern emigrants, from the Border States to the Deep South, expressed their unionist devotions as southern unionists with deep ties to the South, rather than as northerners caught in an alien and hostile environment. The fact that those in the Border States tended to support the Union came as little surprise, since their adopted states did not secede. Yet instead of taking their place among their northern families and communities, they joined the ranks of Marylanders, Kentuckians, and other native white southerners who retained their southern identities without giving up their love for the Union. For instance, John H. B. Latrobe, a native Pennsylvanian, lived in Maryland during the secession crisis and supported the Union. Latrobe outlined his own arguments as a southern slaveholder, claiming that Maryland did not have any reason to join the Confederacy because the latter would never hold together, thanks to different interests among the southern states. He also argued that leaving the Union made slaveholders vulnerable to the uncertainties of war.[17]

Farther west, Abiel Leonard, a Vermont native and adopted Missourian, also made pro-slavery arguments in favor of the Union. Having organized a unionist meeting in St. Louis as early as December 1860, Leonard viewed himself as both an American and a southerner, never hinting at his northern past. Laying out his arguments in favor of Missouri staying in the Union,

Margaret Junkin Preston. A native Pennsylvanian, Preston was the daughter of Washington College President George Junkin, married to John Preston, the founder of the Virginia Military Institute, and was General Stonewall Jackson's sister-in-law. She also became an effective poet and propagandist for the Confederacy while her father returned to Pennsylvania to support the Union. Courtesy of Virginia Historical Society.

Leonard wrote, "A border state united with the seceding states we should of course be subject to constant incursions from the free states that surround us on three sides until after being impoverished & desolated for a few years our slaves would be gradually drawn off to the states affording greater security to such property, & in the end we *should be* where we had better *remain*, with the old confederacy, connected with the great states of the West . . . ." Leonard understood, like any other southern unionist, that if the Border States allied with the Confederacy, they stood to lose far more than the Deep South. Adoptive southerners like Latrobe and Leonard revealed how close proximity to a native section did not automatically mean a continued identification with that section, regardless of their views on the Union.[18]

Several adoptive southerners in the Upper South added their own unionist sentiments to the debate as well. Isaac Murphy, a native of Massachusetts, was one of the strongest unionists in Arkansas. Unlike his fellow adopted Arkansan Albert Pike, who publicly changed his views from pro-union to pro-secession, Murphy never gave up his unionism regardless of the pressure. During the Arkansas secession convention, Murphy voted against secession and defended his stance because of his love for the South. As his biographer recounted, "Calmly and clearly he spoke of his Southern life. 'My principles are all Southern,' said he; 'If necessary, I would lay down my life for the benefit of the Southern States, but I would rather lose a thousand lives than aid in bringing about the untold evils that would assuredly follow in the train of secession. Again I say, to the passage of this ordinance, 'No.'" In Murphy's view, preserving his adopted section from the follies of secession meant backing the Union above all else.[19]

Even after Fort Sumter, when so many other Arkansas delegates changed their minds, Murphy refused to budge. He cast one of only five nay votes in the final vote to approve Arkansas's secession from the Union. And when four of those nay votes changed to yeas, Murphy became the lone delegate to maintain his opposition to the very end. His stubbornness forced him to flee into northwest Arkansas and Missouri after threats against his life by secessionists. Despite his exile, Murphy never wanted to leave the South. When the Union army occupied Arkansas later in the war, Murphy returned to work for a smooth reconstruction for his adopted state by serving as provisional governor.[20] At a time when he had every reason to return to his native region because of his die-hard unionism, Murphy chose to remain in the South, which indicated that he thought of himself much more as a southern unionist than a native northerner.

Even in the Deep South, where unionists faced trouble regardless of their origins, adoptive southern unionists still found a niche. Over in Texas, former governor Elisha Pease, a native of Connecticut, served as a rallying point for Texas unionists. He even helped organize a Unionist militia regiment in Austin, while pleading with his fellow Texans to not rush into secession. Although this made him a friend of powerful figures like Governor Sam Houston, his views put him outside the mainstream of the Texas population. His pleas failed and even some of the men he recruited switched sides. He considered moving back to Connecticut but decided to retire to his home and spent the rest of the war as a well-known unionist who consistently refused to take an oath of allegiance to the Confederacy. His law practice suffered considerably, and he was largely isolated, his correspondence with his relatives in Connecticut significantly curtailed. Unlike in New Orleans, no Union army ever appeared to give him cover for his views. Pease remained a unionist as well as a Texan throughout the war, deep in the heart of Confederate territory.[21]

Throughout the entire ordeal, however, Pease remained steadfast in his adopted southern identity along with his unionist sympathies. His friends and neighbors did not consider him a traitor so much as a lost son. On several occasions, they attempted without success to convert Pease to the Confederate cause, because they respected him as an adopted Texan. Their efforts indicated that only Pease's unionism, and not his background, kept him isolated. His biographer claimed he stayed in Texas mainly to protect his property, even though it made him "an alien in his adopted state." Though that may have happened, Pease found himself sidelined because of his unionism, and not because of his northern roots or perceived northern values.[22] As a unionist, he stood as much of a chance of losing his property staying in Texas as moving to Connecticut. A much more compelling reason to stay lay in his connection with Texas and his support of southern institutions. As his biographer even admitted, "Pease feared that civil war was sure to follow secession and believed that the conflict would endanger civil liberties and southern institutions, to which he was attached as sincerely as most native southerners, more than would continuation in the Union."[23] Pease, and others like him, chose to stay in their adoptive states rather than return to the North, where they would find a much warmer reception for their unionist views, thanks to the strength of their adopted southern identities.

At the same time, a few adoptive southerners followed the path of William Sherman by returning to the North at the outbreak of war. If a native northerner felt a strong connection to the Union in a state that seceded, and they then returned to a northern state, as Sherman did, logic dictates they did so because they still thought of themselves as northerners. In fact, adoptive southerners who chose this option largely followed the patterns of their compatriots who remained behind in the South. Though they decided to leave the South, that did not mean they had given up their southern identity. Even when they lived in the North again, they still did not consider themselves northerners as much as exiled southerners.

This small group included a few individuals who had returned to the North several years before the secession crisis erupted. Such an extended time back in the North provided an opportunity for these men and women to revert back to their northern identities. The fact that they did not do so revealed how much had changed since they first left their northern homes in search of opportunity in the South. For instance, at the time of Abraham Lincoln's election, William Plumer had left his adopted state and lived in Philadelphia to run a Pennsylvania church. With the country tearing itself apart, Plumer sound more like a southern unionist than a native northerner. He wrote to one of his friends that he lamented the loss of the Union and was convinced nothing could prevent secession or civil war. At the same time, unlike most of his neighbors, Plumer put most of the blame on the North. "I am free to say the South has been very badly treated," he wrote to one of his acquaintances. "Have you noticed that all aggressions come from the North? Have you any light? Is there to be (?) an able, conservative, anti-sectional paper in Washn [sic] this winter?"[24] Not even a return to the North managed to reconvert Plumer fully to his northern roots.

A similar situation happened with one of the more famous adoptive southerners, Gail Borden. A native New Yorker, Borden had made a name for himself through different inventions, including condensed milk, while living in Texas. In the early 1850s, Borden moved back to New York to pursue a patent for his inventions and to market them around the country. He thus found himself still in New York when the war broke out, while his property and some of his family remained in Texas. Borden himself and one of his sons stayed in New York, with the son joining the Union army and Borden supplying milk and biscuits to the Union war department. Back in Texas, his other sons and nephews fought in the Confederate armies. Faced with the decision of returning to Texas or staying in New York, Borden opted for the latter.[25] At first glance, it might seem that Borden made his choice based on his current residence, pressure from northern associates, or perhaps a renewed sense of northern identity. In reality, he simply felt that maintaining the Union was the most important goal of all Americans, regardless of section. Everything he owned and loved was in Texas, but he could not return because his adopted state joined the Confederacy.[26] As further proof of his attachments to the South, when the war ended, Borden returned to Texas and managed to rejoin his community with little opposition.[27]

Even those who thought about remaining neutral eventually revealed their attachments to the South. For example, Henry Watson, an adopted Alabamian, had strong connections in both Massachusetts and Alabama and did not wish to let go of either one. In 1860, he spoke out in favor of slavery and supported the Democrats but also moved his children back to Massachusetts for their health and education. In terms of secession itself, he gave an ambiguous analysis. In January 1861, though he considered the creation of the Confederacy a foregone conclusion, he did not indicate which side he favored. He actually expressed more concern about what secession might do to his business, instead of the country. Watson hoped the Union could be preserved, "Yet if we are to be always quarrelling, backbiting & abusing each other as we have been since my earliest recollection I think it would be pleasanter and better to live apart than together." Based on these contradictory actions and statements, Watson never made clear which side he would support once war erupted.[28]

Even after the firing on Fort Sumter and President Lincoln's call for troops, Watson still vacillated. On the one hand, Watson demonstrated his support of the Confederacy when he wrote to the captain of a local militia company, "War has at last been declared against us and Hostilities have actually commenced. It become the duty of every good citizen now to render his state such service as lies in his power. . . . I desire to assist in the cause and beg to offer you on behalf of the company Five Hundred Dollars for that purpose . . ."[29] Despite this show of support, however, Watson refused to enlist in the Confederate armies. He preferred to remain on the sidelines. Ultimately, he avoided making a clear decision by returning to Massachusetts and then leaving the country to live abroad for most of the war. In his case, neutrality remained preferable to taking sides in a war in which his native and adopted sections met on the battlefield.

Due to Watson's vacillation, biographer J. Parker Mason argues that Watson pursued neutrality mainly for business interests. Mason claims that Watson had most of his business contacts in the North and felt a new southern nation put his entire livelihood in jeopardy. Mason also shows that Watson's neighbors in Greensboro no longer trusted him because of his northern background. In this interpretation, Watson was always a northerner who went to the South for financial reasons and then left immediately when financial opportunities dried up. Though Mason does not mention it, this interpretation seems to get a boost from one of Watson's letters to his mother, in which he assures her that northerners are not in any danger. Watson thus did not have real connections to the South, as evidenced by his quick return to Massachusetts once the country fell apart.[30]

A closer look at Watson's actions, however, reveals a much more complex picture. He did have a financial stake in his adopted state of Alabama, but his connections to his community in Greensboro ran much deeper than dollars and cents. First of all, Mason admits that, before Watson left Greensboro, he contributed half his crop to the town's military expenses, as well as donating money to the Greensboro Light Artillery. An outsider who had little connection to his community would hardly go to such lengths to aid his neighbors and then abandon them.[31] Even if he did not pledge such contributions, Watson's own correspondence during the crisis attested to his adopted southern identity. The full text of the letter he wrote to his mother in December 1860 reads, "Neither Sereno nor myself are in any danger because we are 'Northerners' and everything is going on here as quietly as it ever did." The fact that he placed quotation marks around the word "northerners" indicates he was merely playing to his mother's assumptions and does not reflect his true understanding of his own identity.[32] In March, he wrote to one of his friends about his impending move to Massachusetts, but said little about his financial affairs. Telling his acquaintance not to allow tax assessors to assume he was now a resident of Massachusetts, Watson elaborated, "But I am not a *resident* of that state nor domiciled there. This is my *home* and I have never yet made up my mind to remove from it or change it."[33] Even while not wishing to fight for the Confederacy, Watson did not want anyone confusing his actions with a renewed northern identity. In fact, a month later, he told his cousin he intended to leave his property in the care of his slaves until the South came back to its senses, rejoined the Union, and allowed him to return to Alabama, which he figured would happen by the fall of 1861.[34] Clearly, Watson saw secession and war merely as a temporary inconvenience soon to be corrected so he could return to his life in Alabama.

Following Watson's example, other adoptive southerners appeared to hesitate before ultimately staying with their adopted section. Thomas Wharton, an adopted Louisianan who took over the superintendence of the New Orleans custom house after General Pierre G. T. Beauregard left for Charleston, tried to take a neutral stance in the early months of secession. As he recorded in his diary in January, "Every thing financially, politically, and socially, is resolved into an aggregate of utter incertitude; I, therefore, have no record to make, no opinion! but simply fill my daily round of duty as Constructional Officer in charge of important Federal works . . . ." As long as the situation remained fluid, Wharton preferred to stay on the sidelines. Once war erupted, however, he threw his support to the Confederacy.[35] Caroline Seabury, a Massachusetts native living in Mississippi, revealed even more ambiguity. First of all, in October 1860, Seabury visited the North and attended Republican torchlight parades, which reflected her hatred of slavery. Yet she decided to return to the South because, as she noted in her diary, "I have come back—loving my friends here, loving the spot where my dear Martha lies, and all the sacred associations connected with it."[36] Even though she did not agree with many of the South's institutions, Seabury still felt an attachment to the region that made her stay when secession erupted. Even a plea from her uncle did not work, though she did admit the decision left her torn between love of the North and attachments in the South. She admitted to herself, "Had I a father or mother not a moment's delay would keep one from going to them—Without a home except one of dependence—I had rather work & suffer here."[37]

One of the most interesting cases involving the trials and tribulations of an adoptive southern unionist occurred with Frederick Barnard, a native of Massachusetts and president of the University of Mississippi. Barnard seemed like the ultimate contradiction. A product of New England, Barnard made a career for himself as an educator in Alabama and Mississippi. He attained the status of a slaveholder yet defended slaves against attacks by whites. In one celebrated case, the Board of Trustees at the University of Mississippi put him on trial because he defended one of his female slaves who claimed a white student had assaulted her. Beyond his racial views, throughout his life, including nearly a quarter of a century in the Deep South, Barnard maintained solid support for the Union. When his students rebelled against him and ended up joining local militia companies, Barnard felt a further teaching career in the South was hopeless and offered to resign. The Board of Regents then begged him to stay on, which he did on condition that the university would open again in the fall of 1861. When that did not happen, Barnard and his wife left for Virginia to live in Norfolk. Jefferson Davis himself called on Barnard to serve the Confederacy, but Barnard refused to give up his neutrality. Finally, in 1862, after the Union navy captured Norfolk, Barnard moved back to the North to take up a teaching position at Princeton University and continue his vocal support of the Union.[38]

A few of Barnard's biographers point to attacks against him as proof of his northern identity, as well as his unionism. First of all, they cite the University of Mississippi Board of Trustees decision to put Barnard on trial in 1860 on charges of holding antislavery views. He had to consistently defend his stance on slavery, even though he owned two slaves and had not voiced opposition to slavery during his entire time in the South. They also note how his students rebelled against him, that he belonged to the Republican Party, that he refused to serve in any capacity with the Confederacy, and that he returned to the North at his first opportunity. His actions indicate that he never gave up his northern identity. As his biographer Charles Davenport wrote, "Barnard was a northerner, though a slaveholder, caught in the South at the outbreak of secession, of which he disapproved."[39] Though he did not mention it, Davenport could have also pointed to a letter Barnard wrote to President Lincoln in 1863 warning him to beware of traitors on the northern home front, just like he had seen in Mississippi. He knew from experience that not all loyalists came from the North, nor all rebels from the South. To all appearances, Barnard was a stout unionist who never abandoned his northern sectional identity.[40]

Barnard gave equal emphasis, however, to his attachments to the South and to maintaining an adopted southern identity. During his trial before the Board of Trustees, Barnard urged his accusers to look "not only for the period of twenty-two years that I have spent in unwearied devotion to the cause of Southern education, but for that earlier period of youth when I had not yet expected ever to be a resident of a Southern State; but in regard to which I have, providentially, in my possession, testimonials by Southern men, of the most unexceptionable character."[41] Even though he never expected to live in the South, he had his friends and employment record as evidence of his transition to a southern identity. He never subscribed to secession or gave an indication he wanted to join the Confederacy, but that did not necessarily mean he still thought of himself as a northerner. If anything, he hoped for the quick defeat of the secessionists so that the South could return to its proper standing in the Union. The fact that he agreed to stay on at the University of Mississippi as long as they opened classes in the autumn indicates that Barnard did not abandon his Mississippi home lightly.

In addition, both the University of Mississippi Board of Trustees and the president of the Confederacy himself begged Barnard to stay, which they likely would not have done if convinced that Barnard retained a northern identity as well as unionist sentiment. Barnard himself explained to Davis that he wanted a pass between the lines because he still had family in the North and no educational job in the South anymore. If only Barnard had found a job as an educator for a unionist community somewhere in Mississippi or Alabama, in all likelihood he would have elected to stay. As biographer William Chute explained, "Barnard was actually a staunch Union man through the years preceding the conflict. . . . Although a Southerner at heart, he was a nationalist in principle and purpose." Such a description, backed up by his actions during the secession crisis, categorized Barnard much more as a southern unionist than as a northerner returning home.[42]

Mississippi plantation owner Stephen Duncan ultimately came to the same conclusion. Duncan had managed to transform himself from a native Pennsylvanian into a respected Mississippi gentleman with thousands of acres and hundreds of slaves. When the war erupted, Duncan was torn between his devotion to the Union, his hard-earned economic assets, and his status as an adoptive southerner. He originally hoped that taking a neutral stance would protect both himself and his property, so he stayed on his plantation in Natchez without giving any speeches or openly supporting either side. This strategy worked well enough until 1863, when Union forces occupied Natchez. At that point, Duncan felt secure enough to express his unionist views. No less an authority than Admiral David Dixon Porter expressed his confidence in Duncan when he wrote to Secretary of the Navy Gideon Wells, "I think there is no man in the South who deserves as much consideration as Mr. Stephen Duncan, and he is clearly entitled to his cotton or the proceeds of it."[43] Unfortunately for Duncan, neither his northern roots nor his professed unionism secured his safety or his property. On several occasions, Union raids damaged his plantation and burned his cotton crop.[44] As a result, Duncan decided to abandon Mississippi altogether at the end of 1863 and move to his summer home in New York City. He still hoped to retain some control over his finances and eventually return to Mississippi, because before he left he sold his remaining cotton and left his property with his children.[45] Nevertheless, Duncan's attempts to remain a neutral southern unionist in his adopted state failed in the face of both Confederate and Union attacks.

Not content to remain quiet, some adoptive southern unionists achieved high positions in Union governments in captured territory. Calvin Robinson became chairman for the Union committee in Jacksonville and helped draw up a petition to form a Reconstruction government in Florida. He also assisted Colonel Latta in taking possession of abandoned property in the city. His position only lasted until the Union gunboats left after a few months, and he ended up establishing a business in Fernandina.[46] Horace Maynard, a Massachusetts native, continued his service as a congressman from East Tennessee and its largely unionist population. In that capacity, he tried in various speeches to explain to northern audiences the commitment and dedication of southern unionists. Maynard himself never acknowledged his northern roots in his speeches, referring several times to "our northern friends" and declaring, "What I have said of the people in my own State . . . is true to a greater or lesser extent of all portions of the southern States . . . ."[47] In an ironic twist, Maynard denounced the comments of a New Yorker sympathetic to southern secessionists and insisted all such individuals were traitors, not only to the Union, but also to the South.[48]

In Louisiana, a full-scale political war nearly erupted over who should occupy the governor's chair, with an adoptive southern unionist in the thick of the fight. The battle took place between Michael Hahn, a native Louisianan, and Benjamin Flanders, who came from New Hampshire but spent his adulthood in New Orleans. Flanders had fled to the North at the start of the war but in 1863 returned to New Orleans to resume his business ventures and join the unionist community. He ended up as an agent for the Treasury Department and president of the National Bank in the city. In all likelihood, Flanders did not envision a political career, but his ties to Radical Republicans put him in the center of Louisiana's Reconstruction saga.[49]

The drama began when unionists met in the city to set up a new pro-Union government at the urging of the Lincoln administration. The convention initially favored Hahn because of his moderate views. More radical members, however, looked for a more suitable candidate for their interests, and they urged Flanders to run. One observer, George Denison, reported the proceedings to Secretary of the Treasury Salmon P. Chase: "Unexpectedly and just before the meeting of the Union nominating convention, he [Flanders] was announced as a candidate. The convention was about equally divided between Hahn and Flanders, and ended in the nomination of Mr. Hahn — the friends of Mr. Flanders having bolted formed another convention which nominated Mr. F. We have therefore two Union candidates in the field."[50] Denison went on to report numerous times on Flanders, largely in an unfavorable light because he claimed Flanders engaged in corruption and divided the Union camp.[51] Denison's diatribes were biased, however, because he viewed Flanders as a threat to his own relationship with Chase. In any case, Hahn's election as governor held and Flanders continued his services as a treasury agent before resigning to take over the National Bank.

During the entire episode, however, Flanders's standing was never affected one way or the other by his status as a native northerner. Anyone who mentioned Flanders in or out of New Orleans did not invoke his background as a reason to support or oppose him. George Denison admitted that Flanders had many good qualities, "But to you I say that I think he confuses his principles with his interests and desire for personal advancement . . . he greatly overestimates his own personal influence—he makes no friends and alienates many once his friends."[52] Gideon Welles, the secretary of the Navy, recorded in his own diary his concern that Flanders took over fifty plantations in his status as a treasury agent. His actions sparked a heated cabinet debate over which department, War or Treasury, had control over Louisiana's Reconstruction policies.[53] His supporter, Salmon Chase, loved what Flanders did because it buttressed his own power base. Upon hearing that Flanders resigned as a treasury agent, Chase wrote to him, "I feel much indebted to you for accepting the difficult and responsible position you now fill. It has been my endeavor to put none but good men in office, and I am glad to find that the unanimous voice of the loyal people confirms my judgment in your appointment."[54] Finally, in the lead-up to the election for governor, Flanders received both support and ridicule from two different anonymous authors. The pro-Flanders pamphlet mentioned his stout unionist credentials and willingness to speak out on the slavery question. The anti-Flanders pamphlet claimed he was a dangerous radical who would alienate moderate Louisiana unionists.[55] In all of these comments, everyone concentrated on his personal qualities, unionist credentials, or his assistance to the Treasury Department. His New Hampshire roots remained a non-issue. As far as the unionist community of New Orleans was concerned, Flanders belonged to Louisiana.

Despite the high profile of men like Flanders, they represented a small minority of northern emigrants. The vast majority fought for the Confederacy in one capacity or another to protect their adopted families, homes, and identities. Viewing themselves as Confederates came naturally, yet that allegiance had profound consequences. In the past, native northerners always had the option to abandon the South and return to their native region, just as adoptive southern unionists often did. Thanks to the Civil War, newly minted Northern Confederates would forever be associated with the Confederacy.

6

Northern Confederates in War

Now that newly minted Northern Confederates had made their decisions, they quickly blended in with the hundreds of thousands of native southerners who joined the infant Confederate armies. In the process, they contributed to both the successes and failures of their new country far out of proportion to their numbers. At no time did they ever comprise more than a small percentage of the Confederate armies or the home front, yet they commanded the defenses of some of the most important cities in the Confederacy, including Charleston and Vicksburg. This did not happen by chance. Thanks to their years of assimilation into their adopted homes, these men had already established themselves as important figures in their southern communities and as firm supporters of the Confederate cause. As a result, despite their backgrounds, Northern Confederates had little trouble serving in the ranks of their new country. Their dedication to the cause revealed the strength of the Confederate nation, since individuals who did not have native ties to the region still willingly gave their lives for its survival.

Not surprisingly, Northern Confederates made their greatest contributions to Confederate survival on the battlefield. Out of the two hundred and fifty-three individuals in this study who supported the Confederacy, one hundred and sixty-six, or nearly two-thirds, answered the call to arms. Over the course of the war, they served in every capacity, from private to general and from front-line soldier to staff officer. At least thirteen served for the entire war as privates, five as corporals or sergeants, and thirty-one with an unknown status but likely serving with the same ranks. The other 70 percent achieved much higher ranks. Nine ended their service as lieutenants, seventeen as captains, nineteen as majors, and thirty-four as colonels. And in the greatest display of the importance of Northern Confederates in the ranks, thirty served as brigadier generals, six as major generals, two as lieutenant generals, and one as a full general. In other words, nearly 10 percent of all Confederate generals hailed from a northern state, far out of proportion to the overall numbers of native northerners in the South at the time of the Civil War.[1]

Similar to every other ambitious soldier at the time, prominent Northern Confederates did everything possible to obtain an officer commission in a front-line command. They ended up succeeding at a phenomenal rate. In just one example, in the Washington Artillery, a militia regiment with a long history in Louisiana, the colonel, captain, and major all came from northern states. Adopted Texan Walter Lane served as a captain of artillery in a Georgia regiment in General D. H. Hill's division. Charles Quintard, at the insistence of his friends, joined a Tennessee regiment as their chaplain and eventually achieved the rank of major. Connecticut native Thomas Hinsdale started off in the reserve state troops in North Carolina until 1865, when he became the elected colonel of the Seventy-Second North Carolina regiment.[2] General Thomas J. "Stonewall" Jackson's brilliant mapmaker, native New Yorker Jedediah Hotchkiss, served as one of Jackson's most trusted staff officers and continued his service in the Second Corps of the Army of Northern Virginia after Jackson's death. Hotchkiss played a major role in enabling Jackson to achieve numerous victories in the Shenandoah Valley based on his excellent maps of the region.[3]

Along with majors and colonels, every Confederate state witnessed one of its adopted sons achieve the coveted rank of general. When Mississippi seceded, the governor appointed four men as generals for the army in Mississippi before the incorporation of state forces into the Confederacy. Two of those four came from Illinois and Ohio respectively.[4] A fellow adopted Mississippian, Samuel French, received his promotion to brigadier general in October 1861 and then major general in August 1862. In August 1861, Daniel Ruggles received a promotion to brigadier general and a post in Virginia. A year later he commanded a division in Louisiana. Further east, the Fifty-Ninth Alabama came under the command of two Northern Confederate generals in succession, Archibald Gracie and Bushrod Rust Johnson, originally from New York and Ohio respectively. In probably the biggest coup for the standing of Northern Confederates, President Davis appointed New Jersey native Samuel Cooper as Adjutant General of the Confederacy, the highest rank of any Confederate soldier.[5] The presence of these northern-born officers symbolized the regional inclusiveness of the Confederate high command. The fight for independence did not just extend to native southerners; anyone who wished to further the cause of the Confederacy had the chance to participate. The Union could boast of having four southern states in its column, but the Confederacy had its cross-border representatives as well.[6]

Incredibly, at times it appeared that entire sectors of the Confederate frontlines depended on the decisions of Northern Confederates. Charleston, the epicenter of anti-northern rhetoric, had a succession of native northerners commanding the forts around the city. After the transfer of General Pierre G. T. Beauregard, the popular hero of Fort Sumter, native Pennsylvanian John C. Pemberton took over the command. When he left for Mississippi in 1862, native Ohioan Roswell Ripley, who made South Carolina his adopted state and helped shell Fort Sumter into submission, assumed command. All three succeeded in preventing the city's capture until the very end of the war. As a result, the Union failed to take the instigator of secession for years, thanks to their own native sons whom they had lost to the Confederacy.[7]

Still, with the exception of Charleston, Northern Confederates were few and far between in the top field commands along the Confederacy's eastern coast. In the Western Theater, on the other hand, Northern Confederates oversaw a large part of the command structure. The Mississippi River especially witnessed a parade of Confederate generals who did not originally come from a southern state. During the battle for New Orleans, the most populous city in the Confederacy, Americans witnessed the unusual circumstance of a southern unionist seeking to capture a Confederate city defended by several native northerners. Tennessean David Farragut led the Union fleet against Forts Jackson and St. Philip under the command of Northern Confederate generals Mansfield Lovell, Johnson Kelly Duncan, and Daniel Ruggles. A few months later, the four generals in charge of defending Baton Rouge included John C. Breckinridge, Mansfield Lovell, Daniel Ruggles, and Charles Clark. Only Breckinridge did not qualify as a Northern Confederate.[8]

Further to the north, native northerners commanded several other important posts. After the Union navy captured nearly every strategic point along the Mississippi River in 1862, only two cities remained in Confederate hands. At Port Hudson, a critical juncture north of Baton Rouge, Daniel Ruggles first assumed the command in 1862, followed by New York native Franklin Gardner, who defended the town against a siege by Union troops

Battle of New Orleans. One of the most critical naval battles of the war, this engagement featured Union admiral and native Tennessean David Farragut leading his ships against the forts of New Orleans, commanded by native Pennsylvanian Johnson Kelly Duncan. Library of Congress.

under General Nathaniel Banks in 1863.[9] North of Port Hudson stood the other major Confederate stronghold, Vicksburg. President Davis, himself a Mississippian, first ordered Martin L. Smith, a native New Yorker, to defend the city. He succeeded in defending the city against assaults made by Admiral Farragut in the spring of 1862. A few months later, Davis gave the command to General Pemberton, formerly the commander of Charleston. He stayed in that command until General Ulysses S. Grant captured the city in 1863.[10]

Therefore, in the critical years of 1862 and 1863, when the Confederacy fought to keep the Mississippi River open, Northern Confederates commanded the major armies assigned to carry out that mission. Had anyone at the time stopped to ponder the situation, they might have marveled that native northerners determined the course of the campaign for the Mississippi River for both sides. Instead of a fight between North and South, at least where the commanders were concerned, the outcome depended on a fight between Union and Confederate supporters of northern origin. Despite their backgrounds, Northern Confederates worked hard to frustrate the will of their native section to ensure the survival of the new nation.

Along with major commands, Northern Confederates also occupied a number of important staff positions. In just a few examples, Colonel Walton, an adopted Louisianan formerly of the Washington Artillery, served as General James Longstreet's chief of artillery during the Gettysburg campaign. John S. Preston, an adopted South Carolinian, served as an aide de camp to General Beauregard before getting promoted to adjutant assistant general on his staff. John Hinsdale, a native of Connecticut, served on the staffs of Generals Johnston Pettigrew, William Pender, and John Bell Hood. General Robert E. Lee himself briefly had a Northern Confederate, adopted Tennessean Charles Quintard, on his staff when Quintard's regiment was stationed in Virginia. In both the East and the West, Confederate generals at times relied on the skills of non-native southerners to carry out their orders.[11]

Even when they did not reach such lofty heights, Northern Confederates still risked their lives alongside native southerners in major battles and skirmishes across the continent. War records, diaries, correspondence, memoirs, and biographies reveal extensive war careers for many of these men. For example, native Ohioan Henry Handerson fought in nearly every major engagement in the Virginia Theater while serving with the Ninth Louisiana Regiment. He saw action at First Manassas, the Valley Campaign, Gaines Mill, Malvern Hill, Second Manassas, Antietam, Fredericksburg, Chancellorsville, Gettysburg, and the Wilderness Campaign before getting captured.[12] Another native Ohioan in the east, Edmund DeWitt Patterson, joined the Ninth Alabama Infantry. His regiment arrived too late to participate at First Manassas, but he did see action at Williamsburg, Seven Pines, Seven Days (where he was wounded), Fredericksburg, Chancellorsville, and Gettysburg, where he was captured and taken to a prison camp in Sandusky, Ohio.[13] Native Pennsylvanian Samuel Myers also served in the Valley Campaign, Antietam, and the Wilderness in a Virginia cavalry regiment until disease forced him to retire.[14] Adopted Floridian Edward Perry fought at Chancellorsville, missed Gettysburg because of typhoid fever, rejoined the army to fight at Bristoe Station, and finally had to leave the service after receiving a severe wound in the Wilderness Campaign.[15]

The Western Theater had an equal if not larger share of Northern Confederates with long careers in combat. Native New Yorker Archibald Gracie commanded several Alabama regiments while serving in Kentucky and East Tennessee, leading charges at Perryville, Chickamauga, and Knoxville. After recuperating from wounds received at Bean's Station in East Tennessee, he rejoined his regiments to defend Drewry's Bluff and Petersburg in 1864. Gracie lost his life in the Petersburg trenches in December of that year.[16] Maine native Edward Drummond started his career at Fort Pulaski and spent several years in prison after the Union navy captured Savannah. After his exchange, he returned to Savannah to join the First Georgia Regiment. In 1864, he fought in the Atlanta campaign, Franklin, and Nashville, ending the war serving under General Joseph E. Johnston at Bentonville.[17] General Frank C. Armstrong, who grew up on the frontier and in Massachusetts, served in a cavalry regiment in Tennessee and fought in the Chickamauga and Chattanooga campaigns. He ended the war fighting with Nathan Bedford Forrest at Selma.[18] Francis Shoup, a native of Indiana, served in Vicksburg during the siege and then participated in the Meridian campaign. Appointed by President Davis as chief of artillery for the Army of Tennessee, he also helped build defensive lines around Atlanta. When that city fell, Shoup was accused of disobeying orders, whereupon he resigned and returned to Richmond.[19]

These men represent just a sample of the exploits of Northern Confederates in the Confederate armies. In this study, one hundred and eleven served in the infantry, twenty-four in the cavalry, thirteen in the artillery, one in the navy, and thirty-one in the state militias. Together they marched and fought alongside their native southern comrades on nearly every major battlefield. In all likelihood, thousands more undocumented native northerners made their own sacrifices from Pennsylvania to Florida and from Kentucky to Texas. Just like native southerners, they willingly risked their lives so that their new nation might live. It did not matter that they did not have the same ties of blood as most of their comrades. Their blood ties came from the blood they spilled while wearing Confederate gray.

In one of the most unusual twists, a few Northern Confederates even began their careers in the North before joining the Confederate armies. General Frank C. Armstrong actually joined the Union army at the beginning of the war and commanded a regiment at First Bull Run. After that battle, inexplicably, he deserted and joined the Confederate cavalry. Armstrong left behind no record or even a hint of why he switched sides. He was born in Indian Territory and grew up in New Mexico and Massachusetts before joining the cavalry in 1855 and taking part in the Utah expedition in 1858. In one of the rarest instances of any non-native southerner, Armstrong had no obvious ties to the South yet fought in a Confederate cavalry regiment for nearly four years.[20]

And Armstrong was not alone. The Fifteenth Tennessee Regiment had an entire company of volunteers who lived in the southern districts of Illinois and Indiana at the start of the war, with seven of these volunteers known to have never left the North until they joined the Confederacy. Though rare, these men showed that native northerners could offer valuable service to the Confederacy without any apparent ties to the southern states. They obviously did not represent a decisive factor, but their willingness to serve indicates that the Confederacy drew support not just from native white southerners, but also from those who, even without any obvious attachments to the South, believed in its ideology and struggle for independence.[21]

In addition to conventional combat, several Northern Confederates also undertook special missions to further the cause. After the firing on Fort Sumter, and just before Virginia officially seceded, secessionists plotted to send troops up to Harpers Ferry to secure the weapons at the armory. Charles Dimmock and Kenton Harper, Massachusetts and Pennsylvania natives respectively, participated in the plan. As one participant recalled, "Captain Charles Dimmock, a Northern man by birth and a West Point graduate, was in full sympathy with us, and that night filled our requisitions for ammunition and moved it to the railway station before sunrise." He continued his description by mentioning Harper, "a native of Pennsylvania, 'a born soldier,' and Brigadier-General William H. Harman, both holding commissions in the Virginia militia, — and both of whom had won their spurs in the regiment the State had sent to the Mexican war . . ."[22] They both joined their adopted state in seizing the armory at the expense of their native section.

A few months later, native Pennsylvanian George W. Alexander carried out an even more daring mission in Union territory. When Virginia seceded, Alexander offered his services to Governor John Letcher, who assigned him a mission to take the island of Sombrero in the West Indies. That mission foundered when Alexander's ship and crew got caught in a storm and shipwrecked at Point Lookout in Maryland. After recovering, Alexander launched a new mission by traveling to Baltimore with the intention of recruiting a company of Maryland secessionists. Along with a friend, Alexander succeeded in putting together sixty-two recruits, who elected him as their lieutenant. He then planned to capture Union ships in Baltimore harbor. The company targeted a ship called the *St. Nicholas,* which made runs between Baltimore and Washington. One detachment boarded the ship disguised as passengers in Baltimore, while Alexander led a second detachment that boarded at Point Lookout.[23] Together the two squads seized the ship and sailed it into Fredericksburg. Along the way, they captured three more Union ships and forty Union prisoners, yielding a total cargo of over three hundred thousand dollars.[24] The raid did not create any lasting damage, but it revealed the risks Alexander and others like him took to dent the Union war machine.[25]

Native New Yorker Edward Wells made his contributions to Confederate victory in an equally dramatic fashion. His account almost reads like a spy novel. At the start of the war, he appeared to abandon his adopted state of South Carolina by leaving the Confederacy and rejoining his family back in New York. He stayed in his native state for three years as an apparent Union supporter. In reality, he hoped to conduct spy work on behalf of the Confederate government. According to his postwar account, Wells traveled to Montgomery in 1861 asking Confederate officials how he could help. Because of his northern background, they asked him to go back to the North to gather intelligence. He did not say what information he obtained, but he confessed that by 1863, especially after the disasters at Gettysburg and Vicksburg and the failures of the New York City draft riots to foster more anti-war rioting, he felt he could make more of a contribution in the South than in the North. In early 1864, he sailed out of New York City on a British steamer, transferred to a blockade runner, and sailed into Wilmington.[26] Free to finally serve in the field, Wells enlisted in a South Carolina cavalry regiment under General Wade Hampton.[27]

Although not all Northern Confederates had such an adventurous career, others still made contributions to the Confederate war effort in non-combat roles. Several of them oversaw prison camps. For example, Elias Griswold, originally a provost marshal under General Winder, was sent to Americus, Georgia, in 1864 to work as second in command of the prison in that city. That same year, Samuel Cooper suggested that fellow Northern Confederate Mansfield Lovell command all prisons in the Confederacy. In addition, George W. Alexander, after his own imprisonment in Fort McHenry, served as commandant of Salisbury Prison in Virginia and then as commandant of Castle Thunder.[28]

In a more crucial role, native Pennsylvanian Josiah Gorgas led the Confederate Ordnance Bureau, achieving near-miracles over four years to keep the Confederacy supplied with guns and ammunition. When the Civil War began, the Confederacy faced a huge disadvantage when it came to weapons, because nearly all of the powder mills, arsenals, and manufacturing plants remained in the Union. Gorgas did not eliminate the discrepancy, but he did manage to at least give Confederate armies the ability to remain supplied in the field. He created a Nitre and Mining Bureau to search for critical supplies like saltpeter, built a large gunpowder mill in Georgia, and sent agents around the Confederacy to scrounge for scrap metal, including church bells, to make into cannon. He even bought blockade runners for the exclusive use of the Ordnance Bureau to smuggle in supplies from Europe through the tightening blockade. By the end of the war, Gorgas arguably had the greatest success in carrying out his mission among Confederate suppliers. In fact, when General Lee retreated from Petersburg on his way to Appomattox, his army stopped at Dinwiddie Court House hoping to find supplies of food before he turned south to join General Johnston. Instead, his men found the trains loaded with ammunition, courtesy of Gorgas' Ordnance Bureau. The Confederacy held on as long as it did partly because an able planner of northern origin headed a department crucial to the maintenance of the armies in the field.[29]

As Gorgas knew all too well, since he relied on one of them for supplies abroad, a few Northern Confederates worked overseas in the all-important mission of obtaining recognition from European governments or securing supplies. When President Davis sent a three-man commission to England to meet with the British government, a fourth agent went along as a special commissioner. That man was Thomas Butler King, an adopted Georgian originally from Massachusetts. As a result, a quarter of the team initially sent to obtain recognition originally came from the North. Unfortunately for the Confederacy, that same team failed to sway the British and they returned empty-handed. King stayed behind to try to obtain supplies, but he foundered in that endeavor as well. The *New York Herald* gleefully reported in 1862, "T. Butler King, of Georgia, who has been in Europe for several months, as a Southern Commissioner, has arrived at New Orleans. . . . His mission to obtain European recognition of the rebel confederacy has proved a total failure." Although the mission failed, one native northerner at least tried to bring Britain on the Confederate side.[30]

Shortly afterwards, a fellow Northern Confederate had a much greater role to play in Europe. President Davis appointed two ambassadors to Britain and France to continue to lobby for recognition. Virginian James Mason received the British assignment, but the French assignment went to native New Yorker and adopted Louisianan John Slidell. Slidell already had plenty of experience for such an assignment. He originally emigrated to Louisiana after his family's merchant business failed and to avoid prosecution for fighting a duel and severely wounding his opponent. After settling in New Orleans, Slidell became a lawyer and politician, serving as district attorney and a member of the Louisiana legislature. He won election to Congress in 1842 and then to the Senate in 1853. In the interim, President James Polk selected Slidell to serve as a minister to Mexico to negotiate border disputes around the Rio Grande River. This assignment, along with his political experience, served him well when he reached the Quai d'Orsay.[31]

Slidell spent three years in Paris securing interviews with French officials on the subject of recognition. Since he technically held an unofficial status, Slidell corresponded through an intermediary named Count Wolneski. In one particular letter, Slidell insisted the Confederacy functioned as a legitimate nation and would never submit to northern domination. He argued that the North had started the war because of "envy at Southern ease and affluence, the results of industry. Then to sever our last bond connection the Constitution was disregarded and our homes invaded to compel us to acquiesce to their authority."[32] Like his counterpart in Britain, Slidell failed to secure recognition, but he presented his nation's case as forcefully as possible. Though he considered himself an adoptive southerner, he might have bolstered his case if he had highlighted his origins, rather than suppressing them. The image of a native northerner working on behalf of a country with no northern states in the pursuit of independence gave at least some evidence of the power and endurance of Confederate nationalism among its adopted, as well as native, citizens.

One other Northern Confederate working in Europe was Caleb Huse, a native of Massachusetts. While King and Slidell concentrated on obtaining recognition, Huse served as a Confederate supply agent. He negotiated with European agents to purchase saltpeter and other supplies for the Ordnance Bureau. He also tried to procure blockade runners to prey on Union shipping. In the process, Huse likely worked with the Confederacy's chief blockade-runner agent, James Bulloch, who commissioned the raiders CSS

Florida and CSS *Alabama*. Huse himself did not pull off nearly as big a coup, but his efforts in obtaining supplies still contributed to the Confederacy's blockade-running trade with Europe. Gorgas certainly would not have had the level of success that he did without the assistance of his fellow Northern Confederate.[33]

Ironically, in order to carry out his mission, Huse needed to travel to the North from Richmond for a short period to find a suitable ship for passage to Europe. He took a train to New York to visit with an English trading company to secure funds for his voyage. After borrowing approximately five hundred dollars worth of gold, he then boarded another train bound for Canada. He never made it to Canada, because he boarded a ship in Portland, Maine, for passage to Liverpool. Either Huse thought the border might be guarded, or he simply found what he needed in Maine. In either case, Huse had ample opportunity to abandon everything and return to his native home in Massachusetts, especially since the train made stops in that state. Instead, Huse left his old home behind, as so many other Northern Confederates did, to carry out his mission for his new nation.[34]

Along with agents in Europe, the Confederacy also relied on native northerners within the national and state governments. Over twenty held positions in the Confederate government in one capacity or another. For instance, William Montague Browne, a native Englishman who spent nearly ten years in New York before moving to the District of Columbia, was a fervent supporter of the Democratic Party and southern sympathizer. After the secession crisis, President Davis appointed him as assistant secretary of state. Later in the war, he served as a personal aide to Davis with the rank of colonel.[35]

Surprisingly, considering their numbers in the Confederate armies and diplomatic corps, only four Northern Confederates served in the Confederate Congress. Three of them represented the Deep South, while the fourth actually represented the border state of Missouri.[36] For the most part, each of these men demonstrated their steadfast support for their adopted homeland by advocating for any means necessary to secure Confederate independence. Edward Sparrow encouraged such policies while representing Louisiana. A native Irishman, Sparrow immigrated to the United States with his family as an infant and grew up in Ohio. In 1831, at the age of twenty-one, he moved to Louisiana to work as a lawyer and eventually as a planter, reportedly acquiring over a million dollars in assets by 1860, including sixty-seven slaves.

During the secession crisis, Sparrow initially served as an immediate secessionist delegate to the secession convention and then worked as a delegate to the Confederate constitutional convention in Montgomery. Following the completion of that convention, the Louisiana legislature elected him as a senator, a capacity in which he served for the remainder of the war. He eventually rose to chairman of the Naval Affairs Committee and the Committee of Military Affairs. During his time in office, he consistently voted in favor of the draft, suspending the writ of habeas corpus, and other measures designed to win the war at any cost.[37]

The other two Deep South legislators did not have as much of an impact as Sparrow, because of their extremely short tenures, yet they still demonstrated their commitment to sacrifice for the cause. John Sanderson, a native of Vermont, moved to Florida to practice law and eventually acquired a plantation. He also served in the Florida legislature as a Democrat and operated several railroads. As a member of the Florida secession convention, Sanderson supported immediate secession and signed the state's secession ordinance. In 1862, the legislature selected him to fill the seat vacated by George Ward in the provisional Congress. He only served for thirteen days and then went back to his law practice for the rest of the war, though he later worked as a clerk for the Quartermaster Corps for six months and then as an appraiser of property for the Conscript Bureau in 1864. Porter Ingram, another native of Vermont, became a lawyer and planter in Georgia. Unlike Sparrow and Sanderson, Ingram ran as a unionist candidate for the secession convention but went with Georgia when the state seceded. Too old to serve, he sat out the war until 1864, when the legislature selected him to complete the House term of Hines Holt. During his five weeks as a congressman, he supported all major war programs and served on the Medical Department Committee. After leaving Congress, he stayed at his home until April 1865, when he enlisted in the home guard to fend off a Union cavalry attack against Columbus.[38]

Farther north, Andrew Conrow, a native Ohioan, moved to Missouri before the war as a lawyer and judge. Elected to the legislature as a Democrat in 1860, Conrow supported immediate secession for his adopted state. He recruited a Confederate company and received an appointment as a colonel in the Missouri State Guards, which he helped create. After Union forces drove Governor Claiborne "Fox" Jackson and the secessionist legislature to the border of Arkansas at Neosho, Conrow received an appointment from that legislature as a Confederate congressman. A firm supporter of President Davis, Conrow advocated total war and voted for such unpopular measures as an extension of the draft and higher taxes. It certainly helped that his own district, largely occupied by Union troops, did not have to pay the taxes or endure the conscription measures. In 1864, he won reelection in a purely symbolic vote from Missouri troops stationed in Texas, since the Union occupied all of Missouri by that point.[39]

Conrow stood out because he neither originally came from the South nor did his adopted state secede. He appeared to have little reason to abandon the Union, but did so anyway because he believed in the righteousness of the Confederate cause. At any time, he had the opportunity to return to either his native or adopted state and rejoin the Union. Instead, Conrow retreated from both and traveled to Richmond to assist the Confederacy in its struggle for survival. And like many of his fellow congressmen, he urged Confederates to make any sacrifice necessary to make that happen.

On a more local level, Mississippi and Arkansas placed their faith in Northern Confederates to run their state governments.[40] Ohio native Charles Clark initially served for two years on the front lines as a general for a Mississippi regiment. Injuries sent him home but the state's residents, grateful for his past service, elected him as wartime governor. In the process, Clark followed the tradition of John Quitman as a native northerner ascending to the highest state office of Mississippi. In this case, his job was much more difficult because, by the time he took office, the Union armies had overrun much of the state, including the capitol. Nevertheless, Clark remained at his post for the remainder of the war and even refused to yield the office when a Union army commander demanded his surrender. Frank Montgomery, a Mississippi resident, recalled in later years his appreciation of Clark's conduct: "At the election of 1863, he was elected governor, and this trying position he held till forced by federal bayonets to yield. He was literally ejected from his office by force, refusing to give it up on demand, for he said he had received it from the people of the state and to them alone would he surrender it."[41]

New Jersey native Harris Flanagin had a similar opportunity to show his devotion in his adopted state of Arkansas. A lawyer and plantation owner, Flanagin served in the secession convention in 1860 as a unionist delegate and originally voted against secession. After Fort Sumter, however, he changed his mind and supported his state's withdrawal from the Union. He began the war as a captain in the Second Arkansas Mounted Rifles, eventually getting promoted to colonel. After a year of serving in that regiment, the residents of Arkansas elected Flanagin as their wartime governor in 1862. He remained in office for the rest of the war, even after Union troops captured Little Rock. During his tenure he helped raise state troops for Confederate service and later assisted in recruiting efforts in the Trans-Mississippi region.[42] Flanagin and Clark together represented the Northern Confederate population in the elite group of southern wartime governors. In the process, they continued the pattern of Northern Confederate leaders maintaining a defiant stance toward their native section in the pursuit of Confederate independence.

One did not have to fight on the battlefield or roam the halls of power, however, to have an impact. In fact, the battlefield did not exist without the home front, as each one supported the other in a symbiotic relationship. Northern Confederates, especially women, participated in the same trials as native southerners caught in the crossfire of the Confederate home front. At least ninety-four individuals in this study spent the entire war on the home front, along with others who participated in both the army and the home front. They existed in relative obscurity, except among the local communities and families they cared for and assisted.

In South Carolina, Caroline Gilman, whose husband died a couple of years before the war, lived with her children in Charleston until 1862. During one of the Union navy's bombardments of the city, a shell hit her house, and she felt unsafe staying in her home thereafter. She then packed up her belongings and moved west to Greenville, where she stayed for the remainder of the war. At no time did she consider returning to Massachusetts, though she had the option, especially after the Union navy occupied various South Carolina ports. In fact, while in Greenville, Gilman invested five hundred dollars in Confederate treasury bonds in 1864, indicating she committed herself to the new nation economically as well as ideologically.[43]

Down in Georgia, Maine native Dolly Burge operated a plantation without help from either a husband or children. She grew cotton and managed her slaves until 1864, when the left wing of General Sherman's army stripped her plantation clean in the March to the Sea. Throughout the war, she kept a diary but rarely mentioned the war itself. Most of the time she wrote about prices, shortages, and anything else that might affect her livelihood.[44] Through it all, she identified with the Confederacy. As she wrote in December 1861, "Our once united & prosperous country is in the midst of civil war. Battle after battle has been fought & it still goes on. The enemy has blockaded our coasts so that we can neither export our produce or import our needful. Some of the best blood of the country has been spilled. O the horrors of war."[45] Burge lamented the death and destruction, and missed her family, but she still did not consider returning to the Union.

Farther to the west, Amanda Trulock and Caroline Seabury fought their own private wars to keep families intact and contribute to the Confederacy at the same time. Staying on her plantation in Arkansas, Trulock tended crops and tried to keep her sons out of the army. She even paid three thousand dollars to hire a substitute. Her attempts did not work in the long run, because one of her sons was conscripted in 1864.[46] Nevertheless, despite the fact that both Union and Confederate raiders struck her plantation at various times, she refused to leave. In the process, like so many other southern plantation mistresses, Trulock ended up losing most of her slaves, either from flight or removal by Union soldiers. She lost her private war to keep her family and home together, yet still she did not give up. Many of her neighbors fled, but she chose to remain in her adopted home whatever the cost. Caroline Seabury echoed this determination by volunteering for various positions in Mississippi, including working as a nurse in an army hospital and tutoring for other families in the area.[47]

Along with women, some Northern Confederate men either never entered the army or returned home at various times after receiving wounds or while on furlough. Their actions on the home front ranged from business to convalescence to charity work. For example, native Pennsylvanian Charles Dahlgren initially served in the Mississippi state militia but then retired to his plantation for the first two years of the war. He worked as a recruiter and advised other Confederate generals, including Pemberton, on erecting defenses in the area. When the Union navy ascended the Mississippi River in 1862, Dahlgren urged planters within a ten mile radius to burn all their cotton rather than allow it to fall into Union hands.[48] Similar to many other die-hard Confederates, Dahlgren favored nearly any step, even if it meant his own ruin, to achieve victory. After General Grant captured Vicksburg, Dahlgren fled Mississippi with his family and settled in Georgia. In the process, he left behind two sons, one who fought in the Jeff Davis Legion in Virginia and another who was taken prisoner in Vicksburg. Fellow Northern Confederate General Samuel French also retired to Georgia to recover from wounds sustained after the Battle of Nashville in early 1865. He ended up marrying his second wife, the daughter of a wealthy Alabama planter, during his convalescence, which helped him recover losses from his own plantation back in Mississippi.[49]

Charles Quintard engaged in more charitable work in his time away from the army. As a preacher, Quintard visited hospitals and raised funds for churches in various states. Mississippi resident Kate Cumming recalled one of his efforts to restore a small church in a rural part of the state. She wrote in the summer of 1863, "I went to the church this afternoon to practice for the choir, and there I found Dr. Quintard and Dr. Cannon enveloped in a cloud of dust. They were both sweeping, trying to make the church look as clean as possible. . . . Dr. Quintard is a man of great energy. He has already collected twenty-five hundred dollars, and contracted for seats for the church."[50] A month later, with the chapel still under repair, Quintard held services outside under an oak tree, even in the dark. Cumming likely spoke for the rest of the community when she wrote, "I can now understand how it is that he is so popular and does so much good in the army. He suits himself and all he does to the times."[51] Both on and off the battlefield, Quintard did everything possible in his role as a pastor to cater to the religious needs of his fellow countrymen. And unlike Dahlgren and French, Quintard rarely if ever had a profit motive in mind for his work. In fact, in 1864 he traveled to Atlanta to organize a new parish. In order to pay for the materials for a new church, he went to a nail factory, conducted services and baptisms, and then accepted lumber and nails as payment.[52]

Other Northern Confederates engaged in more mundane tasks behind the lines. Massachusetts native Moses Curtis saw his sons go off to war but stayed behind with his wife in their home in Hillsborough, North Carolina. Together they made clothes for Confederate soldiers, invested in Confederate bonds, and watched the Confederacy fall apart when General Sherman's army came within six miles of the town before General Johnston surrendered. George Kendall, a native of New Hampshire, cited age as a reason for not enlisting and largely stayed out of the war on his ranch in Texas. His one contribution involved raising money for equipping Texas Rangers to defend against Native American attacks, a greater threat thanks to so many young white men in the armies.[53] Adopted Virginian George D. Armstrong actually had to accommodate other northerners because he remained in Norfolk after the city's capture in 1862. For the next two years, Armstrong administered his church alongside Union missionaries, somewhat ironic since Armstrong himself originally came to Virginia as a northern missionary. Apparently his conduct did not suit the occupying forces, because General Benjamin F. Butler expelled Armstrong in 1864; he went on to join the Army of Northern Virginia as a pastor.[54]

Eugene Hilgard and Ebenezer Emmons used science rather than religion to further the cause. Hilgard, a native German who grew up in Illinois before emigrating to Mississippi, had developed a reputation as a respected geologist throughout the Southwest, even rising to the position of state geologist in Mississippi. When the war erupted, Hilgard turned his geological knowledge toward Confederate defenses. He wrote a report on possible nitrate finds in the state, attempted to invent a turpentine lamp to make up for the lack of kerosene, and even drew up plans to set up calcium lights on the Vicksburg bluffs to illuminate Union gunboats. Unfortunately for Hilgard, none of these ideas ever left the drawing board.[55] Emmons also used geological knowledge to help the Confederacy. A native of Massachusetts who emigrated to North Carolina only three years before the war, Emmons taught geology at a North Carolina university. Jonathan Worth, a member of the war department, wrote to Emmons in 1862 about the desperate salt shortages in the region. Since Emmons knew the area, Worth asked him to travel to Wadesboro to investigate possible salt deposits. Although he never donned a uniform, Emmons still found a way to assist his adopted region and country.[56]

In fact, the Confederacy relied on several other civilians to assist the war effort behind the lines. Thomas Clemson, a native Pennsylvanian who lived in South Carolina and Maryland before the war, worked on behalf of the Confederate government in both an unofficial and official capacity. From 1861 to 1862, Clemson lived in South Carolina and engaged in business investments for the government, including a failed attempt to send cotton to Europe to pay for supplies. He also gave a speech calling for the creation of a national agricultural department, though the Confederate Congress did not act on the suggestion. Finally, in 1863, the government called on Clemson to join the Trans-Mississippi division of the Nitre and Mining Bureau. He ended up in Texas, in charge of iron works and furnaces in the state, nearly acting as an independent agent because of the lack of communication between Texas and Richmond. The appointment lasted for nine months, until he was relieved for unknown reasons. Not content to go back to South Carolina,

Clemson stayed in Texas to serve as an inspector for scientific surveys looking for scarce minerals throughout the state.[57]

Further to the east, native New Yorker Rufus Bullock utilized his own organizational skills on behalf of the Confederate transportation and communication systems. Specifically, Bullock worked as the superintendant of the Southern Express Company's eastern operations, appropriate considering his background as a telegraph operator. In that capacity, he built telegraph lines across the Atlantic Coast and directed railroad transportation through Georgia, his adopted state. He also helped turn Augusta into a major war center. In 1865, with General Sherman's army on the march, Bullock personally oversaw the shipment of over a million dollars worth of gold from Columbia to Augusta for safekeeping. Bullock stayed at his post until General Lee's surrender at Appomattox.[58]

These displays of support for the Confederate nation occurred thousands of times among Northern Confederates throughout the war. Collectively, they all revealed just how much the Confederacy meant to native northerners who seemingly had no stake in the survival of a country that did not include any northern states. In the process, they not only thought of themselves as southerners but also came to identify with the Confederacy. Viewing themselves as Confederates came naturally, yet that allegiance had profound consequences for their future.

7

Emergence of a Confederate Identity and Nationalism

While Northern Confederates did everything in their power to ensure the overthrow of the Union on the battlefield and the home front, something even more significant occurred. Serving in the Confederate forces solidified what it meant for adoptive southerners to identify as Confederates. They generally did not see themselves as northern mercenaries, but rather as genuine Confederates, with the same practical and ideological motivations as every other Confederate citizen. Specifically, fighting as Confederate soldiers meant protecting their adopted southern homes, distancing themselves as much as possible from their native section, and upholding the right of their new Confederate nation to exist free from the tyranny of northern aggression. Their participation in the Confederate forces thus provided a unifying experience with native southerners and made Northern Confederates equal to native southerners in the forging of the new nation. Once they enlisted in the Confederate cause, these men and women made the transition from adoptive southerners into Northern Confederates and forever became associated with the Confederacy.

As a result, the Civil War itself marked a major turning point for sectional identity among adoptive southerners. For the entire antebellum era, native northerners had few problems in emigrating to the South and setting up new lives in an adopted state if they so chose. Many changed their sectional identities, while others chose to still see themselves as northerners living in the South. They always had the option to abandon the South and return to their native region at any time. That option existed because sectional and national identity remained fluid and flexible in American society. Once the Civil War erupted, that fluidity and flexibility effectively ended. Service in the Confederate armies and living on the Confederate home front forced these native northerners to think of themselves as both Confederates and southerners. The North now represented the enemy and invader instead of their childhood home. Unlike in the past, when they had the option of keeping their northern identities, the Civil War made such a choice nearly impossible.

This chapter analyzes this transition among Northern Confederates and the ways they expressed it. We cannot pretend to know everything that went on in the minds of all Northern Confederates as their past and present collided on the battlefield. The remarks many of them made in their journals and letters, and the few who did try to justify themselves to their families and peers, provide at least a glimpse of what the transition may have felt like for other Northern Confederates as well. Even those who only moved to the South a few years before the war, and thus did not have much time to develop an adopted southern identity, still made statements that aligned them with the Confederacy, the South, and their adopted states.

The declarations made by Northern Confederates also spoke to the enduring viability of Confederate nationalism. Historians have engaged in extensive debate about whether Confederates felt a strong connection to their nation or abandoned it once the war turned against them. Skeptics have traditionally pointed to the collapse of Confederate morale in the later years of the war, as well as internal opposition between slaveholders and nonslaveholders over measures like draft exemptions. More recent scholarship tilts toward the acceptance of the Confederacy having a strong nationalist spirit among its people even in the face of adversity. The reactions of Northern Confederates in this study reinforce the latter interpretation because, if native northerners who did not always have firm attachments to the South could fight and die for the Confederacy up until its surrender, then Confederate nationhood had cross-sectional appeal. The commitment of Northern Confederates to the cause, as expressed through the protection of their adopted homes and their support of the right of the Confederacy to resist subjugation by the North, reinforced the foundation of Confederate nationalism through both success and failure.[1]

Northern Confederates unveiled their transition to a Confederate identity in many ways, but few as revealing as the phrasing used when referring to both sides. Soldiers and civilians used specific words linking them to the Confederacy, their comrades, and their adopted communities, including "our," "us," "comrades," "friends," "we," and other terms of endearment. For instance, in letters to his daughter, adopted Virginian Jedediah Hotchkiss asked her to pray for the success of the Confederate armies in order to protect their family and country. After the battle of Fredericksburg, Hotchkiss told her "we must thank the good Lord that he enabled us to whip them and drive them away, for they would come and destroy us and our country if they could." A few months later, he urged her to continue to pray that God would "drive away our enemy and bring peace so that we may all go home & stay there."[2] Similarly, adopted Louisianan John Slidell constantly referred in his dispatches from Paris to his hope that France would recognize "us;" if not, then "our people" needed to achieve victory with "our own resources."[3] In Georgia, Edward Drummond spent his first six months of service stationed at Fort Pulaski. Throughout his diary, Drummond referred to "our boats," "our picket," and "we" when describing the Confederate forces.[4] In February 1862, Drummond made his commitment more explicit when he wrote, "Tomorrow our Congress meets to sign the declaration of our independence and the foundation of a permanent government."[5] Even after his capture and imprisonment in the North, Drummond did not express any connection to his native region. If anything, he prided himself on being called a "Secesh" by northern onlookers.[6]

This pattern continued in other letters and diaries written by Northern Confederates. Henry Handerson wrote to his uncle about the actions of "our southern Congress" and complained that "we are forced to endure a winter campaign." Edmund Dewitt Patterson consistently wrote about "our friend," "our camp," "our little band," and "our Country." Jedediah Hotchkiss referred to his regiment as "our Valley men." Robert Hatton called the southern armies "our forces" striving for "our success." Edward Wells wrote to his sister and mother calling his fellow soldiers "my comrades." Thomas Butler King, writing about the Confederate Congress, complained that congressmen did not devote enough attention to defending "our coast," "our gallant armies," "our people," and "our citizens."[7] In each case, a native northerner labeled Confederates his natural friends and comrades through the simplest words and phrases.[8]

At times such declarations of identification with the new nation went into much greater detail. For example, Joseph Garey, who only emigrated to

Mississippi in 1860, nevertheless considered himself a loyal Confederate. In November 1861, he wrote in his diary, "Should the war last a few years we will certainly become a manufacturing people & depend alone upon ourselves for the goods once imported." A couple of months later, Garey reiterated his views when he said, "To their [Federals'] vaunting hosts are opposed our brave southern boys . . . prepared to meet them at any front. On the Potomac or the Mississippi—at Manassas or Bowling Green—in Virginia or Kentucky we stand waiting to meet & repel them from our soil. 'We're eager for the fray.'"[9] In a similar vein, adopted Louisianan Thomas Wharton believed the Union navy did not pose any real threat to his home in New Orleans and hailed their criticisms as a mark of pride. As Wharton wrote in his diary, "and in spite of the menacing attitude of the North, and their terrible denunciations of us 'rebels' we treat their flippant threats, their promises to annihilate us! to subjugate us! their men? [sic] their money? [sic] all that belongs to them? [sic] if *anything;* with supreme derision and contempt."[10] In a grander and more public statement, New Jersey native George D. Armstrong delivered a sermon in his Virginia church praising the Confederacy's first major victory at Manassas. Armstrong, exactly like native southern preachers, interpreted the victory as the will of God and touted the inevitable certainty of independence. In the course of his sermon, Armstrong used the same language as every other adopted southerner who now embraced the Confederacy as his own. "Call to mind now the character of our army, made up, as it is, from all classes of our community—our fathers—our husbands—our sons—our brothers—the very flower of our Southern people—and I can conceive of no more emphatic declaration than this, that, in the judgment of the people, our President is 'the right man in the right place.'"[11]

One might argue that the use of such language was merely artificial and masked their continued secret devotion to their native section. Certainly some native southerners questioned the inclusion of such men in the armed forces. John Beauchamp Jones, a clerk in the war department in Richmond, referred to them as "hybrid Yankees" and other derogatory names.[12] Even a few Northern Confederates noted how, though they felt connected to the Confederate army, the southern population itself remained distant. Silas Grisamore, a Confederate officer and native of Indiana, commented on how the hospitality of the local population in Louisiana made life "among the Southern people" a positive experience. Despite that experience, he still felt distant from the local population, because he referred to them as a separate people.[13]

Part of that distance stemmed from the persistent idea that sectionalism came from ancestry. Felix de Fontaine, a Massachusetts native who worked as a correspondent for South Carolina newspapers, related an incident where a southern soldier talked down to his Union captors. The soldiers warned the prisoner to watch his tone, but the prisoner defiantly proclaimed, "'I am not bolder or more frankly spoken than every man with Southern blood in his veins, and I do not hesitate to tell the truth anywhere.'"[14] Such statements contribute to the idea that, although many native northerners fought for the Confederacy, only rarely did they quickly convert to the Confederate cause. In this interpretation, native northerners may have backed the Confederacy's bid for independence, but they still did not have the same stake in its outcome because they did not have the same connection as native southerners. The Confederacy, born from the southern states and its native sons, could only truly survive through the efforts of those who would lose everything if it failed.

In reality, from the earliest days of the war to the final surrender, Northern Confederates eagerly aligned themselves with the Confederate cause and made tremendous sacrifices in pursuit of its success. "Southern blood" did not flow through their veins, but their attachments to the region and determination to prevent its subjugation provided more than enough of a foundation for their support.[15] The editor of Edmund Dewitt Patterson's journal, for example, summed up his introduction by writing, "Seldom did one so young become so quickly such a strong believer in the southern cause."[16] In addition, because Confederates needed to create their nation from scratch, ancestry did not matter because everyone involved had to alter their identities in the midst of war. Since Northern Confederates participated in the creation of the Confederacy from its inception, they had as much claim to it as any native southerner. Previous lives in the North meant nothing when compared to the camaraderie of the Confederate army and the protection of the nation they now considered their own.

Edmund Dewitt Patterson himself prominently displayed such a commitment from the time he received his baptism of fire. He originally left Ohio in 1859 to try his luck in Alabama as a bookseller, teacher, and clerk. When war erupted, he had little financial stake in the state, remained unmarried, had no prospects of achieving high rank in either army, and had a family back in Ohio who eagerly supported the Union. Despite all this, Patterson wasted little time in joining the Confederate army because of his certainty of the righteousness of the Confederate cause. As he toured the carnage after the Confederate victory at First Manassas, he reflected on how the outcome would send the perfect message to his enemies. "The result of this battle will teach the North a lesson that will not soon be forgotten. It will show to them, and the world, that we are in earnest and that we mean what we say and that in attempting our subjugation [they] have undertaken an herculean task."[17] The fact that Patterson had a family in the North and had lived in Ohio a mere two years earlier did not appear to have entered his mind. Within only a few months, the North had transformed from his childhood home into the ultimate threat that needed neutralization.

By the end of the year, he looked back on his time in the army with pride and happiness. The last entry in his diary for 1861 reflected his complete transformation into a die-hard Confederate. "It will be remembered as the year in which the Southern people, unable longer to bear the tyranny of the North, or rather of Northern fanaticism, determined to exercise those rights guaranteed to them by the constitution [sic] and, following the example of the colonies, years ago, separated themselves from the old government and set up for themselves another in which there will not be so many conflicting interests," he boasted to himself. "The cause of the South is growing brighter and I believe that ere long the Confederate States will be a free and independent government, loved at home, respected abroad."[18] Harkening back to the Founding Fathers, Patterson presented a justification for southern independence worthy of a native Alabamian. He used the same references to the Revolution, liberty, and justice as expressed by the Union to justify his stance for the Confederacy. Following Patterson's logic, Northern Confederates of all ages believed upholding the sanctity of Confederate nationhood along with their own adopted homes, and labeling their native section as the epicenter of tyranny and oppression, symbolized the very definition of a Confederate warrior.

Patterson even acknowledged the unusual situation he faced as a native northerner fighting in the Confederate army. Since he moved to Alabama only a short time before secession, he could not completely forget his past. On his birthday in March 1862, he recalled how twenty years earlier the state of Ohio welcomed him into the world and provided him with a bright home and a bright future. Thanks to twists of fate, "now I am a soldier in the army of the Confederate States, and 'I am become a stranger unto my brethren, and an alien unto my mother's children.' But I am engaged in the glorious cause of liberty and justice, fighting for the rights of man—fighting for all that we of the South hold dear."[19] He never intended to become an adoptive southerner or a Confederate, but now he felt like a stranger toward his own family. His entries implied that his fate could have happened to anyone from the North. A few months later, in the aftermath of the Battle of Second Manassas, he even tried to explain how such a transition occurred. "That line of skirmishers made me feel that friends were at hand, and then I knew that with them our cause was advancing. This kindred of common cause—common hope—common fears, and common suffering—is it not sometimes stronger than the ties of nature?"[20]

His devotion to his new nation only grew as the years passed. While recovering from sickness in the summer of 1862, he stayed in Richmond hospitals and toured the city. He also had the opportunity to see Jefferson Davis and the Confederate Congress and liked what he saw. Patterson especially appreciated that former unionists in the Congress worked arm in arm with secessionists, with the Union by that time symbolizing tyranny and oppression. Even upon returning to northern soil after rejoining his regiment in the fall, he kept to his convictions and regarded that soil as alien country rather than a home. In describing the upcoming attacks on the second day of Gettysburg, Patterson steeled his nerve by writing in his journal, "The time to try our manhood, the long looked for hour when we should meet the enemy on his own soil. I prayed God in that hour to assist me to do my whole duty to my country."[21] His dedication to his new nation, combined with his alienation from his native region, defined Patterson as a Confederate soldier.

Patterson's experience was by no means unique. Throughout the first year of the war, in evidence of a rapid transition, other Northern Confederates across the South expressed the same kind of dedication. In spite of their vastly different backgrounds, they joined native southerners with the same motivations to protect home, family, slavery, and country against invasion from an alien North. In the process, their transformation to a Confederate identity mirrored those of their comrades. Henry Handerson wrote to his uncle in the Midwest explaining his training in preparation for the first land battles and expressed confidence in a quick Confederate victory. In case his uncle had any illusions about his ultimate intentions, Handerson said that, should he survive the war, "I shall try to pay you a short visit on my return to Louisiana."[22] General Daniel Ruggles, a native of Massachusetts, issued a proclamation from his headquarters in Fredericksburg claiming that Confederate troops, himself included, had to take up arms to protect their homes and families against tyrants who unleashed death and destruction against the southern homeland.[23]

Adopted Louisianans John Slidell and Thomas Wharton wrote similar statements about the durability of the Confederacy. Slidell, before departing on his mission to France, predicted that the Confederacy could overcome any setbacks or difficulties. He noted that the recruiting officers already needed to turn away some of the flood of volunteers, which demonstrated "our people thoroughly united, & require no stimulus." In addition, he predicted that the country would suffer some hardship for a few months, but once Europe broke the blockade "we shall get into smoother water."[24] Wharton also vividly displayed his own nationalism early in the war when he wrote in July 1861, "The impudent 'Lincoln blockade' is acting in our favor by keeping out yellow fever, and stimulating our heretofore dormant industry and self reliance. . . . But we can readily dispense with them [fish from the Gulf] for one Season, in view of the happiness & prosperity that will inure to the South from the establishment of her *Nationality.*"[25]

Such opinions only solidified over the next four years during both the highs and lows of Confederate fortunes. Commanders especially did everything in their power to stoke the fire of patriotism at every opportunity. The proclamations given by Northern Confederate generals at New Orleans and Vicksburg provided a glimpse into these efforts. Nowhere in these proclamations did the generals equivocate or express uncertainty about the duty expected of them and their men. In New Orleans, General Mansfield Lovell urged his troops to stand fast because southern families depended on their skills and fortitude. His subordinate, native Pennsylvanian General Johnson Kelly Duncan, published his own declaration in the city papers not only backing up his men but also revealing his own dedication to the cause. On the eve of the battle, Duncan told the population, "We are all Cheerful, and have an abiding faith in our ultimate success, which I deeply regret is not altogether the case in the city. A people in earnest, in a good cause, should have more fortitude . . . They [the Union navy] must soon exhaust themselves. If not, we can stand it, with God's blessing, as long as they can."[26]

A year later, General John C. Pemberton found himself in even greater danger when General Ulysses S. Grant's army surrounded Vicksburg. Despite his predicament, Pemberton vowed to both his men and the rest of the Confederacy that he would not surrender Vicksburg without a fight. Answering his critics, Pemberton declared, "'You have heard . . . that it was my intention to sell Vicksburg. Follow me, and you will see the cost at which I will sell Vicksburg. When the last pound of beef, bacon and flour; the last grain of corn, the last cow, and hog, and horse, and dog shall have been consumed, and the last man shall have perished in the trenches, then, and only then, will I sell Vicksburg."[27] Any native southerner reading these words would not have guessed that commanders like Pemberton did not grow up in the South. Most Confederate generals issued similar statements, and they all had the same purpose: to gird their soldiers to accept any sacrifice in the pursuit of independence and the protection of their homes and families.

Northern Confederate General Daniel Ruggles also used his correspondence with opposing generals to outline his new nation's position. In the summer of 1862, Ruggles commanded the department of East Louisiana and Mississippi. The Union navy had captured New Orleans months earlier, and the occupation forces fell under the command of General Benjamin F. Butler, who later earned the wrath of the white southern population for his hard-handed tactics against white southern civilians. Both generals happened to have grown up in Massachusetts, but fate placed them on opposite sides of the battlefield. They corresponded frequently over military affairs and in the process spelled out the views of their respective sides. Ruggles especially hated Butler's orders to execute partisan soldiers operating in the Louisiana swamps. In one of his letters, Ruggles declared guerilla warfare perfectly legitimate because, "Our own revolution; that revolution which successfully established the great principle for which the Confederate States are now contending 'that all Governments derive their just powers from the consent of the governed,' was mainly fought out by men who left the plow at the news of the Enemy's approach, and returned to it when he had been driven back."[28]

Ruggles's justification compared the Confederacy's efforts to those of every other freedom movement throughout history, including the revolution his native state started more than eighty years earlier. Linking such movements together enabled Ruggles, along with many other native northerners, to view their resistance as a natural right to combat foreign invaders, in this case their native section. George D. Armstrong continued this tradition when he told his Virginia congregation, "The members of our Confederate Congress have exhibited a statesmanship and a pure and lofty patriotism which, in all coming time, will associate their memory with that of the fathers of our first revolution." Adopted Floridian Samuel Pasco, reflecting on the symbolism of the Fourth of July, altered its meaning to include the resistance of his adopted section. He wrote in his journal in 1863, "the importance of the contest we are now engaged in causes the importance of former success to pale into insignificance; for of what avail is the Declaration of 1776 to us if we are now to be enslaved by the minions of Lincoln. God grant that the success of our present terrible struggle may soon be established." Edmund Dewitt Patterson made similar comments on the same day in his own journal: "Today the South contends for the same principles which fired the hearts of our ancestors in the revolutionary struggle, and as sure as right and justice prevail, so surely will we finally triumph." Toward the end of the war, while returning to Louisiana from a northern prison, Henry Richardson wrote a letter to his parents in Maine saying how he felt like his ancestors in the War for Independence, "as much as if the period had been eighty-five or six years earlier, and the rebellious cause that of colonies against a mother country, instead of Sovereign States against a government with no claim to dominion other than those it seeks to crush."[29] For these men, the Confederacy represented the continuation of protecting freedoms first laid down by the Founding Fathers and held dear by all Americans, which required all of their efforts.[30]

Girded by this conviction, several Northern Confederate commanders even chose to keep fighting when they lost their commands or did not receive promotions. After the fall of Vicksburg, General Pemberton became the perfect scapegoat for the failures of the Confederate high command. Newspapers and civilians alike called for Pemberton's removal or even his head for his supposed incompetency. Some of them even brought up the general's background and claimed he acted as a traitor who unnecessarily gave up Vicksburg to further the cause of his native North. Upset that people questioned his patriotism, Pemberton resigned his commission as a lieutenant general and offered his services to President Jefferson Davis at any rank his commander-in-chief saw fit. Few other acts of contrition could have confirmed Pemberton's dedication to serve in whatever capacity necessary for the success of his country.[31] Further to the east, the *Charleston Mercury* commented on how adopted South Carolinian Roswell Ripley had helped defend Charleston for several years yet had not received a promotion to major general. The correspondent thought the high command had dishonored Ripley, since his superior had sent in numerous recommendations, but he admired Ripley even more when he chose to stay at his post rather than resign in disgust. As the writer summarized, "But this is the hour of our country, and General RIPLEY, we learn, deems that he can serve the country."[32]

Northern Confederates from all walks of life showed equal dedication. In 1863, Josiah Gorgas heard rumors that General Jubal Early's corps destroyed Harrisburg, the capitol of his native state. In his journal, Gorgas mentioned the news in a very matter-of-fact manner, even adding, "If not true now, I presume it will be."[33] No hints of remorse or regret appeared here because Gorgas now saw Pennsylvania as enemy country. Henry Handerson, who

Generals Pemberton and Grant at Vicksburg. On July 3, 1863, two northern-born generals, native Ohioan Ulysses S. Grant and native Pennsylvanian John C. Pemberton, met to discuss the surrender of Vicksburg. Utilizing his background, Pemberton managed to obtain favorable surrender terms from Grant by agreeing to surrender on July 4, Independence Day. Library of Congress.

Emergence of a Confederate Identity and Nationalism

during the secession crisis considered himself a conditional unionist, later despised any hint of unionism around him. When his regiment passed by the house of Parson Brownlow, a prominent Union sympathizer in Tennessee, Handerson commented that Brownlow's conduct "had won for him our cordial hatred."[34] Ashbel Smith confidently told the Texas governor that "our climate and institutions give us an incalculable superiority over our enemies . . . we may present such a bristling front of power for defence or aggression that our enemies may well heed ere they assail our territory or our institutions."[35] Doctor and preacher Charles Quintard uttered similar remarks in a sermon he delivered to his church in Tennessee. "We may soon become not only a separate and indifferent people," Quintard declared, "but a holy nation, a peculiar people, realizers of good works, and in all things devolved of thy service."[36]

Maine native Henry Richardson went even further than most of his comrades by writing a lengthy justification of his conduct to his parents in March 1865. Although few others followed Richardson's example, his comments still provide a window into the soul of a native northerner converted to a Confederate identity through the crucible of war. At the beginning of the conflict, he believed in the right of secession in theory but did not think it represented the best option for redressing the South's grievances. Two years on the battlefield and two years in a prison camp, however, made the theory a reality. Much of that change occurred because of what the Union armies did to the white southern population. As he wrote to his parents, "separation from such a people as a majority of those of the U.S. have shown themselves to be, is worth any price and ought to have been accomplished long years ago. I did not then believe that, as a class, they were lost to all sense of honor and humanity. . . ."[37] In a story familiar to many other Confederates, the realities of war had turned a formerly reluctant unionist into a die-hard secessionist wishing to protect the nation that represented the best hope for freedom and righteousness against an enemy ready to subject its population to virtual slavery.

Richardson continued his narrative by establishing the special connection he felt for his adopted state. In fact, he felt insulted that his family believed his connection to the Confederacy remained superficial. "Now I believe you have thought very little about my circumstances and position at that time," he remarked, "else you would see, as I felt I did then, and am certain I do now, that if I owed allegiance to any government (as I doubtless did) it was to that of the State of Louisiana." In his mind, Richardson's family should have seen what he himself easily saw: his adopted state and country counted more than anything else. As the Union represented their country, so Louisiana, and by extension the Confederacy, represented his. He even acknowledged that his decision caused his family grief and pain, but while he regretted hurting their feelings, he refused to abandon his chosen path.[38]

Just so his parents did not have any further doubts, Richardson also took the time to directly address his own background. He admitted that his roots came from Maine, and that Louisiana only represented his adopted state, yet he questioned whether a native state necessarily meant automatic loyalty. "I was legally a citizen of Louisiana," he wrote. "I intended to make it my home as long as I lived; to obey its laws and support its interests. True I was not born there, but does the accident of birth necessarily determine where allegiance is due?" Building on this argument, Richardson then went on to cite such figures as John Hancock and George Washington, who abandoned their own previous loyalties to England to lead their states into rebellion. He considered himself a continuation of the Founders' legacy because he too had abandoned his roots in favor of a just and noble cause against his former home.

Richardson summed up his justification by explaining what it meant for him to be a Confederate. He acknowledged the pain his choices caused his family yet did not regret anything, because he believed in the righteousness of the Confederacy and his duty to protect his adopted home. Blaming the Union for unleashing the war, Richardson asked his parents, "if she [Maine] chooses to join in a wicked war against Louisiana, am I bound to turn against the country of my adoption—the country of which I have in good faith become a citizen?" In Richardson's opinion, nativity meant far less than the place where an individual chose to remake his or her life. Since Louisiana offered him the chance to do just that, he felt it only natural to return the favor when Louisiana called on her sons, both native and adopted, to fight in her defense. Louisiana thus bred in Richardson an adopted southern identity that later translated into a Confederate identity. Such a transition could not be undone, even by an attack against a native section.

Richardson closed his letter with the hope that his family now understood what he himself considered natural: "I doubt my having arrived at the conclusion that my parents would be pleased to see their son sneak away from a country he had adopted—from people toward whom he held the relation of a fellow-citizen—from the share of the burden of defense against a wrong-headed, over-grown, boasting foe, who proposed to give all their carcasses to the fowls of the air in less than sixty days!"[39] Although few attempted to describe their transformation as bluntly as Richardson, other Northern Confederates likely would have agreed with much of what he said. They considered the Confederacy their nation, the center of their home and identity, and defended it to the best of their ability, both on the battlefield and on paper.

In a more subtle yet no less dramatic demonstration of their Confederate identity, some Northern Confederates went to extreme lengths to ensure success, even if it meant the sacrifice of cherished rights. For example, adopted Texan Ashbel Smith wrote to the governor in 1862 giving his own opinions on the measures necessary for the prosecution of the war. In his view, neither Texas nor the Confederacy had enacted strong enough policies to bring the war to a successful conclusion. First of all, he hinted that the government should utilize slave labor to work the farms in order to free up more white manpower. Secondly, he contemplated the possible need for a military republic, because the war would last a long time and every man and woman had to make sacrifices.[40] After only a year of conflict, Smith actually considered ending democracy itself for the sake of independence. That same year, Thomas Wharton applauded the passing of martial law in New Orleans because it would root out potential disloyalty.[41] Apparently, both Smith and Wharton missed the irony that their fellow white southern citizens might easily have looked upon them as potential traitors because of their background. They did not consider such a possibility because they felt the same alienation toward the Union as anyone else in the Confederacy. At the end of his letter, Smith insisted that Texans needed to become a warrior people, not just to win the war but to secure the peace as well. "If we are not warlike, if we are only brave individually, we shall, after peace be harassed by John Brown forays and slave stealing expeditions, until our condition on the border especially, will be intolerable, nay worse, pitiable. . . ."[42]

Despite such fiery rhetoric, all Confederates, native northerners included, faced tests of their resolve over the course of the war. One such test occurred in the first half of 1862. Nearly three quarters of a year had passed since the victory at Manassas, and the Confederacy faced threats from multiple directions. In the West, Generals Grant and Halleck, along with the Union navy, secured Kentucky, captured the western half of Tennessee, subdued the vital port of New Orleans, and controlled nearly the entire Mississippi River. In the East, the navy captured multiple ports along the Atlantic Coast, while General George B. McClellan prepared his massive army for the final push to Richmond. The war seemed destined to end in Union victory by the time of the summer solstice.

Even though the cause appeared doomed, many Northern Confederates only chose to see the positive side of such news. Edward Drummond, when he heard that General David Hunter declared emancipation and martial law in the Carolinas, actually thought the Union made a terrible blunder. As he wrote in his journal, "It is the best thing that could have happened for the South as it will make the determination more strong for resistance and will have a tendency to make a division at the North and in a measure demoralize the Federal Army."[43] Likewise, Henry Handerson told his uncle that, though Tennessee had to endure "Lincoln rule," he hoped "the South, aroused from her torpidity by her recent reverses, may arise in her strength and expel the invader from every foot of her territory."[44] In New Orleans, after many of his own men mutinied and forced him to surrender the forts after the Union navy sailed past them, General Johnson Kelly Duncan still urged his remaining soldiers to put up as much symbolic resistance as possible. Union admiral David Dixon Porter noted, "their being was that of men who had gained a victory, instead of undergoing defeat."[45] On the home front, Dolly Burge remarked just before the Peninsular Campaign began, "The blessing of God is on our arms & may His Spirit incline all Hearts to Peace."[46]

Their optimism paid off as General Lee reversed the nation's fortunes and embarked on a year-long campaign of success. Within a few months, the Confederate armies had not only pushed back the Union drive to take Richmond but launched a double invasion of the Union through Maryland and Kentucky, swinging the momentum back in the Confederacy's favor. Military reversals did not cause a permanent drop in morale but merely a temporary one coupled with renewed determination.[47]

The next major reverses occurred in the summer of 1863, with the double disasters of Gettysburg and Vicksburg. Northerners and Union sympathizers rejoiced, since the battles had given the mighty General Lee a decisive defeat and left the Confederacy cut in twain with the complete loss of the Mississippi River. An entire army had surrendered at Vicksburg, and the blow at Gettysburg prevented Lee from ever unleashing a major offensive into the North. Confederate hopes of victory on the battlefield plummeted as the best chance for independence now lay in destroying Union morale rather than Union armies.

Nevertheless, reactions among Northern Confederates generally followed the same pattern as those observed a year earlier. Samuel Pasco, instead of giving up all hope, wrote in his journal, "God grant that the success of our present terrible struggle may soon be established." A few weeks later, Pasco reiterated his optimism by claiming that, though people remained dejected back in Florida, they could not always expect victories and needed to stay the course. He also mentioned the New York draft riots as a way to counter the impression that the Confederacy had no hopes for success.[48]

Edmund DeWitt Patterson, after his capture at Gettysburg, recorded his own impressions of the significance of the recent battles. On his way to prison, and knowing the Confederacy had failed in its invasions, he could have felt dejected, especially since his captors tormented him with the prospect of inevitable Union victory.[49] Instead, like Pasco, he looked for inspiration to rebuild his confidence. As he wrote in his journal, "as sure as right and justice prevail, so surely will we finally triumph. Men of the North tell us that our cause is a doomed one. . . . I might believe this if I did not know that the race is not always to the swift, nor the battle to the strong. There is a God above us that holds the destinies of Nations in his hands, and who in his own good time will bring us safely out of the fiery ordeal through which we are now passing."[50] Similar to other Confederates undergoing the same trials, Patterson looked to God, the past, and his own resolve to help him through times of uncertainty.

On the home front, Caroline Gilman, upon hearing of the capture of Vicksburg and Port Hudson, countered by noting the harassment of Union forces by guerillas all along the Mississippi River. She added, "So it will be in South Carolina; let Charleston be annihilated (for it never will be taken) and resistance will spring up in every new form that valor and ingenuity can devise."[51] Even at the end of the war, with both the Confederacy and her beloved South Carolina crushed under the weight of the Union army, Gilman wrote to her friend, "We are glad to leave . . . early in the morning for home, *Home!* In 1858 I journeyed with a coffin, where was laid my love and earthly hope, and came *home*. In 1865 I journeyed with the dead South and came *home*."[52] In this case, home for Gilman was the one she had created with her husband in their adopted state of South Carolina, rather than her native state of Massachusetts. Even at their seemingly lowest point of morale, at least some Northern Confederate soldiers and civilians alike found ways to cope with major setbacks on the battlefield. Their resilience reflected the strength of Confederate nationalism among adoptive southerners as well as native southerners.

By 1864, Confederate morale rose and fell again as Confederate citizens realized they just needed to hold out long enough to wear down northern willpower. Over the spring and summer, General Grant battled General Lee in a long campaign that led to the siege of Petersburg, while General Sherman faced General Johnston in a push for Atlanta. July and August seemed to mark a turn in Confederate chances; neither Grant nor Sherman succeeded in taking Richmond or Atlanta, and the Democrats proceeded to enact a largely antiwar platform at their convention in Chicago. Several southern newspapers reported that, as long as the Confederate armies prevented any more major Union victories, then George McClellan and his Democratic allies would sweep the election and bring about peace and independence. All such hopes evaporated after Sherman conquered Atlanta in early September and caused northern morale to skyrocket. The rest of the year saw the destruction of Confederate forces in the Shenandoah Valley, the successful reelection of President Lincoln, and the destruction of another major Confederate army at Nashville. Rational observers recognized that the Union had gained all the momentum. If native northerners ever felt a need to return to their native section, the last few months of the war seemed ideal.[53]

Nevertheless, by that point of the war, Confederate identities and nationalism among Northern Confederates had sunk roots too deep to dislodge so easily. They understandably expressed sorrow and hopelessness in the wake of relentless Union attacks, but their commitment to independence had not died. For example, a few days after the loss of Atlanta, Josiah Gorgas argued that the Confederacy could not rely on the election alone to ensure victory. He acknowledged the weakened state of the country's morale, but the populace still had a solemn duty to hold out to the end. "We must make of our means to fight until we have convinced the north that we can beat back their armies & feed & support ourselves," he told an acquaintance. "Still nations like individuals are liable to impulses & the tendency is doubtless toward a cessation of the war but the *terms* will not I fear help us & we cannot stop fighting until their people are weakened and a cessation of hostilities will be felt . . ." In October, Gorgas reiterated his stand by claiming that Grant's attacks had stalled, and the Confederate ordnance department continued to send out a steady supply of munitions. Even if others did not share his optimism, Gorgas himself had the utmost confidence in the war effort and upcoming independence.[54]

Samuel Cooper held the same assessment of the war's outlook in his own letters to his wife that same month. He admitted that the fortunes of the nation had fallen further thanks to the loss of Fort Harrison, situated only a few miles from Richmond, and increasing desertion rates. Yet Cooper still insisted that "we do not despond" because, despite the threats, the war would end in Confederate victory in less than two months if only all the deserters rejoined the ranks. Again, whether true or not, Cooper believed it and thus showed his own undying commitment in the face of a quickly deteriorating situation.[55]

Charles Quintard expressed that theme repeatedly in December 1864. By that time, along with other disasters, General Sherman's army was rampaging through Georgia, while General Grant tightened his grip on Petersburg and Richmond. In spite of all that, Quintard looked for any silver lining available to keep up his morale. For instance, Quintard responded to an article in a northern newspaper claiming the South was on its last legs by pointing out that General Lee still held onto his lines around Petersburg and General John Bell Hood's army had moved north "with Tennessee rescued from the grasp of invaders."[56] Quintard kept detailed accounts over the course of Hood's campaign and tried to record the outcome as positively as possible. After the battle of Franklin, when Hood's army suffered enormous casualties, Quintard simply said the enemy retreated in confusion. Incredibly, he even managed to find good news after the disastrous defeat at Nashville, when for the only time in the war a Union army nearly destroyed a Confederate army on the field. Quintard was initially shocked when he heard the news, but only a couple of days later recovered by calling the defeat a temporary setback. He still believed the Army of Tennessee could hold the line and allow the Confederacy to survive. Only after the army completely dissolved, with just a small remnant left in Mississippi, did he truly believe his beloved Confederate nation might lose.[57]

All of these statements, both public and private, revealed the solidification of a Confederate identity among former northerners. Military reversals alone were not enough to erase that attachment. As Caroline Gilman told her daughter after the loss of Savannah and the threat of the loss of Charleston, "they are not *the* Confederacy."[58] The Confederate nation represented more than just cities and towns and armies; its survival depended just as much on the determination of the people who supported it. Since the citizens of the southern states represented the pioneer generation for the new nation, anyone who participated in its creation belonged to the nation. As Henry Richardson had shown earlier, Northern Confederates could also consider themselves as citizens of a southern state and thus join that pioneer generation.

Nevertheless, their transition still did not blind them to the deteriorating condition of the Confederacy. In 1865, when more and more people recognized the inevitable victory of the Union, Northern Confederates also bowed to the probability of defeat. For example, Josiah Gorgas recorded in March that the Confederacy might still have a chance if Sherman failed to link up with Grant, but he did not think such an outcome likely. "We seem to be on the brink of despair and ruin," he recorded despondently.[59] Charles Quintard saw the same situation in Tennessee with the near total destruction of Hood's army. He lamented that, "Our lands are laid waste with fire and sword. Our slaves are carried off and withdrawn from the cultivation of our rich plantations. The enemy is victorious in almost every quarter except in glorious old Virginia. Our people are disheartened . . . ."[60] News of the loss of Richmond only heightened his grief. Over in France, John Slidell knew the war was over as soon as General Lee surrendered his army in Virginia. He dismissed reports of guerilla warfare as unfeasible and prepared for the worst.[61] The threatened collapse of the Confederate nation represented as much a personal disaster for them as for any native white southerner.

Yet even in the darkest moments of the war, those who wished to do so still found ways to maintain a defiant stance. Despite the certainty of Confederate defeat, Quintard insisted that later generations would look kindly on the doomed Confederacy because, "It has been gallantly defended by the wisest & most rapacious of generals by the bravest & most determined body of troops. History will delight to linger over the record of noble deeds done by our noble arm. . . ."[62] Quintard, like so many other Confederates, believed he had served a noble cause and had every right to stand proud. Henry Richardson offered his own appraisal of the Confederate people's struggle. In one of the more thorough reflections on the subject, Richardson wrote, "That confidence is inspired alike by the precedents of history and the spirit and determination of our people. . . . True, there are a few malcontents and those sewers, who would do anything to save a little filthy lucre; but the most of the people are prepared for extermination in preference to submission. . . . Even now, in the darkest hour, I look forward to a triumphant end."[63] Even Ambassador Slidell refused to let the North have a complete victory. As he wrote to his counterpart in England, "Our children must bide their time for vengeance, but you and I will never revisit our homes under our glorious flag. For myself I shall never put my foot on a soil over which flaunts the hated stars and stripes."[64] In a tone that would echo into Reconstruction, Slidell might bow to defeat, but he refused to give up his Confederate identity. The experiences of war prevented him from accepting the Union the same way ever again.

Refusing to accept any talk of defeat, other Northern Confederates preferred to fight until the very end. Edward Wells, still serving in the cavalry against General Sherman's army as it made its way through South Carolina and North Carolina, informed his aunt that his dedication to the Confederacy remained unbroken. In fact, he found reasons for hope when so many others had given up. "Charleston has gone, Savannah has gone, Columbia is gone, Wilmington is gone," he admitted, "but rest assured we will redeem them in the blood of our enemies. . . . Sherman will find us different customers from the Western Army & rather harder to run."[65] Such a statement might have come from Jefferson Davis himself, and yet this one came from a native New Yorker. Correspondent Felix de Fontaine, reporting on the fall of Richmond, also issued a Davis-worthy report on the devastating news. He told his readers, "Now Richmond is given up . . . it was too heavy a load to carry, and we are stronger than ever." Davis, in comparison, claimed that since General Lee's army no longer needed to stay in one place, nothing stood in the way of total victory except "our own unquenchable resolve."[66]

As a result, several native northerners displayed just as much resolve as the Confederate president himself. They took his call for never-ending war as seriously as possible. In May, more than a month after General Lee surrendered, Ashbel Smith ordered his men to fight to the last at Galveston. When his troops started deserting at an alarming rate, he doubled his guards and issued a proclamation listing all the advantages they still held against the Yankee forces. Only when Confederate general Edmund Kirby-Smith, the commander of the Trans-Mississippi region, ordered him to lay down his arms did he finally evacuate Galveston and travel to New Orleans to seek terms. Likewise, Henry Handerson refused to accept a pardon while in prison in May 1865 until he felt certain the Confederate government no longer functioned. Although they accepted the reality of Union victory, both men made sure they exhausted every possible means of resistance before giving up.[67]

Along with protestations of support, love, and undying commitment for the Confederacy throughout the war, Northern Confederates also demonstrated their Confederate identity by distancing themselves as much as possible from the North. Just as they used "our" and "us" to describe the Confederate army and people, they used words like "Yankee" and "foreigner" to describe the Union army and northern populace. The use of such terms by Confederates came as no surprise, since the Union soldiers represented invaders, marauders, tyrants, and the like. The fact that Northern Confederates used the same vocabulary, however, showed just how much they had aligned themselves with southern society. As native northerners, they had grown up in the North and so knew that northerners, their own families included, were not one-dimensional. Yet they had no problem using the same vocabulary of derision prevalent in the Confederate ranks. For this reason, what Northern Confederates said about their former section revealed as much about their identities as what they said about their adopted section.

Several different terms, including "enemy" and "Yankee," permeated the writings of northern-born soldiers and civilians when describing their former neighbors. Few Northern Confederates failed to use these terms in some form or another. In just one example, Charles Quintard referred to the Union armies throughout his diary as "the enemy." Jedediah Hotchkiss used the term "enemy" constantly in his correspondence with his family in Virginia. Felix de Fontaine preferred the term "Yankees" in propaganda tracts while working as a correspondent in South Carolina.[68]

In the process, Northern Confederates refused to occupy any middle ground, as some of them did in the secession crisis. They identified themselves completely with their new nation, regarding the North as a foreign country and anything associated with the region as contemptible. Edward Drummond insisted that Union soldiers did not have the willpower to withstand southern weather. Henry Handerson, while describing a deserter in his regiment, wrote, "In Yankee parlance my man skedaddled."[69] Robert Hatton even tried to erase all memories of his childhood in the North by telling his family he actually saw a "real live Yankee" and was upset that northern soldiers had invaded their home in Tennessee. Using these terms appeared second nature to Northern Confederates, and not once did they see Union soldiers as anything but alien.[70]

Such a pattern existed throughout the war. Northern Confederates managed to distance themselves so much from their past because the secession crisis and experiences of war increased their feelings of alienation. The conduct of northern soldiers against the South provided further evidence for Northern Confederates that the North they left behind all those years ago had turned into a tyrannical government out to destroy the very freedoms and liberties with which they had grown up. As a result, even though they had first-hand experience in the North, these individuals chose to focus only on the negative aspects of nearly every northerner they encountered. Branding northerners as aliens and enemies helped them define themselves as members of the new nation.

Another way Northern Confederates managed to distance themselves from their native section involved stereotyping a part of the North where they never lived. Specifically, New England provided a useful foil for hatred against the Union. As a base of support for abolitionism, Radical Republicans, and industrialization, New England represented many of the perceived threats against the southern heartland and its values. Immersed in southern culture, adoptive southerners, especially those from outside New England, had no trouble sharing the same prejudices. Adopted Louisianan Thomas Wharton asked what the South should do, "when a savage and demoniac war is waged against us at our very doors by the immaculate and supremely pious!! [sic] puritans of New England, and the refined? and polished!! [sic] powers of the North." Native Ohioan Edmund DeWitt Patterson wrote sarcastically, "Yes, we ought to return to the fold and receive remission of our sins, through the mercy of the sanctified cut-throats of New England who uphold this warfare in the name of our blessed Savior." New Jersey native Samuel French in later years also equated the term "Yankee" with New England.[71]

Descriptions of actual Union soldiers sometimes evoked a more creative and colorful tone. For instance, in the early months of the war, Wharton claimed most of the Border States "are presenting an unbroken front against Northern aggression" and that New Orleans set up defenses "against the savage hordes of the North."[72] French went further by comparing Union soldiers, especially Sherman, to "heathen" Native Americans. He noted that Sherman had the same middle name as a famous native leader of the early nineteenth century and thus must share his nature. As he wrote in his diary, "The one is wicked by nature; the other, I fear, is becoming so by habit." The "habit" he referred to included the policy of "hard war," as historian Charles Royster coined the term, adopted by the Union armies against the southern population.[73] Adjutant General Samuel Cooper, commenting on the great victory at Manassas, picked up this theme of uncivilized northerners when he told a colleague, "You would scarcely know it from the ravage, which have been committed on her soil by a ruthless foe."[74]

In addition, sometimes these men echoed stereotypes typical of the most extreme secessionists. Edward Drummond recalled an incident where the Union navy sent down two vessels, one bearing a flag of truce, toward Confederate lines. He assumed the sailors wished to lure the Confederates into a trap to kill or capture them, because the Union did not have a sense of decency and fair play. A few months later, he contrasted the strong patriotic spirit among his own army with the shallow patriotism of his opponents. Drummond even claimed that the Lincoln government depended on bounties to entice men to enlist, in contrast to the volunteers of the Confederate armies.[75] Josiah Gorgas, along the same lines, believed the Union army only employed foreigners to do their fighting for them. Such a charge implied that the Union had no honor and that northerners did not wish to engage with Confederates, himself included, on equal terms. Nor did Gorgas see northerners as kindred souls. In fact, he preferred immigrants when it came to prisoners his department might employ as workers. "They should be kept under surveillance until they prove their new fruits by their good works," he wrote. "Native born I would not have at all—the foreigners may in time become good citizens."[76] Considering his own background in Pennsylvania, Gorgas's declarations verged on hypocrisy.

Jedediah Hotchkiss and Samuel Pasco echoed Drummond and Gorgas in their refusal to draw on their childhood memories to create an accurate description of northerners. In fact, while serving in General Early's army in the Shenandoah Valley in 1864, Hotchkiss actually described Union society as though he had never seen it before. He told his wife, "I have seen enough of Northern society in our visits to PA & MD to satisfy me that any one holding Southern sentiments, there would be uncomfortable." Rather than base such an assessment on his own childhood in New York, Hotchkiss instead focused on his brief time along the Pennsylvania and Maryland border. He also based his observations mostly on the conduct of the Union army. In a letter to his daughter, he wrote that the Confederate army needed to carry on the war, "for the Yankees have torn down or burn up nearly all the houses

& driven the people away and you can go miles and miles and see no living thing but the wild birds & rabbits."[77] Samuel Pasco witnessed the same kind of deprivations in Mississippi during the Vicksburg campaign. He noted in his journal, "The Yankees have played terrible havoc with the place burning the palings around the beautiful gardens of the fine mansions about the suburbs . . . our enemies have taught us a fearful lesson in the work of destruction which may come down upon their own pates some day."[78] The defiant tone toward the end of this entry indicated the revenge he wished to wreak against his former section. It appeared that if he came upon his own childhood home in Massachusetts, he would have no problem burning it to the ground if such an action would stop the devastation to his adopted section.

Based on these prejudices and stereotypes, several of these men vowed to never reconcile with such a hated people. As late as 1864, while in virtual exile in the Ozarks, Albert Pike continued to vouch for the validity of states' rights and the freedom to leave the Union. Pike wrote in one of his political tracts, "A State is free like an individual in any government worthy of the name. . . . So, in a union of States, the freedom of the States is consistent with the supremacy of the nation."[79] Samuel French, who previously served in the United States Army, wanted all such memories erased, and his sisters helped him accomplish that end. When a squad of Union troops raided his Mississippi home and took his former Army uniform as contraband, his sisters said they could have it. French quoted his sisters in his memoirs as saying, "'I know you are going to steal it, and to relieve your conscience from remorse I will give you the coat. It is my brother's, but he would scorn to wear it with those badges on it.'"[80] Even if his sisters did not utter those precise words, French's recollections reflected his own feelings at the time.

Also on the home front, Maine native Dolly Burge wondered why Union soldiers thought Confederates would return peacefully, considering that the former stole everything from southern civilians. "Is this the way to make us love them & their union?," she asked. "Let the poor people answer whom they have deprived of every mouthful of meat & of their stock to make any."[81] Pastor George D. Armstrong also warned his fellow Confederates to continue resistance because if the Union won, they intended to reduce the South to territories ruled over by fanatical governors and judges.[82] Thomas Wharton likely said it best when he wrote in his diary at the end of 1861, "every thing pleasant in spite of the imbecile but arrogant Northern foe, whom I have learned to condemn more intensely than the meanest reptile that crawls on earth's surface. . . ."[83] All of these statements show a hatred and contempt for the Union invader among native northerners equal to anything native southerners felt.

Still, despite such seemingly universal condemnations, some Northern Confederates, along with native southerners, did not see all northern soldiers and civilians in such a one-dimensional manner. In fact, "Yankee" and "northerner" had far different meanings among Confederates. A "Yankee" usually meant someone in the Union army who destroyed white southern homes, made life miserable for Confederate civilians, or occupied the power centers in Washington, D.C., out to usurp freedom and liberty. "Northerners," on the other hand, did not receive the same levels of condemnation. These individuals usually included white northern civilians, soldiers wounded on the field of battle, and others whom white southerners might look upon with a kinder eye.

Northern Confederates saw such individuals as the personification of the North they left behind, and so did not demonize them in the same way. The difference between "Yankee" and "northerner" became clear when northern-born soldiers wished to separate the worst excesses of the Union army from the rest of northern society. Felix de Fontaine illustrated the point by isolating the conduct of General Butler, whose administration of New Orleans white southerners loathed, from the rest of the Union. Fontaine recorded in his publication, "The North, even—we mean the honest, conservative portion of the people—are put to shame at the infamy and atrocities of some of her military tyrants."[84] As much as he hated the Union army, and Butler in particular, Fontaine knew the entire North did not condone Butler's policies. As with the John Brown raid in 1859, the extremes spoke the loudest, but the larger majority favored a more moderate approach, and Fontaine, a native New Englander himself, understood that. In the same publication, while describing a Confederate attack on a Union position, he told his readers, "The Yankees fought with pluck to the last, but the vigor and vim of the attack was too much for them. They were Michigan men, and were quite indignant at being called 'Yankees.'"[85] Again, "Yankee" held a specific meaning and not everyone fit the profile.[86]

In addition, Jedediah Hotchkiss, who so often excoriated Yankee depredations, at least once wanted to extend a helping hand to a native northerner in need, even though she supported the Union. In August 1863, a family friend from New York, who found herself stuck in Virginia, wanted to return to New York and asked Hotchkiss for help. He sympathized with her plight and truly wished to help her, but in the end he decided not to because of the negative perception of helping a northern unionist. As he wrote to his brother, "It is far better to have no passing to or from the north now. It creates suspicions and looks badly to the army and those engaged in fighting against our cruel and outrageous enemies."[87] In all likelihood, if Hotchkiss had a chance to help her secretly he would have; the problem was that his unit would immediately know about it, and he did not wish to tarnish his own reputation.

Limited acts of mutual respect also occurred when enlisted men met each other face to face in non-combat situations. When soldiers realized their enemy had the same qualities as themselves, they interacted with each other to some degree. These interactions included talking across picket lines, exchanging newspapers, tobacco, and other goods, and administering aid to wounded men on the battlefield.[88] Northern Confederates followed those traditions as well. Samuel Pasco, for example, spent time in a Chattanooga hospital with both Union and Confederate wounded. He talked all day with an Indiana lieutenant who occupied the bed next to him and wrote letters for illiterate Confederate and Union soldiers. In the process, Pasco developed close attachments with several soldiers, especially a private in a Wisconsin regiment. When that soldier died, Pasco wrote, "He belonged to the 24th Wisconsin but we have suffered so long to-gether that it seems like losing an old acquaintance." He also gained a lot of respect for the surgeon who tended to his wounds. Pasco commented, "I like him very much though we differ very widely in our views on the condition of affairs." Whether he referred to the war or differences in society did not matter, since in either case he remembered that not everyone from the North ranked among the worst of Yankees.[89]

Dolly Burge came to the same realization when she found her home and family in the middle of General Sherman's March to the Sea. Rumors spread all across Georgia about Sherman's men's desire for destroying homes, stealing everything in sight, and raping white southern women. Burge, however, reassured her daughters that, though they needed to hide valuables, they did not need to fear Union soldiers as uncontrollable beasts. Her predictions proved somewhat accurate, since Sherman's men did slaughter her livestock, take her food stores, and set her slaves free, yet left the house itself and her family untouched.[90]

More importantly, while stigmatizing a faceless enemy required little effort, applying the same attitude to close friends and relatives was much more difficult. Unlike the vast majority of northern soldiers they encountered during the war, Northern Confederates understood that applying a generalized "Yankee" characterization did not work with family and friends, because they had close personal relationships with them. Family normally represented the last major link these men and women had with their past lives as well as northern society. As much as they hated the Union army, the Republican Party, and abolitionists, they sometimes still tried to keep in contact with their fathers, mothers, siblings, and extended families. No one else reminded them more of their history and past identity. As a result, Northern Confederates faced a conundrum if they wanted to simultaneously uphold their adopted identities and prevent a complete break with their northern families. Such a task was easy in the antebellum period but presented more challenges in a war that seemed to have no middle ground between the sections.

Nevertheless, individuals who so desired both expressed their love for their families and kept their distance from what those families supported. Instead of pushing aside or cutting off communication with their families, as they might easily have done, at least some Northern Confederates attempted to maintain correspondence, mention their families in personal writings, or both. For instance, Jedediah Hotchkiss wrote several letters to his brother in New York to keep up with family news. In 1864, he told his brother about the death of their sister, who lived in Hotchkiss's house in Virginia. He remarked that the news would likely have a devastating effect on their mother.[91] Amanda Trulock utilized the Union occupation of Arkansas to restart her interrupted correspondence with her own family in Connecticut.[92] She mentioned numerous times her gratitude for the opportunity to reestablish the contact they had enjoyed before the war, even though Union victory allowed it to happen. Similarly, when Union soldiers stopped by Dolly Burge's house during their march through Georgia, she inquired about her brother in Chicago after talking with a captain from Illinois.[93] Ashbel Smith did not have the same luck because he lived in Texas, far from his own family in Connecticut. In a letter he wrote to his nephew in February 1861, Smith lamented the certainty of an interruption in their correspondence, adding, "When I think of your grandmother, my dear old mother, from whom I am separated my heart seems ready to break."[94]

In the course of their separation, Northern Confederates sometimes expressed nostalgia for the North they remembered as children. Charles Quintard mentioned in his journal how he longed to reconnect with his northern family. "I think upon my early home, my beloved parents from whom I have been so long separated, my brothers and sisters around whom the tendrils of my heart are turned . . ."[95] Dolly Burge reflected on her old home in Maine when she heard through a flag of truce that her father and stepmother had died from disease. She hated that the war kept her from seeing them and attending the funeral, "that away in Maine my native state friends & relatives were laying in the grave my father & stepmother."[96] Rarely did Northern Confederates actually mention their native state, but in this case she needed to in order to properly reflect on the role her parents played in her life. A year after their deaths, she reiterated her nostalgia when she wrote, "What scenes were enacting in that distant home & here I so totally unconscious of it. It is my hearts desire to meet them in the Heavenly Mansions where I trust they are at rest!"[97] Even Edmund Dewitt Patterson, whose diary entries constantly reflected hatred against the Union enemy, still had a soft spot for his childhood home. After getting wounded in the Seven Days Campaign, his first thought was the prospect of dying alone without family. He recorded after his recovery, "I thought of a home far away in the North-land, and of those dear ones there who will never know how much I loved them, and I wondered if my fate would ever be known to them. . . ."[98] As much as they tried to forget their pasts entirely, such a task proved more difficult than it seemed at first glance.

As Patterson indicated, however, northern families remained separate from the faceless enemy. For this reason, he and others like him had little trouble fighting against their native section while also missing their parents and siblings. In the spring of 1863, Patterson professed his undying love and compassion for his family, and felt relieved when he heard good news from them. Especially since he did not have a southern wife or children, the letters he received kept him in contact with the only family he still had. One diary entry went into great detail on the subject after he received a letter from his sister. "I feared that some of the loved ones were gone, that the home circle was broken. But no, all are well at home. . . . It seems to me that I love them better now than ever I did in my life before the war, and oh, will I live through this miserable war and revisit the scenes of my boyhood home. I pray that I may."[99] Two years in the South was enough to turn his heart to the Confederacy but not enough to alienate him completely from his kin or memories of his earlier life.

Others felt the same way. Sally Baxter Hampton gave up everything to stay in South Carolina with her husband, but she still regretted the required separation from those she loved. As she lay dying of disease, unable to communicate directly with her family, she wrote to one of her friends that her parents and sister did not even know if she still lived.[100] She hoped he would forward her last thoughts on to them after she passed away. To the very end, Hampton kept as close to her northern family as possible in the midst of war. Henry Richardson only reconnected with his own family in the closing days of the war but did not harbor ill will towards them. He vowed never to return to the North again (he claimed he would rather go to Mexico if need be) but hoped he and his parents could still meet together amicably. Richardson also offered to help his parents if they needed assistance, even though he admitted the war had largely ruined his own fortunes.[101]

Edward Wells and Samuel Pasco went to more unusual lengths to maintain contact with their own families while simultaneously keeping their distance from the North in general. Aware of the state of communication between the two sections, after Wells reached South Carolina he promised his mother he would tell her about his condition through Richmond newspapers, which he claimed were easier to smuggle through the lines than letters. Several times Wells wished for the return of peace so the whole family could reunite.[102] Nowhere, however, did Wells indicate he wanted to return to New York. In fact, he made clear he hated the members of his extended family who supported the extreme measures of the abolitionists. As he told his mother, "I suppose my relatives of the nigger-worshiping order consider me as a dreadful devil to resist the will of the 'Descendants of the Puritans.' What do they say? I would like to see their sanctimonious, hypocritical, Yankee upturnings of the eyes."[103] In a sense, Wells wanted to remain close to the family that either shared his views or did not align with the worst excesses of the Union's policies against the Confederacy. Pasco went further by entrusting his northern family with his possessions in case he died from wounds or disease. Specifically, he instructed whoever found his remains to send his journal to his mother in Massachusetts for her comfort. In return, he continued to receive letters from his siblings along with copies of his favorite Boston newspaper. Nevertheless, Pasco still laid out his plans for returning to Florida with honor after the war. Again, devotion to family coincided with unbroken commitment to their new nation.[104]

Through all of these various measures and expressions, Northern Confederates who left behind their thoughts on the subject made a relatively smooth transition into their roles as Confederate patriots and citizens. Although we cannot know, based on the relatively few individuals in this study, whether they represented the opinions of all native northerners in the Confederacy, they at least provide evidence that adoptive southerners from all walks of life had the ability to transform their identities once again. Regarding themselves as equal members of the new nation, they directed all of their energies to the success of the Confederacy. Their contributions not only had a noticeable effect on the battlefield; they also provided yet another foundation stone for Confederate nationalism. Without the same ties of blood and lifelong associations that guided native southern Confederates, these men and women still thought of themselves as Confederates and as adoptive southerners with the same stake in the conflict as their native southern peers. Victory meant security for their adopted homes and families along with the preservation of freedom and liberty. Failure meant humiliation and subjugation by a region they disowned.

Expressions of support for and identification with the Confederacy came naturally while soldiers and civilians remained within the South among likeminded comrades. A select few of these soldiers, however, faced an extreme test of their resolve when they found themselves back on northern soil in Union prison camps. The challenges these men faced to their adopted identity and their responses to those challenges would show whether their loyalty to the Confederacy arose from true conviction or merely served as a pretext for survival until they had a chance to reconnect with their native section.

8

Northern Confederate Prisoners of War

One of the most significant tests Northern Confederates faced in terms of preserving their adopted identities and defining what it meant to be a Confederate occurred when they became prisoners of war. As members of the Confederate forces, they had the opportunity to strike a blow against an abstract "invader" and "enemy." They remained surrounded by southern family, acquaintances, and comrades-in-arms. Maintaining allegiance to their adopted country was relatively easy in such situations because of reinforcement from like-minded patriots. If Union soldiers happened to capture them, however, these individuals made an unexpected trip back to their native section, albeit unwillingly. At that point, Northern Confederates had every opportunity to renounce their allegiance and support the Union. The links they tried to maintain with their families and the nostalgia for a North they once called their own provided a potential opening for these individuals to return to their loved ones once they re-crossed the Mason-Dixon Line. Did a reunion with the North crack the façade of pressured nationalism and reestablish them in their rightful place in their native section? Or did they prove once and for all that their status as Confederates remained steadfast and genuine?

When Northern Confederates faced this choice, more often than not they proved their allegiance to the Confederacy by enduring captivity with the same determination as native southerners. Available records indicate that out of the three hundred and three individuals documented in this study, approximately thirty of them, or 10 percent, were confirmed as prisoners at some point during the war. Some received a parole immediately, others spent a little time in prison before passing through the prisoner exchange system, and still others spent years in northern prisons before the end of the war released them all. Unfortunately, not all of these prisoners left behind surviving records of their experiences and/or thoughts of confinement. For these reasons, with a few exceptions, a select group of six prisoners, who left behind detailed records of their time in confinement, will receive the most attention in this chapter: George Junkin, Edward Drummond, Samuel Pasco, Henry Richardson, Edmund DeWitt Patterson, and Henry Handerson. Together they represented a range of geographical origins, time spent in prison, and prison locations. In addition, they all emigrated to the South in the 1850s, meaning they had spent less time in the region and had fewer connections than many other Northern Confederates. Although they likely did not speak for all Northern Confederate prisoners, their experiences and opinions still provide a glimpse into the minds of those faced with the ultimate paradox of returning to their native section as members of an enemy army.

Each of these prisoners dealt with prison life in their own way, but they all faced similar challenges to their adopted identities from families, Union authorities, and war news. As native northerners confined in northern prison camps, Northern Confederate prisoners had the opportunity to reestablish contact with their northern families and benefit from their close proximity to them. This unusual reality provided an opening for families to bring back their wayward sons. Fathers, mothers, and siblings wanted nothing more than to make them see the error of their ways and renounce their treason. Convinced that white southerners had brainwashed their family members into joining the Confederacy, these parents and siblings worked hard to reverse the effect by convincing their victimized sons and brothers to return to their rightful place in the North and the Union. Union prison authorities offered another incentive by promising pardons to any Confederate prisoners who took an oath of allegiance. Native northerners seemed especially susceptible to this offer because it represented an easy way to escape prison and return to established homes in the North without further fears of invasion and destruction. Finally, the reversals in Confederate military fortunes at various times of their imprisonment provided them more evidence of the futility of further resistance and offered yet another excuse to abandon a failed cause.

Despite these incentives, however, all six of these men, along with nearly all of their known fellow Northern Confederate prisoners, rebuffed all efforts to entice them back into the Union. Instead, they utilized their time in prison to rededicate themselves to the Confederate cause and their own standing as both Confederates and southerners. Through their trials and dedication, these six soldiers personified the strength of Northern Confederates' adopted identities by holding onto them even while ensconced in the land of their birth.

The amount of time they spent in prison to further these goals depended on when they became prisoners. Early in the war, captured soldiers did not spend too much time in captivity because of the prisoner exchange policies worked out between the two armies. Union and Confederate representatives created an elaborate system whereby men were released and exchanged according to their rank, with officers worth a certain number of privates and privates traded man for man. The system worked reasonably well until the Union started utilizing blacks as soldiers. Confederate officials refused to include blacks in exchanges because they viewed black soldiers, along with their white officers, as insurrectionists rather than legitimate fighting men. In 1863, the Union armies responded by ending the entire exchange system until the Confederacy gave in to demands for equal treatment of black and white prisoners.[1] Officials on both sides convinced themselves that the other would give in eventually, and so neither the Union nor the Confederacy came up with viable plans for holding large numbers of prisoners for long periods of time. The problem multiplied exponentially during the Wilderness and Atlanta Campaigns in 1864, with tens of thousands of men in both armies captured within a few months and no prospect for quick exchanges.

As a result, soldiers suffered months or even years of confinement in overcrowded compounds with little food or creature comforts. Prisoners constantly complained of ill treatment, starvation, disease, and many other challenges. Some of the prisons became notorious for poor treatment, especially Elmira in New York, Johnson's Island in Ohio, Libby Prison in Richmond, and Andersonville in Georgia. In fact, the only man to suffer the death penalty after the war, Henry Wirz, commanded the prison at Andersonville. Such conditions tested the resolve of captured soldiers on both sides in their quest to save the Union or ensure independence for the Confederacy.[2]

Northern Confederate prisoners went through the same trials but with unique twists. Usually, when a northern-born soldier became a prisoner, he spent his captivity in the South. Conversely, when a southern-born soldier became a prisoner, with the exception of southern unionists, he spent his captivity in the North. Northern Confederates, on the other hand, endured their captivity in their native sections, sometimes even close to their childhood homes. This presented some unusual circumstances, especially since their northern families had the possibility of visiting them to urge their sons and brothers to rejoin the Union. These pleas put further pressure on Northern Confederates and potentially strained their commitment to the Confederacy.

Several Northern Confederate prisoners could not handle the pressure and ended up fulfilling the wishes of their families by taking an oath to rejoin the Union. Union prison officials offered pardons and freedom to Confederate prisoners who took these oaths. Although most prisoners rejected the offer, a few braved the wrath of their comrades to escape the hell of prison life. Northern Confederates were in the best position to do so because they had homes in the North to return to if they so chose. For example, Joseph Lyman, a Massachusetts native who fought in a Louisiana cavalry regiment, was captured in the fall of 1863 and imprisoned in Louisville, Kentucky. A few months later, for reasons he did not elaborate, he took the loyalty oath and returned to his native state to start a farm. He later moved to New York and stayed there for the rest of his life. Edward Tucker, a New Hampshire native serving in General J. E. B. Stuart's cavalry as a lieutenant, became a prisoner during the Gettysburg campaign. After a few months on Johnson's Island, he too took the oath and claimed he only joined the Confederacy under duress. Pennsylvania native George Junkin took the oath when he learned that his dying mother wanted her son back home.[3] Lyman, Tucker, and Junkin together represented one possible response for Northern Confederates brought back to their native homes. If every Northern Confederate prisoner followed their example, the image of native northerners in the Confederate ranks as Yankee traitors would gain credence.[4]

That image did not materialize, however, because Lyman, Tucker, and Junkin represented the exception rather than the rule. Out of the approximately thirty men in this study known to have spent time in prison camps, only these three actually took the oath, with one of them later breaking it. Several more who received paroles without enduring prison time either rejoined the ranks once they received the proper exchange or returned to their adopted homes in the South. Northern Confederates put much more emphasis on their Confederate identities than their relatives realized. They had sworn an oath to defend the Confederacy, and they took those oaths seriously. In the secession crisis, these men had eagerly or reluctantly sided with their adopted states and, like most of their native southern comrades, vowed to fight to the death to secure the independence of their new country and protect their adopted homes. Although Northern Confederate prisoners now found themselves back in their native sections, they were held there against their will. These former northerners rarely had such an opportunity to demonstrate their loyalties and identification to adopted home and country in such a dramatic fashion, and they utilized that opportunity to the utmost. Average northerners in the Union might find such actions treasonous, ill-advised, even against self-interest, but Northern Confederates saw it as a reinforcement of their own understandings of what it meant to serve as a Confederate.

A few Northern Confederate prisoners decided to highlight their loyalty in the most dramatic way possible by planning and executing escape attempts. As with most prisoners, these efforts usually failed, but those failures did not diminish the risks they took to get out of the North and return to their regiments. One such escape attempt involved Julius Adolph de Lagnel, a New Jersey native serving in a Virginia regiment during General Robert E. Lee's failed attempt to retake western Virginia against General George B. McClellan in 1861. As told by his fellow prisoner Lawrence Sangston, de Lagnel received a severe wound leading the rear guard of his brigade, got separated from his men, and sought shelter in the home of a Confederate sympathizer. After a month of recovery, de Lagnel decided to risk traveling across enemy territory to make it back to eastern Virginia. He wandered along unfamiliar mountain trails for six days before stumbling into a Union picket line. In an effort to fool his captors, de Lagnel claimed to be a cattle driver searching for strays. The pickets did not believe his story because they noticed he wore expensive boots and spoke with an advanced vocabulary. Asked for his real name, de Lagnel defiantly replied, "Then I am Captain De Lagnel of the Confederate Army," and resigned himself to six months in several prison camps.[5] His effort to escape capture failed, but the mere attempt meant de Lagnel never considered backing out of his commitment and returning to his native section to sit out the war in peace. Immediately after his exchange, he returned to Virginia to carry out his duty to his adopted nation.

Unlike de Lagnel, native Pennsylvanian George W. Alexander actually succeeded in breaking out of prison with the help of his wife. Alexander spent the early months of the war attempting to recruit Confederate soldiers in Maryland and launching raids on Union shipping. On one such raid, Union soldiers captured him and sent him to Fort McHenry in Baltimore. His wife, who lived in Maryland, requested and received permission from the Union guards to visit her husband. Unbeknownst to the guards, Alexander's wife somehow managed to smuggle in a life preserver, waistcoat, clothesline, blue uniform and a map of Fort McHenry and the surrounding area. A few nights later Alexander donned the uniform, got his cellmate to distract the guards, and proceeded to walk out of the prison compound, run to the parapets, and leap out of the fort into the river. Alexander injured his right leg in the process, but he managed to swim to shore and receive help from a local family. Eventually, Alexander completed his escape to Virginia, where he ultimately took a post, ironically, as commandant of a Confederate prison for Union soldiers.[6]

Most of the time, however, escape remained elusive, and so Northern Confederates generally had to find other ways to reinforce their adopted identities. George G. Junkin provided one such dramatic example. Having moved to Virginia in 1855 at the age of eighteen, Junkin attended Washington College and later taught at the Montgomery Male Academy in Christiansburg. When Virginia seceded, he joined the Fourth Virginia Infantry. Captured at the Battle of Kernstown in the spring of 1862, Junkin spent several months in a prison camp waiting for an exchange.[7] As mentioned above, he appeared to have given up on the Confederacy when he took the oath of allegiance after hearing that his dying mother's last wish was to have her son return to her side at her deathbed. Despite his apparent return to the Union, however, he remained a Confederate at heart. Junkin originally took the oath of allegiance only because his father told him that his dying mother needed her son. He even called his decision necessary yet "an insult to me as an officer and a gentleman." The pleas of his father alone never would have worked; only a mother's illness tipped the balance. When Junkin returned home, however, he learned to his chagrin that his mother was perfectly healthy, and that his father had deceived him. The elder Junkin apparently believed that since his son had now sworn an oath to support the Union, albeit based on false information, he needed to uphold it. Much to his father's dismay, the younger Junkin did not view the situation that way. Claiming that his father coerced him under false pretenses and proclaiming his loyalty to the Confederacy, Junkin renounced his oath, ran away from his parent's home in 1863, and returned to Virginia to join a cavalry regiment for the rest of the war.[8]

Although not in such a spectacular fashion, other Northern Confederate prisoners also resisted efforts to bring them back into the Union. Edward Drummond, a native of Maine, moved to Georgia in 1859 to work in a commission house as a bookkeeper. He enlisted in the First Georgia Regiment at the start of the war and helped defend Fort Pulaski. When the Union navy captured the fort in April 1862, Drummond and his comrades ended up as prisoners on Governor's Island in New York before moving to Johnson's Island in Ohio. Fortunately for Drummond, he arrived while the exchange system still operated and so only spent a few months in prison before getting exchanged. During his time in prison, Drummond kept a detailed journal of his experiences. His thoughts and opinions revealed that he never thought about abandoning the Confederacy and resolved to endure prison until he could once again serve his adopted nation.[9]

In the meantime, Drummond engaged in activities that became a standard pattern for later Northern Confederate prisoners. First of all, he wanted to reestablish contact with his family back in Maine. Upon his arrival, he wrote letters to both his wife and father. A week later, he received replies from his father, mother, and sister, who informed him about family news and even included a photograph of his father as a keepsake. Drummond noted in his diary that "All are well" and appreciated the efforts of his northern family to keep in touch.[10]

In this instance, he also showed the advantages a Northern Confederate soldier had in terms of having relatives close at hand. While he received a reply from his family within a week, he never indicated whether he ever received a similar reply from his wife in Georgia. Generally, native southern prisoners had a harder time maintaining contact with their own families because of the deteriorating state of the Confederate transportation system. Northern Confederates did not have that problem because they sent their letters within the North. Thus, they had more opportunities for outside contacts than many of their comrades. In fact, Drummond recorded that a week after his transfer to Governor's Island, his uncle traveled from Maine to visit him. The guards refused to let them see each other, but the uncle's ability to get that close reflected the fact that Drummond symbolically came home again.[11]

Hoping to capitalize on that fact, Drummond's relatives tried to convince him to take the next step by returning to Maine. They even offered to secure a full pardon for him in return for rejoining his family and supporting the Union. Drummond mentioned that his sisters worked hard in the spring of 1862 to secure a parole for him from the government. It certainly helped that Drummond's cousin served as Maine's attorney general and remained a close friend of Vice President Hannibal Hamlin. In all likelihood, they would have succeeded if Drummond had agreed to take the oath.[12] The time seemed ripe for this Northern Confederate to shed his supposedly superficial southern identity and return to his true roots in the North.

Such pleas, however, fell on deaf ears. Although a couple of Northern Confederate prisoners did take the oath, Drummond joined his native southern comrades in rejecting any hint of betrayal of the Confederacy.[13] He especially hated Union authorities who offered pardons and immediate release for anyone who accepted the oath. In one of his diary entries in August 1862, Drummond denounced all those who accepted the offer as useless to the Confederate cause and best returned to the North. In his mind, anyone who betrayed the oath to their country, whether Union or Confederate, deserved the ultimate scorn, since they did not remain true to their principles and ideals. Oaths of allegiance represented nothing more than bribes designed not only to divide prisoners from each other but also to undermine the legitimacy of the Confederacy as a nation. By rejecting such oaths, Northern Confederates like Drummond symbolically reinforced their own understanding of themselves as Confederate patriots by snubbing authorities from their native section, whom they now considered tyrannical foreigners. Despite the efforts of both his family and Union prison officials, Drummond never considered betraying the country he had adopted as his own.[14]

Along with his decision to remain in prison, Drummond also professed faith in the Confederacy through reactions to war news. Generally, morale on the respective home fronts rose and fell in direct relation to news of military victories and defeats. Both sides faced both elation and despair as the war progressed, and all had a chance to either rededicate themselves to their cause or give it up as doomed or too high a cost in blood. Northern Confederate prisoners seemed especially susceptible to this cycle of morale because their ties to the North always offered a way out. Drummond was no exception; he reached prison in the midst of General McClellan's seemingly unstoppable drive toward Richmond. Throughout the spring, news reached the camp of the imminent capture of Richmond and the expected end of the war. The time seemed ideal to abandon a failed cause and rejoin the Union just in time to celebrate its expected total victory.

In all of his diary entries, however, Drummond refused to concede one iota of confidence in the ultimate victory of his beloved Confederacy. He wrote off all reports of Union victories as malicious propaganda while believing any news of Confederate victory.[15] His reactions mirrored those of many other Confederates yearning for the success of their armies and their nation. By the end of June, with General McClellan's army still on the outskirts of Richmond, Drummond seized on the rumor of imminent British and French recognition as cause for hope. He even kept up his spirits when one of the prisoners reported that recent negotiations regarding prisoner exchanges had temporarily shut down. As Drummond wrote, "The C.S. is now so situated as to be able to hold out for fair and honorable measure and will have them. We are perfectly satisfied and would rather wait here until the end of the War than have our Government knuckle an inch."[16]

Along with most of his fellow soldiers, Drummond had full confidence in both his army and his government to bring about an honorable end to the war and was prepared to wait for that outcome. Only a few days later, the prisoners at Johnson's Island learned of General Lee's victories in the Seven Days Campaign, thus fulfilling their hopes of a reversal of fortune. Drummond joined in the shouts of joy, singing "Dixie" and reveling in the victory over "Yankeedom" and "the whole North." He closed out his entry by saying, "The losses on both sides must be terrible and we feel that we have lost many friends. If so, they have died in good cause and I do not think there is a Man here that would not have given his all to have been there no matter what the consequences might have been. All well."[17]

Drummond thus continued the tradition among Northern Confederate soldiers and civilians of using a distinct vocabulary to reinforce his adopted identity. For example, when Drummond referred to news about the Seven Days, he commented on how "our forces" pursued the Union army up the Peninsula and "The Yankees as usual have fled to their Gun Boats and hope for protection . . ."[18] He also recorded how northern civilians came by the prison to "see the Rebels, as they call us" and how they "played their National airs such as Yankee Doodle, Red White & Blue &c&c."[19] In later entries, he even made comments about the weather and its effects on morale. As a young man growing up in Maine, Drummond lived through some of the coldest winters in the country. Yet once the war began in earnest, Drummond made it appear as though he always enjoyed southern weather in a way northerners did not understand. As he wrote in June 1862, "We look for an exchange very soon as our Government now by report has the ascendancy in numbers and will exchange whenever fair offers are made, which we are inclined to think will be, for the Yanks do not like sweltering under our Southern Sun."[20] In reality, Drummond likely had less experience with southern summers than older northern soldiers who made frequent trips to the South for business or pleasure before the war. It did not matter because, in Drummond's mind, his transformation into a Confederate made him an expert on the effects of southern weather on ignorant Yankees.

By the end of his imprisonment, Drummond showed one last time his devotion to the Confederacy while on northern soil. In the final entry of his journal in prison, he closed his unexpected and unwanted return to the North by declaring, "Ho for Dixie. We shall soon be among our People."[21] As soon as he returned to Georgia after his exchange, Drummond rejoined his comrades and returned to the field, as did more than twenty other Northern Confederate prisoners in the same situation. The mere fact that they wanted to rejoin their units so quickly revealed their loyalties to their comrades, as well as to their adopted section and nation. And as Drummond indicated, turning their backs on a North they no longer felt connected with to return to an adopted section they could refer to as "our People" embodied their espousal of a Confederate identity.

Nevertheless, Drummond had a relatively easier time than many of his fellow prisoners because he managed to get exchanged fairly quickly. Others either arrived in prison after the breakdown of prisoner exchanges or did not get exchanged before the system broke down. They potentially faced more challenges because they did not have the certainty of an exchange to keep up their morale. Northern Confederates in this situation remained in prison for various amounts of time, until the last year of the war, in much more overcrowded conditions. In spite of their increased hardships, each of them went through patterns similar to those experienced by Drummond, including reconnecting with family members, refusing to take an oath, keeping up morale in the face of negative war news, and openly expressing their identification with the Confederacy.

Samuel Pasco spent relatively little time in prison yet still had ample opportunity to reveal his adopted identity within northern territory. A native

Englishman, Pasco immigrated to Massachusetts with his family as a child and grew up there. After graduating from Harvard in 1858, he moved to Florida in 1859 and enlisted in a Florida regiment when the state seceded. Serving in Florida and the Western Theater, Pasco became a prisoner after receiving a wound at Chattanooga. After recovering in a Union hospital in Nashville, he spent nine months in prison camps in Kentucky and at Camp Morton in Indiana, before getting exchanged in February 1865, when the exchange system restarted in the closing months of the war.[22]

Similar to Drummond, Pasco wanted to stay close with his family back in Massachusetts. At the end of the summer of 1864, when he realized exchanges would not happen before the end of the year, Pasco steeled himself for another dreaded winter in northern territory by relying on "a strong constitution, a stout heart, dear parents and loving brothers and sisters to live for and a firm trust in God's goodness and mercy to help me through with all I have to endure."[23] These reflections indicate a continued tendency among Northern Confederates to separate family from the Union. Their adopted southern identities may have driven them to don Confederate gray, but ties of blood still held strong, especially since many of these men, Pasco included, had only left their native region behind a few years earlier.

At the same time, despite the war having dragged on for over three years with no end in sight, Pasco rejected all efforts to take an oath. In fact, Pasco mentioned the subject many times during his stay at Camp Morton. Every time Pasco witnessed prisoners accepting the oath, he expressed nothing but disgust, both for those who offered the deals and those who accepted them. In January and February 1864, while recovering in a prison hospital from wounds received in his last battle, Pasco resented the chaplains who went to the hospital urging the wounded to take an oath to ease their condition. The only chaplain he respected concentrated solely on his ministering duties without engaging in what Pasco considered treasonous activities. As he recorded in his diary, "He is a young man, a German I think, but he attends to his work and does not insult us by trying to persuade us to become traitors and accept Lincoln's Amnesty."[24] Pasco despised the other religious figures that preyed on men in their weak moments to give up what they held most dear. In an attempt to explain away those who did accept the oath, Pasco insisted they must have caved to pressure from Union authorities manipulating them against their better judgment. "Much to our astonishment Avner went off this morning without saying a word to any of us to take the oath of allegiance," Pasco wrote about one such turncoat. "He is a good-natured fellow and has no doubt been over-persuaded by the men at the kitchen where he has been working for some time."[25]

Pasco especially hated to see other native northerners flirt with the idea of renouncing their ties to the Confederacy. In July and August 1864, Pasco twice described incidents where two prisoners, both raised in New York, considered accepting an oath. Both times Pasco went out of his way to denounce their actions. He described one of the prisoners talking with a friend whose brother-in-law was a Union colonel and who offered to secure their release if they took the oath. Though he did not say whether the two men accepted or not, Pasco closed his description by writing, "I suspect that both are deserters," indicating he believed they did not belong in the same ranks as true Confederates like himself.[26] A month later, reinforcing his initial impression, he wrote about another encounter with the second New Yorker, who speculated that perhaps a reunited Union might still keep slavery intact. Pasco considered such thinking ludicrous. "I have no patience with traitors. Why did he join our army if he did not mean to go through with the undertaking? He has already lost the confidence of his Northern friends, and by his proposed course will make bitter enemies of those with whom he has been acting in concert for more than three years without regaining his position among his former friends in the North."[27]

Such invective reflected not only his own convictions as a Confederate but also the reality of his own situation. Pasco knew about the temptations of returning to the North and understood that prison presented an ideal environment for pushing those like him in that direction. In addition, although confident of his own loyalty, he may have believed his comrades might use such defections as proof that white southerners could not trust anyone with a northern background. Pasco's scathing response in both instances thus makes perfect sense. In his mind, anyone in his own position who thought about taking the oath never had his heart in the conflict in the first place. Even acknowledging the possibility of returning to the Union represented nothing less than treason. Therefore, Pasco went out of his way to distance himself from anyone not willing to endure sacrifices for the cause.

In addition, like Drummond in 1862, Pasco had the opportunity to demonstrate his unwavering loyalty through his response to the crucial military campaigns of 1864. In that year, the Confederacy fought bitter defensive battles in Virginia and Georgia while hoping for the election of a Democratic president to usher in the end of the war. Confederates experienced a lower point of morale at the start of the campaign in the spring, one of its highest periods of morale during the summer, and a crushing defeat at Atlanta in September. In that time, Pasco remarked constantly on both military and political news, all of which revealed his determination to fight the invader of his adopted home as long as possible, even in the confines of prison. For example, throughout March, Pasco recorded his thoughts on the constitutional grounds for secession, citing arguments made by Kentucky newspapers that Lincoln consistently violated the sanctity of the Constitution. He wrote in one such entry, "Borrowed some papers this morning . . . which I like much for its bold language in maintaining the case for the . . . constitutional rights of the South." He also read the works of Thomas Hart Benton, a Missouri politician who served as one of Andrew Jackson's close advisors, which highlighted the importance of states' rights in the success of a republican form of government.[28] These musings kept him occupied in the next few months as further news came in of Union frustrations in the sieges of Petersburg and Atlanta.

Pasco's greatest cause for hope, other than possibly restarting prisoner exchanges, came in late August with the Democratic convention in Chicago. Like so many other Confederates, Pasco took comfort from the large turnout of support in Chicago and wished for a favorable outcome in the future. In his own unique twist stemming from his northern background, Pasco predicted a Democratic victory would prove beneficial not just for the South but also for the North. "If the Democrats act harmoniously in the Convention and can get a fair election," he wrote, "I think they will probably elect their candidate and the North will be saved from the horrors of civil war which are now so imminent."[29] He recognized the impact a Democratic victory would have on the chances for Confederate victory and seemed to give a warning to his former section: come to the same conclusion or suffer the destruction already inflicted on the South.

Sadly for Pasco and his comrades, the hopes of the Democratic Convention were quickly overshadowed by the reported victory of General Sherman's army at Atlanta. Even that crushing blow, however, failed to dent Pasco's determination. Similar to Drummond, he either questioned the accuracy of the news or called for a renewed commitment. "The Camp is still full of rumors in regard to the fall of Atlanta. . . . I am not satisfied yet but fear it may be true; if so it only remains for us to keep up a stout heart and a firm reliance upon God," he insisted. "It is not our territory they are trying to conquer it is the spirit of our people the possession of another town and a few more miles of territory must not crush our spirits [*sic*] we must still show a firm front to the invader."[30] Even in the wake of Union victories, when reasons for rejoining their native section might appear strongest, no such thoughts entered the minds of Drummond, Pasco, or most other Northern Confederate prisoners. Instead, they continued to reaffirm their dedication to a weakened but steadfast Confederacy and defy an all but victorious North they had once called home.

While all of these events occurred, Pasco utilized the vocabulary of Northern Confederates as further proof of his unwavering conviction. In one diary entry, he expressed pity for prisoners who suffered through years of confinement, writing that "they almost despair of ever getting back to our beloved South."[31] Conversely, while talking about religion, Pasco drew distinctions between southerners like himself and northern outsiders. Prisoners sometimes did not have the luxury of praying with their own chaplains but instead were forced to listen to sermons given by their enemies. Pasco wrote in his journal that Union chaplains passed out a pamphlet entitled "The Christian Banner," which he claimed maligned white southerners by describing southern refugees as not knowing how to read or write. He responded by mocking the chaplains, even the kind ones, for not recognizing "the impiety of calling this the *Christian* Banner, this the symbol of oppression, tyranny and barbarity to a whole nation of freemen."[32]

Such comments echoed those of native southerners suffering the same conditions. One southern soldier commented on the different styles of authority between northerners and southerners and naturally found southerners superior because of their association with slavery. As he remarked in his notes, "To the Southern people their education and labor-system gives the habit of command. . . . But most of the Yankee centurions never before had the power to say to this one, 'go,' and to that one, 'come,' and to the other, 'do this,' and as all essentially vulgar minds take delight in the parade of such a power . . ."[33] Selecting randomly from such quotations, a neutral observer could not distinguish between native southern and Northern Confederate prisoners. They used the same language and held the same contempt for their common enemies in the Union.

Significantly, as had happened before their imprisonment, men like Pasco did not reach such conclusions by denying their past. Pasco made no secret of his heritage and how it affected him. He spent part of his free time as a prisoner reading the exploits of a British soldier serving in India for over a decade. He recorded in his journal how he admired the soldier and saw a lot of similarities between himself and the protagonist. Pasco then went on to say, "Would that I could have followed such a career in India under the flag of my own beloved native land. . . . In that case my own family would have rejoiced at my successes and I could always have had opportunity to share my joys and trials with them."[34] In this instance, he hinted at the immense gulf created between himself and his roots because of the war. Pasco well understood the distance separating him from native southerners and his own family and heritage. In his case, Pasco did not even technically belong to either side because of his birth in England, despite his childhood spent in New England. In spite of that awareness, Pasco did not allow such distance to overwhelm his commitment to the Confederate cause. At no time did he consider taking an oath to return to his childhood home in Massachusetts or even applying for a pardon to travel to his native England. The Confederate nation meant everything to him, and he would triumph or fall alongside it.

Whatever their past associations, serving in defense of the Confederacy gave soldiers like Pasco as much right to be called a southerner as anyone actually born in the South. For Northern Confederate prisoners especially, that belief resonated in light of their proximity to their native state and northern families putting constant pressure on them to renounce their loyalty to the Confederacy. For example, while Pasco lamented the distance between himself and his family in the North, he also remained convinced they would eventually see the justice of his actions. Comparing himself to the British soldier he so admired, Pasco declared, "But the day will come when we shall enjoy the same honor for defeating these Yankee hirelings who put themselves side by side with the African negro to put down free men that the English gained by defeating the barbarians of India."[35] Reflecting on his service in the army, Pasco remarked that by the summer of 1864 he had served for three years, almost a third of that time spent in prison. At least technically, he had paid his debt to the Confederacy in terms of his initial enlistment, which meant he could take the oath and return to his family. Instead of feeling relieved, Pasco did not wish to leave until his country achieved its goals.

"I feel conscious that I have served my country faithfully during this period and I do not for a moment regret what I have had to suffer and endure," he wrote in his journal. "I only lament the anxiety and pain the dear ones at home have suffered upon my account but I have followed the path duty seemed to point out . . . ."[36]

Another Northern Confederate prisoner, Edmund DeWitt Patterson, followed the same patterns as Drummond and Pasco but with even greater challenges, thanks to his location. A native Ohioan, Patterson moved to Alabama in 1859 and joined the Ninth Alabama Regiment at the start of the war. After fighting with his regiment in battles across Virginia and Maryland, he was taken prisoner at Gettysburg and transferred to Fort Delaware and then Johnson's Island. He spent nearly two years in prison before getting exchanged in March 1865. As it turned out, Patterson's family lived only a few miles away from Johnson's Island. That proximity gave Patterson a unique perspective as a prisoner who truly came close to home.[37]

Patterson's family certainly tried to take advantage of the situation. For two years, Patterson received packages, letters, and visits from his family.[38] Shortly after his imprisonment in 1863, the whole family came to see him, though Union guards did not allow them into the prison itself. Nevertheless, Patterson appreciated that he could shout to them over the walls.[39] They hoped that such displays of familial affection might get their rebel son to rejoin his family and give up what they considered a useless and treasonous struggle. As Patterson recorded in his diary in August 1863, "He [his father] urges me to give up the cause of the South which he pronounces a doomed one and one which he is willing and anxious to see put down even though it should take years to accomplish and all the treasure and blood both North and South have."[40]

Yet Patterson, like so many before him, considered these oaths as a betrayal of himself and his nation. In just one example, Patterson recalled an incident in October 1863 when thirty prisoners obtained their freedom by taking the oath. "Last Friday about thirty of the privates who were confined here took the oath of allegiance to the Yankee government, and went out amid the taunts and jeers of their loyal companions in arms. We are glad to get rid of such men; they are worth nothing to either side and are despised by both Yankee and Southern men."[41]

Patterson's family learned this the hard way when their son rejected all their appeals, even as they stood at the base of the prison wall shouting for him to return home. His father repeatedly came to Johnson's Island to persuade his son to rejoin his rightful place in the Union, citing the recent battle at Gettysburg and other Union victories as evidence of the hopelessness of the Confederate cause. Patterson angrily refused and took the opportunity to detail his expectations of the sacrifices needed to create a new nation. Dismissing lofty rhetoric, he understood that defeating the Union might take years and possibly even destroy slavery itself. Patterson admitted he had no idea what such a step might do to the South; perhaps it might even bankrupt the region. He also knew that, "Years must pass before this war will be settled and thousands upon thousands of noble forms must lie cold in death, and I may be among the number . . . Present appearances indicate that a large portion of our country will be overrun by the invaders and will become a desert waste." Despite the gloomy prospects, Patterson felt a deeper connection than ever to his army and his nation. If slavery collapsed or his own life were taken, he considered those outcomes acceptable sacrifices. As he summarized in his journal, "I pray . . . that my life may be spared. I wish to live to see the Confederate States an independent Nation, loved at home and respected abroad, and at peace with all the world."[42]

Patterson felt alienated, not just from the North, but from his own family thanks to his convictions. Considering his family's hostile reaction to his decisions, Patterson sadly came to the conclusion that he no longer had a real family anymore. "I can scarcely consider myself a member of the family—we have nothing in common," he wrote despondently after his father demanded his return to the Union. "They pray Almighty God to visit the Confederate States with swift destruction while I am risking my life in defence of the South and am willing if necessary to lay down my life in defense of her principles . . . although I have the proud consciousness of right within my own bosom, I cannot help thinking of those far away in the North who are praying for the success of our foes."[43]

With no family to support him, Patterson relied on himself to get through the trying times in prison. Though rarely commenting on the outcomes of battles, he still consistently wrote of his hope for the success of the Confederacy as an independent country. By the end of 1863, shortly after rejecting his father's demands that he take an oath, Patterson looked back over the events of the war up to that point and became convinced of the inevitable triumph of the Confederacy, leaving no doubts about his alienation from a Union in which he used to belong. He lamented that his time in prison prevented him from furthering Confederate victory, grieving that he was "entirely separated and cut off from the outside world, unable to take any active part in the struggle which is still going on between justice and injustice, right and wrong, freedom and oppression, unable to strike a blow in the glorious cause of Southern independence." Patterson went on to say, "And we *will* succeed. Who will say that a country such as ours . . . inhabited by eight millions of brave people determined to be free and willing to sacrifice everything even life itself upon the altar of their country, united as no people ever were before, I ask, who will say, in view of all this, that the South will not be free."[44] As shown many times before, Northern Confederates like Patterson prepared to lay down their lives to uphold the Confederacy's promise of justice and freedom for their adopted section.

In the same entry, Patterson reiterated his firm belief that the South would prevail regardless of setbacks or hardships. "I engaged in this war firmly believing that the South would be successful," he insisted, "and now after nearly three years of war, I find that time has only served to strengthen that opinion." It did not matter if Union armies occupied every city and county in every southern state; his beloved Confederacy would continue to fight as their ancestors had done in the War for Independence. He even admitted the military shortcomings of the Confederate armies compared to their Union counterparts, yet the stubbornness of the southern people, himself included, would tip the balance in the end. As he said towards the end of his monologue, "We have met with many reverses during the year, but the spirit of our people remains unbroken . . . and the Yankees will soon find that it will require a standing army in every Southern state to enforce their laws. A great party will be raised up in the North who will demand that the war shall cease, and it will cease."[45] Few native southerners could have made a stronger defense of the Confederacy and the sacrifice of its people.

Similar to Junkin and Drummond and Pasco, Patterson regarded his association with the southern population as natural, and his language reflected that sentiment. In the summer of 1863, shortly after his arrival in prison, Patterson heard that Alabama's legislature passed resolutions pledging to fight to the bitter end. He expressed overwhelming pride for his adopted state, writing in his diary, "I am glad to think of the glorious record my Alabama, my sunny home, will have . . . our legislature has passed a series of resolutions pledging the last man and the last dollar in the state toward the carrying on the war until every invader is driven from our soil." A month later he reiterated his earlier support by calling Alabama and the South "the land I love best."[46] At the same time, as he had done before he went to prison, Patterson used derogatory language to describe northerners. At one point he recounted an incident where a prisoner bribed a guard to allow him to escape, but the guard kept the money and alerted the sentries anyway. Patterson chastised the guard's conduct as a typical "yankee trick."[47] Echoing Pasco, Patterson also denounced northern preachers in the prison camps. He noted in his diary that he refused to have anything to do with such preachers because "their Yankee religion" was foreign to southerners.[48] In the crucible of war, these men regarded religion itself as symbolic of sectional differences, and they made sure to place themselves on the southern side even while surrounded by their native section.

Still, Patterson did not escape his past. If anything, he appreciated the irony of his situation as a native Ohioan in an Ohio prison camp just a few miles from his childhood home. In one of his journal entries, Patterson reflected on his age and realized he had spent eighteen years in Ohio, two years in Alabama, one year in Virginia, and one year in prison, which meant a total of nineteen years in the North versus only three years in the South. Patterson even deemed his whole life a failure because of missed educational opportunities in Ohio, still calling it his "native state."[49] He wrote, earlier in his journal, "Here I am near the spot where I passed the sunny hours of childhood and the golden dreaming days of youth and under what circumstances—a prisoner of war."[50] Patterson clearly recognized that his status as a Confederate soldier did not come from a southern heritage. And he understood that his refusal to abandon the Confederacy alienated him from the family he cared about deeply. They only visited him to urge him to take an oath, and when that effort failed, one cousin vowed to never see him again because of his status as a rebel.[51] As a result, Patterson's decision to side with the Confederacy left him without a family, since he never married while in Alabama. The pain Patterson endured from that situation was best reflected when he read the letters from his parents and siblings. He believed that they all loved him, "yet all regard me as forever disgraced and dishonored. They consider my course a stain on the family name and with their every prayer for my safety is mingled a prayer for the speedy overthrow of the Southern cause. Their letters, too, give me much more pain than pleasure, telling me that I am worse than wasting the early years of my manhood...."[52]

Trying to find an alternative, Patterson turned to his friends and acquaintances in Alabama and Virginia. Toward the end of 1863, he spent one night recalling happy memories of his childhood in Ohio but then immediately transitioned to even happier times in his adopted state of Alabama and his first year in the army in Virginia. "Yes, I would like to be once again in my little room at Mr. Whitsett's and feel myself at home. At home, did I say?—I am at home anywhere. (Northern prisons excepted). Richmond has become one of my homes, and so has Inglewood and Belle Monte. If ever again sick or wounded, let my lot be cast in no pleasanter place than Alabama or Virginia."[53] In Patterson's mind, the Civil War represented the final break between his past life and his present one. Although he might have technically returned home, his status as a Confederate meant he could never really return home the same way again. Rather than bring them closer to their roots, time spent in northern prison camps merely solidified an identity nurtured in the antebellum period and forged in the fires of war. As Patterson succinctly wrote, "'Is not the kindred of common fate a closer tie than that of birth?'"[54]

Such displays of connection with the Confederate nation only grew in strength as the years passed. By the beginning of 1864, with the end still nowhere in sight, Patterson had further cause for celebration thanks to the anniversary of Alabama's secession from the Union. He wrote in the middle of January, "Anniversary of the secession of Alabama, and gloriously has she sustained herself during the last three years of trial. The fires of patriotism still glow unquenchably in the bosom of every true son and daughter of that lovely, noble state."[55] He carried that conviction with him throughout his prison term until he finally managed to return to his beloved South in March 1865. Despite nearly two years of living within a stone's throw of his childhood home, Patterson never felt more distant from it in his life. His experiences both in the army and in prison, especially his unwavering commitment to the Confederate cause and fiery hatred of a Union he had only left a few years earlier, had made his transition to a Confederate identity permanent.

Adopted Louisianan Henry Richardson went even further than his peers by not only affirming his adopted identity but also giving an elaborate justification for it. A native of Maine, Richardson originally moved to Louisiana in the 1850s to work as a civil engineer. Following his adopted state into secession, he served in Virginia before becoming a prisoner on the second day of Gettysburg. He eventually found himself on Johnson's Island for two years, until the final months of the war.[56] Like his peers, Richardson took advantage of his unintended residence in the North to reconnect with his family. He exchanged letters with his parents for a year, talking about a variety of topics, especially his condition as a prisoner. In general, he assured them that his health remained strong and that he missed everyone back in New England. He also thanked them for the money they had sent him to purchase supplies from the prison commissary. In several of the letters, he signed off as "your affectionate son," and at one point even wished he could send them something as a token of his appreciation.[57]

As happened so often before among Northern Confederate prisoners, however, Richardson had to disabuse his family of any ideas that he might renounce his allegiance to the Confederacy. He wrote that his own parents and friends, "doubtless with the kindest intentions, have recommended me to damnation, by advising me to break my solemn oath and perjure myself with new ones. . . . I have been told as a further inducement, that the cause for which I suffer and scruple to betray is 'hopeless'; 'the rebellion is crushed'; 'you will be imprisoned for life if you do not come to terms'; 'your leaders are wicked and are deluding you', etc. etc."[58] Reflecting on his time in prison, Richardson lamented that the worst times came when his friends and relatives in the North begged him to renounce the Confederacy. He did not blame the Union government for similar attempts, but pleas from families were far more personal. Despite his knowledge of the heartache he caused them, and their attempts to convince him of the hopelessness of the Confederate cause, Richardson did not agonize over the decision because, in his mind, the success of the Confederacy overshadowed everything else. Prisoners like Richardson required no other explanation and thus usually did not see the need to justify themselves either in public or in private.[59]

Richardson, on the other hand, actually took the time to explain to his parents on the eve of his exchange in 1865 why he refused to take an oath. Knowing that his family likely thought the worst of him, and hoping to make them see reason, Richardson outlined a detailed defense of his actions. In the process, he provided arguments that spoke for others in his position. First of all, he put forward a hypothetical scenario wherein he married a woman his parents did not approve of, and they asked him to give her up. Richardson argued he could never agree to such a request, because he knew her better than they did and loved them both. Therefore, though he did not want to give up either one, if forced to choose he would betray his family because of the greater love for his wife. The wife, in this case, represented the Confederacy, to which he had wedded himself. In addition, Richardson refused to take the oath because doing so would make him a failure and a traitor to his conscience. "The world would say of me: 'Here is a man who when all went smoothly could boast as defiantly as any, but once in trouble, in prison, and the cause he had sworn to support and defend even to death—that cause once under a cloud, deserts his companions in arms, renounces his solemn protestations and licks the dust from the feet of those who spurn him.'"[60]

Union soldiers themselves would have a hard time refuting such logic. All wars involved highs and lows and abandoning one's cause in a time of low morale represented the ultimate betrayal for any soldier. Richardson emphasized that theme and put the onus on his parents for asking for such a betrayal for the sake of family. He missed them, but until the war ended, his devotion to the Confederacy remained paramount. "I know that you would not willingly see me violate an oath, unless you had juggled your consciences into the belief that it was morally right to do so, and that you would not have me take one that there was no probability of my keeping in its spirit, as well as in its letter," he summarized in the rest of his letter. "But, still, in some inexplicable way I find you counseling me to do these things . . . I am mortified alike that I should be thought base enough to receive them, and that those I love so well can stoop to make them . . . ."[61] As Richardson indicated, the experience of incarceration, rather than weakening his devotion to the Confederacy, actually enhanced it.

Many northerners, including Abraham Lincoln, convinced themselves that a majority of southerners only joined the Confederacy under pressure or coercion and thus wanted to rejoin their rightful place in the Union. The families of Northern Confederates likely felt the same, especially since it seemed these misguided sons had little reason to continue their allegiance to traitorous states once they came back to the North. Instead, these men not only spurned attempts to take an oath of allegiance; they also provided more evidence of their transformation into Confederates and southerners. The convictions that originally led them into the Confederate forces, and sustained them through multiple campaigns, now kept their focus clear within the confines of their native section.

In addition, like Drummond and Pasco and Patterson before him, Richardson was also fully aware of his limited residence in the South in comparison with his earlier life. In justifying his decision to fight for the Confederacy, Richardson readily admitted to his roots in Maine but did not feel an accident of birth required him to fight for the Union. As he wrote to his parents, "I was born in Maine; but if Maine had seceded and joined the Canadian Confederacy, was I therefore bound to go with her? Or, if she chooses to join in a wicked war against Louisiana, am I bound to turn against the country of my adoption—the country of which I have in good faith become a citizen? No! No!" Although he had spent nearly his whole life in Maine and but a few years in his adopted state of Louisiana, Richardson believed the latter deserved his allegiance because he considered himself one of its loyal citizens. He did not see any hypocrisy in his stance because of the example of the Founding Fathers. Referring to Louisiana, he explained, "True I was not born there, but does the accident of birth necessarily determine where allegiance is due? If so, what must we say of numberless men of the Revolution—John Paul Jones, Chas. Lee, and the like? . . . I was born in the U.S., but if for that reason I owe allegiance to its government, so did Hancock and Washington owe theirs for the same reason to the government of England."[62] If the men who fought the first war for independence could subordinate their roots in support of a new ideal, then Richardson felt entitled to do the same.[63]

Finally, native Ohioan Henry Handerson added his voice to the chorus of transformed identity among Northern Confederates. Originally moving to Tennessee with his family in 1852, at the age of seventeen, Handerson returned to his native Ohio two years later only to accept a job as a tutor at a Louisiana plantation by 1858. Although a conditional unionist in the secession crisis, he ultimately joined the Confederacy and fought in many battles throughout Virginia. His luck ran out in 1864 when he was taken prisoner in the Wilderness Campaign and sent to Fort Delaware. In the process, he gained the distinction of being one of the last prisoners released from that prison in May 1865. He did not suffer from bad luck but instead chose to remain in prison as long as the Confederacy survived, reflecting his own unbreakable commitment to his new nation.[64]

Handerson exploited the advantage of his incarceration in the North as much as he could. As he recalled after the war, "Soon after my arrival at Fort Delaware I wrote to Mr. E.W. Palmer of Cleveland, asking him to lend me a small sum of money for my immediate necessities . . . ." He went on to note his surprise when he learned his uncle, living in Tennessee when the war began, had returned to Ohio. He wrote to his uncle in August, telling him that the guards restricted mail to family members, which meant he was lucky to have relatives in the North, since he could write without having to worry as much about censorship.[65]

Yet Handerson made his ultimate mark by refusing to submit until all hope had vanished. By the end of April 1865, several weeks after the surrender of General Lee and the assassination of President Lincoln, Handerson remained imprisoned at Fort Delaware. Most Confederate prisoners by then understood that the war had ended and sought to receive their paroles. Handerson, however, insisted in his postwar memoirs that as long as the Confederate government survived, he still owed his allegiance to it. He wrote in his memoirs that he maintained that stance even after hearing about the surrender of General Lee to General Grant at Appomattox and the surrender of General Joseph Johnston to General Sherman in North Carolina. Only after learning of President Davis' capture in Georgia in the middle of May did he finally agree to take the oath.[66]

Lest readers interpret Handerson's description as postwar bravado, he included in his memoirs three letters he wrote to his uncle at the end of April and beginning of May 1865 explaining his decision. The first letter described how a Union official came to Fort Delaware in the last week of April ready to dispense pardons to the remaining prisoners. Handerson freely admitted that most of his fellow officers did so immediately but felt his own obligations to the Confederacy prevented him from doing the same. As he told his uncle, "When the war broke out I was a citizen of one of the Southern States. The citizens of that state, by their representatives in convention assembled, withdrew from the U.S. government and united themselves with their sister states of the South. . . . An independent government was formed, having its seat first at Montgomery, then at Richmond. To that government I swore allegiance; not only to obey its orders, but to support it against all its enemies." He went on to say that since the Confederacy still had armies in the field, and that Union officials still engaged in prisoner exchanges, the Confederacy itself still existed in body and in soul. As long as the war continued, Handerson felt obligated to maintain his allegiance to the nation he swore to protect.[67]

Incredibly, Handerson acknowledged the Confederacy had no chance to succeed at that point yet still refused to accept surrender until the Confederate government, not just its armies, released him from his obligations. "Indeed I can no longer hope that the cause in which I am embarked is not hopeless," he informed his uncle in late April, "and, had I consulted feelings alone, I should have taken the oath when offered. I expect, when the Confederate government ceases to be, to take the oath of allegiance to the U.S., if permitted, and to become at once a law-abiding citizen."[68] Whereas most other Confederates by 1865 viewed General Lee as the symbol of the Confederacy, Handerson, who only a decade earlier lived in the North, considered the Confederacy greater than any one man. Not even the surrender of General Johnston, which effectively eliminated all meaningful military resistance, changed his mind. He informed his uncle he might hold out until he heard that General Edmund Kirby Smith's command in Texas surrendered. Finally, at the beginning of May, Handerson agreed to take the oath because, "The simple question with me was, are Mr. Davis & his Cabinet still exercising, as far as lies in their power, the functions of government appertaining to each. I had no reliable news to the contrary, until the voluntary surrender of Mr. Mallory, our Sec. of Navy. *His* action convinced me that it was time for *every one* to take care of himself, if possible."[69] In this case, Handerson, a native northerner, held out longer than most native southerners for the survival of the Confederacy. He demonstrated that Northern Confederates had the same devotion to the Confederate cause as any native southerner.

And so Northern Confederate prisoners joined their comrades in enduring the searing heat of northern summers, bitter cold of northern winters, mocking from Union civilians, and the confinement of Union prison walls. They waited patiently for the day when they could return to their beloved Confederacy. They did so, not as northerners unduly pressured into the Confederate armies, but as adoptive southerners determined to preserve their section and their newly created nation. Their experiences in prison solidified their determination at every turn, rarely if ever wavering. Union authorities and northern families tried different tactics to persuade these erstwhile sons of the North to return to their true allegiance, but they encountered individuals who had already experienced a symbolic rebirth. The process by which their identities transformed began before the war yet did not reach its full fruition until the rigors of both the battlefield and prison life tested that transformation. Patterson best summed up the outcome when, only a few weeks after the defeat at Gettysburg, he wrote in his journal, "As for myself, I see before us as citizens of the confederate states, *war* for years to come. And although we have suffered much, I believe it has been nothing compared to what is yet in store for us. It is not for us to pretend to say when peace shall be made, but it is our duty to fight on and on, until our enemies shall find that they are making a losing business of it and conclude to terminate it."[70]

The core of these men's identities depended upon the success or failure of the Confederacy. Even if they returned to the North at some future date, they could never do so again as northerners. The Civil War solidified their status as southerners and Confederates, and they would carry that legacy for the rest of their lives.

9

Native Southern Reactions toward Northern Confederates

At the same time that Northern Confederates demonstrated their identification with the Confederacy and contributed to the strength of its nationalism, they neither lived in a vacuum nor remained invisible. Because they obtained high ranks in political, military, and social circles far out of proportion to their numbers, many native white southerners were fully aware of the presence of Northern Confederates in their midst and had ample opportunity to express their feelings toward them. These reactions speak volumes about the theory versus reality of antebellum sectional thinking and the strength of Confederate nationalism. In a sense, Northern Confederate efforts to remake their identities said as much about those around them as it did about themselves.

In the context of the secession crisis and the Civil War especially, the possibility of suspicion or outright hostility between native and adoptive southerners was quite real. Many Americans in both sections considered a person's state of birth as the prime factor of that individual's character. Under this interpretation, no matter where they actually settled, native northerners supposedly carried their northern upbringing with them permanently. As a result, the likely reactions among native southerners should have included suspicion, paranoia, and even rage. Thanks to decades of propaganda from white southern leaders, any native northerner, regardless of their contributions to southern society, potentially carried the label of an inherent traitor, ready to sell out the Confederacy on behalf of the North.

In reality, and somewhat surprisingly, native white southerners largely accepted their northern-born neighbors into the Confederate ranks. Soldiers and civilians across the Confederacy expressed their confidence and admiration for fellow soldiers who originated from enemy territory. The Confederate nation, although composed entirely of southern states, relied on all of its soldiers and civilians for survival. In fact, given the apparent odds against Confederate military victory throughout the war, native southerners welcomed any kind of support from nearly any quarter. Northern Confederates fit the criteria perfectly. They espoused the Confederate cause, damned the North as tyrants, and fought in the Confederate armies. They did not always rank as the best soldiers, but nearly all of them fought, died, and endured privations with the same dedication as native southerners. No matter what the latter may have believed in theory of an abstract Yankee demon, native northerners in the Confederate ranks continuously fell within the category of trusted comrades. That trust and acceptance not only reinforced Northern Confederates' own perceptions of themselves as dedicated Confederates, but also the viability of Confederate nationalism itself. Just as the Union included southern unionists in its national identity, so did the Confederacy accept native northerners in its own bid for nationhood.

The groundwork for this bi-sectional effort began long before the first shots of the war erupted. As soon as most northern emigrants arrived in the South, they did everything in their power to blend into their new surroundings and obtain the acceptance of their adopted communities. Those communities in turn appreciated that most northern emigrants did not seek to upset the status quo. The respect and praise only increased as time passed and these individuals started new careers, married southern spouses, and participated in local organizations. For instance, New York native John Quitman organized a local militia unit in Mississippi and served as its commander. Massachusetts native Charles Dimmock became a popular captain in the Virginia militia, with one newspaper correspondent commenting, "This veteran corps turned out on Monday last in excellent style, under their new and highly popular commander, Captain Charles Dimmock—than whom there is not probably a more efficient officer in the state."[1] Not all northern emigrants joined militias, but the very fact that they made the effort to engage with their adopted region brought them respect and trust.[2]

Personal contacts in particular allowed white southerners to accept northern emigrants as neighbors and friends. In places like the Southwest and Texas, where established social circles had not fully developed, people from across the country came to build new communities from scratch. Northerners who emigrated before the 1830s especially found a welcoming environment because of increased national unity in the wake of the War of 1812 and the lack of extreme anti-slavery views in the North at the time. Geographical borders remained fluid for much of the antebellum era, and so sectional identity remained fluid as well. Only after the rise of abolitionism did fears of the potential influence of Yankees spread among the southern populace. Even then, while southern propaganda perpetuated the stereotype of Yankees as greedy radicals out to overthrow southern society, few northern emigrants actually held those views. Instead, these men and women defended southern institutions to their northern families and friends, and scores became slave-owners themselves. As long as these native northerners avoided acting like abolitionists and accepted southern cultural norms, native southerners had little reason to link them with their perceptions of abstract Yankee demons.

In fact, several northern emigrants originally moved to the South because white southerners invited them. Thanks to the North's reputation for top quality education, many southerners insisted on bringing in northern teachers, tutors, orators, and others to bolster their own institutions. Massachusetts native Theodore Clapp, after giving several sermons in Louisville, received an offer to take over the Presbyterian Church in New Orleans. Although hesitant to leave his home state of Massachusetts, and after twice rejecting the offer, Clapp finally agreed to assume the post because the members so eagerly wanted his services. When he arrived, he marveled at the extent of southern hospitality toward non-southerners: "In almost every parish of Louisiana are persons living born in New England, whom the generous encouragement of their Creole neighbors has raised from indigence and obscurity to the possession of wealth, honor, and usefulness."[3]

Fellow Massachusetts native Frederick Barnard received a similar endorsement when professors from the University of Alabama offered him a position in the 1830s. The professors wanted Barnard for their college partly because they believed he would bring not only northern educational expertise but also an open mind regarding southern customs. Professor J. W. Stuart commented to a colleague that Barnard "is fond of the South, a warm supporter of its Institutions, and of manners highly affable and gentlemanly."[4] Another observer, O. E. Carmichael, went even further by saying that, although Barnard came from New England, and therefore possibly held negative views of southern society, he would fit in perfectly with the community. "I can with safety," he assured his colleagues, "speak of him as a gentleman possessing all the qualifications that a Southerner could wish in one who designed becoming one of their society, and that on all important questions . . . his actions and feelings will be truly Southern."[5] Even though Barnard had never set foot in the South before, both of these professors already believed he would eventually adopt a southern lifestyle and possibly even a southern identity. Teachers like Barnard may have started out as outsiders, but the warm embrace of their colleagues afforded them the opportunity to switch their sectional identities if they so chose.[6]

The experiences of Clapp and Barnard were not exceptional. Across the South, native northerners of all occupations consistently expressed admiration for how white southerners treated them. Native Pennsylvanian Stephen Duncan received numerous letters thanking him for his work as president of the Bank of Mississippi, as well as for the local charities he supported. Dennis Heartt, a Connecticut native and the owner of the *Hillsboro Recorder* in North Carolina, gained the full acceptance of his small community, and his newspaper quickly became one of the most popular papers in central North Carolina. Another Connecticut native, Amanda Trulock, wrote to her family after moving with her husband to Georgia that her in-laws "appeared to be very much pleased with me, which I have not the least reason to doubt, for they have a very exalted opinion of the Yankees." Native Pennsylvanian Emily Sinkler passed along similar news from Charleston to her own mother by saying how all her neighbors treated her kindly and constantly invited her to various social events.[7] If suspicion or hatred lurked beneath the surface toward all "Yankees," these northern emigrants certainly did not witness it. Despite a growing isolationist mentality in the nineteenth century, white southerners did not shut their doors completely to outsiders.[8]

That kindness did not mean, however, that white southerners immediately viewed native northerners as anything except outsiders. Southerners extended the same hospitality to most visitors as a sign of respect and a mark of pride for the region. Northern visitors and foreign travelers repeatedly commented on the famed southern hospitality prevalent throughout the region.[9] At the same time, newly arrived northern emigrants often felt like aliens in a strange land as they adjusted to southern society, while white southern propagandists claimed true southern character only arose from proper birth.[10]

Connecticut native Henry Watson likely said it best when he wrote during the secession crisis, "the people here are not intolerant of Northern men whom they know."[11] Although many of these emigrants eventually viewed themselves as southerners, no guarantees existed that their neighbors would ever see them as anything other than transplanted Yankees.

Yet over time, the warm welcomes initially given to outsiders grew into full-fledged acceptance of adoptive southerners as part of the white southern population. The longer native northerners remained in the South and blended into local communities, the more their neighbors came to see them as their own. An editor from the Lebanon *Herald* in Tennessee referred to Robert Hatton, an Ohio native, as a "fellow citizen" and "fellow townsman."[12] In 1857 adoptive southerner Hugh Buchannan received an appointment to the Board of Trustees of Oglethorpe Medical College in Georgia, in which the correspondent stated the positions only went to "the most distinguished Southern Gentlemen of our Country," implying that Buchannan belonged in that category.[13] Acquaintances of Stephen Duncan usually addressed him as "Stephen Duncan of Natchez," reflecting his long residence in the city.[14] In addition, Texans consistently referred to native northerners who had fought in the Texas Revolution as "Old Texians," for their service.[15] When Elisha Pease initially ran for governor in 1853, several newspapers urged Democrats to unite behind him. They outlined his contributions to the state in both the military and legislative spheres. Significantly, while extolling his past accomplishments, one editor wrote, "In the dark hour of the Lone Star, penniless and unknown, he landed on our soil to contribute all he had to the accomplishment of her independence—his energies, his talents, and if need be, his blood."[16]

The clearest instances of native southerners accepting northern emigrants as genuine southerners occurred with the eulogies of John Quitman in Mississippi and Samuel Gilman in South Carolina. Although neither survived to see the Civil War, the eulogies given by their colleagues revealed their status among their peers. Quitman originally came from New York but achieved a stellar reputation as a lawyer, governor, and Mexican War hero in his adopted state of Mississippi. Upon his death, white northerners and southerners alike praised him for his services as well as his attachments to the South. One Tennessee representative noted that Quitman represented a state not of his birth but nevertheless earned the hearts and minds of everyone there, as well as falling in love and identifying with his adopted state. Even New

Yorkers recognized the change that took place, with one New York representative declaring "New York may claim the honor of his nativity . . . but at an early age he adopted Mississippi for his home, and was warmly attached to her institutions, and earnestly labored for her development and prosperity."[17]

Similarly, Samuel Gilman, a native of Massachusetts who earned a reputation as an inspiring pastor in South Carolina, had achieved full acceptance into his adopted community at the time of his death in 1858. He died while visiting his native state, but Charlestonians insisted that his final resting place belonged in South Carolina.[18] Thousands of people attended his funeral, and Charleston newspapers lamented the passing of so great an adopted son. The Charleston *Daily Courier* wrote "'[It] was far from home . . . that he ended his gentle, useful and enviable career; far from us who loved and honored him so truly," and claimed Charleston had not seen such a funeral since that of John C. Calhoun.[19] In an even more revealing statement, another Charleston paper stated, "We of Charleston all knew and loved him, and we had grown to think him so utterly and entirely our own, that we had hoped, unconsciously, that even the inevitable message would have found and reached him in our midst . . . ."[20] Two native northerners, living on opposite sides of the South and with vastly different backgrounds and careers, received the same acknowledgement as former northerners now at one with their fellow southerners.

Birthplace alone did not determine the ultimate basis of sectional identity, which helps explain why white southerners did not immediately cast suspicion on every native northerner in their midst. In states like Mississippi, Alabama, and Texas, which came into the Union after the eighteenth century, most of the white population came from other states as emigrants. Most of them admittedly came from the South, but they still had to forge a new state identity that incorporated a mix of people from the eastern and western portions of the South within what was essentially wilderness. At that stage, men from the North could arrive in a territory and have a direct impact on its formation into statehood. They made favorable impressions among their neighbors by making the South their home, adopting southern customs, raising southern families, and even ascending into the ranks of slave-owners. Once native northerners established themselves in their adopted communities, they shed their "Yankee" image in the eyes of their neighbors. As a result, adoptive southerners did not fall into the category of "Yankee" as envisioned by secessionist doomsday prophets. Native white southerners understood, consciously or unconsciously, the flexible nature of antebellum sectional identity.[21]

Not all historians, however, agree with this interpretation. Several claim that southern sectional hatred extended to most native northerners and reflected longstanding southern opposition to its non-native population. Joseph Rainer argues that northern traders reinforced stereotypes of northerners as commercial, greedy, dishonest wanderers. By the 1830s, when abolitionists began calling for the immediate elimination of slavery, white southerners faced the additional fear of northern emigrants arriving to disseminate such ideas in order to destabilize the entire southern social structure.[22] Similarly, historian Dennis Rousey points out that southerners felt increasingly threatened because of their decreasing population in comparison to the North and the fact that most of the rest of the world disapproved of slavery. As a consequence, native northerners in the South faced much greater suspicion than native southerners in the North.[23]

In order to reinforce their claims, these historians argue that, regardless of how white southerners responded to northerners in the early decades of the nineteenth century, by the 1850s sectional hatred had hardened to such a degree that most native northerners, even those who lived in the South for years, seemed dangerous and unwelcome. The secession crisis provided the perfect environment for suspicions against all native northerners. James McPherson quotes several Upper South politicians seeking to align their states with the Confederacy during the secession crisis, with each of their statements referring to ties of blood, kin, and race. McPherson writes, "'We must go with 'our Southern brothers,' declared the governor of Tennessee. 'Blood is thicker than water,' echoed a North Carolina newspaper editor. The attorney general of Virginia chimed in with an assertion that Virginians were 'homogeneous with the [people of the Confederate] States in race. . . .'"[24] Adoptive southerners had none of these ties to link them to the South. If native southerners truly believed only in these ties as qualifiers for Confederate nationalism, then native northerners simply did not, and could not, belong.

It certainly appeared that way to some adoptive southerners, especially those who emigrated to the South less than a decade before the Civil War. Massachusetts native Tryphena Blanche Holder Fox told her mother in 1856 that the nomination of Republican John C. Fremont for president stirred a lot more opposition to native northern teachers in Mississippi. In the same state, Joseph Ingraham claimed one county called for new resolutions barring any native northerners from teaching southern students. New England native Calvin Robinson, a resident of Florida in the 1850s, found himself accused as a closet abolitionist in the wake of the John Brown raid in 1859.[25] Even a stalwart like Elisha Pease, a former governor of Texas, came under suspicion when he ran for the Senate in 1857. During the campaign one of Pease's friends warned him that, despite his reputation and history in Texas, several Democratic colleagues had "an apprehension that you are not sufficiently Southern in your feelings."[26] In each case, increasing sectional hostility, fed by the rise of the Republican Party and attacks against slavery, made the South a less welcoming environment for native northerners. It seemed that not even a long residence there put someone above suspicion. Sylvanus Lines, a New Englander who lived for over a decade in Georgia, likely said it best when he wrote to his northern-born wife in 1858, "when once their [southerners'] displeasure is aroused there is scarcely any bounds to the malignity of their disposition. They look with an eye of criticism upon strangers and for this reason no doubt you have found it very unpleasant."[27]

Even in the 1850s, however, such threats and rhetoric usually applied to unnamed Yankees and abolitionists, rather than those who actually lived in the South. As long as they did not cause trouble or express controversial statements, even newly arrived emigrants in the 1850s discovered a fairly hospitable environment. Tutors like Caroline Seabury and Henry Handerson felt grateful for the generally warm welcome they received from their employers and neighbors. Maine native Arthur McArthur, who arrived in Louisiana in 1860, wrote to his father, "I like the people very well & they seem to like me, & as you say it is best to 'let well enough alone.'"[28] At a time when New Englanders were supposedly all viewed as dangerous abolitionists, McArthur found that personal relationships helped neutralized negative stereotypes.

Even adoptive southerners who expressed apprehensions about the South admitted that, despite character attacks from strangers, they still found support from those who knew them well. Fox informed her grandmother that the family she tutored never wanted to let her leave. When Robinson faced accusations of harboring abolitionist sentiments, his friends in Florida vigorously denied the charges. And Sylvanus Lines's wife, Amelia, while claiming she could never feel at home in the South, wrote in her diary when she first arrived in Georgia in 1857, "The people seem very kind. Mrs. Gleasoner does all she can to make me happy . . . the kindness of the people will do much to reconcile me to such a way of living or staying rather."[29] The closer secession loomed over the horizon, the more conditions seemed to stay the same for any northerner wishing to remake his or her life in the South.[30]

Not even the secession crisis itself managed to erode southern confidence in adoptive southerners completely. Considering that over 80 percent of the individuals in this study eventually joined the Confederacy, native southerners did not go out of their way to persecute anyone with a northern heritage. For example, an editor of the *Richmond Enquirer* gave a report on Governor Letcher's tour of the Virginia armories in February 1861, and in the process mentioned the superintendant of the armories, Charles Dimmock. Though aware of Dimmock's past in the North, having mentioned it in previous articles, the editor instead focused on his career as a West Point officer and his efficient service for the state. Nowhere did Dimmock's ties to the North appear in the paper because, by that time, his contributions to Virginia made him a fully accepted citizen.[31] In Arkansas, Isaac Murphy, a native New Englander, ran into potentially more trouble when he gained a reputation as one of the few unionist members of the Arkansas secession convention. While many newspapers called him a traitor, they did so only because of his unionist stance and not explicitly for his northern background. The *Arkansas Gazette* even came to his defense, describing Murphy as "a true and a brave man, and Arkansas has no citizen upon her soil who will be more ready to respond to her call when necessity and public safety demands that her sons shall offer their services, or their lives, in her defense."[32]

The experiences of Frederick Barnard in Mississippi and Caleb Huse in Alabama further reveal the confidence many native southerners held for their northern-born colleagues. Their supporters insisted that background alone did not automatically make them enemies of the South. Barnard went through his ordeal by fire when the board of the University of Mississippi put him on trial in 1860 for unsoundness on the slavery question. His critics claimed that, since Barnard wanted to use a slave's testimony to expel a student, he must have abolitionist leanings. One of the professors even charged that Barnard betrayed both the university and the South by wanting to print the school catalogues in the North. Despite what these critics claimed, in reality the charges of northern collusion merely served as a front for other lingering issues from Barnard's teaching career. His advocacy for reforming the educational process, including requiring science courses, and his reputation as an Episcopalian and former Whig upset many of the Baptist and Democratic professors and students. Barnard's northern background played little role in the whole affair.[33]

Despite the accusations, Barnard received critical assistance from the rest of the faculty, who appreciated his efforts to bring better education to the state. During the trial, Barnard produced several letters and pamphlets written by his supporters defending his character against what they perceived as personal attacks. Colonel A. H. Pegues admitted that Barnard was "a Northern man by birth" but pointed out that Barnard's past speeches revealed his loyalty to his adopted section. Two other professors added that, over the many years they had known him, they never saw anything "to induce a suspicion that he was not entirely identified with the South and attached to her institutions . . . and therefore we do not doubt he is a loyal Southern man."[34] In the end, Barnard achieved full vindication when the board voted eleven to zero to acquit him of all charges.[35]

More remarkably, Caleb Huse, also a native of Massachusetts, managed to obtain the same confidence from his southern peers even without a long residence in the South. Unlike Barnard, who spent decades living in Alabama and Mississippi, Huse only spent a year in Florida as a soldier before returning to New York to work as an instructor at West Point. In 1860, after a short leave of absence in Europe, the University of Alabama appointed him as a professor of chemistry and commandant of the corps of cadets. Huse accepted but immediately came under suspicion by the students because of his New England background. The president of the university warned him that rumors circulated of a mutiny among the student body because, as Huse recalled, "I was a northern-born man; that they called me a d———d Yankee, and intended running me out of the State."[36]

Nevertheless, when Huse offered to resign, the administration refused to even consider it and offered him their full backing. Buoyed by this support, Huse arrived at the university determined to face his critics and ultimately found the rumors groundless. "The cadets, backed by their families, had threatened to run me out of the State; I should put upon them the responsibility of executing their threat; I should not resign. I went back to camp and never heard anything more about the 'mutiny.'"[37] Huse realized that even at the height of anti-northern sentiment in the Deep South, native northerners could still find defenders on a personal level. The fact that no mutiny ever materialized suggests that, once the students realized Huse was not actually an abolitionist (though he did describe himself as Massachusetts-born and Puritan-bred), they had no other personal quarrels with him. As long as native northerners either did not cause trouble or voiced support for southern society, native southerners generally treated them with respect, confidence, and friendship.

Even so, despite the generally positive receptions, nothing guaranteed such feelings would persist once tens of thousands more native northerners entered the South intent on destruction. After the firing on Fort Sumter and President Lincoln's call for troops, all thoughts of moderation disappeared as the vast majority of white southerners joined the Confederate ranks to defend their homes from northern invaders. In such a charged atmosphere, everything that adoptive southerners had worked for appeared ready to dissolve under the tsunami of sectional hatred. The negative attitudes of a minority of southerners in the past now threatened to shift into the majority against all native northerners, foreign and domestic.

Observers across the country recorded their impressions of this turn toward unyielding sectional mistrust. The *Charleston Mercury* mocked northern soldiers for attempting to survive under the southern sun.[38] A correspondent for the *New York Times* remarked that during a trip through Georgia he found the population yearning to kill every northerner they could find. He told his readers, "They spoke of hanging the Northern people with as much confidence as though it were a feat easy of accomplishment . . . [they] seemed to look upon Northerners, of whatever political sentiments, in the light of radical abolitionists, not to be tolerated nor permitted to live."[39] Several civilians repeated the opinions recorded by newspaper reporters. On a trip back from England, a passenger wrote in her diary that the ship she sailed on contained a large number of Union officers and, though everyone tried to treat each other politely, she sensed "an impossible gulf between every Northern and Southern man and woman."[40] Julia Tyler, a former first lady and native New Yorker, expressed her own unease to her family back in New York. She told her mother, "oh! how the wickedness of the North is stamped upon their [southerners'] very souls! It is a perfect surprise to them when I assure them there is some good feeling there. They are hardly prepared to believe in the exceptions."[41]

With such animosity, it only made sense that native northerners in the South would come under the same scrutiny. The sin of northern birth, northern upbringing, even association with a northerner condemned a person in the eyes of many Confederates. For example, Sallie Putnam, a resident of Richmond, related in her memoirs a story about how "Little girls learned to dread and fear the Yankee above all tame or wild animals, and amusing lessons were often gleaned by those who paid attention to the innocent sports of the children." She recorded one such incident when a group of girls mocked and derided two of their playmates for "being Yankees" simply because their parents came from the North.[42] The children's accusations reflected their parents' growing suspicions about the supposed evil deeds of native northerners in their midst.

Similar incidents prevailed in other areas outside the Confederate capitol. Calvin Robinson recalled that in Jacksonville, Florida, "ruffians and thugs" threatened northern-born merchants unless the latter paid bribes to stop the harassment. Robinson's wife, Elizabeth, wrote to her sister, "In the first place they call every person born north of Mason and Dixon's line by the meanest name they can command. With the confederates or secessionists, 'Yankee' is meaner than 'nigger,' the lowest name a person can have. Until the Federalists came, there was in our very midst a company of desperadoes calling themselves Guerrillas, whose avowed intention was to destroy the property and kill every northern man, particularly Unionists. . . ."[43] The potential threat of native northerners agitated a swath of the Confederate population who equated any northerner as a unionist traitor. Franklin and Phoebe Farmer, along with their daughter Alice, felt even more terrified by their neighbors in Louisiana. As natives of Massachusetts, the Farmer family endured derision, accusations of treachery, and death threats. Alice Farmer vividly recalled those experiences after the war when she wrote in her memoirs, "Families that had been the most intimate with us, that had been entertained in our home and we in theirs refused to recognize us. These same friends were the ones who finally flatly accused mother and father of being spies—which they were not—and threatened to kill them."[44]

Other attacks against native northerners occurred in a more low key setting but still revealed much about native white southern anxiety. Several southern commentators yearned to make the Confederacy a purely southern nation, free from outside influence. The Richmond *Enquirer,* describing northern-born men living in the state, exclaimed, "These men are not of us, nor with us. . . . They are illegitimate Virginians."[45] The *Charleston Mercury,* in trying to explain the prevalence of unionism in East Tennessee, cited a plot by New Englanders and Europeans as the cause. "For many years past the Yankees have systematically sent into East Tennessee hordes of New Englanders," the editor told his readers. "They have sent us, too, thousands of Dutch and Swiss, who dwell amid the vine clad hills and in secluded valleys. All these are original Abolitionists."[46] In the Confederate Congress, Missouri senator John Clark declared that he "'hoped our laws would go even further than to exclude them [northerners] from citizenship'" and warned any man who married a northern woman, "'Go out of the country—we want none of your breed. We will have a pure blooded nation.'"[47] In their pursuit of a purely southern nation, these leaders saw native northerners as the perfect foil for stimulating southern nationalism.

Thanks to such propaganda, even Northern Confederates with long ties to the South did not always escape these stereotypes. In March 1862, Mary Chesnut of Charleston described a party she attended with several of her friends and General Samuel Cooper, on his way down for an inspection tour of the city. In the course of the evening, one of her friends, Mrs. Pickens, complained about how Jefferson Davis kept sending men of northern birth to Charleston. Chesnut remarked, "Some one crossed the room, stood back of Mrs. Pickens, and murmured in her ear, 'General Cooper was born in New York.' Sudden silence."[48] Mrs. Pickens was obviously embarrassed by her faux pas, but it still represented a willingness to believe the worst of native northerners.[49]

Such beliefs only gained strength as the war dragged on and white southerners looked for scapegoats. The *Charleston Mercury* printed a story in 1863 about the arrest of a Mrs. Pat Allan, whom the editor described as an Ohio woman married to a southern officer who betrayed the Confederacy by corresponding with Union general John A. Dix. Though no other papers reported the story, the *Mercury* editor claimed the government wanted to hush up the affair, because Mrs. Allan had a high social position and because government officials wanted to intercept more of her letters. In addition, Charles Dahlgren, a Pennsylvania emigrant who lived in the South for decades, nevertheless came under attack for supposedly corresponding with his brother John, a Union admiral. Rufus Bullock, who worked as a telegraph operator for the Confederate government, was criticized for receiving letters from his native state of New York.[50]

A clerk in the War Department in Richmond named John Beauchamp Jones represented an extreme example of the obsession by some southerners with blaming all the Confederacy's ills on Northern Confederates. Jones kept an extensive diary during the war, in which he complained constantly about the malign influence of native northerners in the Confederate government and its armies. In his mind, a person's state of origin counted as much as anything else in determining that person's loyalties and fitness for command. As a result, Jones rarely failed to mention a soldier's origins if they hailed from anywhere other than the South. He called Albert Blanchard "another general from Massachusetts" and Mansfield Lovell as a New York politician and street commissioner. Commenting on the appointment of a non-Virginian to head the Richmond Department in December 1862, Jones wrote, "it is said this appointment was made by Gen. S. Cooper (another Yankee) to insult Virginia by preventing the capital from being in the hands of a Virginian."[51] In Jones' opinion, the Confederacy had little chance of surviving as a nation unless the southern population closed ranks against northerners. In a perfect world, the whole country would consist solely of native southerners. As he recorded in 1861, "And there are several Northern men here wanting to be generals. This does not look much like Southern homogeneity. God save us, if we are not to save ourselves."[52]

In fact, the biggest problem for the Confederacy, according to Jones, lay in the appointment of native northerners over southerners for top assignments. Time and again, Jones cited commands in the Confederacy led by northern-born major generals while white southern generals languished as brigadiers. One of his criticisms included Jefferson Davis' tendency "for lifting up Yankees and keeping down great Southern men. Wise, Floyd, etc. are kept in obscurity; while Pemberton, who commanded the Massachusetts troops, under Lincoln, in April, 1861, is made a lieutenant general."[53] He also faulted General Cooper for placing General Samuel French, a New Jersey native, in command of Confederate forces at Petersburg, only thirty miles south of the capitol.[54] Nine months later, with the loss of New Orleans and Vicksburg, Jones felt vindicated in his prediction and renewed his objections to putting native northerners in top commands. As he wrote in July 1863, "Altogether, this is another dark day in our history. It has been officially ascertained that Pemberton surrendered, with Vicksburg, 22,000 men! He has lost, during the year, not less than 40,000! And Lovell [another Northern Confederate general] lost Fort Jackson and New Orleans. When will the government put 'none but Southerners on guard?'"[55] As long as native northerners retained their commands, according to Jones, the new nation remained vulnerable to disaster.

By the end of the war, Jones did not even limit his suspicions to military men. A month before Richmond fell, Jones expressed concern that northern-born preachers might betray the cause. "A large per cent of these preachers is of Northern birth," he insisted, "and some of them may possibly betray the cause if they deem it desperate. This is the history of such men in the South so far."[56] If all native white southerners in the Confederacy felt like Jones, then no one had any reason to trust Northern Confederates. The government should have rounded up every native northerner and banished them to the North at the first opportunity.

Yet such banishments did not occur. Jones may have taken every opportunity to disparage Northern Confederates and drive them out of top commands, but his wishes rarely came to fruition. In correspondence, diaries, speeches, and newspaper stories, most of the time native southerners either did not mention Northern Confederates, talked about them without mentioning their origins, or came to their defense. As long as someone expressed support for the Confederacy, few people had reason to doubt his or her intentions. A foreign observer, William Russell of England, noticed this pattern in his own travels in the South. While in Louisiana, he recorded his observations of one of the senators from the state, John Slidell. Russell said that Slidell, "though born in a Northern State, is perhaps one of the most determined disunionists in the Southern Confederacy . . . he is quite satisfied, the government and independence of the Southern Confederacy are as completely established as those of any power in the world."[57] If Russell had not mentioned Slidell's birthplace, few could have guessed that he did not come from Louisiana. By the time of the secession crisis, native northerners in the South had the same choices as native southerners on the question of the Union, and their decisions on that question served as the main criteria for how the Confederacy perceived them.

Beyond acceptance of adoptive southerners in the past, native southerners found more reasons to grant their support once the Civil War erupted. The Confederacy faced a daunting manpower shortage that only got worse as the war progressed. Considering that the Union held onto the Border States and the support of both white and black unionists across the South, their opponents did not have the luxury of chastising anyone who supported the Confederacy, even if they hailed from the hated North. Governor Thomas Moore of Louisiana wrote to Secretary of War Judah Benjamin begging for qualified officers, stressing that "A gentleman by the name of Smith, I believe from New York, is much desired here . . ."[58] Moore did not care where an officer came from as long as he brought military expertise to the battlefield.

Confederate president Jefferson Davis himself ranked among the staunchest supporters of northern-born men in the Confederate armies. As a West Point graduate and former soldier in the United States Army, Davis knew many Northern Confederate generals and considered them among his close friends and associates. He also developed a reputation for keeping his friends in high positions regardless of their conduct, either out of deep loyalty or as a way to deflect questions about his judgment. Once he appointed a man to a military command, Davis supported him with fanatical dedication.[59] He thus had no qualms in appointing such men as Samuel Cooper, John C. Pemberton, Samuel French, and many others.

For the most part, Davis did not consider these men as northerners fighting in the Confederate armies but rather as dedicated southerners defending their homes and nation. One address he gave to the Confederate Congress in 1861 described efforts to negotiate treaties with Native American tribes in the Trans-Mississippi region. He selected Albert Pike for this mission because Pike had worked with Native Americans in the past and was, as Davis described him, "a citizen of Arkansas." The fact that Pike originally came from Massachusetts, a fact well known because of his published writings and ties to the Masons before the war, did not deter Davis. He used the same logic when he forwarded to Congress his recommendations for promotions to full general, which included New Jersey native Samuel Cooper. Davis listed him as "General Samuel Cooper of Virginia," since Cooper made his home in that state. In 1864, Davis decided to settle a command dispute in Mississippi by sending General Samuel French to the state. The president defended his decision by saying, "Saml. French is a citizen of Misspi [sic]. and acquainted with the topography of the Country." In each of these cases, Davis regarded all residents of southern states as genuine Confederates who belonged with their adopted states regardless of origin.[60]

When critics objected to some of Davis' appointments because the chosen commanders happened to have northern backgrounds, Davis rarely if ever acknowledged any problems arising out of such accusations. For instance, General Joseph Johnston once wrote to Davis during the Vicksburg campaign expressing concern that some of the enlisted men did not feel comfortable serving under northern-born officers, particularly General French. Davis, according to French's memoirs, replied, "Those who suggest that the arrival

General Mansfield Lovell. A West Point graduate, Lovell grew up in New York and later worked as New York City's deputy street commissioner before leaving for the Confederacy to serve as a Major General. He commanded the garrison at New Orleans and ultimately failed to protect the city from the Union navy. Library of Congress.

of Gen. French will produce discontent among the troops because of his Northern birth are not probably aware that he is a citizen of Mississippi . . . [and] was the chief of ordnance and artillery in the force Mississippi raised to maintain her right of secession . . . and has frequently been before the enemy where he was the senior officer."[61] Davis did not believe that a general's birthplace should cause discontent. He lauded French's service to Mississippi and regarded him as a loyal citizen of that state and to the Confederacy.

The most significant example of Davis's undying support of Northern Confederates occurred with the commander of Vicksburg, General John C. Pemberton. In the summer of 1863, Pemberton surrendered not only the city of Vicksburg but his entire army to General Ulysses S. Grant, which represented one of the worst defeats in the history of the Confederacy. Any general would have faced the severest criticism from such a debacle, but since Pemberton happened to come from Pennsylvania and still had family there, his conduct looked like treason. Davis could have easily joined in the condemnation, especially since Pemberton failed to defend Davis's home state from Union occupation.

Davis's subsequent support of, and confidence in, this highly controversial Northern Confederate seems astonishing. In August 1863, barely a month after the double disaster at Vicksburg and Gettysburg, Davis said that both Pemberton and General Lee were on the same level because they both suffered recent defeats. Just as he still put his trust in Lee, Davis wanted Pemberton to know that "my confidence in both has not diminished because 'letter writers' have not sent forth your praise on the wings of the press."[62] For the rest of the year, Davis tried several times to give Pemberton another command suitable to his rank but always had to back off because other generals said nobody wanted to serve under him again.[63] When Pemberton finally resigned his general's commission, Davis promoted him to lieutenant-colonel of artillery as a symbol of his continued trust in the native Pennsylvanian. In March 1864, Davis wrote to Pemberton, "Your devotion to our country's cause has enabled you to rise above personal and professional pride; and in the manner you have found disappointment I find proof of the injustice of the prejudice which has existed against you, and sincerely hope you rightly believe that it is subsiding."[64] Through everything that happened, Davis never lost his confidence in Pemberton's dedication to the cause. The fact that the highest Confederate official expressed his ironclad support of even the most vulnerable of northern-born generals gave all Northern Confederates a justification for their devotion to their adopted nation.

Along with Davis, many other native southerners expressed their own confidence in their northern-born comrades. Interestingly enough, they often spoke about Northern Confederates without mentioning the latter's origins. Some northern emigrants had lived in the South for so long, and become such an integral part of their communities, that people either forgot that some of their neighbors came from the North or did not consider it important enough to mention. Even for those who came to the South in the 1850s or later, not everyone knew about their origins, especially not soldiers and civilians who never previously met them.[65]

Whether they knew about their comrades' backgrounds or not, many native southerners chose to focus mainly on an individual's military or personal accomplishments in gauging their contributions to Confederate victory. In the summer of 1863, the *Charleston Mercury* reported on the exploits of General Franklin Gardner, a New York native and commander of

Port Hudson, without ever mentioning his origins.[66] Henry McCay, a native Pennsylvanian who spent twenty years in Georgia and served as a captain in the Twelfth Georgia Regiment, received a vote of confidence from a Georgia civilian, who declared, "Leut. McCay has done a great deal for the company since we left home. He spares no pains for the benefit of the company and is allways [sic] at work, & the other officers are all attentive."[67] The editor of the Richmond *Dispatch,* reporting on the defenses of New Orleans in 1862, wrote, "In New Orleans we have 32,000 infantry and others encamped in the vicinity. In point of discipline and the manual of arms they are very superior to the Yankees. We have two generals, very able and active, who possess our entire confidence—General Mansfield Lovell and Brigadier General Ruggles."[68] Ironically, the commanders of the infantry whom the editor labeled superior to the "Yankees" were in fact native northerners. These commentators either did not know or did not care about a soldier's origins, as long as he performed well on the battlefield on behalf of the Confederacy.

In Tennessee, Connecticut native Charles Quintard gained the admiration of all the soldiers in the First Tennessee Regiment for his work as their chaplain. His reputation among the men reached such high levels they became despondent whenever he took leave to work in hospitals or give services on the home front. In June 1862, over two hundred soldiers from four different companies in the regiment wrote letters begging Quintard to return to his old post as chaplain.[69] Quintard received similar correspondence from other soldiers and civilians throughout the war asking for his services.[70] Nowhere did these soldiers indicate they knew or cared Quintard did not originally hail from the South.

Patriotic devotion to the cause at the expense of personal gain brought welcome attention from Confederate participants as well. For instance, several authors, in an exposé on Confederate generals, singled out General Martin Luther Smith, a native New Yorker, for exceptional conduct. "With him the success of our glorious cause is paramount to *self* or any other consideration," they proclaimed. "In reply to a telegraphic dispatch from President Davis, expressing some concern about Vicksburg and asking what more was particularly needed for its successful defence, General Smith replied: * * * * More infantry is desired *and another general officer, whether ranking me or not is immaterial, so we succeed.*"[71] Unlike so many other generals on both sides, Smith did not care whether he served as a commander or as a subordinate; either one would do as long as enough men arrived to defend the post. The authors also believed Smith belonged with the South because he married a southern woman and had family in the South, as well as the North and West. They especially thought Smith was the perfect man to defend Vicksburg because of "the homes of those who are bound to him by the most sacred ties of blood and friendship."[72]

Even when white southerners knew about the origins of their Northern Confederate comrades, they did not always feel the information sufficiently worthy of mention or elaboration. As long as these individuals served in the Confederate armies, nothing else mattered. For example, one Confederate officer mentioned in passing that his fellow officer, W. C. Duxbury, worked in a drugstore in Montgomery "and that he was born somewhere in Massachusetts." The editor of the *Charleston Mercury* mentioned General Lovell's past service in the New York City Guards militia but did not give any indication he disapproved of Lovell's appointment as commander of New Orleans.[73]

Generals who had served in the prewar army with Northern Confederates especially regarded such matters as irrelevant to the latter's performance on the battlefield or identification with the Confederacy. When General James Longstreet mentioned a Northern Confederate in his memoirs, he concentrated on the person's military achievements without speculating on any suspected treason.[74] General Joseph Johnston did the same in his own wartime correspondence. Johnston had numerous opportunities to place blame on others, especially Generals Lovell and Pemberton, for the failures the Confederacy suffered in the Western Theater. He ended up praising Lovell for his conduct at New Orleans and criticizing Pemberton for the debacle at Vicksburg. Johnston, like Longstreet, did not attribute success or failure to northern origins.[75]

The fact that native southerners could dismiss northern origins in fellow Confederates as irrelevant revealed the nuances of southern sectionalism. For decades, white southern leaders and propagandists claimed that white southerners shared a separate nationalism, and the Civil War provided them with the perfect environment for solidifying that nationalism. For instance, a civilian in Louisiana, Sarah Dawson, wrote in her diary in 1862 that though she respected northerners, and even had relatives in the Union armies, she still considered them a separate race out to subjugate the southern people. "We, the natives of this loved soil, will be beggars in a foreign land; we will not submit to despotism under the garb of Liberty. The North will find herself burdened with an unparalleled debt, with nothing to show for it except deserted towns, burning homes, a standing army which will govern with no small caprice, and an impoverished land."[76] If any moment existed for a true break between the North and South, the Civil War gave white southerners the best chance to accomplish that goal. Confederate propagandists especially attempted to solidify the Confederacy as a purely native-born southern nation.[77]

Despite the favorable environment for such a project, however, Confederates themselves admitted that Confederate nationalism actually depended on the devotions of everyone, northern as well as southern, who espoused Confederate nationhood. White southerners understood that Northern Confederate soldiers and civilians were fellow comrades entirely different from the perceived Yankee hordes of the Union. Only northerners who supported the Union deserved the pejorative term "Yankee." The viability of Confederate nationalism required the recognition of every individual who fought for its survival, regardless of origin, as equal members.[78]

Native southerners who came into contact with northern-born soldiers in their ranks made both direct and indirect comments that showed how they differentiated between Union soldiers and Northern Confederates. Charles Quintard, who had a loyal following among his men, received one such endorsement from one of his acquaintances in the secession crisis. Hoping that Tennessee would "vindicate her right of independence of all Yankeedom," he assured Quintard "I know you are from N.Y. but I don't include that as a part of that [mass] Puritanical land."[79] Since Quintard went along with secession, his background did not count against him. The acquaintance did not even realize Quintard actually came from Connecticut, part of the "Puritanical land" of New England he mentioned. He simply assumed that Quintard had to come from the Mid-Atlantic, because no one from New England could ever join the Confederacy as Quintard had done.

In Mississippi, General Charles Dahlgren had northern relatives who fought in the Union forces, most notably his brother John, an admiral in the Union navy, and his other brother Ulrich, who served in the Union cavalry. Such an association could easily have turned native southerners against Dahlgren. Instead, his associates understood that having family members in the Union armies did not make one guilty by association. While Dahlgren stayed in Atlanta in 1864, one of his neighbors wrote to her mother, "A General Dahlgren, said to be brother of the commodore, has been attending our church regularly for some Sabbaths past with his family. They are very genteel, attractive persons in their appearance. . . . It is said this brother gave our government the pattern of the Dahlgren guns invented by his Yankee brother."[80] While she admitted Dahlgren's relations with the famous Dahlgren family, Mary only called his brother a "Yankee" and even credited Dahlgren with providing gun designs for the Confederacy. Georgia resident Eliza Andrews also recorded her impressions of Dahlgren in her own diary, though not nearly as positively. Andrews thought he was pompous and took too much credit for others' accomplishments, including his claim to have invented the Dahlgren gun. She believed his brother, the "Yankee admiral" as she called him, actually developed the design.[81] Regardless of her negative views of him, Andrews did not call Dahlgren himself a "Yankee." Whether his acquaintances liked or hated him, they still thought of him as one of their own.

Native white southerners thus did not have to view every native northerner as a potential traitor. Exclamations of support for southern rights and the viability of secession brought a lot of credibility for Northern Confederates among their peers. Indeed, native northerners siding with the Confederacy only bolstered the case for secession, since it challenged the image of a united North. Virginia representative James Mason said as much when he heard that Samuel Cooper resigned from the army and accepted a post in Virginia. Mason told Cooper he congratulated him on the "patriotic determination to which you have come. . . . I trust, that your noble position will have its deserved influence on . . . your Brother officers; of that we shall soon see the whole heart & soul of the Army & Navy too, always in his defence of justice & right."[82] Rank and file Confederate soldiers also appreciated the convictions of their Northern Confederate comrades. For example, James Langhorne, a soldier in a Virginia regiment, expressed such an opinion toward one of his fellow soldiers, native Pennsylvanian George Junkin. Langhorne was impressed that, despite pleas from his family to join the Union, Junkin felt that his destiny lay with the Confederacy. As Langhorne commented, "He is fighting against the S[t]ate that gave him birth, Father, Mother, Bro. & Sister, and for what [?] because he thinks our cause is just . . . he was not to be persuaded, he could not give up the loyal principles of his noble heart & made the sacrifice of all family connection . . . ."[83] Langhorne knew, like so many others, that northern birth did not preclude someone from professing die-hard support for the Confederate cause. For that reason, regular soldiers from both the South and North fought side by side for the same goals.[84]

More importantly, many native southerners did not just tolerate Northern Confederates as fellow ideologues but also as genuine Confederates. Native southerners appreciated the extra manpower and reinforcement of their own ideology, but that did not mean they had to accept native northerners on the same level as themselves. They could have easily dismissed this relatively small minority as a novelty and concentrated on perpetuating the image of a pure-blood southern nation. Instead, many Confederates went out of their way to link their Northern Confederate comrades with Confederate nationalism and, in some cases, a southern identity.

Some Confederates simply acknowledged their northern-born comrades as fellow Confederates without considering them southerners. Though they remained outsiders in the sense of not claiming the South as the land of their birth, in these cases Northern Confederates still received recognition as equal members of the Confederate nation. A South Carolina editor described Josiah Gorgas as "the distinguished and very able head of the Ordnance Department of the Confederate States."[85] A Richmond socialite named Constance Harrison wrote fondly in her memoirs about her friends Mr. and Mrs. Cooper. She recalled how "Our good neighbors at Vaucluse, the Samuel Coopers, had removed to Richmond, where the general, albeit of Northern birth, had elected to serve the South. Made adjutant-general of the Confederate Government, he was much esteemed by his confreres and the public."[86] Colonel Arthur J. Fremantle, a British soldier traveling through the Confederacy in 1863, recorded his impression of General Roswell Ripley in Charleston: "He has the reputation of being an excellent artillery officer, and although by birth a Northerner, he is a red-hot and indefatigable rebel."[87] General Henry Heth expressed a lot more emotion in his eulogy of native Pennsylvanian General Johnson Kelly Duncan, who died in December 1862. Recalling his service in New Orleans, Heth declared, "His distinguished gallantry and courage, his energy and self sacrificing devotion in the maintenance of right and justice, fill the measure of a soldier's and a patriot's fame. As a brother in a common cause, we mourn him with heartfelt sorrow . . ."[88]

Others went much further by trying to link their comrades not just with the Confederacy but also with the South. Just as Northern Confederates often viewed themselves as adoptive southerners fighting to protect their homes, so did their neighbors extend the same recognition. For example,

Ashbel Smith received several letters reaffirming his status as a Texan. One Texas officer told him, "The fire of the old Texan state burns in your breast," while a civilian lauded Smith's efforts to protect Galveston at the end of the war, reminding him of the glory days when Texas first declared independence with Smith's help. Smith's past service and identification with Texas carried over into the Confederacy without any suspicion he still might have held sympathy for his native Connecticut.[89] Similarly, friends of native New Yorker Jedediah Hotchkiss did not see him as anything except a Virginian. When General J. E. B. Stuart recommended Hotchkiss for a promotion, the chief of the Bureau of Engineers, Colonel J. F. Gilmer, regretted that no openings were available. As Hotchkiss's biographer summarized, "Gilmer was sorry that he could not grant Hotchkiss a regular commission. The chief stumbling block was still the fact that Hotchkiss was from Virginia, and, as he lamented, 'they all make such a fuss about appointments from Virginia.'"[90]

Even when these friends and associates acknowledged a Northern Confederate's background, they often tried to dismiss it as a part of the distant past with little to no relevance to a person's actual identity. For example, in January 1861 the governor of Florida appointed William Chase, a native of Massachusetts and former engineer officer in the United States Army, as commander of Pensacola. The editor of the *Charleston Mercury* provided details of Chase's military accomplishments, from his West Point graduation to his retirement in 1856. In the process, the editor wrote, "He was formerly a resident of Massachusetts," as well as "a man of indomitable perseverance and courage, and ranks high as a military engineer and strategist."[91] In the same breath, the editor lauded the exploits of a commander in Florida while simultaneously declaring that this commander came from the most hated New England state. Yet the editor did not really consider Chase to be part of Massachusetts, because he called Chase a former resident. When Florida called upon her citizens to defend the state, Chase answered that call as a son of Florida instead of New England.

Friends of another Northern Confederate, Robert Hatton, even tried to deny that he had any connections other than to his adopted state of Tennessee. Upon Hatton's death in battle in 1862, several Tennessee newspapers went out of their way to praise Hatton for his services to the state and to the Confederacy. The editors also insisted Hatton belonged to Tennessee as a native son, even though they knew Hatton originally came from Ohio. The

Richmond *Dispatch* noted this fact in its own eulogy by describing Hatton as a "native of Ohio and citizen of Tennessee."[92] Such a description in itself afforded Hatton due respect as a patriot of the South. Yet his fellow citizens admired him so much they desired to see him remembered as a native of Tennessee. The Memphis *Daily Commercial* said Hatton's death "cast a gloom over his native and beloved Tennessee." The editor went on to write that, when all hopes of compromise in the Union failed, "he joined forces with his people of the South, and raised one of the finest regiments in either service." Hatton saw himself as a southerner, and his compatriots acknowledged him as such. In this case, the distinction between Northern Confederate and native southerner faded to the point of irrelevancy over the course of the war.[93]

A vital test of that image occurred with high profile Northern Confederate officers who suffered military setbacks. Unionists and Confederates alike scrutinized the military capability of their soldiers, particularly their generals. As long as their commanders had success, both soldiers and civilians willingly gave them their enthusiastic support. If a general suffered a major defeat, however, he faced a potential backlash from which he might not recover. For example, Union generals Ambrose Burnside and Joseph Hooker, one time commanders of the Army of the Potomac, lost a lot of respect after their defeats at Fredericksburg and Chancellorsville respectively. On the Confederate side, General Braxton Bragg drew the ire of the Confederate populace after he squandered his victory at Chickamauga and subsequently retreated from Chattanooga at the end of 1863. Even General Robert E. Lee did not escape censure after Gettysburg, and he offered to resign because he feared the population had lost confidence in him.[94] Northern Confederates labored under the same standards but with the potential added burden of their backgrounds resurfacing. Few other situations so threatened to tarnish the reputations of these soldiers and give credibility to the image of native northerners as traitors.

As it turned out, Confederate public opinion generally either supported or criticized Northern Confederates based on their military records rather than their northern backgrounds. While some native southerners never trusted them at all, many more gave them a chance as long as they produced results on the battlefield. When they achieved success, Northern Confederates received just as much praise as native southerners. When they suffered defeat, the populace faulted them for poor leadership. In either case, the fact that they originally came from the North usually did not change people's opinion of their status as Confederates and/or southerners. If commentators did accuse a native northerner in the ranks of treason or doubtful loyalty because of his origins, they commonly did so only after a catastrophic defeat. Military success helped to blunt whatever doubts existed about supposed loyalties to native sections. What a soldier contributed on the battlefield counted for far more than his birthplace.

The careers of several highly visible Northern Confederate generals provide evidence for this pattern. Roswell Ripley, a native Ohioan and adopted South Carolinian, served as commander of Charleston for much of the war. Ripley faced possible scrutiny because of his status as a native northerner overseeing the focal point of southern secessionism. Few other places in the Confederacy seemed less hospitable to anyone with northern contacts, much less northern heritage. Although an adopted South Carolinian, Ripley grew up in Ohio and accepted his appointment to West Point from that state. Regardless of his accomplishments, the reality of his heritage had the potential to damn him in the eyes of South Carolinians practically bred on hatred for abolitionist northerners.

Over the course of his command, however, Ripley received not only acceptance but praise for his services. As an adopted South Carolinian and committed secessionist, Ripley helped organize the state's militia, drilled artillerists in Charleston, helped site batteries in the harbor, and participated in the firing on Fort Sumter. His conduct during the engagement, where not a single soldier died, marked him as a rising success story for his adopted state. The *Charleston Mercury,* a mouthpiece of extremist secessionist mentality, lauded Ripley's achievements and claimed he made South Carolina proud. Focusing on his skill as an artillery officer, one editor proclaimed, "thanks to the knowledge, ability, skill and energy of the gallant and popular RIPLEY, the fort was able to do effective service without the loss of a single life. All honor to its noble commander and his dauntless officers and men."[95] More than anything, his successful efforts to prevent a Union invasion of Charleston helped Ripley maintain his reputation. In the spring of 1862, Richmond authorities ordered Ripley to serve in Virginia but returned him to Charleston later that year to recover from wounds. The city's newspapers gave him a fond farewell when he left and were overjoyed when he returned. For the next two years, he improved the defenses of the city and

General Roswell Ripley. A native Ohioan, Ripley became an adopted South Carolinian and directed the cannon fire from Fort Moultrie during the attack on Fort Sumter in 1861. He then became one of two northern-born generals, along with John C. Pemberton, to command Confederate forces at Charleston. Library of Congress.

successfully protected it until 1865, when General Sherman's army forced its evacuation.[96]

Thanks to his successes in Charleston, Ripley's superiors and subordinates rarely expressed anything except admiration for his skills and dedication. While passing through the city in 1863, British colonel Arthur Fremantle remarked that, despite his northern birth, Ripley remained popular in the city for his military exploits and skills. An editor for the *Columbia Carolinian* reported in 1864 on the Union attacks against the Charleston forts and told his readers, "they are all under the command—to give them their greatest efficiency—of the skillful, well tried, devoted veteran, General Ripley, who at the commencement of the war dedicated himself to the cause, and signalized his patriotism, valor and skill by his gallant defence of Fort Moultrie." The *Charleston Mercury* called him "a most useful son" and explained that "Having no sympathies for Abolitionism, and having married a Carolina woman, with interest here, his place was naturally and appropriately among us." In fact, when anonymous sources called for Ripley's removal because of his northern origins, he received the full endorsement of Senator James Orr of South Carolina, Secretary of War James Seddon, and President Jefferson Davis.[97] Nevertheless, one might argue that Ripley rarely came under suspicion only because he never suffered any catastrophic defeats. Under his watch, Charleston withstood years of Union bombardments and remained defiant until nearly the end of the war.

Not all Northern Confederate commanders had the same good fortune. Specifically, Northern Confederate generals along the Mississippi River failed in the tasks assigned to them. In New Orleans in 1862, Generals Mansfield Lovell and Johnson Kelly Duncan, who grew up in New York and Pennsylvania respectively, failed to keep the Union navy out of the city. The next year, Franklin Gardner and John C. Pemberton, also from New York and Pennsylvania, surrendered the vital cities of Port Hudson and Vicksburg. If considerations about their northern roots guided people's views of them, then they should have encountered hostility and charges of treason from civilians and soldiers from the time of their arrival at their commands. Instead, the civilians and soldiers in the area and across the rest of the Confederacy seemed to base their opinions on the generals' effectiveness on the battlefield, with positive feedback during victories and harsh criticism only after a military disaster. This pattern indicates that military considerations played a key role in determining how native southerners reacted to Northern Confederate officers, with northern heritage only a secondary consideration.

The first test of this pattern came when the Union navy targeted New Orleans in the spring of 1862. The largest city in the Confederacy, its capture would enable Union forces to cut off a major supply center while simultaneously tightening the blockade of the Confederacy's coastline. Although General Pierre G. T. Beauregard held overall command of southern Louisiana, Generals Mansfield Lovell and Johnson Kelly Duncan commanded the city's immediate defenses. Since their backgrounds were no secret to the general population, civilians in the area had plenty of opportunity to express their praise or outrage for having non-native southerners leading them. Duncan had the full support of the city because he had lived there for five years, served as Chief Engineer of the Louisiana Board of Public Works, and joined the Confederacy immediately after Louisiana seceded. Lovell, on the other hand, came under more scrutiny because of his work as a street commissioner in New York City, and the fact that he did not arrive in the Confederacy until after secession became a reality.[98] As the weeks passed, Lovell received more respect from citizens thanks to his tireless efforts to prepare the city for defense. For instance, New Orleans resident George Washington Cable recalled how crowds lined the wharves to watch Lovell ride aboard a transport to inspect the forts every day after the Union fleet appeared in the gulf. He also said the crowd loved to see Lovell board his inspection ship, presumably because they believed he wanted to do everything possible to protect the city. As long as both generals did their jobs, few people had any reason to suspect their loyalties.[99]

Once the Union navy successfully captured New Orleans, however, Lovell faced recriminations for the failure of Confederate defenses. People naturally looked for a scapegoat to explain how the Union ships ran past the batteries of the city's forts so easily, and Lovell, as the commander, provided a perfect target. Julia Legrand Waitz, who witnessed the battle, recorded her impressions of Lovell shortly after the city's capture. "In the first place, Lovell, a most worthless creature, was sent here by Davis to superintend the defense of this city. He did little or nothing, and the little he did was all wrong. . . . Lovell knew not what to do; some say he was intoxicated, some say frightened."[100] Mississippian Kate Cumming noted that Lovell faced heavy criticism from her neighbors for his failures. Increasing the speculation, John B. Jones wrote in his diary that the populace blamed Lovell for the disaster, "some to his incompetency, and others to treason." The loss of such an important city, combined with the other recent failures of Confederate forces that year, depressed Confederate morale and left Lovell open to such charges.[101]

Nevertheless, for all his faults, few people actually questioned Lovell's status as a Confederate. Instead, they chastised their commander mainly for his failure to resist the Union attack. Julia Waitz leveled every charge at Lovell, including drunkenness, cowardice, and general incompetence, yet never actually cited his background as a reason for suspicion. She was mainly upset because Lovell had fled the city after the Union gunboats sailed past the forts. Another resident credited Lovell with evacuating all the machinery from the city to save it from falling into Union hands, but still believed Lovell accomplished little, either because of his own shortcomings or because the government did not help him enough. Even Jones, who usually went out of his way to condemn native northerners, instead noted that the city's outrage mainly stemmed from Davis keeping a failed commander in place after so devastating a loss.[102] Lovell's critics concentrated on his military failures rather than his background as the reason for condemnation.[103]

In fact, even after the disaster, Lovell had his defenders, thanks to his defiance of Union authorities. One reporter described how Lovell boarded a steamboat and directed artillery fire onto the Union fleet as it neared the city, despite his lack of guns and useable ships. Returning to the city center, he originally vowed to remain with his troops, but city officials asked him to leave to prevent a Union bombardment. Lovell agreed and retreated seventy miles north to Camp Moore, though not before warning Union admiral David Farragut that any attempt to land troops in the city would be met with musket and artillery fire. A couple of days later, with some of the forts still holding on, city officials changed their minds and contemplated further resistance. Upon hearing the news, Lovell immediately returned and told the mayor he would gladly order his army back to fight to the last man. By then, the mayor had changed his mind again and urged the general to keep his men out of harm's way against a certain Union takeover.[104]

Thanks to his repeated willingness to confront Union troops, Lovell regained some of the respect he had lost after the initial Union ascent up the Mississippi River. The New Orleans *Delta* recorded its admiration when Lovell met with the Union officers and dared them to shell a defenseless city full of women and children. After leaving the meeting, the reporter summarized, "General Lovell . . . was also loudly cheered. He addressed the multitude in a short speech declaring his purpose not to surrender the city, but to retire with his army and fight the Lincolnites, whom they could always whip on land."[105] At least according to this account, Lovell made an excellent show of defiance to the Union forces before evacuating the city. His remarks about standing up to the "Lincolnites" especially helped soothe the populace and win their gratitude.

Later on, after facing a court of inquiry, Lovell bowed to public opinion, resigned his generalship, and rejoined the ranks as a volunteer soldier, showing his willingness to put the Confederacy's needs over his own.[106] Such an act of contrition left no doubt that his ultimate loyalties and identity remained tied with the success of the Confederate armies. One observer even mentioned Lovell's original links with New York but only as a way to reinforce the general's connection with the Confederacy. "When the revolution commenced, he was a citizen of New York. . . . But, abandoning friends, position, fortune and all, he came and offered his great abilities to our people . . . the Southern people will not, when the truth is known, tolerate any wrong or injustice to as true a friend as ever led their sons to battle."[107]

Lovell's subordinate, General Johnson Kelly Duncan, who commanded Fort Jackson below New Orleans, generated even more support from the general populace. After the Union ships sailed past Fort Jackson, Duncan rejected a surrender demand from Admiral David Dixon Porter and vowed to defend the forts to the last man. Unfortunately, the men saw this as an indication that Duncan wanted to sacrifice them for no purpose. Over half of his men ended up mutinying, spiking the guns, and fleeing the fort. Faced with total annihilation, Duncan finally met with Porter to surrender, managing to secure terms allowing his remaining men to return home under parole. As Porter later described the meeting, "'their being was that of men who had gained a victory, instead of undergoing defeat.'"[108]

Duncan's stubbornness largely absolved him of any blame leveled against his superiors and elevated him to hero status. When he reached city hall as a paroled prisoner, the population turned out to cheer him for his determined stand. The city council passed a series of resolutions honoring his dedication to the cause. One of those resolutions insisted, "That Gen. Duncan has well merited of his country, and this city and this State plead for him before the Government of the country the highest rewards that can be offered to bravery and patriotism."[109] Despite his well-known background as a Pennsylvanian, the entire city at that moment linked Duncan with New Orleans, Louisiana, and the Confederacy. The New Orleans *Picayune* wrote that when Duncan reached the city, "he was most enthusiastically greeted by the welcomes of his friends and the cheers of the multitude."[110] The Richmond *Enquirer* went into even more detail on his transformation into an adoptive southern patriot after Duncan's sudden death from illness in December 1862. "General Duncan was by birth, we believe, a Pensylvanian [*sic*], but stern conviction of the right and a sagacious perception of the eternal principles on which only society can be organized, States founded and nations prosper, had made him in heart and soul a Southern soldier."[111] Thanks to his connections to Louisiana and his patriotic defense of a Confederate fort in the face of certain defeat, Duncan never suffered for his northern roots, even though he returned to New Orleans as a defeated prisoner. His personal transition to an adoptive southern identity was confirmed and reinforced by his fellow Confederates fighting a common enemy.

Besides New Orleans, Northern Confederate officers also faced significant challenges farther up the river at Vicksburg and Port Hudson. By the beginning of 1863, both cities represented the last Confederate strongholds connecting the eastern and western halves of the country. If the Union captured them, they would cut the Confederacy in half. In an ironic twist, the fate of both Vicksburg and Port Hudson rested on the efforts of four native northerners. On the Union side, General Ulysses S. Grant of Illinois directed operations against Vicksburg while General Nathaniel Banks of Massachusetts attacked Port Hudson. On the Confederate side, General John Clifford Pemberton of Pennsylvania defended Vicksburg and General Franklin Gardner of New York held the ground at Port Hudson. In few other places did the reality of Northern Confederate commanders hit the Confederate populace with such clarity.

Out of these two commanders, Pemberton faced the greatest challenge to his reputation. Vicksburg held as much, if not more, strategic significance as Richmond, and so Pemberton came under far more scrutiny than nearly any other Northern Confederate during the war. Any Confederate commander would have faced a difficult challenge commanding an army in such a strategically vital location, but Pemberton's background, and the fact that he made several major errors, exposed him to severe criticism and even charges of treason. As a result, he acquired an image as a northern traitor fulfilling the warnings of men like John B. Jones, who said all Northern Confederate acted as fifth columnists.[112]

Despite his popular reputation as the Confederate Benedict Arnold, Pemberton actually faced criticism more for his personality than his heritage. President Davis originally assigned Pemberton to help defend the coastlines of South Carolina and Georgia in 1861. Pemberton then became commander of the department, with his headquarters at Charleston, after General Lee went back to Virginia as Davis's military advisor. When he took over the command, the city did not rise up in arms over the appointment of a Northern Confederate. As Ripley already knew, dedication to the Confederacy and military competence counted for much more in the eyes of the populace.[113] Admittedly, Pemberton did not make many friends because of his no-nonsense style of command and his habit of arguing with his subordinate generals, including putting several under arrest for allegedly disobeying orders. Out of frustration, Governor Francis Pickens demanded that Davis remove Pemberton from command. Davis ultimately bowed to the pressure and reassigned Pemberton to Mississippi at the end of 1862.[114]

Yet Pemberton did not leave his first command under a dark cloud. Although Pickens and many of the soldiers appreciated his departure, others expressed their confidence in Pemberton's abilities and loyalties. Under Pemberton's watch, Charleston remained free from Union invasion, which meant his initial command ranked as a success. Secretary of War George Randolph told Pemberton that his reassignment had nothing to do with either his military ability or suspected loyalties. If anything, it seemed that Pickens simply wanted General Pierre G. T. Beauregard, South Carolina's favorite Fort Sumter hero, back in the state. Randolph assured Pemberton that he and Davis were "satisfied that you were doing everything that could be effected, but if any misfortune should occur it will be impossible to obtain a fair judgment of the case and it will be imputed to you in spite of all proofs to the contrary."[115] Obeying his orders, Pemberton handed over command to Beauregard and headed to Mississippi. When he left, the editors of Charleston's leading newspaper expressed their appreciation for what Pemberton did for the city and affirmed his status as a committed Confederate. As one of the articles proclaimed in its send-off, "He has associated his destinies with us, lived with us, and served us faithfully, and we deem it due to his ardent and unremitting exertions to express our appreciation of his merits as an officer. . . . For he is a soldier—a thorough soldier—and the character of the soldier has stamped itself upon his whole mind and bearing."[116] Similar to Ripley and Duncan and Lovell, Pemberton's efforts on behalf of the Confederacy made him a genuine Confederate in the eyes of his peers, regardless of what they thought about his personality.

Pemberton's reputation only increased once he arrived in Mississippi. His new department was in a state of disarray after the Union navy scored victories at New Orleans and Memphis in the spring and summer of 1862. The previous commander, Mississippian Earl Van Dorn, had declared martial law and provoked uproar among the civilian population, which caused Davis to appoint Pemberton to the post.[117] Despite these difficulties, Pemberton worked tirelessly to shore up the defenses around Vicksburg and bring order back to the command. His efforts bore fruit when Generals Grant and Sherman failed in their first attempt to seize Vicksburg with a frontal assault in the fall of 1862.

Little wonder, then, that Mississippians felt they finally received a commander who could protect them. One eyewitness declared, "Since the appointment of General Pemberton to this command order has been brought out of chaos, and new life, new energy infused into the army and the people. Whatever may be said of the inexperience of General Pemberton as an officer in the field, he has given ample evidence of rare military administrative tact, and proved himself a superior departmental commander."[118] Another observer found him "worthy of trust and confidence" and argued that, since Pemberton came with the full endorsement of both General Lee and President Davis, he received the backing of the local population, especially since Davis, so the thinking went, would never send an inferior general to defend his home state. Although lingering doubts existed, his success on the battlefield earned him the respect and trust he needed to continue with his command.[119] An editor for a Mississippi paper seconded this opinion in the spring of 1863 when he wrote, "Last year, when Gen. Pemberton assumed control of this department, we were menaced by 150,000 Federals. Yet, with not more than 25,000, he so maneuvered his little band that this immense host was kept at bay. He managed to hold Vicksburg and Port Hudson and to stop the enemy's advance from North Mississippi."[120]

Only when the Vicksburg campaign began to unravel did Pemberton feel the full wrath of an angered Confederacy. His losses increased as General Grant defeated him in five separate engagements before encircling the entire Confederate army in Vicksburg by late May 1863. These failures, coupled with earlier suspicions linked to his northern birth, turned public opinion against him. Charges of everything from incompetency to treason circulated widely. In one instance, a correspondent from an Alabama newspaper wrote that, "A general gloom prevails here and people are despondent. The criminations and denunciation of Gen. Pemberton are painful and humiliating. Not a man has a good word for him. The more moderate say that he wants capacity. Bitter, bitter, indeed is the feeling against him." Another correspondent recorded that quartermasters and commissaries in Pemberton's army accused the general of wasting supplies by not ordering their removal before the Union army seized the state capitol at Jackson. He claimed that such missteps caused both soldiers and civilians to "openly accuse him of bad faith." Closer to the front lines, a civilian along the Big Black River recorded the remarks of two soldiers who stopped at her place during the retreat from Jackson. They both blamed Pemberton for the disasters, claiming their regiments never retreated before they came under Pemberton's leadership.[121]

Despite these harsh comments, for most of the siege Pemberton continued to enjoy the confidence and respect of both his soldiers and outside observers alike. His earlier failures tarnished his image, but once Pemberton made clear he would hold Vicksburg until either his whole force starved to death or General Johnston's army rescued the surrounded garrison, opinion began to turn around again. Pemberton's defenders openly chastised those who questioned his patriotism and cited his conduct during the siege as proof of his reliability. For example, one private wrote to his mother at the end of May, "complaints are made of our Comg Genl Pemberton [sic]. which is very wrong & in many instances untrue . . . he has piled Yankee dead upon yankee dead in the ditches before Vicksburg. he risks his own life in the defence of our cause; it is apparent that he now is doing all in his power for us." Another soldier claimed Pemberton boosted morale through his fiery declarations and promises of reinforcements. Just as General Lee maintained the inspiration of his own soldiers after his setbacks at Antietam and Gettysburg, so Pemberton seemed able to accomplish the same feat while awaiting rescue at Vicksburg.[122]

In addition, civilians weighed in with their own renewed confidence for a positive outcome as the siege continued. A reporter for the *Charleston Mercury,* who in May criticized Pemberton several times for getting outmaneuvered by Grant, changed his tone in June thanks to Pemberton's stubbornness. The reporter told his readers, "Confidence in General PEMBERTON since his reply to GRANT'S demand for a surrender, is fully restored. No fears are felt for the result, either at Vicksburg or Port Hudson."[123] Other reporters agreed when they wrote about how Pemberton's refusal to surrender raised his standing among Mississippi's civilians, who only weeks earlier had looked upon him with contempt. In the process, they recognized his status as a fellow Confederate patriot. One reporter said, "The words, that fell from the lips of that Chief, in vindication of himself against the slanderous charge of disloyalty, justly entitle him to our unbounded confidence and our glowing admiration." Another correspondent from Tennessee followed up with his own words of praise: "It has been asserted that he was the spawn of Northern corruption, and, therefore, capable of perfidity or any kind of baseness. . . . This noble patriot can now afford to scorn his traducers and to smile at even death, since he has lived long enough to rescue his name from infamy and to leave it a rich inheritance to his country and his children."[124] As long as Pemberton had the chance for military success, his standing as a Confederate patriot remained intact.[125] The severest criticism Pemberton suffered came when, after only six weeks under siege, Pemberton felt that his men could not endure any longer and surrendered both the city and his army to General Grant's forces.

Once Pemberton surrendered, opinions about him not surprisingly swung against him yet again. Along with losing such a vital city, the timing of the surrender hurt Pemberton's reputation even more. General Lee suffered his famous defeat at Gettysburg at nearly the same time, so news of the fall of Vicksburg only sank Confederate morale further. Pemberton's worst sin, however, occurred when he decided to give up Vicksburg on the Fourth of July. The fact that he surrendered his army on Independence Day seemed to provide proof of a northern-born traitor colluding with fellow northerners to undermine the Confederacy. Many Confederates then believed Pemberton sold out their hopes for maximum Union propaganda, which cemented Pemberton's image as the Confederate Benedict Arnold.[126]

Any support he had in the past seemed to vanish. John B. Jones recorded in his diary three weeks after the surrender, "But all the waters of Lethe will not obliterate the conviction of the people that he gave his army in the West to the enemy. If he had not been Northern born, they would have deemed him merely incompetent. Hence the impolicy of the government elevating Northern over Southern."[127] Mississippi resident Franklin Montgomery recalled, "Some thought he was a traitor then. . . . Surrendering on the 4th day of July, the day of all others which would most fire the northern heart, and nerve it to new efforts to conquer the confederacy . . ." A young Mississippi captain added that many of his comrades started calling Pemberton a traitor. Even one of Pemberton's close friends and defenders, General Richard Taylor, admitted that a large part of the population believed "He had joined the South for the express purpose of betraying it, and this was clearly proven by the fact that he surrendered on the 4th of July, a day sacred to the Yankees."[128] Several others made the same charge and became convinced that Pemberton was nothing but a northern-born fifth columnist who never really supported the Confederacy. Native southerners had the perfect scapegoat for their misfortunes, assigning all blame to northern-born traitors as personified by Pemberton.

Calls for Pemberton's removal increased substantially in the ensuing months. The complaints included Pemberton's relative swiftness in giving up the city, his unfitness for top command, and especially the fact that his men refused to serve under him anymore. Even his supporters admitted that Pemberton had to give up his position, because the stain of Vicksburg would forever tarnish him. Georgia governor Joseph E. Brown likely said it best when he wrote to Secretary of War James Seddon in August 1863, "I have no charge to make against General Pemberton. He may be a good General. But as I have seen a great many of the officers and men who were under him at Vicksburg and have conversed freely with them, and have never yet found a single one of them who has confidence in him . . . ."[129] Brown's words were prophetic because, whenever Davis tried to appoint Pemberton to another command, soldiers threatened to mutiny. Bowing to the pressure, Pemberton resigned his commission in 1864 and never held a significant command again.[130]

Despite what Pemberton's critics said about his traitorous motivations, however, much of the criticism leveled against him actually involved his conduct as a general. Denunciations of Pemberton more often than not focused on military incompetence, rather than suspected treason. Since his failures came on the battlefield, he received the same criticism as any other general who suffered a major defeat. For example, one soldier recounted all the missteps made by Pemberton and how his men lost confidence in his leadership by late June. He claimed Pemberton neglected to reinforce divisions at critical moments and lacked the drive to respond effectively to the crisis. Nowhere in this critique did the soldier bring up Pemberton's background or suspect his loyalty to the cause. Everything he mentioned had to do with military maneuvers.[131] Another private in Mississippi understood the motivations behind the anger against Pemberton as revolving around his military failures. He admitted that Pemberton needed to step down for the good of the army, but he also wrote to a friend, "public opinion, both among the troops and the people, is strongly in prejudice of Genl. Pemberton. . . . I find no one of any consequence expressing the silly opinion that he is a traitor."[132] Even John B. Jones, in his own scathing critique, mainly focused on Pemberton's failure to destroy his remaining supplies to keep them from falling into the hands of the Union.[133] These comments continued the pattern seen repeatedly for Northern Confederate officers. In Pemberton's case, his reputation rose when he succeeded on the battlefield and fell when he failed, with his background only a secondary consideration.

As time passed, his reputation among his fellow Confederates fluctuated yet again. Pemberton's continued devotion to the cause, symbolized by his willingness to give up his high rank and reenlist as a regular soldier, reestablished the admiration many native southerners had for him, even though they continued to criticize his military capability. One newspaper editor reported in 1864, "Pemberton is in command of all the artillery in the fortifications north of the James. We admire his patriotism, in coming down from Lieutenant General to Lieutenant Colonel of artillery, but we would prefer another man."[134] Others came out more forcefully in linking Pemberton with Confederate nationalism. A colonel who served under him at Vicksburg lamented "the unparalleled warfare which has been so violently waged against you by your *countrymen;* for you & I cannot be regarded in any other light than as of the same country as those we are laboring & fighting for." Another one of Pemberton's former officers hoped he would one day receive another command, and if so the men in his Georgia regiment stood ready to fight once again under Pemberton's leadership. In later years, Franklin Montgomery looked back on Pemberton's conduct after Vicksburg and concluded, "he died, I believe, poor and obscure, which goes far to relieve him of the suspicion of treason, which many entertained."[135]

The most detailed defense of Pemberton in the wake of the Vicksburg surrender came from a contributor to a Mississippi paper sometime in the latter half of 1863. Not only did this contributor regard Pemberton as a citizen of the Confederacy; he also described him as an honorary southerner. "He happened to have been born, as remarks the Richmond Dispatch, in a Northern State, and although he had married in Virginia, had reared his children as Southern people, had resided many years among us, and had rejected the offer of a fortune to cast in his lot with the North," the contributor proclaimed. "Those who were wide-mouthed against him are already ashamed of themselves for having reviled a hero. Those who were a little less vehement have veered around, and begin to praise him. . . . Six weeks ago he could not have received common justice from the body of his countrymen.—To-day, he is something very much like an idol."[136] In just one paragraph, the author cited multiple reasons for supporting Pemberton as a patriot, including marrying a southern wife, raising his children in the South, rejecting offers to fight for his native section, having the full confidence of Confederate leaders, and fighting valiantly on the battlefield. Since few native southerners could offer more to the new nation, the contributor felt that Pemberton, and others like him, deserved as much respect as any other Confederate.

The patterns shown in the reactions toward Generals Ripley, Lovell, Duncan, and Pemberton reveal the general perceptions native white southerners held toward most Northern Confederates. Instead of judging them solely on their backgrounds, Confederate public opinion more commonly looked at military accomplishments and personal conduct to decide how to treat these northern-born soldiers. The blind prejudice that could have easily materialized, especially in the wake of catastrophic defeat, did not always happen. Implicitly at least, most native white southerners recognized northern-born soldiers as zealous Confederates fighting for the common goal of independence.

That perception carried over into the postwar period as well. Union soldiers followed the long American tradition of victory in war, while Confederates suffered humiliation as the first Americans to lose a major war. Four years of death and destruction managed to bring the country back together, yet also created a gulf that separated veterans of both sides for the rest of the century. Northern Confederates ended up carrying their newly solidified identities as Confederate veterans into Reconstruction and beyond, which enabled them to largely avoid the hatred and rage directed towards most native northerners. Options formerly available for native northern emigrants to transform their identities disappeared as the newly reunited country entered a new era of increased nationalism coupled with a solidification of sectional identity.

10

The End of an Era: Northern Confederates in Reconstruction and Beyond

The surrender ceremonies at Appomattox Courthouse in Virginia, Durham Station in North Carolina, and elsewhere in 1865 ushered in a new era for all Americans. Four years of war left hundreds of thousands of American lives lost, hundreds of thousands more wrecked in body and soul, thousands of towns and farms ransacked, billions of dollars in wealth eliminated, and a young nation destroyed, never to rise again. Not one person in either the Union or the Confederacy remained unaffected, physically and/or psychologically. For Confederates, the end of the war presented a future more uncertain than any they had ever known. With their nation gone, their destinies lay in the hands of men who for years had trumpeted their subjugation. Yet northerners also faced an uncertain, albeit less shocking, future. They may have won the war, but stitching the nation back together seemed an equally difficult, if not even more daunting, task. Major questions loomed, including the tone of Reconstruction, the rights and opportunities open to freed blacks, the future of former Confederate soldiers, and the amount of time and effort required to complete the healing process.

Northern Confederates potentially faced even more obstacles than their native southern comrades once the war ended. In a way, these individuals ended up as the worst losers. Their native section, which they had shunned, now stood triumphant. All of the warnings of northern families and friends came to pass. The lives they had built in the South appeared utterly destroyed. Even more devastating, the Confederacy itself, the nation they had an equal hand in creating and defending, had disappeared. Theoretically at least, Northern Confederates had no place to return to that they could truly call home. No matter where they turned, these men and women faced potential hostility from both white northerners, who felt they had betrayed their heritage, and white southerners, who might lump them together with all other native northerners despite the sacrifices they made over the previous four years.

Fortunately for these veterans, the Northern Confederates documented in this study not only survived but often thrived in the postwar era, thanks largely to those sacrifices. Most Northern Confederate veterans shared with native southerners a continued expression of a common identity as white southerners and Confederates. Those identities did not crumble with the Confederacy but, rather, hardened precisely because of its failure. All of them had spent part or most of their adult lives in the South, along with four years fighting for Confederate independence. The Union may have destroyed their adopted section, but that did not mean they wished to resume their status as northerners. If anything, Northern Confederate veterans simply wished to follow the path of any other white southerner by salvaging as much as they could from the wreckage of war. Most of them managed to rebuild their lives one way or another in the postwar South. Some achieved even more success than when they first moved to the South, others failed to rebuild their shattered fortunes, and still others fell somewhere in between. Regardless of success or failure, they all made a conscious decision to rededicate themselves to their adopted section.

In the process, a major shift occurred that profoundly altered the dynamics of sectional identity and nationalism throughout the country. Before the war, native white northerners and southerners alike had the option of crossing sectional borders to start a new life and potentially transform their sectional identity. Once the war ended, however, crossing the old line between free and slave states no longer worked in the same way, not least because slavery no longer existed. Thousands of northerners continued to move to the southern states, but after the war white southerners viewed all such emigrants as alien trespassers and occupiers. Regardless of their motives, northern emigrants now carried the moniker of "Yankee," "Carpet-bagger," or other label to set them apart. Nor did these newcomers ever really perceive themselves as southerners. Instead, they viewed their relocation merely as a way for inspired northerners to help the South back on its feet or profit from the destruction around them. The Civil War thus represented the cut-off point for the kind of cross-sectional emigration enjoyed by previous generations.[1]

In a time when sectional identity supposedly weakened, native southern and Northern Confederate veterans together actively worked to build another invisible, though no less potent, wall of separation between the sections. Despite efforts by people on both sides to bring about reunification and reconciliation, the South emerged with its sectional character not only intact but strengthened. The Confederate nation, though short-lived, provided a blue-print for the survival of a postwar collective southern identity. Just as Union veterans shared a common bond through their efforts to save the Union, so did Confederate veterans remain linked through a common bond of sacrifice for independence. Northern Confederates shared that bond and so became the final generation of adoptive southerners in the nineteenth century. While no one called for a renewal of Confederate independence, identification with the South gained strength among native and adoptive southern whites through the collective memory of the recent conflict.

These insights contribute to our understanding of the other transitions that took place once Confederates laid down their arms. The conclusion of the Civil War thoroughly transformed the nature of the United States and the lives of its citizens. The most obvious change involved the total elimination of slavery and a culture based upon that institution. Although white southerners eventually created a new racial system in the form of segregation, the battle waged between the free-labor North and slave-labor South had ended with the total victory of the North's vision. In addition, civilian interaction with the federal government had changed dramatically. Before the war, civilians normally encountered the federal government only through the post office and national elections and relied much more heavily on local and state governments for their everyday lives. Both the Union and Confederate governments changed that relationship by passing income taxes, enforcing drafts, and taking over certain industries. After the war, Congress increased federal power further with the passage of the Thirteenth, Fourteenth, and Fifteenth Amendments to the Constitution, which symbolized a major shift in power from the states to the federal government.

On a more fundamental level, the conflict permanently ended the "compact theory" of Union created by John C. Calhoun, which represented a major justification for the legality of secession. As historian James McPherson has argued, before the war Americans wrote that the United States "are a country;" after the war that phrase changed to the United States "is a country." In other words, the war allowed a collection of separate states to finally emerge as a united nation. President Lincoln himself referred mostly to the Union in his First Inaugural Address, whereas in the Gettysburg Address and his Second Inaugural Address he referred much more often to the nation.[2] All of these events, and many others, symbolized the transition of the United States from its antebellum roots into the late nineteenth- and early twentieth-century powerhouse of the Western Hemisphere.

Many historians argue that the North successfully reincorporated the South into this new nation, with state and sectional identity weakened in favor of national unity.[3] They cite such events as the Spanish-American War, where former Confederate general Joseph Wheeler led troops into battle wearing the Union blue, and the fiftieth anniversary of Gettysburg in 1913, when veterans reenacting Pickett's Charge shook hands at the stone wall on Cemetery Ridge.[4] They also point to the creation of the myth of the Lost Cause and other forms of collective memory that allowed southern whites to celebrate their past while also contributing to the greater good of the nation.[5]

Despite these examples of reconciliation, however, several counter-examples demonstrate the reluctance of the South to abandon its sectional character. White southerners especially looked for any way to limit the changes wrought by the war and reestablish the South's supposed glory days. The experiment of Reconstruction ended in failure partly because of resistance from former Confederates, who allowed Redeemer Democrats to recapture state legislatures and initiate the one-party rule that dominated the South for generations.[6]

The myth of the Lost Cause assisted in this endeavor. Organizations like the Sons of Confederate Veterans and United Daughters of the Confederacy worked tirelessly to promote the Lost Cause interpretation of the Civil War through speeches, fundraisers, and monuments. The United Daughters were so successful that they actually managed to erect memorials to Confederate soldiers in the states of Wisconsin and Montana.[7] Kentucky, though officially a part of the Union during the war, in the ensuing years identified far more with the Lost Cause South than with the victorious North, making it effectively what historian Jack Hutchinson calls "the last Confederate state."[8] In the most shocking example, some white citizens in Vicksburg refused to celebrate the Fourth of July, one of the most revered national holidays, because General Grant captured the city on that day. These residents maintained the boycott for over eighty years, until the end of World War II, when they finally joined the rest of the city in launching fireworks to celebrate the signing of the Declaration of Independence once again.[9]

Into this environment stepped Northern Confederate veterans and adoptive southern unionists. The first task they faced involved where to go once the guns ceased firing. Out of the original three hundred and three individuals documented, thirty-nine did not survive the war and an additional seventeen did not leave sufficient records to determine their whereabouts, leaving a total of two hundred and forty-seven to analyze. They faced three viable options: stay in the South, return to the North, or abandon the United States altogether for a fresh start abroad. Nearly three quarters, one hundred and eighty-one of the survivors, remained in the South for the rest of their lives. An additional thirty-one lived in both the South and the North at different times. Only twenty opted to return to the North without ever living in the South again. Finally, nine lived abroad and six more lived in both the South and a foreign country at different times. Clearly, both Northern Confederate veterans and their adoptive southern unionist counterparts mainly wanted to stay with their adopted section and maintain their adopted identities.[10]

Having decided to remain in the devastated South, these men and women worked hard to rebuild their lives. Some of them returned to their adopted states, while others struck out for new opportunities across the South, as they had done when they first crossed the Mason-Dixon Line so many years earlier. In a way, their new journey mirrored their initial emigration, because they often started out with very little thanks to the destruction inflicted by the Union armies. As though drawing on that inspiration, they once again blended into southern society by starting new careers or reviving old ones. Postwar occupations included, but were not limited to, the law, teaching, government, politics, business, manufacturing, farming, and writing. The most popular of these occupations among Northern Confederate veterans were almost identical to what they did before the war. Fifty worked in the educational field for different periods of time as teachers, professors, or administrators. Forty-seven worked as lawyers or judges. Around fifty created or restarted their own businesses or manufacturing firms. Forty worked as farmers or planters. Fifteen continued work in the church, ten as doctors, and fifteen as newspaper editors. Basically, they returned to the professional ranks that had first propelled them into southern society.

A sampling of biographical information provides a general picture of postwar life for Northern Confederate veterans. Edward Drummond returned to his adopted state of Georgia upon his parole. He immediately started work as a cotton broker for a commission house in Savannah and raised his family there. Although he reestablished contact with his family back in Maine, he never thought about moving back to New England and even persuaded his brother to move to Georgia to join him in the business.[11] Another native New Englander, General Albert Pike, initially faced indictment for treason, but when the federal government dropped the charges, he left behind his adopted state of Arkansas to settle in Memphis and later Washington, D. C. He resumed his prewar career as a lawyer, author, and advocate for Native Americans.[12] Adopted Georgian George P. Swift set up a partnership back in Georgia dealing in cotton and cloth trading.[13] Prewar newspaper editor George Kendall, who originally settled in New Orleans, acquired a sheep ranch in Texas.[14] Edward Wells stayed in South Carolina after the war to work in an office. Like Drummond, he reestablished contact with his family back in New York but remained in South Carolina for the rest of his life.[15] Edward Sparrow, a former Confederate congressman, was more fortunate than most because, when he returned to his home in Louisiana, it remained largely intact. He managed to sell his plantation for over eighty thousand dollars the next year.[16] Each of these men displayed the general pattern for postwar Northern Confederate veterans: returning to their adopted section, finding work, building or rebuilding fortunes, and seeking new opportunities in other southern states when appropriate.[17]

The educational field in the South especially witnessed a mass return of Northern Confederate veterans at both the local and college level. Henry B. McClellan, who first moved to the South as a teacher, moved to Kentucky to work as a professor at Sayre Female Institute in Lexington from 1869 until his death in 1904. Another native Pennsylvanian, Robert McClellan, who ran a boys school in Georgia before the war, opened a new school in Macon and taught there until 1871. Jedediah Hotchkiss reopened his old school at Loch Willow immediately after the war and later taught at Washington College. Massachusetts native and Confederate veteran William Arthur Sheppard returned to his post as a professor at Randolph Macon College in Virginia, serving there for the rest of his life.[18] The University of the South in Tennessee hosted several Northern Confederates during Reconstruction, including the former head of the Confederate Ordnance Bureau, Josiah Gorgas. Gorgas initially attempted to remain in his wife's home state of Alabama by working as a superintendant at the Briarfield Iron Furnace, but the business failed after a few years. Facing bankruptcy, he felt lucky when the university offered him a job as a professor and vice-chancellor. Gorgas remained at that post for nearly a decade. At the same time, another Northern Confederate veteran, Charles Quintard, also accepted a position at that university in the early 1870s, while serving as Episcopal Bishop of Tennessee.[19] Gorgas worked to create the best accommodations for the next generation of southern students and Quintard acted as the university's chief fundraiser, seeking contributions and endowments around the country.[20]

Other Northern Confederate veterans engaged in politics and government. On the state level, seven served in their city governments, twelve in their state's legislature, and five as a mayor. On the national level, nine were elected as congressmen and senators, while an additional two, one a unionist and the other a Confederate veteran, served in the cabinets of President Ulysses S. Grant.

In just a few examples, adopted Texan Ashbel Smith took his oath of amnesty in March 1865 and immediately stood for election to the Texas legislature. For the next decade Smith participated as an unapologetic critic of all Republican Reconstruction policies and as a Texas delegate to every national Democratic presidential convention.[21] Albert Blanchard worked as a city surveyor in the city of New Orleans.[22] Jonathan Clark Greely, a Maine native and adopted Floridian who served in the Florida legislature during the war, continued his public life, only this time as a Republican mayor of Jacksonville in 1872. Similarly, native New Yorker Samuel Phillips served in the wartime legislature of North Carolina as a peace candidate and then became a Republican speaker of the legislature in 1865.[23] Fellow native New Yorker and adopted Texan Christopher Upson started his postwar career as a lawyer and remained active in politics. In 1877, he filled a vacancy in his Texas district as a congressman. He stood for election the next year and served in Congress as a Democrat from 1879 to 1883.[24] President Grant selected Horace Maynard, an adoptive southern unionist in Tennessee, as his postmaster general. Grant later selected a Northern Confederate veteran, New Hampshire native and adopted Georgian Amos Akerman, as his attorney general; he served for a year and played a leading role in prosecuting Ku Klux Klan members.[25] Across the political spectrum, these men attempted to rebuild their adopted states directly as elected officials for the people they had fought beside in the war.[26]

Along with efforts to restart their careers, Northern Confederate veterans faced potential challenges to their adopted identities as the country maneuvered through the difficulties of Reconstruction and reconciliation. Throughout the latter half of the nineteenth century, both white northerners and white southerners attempted to heal the wounds of the recent war through collective symbolism and patriotism.[27] Yet even as these projects materialized, neither section felt similar to the other, which presented obstacles to full reconciliation. Ashbel Smith heard from some of his northern relatives about this problem toward the end of Reconstruction. Smith's cousin, J. H. Williams, hoped that cross-sectional harmony might prevail but lamented that others in his community did not think so. Williams told Smith that people in Connecticut heard that southerners did not distinguish "between a Northern man South who holds to principles and one who allies himself to a miserable horde of thieves and carpet baggers." Williams feared that, based on those assumptions, vengeful northerners might even find a pretense for reinvading places like Georgia and Texas, because of all the supposed attacks by white southerners against northerners living in those states.[28] As a result, those like Smith's cousin wished for reconciliation but feared that negative perceptions of the South by northerners might hinder those efforts, as well as provide challenges for Confederate veterans with northern roots.[29]

White northerners were not the only ones who came to this conclusion. Native southerners, both during and after Reconstruction, commented on the continued difficulties in reconciliation thanks to strengthening sectional identities. In some instances, the myth of southern superiority over inferior Yankees lived on in the minds of veterans. For example, Confederate veteran Hunter McGuire wrote several letters to his friend Jedediah Hotchkiss reminiscing about the glory days of the Army of Northern Virginia and its soldiers. McGuire declared, "I am glad to see that they [northerners] at last recognize and are obliged to confess the superiority of the Southern soldier. . . . The whole explanation can be given in a nutshell. The Southern soldiers were a different breed of people from the Northern."[30] A few months later, McGuire sent a similar letter to Hotchkiss expanding on his views by insisting that upbringing and lack of immigrants accounted for southern stubbornness on the battlefield.[31] Such expressions of superiority were common among white southerners in the lead-up to war, but McGuire wrote these opinions in 1897, long after both the war and Reconstruction rendered such boasting obsolete. In a similar line of reasoning, General Richard Taylor, who had commanded much of the Trans-Mississippi Department, also recalled in his memoirs the outcome of First Manassas and his own theory about why the Union lost that battle. "The first skirmishes and actions of the war," Taylor declared, "proved that the Southron, untrained, was a better fighter than the Northerner—not because of more courage, but of the social and economic conditions by which he was surrounded . . . ."[32]

Even at the turn of the twentieth century, myths of white southern superiority appeared to live on in the collective memory of white southern society. The continued insistence of Confederate exceptionalism affected white southern views of northerners throughout the postwar era. By the end of the war, white southern attitudes toward northerners ranged from indifference to outright hostility. Sydney Andrews of Charleston recalled how, at the beginning of Reconstruction, northern men came down to the city and were immediately met with hostility by the city's population. A New York woman taking a trip to New Orleans remarked that southerners on board her ship used disrespectful language toward northern passengers and remained opposed "to this movement of the 'Yankees' south . . . ." In Arkansas, a unionist foreman of a grand jury in Randolph County testified on the prevalence of die-hard secessionist sentiment among the population. One man even swore "that he would shoot any man who would raise the U. States flag in Jonesboro." Clearly, the postwar environment bred a persistent suspicion between the sections, along with a hardening of southern identity in the face of defeat.[33]

Despite this hostile and volatile environment, most Northern Confederate veterans managed to avoid such negative associations. Though they shared the northern heritage and families of carpetbaggers and "Yankees," thanks to their service in the Confederacy they claimed as much right to call themselves southerners as those born in the region, and they defended that claim vociferously. Whether they supported or resisted efforts at reconciliation, they all shared a core identity built in the prewar South and solidified in the fires of the Civil War. Other northern emigrants in the latter half of the nineteenth century may have poured into the South searching for opportunity, but they remained northerners in their own eyes and those of their communities. Northern Confederates represented the last generation of native northerners in the nineteenth century with the ability to assimilate completely into southern society and avoid the negative imagery associated with their native section.

When discussing sectional identity, therefore, Northern Confederates mainly reacted in the same manner as native white southerners in the postwar era. Since they shared in the culture of defeat bred by the Confederacy's downfall, these men and women had little trouble extending the associations forged during the war into its aftermath. For instance, in the 1890s, Northern Confederate veteran Edward Wells sought to publish his own history of General Wade Hampton's cavalry. Wells especially feared bias from publishing houses in the North that might not advertise books written by Confederate veterans. As he wrote to a friend asking for advice, "This is, I think, especially likely to be the case, where the book is candidly written from a Southern ('unrepentant') stand-point." He went on to request information on any publishing houses willing to publish a "Southern book," so he did not risk being "gouged" by a northern publisher.[34] Josiah Gorgas wrote letters to Jefferson Davis after Reconstruction addressing him as "My Dear President," while dismissing the ineffectiveness of a Congress dominated by northerners.[35] In a time when a broader American nationalism should have manifested itself, Northern Confederate veterans merely added to the desire to maintain sectional differentiation.[36]

Ashbel Smith took this type of rhetoric to another level. Smith, though a firm opponent of Reconstruction and Republicans, did support efforts at industrialization and other reforms. Like many other Confederate veterans, Smith knew the Old South could not return, but he still hoped to retain some semblance of state and sectional distinctiveness against the growing power of the federal government. Toward the end of Reconstruction, Smith wrote to the governor of Texas pressing for more internal improvements, especially the completion of a new transcontinental railroad, because of its importance to "ourselves, Texas and the whole South . . . ." In the same letter, in veiled language meant to address the North, Smith described a county convention he attended where he spoke on the same issues, which he considered vital "to the whole southern country involving a question of justice on one side and of a gross wrong attempted to be perpetrated by the other injurious to our people by parties living elsewhere . . . ."[37] Even with the South fully reintegrated into the Union, Smith still considered the region to be almost a separate country in need of protection from outsiders.

Several years later, Smith reiterated those feelings in a speech he gave in support of better education for Texas students. He wanted the University of Texas to provide a home-grown education for Texas youth since, in his mind, students that went elsewhere for education brought back ideas unfavorable to fellow citizens. Smith also said that if all young Texans went to the state university, they would "unify the people of the State, make them one homogeneous community. They unify all the sentiments of all sections; make the citizens of these various sections to understand each other, to esteem each other, and all of us to feel that all our great interests are in common—one and the same, including the existence of the State one and indivisible." Smith's rhetoric sounded much like Frederick Barnard's appeal to Mississippians before the war to keep their educated youth within the state. The experiences of war did not destroy such thinking; they reinforced it.[38]

Throughout the postwar period, some veterans and civilians even refused to utilize their associations with the North when it might have helped them rebuild their shattered lives. For example, Union agents in South Carolina set up a claims commission after the war designed to cover damages inflicted on unionists in the state. Anyone could appear before the commission, proclaim their unionist sympathies, and possibly receive compensation for some or even all of their claims. Northern officials had a sympathetic ear for such testimony, because it reinforced their theories about the prevalence of unionists in the South who only seceded because of manipulation by secessionist radicals. Where better to prove that theory than in South Carolina, the most radical state of them all? Adoptive southerners, especially if they had not served in the Confederate armies, theoretically stood to gain the most, because commission members would love to hear of native northerners in the South seeking to maintain their unionism amidst radical southerners.

The 1860 census recorded over thirteen hundred native northerners in South Carolina who could have potentially submitted claims through the commission. The actual results, however, highlighted these individuals' desire either to maintain their allegiance to the state or, if they filed for claims, to ignore their northern heritage. According to the commission records, out of five hundred and seventy-eight cases brought before the commission in the 1870s, only four claimants mentioned a northern background. The other roughly thirteen hundred native northerners in the state either served in the Confederate army, and therefore disqualified themselves, or made their pleas as southern unionists. In a situation where a northern background might help their case financially, nearly all native northerners in the state chose not to betray their adopted southern identity in that manner.[39]

More than anyone else, former Confederate general Samuel Gibbs French provided a detailed look at the personal views of like-minded Northern Confederate veterans in the postwar period. French published a lengthy memoir detailing his experiences as a soldier in the Mexican War, where he served as a West Point graduate from New Jersey, and the Civil War, where he joined the Confederacy as an adopted Mississippian. Writing several decades after both conflicts, French showed how much the Civil War and its aftermath affected his identity. He provided a vigorous defense of the Confederacy and perpetuated the idea of sectional distinctiveness. In the process, he demonstrated how Northern Confederate veterans still had the ability, unlike postwar northern emigrants, to regard themselves as southerners. He never again considered himself part of the North, living the rest of his life as an unreconstructed Confederate.[40]

Throughout his memoir, following the same patterns utilized by Northern Confederates during the war to define themselves as Confederate soldiers, French went out of his way to align himself with the South, while branding the North an alien and even dangerous region. In his descriptions about his early life, French mentioned his home and family in New Jersey, but his prose reflected that of a displaced planter longing for the Old South more than a northern-born soldier fondly remembering his prewar service. French declared early in the first chapter, "When I was young it was not considered complimentary or prudent to call a boy of your own size a 'Yankee' . . . *All your life* you have heard the people of this country north of the slave States called Yankees, and the people south Confederates, which is not true, but only an incident of war."[41] Knowing that the term "Yankee" carried a negative connotation among his white southern brethren, French sought to distance himself from that moniker. By his assessment, only New England fell within the perimeter of "Yankee" character, which excluded himself because of his heritage in the Mid-Atlantic.

The latter half of French's memoir provided even more insights. Within the battlefield descriptions and apologias common in the postwar writings of ex-Confederates, French wanted to declare his pride as a Confederate veteran. At one point in his prose, French fondly remembered that, by the end of 1864, "the men in the army had become the *Confederacy,* and to them the power was virtually transmitted, and the commanders of armies held the destiny of the nation in their hands."[42] French counted himself among those men. Nowhere did French reveal himself as more of a committed southerner, however, than in his treatment of Reconstruction. Adopting Lost Cause themes, French portrayed life in the South during Reconstruction as horrific, with honest white southern laborers overwhelmed by the greed and corruption of northerners and blacks. At one point he equated Reconstruction with "annexation," implying the Union forcefully took over a foreign nation.[43] While not always so blatant, much of his rhetoric involved carpetbaggers bankrupting the South for their own ends. The generic carpetbagger, in his mind, mainly came "from the Eastern States," meaning New England. French did not seem to notice that many native southerners considered all northerners, which would have included himself a decade earlier, to be hated carpetbaggers. It did not matter because he counted himself as a part of the South, or at least as a foe of the negative traits of "Yankees."[44]

Finally, at the close of his memoirs, French all but declared the continued existence of the Confederacy. Despite his professions of loyalty to the reconstructed United States, his closing words indicated that no amount of reconciliation would ever erase the bond among Confederate veterans produced by the war. "For this inalienable right—a right that has been exercised by almost every nation on earth, and for which millions and millions of lives have been sacrificed—the States seceded, and it will never die. . . , " he wrote, "Their achievements were great, but their cause was greater; their deeds are immortal, their cause eternal, and paid for in blood."[45]

As French indicated, service in the Confederate armies provided Northern Confederates with all the justification required to call themselves southerners. These men had already established new lives in the southern states but, as veterans in the fight for southern freedom, they grew that much closer to their adopted section. Returning to the North was still possible, but reestablishing themselves as part of the North seemed ever more remote. The day they entered Confederate service was the day they established once and for all their identity as adoptive southerners. As an Englishman who served in the Army of Northern Virginia described in his memoirs about his efforts to obtain American citizenship, "The officer in command at Petersburg told me that my claim would not be considered, unless I could show that I was an American citizen, or intended to become one. As a matter of fact, I had become a citizen of Virginia, by my service in the Confederate Army." The Englishman eventually received his citizenship in 1867, but in his mind his true claim to citizenship came with his connection to the Confederate forces.[46]

Northern Confederate veterans felt the same way. Charles Dahlgren made such a case in 1868 when he wrote to his son explaining his decision to stay in Mississippi rather than return to Pennsylvania, as his father and brothers urged him to do. He claimed that the righteousness of the Confederate cause, as well his own ties to Mississippi, drove him into the Confederate ranks. Dahlgren even admitted that he would have received better rank, privilege and wealth in the Union forces. Nevertheless, as he told his son, "it had no influence with me to possess those things. I believed the South was right and I remained true to my principles and now after all my trials & hardships, after my reduction from wealth to poverty & compelled to live in a conquered country, I stand as firm, unflinching, & unchanged as at first. I would unhesitatingly do the same thing."[47] Similar to prewar southern army officers, Dahlgren turned down lucrative appointments in the Union army for the much greater risk of Confederate independence and the protection of his adopted state and nation. The passage of time did nothing to change his mind about the wisdom of his original choice.

Northern Confederate veteran Edward Wells expressed the same convictions. He recalled in one of his postwar letters, "I believed the South was in the right—believe so now—always have—I had made many warm friendships of both sexes. I wished to go with the Confederate Army . . . But friends represented to me, that I would be of more use to the cause—The cause of Civil liberty—at the north."[48] Wells took that advice and returned to New York, graduated from law school, and opened a law office. He kept expecting others to come around to his point of view but after two years grew impatient. The New York draft riots in 1863 seemed like the perfect spark for a general revolt, but nothing came of it. Even his father, whom he considered a firm states' rights Democrat, still told his son that his ultimate allegiance belonged with New York, his native state, no matter where she turned. Faced with such pressure, Wells might have easily given in and sworn allegiance to the Union. Instead, he immediately made plans to abandon New York and enlist in a South Carolina cavalry regiment.

Wells argued that he returned to South Carolina because he always believed in the justice of the Confederate cause. He considered his mission to his native state a failure, yet did not let that failure dissuade him from his greater purpose. As he wrote toward the end of his correspondence, "I at once made up my mind, that this consideration [getting drafted into the Union army] absolved me from all obligation of duty to the North, & permitted, nay, necessitated, my going to fight on the side of the right, in the Confederate Army. I believed this, *then,* & believe *now* that I was entirely right in my decision, which I have never since, at any time, for one second, regretted."[49] Wells defended his conduct as zealously as any other Confederate veteran, sealing his own identity as both a Confederate and a southerner. Serving in the Confederate ranks had allowed him to transform his identity.[50]

A similar situation occurred with Amelia Lines. Lines, who grew up in New York but lived in Georgia during the war, initially moved to Connecticut with her husband and children at the beginning of Reconstruction for financial reasons. She nevertheless yearned to return to her home in Georgia. She wrote to her sister in September 1865, "We should not be laying plans to get out of 'Dixie.' People from the South meet with very little sympathy here. They seem to think we have had little to eat and wear during the war and ought to be very humble in our aspirations and desires when we come to reside in the land of our *conquerors.*"[51] By 1871, Lines and her family managed to return to Georgia and spent the rest of their lives there. She considered herself a southerner the entire time. As she recorded in her diary, "Ladies at the North think Southern ladies have nothing to do because they keep servants to do their work, but if we perform less labor we have more care and anxiety, so our lot is not so much easier after all."[52]

Assertions of an adopted southern identity appeared in letters, diaries, and speeches from other Northern Confederate veterans as well. Some of these men and women took their identity for granted by this point, so they did not feel the need to stress the theme repeatedly in their writings. Still, the instances when they did mention the subject left little doubt of where they stood. As southern diarist Susan Eppes remarked in 1866, "The Sprague girls, Maggie and Mary . . . are such nice, pleasant young ladies. When I had known them a few days I said I would not have imagined they were from the North. They laughed and said they had been almost raised in the South."[53] Edmund Dewitt Patterson's grandson wrote that his grandfather, though rarely talking about the war during his lifetime, always insisted that "he had been a rebel and had never been reconstructed," and never fully reconciled with his family back in Ohio.[54] Jedediah Hotchkiss expressed his constant love for Virginia in his postwar correspondence. When he took the stand as a witness for a trial in Kentucky, a prosecutor asked where he came from and he replied, "Virginia, Sir, Augusta County, VA." Hotchkiss knew that was not the case because in other letters he referred to his childhood home in Windsor, New York, and the happy times spent at Windsor schools. He even recalled that some of the Union troops who captured Harpers Ferry likely came from New York, and therefore he had a decent chance to run into someone "from my native county." Still, Virginia remained the only place where he truly felt at home, and references to his native state of New York were merely wistful remembrances of another life.[55]

As a respected veteran, as well as geographical and mineralogical expert, Hotchkiss traveled frequently to dispense advice yet always felt reluctant to stray too far from his Virginia home. At the end of Reconstruction, when an acquaintance asked him to join a new mining enterprise in Brazil, Hotchkiss told his daughter, "but I cannot see my way in that direction—& feel like Gen. Lee when asked to go to Mexico after the war—when he replied—'I love the mountains of Virginia still.'" His attachments ran so deep that he did not even want his children following in his footsteps. Before the war, he eagerly found a new life outside his native state, but with his family settled, he wanted everyone to remain in the valleys that he loved. Hotchkiss stressed that theme several times to his daughters when they thought about marrying outside Virginia. His daughter Nellie courted a Georgia gentleman, and Hotchkiss replied that, while he liked Georgians, the Shenandoah Valley still ranked as the most beautiful place in the world, in his opinion, and so wondered why she should give that up. An even more telling piece of advice came from a trip he made to England, when he described how so many Virginia families traced their roots back to Yorkshire. Implicitly, he attempted to stake his claim to such roots even though his own family still resided in New York.[56]

Northern Confederate veterans in Texas echoed Hotchkiss's love for an adopted state. In a letter written in the last year of his life, in 1867, New Hampshire native George Kendall confided to a friend, "With Texas air, Texas exercise and Texas habits generally—active, out-door and bracing—and I can go on for years barring accidents and ordinary ills . . . ."[57] Kendall did not last that long, but Texas still represented the last place he ever wished to reside. Ashbel Smith lauded the characteristics of Texans defending Galveston. Insisting that his men fought to the last, Smith wrote to an acquaintance about his great admiration "for the patience and obedience of our Texian soldiers . . . under the restraints of military discipline in those trying circumstances."[58] The Confederacy might have died, but the spirit of Texas soldiers lived on in the memory of their accomplishments in protecting their native state. Smith and Kendall latched onto that legacy through their own accomplishments in defense of their adopted state.

Such declarations also appeared in connection with the southern region as a whole. Joseph Garey recalled how, on the advice of his brother and in response to the general deterioration of the Confederacy, he actually abandoned his Confederate regiment to make his way to Pennsylvania to rejoin his family in 1864. Despite this betrayal of his duty, by 1866 Garey missed the South so much that he decided to go back, settling in Memphis. The hazards of war pushed him out of the Confederate army, but his attachment to the South ensured his eventual return.[59] Massachusetts native Caroline Gilman made an even more explicit statement when she described the similarities between bringing her husband's body to Charleston for burial and her own return to Charleston after the war: "In 1858 I journeyed with a coffin, where was laid my love and earthly hope, and came *home*. In 1865 I journeyed with the dead South, and came *home*."[60] In the first case, she escorted her deceased husband, who also grew up in Massachusetts, to the place they both considered their true home. Seven years later a much greater death occurred, in the form of the Confederacy, yet Gilman felt more attached to the South than ever.

Others displayed their adopted identities through unmitigated hatred of their native section. Like so many other Confederate veterans, these men regarded the North's subjugation of the South as barbaric. For example, Thomas Clemson, a former mining agent for the Confederate government, spent the first couple of years of Reconstruction attempting to redeem his properties, even traveling to Washington and New York to obtain a pardon and financial backers. Rather than view the trip as a chance to reconnect, Clemson reacted with nothing but despair. The contrast between northern wealth and southern poverty disgusted him, and he vowed not to spend one minute longer in the region than necessary. As his biographer summarized, "he told James Edward that 'the North is no place for a Confederate.' He was pleased to return to the South 'where the majority is poor.'"[61] Similarly, Charles Dahlgren ultimately turned to the North to rebuild his shattered fortunes but never felt reconnected with his boyhood home. He wanted to return to Mississippi as quickly as possible and knew others felt the same way. In fact, when state elections in New York and New Jersey favored

Republicans in late 1865, Dahlgren noted that all the white southerners he knew in those states immediately left, certain that no one other than native northerners could successfully live there any longer.[62]

In a more extreme example, former ambassador John Slidell wanted to stay as far away from the North as possible so long as northerners, especially Republicans, dominated the country. With his assets in Louisiana seized and his salary as a Confederate ambassador eliminated, Slidell faced extreme hardship and poverty in Paris; yet the thought of bowing to Union demands sickened him. He wrote to fellow ex-Confederate diplomat James Mason in 1866, "Nothing would induce me ever to become a citizen of the U. S. nor will any of my children, I trust, ever establish themselves there. Indeed could I return tomorrow to Louisiana, be elected by acclamation to the Senate and received without contradiction at Washington, I would shrink with disgust from any association with those who now pollute the Capitol."[63] He did not wish to return to his adopted state as long as northerners remained in power there, preferring to come back only when southerners like himself controlled it once again. As a result, Slidell endured exile as a potent symbol of his desire to never reconcile with his native section.

At least a dozen other Northern Confederate veterans viewed living in exile as preferable to living under perceived enemy occupation. They spent years, sometimes the rest of their lives, in places like Canada, Mexico, or Europe. The reasons for such a decision varied but usually involved fears of Union retaliation and vengeance. Slidell himself remained in France for several years to see how events played out. Part of his correspondence in those years revealed his worries. He wrote to his friend Edward Butler in December 1867, "I have had but very scanty correspondence with my old friends in Louisiana because I feared to compromise them by any communication from such adverse traitor as I am [appear] to be in after the cessation of hostilities."[64] Though he may have appeared overly cautious, especially since President Andrew Johnson had issued thousands of pardons, recollections of Union officials showed the wisdom of Slidell's course, at least in the short term. When Slidell sent an official letter to the government in 1866 requesting a temporary visit to the United States to take care of some business affairs, Secretary of War Edwin Stanton urged President Johnson to approve the request and then arrest Slidell as soon as he reached American shores.[65] Although the threat was never carried out, high-ranking Confederates abroad clearly faced possible hostility should they ever return.[66] Several

Northern Confederate veterans had similar fears. Caleb Huse remained in France for several years before he felt safe enough to return to the United States. George Alexander, the commander of Castle Thunder Prison, learned the Union government placed him on a list of war criminals for alleged abuses of Union prisoners. Rather than submit to a trial and possibly face execution, Alexander fled and eluded Union authorities as he traveled up the Mississippi River to Canada, where he found a job as a French tutor.[67]

A few expatriates never made it back to either their native or adopted sections. Aaron Conrow, the Ohio-born representative from Missouri in the Confederate Congress, fled Richmond and made his way west, where he hoped to eventually board a ship in California for England. Instead, in August 1865 he and his riding party were ambushed and killed by Mexican irregulars along the border. General Danville Leadbetter, a Maine native, fared a little better when he escaped to Mexico and eventually made his way through the territories to Canada, where he died in 1866.[68] Walter Husted Stevens, a native New Yorker who fought as a colonel in the Army of Northern Virginia, fled to Mexico after Appomattox and determined to make his new home there rather than in a reconstructed Union. He ended up working for the newly reinstalled government of President Benito Juarez as a railroad superintendant for two years, before dying in 1867. He could have easily stopped in Texas to work on railroads, but Stevens instead found a new life south of the border more to his liking.[69]

The Northern Confederate veteran who likely spent the most time abroad was John Taylor Wood. A native of Minnesota and son of an army officer, Wood grew up in the territories and New York before enlisting in the navy. After secession occurred he offered his services to the Confederacy. He accumulated a stellar career as a member of the crew of the CSS *Virginia* and later as commander of the CSS *Tallahassee*. By the end of the war, Wood worked for Jefferson Davis and followed him during the president's flight through the Carolinas. When Davis's advisors scattered, Wood managed to follow Secretary of State Judah P. Benjamin to Florida, where they both boarded a blockade-runner for Cuba. Wood then boarded another ship to Canada, where he eventually settled in Halifax. For the next half century Wood excelled as a businessman, merchant, real estate agent, and one of the first producers of cotton manufacturing plants in Nova Scotia. He even served as a longtime member of the Halifax Chamber of Commerce. The residents of Halifax praised him as a hero and honorary citizen of Canada.

In fact, Wood ended up spending more years in Canada than in either the North or the South.[70]

Nevertheless, only a few Northern Confederates stayed out of the United States for such an extended period of time. Most of the exiles either died a few years after the war or yearned to return to the country at some point in the future. For instance, John Slidell, who opted to stay in Paris and then England rather than risk arrest and the vengeance of men like Edwin Stanton, still hoped to one day return to Louisiana to tend to his children and property. He considered his exile temporary rather than permanent.[71] Similarly, George Alexander only remained in Canada until 1872, returning to Maryland when Congress removed all restrictions on former Confederates. Native New Yorker Daniel Frost originally moved to Canada to escape the war but reclaimed his farm in Missouri during Reconstruction. Former Confederate supply agent Caleb Huse, who joined Slidell in exile in Paris, returned to the United States in the 1870s after receiving a pardon. Wood thus represented the exception rather than the rule. Nearly all exiles still considered themselves proud southerners and ex-Confederates wishing to return to their beloved adopted homeland.[72]

Instead of enduring life-long or even short-term exile, native northerners also had the option of returning to their native section. A few dozen had already moved back to the North before the war but had done so as unionists. Those who chose this option after the war faced an unknown response because of their recent ties to the Confederacy. Approximately fifty individuals in this study decided to risk spending some or all of their postwar lives back in the land of their birth.

One major motivation for such a decision was economic. Union soldiers had damaged or destroyed their farms, plantations, homes, and businesses. When their efforts to rebuild failed, these native northerners felt they had no choice but to try again in the largely untouched North. Charles Dahlgren, for example, attempted to rebuild his shattered Mississippi plantations for five years but finally gave up and moved to New York for better opportunities.[73] Northern Confederate plantation owner Stephen Duncan encountered a similar situation. With his plantations in Mississippi harassed by Union troops during the war, Duncan applied for passage to the North, received permission, and made his way to New York City. He hoped to meet contacts in the city, rebuild his finances, and obtain pardons for his family. He was still working at it when he passed away in New York in 1867.[74]

Others who returned to the North hoped to restart the careers they began in that region as young men. David Bridgeford, a veteran of the First Virginia Battalion, immediately moved to New York at the close of the war to restart his business ventures.[75] Felix de Fontaine, a prewar reporter in New York who moved to South Carolina and covered the war from there, eventually moved back to New York, where he resumed his work as an editor and author for several newspapers.[76] Eugene Hilgard, a geologist in Mississippi, continued his teaching career from the 1870s onward at the University of Michigan and the University of California at Berkeley in the fields of agriculture and soil science.[77] General Mansfield Lovell, a former street commissioner in New York City before the war, returned to that city to work on engineering projects.[78] Moving back to the North helped them restart their lives in more favorable conditions than offered in the ruins of the South. In a way, these men tapped into the same motivations that brought them to the South in the first place: better opportunities for success than their current environment.[79]

Those who made this decision appeared to have abandoned everything they had fought for during the war, including their adopted identities. Evidence does point to at least a few of these native northerners who actually made a complete break with both their southern and Confederate heritage. One of the most prominent examples was native Ohioan Henry Handerson. Handerson had originally vowed not to take an oath of allegiance as long as the Confederate government still existed. Nevertheless, by 1865, his ties to his adopted state had weakened to such a degree he sought help from his relatives to return to the North. As he explained to his uncle, "Indeed Louisiana is now almost a wilderness, and most of my acquaintances and friends are either dead on the battle field or driven from their homes; so that I have very few inducements to return there." Believing that he had lost the connections that formerly bound him to the South, Handerson planned to travel to either Pennsylvania or Ohio to continue his medical studies. In an indication of how much he tried to distance himself from that region, Handerson even claimed soon after the war that he never actually believed in states' rights. Rather than boast of his wartime accomplishments, Handerson almost wished to forget those years. He ended up spending the rest of his life in Cleveland and New York without ever returning to the South again. The Confederacy might have commanded his deepest loyalties, but his connections to the South were destroyed once the Confederacy itself died.[80]

Though not to the same degree, a couple of other adoptive southerners at one time or another followed Handerson's example. For instance, Henry Watson, who sat out the war in Europe, returned to Alabama to restart his business dealings but kept his family in his native Massachusetts. After a few years, Watson felt alienated by his community for not enlisting in the Confederate army and so joined his family in Massachusetts for the rest of his life. As a result, as his biographer argued, Watson renounced his southern identity completely.[81] Amanda Trulock, a plantation mistress in Arkansas during the war, left the plantation to her children and moved back to her native Connecticut after the war, where she remained for the rest of her life. Gail Borden, an adoptive southern unionist who stayed in New York during the war, listed Texas as his temporary residence, implying that he viewed his native New York as his true home.[82]

Such breaks with adopted identities, however, were the exception rather than the rule. Over three quarters of the individuals in this study remained in the South for the entire postwar period. Out of the fifty who moved back to the North, less than half did so for the rest of their lives. More commonly, these men returned to the North out of necessity or desperation rather than a desire to reconnect with their native section. As shown earlier, Charles Dahlgren and Stephen Duncan both tried to maintain their Mississippi plantations as long as possible before giving in to financial necessity. In addition, Rufus Bullock, a native New Yorker who worked on Confederate railroads and telegraphs in Georgia, joined the Republican Party during Reconstruction and actually served as one of Georgia's Reconstruction governors. Plagued by fiscal troubles and constant white southern opposition, Bullock resigned in 1871 and fled with his family to New York City. As both a native northerner and a member of the southern Republican Party, Bullock quite literally had no friends by the time he left.[83] Even Handerson, by his own admission, abandoned his adopted state only because it lay in ruins and he did not believe he could rebuild his life there. As for Watson and Borden, they did not join the Confederacy and so had no Confederate identity to lose.

Other Northern Confederate veterans returned to the North only at the end of their lives, representing more of a symbolic reconnection with their families than a desire to give up their adopted identity. Native Ohioan Bushrod Johnson spent most of his postwar years running the University of Nashville in his adopted state of Tennessee and pursuing a failed endeavor to start a prep school in that state. Only when he retired did he decide to spend his final years working in Illinois as a farmer, to be closer to his relatives.[84] Caroline Gilman spent the first half of Reconstruction in her adopted state of South Carolina to live close to one of her daughters. When that daughter passed away in 1873, Gilman moved back to New England to stay near her other daughter.[85] John C. Pemberton initially hoped to spend the rest of his days with his wife at their farm in Virginia but later decided, after having reconciled with his northern family, to move back to his home state of Pennsylvania in 1875, staying until his death in 1881.[86] Returning to the North did not mean these individuals explicitly rejected their adopted southern identities; they simply wanted to remain close to their families, as they had throughout their lives.[87]

The solidification of southern identities among Northern Confederate veterans received further confirmation from native southerners. Faced with so much destruction, white southerners clung to memories of the Confederacy as a way to unite against the growing power of the North in the postwar Union. They especially hated any reminders of the recent Union victory, which meant postwar northern emigrants felt their wrath more than anyone. Historian Nina Silber implies that in the midst of reconciliation, white southerners, even while appreciating northern efforts to lessen animosity between the sections, viewed northerners, including carpetbaggers and other postwar northern emigrants, as aliens. She even gave an example of a New Hampshire veteran marrying a Virginia woman against the wishes of her father, highlighting the simultaneous growth of reconciliation rhetoric combined with strengthened sectional identity.[88] Yet unlike other native northerners, Northern Confederate veterans had experienced the war from the Confederate perspective, fought in its armies, and given up their prosperity and sometimes their lives in the struggle for independence. Such conduct put them on the same level as native southerners, and so the latter naturally treated them as comrades. In addition, they had time to build up relationships in southern communities, whereas postwar northern emigrants, especially those perceived as carpetbaggers, appeared to arrive solely to pillage the defeated South. The trust built up in the antebellum period and the Civil War carried over into Reconstruction and beyond.

In an environment where the fluidity of sectional identity had diminished, Northern Confederates stood squarely on the southern side in the eyes of their peers. Nativity meant very little when it came to memories of the Civil War and who belonged to which side.[89] General Joseph Johnston, in one section of his memoirs, wrote a lengthy discourse about the Vicksburg campaign that included passages about the defense of Grand Gulf, Mississippi. Two brigades faced nearly five times their number to contest General Grant's crossing of the Mississippi River. General Elisha Tracy, a Connecticut native and adopted Louisianan, commanded one of the two brigades involved in the defense. Without ever mentioning his heritage or questioning his loyalty, Johnston merely noted that "among the first [to fall] was the gallant Tracy, whose death was much regretted by the army." Like so many of his comrades, Tracy led his men into battle without question and gave his life for the cause. That act alone qualified him to join the ranks of Confederate heroes.[90]

Of course, Northern Confederates did not have to die in a blaze of glory to command the respect of their peers. Members of the First Tennessee Regiment never forgot Charles Quintard's contributions as a chaplain and surgeon both on and off the field. Private Sam Watkins loved Quintard for his sermons and medicinal skills. He wrote in his memoirs that every soldier in the regiment fondly remembered Quintard's devotion to the men, the prayer book he prepared for them, and the many times he went out into the countryside to procure clothing and supplies.[91] An unofficial history of the regiment included this description of Quintard's service: "Dr. Charles T. Quintard, who was then Chaplain of the Regiment, but now Bishop, was the first man to administer to the wants of most of these unfortunate men . . . and this love and gratitude for this good man increases as the years roll by." Another veteran, Captain Polk Johnson, described the severe wounding of General Quarles at the Battle of Franklin in Tennessee and credited Quintard with saving the general's life. Quintard's devotion to those around him made his name unforgettable to those who knew him.[92] John Taylor Wood received the same type of gratitude from one of his former pupils at the United States Naval Academy at Annapolis. In a eulogy written for the *Baltimore Sun,* the pupil wrote: "We of the Confederate Navy looked upon John Taylor Wood as a natural born leader. . . . His popularity was such with the enlisted men of the service that when he gave an order twenty men would be on the jump to execute his command, although one man could have done it."[93]

In probably the greatest symbol of acceptance, native southern Confederate veterans often came to the immediate defense of their Northern Confederate brethren when someone questioned the latter's motives in postwar accounts, often taking the accusations as a personal insult. One of these defenses concerned one of the biggest scapegoats of the Confederacy: General John C. Pemberton. The stain of the Vicksburg surrender tarnished his reputation for the rest of his life. The fact that he moved back to Pennsylvania in his later years only provided more circumstantial evidence of his supposedly underhanded motives. The former attorney general of Mississippi, T. J. Wharton, commented on this state of affairs after Pemberton's death. Asked about Pemberton's conduct, Wharton recalled how he never saw a more hard-working or loyal officer, but also acknowledged that many Mississippians distrusted Pemberton and attributed that distrust to his northern birth. In this case, the broadly negative image of northerners prevalent in the postwar South applied to Pemberton as well.[94]

Nevertheless, several Confederate veterans, including prominent generals, came to Pemberton's defense. One postwar friend and correspondent, William Preston Johnson, reassured Pemberton in 1874, "You undervalue the weight of your character and reputation: the discriminating have always done you justice; even the prejudiced will eventually do so too."[95] Jubal Early, one of the biggest proponents of the Lost Cause, wrote a similar defense after hearing about book reviewers who claimed that Pemberton, according to a manuscript written by General Richard Taylor, "joined the South for the express purpose of betraying it." Ready to set the record straight, Early first quoted from the manuscript, showing that, far from chastising Pemberton, Taylor actually praised him by asserting that "Certainly he must have been actuated by principle alone; for he had everything to gain by remaining on the Northern side." Early then contributed his own endorsement of Pemberton. "So foul an aspersion on as true and devoted an adherent of the cause of the South as any who fought for her rights, would have reflected more discredit on the author of it, than on its subject," Early declared. "The Southern man who can permit himself to entertain the slightest suspicion of the want of fidelity in John C. Pemberton to the cause he espoused, either in thought or deed, must have his faculties of both mind and heart obscured by ignorance, prejudice, and all uncharitableness."[96] Clearly, Early took the criticism of Pemberton personally, since he responded to the remarks of a reviewer who did not even comment on Early's own book. Those who believed Pemberton remained in the ranks thanks to his friendship with Jefferson Davis could not discount an endorsement from one of the Army of Northern Virginia's most vocal proponents and apologists.

Decades later, Pemberton's reputation appeared to have reached its zenith when the city of Vicksburg, site of his most devastating failure, considered erecting a monument in his honor. General Stephen D. Lee, when he heard of the rumor, wrote on behalf of the United Confederate Veterans in support of the monument. As Lee argued, "I agree with you, that the Confederacy had no more loyal and true soldier than Gen. Pemberton . . . no one deserved less than he the slanders heaped upon him of disloyalty to the Confederacy."[97] Native southerners like Early and Lee demonstrated that loyal service to the Confederacy provided more than enough reason to come to the defense of their comrades, even if those comrades happened to originate from outside the South.[98]

Along with service in the army, Northern Confederates also received support thanks to their ties to their adopted states. Northern Confederates themselves cited these attachments as a major reason for their adopted southern identities, and native southerners understood the reasoning. As one native southerner summarized in a eulogy of Connecticut native and adopted Alabamian Daniel Pratt, "He came and settled among this people, and shared all their fortunes. He was willing to cast his lot with them."[99] As much as white southerners claimed to value heritage and southern blood above all else, in reality actions on behalf of an adopted state counted equally in their estimation of a person's character.

This phenomenon revealed itself constantly throughout the former Confederacy. Mississippian Frank Montgomery, for example, described in his memoirs his time with Mississippi's wartime governor Charles Clark, a native Ohioan. He recalled how, after the war, Clark was imprisoned at Fort Pulaski "with other distinguished southerners, but was finally permitted to return home," by which he meant Mississippi. At the governor's death bed, not even mentioning Clark's roots, Montgomery insisted that "as long as the history of the state is read, his name and fame will live." Similarly, Jedediah Hotchkiss often received calls for his assistance on various matters in his capacity as a Virginian. One admirer asked Hotchkiss to join a committee of prominent citizens of the state to counter northern textbooks that portrayed the war from a unionist point of view. The National Geographic Society, in its eulogy of Hotchkiss, recalled a time when Hotchkiss "entertained the Society with true Virginia hospitality." Farther south, Floridians waxed praise for one of their own adopted sons, Samuel Pasco. A corporal in Pasco's regiment, Clarence Smith, described how Pasco suffered the humiliations of prison before returning to his Florida home. The citizens of the state rewarded him by electing him senator, "and in placing him there, his constituents had added greater luster to the bright names of Florida and Pasco." Incredibly, on occasion a Northern Confederate veteran did not even have to reside in a state to count among its citizens. Charles Dahlgren lived in Mississippi but held extensive landholdings in Louisiana, as well. Based on those landholdings, when Dahlgren traveled to New York immediately after the war for financial backing, the Reconstruction governor of Louisiana called him "an esteemed citizen of Louisiana."[100]

Occasionally, even adoptive southerners who supported the Union received forgiveness for their actions because of their prewar connections to the South. Frederick Barnard, who fled to the North at the start of the war and became president of Columbia College, still received offers from the University of Alabama to return as their president. When he declined the offer, they showed their continued appreciation by erecting a marble bust of him commemorating his prewar service to the school. Gail Borden had stayed in the Union at the start of the war and had sons who fought for both the Union and the Confederacy. When the war ended, even though he had earlier called Texas his temporary home, he decided to move back to the state. Rather than face accusations of treason, he received a less than laudatory but still respectful welcome when he arrive in the state. His past contributions to Texas allowed his neighbors to partly overlook his support of the Union during the war.[101]

Even more importantly, many native southerners continued another tradition through the postwar era by praising their Northern Confederate comrades with the full knowledge of the latter's background. If anything, the fact that these men turned their backs on their past in favor of protecting ideals shared by white southerners only enhanced their worth. And since these veterans had the same experiences and made the same sacrifices, native white southerners saw no contradiction in including native northerners in the heart of postwar southern life and Confederate memory.

Dr. A. G. Clopton of Texas reflected the tone of southern opinion on the subject in his eulogy of Ashbel Smith in 1886. Unlike other admirers, Clopton made no secret that Smith came from Connecticut and graduated from Yale with a medical degree. He could have stayed in the North as a successful doctor, but Clopton was grateful that he chose otherwise. After outlining his career in Texas, including service as minister to England and as secretary of state, Clopton summed up Texans' gratitude toward him: "he, during the memorable struggle of Texas for independence, united his fortunes with those of the infant republic. The people of Texas were not slow to discern the worth, and employ the services of one willing to serve in any capacity, for the vindication of the sacred principles of self-government." Texans loved him because he helped create the state and, in return, accepted him as a full comrade-in-arms, in spite of his New England background.[102]

Other native southerners echoed Clopton in their own assessments of Northern Confederate veterans. While defending General Pemberton from questions about his Confederate patriotism, Richard Taylor, Stephen D. Lee, and Jubal Early all cited Pemberton's roots in Pennsylvania as yet another reason to admire his convictions. Taylor argued that Pemberton, though born in Pennsylvania, still exhibited support for states' rights rhetoric throughout his career. He cited Pemberton's marriage to a Virginia woman, along with the admiration he showed for John C. Calhoun's nullification arguments in the 1830s while stationed in South Carolina.[103] Taylor found it remarkable that someone not born in the South could nonetheless independently arrive at the same views on states' rights and form the same friendships as native southerners. In Taylor's mind, Pemberton's background, although northern, inevitably turned him into one of the most loyal soldiers in the Confederacy. Stephen D. Lee agreed when he wrote, "He was a Northern man, who had married one of the Southern ladies, and from conviction and from his wife, he liked the South and her cause and knew she had the Constitution and right on her side—He turned his back on his own family & people and gave all he had to the defense. . . ."[104] Native northerners like Pemberton, who fought for the Confederacy out of personal conviction, fit in perfectly with postwar defenders of states' rights and secession.

Efforts to assimilate into southern society confirmed that reality. Writing in 1867, author James Avirrett reflected on this transformation in the case of Samuel Myers, a native Pennsylvanian who became an adopted Virginian. Avirrett argued that Myers worked hard to remake himself as a southerner. "His sympathies and feelings were ever in unison with the great Southern heart. . . ," Avirrett wrote, "He readily adapted himself to the habits and feelings of the people among whom he resided, and soon secured the confidence and esteem of the entire community." Thanks to this adaptation, Myers received the full acceptance of his community and died as a true southerner. Similarly, Samuel Pasco arrived in Florida as a stranger from Massachusetts yet emerged as a committed southern patriot. General B. W. Partridge emphasized that Pasco fought for the Confederacy "without a drop of kindred blood south of the Mason-Dixon line" and "without a penny of investment in the South." Among the people in Pasco's community, "He won their respect and their love. He was their own—their very own."[105]

Newspaper editor Joseph Derry, in another display of this theme, wrote an article for the *Atlanta Constitution* in 1900 giving summaries of over two dozen native northerners who fought for the Confederacy. Most of these summaries merely listed military accomplishments but when Derry mentioned General Stevens, a native New Yorker, he provided more elaboration: "Though of northern birth, his surroundings made him southern." Another newspaper editor in South Carolina described Felix de Fontaine's return to Columbia in 1896 as a homecoming: "[he] has returned from long exile in the north, and making Columbia his home, has begun the publication of a magazine devoted to the reproduction of his war letters and other records of the great struggle for southern independence." The editor also said de Fontaine covered the war from a "South Carolina standpoint."[106] Even though de Fontaine came from New England and spent some of his youth in New York, the editor still considered his sojourn in New York as only temporary. For all of these native southerners, Northern Confederates counted as equals in the southern community because they had successfully assimilated into southern society.[107]

For those who had any more doubts about whether these individuals truly belonged to southern society after the Civil War, they could find proof through the legacies of postwar governors. Several native northerners had governed southern states before and during the war, but the number who occupied governors' mansions reached its zenith after the war. No less than ten of the surviving veterans in this study served as postwar governors in seven southern states, including Alabama, Arkansas, Florida, Georgia, Louisiana, and Texas.[108] This meant that over half of the defeated Confederate states relied on these men to steer them into reunion. Some were appointed by Union authorities, while others were elected by their constituents as Republicans or Democrats. Despite their differences, they all shared the common characteristic of leading their states as adoptive southerners. Their constituents, through both praise and criticism, largely regarded them as such as well.

Those who joined the Democratic Party and called for the end of Republican power in the South not surprisingly received the most support from their white constituents. Since they stood arm-in-arm with ex-rebels to overthrow hated Republican rulers, the majority of white voters had little trouble seeing them as genuine southerners. Florida witnessed the rise of two such governors. The first, Franklin Drew, interestingly enough did not even reside in Florida until after the war. A native of New Hampshire, Drew moved to Georgia as a machinist and served in the Georgia Home Guards. After the war, he decided Florida held more opportunities and so moved further south to establish a lumber mill. Drew mostly maintained a low profile as a local businessman during Reconstruction, although he did support Democratic policies. By 1876, his reputation among white Floridians rose to such an extent that they volunteered his name for the Democratic nomination for governor. In the highly contentious elections in that year, Republican Rutherford B. Hayes won the state's electoral votes for president, but Drew emerged from the controversy with a small margin of victory for the governor's chair. He did not pursue a lengthy political career, wishing only to serve one term before returning to his lumber business in Jacksonville. Ironically, the election of Drew, a native northerner, signaled the end of Reconstruction policies popularly associated with northern rule.[109]

Soon after Drew's departure, another adopted Floridian, Edward Perry, also occupied the governor's mansion in Tallahassee. A native of Massachusetts, Perry worked as a lawyer before the war and served as commander of a Florida brigade in the Army of Northern Virginia. When the war ended he returned to Florida to resume his law practice with his wife and five children. Like Drew, Perry became active in Democratic politics as Reconstruction neared its end. After Drew retired in 1880, Perry's name came up for nomination to replace him, though he lost to the eventual winner William Bloxham.

Nevertheless, Perry's reputation made him the favorite for the nomination four years later. In a unique twist, Perry's main opponent for the nomination was Samuel Pasco, himself a Northern Confederate veteran. Democratic delegates did not appreciate the irony, because they only saw two Confederate veterans concerned for the welfare of their state. Perry ended up besting Pasco and winning election as governor in 1884. His administration mainly dealt with assisting veterans and overseeing the drafting of a new constitution in a state constitutional convention, which happened to have his recent opponent Pasco as its president. Following Drew's example, Perry resigned after one term and returned to private life in Pensacola. In a time when most northerners carried the label of carpetbagger in the postwar South, Florida voted for two governors with northern origins because those men served in the Confederacy, which separated them from the new generation of northern emigrants.[110]

Drew and Perry, however, remained the exception among southern governors born in the North. Half of these governors were unionists appointed by Union authorities to carry out Reconstruction policies.[111] For example, Florida first had a native northern governor in the form of William Marvin, a native New Yorker who served for five months after his appointment by President Johnson. Native Pennsylvanian Isaac Murphy, the only delegate to maintain his nay vote in the Arkansas secession convention back in 1861, received an appointment from President Lincoln as provisional governor of Arkansas after Union armies captured Little Rock. He remained governor until 1868 and helped guide his adopted state through Reconstruction, including the passage of the Fourteenth Amendment. Benjamin Flanders, a New Hampshire native and unionist from Louisiana, came to the attention of Union military officials by serving in a Union regiment and as a congressman from Louisiana's wartime unionist government. By the end of the war, he visited Washington to converse personally with General Grant about the proper administration of Reconstruction policy. In 1867, General Phillip Sheridan replaced the existing governor, whom he deemed as too corrupt, with Flanders, to expedite the transition to civil government in Louisiana.[112]

As governors who aligned with Republicans and did not take office through a popular election, these men faced far more obstacles and resistance from white southerners. Those obstacles, however, rarely involved challenges to their status as southerners. In fact, they accepted the position because they all believed subscribing to the Republican Reconstruction plans offered the best chance to quickly rebuild their adopted states. For example, in Alabama, Lewis Parsons, a native New Yorker, made his position clear when he took over the governorship for six months in 1865. In a proclamation he issued to the state's citizens in July, Parsons praised the state's recent service in the Confederacy but made it clear that his major goal involved protecting loyal unionists and reestablishing civil government in Alabama. Although a unionist during the war, Parsons still considered himself a part of Alabama and hoped the state would follow his lead.[113]

The Republican provisional governor of Texas, Elisha Pease, who served from 1867 until 1869, had similar goals in mind. A Connecticut native and longtime resident of Texas, Pease sided with the Union during the war and knew firsthand the difficulties of securing Union control of the state. As a respected former governor, Pease believed he could steer a moderate course for his adopted state. After his defeat for governor in 1866 in a general election, however, Pease completely changed his opinions and met with Secretary of the Navy Gideon Welles, urging him to persuade President Johnson to send troops to the state to protect loyal unionists. Welles opposed such a move, but he recorded in his diary that Pease warned him that all unionists, including himself, were in danger from unreconstructed secessionists if the status quo continued. Pease even placed his children in northern schools and spent nine months in Connecticut after his defeat before finally returning to Texas.[114] Congress and the military eventually agreed with Pease and appointed him as provisional governor once the Military Reconstruction Acts went into effect in 1867. He made it his mission to ensure only loyal men received government posts, passed an ironclad oath for all Texans to sign if they desired such a post, and expected newly freed blacks to receive voting rights and education.

As a result, Pease made enemies among both ex-Confederates and Radical Republicans for either doing too much or too little. After two years he resigned his position amidst pressure from the Radicals in the state.[115] His decisions also cost Pease a lot of good will among white Texans who used to admire him. As Pease's biographer remarked, "Most Texans saw him as the willing tool of a hated military dictatorship; they believed him to have bartered his own honor and that of the state for political power. As a result, his actions were suspect in most quarters."[116] And at least one newspaper editor tried to use Pease's background against him. The *Austin Southern Intelligencer* expressed shock that "radicals," as the editor referred to liberal Democrats and Republicans in the state, could nominate a "born Yankee" in a state that had just failed to win southern independence.[117]

Pease may have forfeited his prewar reputation by aligning with the Republican Party, but he still maintained his adopted identity in spite of what this editor believed. The power of an acquired southern identity emerged not just among unreconstructed rebels but also among those who occupied positions of authority in unionist governments. Pease insisted he made his choices based on what he believed was best for the South and for Texas. In the process, especially when defending himself against Democratic critics,

Pease revealed himself as a devoted southerner. At no point did he feel akin to other governors like Adelbert Ames in Mississippi, who left his home in Maine for the express purpose of transforming the state along the lines of his native New England. Although he came from the same region, Pease worked for the Republicans, not as a northerner out to remake the South, but rather as a southerner out to protect the South.

During his administration, Pease made several speeches that highlighted his identification with the region. Understandably, he met a lot of resistance, both from unrepentant Confederates and from Democratic generals who resisted Republican policies. Pease especially hated General Winfield Scott Hancock because of the general's Democratic leanings and seeming unwillingness to protect Texas unionists. Although much of his invective against men like Hancock arose from political posturing, one such argument included a revealing commentary on his own sectional identity. Pease told his constituents, "the people of the Northern States understand this matter just as well as we do—they are as intelligent as we are; they are a people not easily to be deceived."[118] As a native of Connecticut, Pease could have easily brought up his familiarity with "the people of the Northern States" as a way to demonstrate his own understanding of the differences between the sections, but he deliberately chose not to do so. Any association with carpetbaggers would have deeply offended Pease, because he did not consider himself part of that category. If anything, he ranked as a scalawag with other native southern Republicans.

Pease continued to maintain this position after he resigned from the governorship. Nearly two decades after his brief tenure, Pease defended himself by saying that, although he did not seek the office, he still did what he thought best for the benefit of his state. As he told his critics, "To these men of yesterday and to-day, who make this charge, I will say that I have been one of the people of Texas since the colonial days of Stephen F. Austin; and that my career in Texas has become part of her history, which it is not in their power to change. . . . As one of the citizens of Texas I felt that their interest was my own."[119] In the process, he also recognized that the sectional divide still prevailed as late as the 1880s. While summarizing the efforts of Democrats to use military generals as standard bearers to win elections, Pease declared, "My Friends there will be a united North so long as we have a united South arrayed in opposition to those great principles that were settled by the defeat of the rebellion."[120] He may have considered himself a scalawag, but he also never wanted anyone else to think of him as anything but a true southerner.

Pease's critics eventually acknowledged his connections to Texas despite their disagreements with him. After he left office, Pease attempted to work with Democrats in 1871 to protest increased taxation in the state. His outreach, as well as his past service to the state, won some of them over to his side. As one Democrat from Dallas wrote, "He is a Republican . . . but an honest, straightforward man . . . been in Texas from the first, and [had always been] devoted to her interests."[121] Pease ranked much more as a southern unionist than a northern-born traitor. As a prewar northern emigrant, Pease's postwar conduct hurt him but did not permanently separate him from his adopted home. Even the Texas editor who slandered Pease as a "born Yankee" implicitly knew this, because he only made that reference once and spent far more space criticizing Pease's decision to join Republicans in military rule.

As difficult as Pease found the landscape in Texas, however, it did not compare to the challenges faced by Rufus Bullock, a native New Yorker and Reconstruction governor of Georgia. Bullock differed from nearly every other governor in the postwar South because he not only won his office through a popular election but also as a Republican Northern Confederate veteran. When the war ended, he quickly returned to Augusta and rebuilt his fortunes through investments in telegraphs and factories. Initially not interested in politics, Bullock decided that cooperating with Republicans represented the best chance for a quick restoration of Georgia, and by extension business opportunities in his adopted state. For the next two years, he helped organize the state Republican Party and served as a delegate to the state constitutional convention in 1867. Carpetbaggers in Georgia saw the value of Bullock's prewar residence in the state and nominated him for the gubernatorial contest in 1868. After a very close election, decided by only seven thousand votes, Bullock eked out a victory against his unrepentant Democratic opponent and assumed his role as Georgia's new governor thanks to a biracial coalition of conservative whites, free blacks, and the support of Georgia's wartime governor, Joseph E. Brown.[122]

Nevertheless, most ex-Confederates refused to accept this Confederate veteran who seemingly betrayed his own people. Though no carpetbagger,

Bullock led an administration that represented everything white southerners hated about Reconstruction. Bullock championed Radical Republican economic policies, promoted internal improvements, and expressed unwavering support for the state's black population. He also called for military assistance to enforce federal law, even chastising General George Gordon Meade for not cracking down hard enough on the Ku Klux Klan in the state. He did all of this even though courting the state's white population would have yielded more political power in the long term. By 1870, hatred for Bullock allowed the state's Democratic Party to achieve overwhelming legislative victories. Stubborn to the end, Bullock tried to prevent the legislature from meeting. His efforts failed thanks to white resistance and the reluctance of the Union military to intervene. In 1871, with a newly emboldened Democratic legislature set to impeach him for perceived illegal activities, Bullock resigned and fled to New York.[123]

Few other Northern Confederates faced such unrelenting opposition or challenges to their association with the South. Several of his critics cited Bullock's background as proof that he was a dangerous outsider. Newspaper editors launched attacks that included descriptions of Bullock as a "carpetbagger," "Yankee adventurer," and other insults. One writer, using the penname "Nemesis," wrote several articles in the *Augusta Chronicle and Sentinel* defaming Bullock as a traitorous Yankee out to destroy the state. A February 1871 article exclaimed, "But your peculiar capacity was underrated by the people of your adopted State (for, thank God, you are not a Georgian)." The same article accused Bullock of dealing "with brutal negroes and every thieving adventurer from the region of your nativity." Confederate service notwithstanding, Bullock did not seem able to erase his past in the eyes of his former comrades.[124]

These types of attacks, however, were misleading. Despite the hatred directed against him, Bullock received much of his criticism not from his status as a native northerner but from his alliance with Republicans. The state's newspaper editors may have described him as a "carpetbagger" on some occasions, but on others they referred to him as a "scalawag." Had they really thought of him as nothing more than a scheming northerner, then the "carpetbagger" label alone would have proven sufficient. Few people even questioned Bullock's loyalties before he decided to run for office as a Republican; only then did such language appear. The campaign itself reflected this reality. In 1868, both parties ran Northern Confederate veterans on their statewide tickets: Bullock for the Republicans and Nelson Tift, a native of Connecticut, for the Democrats. Throughout the campaign, Tift called Bullock a "traitor" but did not do so in the context of him coming from the North. Instead, Tift used the term to refer to Bullock's associating with Radicals and supporting military rule.[125] Similarly, the anonymous contributor "Nemesis," though referring to Bullock's northern roots at times, did so only in passing. The articles he wrote mainly focused on Bullock's acquiescence to Radical Republican policies, especially civil rights for blacks. As one of the articles stated, "you became the vile tool and political pimp of cunning knaves, through whose devices and your opportunities, you have made your name classic in the annals of crime." "Nemesis" did not actually equate Bullock with Radical carpetbaggers; instead he accused the governor of acting as their front man.[126]

Once Bullock left office, the political nature of the attacks against him became obvious. In 1876, after Bullock had lived in New York for several years, the governor of Georgia demanded his return to stand trial for the corruption charges levied against him. Bullock returned willingly to defend his honor and, in a setback for those who wished to see him humiliated, received help from many other Georgians. Some of his friends in Atlanta posted his bond to keep him out of jail, others volunteered to act as legal counsel, and the trial itself got delayed for a year. When it finally occurred, witnesses who testified to corruption years earlier changed their stories. Bullock's biographer argued that Democrats recognized that the slander used against Bullock mainly served to put their own party back in power; continuing the trial would merely expose the slander for its true purpose. Not surprisingly, the jury took only a half hour to find Bullock not guilty, allowing him to remain in Georgia and rebuild his business ventures. In the end, Bullock's enemies hated him much more as a symbol of Radical Republican rule, against which ex-Confederates could vent their frustration at losing the war and at the threatened loss of the traditional way of life in the South. In all likelihood, had Bullock joined the Democrats or stayed out of politics altogether, no one would have questioned his adoptive southern bona-fides.[127]

Bullock himself, although he still maintained his allegiance to the Republican Party, identified as a genuine southerner throughout his ordeal. In one of his speeches, Bullock tried to convince his fellow Georgians that one could act as a patriotic southerner, defend the righteousness of the Confederate cause, and yet still accept the results of the war. As he urged his listeners, "You will rejoice with me that out of the chaos of unsuccessful war has come to us in the South unequalled prosperity, and it is only fair to say that the credit for this condition is due to the master class of our own people. . . ."[128] Bullock exaggerated the prosperity the South enjoyed at the time, but he had high hopes for the future based on what he knew about southern character. His reference to the "master class" indicated that he believed in southern myths of superiority and counted himself as part of that class. Bullock had every reason to abandon a state that had labeled him a traitor and remain in New York. The fact that he returned, and continued to speak on behalf of his fellow Georgians, revealed how deeply entrenched southern identities became among Northern Confederate veterans.

Bullock's passions came out even more clearly in his interactions with the North. White northerners, especially in Republican circles, naturally assumed that Bullock's decision to join the Republican Party meant he occupied the same status as any other northern politician in the South during Reconstruction. He may have fought for the Confederacy, but he did so only because of peer pressure. Upset with such assumptions, Bullock tried several times to make northerners understand his sectional loyalties. One such defense came in 1872, a short time after he fled Georgia for New York. Horace Greeley, the editor of the *New York Tribune,* gave a speech likening Bullock to every other corrupt carpetbagger governor. Bullock in turn sent a letter to Greeley, written for publication, not only defending his conduct as a governor but especially dispelling any description of himself as a carpetbagger. "You know, Mr. Greeley, that I was a resident citizen of Georgia before, during, and after the rebellion; that there all my social and pecuniary interests are centered; that my successful efforts in restoring the negro members to the Legislature against the opposition of Gen. Toombs and his Ku-Klux is the cause for the slanders which they have put in circulation and which have since pursued me . . . ."[129] Bullock accepted criticism but he did not accept judgments on his identity. Though he never abandoned the Republican Party, Bullock did not tolerate anyone calling him a northerner.

In fact, Bullock reiterated this theme over a decade later when he traveled to Boston and New York City to give speeches to manufacturing associations. In both cities he wore a Confederate Survivor's Association button and spoke out against national interference in southern elections. He also urged Republicans to stop "waving the bloody shirt" and start appealing to southerners again if they wanted any hope of rebuilding a southern wing of the party. He made sure to stress that point lest either white southerners or northerners mistake him for an opportunistic carpetbagger.[130]

At every stage of the postwar era, the general narrative for Northern Confederate veterans mimicked that of every other Civil War veteran, but with a twist. Everything they had built in the antebellum era, everything that made them adoptive southerners, lay in ruins. As native northerners, they seemed to have every reason to abandon a losing cause, return to the land of their childhood, and restart their lives there. In reality, that choice normally did not enter the minds of Northern Confederate veterans, simply because the war had increased, rather than decreased, their devotion to the South. Akin to their native southern comrades, most of these veterans returned to their destroyed adopted homeland determined to rebuild what they had lost, with no thought of regressing back to the North.

Conclusion

After all of their travels, challenges, successes, and failures, Northern Confederate men and women died as they had lived. Two hundred and seventeen of the individuals in this study, more than 70 percent, passed away in the South. Only forty-six died in a northern state, and nine while abroad.[1] The fact that so many chose to remain in their adopted section all the way up until their deaths showed how much they valued their association with the South.

Several wanted to prove their devotion to their adopted region one last time. For example, when Thomas Clemson died in 1888, his will left the bulk of his estate toward establishing an agricultural college at Fort Hill for the benefit of South Carolina youth and the advancement of the scientific study of agriculture. More symbolically, Charles Dahlgren made sure that his final resting place did not coincide with his postwar address. Dahlgren spent the last years of his life in New York, where he died in December 1888. Despite his time away from the South, Dahlgren demanded that his children bring his body back to Natchez to be buried in his adopted state of Mississippi. His children complied with his wishes and buried him in the Natchez city cemetery a week after his death. Although he had relocated to the North during Reconstruction, he still desired to spend eternity in the place he regarded as home. The vast majority of Northern Confederates and adoptive southern unionists felt the same way.[2]

In many cases, the passing of a Northern Confederate veteran revealed how much of an impact they had on their adopted communities. As shown in the previous chapter, native southerners sometimes wrote moving eulogies about the accomplishments of their Northern Confederate brethren. Those eulogies continued to appear throughout the nineteenth and early twentieth centuries. For instance, the *Lexington Morning Herald,* reporting on the death of native Pennsylvanian Henry B. McClellan, mentioned his northern roots yet still praised his support for his adopted state. "Major McClellan was a Southerner only by adoption. He was born in Philadelphia and educated in Massachusetts. At the age of eighteen he went to Virginia. . . . During his short stay in Virginia he early fell in love with the generous character of the people and in the war espoused the cause of his adopted home."[3] After Edward Perry, the former governor of Florida, passed away while on vacation in Texas in 1889, his family brought his body back to Florida, where several state organizations held ceremonies praising his service to his adopted home.[4] When Dennis Heartt, a native of Connecticut and adopted North Carolinian, died in 1870, hundreds of people mourned his death, including his former apprentice, Governor William Holden.[5] In South Carolina, the Charleston Bar Association wrote a lengthy eulogy after the death of Benjamin F. Dunkin, an original signer of the Ordinance of Secession. The association praised him as one of the greatest jurists in the state and never regarded him as anything but a genuine South Carolinian.[6] South Carolinian B. F. Perry went even further when he talked about Dunkin. "Though a New Englander by family, and a Philadelphian by birth," Perry declared, "he was a true Carolinian in feeling and character, ever loyal to the State, and possessing all the honor, pride and dignity of the old school of South Carolina gentlemen."[7] Dunkin had made South Carolina his home, and South Carolinians eagerly accepted him as one of their own.

Such sentiments extended to several other adopted sons of the South. General B. W. Partridge, recalling the life of Sergeant Samuel Pasco, revered Pasco's willingness to remain true to the Confederacy and his adopted state of Florida while in a Union prison, rather than his childhood home in Massachusetts. "A prisoner of war—with the temptation to desert the land of his adoption and return to his loved ones in Boston. . . . Turning a deaf ear to persuasion he elected to remain in prison and the close of hostilities found him in prison. Returning to his Southland home with a gray jacket and cap to tell where his heart lived and loved." Partridge then concluded his eulogy by describing Pasco as "Citizen! Soldier! Statesman! Christian Gentleman; Patriot; he lived well; he died well; he sleeps well. Peace to his ashes."[8] In a similar manner, friends of Edward Wells, the man who offered to spy in the North before joining a South Carolina cavalry regiment, ended their eulogy with a revealing prayer: "Watch gently, oh Southland, watch tenderly over his grave; He was not of your Sons, but as gallant, as loyal, as brave; He laid at your feet perfect faith in Your Cause & Your Truth, His sword bared for you."[9] Unrepentant to the end, Pasco and Wells stood among those unreconstructed rebels who refused to apologize for their contributions to Confederate independence, and their colleagues loved them for it.

Over in Tennessee, at the dedication of Confederate general Francis Shoup's memorial at the University of the South, Bishop Gailor continued this trend by imploring southern students to follow Shoup's example by never apologizing or being ashamed of past service to the Confederacy. Afraid that southern youth might forget the sacrifices of their forefathers in an increasingly industrialized world, Gailor believed celebrating the section's Confederate past was a "duty," a "privilege," and an "opportunity" to display southern patriotism. Shoup reflected that duty more than anyone because he arrived at that patriotism from outside the South. As Gailor argued, "Gen. Shoup, like very many other prominent officers in the Confederate armies, was not born in the South, and had absolutely no interest in the contest except that of deep conviction. He had been offered the position of commander in chief of the militia of the State of Indiana . . . but he acted with Gen. Lee, by the dictates of 'his inexorable and pure conscience,' and he never regretted the choice he made."[10] When every advantage seemed to push Shoup back toward his native section, patriotism and conviction bound him with the Confederacy. The fact that Shoup originally raised a Zouave regiment in his native state of Indiana at the start of the conflict meant nothing. As Gailor said when he concluded his eulogy, Shoup "was one of the truest and noblest spirits that ever blessed Sewanee with his devotion, but because he was a Confederate soldier, who, to the day of his death, was not ashamed nor afraid of the principles which for four years he had gallantly defended upon the field of battle."[11] Regardless of anything else, Shoup's service to the Confederacy won him an honored spot among the next generation of white southerners.

Texans especially treasured anyone who fought on behalf of their state, regardless of their origins. Continuing a tradition begun before and during the war, Texans accepted any settler as a genuine Texan, especially when they participated in struggles for independence from Mexico and the Union. As a result, native northerners in Texas fared quite well in the eyes of their fellow Texas citizens. For example, one author recalled Ashbel Smith's contributions to the Texas War for Independence and the Civil War: "He always responded to the call of his State without remuneration or other reward, than the approval of his fellow-citizens. Patriotic in the highest sense, as a representative abroad or a legislator at home, he stood upon the highest plane, and, regardless of self, championed nothing that, in his opinion, was not for good of the people."[12] Another Northern Confederate Texan, Walter P. Lane, followed Smith's example by denouncing Republicans, calling for the restoration of white rule, and participating in relief efforts against yellow fever in his adopted home town. As a result, when he passed away in 1892, thousands of people attended his funeral and newspapers across the state lauded his record and sacrifice for Texas. The state legislature even passed a resolution praising his past accomplishments. One newspaper summed up the population's mood best when it proclaimed, "His history is part of the history of the Lone Star State. For her honor he has periled his life and shed his blood." Similarly, though with less fanfare, a eulogy of New Hampshire native George Kendall said, "'He loved Texas with an absolute devotion. He never was tired of writing or speaking in its praise. . . . Texas will deeply miss and mourn him. Perhaps she had no citizen which she could have so ill afforded to spare.'"[13] For Texans, the theme remained the same: fight on behalf of us, and we recognize you as a full citizen.

One of the best examples of such posthumous praise for a Northern Confederate occurred with New Hampshire native William Wadley. Emigrating to Savannah in 1834 at the age of twenty-one, Wadley worked most of his adult life on Georgia railroads, eventually owning several of them. During the war he served as a railroad supervisor for the Confederate government. He continued his work with railroads in his adopted state during the postwar period, securing the devotion of his workers and his community.[14] Upon his death, his workers commissioned a statue to commemorate his services to the state. It listed the railroads he worked on or founded, along with his birth year and death year, without mentioning his New Hampshire birthplace. One side of the statue contained the inscription, "to Commemorate the Life of a Good Man and the Ability of a Great Railway Manager Who Rose From Their Ranks to the Presidency."[15]

Though the monument itself did not mention his origins, on the day of its dedication Wadley's friends and admirers gave speech after speech that included references to his past. Those references in no way lessened his status as an adoptive southerner. One example came from A. O. Bacon, the mayor of Macon. Bacon said Savannah was not Wadley's native home, but that Georgia "claims him as her own, for while born in a distant State, here was passed his life, and here his work was accomplished. He sleeps beneath her soil, and the summer flowers which to-day bloom around his grave, waive to the breezes of her own sky. His body again is dust, but his form, cast in eternal bronze, will stand here and await the unwearied march of the centuries."[16] The keynote speaker, Joseph Cumming, went even further by showing how Wadley managed to bring the North and South together both literally and figuratively. The railroads Wadley operated symbolized a bridge linking the country together, and as an adoptive southerner Wadley himself helped serve as a bridge between the two sections. As Cumming told his fellow Georgians, Wadley "brought Georgia and New Hampshire nearer together than Macon and Savannah were at the beginning of his life, we seem to live in a different world from that into which the boy was born seventy-two years ago."[17] Wadley had crossed both sections in the past and eventually emerged as one with the South.

Nevertheless, the era of Wadley and his ilk had passed. The Civil War did not just destroy the old Union; it eliminated an era of cross-border transformation for northerners seeking new lives in the South. Although the Mason-Dixon Line acted as a barrier between the free North and the slave South in the antebellum popular imagination, it remained only a line on a map. Anyone who wished to do so could cross that line and embark on a journey that the majority of their childhood friends could only imagine. They arrived as outsiders yet managed to adapt to the point where they often considered themselves adoptive southerners. Those who served in the Confederacy helped solidify that image in the eyes of their native southern peers, as well as their own. Few others managed to have such an intimate knowledge of the diversified societies that coalesced into the Union.

The conduct of Northern Confederate veterans reflected changes in the entire nation in the wake of the war. Veterans and leaders from both sides led the way in creating a reunited nation, yet they only partially succeeded, because the postwar environment ushered in an era of strengthened sectional identity. The power dynamic of the antebellum era had reversed itself, with the North now dominant over the South, but the dynamic itself remained intact. Sectional tension survived Reconstruction and the latter half of the nineteenth century, and Northern Confederates contributed to the preservation of that sectional separation. The Civil War, while ending any dreams of permanent separation, nevertheless provided white southerners with a rallying point for solidarity. Thanks to their service in the Confederate forces, Northern Confederate veterans shared in that solidarity, which helped entrench what they had built years earlier. In this era of strengthened sectional identity, these veterans either explicitly or implicitly affirmed their entrenched southern identity.

The fluidity of sectional identity prevalent before the war all but disappeared in its aftermath. In the halcyon days of northern emigration to the South, native northerners had the opportunity to either hold on to their northern identities or assimilate into a southern one. Once the last Confederate soldiers laid down their arms, any northerner venturing into the South did so as an alien, immediately suspected by his neighbors of being a destructive Yankee. Northern Confederate veterans represented the last generation of northern emigrants in the nineteenth century to escape this label.[18] Their experiences reflected a reversal of what happened to some southerners who relocated to the North after the war. As Daniel Sutherland argued about twentieth century southern emigrants, "Young people born in the North of southern parents or grandparents can boast of a southern heritage but not of southern birth, and the heritage itself seems more historical than real."[19] Northern Confederate veterans, in contrast, disassociated themselves from their native section in favor of their adopted section.

Their experiences were a microcosm of the fluidity and subsequent hardening of sectional identity in the United States. Propagandists on both sides, especially extremists like abolitionists and fire-eaters, insisted that northerners and southerners represented two distinct peoples destined from birth to follow their own section. Adoptive southerners, and later Northern Confederates, show the fallacy of such thinking, since they originated in the North yet made the South their own. Northern Confederates especially did not fight for the Confederacy as northern mercenaries but rather as patriots, with as much commitment and identification with the Confederate nation as any native southerner. The conclusion of the war brought an end to those types of journeys. Northerners still emigrated to the South, but they did not have the same options for identity formation as their forebears. Northern Confederate veterans represented the last generation of cross-border emigrants in the nineteenth century to truly call themselves southerners. In a time when many people considered the divide between the North and South unbridgeable, these men and women proved that they could successfully live, fight, and die in Dixieland.

Appendix 1

TABLES

The following appendix provides statistical data on the three hundred and three individuals utilized in this study. The biographical information used for this study came from several different sources, including biographical registries, individual biographies, published and private journals and diaries, the 1860 United States Census, and many others. Readers may refer to the bibliography for more information.

The first six tables provide statistics on their prewar lives in the North. Each table, unless otherwise indicated, utilizes all three hundred and three individuals as a source base. Table 1 shows their birthplaces and how many came from each area. Along with northern states, this table also includes United States territories and foreign countries, because approximately twenty of the individuals were born outside the United States. Table 2 displays the decade when these individuals first left the North to take up residence in the South, while Table 3 reveals northern emigrants' ages when they first came to the South. Both of these tables include "none" and "unknown" as variables for those who never emigrated to the South before the war and those for whom not enough information was available to determine an accurate age and date.

The next three tables provide data on the subject's lives in the antebellum South. Table 4 lists the states in the South where northern emigrants first took up residence after moving to the region. Many of these individuals eventually moved to other states or even back to the North in later years, but this table reveals where they first experienced the South personally. Tables 5 and 6 deal with slavery, with the former showing the number of slave-owners in 1860 versus non-slave-owners in the study and the latter showing the number of slaves owned by northern emigrant slave-owners in 1860. For Table 6, "none" indicates a non-slave-owner, "1–5" indicates a small slave-owner, "6–20" indicates a mid-level slave-owner, "21–100" indicates a plantation owner, and "100 plus" indicates a major plantation owner. In addition, "unknown" refers to individuals for whom there is either limited or no information about the number of slaves owned.

Tables 7, 8, and 9 provide information for the Civil War and Reconstruction Era. Table 7 shows where these individuals were living during the secession crisis in 1860. Similar to the other tables, this one includes "none" and "unknown" variables. Table 8 displays how many of these individuals supported the Confederacy versus the Union during the war. This table also includes "both" and "neither" variables for those who either supported both sides at various times in the conflict or traveled abroad to remain neutral. Finally, Table 9 highlights the postwar residencies of surviving Northern Confederates, as well as adoptive southerners. The variables in this table include residency in a southern state only, residency in a northern state only, residency outside the United States only, residency in the North, South, and/or abroad at separate times, and those who had no postwar residency because they did not survive the war.

In addition, tables 10, 11, and 12 provide the names of all individuals used in this study, as well as vital information about them as listed in the previous tables. Table 10 highlights their states of origin, decade of migration to the South, and age at the time of migration. Table 11 lists their first adopted state, status as a slave-owner or non-slave-owner, and the number of slaves they owned in 1860. Finally, table 12 highlights their residence in 1860, whether they supported the Union or the Confederacy in the Civil War, and their postwar residence.

TABLE 1

Distribution of Native States among Adoptive Southerners

State	Number	Percentage
Connecticut	42	14
Illinois	3	1
Indiana	6	2
Massachusetts	51	17
Maine	16	5
New Hampshire	14	5
New Jersey	14	5
New York	55	18
Ohio	25	8
Pennsylvania	46	15
Rhode Island	3	1
Vermont	7	2
Territories	2	0.5
Abroad	18	6
District of Columbia	1	0.5

TABLE 2

Distribution of Decade of Migration among Adoptive Southerners

Decade	Number	Percentage
1800–1809	3	1
1810–1819	15	5
1820–1829	29	10
1830–1839	73	24
1840–1849	65	21
1850–1859	97	32
1860	4	1
None	11	4
Unknown	6	2

TABLE 3

Distribution of Age of Migration among Adoptive Southerners

Age	Number	Percentage
Teens	44	15
Twenties	199	66
Thirties	37	12
Forties	4	1
Fifties	2	1
None	11	4
Unknown	3	1

TABLE 4

Distribution of First Adopted State among Adoptive Southerners

State	Number	Percentage
Alabama	16	5
Arkansas	8	3
Delaware	1	0.5
District of Columbia	6	2
Florida	13	4
Georgia	43	14
Kentucky	14	5
Louisiana	37	12
Maryland	7	2
Mississippi	18	6
Missouri	8	3
North Carolina	18	6
South Carolina	16	5
Tennessee	13	4
Texas	23	7.5
Virginia	50	16.5
None	11	4
Unknown	1	0.5

TABLE 5

Distribution of Slave-owners among Adoptive Southerners

Status	Number	Percentage
Slave-owner	109	36
Non-Slave-owner	156	51.5
Unknown	38	12.5

TABLE 6

Status of Slave-owners among Adoptive Southerners (N=109)

Status	Number	Percentage
Small Slave-owner (1–5)	41	38
Mid-level Slave-owner (6–10)	38	35
Plantation Owner (21–100)	21	19
Major Plantation Owner (100+)	9	8

TABLE 7

Residences of Adoptive Southerners in the South in 1860

State	Number	Percentage
Alabama	17	5.5
Arkansas	10	3
Delaware	0	0
District of Columbia	2	0.5
Florida	10	3
Georgia	39	13
Kentucky	8	2.5
Louisiana	39	13
Maryland	6	2
Mississippi	17	5.5
Missouri	8	2.5
North Carolina	17	5.5

(cont.)

TABLE 7 (cont.)

Residences of Adoptive Southerners in the South in 1860

State	Number	Percentage
South Carolina	16	5
Tennessee	12	4
Texas	32	10.5
Virginia	48	16
None (Outside the South)	21	7
Unknown	1	0.5

TABLE 8

Distribution of Confederate versus Union Supporters among Adoptive Southerners

Side	Number	Percentage
Confederacy	247	81.5
Union	47	15.5
Both	6	2
Neither	3	1

TABLE 9

Postwar Residences of Adoptive Southerners

Region	Number	Percentage
South	183	60
North	20	7
Abroad	9	3
North and South	29	9.5
South and Abroad	5	1.5
North, South, and Abroad	1	0.5
None	39	13
Unknown	17	5.5

TABLE 10

Native State, Migration Decade, and Age at Migration of Individuals

Name	Native State	Migration Decade	Age at Migration
Arunah Abell	Rhode Island	1830s	30s
Charles Adams	Massachusetts	1830s	10s
Stephen Adams	New York	1850s	20s
Amos Akerman	New Hampshire	1840s	10s
George Alexander	Pennsylvania	Unknown	Unknown
William Alexander	Scotland	1850s	30s
Ebenezer Allan	New Hampshire	1830s	30s
Frank Armstrong	Choctaw Territory	None	None
George Armstrong	New Jersey	1830s	20s
Lewis Ayers	New Jersey	1830s	30s
John Bachman	New York	1810s	20s
David Bain	Ohio	Unknown	Unknown
William Baldwin	Ohio	None	None
William Barker	Pennsylvania	Unknown	Unknown
Frederick Barnard	Massachusetts	1830s	20s
William Bartlett	Maine	1850s	20s
Gordon Battele	Ohio	1840s	20s
Herman Battles	Massachusetts	1850s	20s
Ezra Bauder	New York	1850s	20s
J. Edwin Belch	Pennsylvania	1850s	20s
Clifford Belcher	Maine	1840s	20s
Noah Benedict	Connecticut	1840s	30s
Daniel Bestor	Connecticut	1810s	20s
Albert Blanchard	Massachusetts	1840s	30s
Spince Blankenship	Indiana	None	None
Gail Borden Jr.	New York	1820s	20s
John Borden	New York	1820s	10s
William Bostwick	Connecticut	1810s	20s
Charles Bradford	Pennsylvania	1850s	30s
Edmund Bradford	Pennsylvania	1840s	30s
David Bridgeford	Canada	1850s	20s

(cont.)

Name	Native State	Migration Decade	Age at Migration
William Brown	Massachusetts	1840s	20s
William Browne	Ireland	1850s	30s
Hugh Buchanan	Scotland	1840s	20s
Samuel Buckley	New York	1830s	20s
Rufus Bullock	New York	1850s	20s
Dolly Burge	Maine	1840s	20s
David Burnet	New Jersey	1810s	20s
Hiram Cassedy	Pennsylvania	1840s	20s
William Cazneau	Massachusetts	1830s	20s
Alvan Chapman	Massachusetts	1830s	20s
William Chase	Massachusetts	1810s	20s
Norman Chester	Connecticut	1820s	10s
Joseph Claghorn	Connecticut	1840s	20s
Theodore Clapp	Massachusetts	1820s	30s
Charles Clark	Ohio	1830s	20s
William Clark Sr.	New York	1820s	20s
Willis Clark	New York	1840s	20s
Thomas Clemson	Pennsylvania	1830s	30s
Jeremiah Clough	New Hampshire	1840s	20s
James Colcord	New Hampshire	1850s	20s
Charles Collins	Pennsylvania	1850s	20s
Edward Cone	Connecticut	1850s	20s
Benjamin Conley	New Jersey	1830s	10s
Aaron Conrow	Ohio	1840s	10s
Charles Cooper	Pennsylvania	1830s	30s
James Cooper	New York	Unknown	Unknown
Samuel Cooper	New Jersey	1810s	20s
George Crane	Ohio	1850s	20s
Wesley Culp	Pennsylvania	1850s	10s
Moses Curtis	Massachusetts	1830s	20s
Charles Dahlgren	Pennsylvania	1830s	20s
Charles Dana	New Hampshire	1820s	10s
Joseph Daniels	Massachusetts	1830s	20s
Amos Darrow	Connecticut	1840s	20s
John Davis	New York	1820s	10s

Name	Native State	Migration Decade	Age at Migration
William Davis	New York	1850s	30s
W. J. Davis	Ohio	None	None
George Deas	Pennsylvania	1840s	20s
Louis Dembinski	Poland	1850s	30s
Charles Dimmock	Massachusetts	1820s	20s
Henry Dimock	Maine	1830s	20s
William Douglas	Connecticut	1850s	20s
Timothy Downie	New York	1850s	20s
Lemeul Downing	Connecticut	1840s	20s
William Drake	Massachusetts	1850s	30s
George Drew	New Hampshire	1840s	20s
Edward Drummond	Maine	1850s	20s
Johnson Duncan	Pennsylvania	1850s	20s
Stephen Duncan	Pennsylvania	1800s	20s
Benjamin Dunkin	Pennsylvania	1810s	10s
Samuel Durand	Connecticut	1830s	10s
George Eggleston	Indiana	1850s	10s
John Ells	New York	1850s	20s
Ebenezer Emmons	Massachusetts	1850s	50s
Franklin Farmer	Massachusetts	1850s	30s
Phoebe Farmer	Massachusetts	1850s	30s
Greenleaf Fisk	New York	1830s	20s
Henry Flanagin	New Jersey	1830s	20s
Benjamin Flanders	New Hampshire	1840s	20s
Felix de Fontaine	Massachusetts	1860	20s
William Foote	Connecticut	1810s	20s
Tryphena Fox	Massachusetts	1850s	10s
George French Sr.	Massachusetts	1820s	10s
Samuel French	New Jersey	1840s	20s
P. A. Frercks	Germany	1850s	30s
Daniel Frost	New York	1850s	30s
Frederick Fuller	Connecticut	1840s	20s
Franklin Gardner	New York	1840s	20s
Joseph Garey	Pennsylvania	1860	20s
William Gere	New York	1830s	30s

(cont.)

Name	Native State	Migration Decade	Age at Migration
William Gilham	Indiana	1840s	20s
Charles Gillette	Connecticut	1840s	20s
Henry Gillette	Connecticut	1830s	20s
Caroline Gilman	Massachusetts	1810s	20s
George Goldthwaite	Massachusetts	1820s	10s
Josiah Gorgas	Pennsylvania	1850s	30s
William Gould	Connecticut	1820s	20s
Archibald Gracie Jr.	New York	1850s	20s
Douglass Gray	Pennsylvania	1850s	20s
Jonathan Greely	Maine	1850s	10s
Richard Griffith	Pennsylvania	1830s	20s
Silas Grisamore	Indiana	1840s	20s
James Hagan	Ireland	1830s	10s
Sally Hampton	New York	1850s	20s
Henry Handerson	Ohio	1850s	10s
Samuel Hanen	Ohio	1850s	20s
Hiram Hanover	Maine	1830s	10s
Kenton Harper	Pennsylvania	1820s	20s
J. George Harris	Connecticut	1830s	30s
Lewis Hatch	New Hampshire	1830s	10s
Robert Hatton	Ohio	1830s	10s
Wells Hawks	Massachusetts	1830s	20s
Dennis Heartt	Connecticut	1810s	30s
William Heyward	New York	1830s	20s
Eugene Hilgard	Germany	1850s	20s
James Hill	Maine	1850s	20s
Oscar Hinricks	Baltic Coast	None	None
Samuel Hinsdale	Connecticut	1840s	20s
Robert Hitt	Illinois	None	None
Jedediah Hotchkiss	New York	1840s	10s
Volney Howard	Maine	1830s	20s
Fred Hull	New York	1850s	10s
Caleb Huse	Massachusetts	1850s	20s
George Hutter	Pennsylvania	1830s	30s
Ross Ihrie	Pennsylvania	1850s	20s

Name	Native State	Migration Decade	Age at Migration
Porter Ingram	Vermont	1830s	20s
Joseph Ives	New York	1850s	20s
Henry Jewett	Connecticut	1830s	10s
Bushrod Johnson	Ohio	1840s	30s
Charles Johnson	Connecticut	1840s	20s
Joseph Johnson	New York	1800s	10s
Oliver Jones	New York	1820s	20s
George Junkin Sr.	Pennsylvania	1840s	50s
George Junkin	Pennsylvania	1850s	10s
Robert Kelly	Illinois	None	None
William Kelly	Pennsylvania	1840s	20s
Amos Kendall	Massachusetts	1810s	20s
George Kendall	New Hampshire	1830s	20s
John Kimberly	New York	1840s	20s
Thomas King	Massachusetts	1820s	20s
Lee Kramer	Pennsylvania	1840s	20s
Julius de Lagnel	New Jersey	1850s	20s
Robert Lane	Ohio	1850s	20s
Walter Lane	Ireland	1830s	10s
John Lathrop	New York	1840s	40s
Danville Leadbetter	Maine	1850s	40s
Abner Leavenworth	Connecticut	1830s	30s
Abiel Leonard	Vermont	1810s	20s
Julius Lewis	Connecticut	1850s	20s
James Lindley	Ohio	1830s	10s
Amelia Lines	England	1850s	30s
John Long	Illinois	1850s	20s
Mansfield Lovell	District of Columbia	None	None
Joseph Lyman	Massachusetts	1850s	20s
William Lyman	New York	1850s	10s
Robert Maclay	Pennsylvania	1840s	30s
Henry Marean	Massachusetts	1850s	20s
Albion Martin	Maine	1850s	20s
Levi Marvin	New Hampshire	1840s	30s
William Marvin	New York	1830s	20s

(cont.)

Name	Native State	Migration Decade	Age at Migration
Horace Maynard	Massachusetts	1830s	20s
Arthur McArthur Jr.	Connecticut	1850s	20s
Henry McCay	Pennsylvania	1840s	20s
Henry McClellan	Pennsylvania	1850s	10s
Robert McClellan	Pennsylvania	1850s	20s
Edward McClure	New Jersey	1850s	20s
William McComb	Pennsylvania	1850s	20s
William McGuffey	Pennsylvania	1840s	40s
Daniel McKay	Maine	1830s	20s
George Meade	Massachusetts	1850s	20s
Edwin Merrick	Massachusetts	1830s	20s
Eli Merriman	Connecticut	1830s	20s
John Mitchell	Vermont	1850s	20s
Francis Moore Jr.	Massachusetts	1830s	20s
Samuel Moore	Pennsylvania	Unknown	Unknown
Isaac Murphy	Pennsylvania	1830s	30s
Samuel Myers	Pennsylvania	1850s	20s
Wilson Nicholas	New York	1850s	20s
James Nixon	New Jersey	1840s	10s
John O'Brien	Ireland	1850s	20s
William Owen	Ohio	1850s	10s
Horatio Parker	New York	1850s	20s
Homer Parsons	Connecticut	1850s	20s
Lewis Parsons	New York	1840s	20s
Samuel Pasco	England	1850s	20s
Spicer Patrick	New York	1810s	20s
Edmund Patterson	Ohio	1850s	20s
James Patterson	Scotland	1850s	20s
J. G. Patterson	Ohio	None	None
Elisha Pease	Connecticut	1830s	20s
Lucadia Pease	Connecticut	1830s	20s
John Pemberton	Pennsylvania	1830s	20s
Edward Perry	Massachusetts	1850s	20s
Richard Peters	Pennsylvania	1830s	20s
Alexander Phillips	New York	1830s	30s

Name	Native State	Migration Decade	Age at Migration
William Pierce	New York	1850s	20s
Aaron Piggot	Pennsylvania	1840s	10s
Albert Pike	Massachusetts	1830s	20s
William Plumer	Pennsylvania	1820s	20s
Daniel Pratt	New Hampshire	1820s	20s
John Pratt	Connecticut	1840s	20s
Nathaniel Pratt	Connecticut	1820s	30s
George Prentice	Connecticut	1830s	20s
Margaret Preston	Pennsylvania	1840s	20s
Edward Pynchon	Massachusetts	1820s	20s
Charles Quintard	Connecticut	1840s	20s
Daniel Reynolds	Ohio	1850s	20s
William Rice	Massachusetts	1830s	20s
Henry Richardson	Maine	1850s	20s
John Riddell	Massachusetts	1830s	20s
William Riddell	New York	1850s	20s
Roswell Ripley	Ohio	1840s	20s
Anna Ritchie	France	1850s	30s
James Robb	Pennsylvania	1820s	10s
Calvin Robinson	Vermont	1850s	20s
Charles Root	Massachusetts	1830s	10s
Daniel Ruggles	Massachusetts	1830s	20s
Charles Rundell	New York	None	None
John Ryan	New York	Unknown	Unknown
James Safford	Ohio	1840s	20s
John Sanderson	Vermont	1840s	20s
Thaddeus Sanford	Connecticut	1820s	30s
Caroline Seabury	Massachusetts	1850s	20s
Claudius Sears	Massachusetts	1840s	20s
Henry Shaw	Rhode Island	1830s	10s
Daniel Shearer	Massachusetts	1840s	20s
George Sheffield	Connecticut	1840s	20s
Reuben Shelby	Pennsylvania	1830s	20s
William Shepard	Massachusetts	1850s	20s
Gardner Sherman	Indiana	None	None

(cont.)

Name	Native State	Migration Decade	Age at Migration
Sidney Sherman	Massachusetts	1830s	20s
William Sherman	Ohio	1850s	30s
Francis Shoup	Indiana	1850s	20s
Emily Sinkler	Pennsylvania	1840s	10s
John Slidell	New York	1810s	20s
Ashbel Smith	Connecticut	1820s	20s
Martin Smith	New York	1840s	20s
Milo Smith	Ohio	1840s	20s
Nelson Smith	New York	1840s	20s
Edward Sparrow	Ireland	1830s	20s
Almon Spencer	Ohio	1850s	20s
Horatio Spencer	Connecticut	1810s	20s
William Steele	New York	1840s	20s
Walter Stevens	New York	1850s	20s
William Stevenson	Pennsylvania	1850s	30s
Otho Strahl	Ohio	1850s	20s
George Swift	Massachusetts	1830s	10s
Otis Tenney	New Hampshire	1840s	20s
George Thatcher	Vermont	1850s	20s
Frederick Thomas	Rhode Island	1830s	20s
William Thompson	Ohio	1830s	10s
Thomas Thorpe	Massachusetts	1830s	20s
Nelson Tift	Connecticut	1820s	10s
Salathiel Tobey	Massachusetts	1850s	20s
Mary Townsend	New York	1850s	20s
Elisha Tracy	Connecticut	1820s	20s
Amanda Trulock	Connecticut	1830s	20s
Edward Tucke	New Hampshire	1850s	30s
Joseph Tucker	Massachusetts	1850s	20s
Amasa Turner	Massachusetts	1820s	20s
David Tuttle	New Jersey	1850s	20s
Julia Tyler	New York	1840s	20s
John Underwood	New York	1830s	20s
Christopher Upson	New York	1850s	20s
Charles Upton	Maine	1830s	20s

Name	Native State	Migration Decade	Age at Migration
John Wade	New York	1830s	20s
William Wadley	New Hampshire	1830s	20s
Robert Walker	Pennsylvania	1820s	20s
Hiram Warner	Massachusetts	1820s	20s
James Waters	New Jersey	1840s	20s
Alfred Watson	New York	1840s	20s
Henry Watson	Connecticut	1830s	20s
William Weaver	Pennsylvania	1820s	40s
William Webster	Connecticut	1850s	20s
Otis Welch	Maine	1840s	20s
Edward Wells	New York	1860	20s
John Westcott	New Jersey	1830s	20s
Killian Whaley	New York	1840s	20s
Thomas Wharton	England	1840s	20s
Charles Wheeler Jr.	Connecticut	1860	20s
Royall Wheeler	Vermont	1830s	20s
Daniel Whitaker	Massachusetts	1820s	20s
John Wilkes	New York	1840s	10s
Henry Williams	New Jersey	1830s	10s
Sarah Williams	New York	1850s	20s
Aaron Wellington	Massachusetts	1800s	20s
Joseph Wilson	Ohio	1850s	20s
John Wood	Minnesota Territory	1850s	20s
James Woodrow	England	1850s	20s
Thomas Woodward	Connecticut	1840s	10s
Zebulon York	Maine	1840s	20s
William Young	New York	1820s	10s

TABLE 11

First Adopted State and Slaveholder Status of Individuals

Name	First Adopted State	Slaveholder	No. of Slaves
Arunah Abell	Maryland	No	0
Charles Adams	Arkansas	Yes	34
Stephen Adams	Virginia	Yes	1
Amos Akerman	South Carolina	No	0
George Alexander	Unknown	No	0
William Alexander	Alabama	Unknown	Unknown
Ebenezer Allan	Texas	Unknown	Unknown
Frank Armstrong	None	No	0
George Armstrong	Virginia	No	0
Lewis Ayers	Texas	No	0
John Bachman	South Carolina	Yes	4
David Bain	Alabama	No	0
William Baldwin	None	No	0
William Barker	District of Columbia	Unknown	Unknown
Frederick Barnard	Alabama	Yes	2
William Bartlett	Mississippi	Unknown	Unknown
Gordon Battele	Virginia	No	0
Herman Battles	Mississippi	No	0
Ezra Bauder	South Carolina	Yes	1
J. Edwin Belch	Missouri	No	0
Clifford Belcher	Louisiana	Unknown	Unknown
Noah Benedict	Louisiana	Unknown	Unknown
Daniel Bestor	Kentucky	Yes	73
Albert Blanchard	Louisiana	Yes	3
Spince Blankenship	None	No	0
Gail Borden Jr.	Mississippi	Unknown	Unknown
John Borden	Texas	Yes	2
William Bostwick	Georgia	Unknown	Unknown
Charles Bradford	Louisiana	Yes	13
Edmund Bradford	Virginia	Unknown	Unknown
David Bridgeford	Virginia	No	0
William Brown	Virginia	Yes	7
William Browne	District of Columbia	No	0

Name	First Adopted State	Slaveholder	No. of Slaves
Hugh Buchanan	Georgia	Yes	23
Samuel Buckley	Alabama	Unknown	Unknown
Rufus Bullock	Georgia	No	0
Dolly Burge	Georgia	Unknown	Unknown
David Burnet	Louisiana	No	0
Hiram Cassedy	Mississippi	Yes	58
William Cazneau	Texas	No	0
Alvan Chapman	Georgia	No	0
William Chase	Louisiana	Yes	11
Norman Chester	Georgia	Yes	4
Joseph Claghorn	Georgia	Yes	12
Theodore Clapp	Kentucky	No	0
Charles Clark	Mississippi	Yes	141
William Clark Sr.	Virginia	Yes	1
Willis Clark	Alabama	No	0
Thomas Clemson	South Carolina	No	0
Jeremiah Clough	Texas	Yes	3
James Colcord	Georgia	No	0
Charles Collins	District of Columbia	No	0
Edward Cone	Virginia	Yes	1
Benjamin Conley	Georgia	No	0
Aaron Conrow	Missouri	No	0
Charles Cooper	Tennessee	Yes	1
James Cooper	Georgia	Yes	17
Samuel Cooper	District of Columbia	Unknown	Unknown
George Crane	Georgia	No	0
Wesley Culp	Virginia	No	0
Moses Curtis	North Carolina	Unknown	Unknown
Charles Dahlgren	Mississippi	Yes	23
Charles Dana	Maryland	Yes	1
Joseph Daniels	Louisiana	Unknown	Unknown
Amos Darrow	Kentucky	No	0
John Davis	Georgia	No	0
William Davis	Virginia	Unknown	Unknown
W. J. Davis	None	No	0
George Deas	Georgia	No	0

(cont.)

Name	First Adopted State	Slaveholder	No. of Slaves
Louis Dembinski	Louisiana	No	0
Charles Dimmock	Virginia	Yes	8
Henry Dimock	North Carolina	No	0
William Douglas	Louisiana	Yes	7
Timothy Downie	Kentucky	No	0
Lemeul Downing	Georgia	Yes	11
William Drake	Tennessee	No	0
George Drew	Georgia	No	0
Edward Drummond	Georgia	No	0
Johnson Duncan	Louisiana	No	0
Stephen Duncan	Mississippi	Yes	2241
Benjamin Dunkin	South Carolina	Yes	237
Samuel Durand	Georgia	No	0
George Eggleston	Virginia	Unknown	Unknown
John Ells	Virginia	Unknown	Unknown
Ebenezer Emmons	North Carolina	No	0
Franklin Farmer	Louisiana	No	0
Phoebe Farmer	Louisiana	No	0
Greenleaf Fisk	Texas	Yes	1
Henry Flanagin	Arkansas	Yes	7
Benjamin Flanders	Louisiana	No	0
Felix de Fontaine	South Carolina	No	0
William Foote	Virginia	Yes	1
Tryphena Fox	Mississippi	Yes	6
George French Sr.	Georgia	Yes	2
Samuel French	North Carolina	Unknown	Unknown
P. A. Frercks	Georgia	No	0
Daniel Frost	Missouri	No	0
Frederick Fuller	Georgia	Yes	1
Franklin Gardner	Florida	Unknown	Unknown
Joseph Garey	Mississippi	No	0
William Gere	Missouri	No	0
William Gilham	Virginia	Unknown	Unknown
Charles Gillette	Virginia	Unknown	Unknown
Henry Gillette	Texas	Yes	28
Caroline Gilman	South Carolina	No	0

Name	First Adopted State	Slaveholder	No. of Slaves
George Goldthwaite	Alabama	Yes	24
Josiah Gorgas	Alabama	Yes	4
William Gould	Georgia	No	0
Archibald Gracie Jr.	Alabama	No	0
Douglass Gray	Virginia	No	0
Jonathan Greely	Florida	Yes	1
Richard Griffith	Mississippi	Yes	36
Silas Grisamore	Louisiana	No	0
James Hagan	Alabama	Yes	6
Sally Hampton	South Carolina	Yes	210
Henry Handerson	Tennessee	No	0
Samuel Hanen	Virginia	No	0
Hiram Hanover	Texas	Yes	2
Kenton Harper	Virginia	Yes	10
J. George Harris	Tennessee	No	0
Lewis Hatch	South Carolina	Yes	12
Robert Hatton	Tennessee	Yes	17
Wells Hawks	Virginia	No	0
Dennis Heartt	North Carolina	No	0
William Heyward	South Carolina	Unknown	Unknown
Eugene Hilgard	Mississippi	No	0
James Hill	North Carolina	No	0
Oscar Hinricks	None	No	0
Samuel Hinsdale	North Carolina	Yes	1
Robert Hitt	None	No	0
Jedediah Hotchkiss	Virginia	Yes	2
Volney Howard	Mississippi	No	0
Fred Hull	Georgia	No	0
Caleb Huse	Florida	No	0
George Hutter	Virginia	Yes	21
Ross Ihrie	North Carolina	No	0
Porter Ingram	Georgia	Yes	39
Joseph Ives	District of Columbia	No	0
Henry Jewett	Georgia	Yes	10
Bushrod Johnson	Kentucky	No	0
Charles Johnson	Louisiana	No	0

(cont.)

Name	First Adopted State	Slaveholder	No. of Slaves
Joseph Johnson	Virginia	Yes	11
Oliver Jones	Texas	Yes	7
George Junkin Sr.	Virginia	Yes	8
George Junkin	Virginia	No	0
Robert Kelly	None	No	0
William Kelly	Kentucky	Yes	13
Amos Kendall	Kentucky	No	0
George Kendall	Louisiana	Unknown	Unknown
John Kimberly	North Carolina	No	0
Thomas King	Georgia	No	0
Lee Kramer	Virginia	No	0
Julius de Lagnel	Virginia	No	0
Robert Lane	Tennessee	No	0
Walter Lane	Kentucky	No	0
John Lathrop	Missouri	No	0
Danville Leadbetter	Alabama	Yes	5
Abner Leavenworth	North Carolina	Yes	1
Abiel Leonard	Missouri	Yes	15
Julius Lewis	North Carolina	No	0
James Lindley	Kentucky	No	0
Amelia Lines	Georgia	No	0
John Long	North Carolina	No	0
Mansfield Lovell	None	No	0
Joseph Lyman	Mississippi	No	0
William Lyman	Louisiana	No	0
Robert Maclay	Texas	Unknown	Unknown
Henry Marean	Arkansas	No	0
Albion Martin	Virginia	No	0
Levi Marvin	Missouri	No	0
William Marvin	Florida	No	0
Horace Maynard	Tennessee	No	0
Arthur McArthur Jr.	Missouri	No	0
Henry McCay	Georgia	Yes	3
Henry McClellan	Virginia	No	0
Robert McClellan	Georgia	No	0
Edward McClure	South Carolina	Yes	111

Name	First Adopted State	Slaveholder	No. of Slaves
William McComb	Tennessee	Unknown	Unknown
William McGuffey	Virginia	Yes	2
Daniel McKay	Texas	Yes	9
George Meade	Arkansas	No	0
Edwin Merrick	Louisiana	Yes	16
Eli Merriman	Texas	No	0
John Mitchell	Texas	No	0
Francis Moore Jr.	Texas	No	0
Samuel Moore	Virginia	Yes	3
Isaac Murphy	Tennessee	No	0
Samuel Myers	Virginia	No	0
Wilson Nicholas	Maryland	No	0
James Nixon	Louisiana	No	0
John O'Brien	Arkansas	No	0
William Owen	Louisiana	No	0
Horatio Parker	Texas	No	0
Homer Parsons	Arkansas	No	0
Lewis Parsons	Alabama	Yes	16
Samuel Pasco	Florida	Unknown	Unknown
Spicer Patrick	Virginia	Yes	22
Edmund Patterson	Alabama	No	0
James Patterson	Kentucky	Unknown	Unknown
J. G. Patterson	None	No	0
Elisha Pease	Texas	Yes	10
Lucadia Pease	Virginia	Yes	10
John Pemberton	Florida	Unknown	Unknown
Edward Perry	Georgia	Unknown	Unknown
Richard Peters	Georgia	Yes	5
Alexander Phillips	Texas	Yes	13
William Pierce	Mississippi	No	0
Aaron Piggot	Virginia	No	0
Albert Pike	Arkansas	Yes	4
William Plumer	Virginia	No	0
Daniel Pratt	Georgia	Yes	107
John Pratt	Louisiana	Yes	78
Nathaniel Pratt	Georgia	Yes	13

(cont.)

Name	First Adopted State	Slaveholder	No. of Slaves
George Prentice	Kentucky	Yes	4
Margaret Preston	Virginia	Yes	3
Edward Pynchon	Georgia	Yes	24
Charles Quintard	Georgia	No	0
Daniel Reynolds	Tennessee	No	0
William Rice	Texas	Yes	18
Henry Richardson	Louisiana	No	0
John Riddell	Louisiana	Yes	9
William Riddell	Louisiana	No	0
Roswell Ripley	South Carolina	Unknown	Unknown
Anna Ritchie	Virginia	Yes	4
James Robb	Virginia	No	0
Calvin Robinson	Florida	No	0
Charles Root	North Carolina	Yes	3
Daniel Ruggles	Virginia	No	0
Charles Rundell	None	No	0
John Ryan	South Carolina	Unknown	Unknown
James Safford	Tennessee	Yes	5
John Sanderson	Florida	Unknown	Unknown
Thaddeus Sanford	Alabama	No	0
Caroline Seabury	Mississippi	No	0
Claudius Sears	Mississippi	No	0
Henry Shaw	North Carolina	Yes	26
Daniel Shearer	Louisiana	No	0
George Sheffield	Virginia	No	0
Reuben Shelby	Texas	Yes	8
William Shepard	Virginia	No	0
Gardner Sherman	None	No	0
Sidney Sherman	Kentucky	Yes	1
William Sherman	Louisiana	No	0
Francis Shoup	Florida	No	0
Emily Sinkler	South Carolina	Yes	90
John Slidell	Louisiana	Yes	1
Ashbel Smith	North Carolina	Yes	20
Martin Smith	Florida	No	0
Milo Smith	Louisiana	Yes	3

Name	First Adopted State	Slaveholder	No. of Slaves
Nelson Smith	Alabama	Yes	3
Edward Sparrow	Louisiana	Yes	67
Almon Spencer	Louisiana	No	0
Horatio Spencer	Georgia	Yes	119
William Steele	Texas	No	0
Walter Stevens	Louisiana	No	0
William Stevenson	Virginia	No	0
Otho Strahl	Tennessee	No	0
George Swift	Georgia	Yes	13
Otis Tenney	Delaware	No	0
George Thatcher	Louisiana	No	0
Frederick Thomas	Maryland	Unknown	Unknown
William Thompson	Florida	No	0
Thomas Thorpe	Louisiana	No	0
Nelson Tift	Florida	Yes	11
Salathiel Tobey	Tennessee	No	0
Mary Townsend	Louisiana	No	0
Elisha Tracy	Louisiana	Unknown	Unknown
Amanda Trulock	Georgia	Yes	62
Edward Tucke	North Carolina	No	0
Joseph Tucker	Kentucky	Yes	5
Amasa Turner	Alabama	Yes	15
David Tuttle	Virginia	No	0
Julia Tyler	District of Columbia	Yes	51
John Underwood	Virginia	No	0
Christopher Upson	Texas	No	0
Charles Upton	Virginia	No	0
John Wade	Texas	No	0
William Wadley	Georgia	Yes	10
Robert Walker	Mississippi	Unknown	Unknown
Hiram Warner	Georgia	Yes	92
James Waters	Virginia	Unknown	Unknown
Alfred Watson	North Carolina	No	0
Henry Watson	Alabama	Yes	122
William Weaver	Virginia	Yes	66
William Webster	Maryland	No	0

(cont.)

Name	First Adopted State	Slaveholder	No. of Slaves
Otis Welch	Texas	No	0
Edward Wells	South Carolina	No	0
John Westcott	Florida	Yes	4
Killian Whaley	Virginia	No	0
Thomas Wharton	Mississippi	No	0
Charles Wheeler Jr.	Louisiana	No	0
Royall Wheeler	Arkansas	No	0
Daniel Whitaker	Georgia	Unknown	Unknown
John Wilkes	Maryland	Yes	4
Henry Williams	Georgia	Yes	11
Sarah Williams	North Carolina	Yes	49
Aaron Wellington	South Carolina	Yes	15
Joseph Wilson	Virginia	No	0
John Wood	Maryland	No	0
James Woodrow	Georgia	Yes	1
Thomas Woodward	Kentucky	Unknown	Unknown
Zebulon York	Louisiana	Yes	1700
William Young	Georgia	Yes	15

TABLE 12

Location of Individuals during Secession, Civil War, and Postwar

Name	Residence in 1860	Civil War Service	Postwar Residence
Arunah Abell	Maryland	Union	South
Charles Adams	Arkansas	Confederate	South
Stephen Adams	Virginia	Confederate	South
Amos Akerman	Georgia	Confederate	South
George Alexander	Unknown	Confederate	South and Abroad
William Alexander	Texas	Confederate	South
Ebenezer Allan	Texas	Confederate	None
Frank Armstrong	None	Both	South
George Armstrong	Virginia	Confederate	South
Lewis Ayers	Alabama	Confederate	South
John Bachman	South Carolina	Confederate	South
David Bain	Alabama	Confederate	None
William Baldwin	None	Confederate	Unknown
William Barker	District of Columbia	Confederate	South
Frederick Barnard	Mississippi	Union	North
William Bartlett	Mississippi	Confederate	South
Gordon Battele	Virginia	Union	None
Herman Battles	Louisiana	Confederate	South
Ezra Bauder	South Carolina	Confederate	North and South
J. Edwin Belch	Missouri	Confederate	South
Clifford Belcher	Louisiana	Confederate	South
Noah Benedict	Louisiana	Confederate	None
Daniel Bestor	Mississippi	Confederate	South
Albert Blanchard	Louisiana	Confederate	South
Spince Blankenship	None	Confederate	North
Gail Borden Jr.	None	Union	North and South
John Borden	Texas	Confederate	South
William Bostwick	None	Union	None
Charles Bradford	Louisiana	Confederate	Unknown
Edmund Bradford	Virginia	Confederate	South
David Bridgeford	Virginia	Confederate	North
William Brown	Virginia	Confederate	South

(cont.)

Name	Residence in 1860	Civil War Service	Postwar Residence
William Browne	Georgia	Confederate	South
Hugh Buchanan	Georgia	Confederate	South
Samuel Buckley	Texas	Union	South
Rufus Bullock	Georgia	Confederate	North and South
Dolly Burge	Georgia	Confederate	South
David Burnet	Texas	Confederate	South
Hiram Cassedy	Mississippi	Confederate	Unknown
William Cazneau	None	Neither	Abroad
Alvan Chapman	Florida	Union	South
William Chase	Florida	Confederate	South
Norman Chester	Georgia	Confederate	South
Joseph Claghorn	Georgia	Confederate	South
Theodore Clapp	Kentucky	Union	South
Charles Clark	Mississippi	Confederate	South
William Clark Sr.	Virginia	Confederate	None
Willis Clark	Alabama	Confederate	South
Thomas Clemson	Maryland	Confederate	South
Jeremiah Clough	Texas	Confederate	None
James Colcord	Georgia	Confederate	Unknown
Charles Collins	Virginia	Both	None
Edward Cone	Virginia	Confederate	South
Benjamin Conley	Georgia	Confederate	South
Aaron Conrow	Missouri	Confederate	Abroad
Charles Cooper	Tennessee	Confederate	None
James Cooper	Georgia	Confederate	South
Samuel Cooper	Virginia	Confederate	South
George Crane	Georgia	Confederate	South
Wesley Culp	Virginia	Confederate	None
Moses Curtis	North Carolina	Confederate	South
Charles Dahlgren	Mississippi	Confederate	North and South
Charles Dana	Mississippi	Confederate	South
Joseph Daniels	None	Union	North
Amos Darrow	Mississippi	Both	North and South
John Davis	Georgia	Confederate	None
William Davis	Virginia	Confederate	South

Name	Residence in 1860	Civil War Service	Postwar Residence
W. J. Davis	None	Confederate	None
George Deas	Georgia	Confederate	North
Louis Dembinski	Louisiana	Confederate	North and South
Charles Dimmock	Virginia	Confederate	None
Henry Dimock	North Carolina	Confederate	None
William Douglas	Mississippi	Confederate	South
Timothy Downie	Georgia	Confederate	North
Lemeul Downing	Georgia	Confederate	South
William Drake	Tennessee	Confederate	South
George Drew	Georgia	Confederate	South
Edward Drummond	Georgia	Confederate	South
Johnson Duncan	Louisiana	Confederate	None
Stephen Duncan	Mississippi	Union	North
Benjamin Dunkin	South Carolina	Confederate	South
Samuel Durand	Georgia	Confederate	South
George Eggleston	Virginia	Confederate	North and South
John Ells	Virginia	Confederate	None
Ebenezer Emmons	North Carolina	Confederate	None
Franklin Farmer	Louisiana	Union	Unknown
Phoebe Farmer	Louisiana	Union	North and South
Greenleaf Fisk	Texas	Confederate	South
Henry Flanagin	Arkansas	Confederate	South
Benjamin Flanders	Louisiana	Union	South
Felix de Fontaine	South Carolina	Confederate	North and South
William Foote	Virginia	Confederate	South
Tryphena Fox	Louisiana	Confederate	South
George French Sr.	North Carolina	Confederate	South
Samuel French	Mississippi	Confederate	South
P. A. Frercks	North Carolina	Confederate	South
Daniel Frost	Missouri	Confederate	South and Abroad
Frederick Fuller	Georgia	Confederate	None
Franklin Gardner	Louisiana	Confederate	South
Joseph Garey	Mississippi	Confederate	North and South
William Gere	Louisiana	Confederate	North
William Gilham	Virginia	Confederate	North and South

(cont.)

Name	Residence in 1860	Civil War Service	Postwar Residence
Charles Gillette	Texas	Confederate	North
Henry Gillette	Texas	Confederate	South
Caroline Gilman	South Carolina	Confederate	North and South
George Goldthwaite	Alabama	Confederate	South
Josiah Gorgas	None	Confederate	South
William Gould	Georgia	Confederate	South
Archibald Gracie Jr.	Alabama	Confederate	None
Douglass Gray	Virginia	Confederate	None
Jonathan Greely	Florida	Confederate	South
Richard Griffith	Mississippi	Confederate	None
Silas Grisamore	Louisiana	Confederate	South
James Hagan	Alabama	Confederate	South
Sally Hampton	South Carolina	Confederate	None
Henry Handerson	Louisiana	Confederate	North
Samuel Hanen	Virginia	Union	Unknown
Hiram Hanover	Texas	Confederate	South
Kenton Harper	Virginia	Confederate	South
J. George Harris	Tennessee	Union	South
Lewis Hatch	South Carolina	Confederate	South
Robert Hatton	Tennessee	Confederate	None
Wells Hawks	Virginia	Confederate	South
Dennis Heartt	North Carolina	Union	South
William Heyward	South Carolina	Confederate	None
Eugene Hilgard	Mississippi	Confederate	North and South
James Hill	North Carolina	Confederate	South
Oscar Hinricks	None	Both	South
Samuel Hinsdale	North Carolina	Confederate	South
Robert Hitt	None	Confederate	None
Jedediah Hotchkiss	Virginia	Confederate	South
Volney Howard	None	Union	North
Fred Hull	Georgia	Confederate	Unknown
Caleb Huse	Alabama	Confederate	North, South, Abroad
George Hutter	Virginia	Confederate	South
Ross Ihrie	North Carolina	Confederate	South

Name	Residence in 1860	Civil War Service	Postwar Residence
Porter Ingram	Georgia	Confederate	South
Joseph Ives	Virginia	Confederate	North
Henry Jewett	Georgia	Confederate	Unknown
Bushrod Johnson	Tennessee	Confederate	North and South
Charles Johnson	Louisiana	Confederate	South and Abroad
Joseph Johnson	Virginia	Confederate	South
Oliver Jones	Texas	Confederate	South
George Junkin Sr.	Virginia	Union	North
George Junkin	Virginia	Confederate	South
Robert Kelly	None	Confederate	North
William Kelly	Kentucky	Union	South
Amos Kendall	Kentucky	Union	South
George Kendall	Texas	Confederate	South
John Kimberly	North Carolina	Confederate	South
Thomas King	Georgia	Confederate	None
Lee Kramer	Virginia	Union	South
Julius de Lagnel	Virginia	Confederate	South
Robert Lane	Tennessee	Confederate	South
Walter Lane	Texas	Confederate	South
John Lathrop	Missouri	Union	South
Danville Leadbetter	Alabama	Confederate	Abroad
Abner Leavenworth	Virginia	Confederate	South
Abiel Leonard	Missouri	Union	None
Julius Lewis	North Carolina	Confederate	South
James Lindley	Missouri	Union	North and South
Amelia Lines	Georgia	Confederate	North and South
John Long	North Carolina	Confederate	Unknown
Mansfield Lovell	None	Confederate	North
Joseph Lyman	Louisiana	Both	North
William Lyman	Louisiana	Confederate	South
Robert Maclay	Louisiana	Confederate	South
Henry Marean	Arkansas	Union	Unknown
Albion Martin	Virginia	Confederate	South
Levi Marvin	Missouri	Union	South
William Marvin	Florida	Union	North and South

(cont.)

Name	Residence in 1860	Civil War Service	Postwar Residence
Horace Maynard	Tennessee	Union	South
Arthur McArthur Jr.	Louisiana	Confederate	None
Henry McCay	Georgia	Confederate	South
Henry McClellan	Virginia	Confederate	South
Robert McClellan	Georgia	Confederate	North and South
Edward McClure	South Carolina	Confederate	Unknown
William McComb	Tennessee	Confederate	South
William McGuffey	Virginia	Confederate	South
Daniel McKay	Texas	Confederate	South
George Meade	Arkansas	Confederate	South
Edwin Merrick	Louisiana	Confederate	South
Eli Merriman	Texas	Confederate	South
John Mitchell	Texas	Confederate	South
Francis Moore Jr.	Texas	Union	None
Samuel Moore	Virginia	Confederate	South
Isaac Murphy	Arkansas	Union	South
Samuel Myers	Virginia	Confederate	None
Wilson Nicholas	Maryland	Confederate	South
James Nixon	Louisiana	Confederate	South
John O'Brien	Arkansas	Confederate	South
William Owen	Louisiana	Confederate	South
Horatio Parker	Texas	Confederate	South
Homer Parsons	Arkansas	Confederate	South
Lewis Parsons	Alabama	Union	South
Samuel Pasco	Florida	Confederate	South
Spicer Patrick	Virginia	Union	South
Edmund Patterson	Alabama	Confederate	South
James Patterson	Kentucky	Union	South
J. G. Patterson	None	Confederate	Unknown
Elisha Pease	Texas	Union	South
Lucadia Pease	Texas	Union	South
John Pemberton	Virginia	Confederate	North and South
Edward Perry	Florida	Confederate	South
Richard Peters	Georgia	Confederate	South
Alexander Phillips	Texas	Confederate	South

Name	Residence in 1860	Civil War Service	Postwar Residence
William Pierce	None	Union	Unknown
Aaron Piggot	Maryland	Confederate	South
Albert Pike	Arkansas	Confederate	South and Abroad
William Plumer	None	Union	North
Daniel Pratt	Alabama	Confederate	South
John Pratt	Louisiana	Confederate	North
Nathaniel Pratt	Georgia	Confederate	South
George Prentice	Kentucky	Union	South
Margaret Preston	Virginia	Confederate	South
Edward Pynchon	Alabama	Confederate	South
Charles Quintard	Tennessee	Confederate	South
Daniel Reynolds	Arkansas	Confederate	South
William Rice	Texas	Confederate	North
Henry Richardson	Louisiana	Confederate	South
John Riddell	Louisiana	Confederate	South
William Riddell	Texas	Confederate	South
Roswell Ripley	South Carolina	Confederate	South and Abroad
Anna Ritchie	Virginia	Neither	Abroad
James Robb	None	Union	North and South
Calvin Robinson	Florida	Union	South
Charles Root	North Carolina	Confederate	South
Daniel Ruggles	Texas	Confederate	South
Charles Rundell	None	Confederate	Abroad
John Ryan	South Carolina	Confederate	South
James Safford	Tennessee	Confederate	South
John Sanderson	Florida	Confederate	South
Thaddeus Sanford	Alabama	Confederate	South
Caroline Seabury	Mississippi	Confederate	North and South
Claudius Sears	Mississippi	Confederate	South
Henry Shaw	North Carolina	Confederate	None
Daniel Shearer	Louisiana	Confederate	North and South
George Sheffield	Virginia	Confederate	South
Reuben Shelby	Missouri	Confederate	Unknown
William Shepard	Virginia	Confederate	South
Gardner Sherman	None	Confederate	Unknown

(cont.)

Name	Residence in 1860	Civil War Service	Postwar Residence
Sidney Sherman	Texas	Confederate	South
William Sherman	Louisiana	Union	North and South
Francis Shoup	Florida	Confederate	South
Emily Sinkler	South Carolina	Confederate	North and South
John Slidell	Louisiana	Confederate	Abroad
Ashbel Smith	Texas	Confederate	South
Martin Smith	Georgia	Confederate	South
Milo Smith	Louisiana	Confederate	South
Nelson Smith	Alabama	Confederate	South
Edward Sparrow	Louisiana	Confederate	South
Almon Spencer	Alabama	Confederate	Unknown
Horatio Spencer	Mississippi	Confederate	South
William Steele	Texas	Confederate	South
Walter Stevens	Louisiana	Confederate	Abroad
William Stevenson	Virginia	Union	South
Otho Strahl	Tennessee	Confederate	None
George Swift	Georgia	Confederate	South
Otis Tenney	Kentucky	Confederate	South
George Thatcher	Louisiana	Confederate	South
Frederick Thomas	Alabama	Confederate	South
William Thompson	Georgia	Confederate	South
Thomas Thorpe	Louisiana	Union	Unknown
Nelson Tift	Georgia	Confederate	South
Salathiel Tobey	Tennessee	Confederate	North and South
Mary Townsend	Louisiana	Confederate	South
Elisha Tracy	Louisiana	Confederate	None
Amanda Trulock	Arkansas	Confederate	North
Edward Tucke	North Carolina	Both	South
Joseph Tucker	Kentucky	Confederate	South
Amasa Turner	Texas	Confederate	South
David Tuttle	Virginia	Confederate	North and South
Julia Tyler	Virginia	Confederate	North and South
John Underwood	None	Union	South
Christopher Upson	Texas	Confederate	South
Charles Upton	Virginia	Union	Abroad

Name	Residence in 1860	Civil War Service	Postwar Residence
John Wade	Texas	Confederate	South
William Wadley	Georgia	Confederate	South
Robert Walker	District of Columbia	Union	South
Hiram Warner	Georgia	Confederate	South
James Waters	Virginia	Confederate	South
Alfred Watson	North Carolina	Confederate	South
Henry Watson	Alabama	Neither	North and South
William Weaver	Virginia	Confederate	None
William Webster	Maryland	Confederate	None
Otis Welch	Texas	Confederate	South
Edward Wells	South Carolina	Confederate	South
John Westcott	Florida	Confederate	South
Killian Whaley	Virginia	Union	South
Thomas Wharton	Louisiana	Confederate	None
Charles Wheeler Jr.	Louisiana	Confederate	South
Royall Wheeler	Texas	Confederate	None
Daniel Whitaker	South Carolina	Confederate	South
John Wilkes	North Carolina	Confederate	South
Henry Williams	Georgia	Confederate	South
Sarah Williams	Georgia	Confederate	South
Aaron Wellington	South Carolina	Confederate	None
Joseph Wilson	Georgia	Confederate	North and South
John Wood	Maryland	Confederate	Abroad
James Woodrow	South Carolina	Confederate	South
Thomas Woodward	Kentucky	Confederate	None
Zebulon York	Louisiana	Confederate	South
William Young	Georgia	Confederate	South

Notes

Introduction

1. Christian B. Keller, "Keystone Confederates: Pennsylvanians Who Fought for Dixie," in William Blair and William Pencack, eds., *Making and Remaking Pennsylvania's Civil War* (University Park, Pa.: Pennsylvania State Univ. Press, 2001), 1–22; Thomas A. Desjardin, *These Honored Dead: How the Story of Gettysburg Shaped American Memory* (Cambridge, Mass.: Da Capo Press, 2003); *Adams Sentinel,* June 3, 1862, http://www.encyclopediavirginia.org/Culp_s_Hill_and_Wesley_Culp_1839–1863.

2. http://www.encyclopediavirginia.org/Culp_s_Hill_and_Wesley_Culp_1839–1863.

3. Fletcher Green, *The Role of the Yankee in the Old South* (Athens: Univ. of Georgia Press, 1972), 5–6, 19.

4. Seargent Prentiss to his mother, June 24, 1829, quoted in George Lewis Prentiss, ed., *A Memoir of S.S. Prentiss,* 2 vols. (New York: Charles Scribner's Sons, 1891), 1:101.

5. For a sample of the literature on this subject, see William W. Freehling, *The South vs. the South: How Anti-Confederate Southerners Shaped the Course of the Civil War* (New York: Oxford Univ. Press, 2001); Richard Nelson Current, *Lincoln's Loyalists: Union Soldiers from the Confederacy* (Boston, Mass.: Northeastern Univ. Press, 1992); Daniel Crofts, *Reluctant Confederates: Upper South Unionists in the Secession Crisis* (Chapel Hill: Univ. of North Carolina Press, 1989); James Alex Baggett, *The Scalawags: Southern Dissenters in the Civil War and Reconstruction* (Baton Rouge: Louisiana State Univ. Press, 2003); Daniel Sutherland, ed., *Guerrillas, Unionists and Violence on the Confederate Home Front* (Fayetteville: Univ. of Arkansas Press, 1999); Edward Ayers, *In the Presence of Mine Enemies: War in the Heart of America, 1859–1863* (New York: W. W. Norton, 2003).

6. When historians do mention these individuals, they tend to regard them as either an anomaly or not really a part of the South at all. See James M. McPherson,

Battle Cry of Freedom: The Civil War Era (New York: Oxford Univ. Press, 1988), 282; William W. Freehling, *The Road to Disunion, Vol. 2: Secessionists Triumphant, 1854–1861* (New York: Oxford Univ. Press, 2007), 237–40; Joseph Rainer, "The Honorable Fraternity of Moving Merchants: Yankee Peddlers in the Old South, 1800–1860" (PhD diss., College of William and Mary, 2000), 51–52; D. Clayton James, *Antebellum Natchez* (Baton Rouge: Louisiana State Univ. Press, 1968), 217.

7. William Gilmore Simms quoted in Peter Parish, *The North and the Nation in the Era of the Civil War,* eds. Adam I. Smith and Susan-Mary Grant (New York: Fordham Univ. Press, 2003), 143; Philip Hone quoted in Susan-Mary Grant, *North Over South: Northern Nationalism and American Identity in the Antebellum Era* (Lawrence: Univ. Press of Kansas, 2000), 68. Reflecting on this relationship further, historians John M. McCardell and David M. Potter argued that American nationalism, instead of being an isolated category, grew directly out of these local loyalties and commitments. See John M. McCardell, *The Idea of a Southern Nation: Southern Nationalists and Southern Nationalism, 1830–1860* (New York: W.W. Norton & Company, 1979), 3–9; Don E. Fehrenbacher, ed., *History and American Society: Essays of David M. Potter* (New York: Oxford Univ. Press, 1973), 75–85.

8. David Potter highlights the period between 1848 and 1861 as the time when national loyalty was fatally weakened by growing sectional loyalties, citing the paradox of the events of the 1850s as simultaneously allowing the Union to survive and threatening its survival. David M. Potter, *The Impending Crisis 1848–1861: Completed and Edited by Don E. Fehrenbacher* (New York: Harper & Row, 1976), 17.

9. McPherson, *Battle Cry of Freedom,* 859–60.

10. *New York Times,* March 1, 1854.

11. Historian James Miller, who generally agrees with this assessment, tracked planter emigration and found that slaveholders mainly moved from Georgia, the Carolinas, and Virginia to Alabama, Mississippi, and Louisiana. He concludes that emigration "was less likely to be into 'the wilderness' but rather toward a landscape that in its broad features resembled 'home.'" James M. Miller, *South by Southwest: Planter Emigration and Identity in the Slave South* (Charlottesville: Univ. of Virginia Press, 2002), 11.

12. U.S. Census Office, *Statistics of the United States (Including Mortality, Property, &c.) in 1860; Compiled from the Original Returns and Being the Final Exhibit of The Eighth Census, Under the Direction of the Secretary of the Interior* (Washington, D.C.: Government Printing Office, 1866), lxi–lxii.

13. Supporters of this interpretation generally point to the 1820s and 1830s as the breaking point between northern and southern sectional identity. Events like the Panic of 1819, the establishment of the Missouri Compromise line, and the Nullification Crisis revealed the different economic systems used by each section,

as well as drawing a new line stretching across the continent that divided them. Slavery had a lot to do with that division because by the end of the 1830s abolitionists waged their campaign in full force, and southerners became much more suspicious of northerners and their intentions. For more analysis on this school of thought, see Grant, *North Over South*, 5–6, 8–20, 35–58, 63–65, 149; Rollin G. Osterweis, *Romanticism and Nationalism in the Old South* (New Haven, Conn.: Yale Univ. Press, 1949), 1–11, 40, 213–16; Charles S. Sydnor, *The Development of Southern Sectionalism 1819–1848* (Baton Rouge: Louisiana State Univ. Press, 1948), ix, 1–6, 20–32, 104–33; Clement Eaton, *The Freedom-of-Thought Struggle in the Old South* (New York: Harper Torchbooks, 1964), 351–52; Robert LeRoy Hilldrup, "Cold War Against the Yankees in the Antebellum Literature of Southern Women," *The North Carolina Historical Review* 31 (July 1954): 378; William Taylor, *Cavalier and Yankee: The Old South and American National Character* (Cambridge, Mass.: Harvard Univ. Press, 1979); Samuel G. French, *Two Wars: An Autobiography of Gen. Samuel G. French, An Officer in the Armies of the United States and the Confederate States, A Graduate from the U.S. Military Academy, West Point 1843. Mexican War; War Between the States, A Diary; Reconstruction Period, His Experience; Incidents, Reminiscences, Etc* (Nashville, Tenn.: Confederate Veteran, 1901); McCardell, *Idea of a Southern Nation*, 3–9; J. Parker Mason, "Henry Watson: Assimilation of a Yankee in the Land of Cotton" (PhD diss., Duke University, 1983), 21; Miller, *South by Southwest*, 22–23, 28; Parish, *The North and the Nation in the Era of the Civil War*, 129–31; Donald Davidson, *Regionalism and Nationalism in the United States: The Attack on the Leviathan* (New Brunswick, Maine: Transaction Publishers, 1991), 323; Frederick Jackson Turner, *The United States 1830–1850: The Nation and Its Sections* (New York: W. W. Norton & Company, 1935), 68; W. J. Cash, *The Mind of the South* (New York: Vintage Books, 1941), 28–29.

14. Some historians, especially Frederick Jackson Turner, Donald Davidson, and William Freehling, take this analysis even further by emphasizing divisions not only between regions but also within regions, especially in the South. In their analyses, the United States of the nineteenth century was divided not just into North and South but also into the sub-regions of New England, Northwest, South Atlantic, Southwest, and Trans-Mississippi. See Frederick Jackson Turner, "New England 1830–1850," *Huntington Library Bulletin* 1 (May 1931): 153–98; Turner, *The United States*, 144–55; Davidson, *Regionalism and Nationalism*, 12–25, 45–48; William Freehling, *The Road to Disunion: Secessionists at Bay 1776–1854* (New York: Oxford Univ. Press, 1990); Freehling, *Road to Disunion: Secessionists Triumphant*; and Freehling, *The South vs. the South*.

15. McCardell, *Idea of a Southern Nation*, 3–9; Potter, *The Impending Crisis*, 8–10, 472; Fehrenbacher, *History and American Society*, 86–87; David Waldstreicher, *In the Midst of Perpetual Fetes: The Making of American Nationalism, 1776–1820*

(Chapel Hill: Univ. of North Carolina Press, 1997), 6, 248–51; Parish, *North and the Nation,* xv, 92–95; Rogan Kersh, *Dreams of a More Perfect Union* (Ithaca, N.Y.: Cornell Univ. Press, 2001), 1–21; Michael F. Holt, *The Rise and Fall of the American Whig Party: Jacksonian Politics and the Onset of the Civil War* (New York: Oxford Univ. Press, 1999), ix–xiv.

16. Parish, *North and the Nation,* chap. 4; Patrick Gerster and Nicholas Cords, "The Northern Origins of Southern Mythology," *Journal of Southern History* 43 (November 1977): 569–70; Carl N. Degler, *Place Over Time: The Continuity of Southern Distinctiveness* (Baton Rouge: Louisiana State Univ. Press, 1977), chap. 3, 90–91.

17. Some authors take this idea further by arguing that we need to look beyond the "Whig interpretation," which views American history as encompassing freedom, national unity, urban growth, and ethnic diversity. Such an interpretation by definition casts southerners as outsiders because the latter defended slavery, launched secession, had fewer large cities, and not as much immigration. Author Carl Degler, along with historians like C. Vann Woodward and Howard Zinn, wrote that the South, though unique, still deserved inclusion in the American saga because southerners were just as interested in profit-making as northerners, and the former's reliance on slave labor and agriculture enabled the North to expand into industry, since the South provided a market for northern manufacturing and helped pay for foreign imports through cotton exports. See Carl N. Degler, "Thesis, Antithesis, Synthesis: The South, the North, and the Nation," *Journal of Southern History* 53 (February 1987): 4–9, 18.

18. For further discussion, see Peter Parish, "Abraham Lincoln and American Nationhood," in *Legacy of Disunion: The Enduring Significance of the American Civil War,* ed. Susan-Mary Grant and Peter Parish (Baton Rouge: Louisiana State Univ. Press, 2003), 116–17; Parish, *North and the Nation,* xiii–xviii, 57–61; Elizabeth R. Varon, *Disunion: The Coming of the American Civil War 1789–1859* (Chapel Hill: Univ. of North Carolina Press, 2008), 1–16; Robert E. Bonner, *Mastering America: Southern Slaveholders and the Crisis of American Nationhood* (New York: Cambridge Univ. Press, 2009), xi–xxii; Brian R. Dirck, *Lincoln & Davis: Imagining America 1809–1865* (Lawrence: Univ. Press of Kansas, 2001), 1–6; Wilbur Zelinsky, *Nation into State: The Shifting Symbolic Foundations of American Nationalism* (Chapel Hill: Univ. of North Carolina Press, 1988), 1–19; William L. Barney, *Battleground for the Union: The Era of the Civil War and Reconstruction 1848–1877* (Englewood Cliffs, N.J.: Prentice-Hall, 1990), ix–x; McCardell, *Idea of a Southern Nation,* 3–9.

19. Within this debate lies the major question of the meaning of nationalism and sectionalism. On the sociological end, authors like Benedict Anderson view nationalism as an "imagined community," (whereby people who have never or will ever meet each other still feel a connection) while others claim nationalism has

existed since ancient times or requires collective memory, myth, and a sense of the past and of a destiny to exist. Yet the United States did not have the general characteristics of the sociological understanding of nationalism, and so American historians have had to tweak their own analyses to account for American distinctiveness. For further analysis, see Benedict Anderson, *Imagined Communities: Reflections on the Origin and Spread of Nationalism* (New York: Verso, 1991); Aviel Roshwald, *The Endurance of Nationalism: Ancient Roots and Modern Dilemmas* (New York: Cambridge Univ. Press, 2006), 1–6; Anthony D. Smith, *The Ethnic Origins of Nations* (Oxford, Eng.: Basil Blackwell Ltd., 1986), 1–5; Osterweis, *Romanticism and Nationalism,* 136–37; Fehrenbacher, *History and American Society,* 61–108; Parish, *North and the Nation,* 114–15; Charles Joyner, "Forget, Hell! The Civil War in Southern Memory," in *Legacy of Disunion*, ed. Grant and Parish, 19; Mitchell Snay, *Fenians, Freedmen, and Southern Whites: Race and Nationality in the Era of Reconstruction* (Baton Rouge: Louisiana State Univ. Press, 2007), 10; Dirck, *Lincoln and Davis,* 241–46.

20. Parish, *North and the Nation,* 63.

21. For the major contributors to this debate, see Drew Faust, *The Creation of Confederate Nationalism: Ideology and Identity in the Civil War South* (Baton Rouge: Louisiana State Univ. Press, 1988); Gary W. Gallagher, *The Confederate War* (Cambridge, Mass.: Harvard Univ. Press, 1997); Freehling, *The South vs. the South;* Potter, *Impending Crisis;* Waldstreicher, *Midst of Perpetual Fetes;* Paul D. Escott, *After Secession: Jefferson Davis and the Failure of Confederate Nationalism* (Baton Rouge: Louisiana State Univ. Press, 1978); Bonner, *Mastering America;* Varon, *Disunion;* Zelinsky, *Nation Into State;* Michael T. Bernath, *Confederate Minds: The Struggle for Intellectual Independence in the Civil War South* (Chapel Hill: Univ. of North Carolina Press, 2010); McCardell, *Idea of a Southern Nation.*

22. Faust, *Creation of Confederate Nationalism,* 6–7, 83–84.

23. Daniel Sutherland, "Southern Fraternal Organizations in the North," *Journal of Southern History* 53 (November 1987): 590; Jan C. Dawson, "The Puritan and the Cavalier: The South's Perception of Contrasting Traditions," *Journal of Southern History* 44 (November 1978): 597–660. See also Robert F. Dalzell, Jr., *Daniel Webster and the Trial of American Nationalism 1843–1852* (Houghton Mifflin Company, 1973), 128–31; French, *Two Wars,* 24–25; Degler, *Place Over Time,* 58–59.

24. Alexis de Tocqueville quoted in Felix G. De Fontaine, *Marginalia, or Gleanings From an Army Notebook* (Columbia, S.C.: Steam Power Press of F.G. De Fontaine & Co., 1864), 2, LV; Anthony M. Keiley, *Prisoner of War, or Five Months Among the Yankees. Being a Narrative of the Crosses, Calamities, and Consolations of a Petersburg Militiaman During an Enforced Summer Residence North* (Richmond, Va.: West & Johnson, 1865), 108; Sally Hampton to Lucy Baxter,

March 23–24, 1859, quoted in Sally Baxter Hampton, *A Divided Heart: Letters of Sally Baxter Hampton 1853–1862*, ed. Ann Frip Hampton (Spartanburg, S.C.: Reprint Co., 1980), 50–51; Sally Hampton to George Baxter, December 22, 1860, quoted in ibid., 83.

25. Quoted in Bonner, *Mastering America,* 47. For more discussion on this theme, see Turner, *The United States,* 210–15, 238–47; Norman Johnson, "Yankees in Gray: A Myriad of Reasons—Some Professional, Others Personal—Impelled 30 Northern-Born Soldiers to Become Generals for the South. With Few Exceptions, They Served Valorously and Unselfishly for the Southern Cause," *American Civil War* 5 (September 1992): 64; Russell Duncan, *Entrepreneur for Equality: Governor Rufus Bullock, Commerce, and Race in Post–Civil War Georgia* (Athens: Univ. of Georgia Press, 1994), 176–77; Curt John Evans, "Daniel Pratt: Yankee Industrialist in the Antebellum South" (master's thesis, Louisiana State Univ., 1993).

26. A few historians and biographers of northern emigrants, on the other hand, offer a more balanced view. Rather than always feeling alienated, these authors argue, northerners found acceptance and a good life in the South if they adapted to southern culture. See Martha Jane Brazy, *An American Planter: Stephen Duncan of Antebellum Natchez and New York* (Baton Rouge: Louisiana State Univ. Press, 2006), 3; Green, *Role of the Yankee,* 5–6; Keller, "Keystone Confederates," in Blair, *Making and Remaking,* 14; Benjamin Hillon Miller, "Elisha Marshall Pease: A Biography" (master's thesis, Univ. of Texas at Austin, 1927), 9–11; Mason, "Henry Watson," 12–16; William H. Baria, "The Poetess: Margaret Junkin Preston of Lexington, Virginia," in *Confederate Women*, ed. Mauriel Phillips Joslyn (Gretna, La.: Pelican Publishing Company, 2004), 133–34.; Michael B. Ballard, *Pemberton: The General Who Lost Vicksburg* (Jackson: Univ. of Mississippi Press, 1999); Robert Lipscomb Duncan, *Reluctant General: Life and Times of Albert Pike* (New York: Dutton, 1961).

27. U.S. Census Office, *Statistics of the United States (Including Mortality, Property, &c.,) in 1860,* lxi–lxii.

28. Historian Christopher Phillips makes a similar argument for Missourians, who he says drew distinctions not from birth but from their views on slavery. See Christopher Phillips, *Missouri's Confederate: Claiborne Fox Jackson and the Creation of Southern Identity in the Border West* (Columbia: Univ. of Missouri Press, 2000), 195, 293–95.

29. Edward Pessen, "How Different From Each Other Were the Antebellum North and South?" *American Historical Review* 85 (December 1980): 1119–20. Even the term "Yankee" itself did not describe all northerners in the way people assumed it did. Author Joseph Rainer argues that "Yankee" referred to someone from New England and did not really encompass anyone from other areas of the North like

New Jersey or Illinois. Rainer, "The Honorable Fraternity of Moving Merchants," 10–11.

30. Waldstreicher, *Midst of Perpetual Fetes*, 78; McCardell, *Idea of a Southern Nation*, 3–9; Bonner, *Mastering America*, 286–89.

31. Fletcher Green used similar criteria in his analysis of the role of northerners in the Old South, but he included any northerner who moved to the South at any time in the eighteenth and nineteenth centuries at any age. Green, *Role of the Yankee*.

32. Daniel Sutherland used a similar strategy in his study of ex-Confederates who carved out new lives in the North during Reconstruction. As he wrote in a footnote, "Little will ever be known about most of the southerners who migrated northward after the war. The people examined here, then, are for the most part the ones who succeeded in the North, people who became respected members of the middle and upper classes of their communities and who have left some record of their lives. They may or may not be typical of other southerners in the North . . . But for the moment, these hearty souls are in their own right an important group and worthy of close inspection." Daniel Sutherland, "Former Confederates in the Post-Civil War North: An Unexplored Aspect of Reconstruction History," *Journal of Southern History* 47 (August 1981): 394.

33. McPherson, *Battle Cry of Freedom*, 560.

34. Ibid., 771–76.

35. U.S. Census Office, *Statistics of the United States (Including Mortality, Property, &c.,) in 1860*, lxi–lxii.

36. For a review of the sources used for biographical information used to put together this study, see Ezra J. Warner and W. Buck Yearns, *Biographical Register of the Confederate Congress* (Baton Rouge: Louisiana State Univ. Press, 1975); Ezra J. Warner, *Generals In Gray: Lives of the Confederate Commanders* (Baton Rouge: Louisiana State Univ. Press, 1959); Robert E. L. Krick, *Staff Officers in Gray: A Biographical Register of the Staff Officers in the Army of Northern Virginia* (Chapel Hill: Univ. of North Carolina Press, 2003); Robert E. L. Krick, *Lee's Colonels: A Biographical Register of the Field Officers of the Army of Northern Virginia* (Dayton, Ohio: Press of Morningside Bookshop, 1979); Bruce A. Allardice, *More Generals in Gray*. (Baton Rouge: Louisiana State Univ. Press, 1995); William C. Davis and Julie Hoffman, *The Confederate General* (Harrisburg, Pa.: National Historical Society, 1991); Nathaniel Cheairs Hughes, *Yale's Confederates: A Biographical Dictionary* (Knoxville: Univ. of Tennessee Press, 2008); Helen Trimpi, *Crimson Confederates: Harvard Men Who Fought for the South* (Knoxville: Univ. of Tennessee Press, 2010).

1. Native Northerners Move South

1. Author Jared Diamond argues that entire civilizations followed that pattern because similar latitudes meant the same crops and livestock would grow in any area along those axes. Crops, ideas, and inventions spread across Europe, Asia, and North Africa much more easily than between North and South America. Jared Diamond, *Guns, Germs, and Steel: The Fates of Human Societies* (New York: W.W. Norton & Company, 1999), 176–91.

2. One major exception to this pattern was a group of 120 families from New York who set up a "colony" near Alexandria, Virginia. The families purchased 24,000 acres and were viewed as a Yankee colony in the state. Green, *The Role of the Yankee*, 112.

3. John Fulton and Margaret Barnard, eds., *Memoirs of Frederick A. P. Barnard, Tenth President of Columbia College in the City of New York* (New York: MacMillan and Co., 1896), 1–9, 17–20; Henry E. Handerson, *Yankee in Gray: The Civil War Memoirs of Henry E. Handerson with a Selection of His Wartime Letters*, ed. Clyde Lottridge Cummer (Cleveland, Ohio: The Press of Western Reserve Univ., 1962), 4; Clarence R. Wharton, *Gail Borden, Pioneer* (San Antonio, Tex.: The Naylor Company, 1941), 2–4; Ballard, *Pemberton*, 4–8; Peter Roper, *Jedediah Hotchkiss: Rebel Mapmaker and Virginia Businessman* (Shippensburg, Pa.: White Mane Publishing Co., 1992), 3–7; Michael Strong, *Keystone Confederate: The Life and Times of General Johnson Kelly Duncan, C.S.A.* (York, Pa.: The Historical Society of York County, 1994), 1–8, 19–22; French, *Two Wars*, 2–4. For more examples of long ancestries in the North among northern emigrants, see Dennis Boman, *Abiel Leonard, Yankee Slaveholder, Eminent Jurist, and Passionate Unionist* (New York: Edwin Mellen Press, 2002), 2–5; Roger Allen Griffin, "Connecticut Yankee in Texas: A Biography of Elisha Marshall Pease" (PhD diss., Univ. of Texas at Austin, 1973), 1–2; Sigsbee C. Prince Jr., "Edward Aylsworth Perry Florida's Thirteen Governor" (master's thesis, Univ. of Florida, 1949), 1–8; Bill Blevins, *Albert Pike, 1809–1891* (Pangburn, Ark.: Tumbling Shoals Publishing Company, 2005), 1–6; Elizabeth Silverthorne, *Ashbel Smith of Texas: Pioneer, Patriot, Statesman, 1805–1886* (College Station: Texas A&M Univ. Press, 1982), 3–4; T. B. Catherwood, *The Life and Labors of William W. Wadley, With an Account of the Wadley Memorial Association, and the Ceremony of Unveiling the Statue* (Savannah, Ga.: Morning News Steam Printing House, 1885), 3–4; Edmund Berkeley and Dorothy Smith Berkeley, *A Yankee Botanist in the Carolinas: The Reverend Moses Ashley Curtis, D.D. (1808–1872)* (Berlin, Pa.: J. Cramer, 1986), 13–19; C. W. Tazewell, ed., *Major Edmund Bradford, U. S. Army and Confederate States Army* (Virginia Beach, Va.: W. S. Dawson Co., 1994), 6–7; Evans, "Daniel Pratt," 8–9; Hampton, *A Divided Heart*, xi; Tryphena Blanche Holder Fox, *A Northern Woman in the Plantation*

South: Letters of Tryphena Blanche Holder Fox 1856–1876, ed. Wilma King (Columbia: Univ. of South Carolina Press, 1993), 1–4; John S. Kendall, "George Wilkins Kendall and the Founding of the New Orleans 'Picayune,'" *The Louisiana Historical Quarterly* 11 (April 1928): 262.

4. Nevertheless, a few adoptive southerners did have ancestors who originally came from the South, including parents who migrated to the North. See Harold J. Koke, "John Taylor Wood, Confederate States Navy" (master's thesis, Humboldt State College, 1963), 2–3; James Vaulx Drake, *Life of General Robert Hatton, Including His Most Important Public Speeches, Together With Much of His Washington & Army Correspondence* (Nashville, Tenn.: Marshall & Bruce, 1867), 3–6.

5. Forty-seven were born in the first decade of the nineteenth century, three in the 1840s, and five had unknown birth years.

6. For a sample of the families and early lives of northern emigrants, see William Joseph Chute, "The Life of Frederick A. P. Barnard To His Election as President of Columbia College in 1864" (PhD diss., Columbia Univ., 1951), 30–31; Strong, *Keystone Confederate,* 1–8; Griffin, "Connecticut Yankee in Texas," 1–5; Blevins, *Albert Pike,* 1–6; Silverthorne, *Ashbel Smith,* 3–4; Catherwood, *Life and Labors of William W. Wadley,* 3–4; Berkeley, *A Yankee Botanist,* 13–19; Koke, "John Taylor Wood," 2–3; Tazewell, *Major Edmund Bradford,* 6–7; Hampton, *A Divided Heart,* xi; Robert Poole, *Thomas G. Clemson: His Influence in Developing Land-Grant Colleges* (Princeton, N.J.: Newcomen Pub., 1957), 7–8; Herschel Gower, *Charles Dahlgren of Natchez: The Civil War and Dynastic Decline* (Washington, D.C.: Brassey's Inc., 2002), 1–3, 6; Brazy, *An American Planter,* 4–6; Fox, *A Northern Woman,* 1–4; Frank Everson Vandiver, *Ploughshares into Swords: Josiah Gorgas and Confederate Ordnance* (Austin: Univ. of Texas Press, 1952), chap. 1; Handerson, *Yankee in Gray,* 15; Roper, *Rebel Mapmaker,* 3–7; Walter Lane, *The Adventures and Recollections of General Walter P. Lane, a San Jacinto Veteran; Containing Sketches of the Texan, Mexican, and Late Wars, with Several Indian Fights Thrown In,* ed. Mary Jane Lane (Marshall, Tex.: News Messenger Publication Company, 1928), 115; Ballard, *Pemberton,* 4–8; Louis Martin Sears, *John Slidell* (Durham, N.C.: Duke Univ. Press, 1925), 6; Joseph D. Shields, *The Life and Times of Seargent Smith Prentiss* (Philadelphia, Pa.: J. B. Lippincott, 1884), 3–4; "Window Panes at 11 Orange St. Tell Part of the Gilman Story," *The News and Courier,* February 24, 1952, Caroline Gilman Papers, Special Collections, Marlene and Nathan Addlestone Library, College of Charleston, Charleston, South Carolina (hereafter cited as CC); Robert C. Black and Gary W. Gallagher, *The Railroads of the Confederacy* (Chapel Hill: Univ. of North Carolina Press, 1998), 108; Theodore Clapp, *Autobiographical Sketches and Recollections During a Thirty-Five Year Residence in New Orleans* (Boston, Mass.: Phillips, Sampson & Co., 1857), 1–26; Mason, "Henry Watson," 8–9; Drake, *Life of General Robert Hatton,* 7–16; Frederick Slate, *Biographical Memoir*

of Eugene Woldemar Hilgard 1833–1916 (City of Washington: National Academy of Sciences, 1919), 95–99; John I. Smith, *The Courage of a Southern Unionist: A Biography of Isaac Murphy, Governor of Arkansas, 1864–68* (Little Rock, Ark.: Rose Publishing Co., 1979), 7–8, 11; Robert Franzetti, "Elisha Marshall Pease and Reconstruction" (master's thesis, Southwest Texas State Univ., 1970), 1, 4; John Bell, *Confederate Seadog: John Taylor Wood in War and Exile* (Jefferson, N.C.: McFarland & Company, Inc., 2002), 12–15; Kendall, "George Wilkins Kendall," *Louisiana Historical Quarterly*, 262; Thomas K. Wharton, *Queen of the South: New Orleans, 1853–1862, The Journal of Thomas K. Wharton*, ed. Samuel Wilson, Jr. (New Orleans, La.: Historic New Orleans Collection and New York Public Library, 1999), xiii–xiv; Evans, "Daniel Pratt," 9–16; Dolly Lunt Burge, *The Diary of Dolly Lunt Burge 1848–1879*, ed. Christine Jacobson Carter (Athens: Univ. of Georgia Press, 1997), xxi–xxiv.

7. Harry L. Watson, *Liberty and Power: The Politics of Jacksonian America* (New York: Hill and Wang, 1990); Carol Sheriff, *The Artificial River: The Erie Canal and the Paradox of Progress 1817–1862* (New York: Hill and Wang, 1996); Louis P. Masur, *1831: Year of Eclipse* (New York: Hill and Wang, 2001); Daniel Walker Howe, *What Hath God Wrought: The Transformation of America, 1815–1848* (New York: Oxford Univ. Press, 2007).

8. French, *Two Wars*, 6; William Wright, *The Secession Movement in the Middle Atlantic States* (Rutherford, N.J.: Fairleigh Dickinson Univ. Press, 1973), 104, 154,156, 200–1, 209–10. A few exceptions did exist, notably Samuel French, who noted that his home state of New Jersey still had several hundred slaves not affected by the gradual emancipation policies. Several areas of New York dealt with the same situation up until the 1850s.

9. Historian Eric Foner articulated this concept best when he showed how the development of free labor ideology helped unite the North in visions of social mobility and economic and territorial expansion versus the seemingly backward lives of southern whites tied to slavery. Eric Foner, *Free Soil, Free Labor, Free Men: The Ideology of the Republican Party Before the Civil War* (New York: Oxford Univ. Press, 1970), vii–xxxix, 1–10.

10. Rainer, "The Honorable Fraternity," 30–31.

11. Grant, *North Over South*, 43–73. Susan-Mary Grant argued that after the Mexican War, sectional tension increased because northerners feared that southerners wanted to encroach on northern territory and northern values.

12. Other contemporary authors like George Eggleston counter that, in the West especially, camaraderie persisted among emigrants from all corners of the country. For further discussion on this theme, and the development and expansion of northern values in the antebellum era, see George Cary Eggleston, *Life in Early*

Indiana (Fort Wayne, Ind.: Public Library of Fort Wayne and Allen County, 1953), 1–12; Parish, *North and the Nation,* 27–30; Turner, *The United States,* 39–51, 92–106; Chute, "The Life of Frederick A. P. Barnard," 27.

13. For further examples of the educational experiences of northern emigrants, see Poole, *Thomas G. Clemson,* 7–8; Brazy, *An American Planter,* 4–6; Sears, *John Slidell,* 6; Fulton, *Memoirs of Frederick A. P. Barnard,* 33–34; Prentiss, *A Memoir of S. S. Prentiss,* 1: 33; Silverthorne, *Ashbel Smith of Texas,* 4–9; Blevins, *Albert Pike,* 7; C. Dana to Charles Dana, Nov. 28, 1828, and Anne Dana to Charles Dana, April 7, 1829, Folder 2, Charles Backus Dana Papers, Dolph Briscoe Center for American History, University of Texas, Austin [repository hereafter cited as UT]. In addition, some of these men attended southern universities after they moved to the South, including Cumberland University, Richmond College, Tennessee College, Transylvania College, University of Louisiana, University of Virginia, and several others.

14. Vandiver, *Ploughshares into Swords,* chap. 1; J. K. Duncan to Pat, September 17, 1847, William Duncan Papers 1847–1868, Rare Book, Manuscripts, and Special Collections, William R. Perkins Library, Duke University, Durham [repository hereafter cited as Duke]; Strong, *Keystone Confederate,* 10–17; French, *Two Wars,* 5, 16, 20. Of course, not all native northerners had to attend college to receive a typical northern education. Many others simply attended local academies or were taught by tutors, especially women. See Fox, *A Northern Woman,* 1–4; Shields, *The Life and Times of Seargent Smith Prentiss,* 3–4; Slate, *Biographical Memoir of Eugene Hilgard,* 95–99; Griffin, "Connecticut Yankee in Texas," 2–5; Franzetti, "Elisha Marshall Pease," 4.

15. Mary Ryan, *Cradle of the Middle Class: The Family in Oneida County New York, 1790–1865* (Cambridge, Eng.: Cambridge Univ. Press, 1981), 92, 141.

16. Stuart Blumin, *The Emergence of the Middle Class: Social Experience in the American City, 1760–1900* (Cambridge, Eng.: Cambridge Univ. Press, 1989), 1–16.

17. Jonathan Daniel Wells, *Origins of the Southern Middle Class 1800–1861* (Chapel Hill: Univ. of North Carolina Press, 2003).

18. William W. Chenault and Robert C. Reinders, "The Northern-born Community of New Orleans in the 1850s," *Journal of American History* 51 (September 1964): 246–47.

19. Richard Lyle Power, "A Crusade to Extend Yankee Culture 1820–1865," *New England Quarterly* 13 (December 1940): 640.

20. Parish, *The North and the Nation,* 139–40; Grant, *North Over South,* 45–46. The emigrants who set up a "colony" in Virginia were also viewed by other northerners as a way to spread northern values and customs into the South.

21. Joe Frantz, *Gail Borden: Dairyman to a Nation* (Norman: Univ. of Oklahoma Press, 1951), 15–16, 32–37; Alice Farmer, *The Times and Journal of Alice*

Farmer: Yankee Visitor to Acadiana-New Orleans, ed. Christopher G. Pena (Thibodaux, La.: C. G. P. Press, 2001), 3–15; Silverthorne, *Ashbel Smith,* 100–101, 106, 109; Wharton, *Queen of the South,* xiii–xiv; Kendall, "George Wilkins Kendall," *Louisiana Historical Quarterly,* 262; Roper, *Rebel Mapmaker,* 3–7.

22. Charles M. Cummings, *Yankee Quaker, Confederate General: The Curious Career of Bushrod Rust Johnson* (Rutherford, N.J.: Fairleigh Dickinson Univ. Press, 1971), 76, 86.

23. Duncan's biographer Michael Strong claims that the relationships forged between northern and southern students at these types of academies, "may help to explain the local sympathy shown a few years later for the Southern Confederacy." Strong, *Keystone Confederate,* 6.

24. Ballard, *Pemberton,* 19–20; Kendall, "George Wilkins Kendall," *Louisiana Historical Quarterly,* 9–10; Chute, "The Life of Frederick A.P. Barnard," 124–26.

25. Roper, *Rebel Mapmaker,* 3–7; Evans, "Daniel Pratt," 9–16; Setsuko Takahashi, "Home of Their Choice: Samuel and Caroline Gilman in Antebellum Charleston, South Carolina" (master's thesis, Univ. of North Carolina, 1981), 31–33; Edward Drummond, *Confederate Yankee: The Journal of Edward William Drummond, a Confederate Soldier From Maine,* ed. Roger S. Durham (Knoxville: Univ. of Tennessee Press, 2004), xxv–xxviii. In addition, some native northerners had contact with the South through the Border States. Those living in the southern counties of Pennsylvania and New Jersey, the southern counties of Ohio, Indiana, and Illinois, or settlers in territories like Kansas had more interaction with southerners thanks to their shared border with slave states. For further information, see Drake, *Life of General Robert Hatton,* 7–12, 15–16; Bell, *Confederate Seadog,* 12–15; Wharton, *Gail Borden,* 8–11; Jimmy Bryan, Jr., *More Zeal Than Discretion: The Westward Adventures of Walter P. Lane* (College Station: Texas A&M Univ. Press, 2008), 8–10; Ballard, *Pemberton,* 4, 8; Wright, *The Secession Movement,* 104, 154,156, 200–1, 209–10; Jack T. Hutchinson, *Divided Loyalties: The Border States of the Upper South, Delaware-Maryland-West Virginia-Kentucky and Missouri, Their Cultural Heritage and Divided Civil War Loyalties* (Loganville, Ga.: Jack Hutchinson and Signature Printing, 2005), 304–5.

26. John C. Pemberton's biographer even disputes the notion that Pemberton favored his southern classmates at West Point, because he rarely mentioned his fellow cadets in his letters home and remained best friends with fellow Pennsylvanian George Gordon Meade. Ballard, *Pemberton,* 20.

27. Even for those who did have pre-emigration contact with the South, their perceptions did not always come out positive. What authors see as evidence of favorable opinions toward the region in the antebellum period actually border on conjecture or assumption. Michael Strong's assertion that Johnson Kelly Duncan formed relationships through the York County Academy has problems because little

evidence exists that Duncan actually attended the school. Edward Perry, despite his close friendship with an Alabama student at Yale, actually moved to Georgia first in 1852 before teaching at a private school in Alabama the following year; only later did he and his friend teach at the same academy. As for cities like Philadelphia and New York, residents there did have connections with the South but that did not mean they liked all southerners. Much of the relations between them came purely from economic considerations with little agreement on social or cultural values.

28. Duncan, *Reluctant General,* chap. 2; Blevins, *Albert Pike,* 8–23, 51.

29. Griffin, "Connecticut Yankee in Texas," 5. Pease's biographer argued that he felt drawn to Texas because it represented a sense of adventure lacking in his Hartford home.

30. Elisha Pease to L. T. Pease, March 4, 1836, quoted in ibid., 23.

31. Bryan, *More Zeal Than Discretion,* 11–27.

32. Frantz, *Dairyman to a Nation,* 49–50; William Pierce to Ellen Pierce, October 15, 1852, Ellen E. Pierce Papers 1849–1857, Duke; Mason, "Henry Watson," 9–10; Kendall, "George Wilkins Kendall," *Louisiana Historical Quarterly,* 262–63; George Kendall to Henry Randall, January 1, 1860, quoted in George Wilkins Kendall, *Letters From a Texas Sheep Ranch: Written in the Years 1860 and 1867 by George Wilkins Kendall to Henry Stephens Randall,* ed. Harry James Brown (Urbana: Univ. of Illinois Press, 1959), 36; George Kendall to Henry Randall, September 10, October 6, 1860, quoted in ibid., 101, 114. On the other hand, some northern emigrants abhorred the weather in the South, claiming it caused even more sickness and oppression. See Sarah Brooke Malloy, "The Health of Our Family: The Correspondence of Amanda Beardsley Trulock, 1837–1868" (master's thesis, Univ. of Arkansas, 2005), 73–74; Rainer, "The Honorable Fraternity," 38–39.

33. Only four first moved to the South in their forties and two in their fifties. Three more are unknown, and eleven never made it to the South at all before joining the Confederacy.

34. Cecil Sumners, *The Governors of Mississippi* (Gretna, La.: Pelican Pub. Co., 1980), 31–32; Jacob Cobb, *The Most Southern Place on Earth: The Mississippi Delta and the Roots of Regional Identity* (New York: Oxford Univ. Press, 1992), 7–13. Nevertheless, Cobb argued that the risks usually outweighed the rewards since disease, floods, and other natural disasters created a high mortality rate in the early years of settlement. The only people who could usually gain the rewards were established planters with enough capital resources to clear the land and start a plantation.

35. John Ingraham, *The Southwest By a Yankee,* 2 vols. (New York: Harper & Brothers, 1835), 2:50; Archie P. McDonald, ed., *"To Live and Die in Dixie": How the South Formed a Nation* (Murfreesboro, Tenn.: Southern Heritage Press, 1999), 41–48.

36. Prentiss, *A Memoir of S. S. Prentiss,* 1: 29–131; Miller, "Elisha Marshall Pease," 9–11. For similar arguments, see Wharton, *Gail Borden,* 26–30; Hutchinson, *Divided Loyalties,* 53–55; Gerster, "The Northern Origins of Southern Mythology," *Journal of Southern History,* 572–73; Pessen, "How Different From Each Other Were the Antebellum North and South?" *American Historical Review,* 1134, 1148; Green, *The Role of the Yankee,* 111–12.

37. Chenault and Reinders, "Northern-born Community of New Orleans," *Journal of American History,* 232–33; Daniel Walker Howe, "A Massachusetts Yankee in Senator Calhoun's Court: Samuel Gilman in South Carolina," *New England Quarterly* 44 (June 1971): 198–99.

38. Not all historians agree with this characterization of the South. Some of them argue that climate, dangers, and non-acceptance from native southerners drove many potential northern emigrants out of the South. For further discussion of this argument, see Degler, *Place Over Time,* 48, 55; Chute, "The Life of Frederick A. P. Barnard," 212; Malloy, "The Health of Our Family," 73–74; Norma B. Cuthbert and O. T. Hammond, "Yankee Preacher-Teacher in Florida, 1838," *Huntington Library Quarterly* 8 (November 1944): 95–96; Rainer, "The Honorable Fraternity," 38–39; Miller, *South by Southwest,* 5–13, 114.

39. Juliet Bestor to her mother and sister, January 5, 1834, quoted in *Connecticut Yankee in Early Alabama: Juliet Bestor Coleman 1833–1850,* ed. Mary Morgan Ward Glass (Alabama: National Society of Colonial Dames of America in the State of Alabama, 1980), 29; Ernest F. Dibble, *Ante-bellum Pensacola and the Military Presence, The Pensacola Series Commemorating the American Revolution Bicentennial,* 3 vols. (Pensacola, Fla.: Mayes Printing Company, 1974), 3: 33; George Catlin quoted in George Catlin, *Letters and Notes on the Manners, Customs, and Condition of the North American Indians,* 2 vols. (London: published by the author, 1841), 2: 103–4; Henry Watson to his uncle, April 30, 1834, Box 2, Folder April–May 1834, Henry Watson Papers, Duke; Sarah Williams to her parents, November 7, 1853, Folder 4, Sarah Francis Hicks Williams Papers, Southern Historical Collection, University of North Carolina Library, Chapel Hill, N.C. [collection hereafter cited as SHC].

40. Gower, *Charles Dahlgren,* 6–8.

41. Drummond, *Confederate Yankee,* xiv; Herbert Gambrell, *Anson Jones: The Last President of Texas* (Austin: Univ. of Texas Press, 1964), 6–12; Jones quoted in ibid., 19. For other examples of native northerners not initially planning to move to the South, see Ernest McPherson Lander, Jr., *The Calhoun Family and Thomas Green Clemson: The Decline of a Southern Patriarchy* (Columbia: Univ. of South Carolina Press, 1983), 7–19; John Quitman to his brother, August 18, 1819, quoted in J. F. H. Claiborne, *Life and Correspondence of John A. Quitman,* 2 vols.

(New York: Harper & Brothers Publications, 1860), 1: 35; John Quitman to F. R. Backus, February 28, 1821, quoted in ibid., 59; John Quitman to his father, May 7, 1821, quoted in ibid., 61.

42. William Henry Hora to Jane Hora, December 22, 1833, Manuscripts Division, South Caroliniana Library, University of South Carolina, Columbia [repository hereafter cited as USC].

43. Pierce quoted in Prentiss, *A Memoir of S. S. Prentiss,* 1: 39.

44. Shields, *The Life and Times of Seargent Smith Prentiss,* 9.

45. Evans, "Daniel Pratt," 17, 21–23; S. F. H. Tarrant, *Hon. Daniel Pratt, a Biography, with Eulogies on his Life and Character* (Richmond, Va.: Whittet & Shepperson, 1904), 24, 42–43, 103–15. Interestingly, Pratt's wife also came from the North.

46. Not all northern emigrants found such immediate success. Thousands of them died in the terrain of the Southwest or suffered more losses than gains. That did not mean, however, that they thought about giving up. For example, native Ohioan Edmund Dewitt Patterson started out as a book agent when he first arrived in Alabama, but his employers let him go after three months. Vowing to redeem himself, he taught at a school before working as a store clerk. For more information, and for similar examples, see Edmund DeWitt Patterson, *Yankee Rebel: The Civil War Journal of Edmund DeWitt Patterson,* ed. John G. Barrett (Knoxville: Univ. of Tennessee Press, 2004), xviii–xix; Marilyn Lavin, *William Bostwick: Connecticut Yankee in Antebellum Georgia* (New York: Arno Press, 1978), 6–11; Green, *The Role of the Yankee,* 125; Sears, *John Slidell,* 8; William Appleton to Seargent Prentiss, June 26, 1827, quoted in Prentiss, *A Memoir of S. S. Prentiss,* 1: 42–45.

47. John Quitman to F. R. Backus, February 28, 1821, quoted in Claiborne, *Life and Correspondence of John Quitman,* 1: 59; John Quitman to his father, May 7, 1821, quoted in ibid., 61.

48. Arthur McArthur to William McArthur, February 22, 1854, Correspondence, 1780–1949, Box 2, Folder 1, McArthur Family Papers, George J. Mitchell Department of Special Collections & Archives, Bowdoin College Library, Brunswick, Maine (hereafter cited as Bowdoin).

49. William Pierce to Ellen Pierce, November 5, 1852, Ellen Pierce Papers, Duke.

50. Ashbel Smith to Adrian, July 11, [1835?], Ashbel Smith Journal 1832–1857, Box 2G234, Ashbel Smith Papers, UT.

51. Ingraham, *Southwest by a Yankee,* 2: 88.

52. Prentiss, *A Memoir of S. S. Prentiss,* 1: 50.

53. In addition, eleven of the individuals never settled in a southern state before joining the Confederacy, and one has too few records to determine his status.

54. Elizabeth Brown Pryor, "An Anomalous Person: The Northern Tutor in Plantation Society, 1773–1860," *Journal of Southern History* 47 (August 1981): 364–68. Pryor went on to explain that young educated northerners who ended up emigrating to the South, rather than the Northwest, did so because tutors averaged a substantial yearly income between two hundred and fifty and five hundred dollars on a plantation, along with full access to the families' private libraries. Norma Cuthbert generally agrees with Pryor's analysis, although Cuthbert places more emphasis on the fact that northern tutors only viewed the job as temporary. Cuthbert, "Yankee Preacher-Teacher in Florida, 1838," *Huntington Library Quarterly*, 95–96.

55. Seargent Prentiss to his mother, October 4, 1827, quoted in Prentiss, *A Memoir of S. S. Prentiss*, 1: 59.

56. *In Memoriam. General Lewis Baldwin Parsons*. Published Privately 1908, 46–47, Albert and Shirley Small Special Collections Library, University of Virginia, Charlottesville, Va. [repository hereafter cited as UVA].

57. William Pierce to Ellen Pierce, February 22, 1853, Ellen Pierce Papers, Duke.

58. Caroline Gilman, *Recollections of a Southern Matron* (New York: Harper and Brothers, 1839), 35–36.

59. Malloy, "The Health of Our Family," 83, 91.

60. Seargent Prentiss to his mother, October 4, 1827, quoted in Prentiss, *Memoir of S. S. Prentiss*, 1: 59; Shields, *The Life and Times of Seargent Smith Prentiss*, 9–15. For further evidence of education as a factor in emigration to the South, see Blevins, *Albert Pike*, 26–30; Robert W. Weathersby, *J. H. Ingraham* (Boston, Mass.: Twayne Publishers, 1980), 17; Prince, "Edward Aylsworth Perry," 11–13, 17; Berkeley, *A Yankee Botanist*, 29–37, 51, 59; Wharton, *Queen of the South*, xiv–xviii; Sylvester Dana to Charles Dana, September 12, 1829, Sarah Kimball to Charles Dana, September 29, 1829, Folder 2, Charles Backus Dana Papers, UT.

61. Silverthorne, *Ashbel Smith*, 9–14; Chute, "The Life of Frederick Barnard," 200–3.

62. William T. Sherman, *Memoirs of General William T. Sherman By Himself*, Foreword by B. H. Liddell Hart (Bloomington: Indiana Univ. Press, 1957), 78–95, 132–41.

63. James I. Robertson, Jr., *Stonewall Jackson: The Man, The Soldier, The Legend* (New York: MacMillan Publishing USA, 1997), 152.

64. Ibid., 117, 144, 147, 336–37.

65. Roper, *Rebel Mapmaker*, 8–9; Clapp, *Autobiographical Sketches and Recollections*, 43; Handerson, *Yankee in Gray*, 16–17. Southern communities also extended invitations to northern ministers, especially those who gave inspiring sermons when they visited their affiliations' southern branches. Despite growing differences between the churches on the slavery issue, twenty-one northern ministers still found

homes in various southern churches. For more information, see Takahashi, "Home of Their Choice," 39, 41; H. Dana to Charles Dana, October 30, 1833, Sylvester Dana to Charles Dana, January 28, 1834, H. Dana to Charles Dana, December 17, 1834, all in Folder 3, Charles Backus Dana Papers, UT; E. P. Humphrey to Charles Dana, August 12, 1834, Folder 7, ibid.; Berkeley, *A Yankee Botanist*, 67; Sarah Williams to her parents, December 10, 1853, Folder 1, Sarah Williams Papers, SHC.

66. Pryor, "An Anomalous Person," *Journal of Southern History*, 367–68.

67. Ingraham, *Southwest by a Yankee*, 1: 233–34.

68. Fox, *A Northern Woman*, 4–5; Caroline Seabury, *The Diary of Caroline Seabury, 1854–1863*, ed. Suzanne Bunkers (Madison: Univ. of Wisconsin Press, 1991), 6–7; Viki Leigh Blanks, "Caroline Lee Hentz: Antebellum Author, Antebellum Woman" (master's thesis, Univ. of West Florida, 1999), 38–46. Hentz's husband also worked as a school administrator and teacher, while Hentz herself engaged in writing as well as teaching.

69. John Quitman to F. R. Backus, February 28, 1821, quoted in Claiborne, *Life and Correspondence of John Quitman*, 1: 59. Quitman made similar comments to his father and brother. John Quitman to his father, May 7, 1821, and John Quitman to his brother, June 10, 1821, quoted in ibid., 61–62.

70. Shields, *The Life and Times of Seargent Smith Prentiss*, 30, 39, 44.

71. Mr. Wright to Seargent Prentiss, March 29, 1852, quoted in Prentiss, *A Memoir of S. S. Prentiss*, 1: 60–61.

72. For further examples, see Mason, "Henry Watson," 12–16; Boman, *Abiel Leonard*, 12–15; Griffin, "Connecticut Yankee in Texas," 5–8; Franzetti, "Elisha Marshall Pease," 2–3; Prince, "Edward Aylsworth Perry," 11–13, 17.

73. Anson Jones, *Memoranda and Official Correspondence Relating to the Republic of Texas, Its History and Annexation, Including a Brief Autobiography of the Author* (New York: D. Appleton and Company, 1859), 7–11; Gambrell, *Anson Jones*, 21–23.

74. Silverthorne, *Ashbel Smith*, 13–17, 30–36. Smith did not stay in North Carolina but instead struck out toward the Southwest for more lucrative areas, eventually settling in Texas.

75. Hughes, *Yale's Confederates*; Robert Sobel and John Raimo, eds., *Biographical Directory of the Governors of the United States, 1789–1978*, 2 vols. (Westport, Conn.: Meckler Books, 1978), 1: 258; *Cyclopedia of Eminent and Representative Men of the Carolinas of the Nineteenth Century*, 2 vols. (1892; reprint, Spartanburg, S.C.: Reprint Company, 1972), 2: 517–19; Krick, *Lee's Colonels*; Charles Dew, "Sam Williams, Forgeman," in J. Morgan Kousser and James M. McPherson, eds., *Region, Race and Reconstruction* (New York: Oxford Univ. Press, 1982), 199–228.

76. Green, *Role of the Yankee*, 68–69; Allardice, *More Generals in Gray*, 117–18; Edward James, Janet Wilson James, and Paul S. Boyer, eds., *Notable American*

Women: A Biographical Dictionary, 3 vols. (Cambridge, Mass.: Belknap Press of Harvard Univ. Press, 1971), 2: 482–83; Trinity College Historical Society, *An Annual Publication of Historical Papers, Reconstruction, and State Biography*, 8 vols. (Durham, N.C.: Trinity College Historical Society, 1897), 2: 34–43; Lyon Gardiner Tyler, LLD, *Encyclopedia of Virginia Biography*, 3 vols. (New York: Lewis Historical Publishing Company, 1915), 3: 300–1; William Way, *History of the New England Society of Charleston, South Carolina for One Hundred Years 1819–1919* (Charleston, S.C.: The Society, 1920), section 2, 18–21; Jon Wakelyn, with Frank Vandiver as Advisory Editor, *Biographical Dictionary of the Confederacy* (Westport, Conn.: Greenwood Press, 1977), 136; Arthur C. Burnett, *Yankees in the Republic of Texas, Some Notes on their Origin and Impact* (Houston, Tex.: Anson Jones Press, 1952), 1–60. Some northern emigrants who had moved to the South for other reasons eventually took up the newspaper profession, as well. In one celebrated instance, Frederick Barnard, while working at the University of Alabama, edited two rival Alabama newspapers at the same time. For further examples, see Chute, "Life of Frederick Barnard," 150–55; William S. Speer, *Sketches of Prominent Tennesseans, Containing Biographies and Records of many of the Families Who Have Attained Prominence in Tennessee* (Easily, S.C.: Southern Historical Press, 1978), 485–89; Green, *Role of the Yankee*, 20–22.

77. Pemberton quoted in Ballard, *Pemberton*, 32; Allardice, *More Generals in Gray*, 56–57; Eugene M. Sanchez-Saavedra, "'The Beau Ideal of a Soldier:' Brigadier General Charles Dimmock" (master's thesis, Univ. of Richmond, 1971), 88–92. Nevertheless, the army itself did not guarantee a love for or residence in the South. The vast majority of northern soldiers, who also served in the same southern and frontier forts, returned to their native states when they retired from the army. Even future Northern Confederates did not always find their initial impressions of the South overwhelming. Strong, *Keystone Confederate*, 18–22; Vandiver, *Ploughshares into Swords*, 36–38.

78. Brazy, *An American Planter*, 6–9; George Cary Eggleston, *A Rebel's Recollections* (New York: The Knickerbocker Press, 1905), xxvi–xxvii; George Cary Eggleston, *Recollections of a Varied Life* (New York: Henry Holt and Co., 1910), 45–46; Wharton, *Gail Borden*, 64–66. In Borden's case, he had already lived in Mississippi for several years before moving to Texas.

79. Chenault and Reinders, "The Northern-born Community of New Orleans," *Journal of American History*, 238–41.

80. Green, *Role of the Yankee*, 61, 68, 130–31; Rainer, "The Honorable Fraternity," 250–51.

81. James, *Antebellum Natchez*, 96, 164–66; Gower, *Charles Dahlgren*, 14–15. Each state had its own variations. The first three governors of Tennessee came

from Pennsylvania, while Louisiana did not have any northern-born governors. William C. Binkley, "The South and the West," *Journal of Southern History* 17 (February 1951): 12; Mary Lilla McLure, *Louisiana Leaders 1830–1860* (Shreveport, La.: Journal Printing Co., 1935), 68–76; Burnett, *Yankees in the Republic of Texas*, iv–viii, 62; Chenault and Reinders, "The Northern-born Community of New Orleans," *Journal of American History*, 233, 236–37; Pryor, "An Anomalous Person," *Journal of Southern History*, 364–75; Turner, *The United States*, 251.

82. For further details and analysis on this subject, see Chapter Three.

83. Fulton, *Memoirs of Frederick A. P. Barnard*, 221–22. Barnard even carried out an inside joke by penning pro-Democratic articles in his paper and then refuting them without people knowing he had written both articles.

84. Sanchez-Saavedra, "The Beau Ideal of a Soldier," 15–18, 39–42, 84–88, 92–94, 100–4, 125–28. Dimmock was not perfect, however, because several of his business ventures failed.

85. Strong, *Keystone Confederate*, 26–27.

86. Blevins, *Albert Pike*, 40–43, 47–48, 51.

87. Evans, "Daniel Pratt," 33–38; Tarrant, *Hon. Daniel Pratt*, 22. For further reiteration of the success of northern emigrants, see Cummings, *Yankee Quaker*, 146–49, 155; Drake, *Life of General Robert Hatton*, 37–38; Catherwood, *The Life and Labors of William W. Wadley*, 4–8; Dibble, *Ante-bellum Pensacola* III: 37–40; Howe, "A Massachusetts Yankee," *New England Quarterly*, 201; Herbert Phinehas Shippey, "William Tappan Thompson, A Biography and Uncollected Fictional Writings" (PhD diss., Univ. of South Carolina, 1991), 99–120; Lander, *The Calhoun Family*, 22–23, 28–29, 46–57, 78–81, 90, 112, 121, 137; Bowman, *Abiel Leonard*, 85–89.

88. Gower, *Charles Dahlgren*, 16–34; Brazy, *An American Planter*, 1–20; French, *Two Wars*, 128–33. Dahlgren actually miscalculated because his first wife brought a lot of debt along with her land, and Dahlgren spent over a decade paying back the creditors.

89. Northern women, in contrast, found marriage to southern men not as a way to get rich, but rather to achieve financial security in an environment where single women had an uncertain future. See Hampton, *A Divided Heart*, xiii–xiv; Fox, *A Northern Woman*, 9; Mildred Allen Butler, *Actress in Spite of Herself: The Life of Anna Cora Mowat* (New York: Funk & Wagnalls Company Inc., 1966), 169–75.

90. Not all native northerners, however, followed such a course. In this study, forty-one individuals had northern spouses before the war, thirteen did not marry, three had foreign wives, and seventy are unknown. For more information about a few of the emigrants who had northern spouses, see Fulton, *Memoirs of Frederick A. P. Barnard*, 104–5, 225–26; Clapp, *Autobiographical Sketches*, 113–14; Lucadia

Pease, *Lucadia Pease & the Governor: Letters 1850–185*, ed. Katherine Hart and Elizabeth Kemp (Austin, Tex.: The Encino Press, 1974), ix–xi; Elisha Pease to Lucadia Pease, August 20, 25, 26, 27, 28, September 2, 1853, and Lucadia Pease to Elisha Pease, August 20, 26, September 2, 1853, quoted in ibid., 135–48.

91. Sarah Woolfolk Wiggins, "The Marriage of Amelia Gayle and Josiah Gorgas," in *Intimate Strategies of the Civil War: Military Commanders and Their Wives*, ed. Carol Bleser and Lesley Gordon (New York: Oxford Univ. Press, 2001), 105; Ballard, *Pemberton*, 39–41; Boman, *Abiel Leonard*, 56–57. See also Cummings, *Yankee Quaker*, 124, 134; Duncan, *Reluctant General*, 134–35; Blevins, *Albert Pike*, 37–38; Tazewell, *Major Edmund Bradford*, 17.

92. Bryan, *More Zeal than Discretion*, 46–76; Blevins, *Albert Pike*, 61–64; Sanchez-Saavedra, "The Beau Ideal of a Soldier," 24. See also Kendall, "George Wilkins Kendall," *Louisiana Historical Quarterly*, 273–75, 278–82; Gower, *Charles Dahlgren*, 14–15.

93. Frantz, *Dairyman to a Nation*, 52–55; Appointment of John Quitman as Brigade Inspector in Mississippi State Militia, January 10, 1823, John Anthony Quitman Papers, UVA; Appointment of John A. Quitman as Chancellor of State of Mississippi, February 3, 1829, ibid.; Appointment of John A. Quitman as Chancellor of State of Mississippi, June 10, 1833, ibid.; Chute, "The Life of Frederick A. P. Barnard," 232–35; Eugene A. Smith, "Memorial of Eugene Woldemar Hilgard," reprinted from the *Bulletin of the Geological Society of America* 28 (March 1917): 41; Catherwood, *The Life and Labors of William W. Wadley*, 4–8.

94. *Governor Joseph Johnson of Virginia: A Brief Sketch of His Life and Character* (Baltimore, Md.: John H. Foster's Steam Printing and Publishing House, 1877), 7–15; Franzetti, "Elisha Marshall Pease," 4–6, 8; Miller, "Elisha Marshall Pease: A Biography," 39–42. In addition, John Quitman served as governor of Mississippi twice over two decades before his death.

95. Jones, *Memoranda*, 18–26. In a sign that Jones had not completely forgotten his past, however, he named his home in Texas "Barrington," after his hometown in Massachusetts.

96. Silverthorne, *Ashbel Smith*, 72–103. For more information on native northerners serving as elected officials in Texas, see Ashbel Smith to Samuel Houston, June 7, 1850, Original Papers I-S, Madge Williams Hearne Collection, UVA; Griffin, "Connecticut Yankee in Texas," 18–21, 90–93; Franzetti, "Elisha Marshall Pease," 4–6, 8; Miller, "Elisha Marshall Pease: A Biography," 39–42; James Robinson to Elisha Pease, April 12, 1838, Box 3G483, Folder 10, Paul C. Crusemann Collection, UT; William P. Scott to E. M. Pease, January 6, 1840, Box 3G483, Folder 13, ibid.; P. W. Gray to E. M. Pease, December 27, 1847, Box

3G483, Folder 21, ibid.; George T. Wood to E. M. Pease, February 22, 1848, Box 3G483, Folder 22, ibid.

97. Smith, *Courage of a Southern Unionist,* 7–13; Drake, *Life of General Robert Hatton,* 37–38. The other congressmen and senators were Thomas King and Hiram Warner in Georgia, Robert J. Walker in Mississippi, James Lindley in Missouri, Henry Shaw in North Carolina, Horace Maynard in Tennessee, Volney Howard in Texas, and Joseph Johnson and Samuel Moore in Virginia. In addition, three individuals served in the cabinet of various presidents, including Kenton Harper as Secretary of the Interior, Amos Kendall as Postmaster General, and Robert J. Walker as Secretary of the Treasury.

2. From Northerner to Southerner

1. Historians have engaged in extensive debate over the magnitude of similarity versus dissimilarity between the North and South and when exactly the two sections started to most visibly diverge. For a sample of the debate, see Degler, *Place Over Time,* 27–29; Potter, *Impending Crisis,* 472.

2. One exception was families in the Border States, because their economic lives often tilted toward the North, while their social and cultural lives often remained cemented in the South.

3. W. J. Cash went so far as to claim that the South was only a step ahead of the wilderness up to around 1840. David Waldstreicher added that, at the beginning of the century, southerners really had no sense of themselves as a region yet, with Virginia considered a middle state, New England as the only established section, and most regional differences occurring between East and West. Cash, *Mind of the South,* 10–11; Waldstreicher, *Midst of Perpetual Fetes,* 266, 270.

4. Power, "A Crusade to Extend Yankee Culture 1820–1865," *New England Quarterly,* 640–46, 652.

5. Charles C. Jones, Jr., to Charles C. Jones, January 28, 1861, quoted in James M. McPherson, "Was Blood Thicker than Water? Ethnic and Civic Nationalism in the American Civil War," *Proceedings of the American Philosophical Society* 143 (March 1999): 105.

6. Grant, *North Over South,* 63–66, 103, 131, 145. For a reiteration of this argument, see Turner, *The United State: 1830–1850,* 68; Cash, *Mind of the South,* vii–x; George Dangerfield, *The Awakening of American Nationalism 1815–1828* (New York: Harper and Row, 1965), 15, 18, 112; Hilldrup, "Cold War Against the Yankees in the Antebellum Literature of Southern Women," *The North Carolina Historical Review,* 370–75. Still, not all historians agree that such a level of hostility existed or why it happened, but they do agree that the two sections solidified as

the nineteenth century progressed. Binkley, "The South and the West," *Journal of Southern History,* 12–14; Parish, *The North and the Nation,* 23–25, 37, 45, 133; Turner, *The United States,* 354–55.

7. Chenault and Reinders, "The Northern-born Community of New Orleans," *Journal of American History,* 234–35, 239. Chenault and Reinders went even further by arguing that northern emigrants in the 1850s maintained a "degree of Yankee self-consciousness" by not marrying southern women as frequently as native southerners, forming their own regional clubs based on their native states, and not seeking to acquire a plantation, as most young southerners did at the time. They also believe northern emigrants helped shape New Orleans's atypical business culture, implying that without northern businessmen, New Orleans would have been indistinguishable from other southern urban centers.

8. Some authors, including biographers, claim that since few native northerners ever had long term plans to stay in the South, they had a hard time assimilating and were eager to return home, denying them any chance to change their identities. For further discussion, and for more arguments about blending northern and southern identity, see Cummings, *Yankee Quaker,* 144; *Obituary Addresses on the Announcement of the Death of Hon. John A. Quitman of Mississippi: in the House of Representatives, January 5, 1859,* 14–15, SHC; Miller, "Elisha Marshall Pease," 32; Pryor, "An Anomalous Person," *Journal of Southern History,* 370–71, 377–80, 389; Turner, *The United States,* 202–3, 260–62; Rainer, "The Honorable Fraternity," 25–27, 44–45, 51–52; James, *Antebellum Natchez,* 217; Brazy, *An American Planter,* 1–20; Howe, "A Massachusetts Yankee," *New England Quarterly,* 215; Takahashi, "Home of Their Choice," 62; Mason, "Henry Watson," 37–38, 49.

9. Many writers even unintentionally acknowledge the success of such adaptation when they refer to prominent adoptive southerners without citing their origins. References include "John Slidell of Louisiana" and "John Quitman of Mississippi."

10. Turner, *The United States,* 190–97, 332–33.

11. Joseph Rainer, who insisted that Yankee peddlers remained Yankees during their time in the South, still admitted, "It was a commonly held opinion that the morals of New England emigrants lapsed when they moved south or west . . . New England culture lost another increment of national influence whenever a young man was converted to 'southern' ways or market values." Rainer, "The Honorable Fraternity," 60–63.

12. *Little Rock Advocate,* April 10, 1836, quoted in Virgil L. Baker, "Albert Pike: Citizen Speechmaker of Arkansas," *Arkansas Historical Quarterly* 10 (Summer 1951): 142.

13. Wharton, *Gail Borden,* 70–135; Jones, *Memoranda and Official Correspondence,* 12–17; Silverthorne, *Ashbel Smith,* 38–49; Bryan, *More Zeal than Discretion,* 33–41.

14. Elisha Pease to Lucadia Pease, September 2, 1853, quoted in Pease, *Lucadia Pease,* 147–48.

15. Gower, *Charles Dahlgren,* 8–12; Bowman, *Abiel Leonard,* 18; Blevins, *Albert Pike,* 66–67. In a revealing twist, Pike selected as his second for the duel Luther Chase, another Massachusetts-born Arkansan. For more instances of adoptive southerners engaging in dueling and the nature of dueling and southern honor itself, see Shields, *The Life and Times of Seargent Smith Prentiss,* 72; Ashbel Smith to Charles Fisher, December 13, 1839, quoted in Silverthorne, *Ashbel Smith,* 63–64; Joanne Freeman, *Affairs of Honor* (New Haven: Yale Univ. Press, 2001).

16. Class Report, February 1860, 9, H. B. McClellan Papers 1857–1904, Virginia Historical Society, Richmond (repository hereafter cited as VHS).

17. Ingraham, *Southwest by a Yankee,* 2: 134, 173. For more expressions of adaptation to southern homes, see Sally Hampton to Lucy Baxter, December 23–24, 1855, quoted in Hampton, *A Divided Heart,* 27–28; Phi Beta Kappa Speech quoted in Ashbel Smith, *Addresses of Doctor Ashbel Smith(An Oration Pronounced Before the Connecticut Alpha of the Phi Beta Kappa at Yale College, New Haven, August 15, 1849, by Hon. Ashbel Smith, of Texas* (New Haven, Conn.: B. L. Hamlen Printer to Yale College, 1849), 3, 27; *Address on the Laying of the Corner Stone of the University of Texas, November 17, 1882,* by the Late Ashbel Smith, First President of the Board of Regents, UT.

18. "Why Is It?" *Southern Miscellany* 2 (September 1843), 3, quoted in Shippey, "William Tappan Thompson," 125. In later years, Thompson went on to defend slavery against what he perceived as growing threats from abolitionists in New England. Ibid., 133–52.

19. Northerners praised De Bow's work because it seemed to vindicate the superiority of northern free labor over southern slave labor. De Bow, however, never intended such an interpretation and in fact only advocated greater industrialization to boost economic growth in the South while maintaining the region's superior society and culture. McPherson, *Battle Cry of Freedom,* 93–103.

20. Barnard quoted in Frederick A. P. Barnard, LL.D., *Letter to the Honorable The Board of Trustees of the University of Mississippi* (Oxford: Univ. of Mississippi, 1858), 82–83.

21. *Address of President F. A. P. Barnard, of the University of Mississippi, to the Senior Class of that Institution, on the Relation of Universities to Popular Education,* 1857, quoted in Chute, "Life of Frederick A. P. Barnard," 307–8. For more information on Barnard's opinion of southern education, see Barnard, *Letter to the Honorable Board of Trustees,* 104–5.

22. *Record of the Testimony and Proceedings, in the Matter of the Investigation by the Trustees of the University of Mississippi, on the 1st and 2nd of March, 1860, of the Charges Made by H. R. Branham, Against the Chancellor of the University*

(Jackson, Miss.: Printed at the Mississippian Office, 1860), 20–23; T. Butler King to the *Savannah Republican,* February 23, 1850, quoted in *Address of Hon. T. Butler King to the People of the First Congressional District* (Savannah, Ga.: Steam Press John M. Cooper & Co., 1859), 20, SHC; Gilman quoted in Takahashi, "Home of Their Choice," 74; Watson quoted in Mason, "Henry Watson," 30–32. See also Claiborne, *Life and Correspondence of John Quitman,* 1: 88–92, 103; *A Discussion on Slaveholding. Three Letters to a Conservative by George D. Armstrong, D.D. of Virginia and Three Conservative Replies by C. Van Rensselaer, D.D. of New Jersey. Together with Two Rejoinders, On Slaveholding, Schemes of Emancipation, Colonization, Etc.* (Philadelphia, Pa.: Joseph M. Wilson, 111 South Tenth Street, 1858), 3–4, 10–13, UVA; *Speech of Mr. Ashbel Smith, on the Public Debt Bill. Delivered in the House of Representatives of the State of Texas, December 11th, 1855* (Austin, Tex.: State Times Job Office, 1856), 20, UT.

23. Elisha Pease quoted in Griffin, "Connecticut Yankee in Texas," 27; Elisha Pease to Lucadia Pease, September 5, 1853, quoted in Pease, *Lucadia Pease,* 150.

24. Amanda Beardsley Trulock to Nicholas, Polly, Bronson, and Marcia Beardsley, November 29, 1837, quoted in Malloy, "The Health of Our Family," 33.

25. *Addresses of Doctor Ashbel Smith,* 4, 8, UT.

26. John Latrobe to John S. Lyson, January 28, 1859, Edward Greenway Papers, Manuscript Division, Sheridan Libraries, Johns Hopkins University, Baltimore.

27. Duncan, *Reluctant General,* 136–37; Pike quoted in Baker, "Albert Pike: Citizen Speechmaker of Arkansas," *Arkansas Historical Quarterly,* 148–49; Albert Pike, *Letters to the People of the Northern States on the Nebraska and Kansas Act, and Southern Slavery* (Washington, D.C.: Dieon Printer, 1856), 4, 12–13, Duke.

28. "Speech of Hon. H. M. Shaw of North Carolina, in the House of Representatives, April 20, 1858," *North Carolina Pamphlets,* 1841–59, Vol. 3, No 2, p. 1, Duke; "Speech of Hon H. M. Shaw, of North Carolina, in the House of Representatives, May 29,1854, " *North Carolina Pamphlets,* 1841–59, Vol. 3, No 1, p. 8, Duke. Other top-ranked northern-born politicians in the South made similar remarks when addressing their constituents. See John A. Quitman, "To the Electors of Adams County," delivered from Monmouth, Miss., August 3, 1832, Rare Book Collection, Southern Pamphlet Folio-2, #6253, SHC; T. Butler King to the *Savannah Republican,* February 23, 1850, quoted in *Address of Hon. T. Butler King,* 20, SHC; Pike quoted in Baker, "Citizen Speechmaker," *Arkansas Historical Quarterly,* 145.

29. Gilman quoted in "Biographical Sketch and Letters of Carolina Howard Gilman," 15, Folder 4, Caroline Howard Gilman Papers, 1810–1880, Manuscripts P, USC.

30. Pike, *Letters to the People of the Northern States,* 4, 12–13, 16, Duke.

31. Quitman quoted in Claiborne, *Life and Correspondence of John Quitman,* 1: 116. Elisha Pease expressed similar feelings. See Elisha Pease to Lucadia Pease, October 25, 1853, quoted in Pease, *Lucadia Pease,* 170.

32. Trulock quoted in Malloy, "Health of Our Family," 40.

33. Barnard quoted in Chute, "The Life of Frederick A. P. Barnard," 218. Chute also showed that Barnard even tried to claim he was actually born in Alabama, but recognized few would believe that since so few people of his age were actually born in the state.

34. *Record of the Testimony and Proceedings,* 27.

35. Gilman quoted in Takahashi, "Home of Their Choice," 69–70. Takahashi does not agree and insists that Gilman still considered herself a northerner, though estranged from the region. Ibid., 97–98.

36. Clapp, *Autobiographical Sketches,* 403–4.

37. J. H. Ingraham, ed., *The Sunny South: Or, the Southerner at Home, Embracing Five Year's Experience of a Northern Governess in the Land of the Sugar and the Cotton* (1860; reprint, New York: Negro Univ. Presses, 1968), 5.

38. Handerson, *Yankee in Gray,* 18.

39. Caroline Seabury Diary, October 7, 1854, quoted in Seabury, *Diary of Caroline Seabury,* 25–36.

40. Sally Baxter Hampton to Sarah Baxter, May 8, 1856, Folder 2, Sally Baxter Hampton Papers 1853–1897, Manuscripts P, USC.

41. Henry Watson to his uncle, April 30, 1834, Box 2, Folder April–May 1834, Henry Watson Papers, Duke. For further evidence of northerners who felt isolated and homesick in their first trips into the South, see Seargent Prentiss to unknown, December 22, 1827, quoted in Prentiss, *Memoir of S. S. Prentiss,* 1: 67; Weathersby, *J. H. Ingraham,* 50–53, 93; Arthur McArthur to his sister, November 8, 1853, Box 15, Folder 61, 1853, McArthur Family Papers 1790–1890, Bowdoin; Henry Watson to Rosanna Reed, April 9, 1834, Folder April–May 1834, Box 2, Henry Watson Papers, Duke; Lucadia Pease to Maria and Augusta Niles, December 22, 1850, quoted in Pease, *Lucadia Pease,* 22–23; Holbrook Diary, April 30, May 15, 18, 25, July 2, 7, 27, 1852, quoted in D. D. Hall, "A Yankee Tutor in the Old South," *New England Quarterly* 33 (March 1960): 88; Sally Baxter to Anna Baxter, April 1–2, 1854, quoted in Hampton, *Divided Heart,* 15, 20.

42. Julius Reed to Henry Watson, Jr., April 3, 1832, quoted in James, *Antebellum Natchez,* 140. Strangely enough, Reed still understood the financial opportunities available for those who wanted to participate in slavery and plantations, and even briefly thought about staying for that reason. Ibid., 143.

43. William Pierce to Ellen Pierce, November 5, 1852, May 17, 1853, February 12, May 6, November 10, 1854, October 18, 1855, all in Ellen Pierce Papers, Duke.

44. William Pierce to Ellen Pierce, November 30, 1855, Ellen Pierce Papers, Duke. Further examples can be found in Caroline S. Davies, "A Yankee in the South in 1833," *New England Quarterly* 10 (March and June 1937), 63–83, 270–289; Larry Gara, "A New Englander's View of Plantation Life: Letters of Edwin Hall to Cyrus Woodman, 1837," *Journal of Southern History* 18 (August 1952): 343.

45. Lander, *Calhoun Family*, 139, 150–51; Lavin, *William Bostwick*, 360–61. Clemson, who moved with his family to New York in 1852, did end up in Maryland a year later.

46. Weathersby, *J. H. Ingraham*, 127–28. Nevertheless, Ingraham on several occasions referred to other northern emigrants who had made a transition to a southern identity, so he knew it could happen.

47. Durwood Dunn, *An Abolitionist in the Appalachian South: Ezekiel Birdseye in Slavery, Capitalism, and Separate Statehood in East Tennessee, 1841–1846* (Knoxville: Univ. of Tennessee Press, 1997), 27. Both of Birdseye's wives were also from Connecticut.

48. Farmer, *The Times and Journal of Alice Farmer*, 17–18.

49. Evans, "Daniel Pratt," 37–38, 44, 108–9.

50. Tryphena Fox to Anna Holder, July 31, November 14, 1857, July 9, 1858, quoted in Fox, *A Northern Woman*, 59, 66, 73.

51. Sally Hampton to Lucy Baxter, March 23–24, 1859, quoted in Hampton, *Divided Heart*, 50–51; Sally Baxter to George Baxter, April 15, 1855, quoted in ibid., 22–23.

52. Caroline Seabury Diary, December 25, 1856, quoted in Seabury, *Diary of Caroline Seabury*, 45–46. Three years later she still wished to see her "native land" again. Caroline Seabury Diary, April 16, 1859, quoted in ibid., 56.

53. Henry Watson to his mother, September 27, 1836, p. 21 of letter to his mother starting May 18, 1834, Folder April–May 1834, Box 2, Henry Watson Papers, Duke.

54. This pattern held regardless of time spent in the South. Some emigrants abandoned the South even after decades of living there, while others identified with the South after only a few years in their adopted states. For more examples of northerners who emigrated in the 1850s, see Drummond, *Confederate Yankee*; Patterson, *Yankee Rebel*; Samuel Pasco, *Private Pasco: A Civil War Diary*, ed. William Pasco (Oak Brook, Ill.: McAdams Multigraphies, 1990); Fox, *A Northern Woman*; Seabury, *Diary of Caroline Seabury*.

55. Fox, *A Northern Woman*, 7–8; Tryphena Fox to Anna Holder, July 7, 1856, quoted in ibid., 30–31; Seabury Diary, June 15–16, 1858, quoted in Seabury, *Diary of Caroline Seabury*, 54.

56. Dibble, *Antebellum Pensacola*, 3: 31, 37–40, 62–67; Sanchez-Saavedra, "The Beau Ideal of a Soldier," 1–24, 39–42, 84–88, 92–94, 100–4.

57. Vandiver, *Ploughshares into Swords*, 42–43. However, in a hint to his future, Gorgas did record in his diary how he hoped to eventually buy a plantation with dozens of slaves to please his wife. Josiah Gorgas Diary, January 28, 1857, quoted in Josiah Gorgas, *The Journals of Josiah Gorgas, 1857–1878*, ed. Sarah Wiggins (Tuscaloosa: Univ. of Alabama Press, 1995), 6.

58. Thomas Clemson to John Calhoun, September 24, 1849, quoted in Lander, *Calhoun Family*, 121–22. In Clemson's case, those needs were mainly economical. William Chute cited this tendency when he quoted a Louisiana congressman talking about South Carolinian anti-protectionists, saying they adopted that position because of personal needs. Chute, "Life of Frederick A. P. Barnard," 20.

59. Tryphena Fox to Anna Holder, June 29, 1856, quoted in Fox, *A Northern Woman*, 27–28. Fox made a similar reference to "home" when she first moved to Mississippi. Tryphena Fox to her grandmother, June 25, 1853, Tryphena Holder Fox Papers 1826–1885, Department of Archives and History, Division of Records Management, State of Mississippi, Jackson, Miss. (repository hereafter cited as SM).

60. William Pierce to Ellen Pierce, November 10, 1854, Ellen Pierce Papers, Duke.

61. Lucadia Pease to Augusta Niles, October 18, 1850, quoted in Pease, *Lucadia Pease*, 3–4. For further evidence of this theme, see Sally Hampton to Lucy Baxter, December 23–25, 1855, quoted in Hampton, *Divided Heart*, 27; Jedediah Hotchkiss to George Hotchkiss, September 24, 1849, quoted in Charles Hotchkiss Osterhout, *Stonewall Jackson's Map-Maker (Jed Hotchkiss): Excerpts From His Letters and Papers* (s.l: s.n., 1977), 20; Elisha Pease to Lucadia Pease, August 25, 1853, quoted in Pease, *Lucadia Pease*, 137–38; Clapp, *Autobiographical Sketches*, 83–94; Dolly Lunt Burge Diary, March 20, 1851, December 25, 1853, October 20, 1854, quoted in Burge, *The Diary of Dolly Lunt Burge*, 60, 79, 86.

62. Jed Hotchkiss to George Hotchkiss, September 24, 1849, quoted in Osterhout, *Stonewall Jackson's Mapmaker*, 20. In this case, Hotchkiss seemed to lean more toward a northern identity, because he talked about receiving mail from "home" in record time, indicating his continuing communication with friends and family in New York.

63. *Record of the Testimony and Proceedings*, 2–3.

64. Malloy, "The Health of Our Family," 56–57, 65–69.

65. Amanda Beardsley Trulock to Nichols Beardsley, March, 1850, quoted in ibid., 92. Ultimately, Trulock remained in Arkansas during the Civil War, but after losing everything, she finally returned to Connecticut during Reconstruction.

66. Lander, *Calhoun Family*, 112–14; Brazy, *An American Planter*, 11–13, 17–18; Tryphena Fox to her mother, July 7, 14, 1856, quoted in Fox, *A Northern Woman*, 33; Ballard, *Pemberton*, chap. 4; Silverthorne, *Ashbel Smith*, 134–38, 144; Berkeley, *A Yankee Botanist*, 75–77, 124–27; Glass, *Connecticut Yankee in Early*

Alabama, 39, 86; Vicki Adams Tongate, "Transcendent Ties: A Northern Girl's Sojourn in Confederate Texas, The Lucy Pier Stevens Diary" (master's thesis, Southern Methodist Univ., 2002), 7–9; Takahashi, "Home of Their Choice," 84–85; Henry Richardson to his parents, January 6, 1861, Henry B. Richardson Materials, Richardson and Farrar Family Papers 1860–1876, #2892-z, SHC; Samuel Gilman to his sister, December 8, 1846, Folder 1, Samuel Gilman Papers, 1828–1961, Manuscripts P, USC; Hampton, *Divided Heart,* xiv; Sally Hampton to Anna Baxter, March 17, 1859, quoted in ibid., 45–47; Sally Hampton to George and Anna Baxter, May 10–12, 1859, quoted in ibid., 57–61; Burge Diary, March 12, 1848, quoted in Burge, *Diary of Dolly Burge,* 15; Tryphena Fox to Anna Holder, March 17, 1860, quoted in Fox, *A Northern Woman,* 100; Ashbel Smith to Mary, March 27, 31, April 9, 17, 23, May 2, 18, 1835, Ashbel Smith Journal 1832–1857, Box 2G234, Ashbel Smith Papers, UT.

    67. William Pierce to Ellen Pierce, May 29, 1853, Ellen Pierce Papers, Duke.

    68. Lucadia Pease to Augusta Niles, November 5, 1850, quoted in Pease, *Lucadia Pease,* 8. Pease made similar remarks in other letters of the same time period. See Lucadia Pease to Augusta Niles, October 18, 23, December 3, 1850, quoted in ibid., 3–12, 18–21.

    69. Tryphena Fox to Anna Holder, April 26, 1857, quoted in Fox, *A Northern Woman,* 49; Ashbel Smith to Cousin Lydia, January 31, 1840, Ashbel Smith Journal, 1832–1857, Box 2G234, UT. See also Hotchkiss to Jedediah Hotchkiss, November 23, 1846, Box 1, Folder 1, Jedediah Hotchkiss Papers, UVA; Sarah Williams to her parents, March 17, 1854, Folder 1, Sarah Williams Letters, #3210, SHC.

    70. Juliet Coleman to Dorcas Bestor, April 12, 1849, August 5, 1850, quoted in Glass, *Connecticut Yankee in Early Alabama,* 57, 83.

    71. John S. Ryan to A. F. Girard, December 13, 1858, John S. Ryan Papers, 1858–1863, Manuscripts P, USC. See also Caroline Lee Hentz to Mrs. Stafford, March 5, 1851, Folder 1, Hentz Family Papers, #332, SHC; Charles Edward Nash, *Biographical Sketches of Gen. Pat Cleburne and Gen. T.C. Hindman, Together with Humorous Anecdotes and Reminiscences of the Late Civil War* (Dayton, Ohio: Morningside Bookshop, 1977), 83–84.

    72. Tryphena Fox to Anna Holder, September 8, 1856, quoted in Fox, *A Northern Woman,* 38–39.

    73. Olin quoted in Green, *Role of the Yankee,* 100–1. Interestingly, despite his assertions, Olin moved back to Connecticut in the 1840s, after twenty years in the Deep South.

    74. Lucadia Pease to Augusta Niles, August 20, 1854, quoted in Pease, *Lucadia Pease,* 205. For more of the letters Lucadia wrote on the subject, see Lucadia Pease to Maria and Augusta Niles, January 21, August 4, 1851, December 28, 1853,

January 13, February 27, April 15, 1854, quoted in ibid., 26–27, 51–52, 175–77, 184–87.

75. Similar events may also have happened for native southerners moving to the North. Much of the North had the same frontier mixing that occurred in the Southwest. The territorial governor of Illinois, a native Virginian, led the drive to keep the entire Northwest free soil by abandoning his own upbringing and calling for making Illinois a free state. The Grimké sisters of South Carolina abandoned their childhood homes and moved to New England as firm opponents of slavery. More study is needed to see if this phenomenon occurred nationally rather than just for northern emigrants.

3. Adoptive Southerners React to Slavery

1. For a review of the literature on sectional divisions over slavery and the lead up to the Civil War, see Freehling, *The Road to Disunion: Secessionists at Bay;* Freehling, *Road to Disunion: Secessionists Triumphant;* Varon, *Disunion;* Bonner, *Mastering America;* Potter, *Impending Crisis;* McPherson, *Battle Cry of Freedom;* Elizabeth Fox-Genovese and Eugene Genovese, *The Mind of the Master Class: History and Faith in the Southern Slaveholder's Worldview* (New York: Cambridge Univ. Press, 2005); William E. Gienapp, *The Origins of the Republican Party 1852–1856* (New York: Oxford Univ. Press, 1987); Holt, *The Rise and Fall of the American Whig Party;* Michael A. Morrison, *Slavery and the American West: The Eclipse of Manifest Destiny and the Coming of Civil War* (Chapel Hill: Univ. of North Carolina Press, 1997); James B. Stewart, *Holy Warriors: Abolitionists and American Slavery* (New York: Hill and Wang, 1976); Adam Goodheart, *1861: The Civil War Awakening* (New York: Alfred A. Knopf, 2011).

2. Foner, *Free Soil,* ix–xxxix.

3. Dennis C. Rousey, "Friends and Foes of Slavery: Foreigners and Northerners in the Old South," *Journal of Social History* 35 (Winter 2001): 373, 380–83.

4. Pryor, "An Anomalous Person," *Journal of Southern History,* 386–87. Pryor, however, did add that northern tutors sometimes espoused proslavery arguments, generally did not like blacks, were curious about slavery, and usually did not see much of the harshness expounded in the North, because they did not actually see slaves all that much.

5. Rousey, "Friends and Foes of Slavery," *Journal of Social History,* 373–83.

6. Takahashi, "Home of Their Choice," 85–94; Peter Gilman Pinckney, *Samuel Gilman,* Senior Term Paper, April 20, 1977, 8, Caroline Gilman Papers, CC; Howe, "A Massachusetts Yankee," *New England Quarterly,* 205–6.

7. Mary Jane Lee Brazy, "The World a Slaveholder Made: Stephen Duncan and Plantation Slavery" (master's thesis, Univ. of Wisconsin-Milwaukee, 1987),

120–25; Boman, *Abiel Leonard,* 28–33, 125–28, 136, 146–47. See also Chute, "Life of Frederick A. P. Barnard," 206–8; Berkeley, *A Yankee Botanist,* 31–32; Rousey, "Friends and Foes of Slavery," *Journal of Social History,* 384–85; Elisha Pease to Lucadia Pease, September 2, 1853, quoted in Pease, *Lucadia Pease & the Governor,* 148.

8. Brazy, "The World a Slaveholder Made," 124–25; Boman, *Abiel Leonard,* 28–33. For further analysis of this interpretation, see Grant, *North Over South,* 47–49, 71; Eaton, *The Freedom-of-Thought Struggle,* 180–83, 190–93, 222.

9. For references to historians who adopt this view, see Green, *Role of the Yankee,* 73–77; Grant, *North Over South,* 88, 93, 95; Eaton, *Freedom-of-Thought Struggle,* 266; Lavin, *William Bostwick,* 17, 24.

10. Eugene Genovese, *Roll Jordan Roll: The World the Slaves Made* (New York: Vintage Books, 1976); Fox-Genovese, *The Mind of the Master Class;* Ira Berlin, *Generations of Captivity: A History of African-American Slaves* (Cambridge, Mass.: Belknap Press of Harvard Univ. Press, 2003).

11. James Oakes, *The Ruling Race: A History of American Slaveholders* (New York: W.W. Norton and Company, 1998), 39–41.

12. Ibid., xv–xviii, 59–79.

13. For more information on emancipation in the North in the antebellum period, see Joanne Pope Mellish, *Disowning Slavery: Gradual Emancipation and Race in New England 1780–1860* (Ithaca: Cornell Univ. Press, 1998); Robin Blackburn, *The American Crucible: Slavery, Emancipation and Human Rights* (New York: Verso, 2011); Arthur Silversmith, *The First Emancipation: The Abolition of Slavery in the North* (Chicago: Univ. of Chicago Press, 1967); Graham Russell Hodges, *Slavery and Freedom in the Rural North: African-Americans in Monmouth County, New Jersey 1665–1865* (Madison, Wis.: Madison House, 1997)

14. Brazy, *An American Planter,* 14–15; Unknown, *A Brief Sketch of the Life, Civil and Military, of John A. Quitman, Major General in the Army of the U.S.* (Washington: Ritchie & Heiss, 1848), Southern Historical Collection, University of North Carolina Library, Chapel Hill (collection hereafter cited as SHC).

15. Dangerfield, *The Awakening of American Nationalism,* 131–32.

16. McPherson, *Battle Cry of Freedom,* 52–55.

17. Tryphena Fox to Anna Holder, July 7, 1856, quoted in Fox, *A Northern Woman in the Plantation South,* 26; Tryphena Fox to Anna Holder, July 14, 1856, quoted in ibid., 35–36. For further examples of Fox's views on free blacks and Creoles, see Tryphena Fox to Anna Holder, June 6 and September 8, 1856, quoted in ibid., 26, 39–40; Tryphena Fox to Anna Holder, January 4, 1857, quoted in ibid., 46–47; Tryphena Fox to Anna Holder, August 16, 1858, quoted in ibid., 76.

18. Sally Hampton to George Baxter, May 10–12, 1859, quoted in Hampton, *A Divided Heart,* 58.

19. Bowman, *Abiel Leonard*, 194–95.

20. Caroline Seabury Diary, November 18, 1854, quoted in Seabury, *Diary of Caroline Seabury*, 36; Calvin L. Robinson, *A Yankee in a Confederate Town: The Journal of Calvin L. Robinson*, ed. Anne Robinson Clancy (Sarasota, Fla.: Pineapple Press Inc., 2002), 103–11.

21. Ingraham, *The Southwest By a Yankee*, 2: 92–93. Ingraham claimed many northerners not only became established planters but even acted more harshly than native southerners because they had not grown up with the institution and thus remained more fearful of blacks than those who had.

22. Green, *The Role of the Yankee*, 35.

23. Caroline Seabury Diary, October 7, 1854, quoted in Seabury, *Diary of Caroline Seabury*, 35.

24. Juliet Bestor to her mother and sister, January 11, 1834, quoted in Glass, *Connecticut Yankee in Early Alabama*, 35–36.

25. Pike quoted in Blevins, *Albert Pike*, 34.

26. Caroline Seabury Diary, February 8 and April 5, 1855, quoted in Seabury, *Diary of Caroline Seabury*, 37–39.

27. Caroline Seabury Diary, January 1, 1856, quoted in ibid., 43.

28. Caroline Seabury Diary, April 5, 1859, quoted in ibid., 56.

29. William Pierce to Ellen Pierce, December 10, 1852, Ellen E. Pierce Papers 1849–1857, Duke. At the same time, reflecting the general racist views of native northerners, Pierce also claimed that slavery was evil because it forced white children to grow up with slave children and possibly even acquire slave dialects.

30. Lucadia Pease to Augusta Niles, March 2, 1851, quoted in Pease, *Lucadia Pease & the Governor*, 33.

31. Charles William Holbrook Diary, September 13, October 1–5, 1852, quoted in Hall, "A Yankee Tutor in the Old South," *New England Quarterly*, 89.

32. Sarah Williams to her parents, February 25, 1855, Folder 1, Sarah Francis Hicks Williams Papers, SHC. For similar rhetoric about the negative effects of slavery, see Edwin Hall to Cyrus Woodman, March 24, June 13, and August 30, 1837, quoted in Gara, "A New Englander's View of Plantation Life," *Journal of Southern History*, 344–51; Seargent Prentiss to mother, February 12, 1828, quoted in Prentiss, *A Memoir of S. S. Prentiss*, 1: 69.

33. James, *Antebellum Natchez*, 175–76; William Ransom Hogan and Edwin Adams Davis, eds., *William Johnson's Natchez: The Ante-Bellum Diary of a Free Negro* (Baton Rouge: Louisiana State Univ. Press, 1951), 130, 210, 231, 343, 411, 546, 589; Stephen Duncan to Josiah S. Johnston, October 11, 1831, quoted in Brazy, "The World a Slaveholder Made," 117. Author William W. Chenault even claimed that, partly because of its northern-born community, cities like New Orleans held an indifferent view of slavery, with few pro-slavery pamphlets sold and *Uncle Tom's*

Cabin freely sold in its bookstores. Chenault and Reinders, "The Northern-born Community of New Orleans in the 1850s," *Journal of American History,* 244.

34. Robinson, *A Yankee in a Confederate Town,* 103–11; Lucadia Pease to Maria Niles, March 30, 1851, quoted in Pease, *Lucadia Pease & the Governor,* 38; Farmer, *The Times and Journal of Alice Farmer,* 30–31; Mason, "Henry Watson," 12–16; Julius Reed to Henry Watson, Jr., April 3, 1832, quoted in James, *Antebellum Natchez,* 140.

35. Trulock quoted in Malloy, "The Health of Our Family," 17–20.

36. Sarah Williams to her parents, December 10, 1853 or 1854, 113, Folder 1, Sarah Francis Hicks Williams Letters, SHC.

37. Emily Sinkler to Frank Wharton, November 22, 1842, quoted in Emily Wharton Sinkler, *Between North and South: The Letters of Emily Wharton Sinkler 1842–1865,* ed. Anne Sinkler Whaley LeClercq (Columbia: Univ. of South Carolina Press, 2001), 11–12. For further references to Sinkler's views on slavery, see Emily Sinkler to Henry Wharton, November 25, 1842, quoted in ibid., 13–14; Emily Sinkler to her father, December 1 and 24, 1842, quoted in ibid., 17, 23–24; Emily Sinkler to Mary Wharton, December 10, 1842, quoted in ibid., 20–21; Emily Sinkler to her mother, February 11, 1843, quoted in ibid., 31–33.

38. Arthur McArthur to his sister, November 8, 1853, Correspondence, 1780–1949, Box 2, Folder 1, McArthur Family Papers, Bowdoin.

39. John Quitman to Colonel Brush, August 23, 1823, in Claiborne, *Life and Correspondence of John A. Quitman,* 1: 84–85.

40. Juliet Bestor to Dorcas Bestor, November 14, 1833, quoted in Glass, *Connecticut Yankee in Early Alabama,* 23. Similar comments can be found in Julia Bestor to Dorcas Bestor, December 2, 1833, quoted in ibid., 27.

41. Admittedly, Coleman may have had a biased view because she was writing to her family about a relative and only witnessed slavery for a relatively short period of time. Still, a year later her views had not changed about her brother or slavery itself. See Juliet Bestor to her mother and sister, January 11, 1834, quoted in ibid., 35–36.

42. Fox-Genovese, *The Mind of the Master Class,* 365–82.

43. Daniel Pratt to Edward Pratt, June 19, 1827, quoted in Evans, "Daniel Pratt," 23–24. Nevertheless, Pratt's biographer argues that Pratt was not ready to accept the South completely, since he really did not believe in slavery or think of the South as his home (claiming he referred to it as another country). He also said Pratt openly disdained life in the South because it was so hard to get cash for his work. As further evidence, Pratt married a New Hampshire woman in 1827 and worked for a Connecticut-born gin manufacturer. See ibid., 23–28.

44. Editors and biographers of adoptive southerners often agree that these motivations helped turn neutral or anti-slavery northerners into pro-slavery defend-

ers. See Fox, *A Northern Woman,* 13; Ballard, *Pemberton,* 74–76; Lavin, *William Bostwick,* 17, 24; James, *Antebellum Natchez,* 176; Floride Clemson, *A Rebel Came Home: The Diary and Letters of Floride Clemson, 1863–1866,* rev. ed., ed. Ernest M. Lander, Jr., and Charles M. McGee, Jr. (Columbia: Univ. of South Carolina Press, 1989), 4; Franzetti, "Elisha Marshall Pease," 7–8; Malloy, "The Health of Our Family," 17–20; Dibble, *Ante-bellum Pensacola,* 3: 62–67; Brazy, *An American Planter,* 14–15, 54–56; Green, *The Role of the Yankee,* 73–74, 77; Bowman, *Abiel Leonard,* 125–28.

45. Caroline Gilman, *Recollections of a Southern Matron* (New York: Harper and Brothers, 1839), 71; Jedediah Hotchkiss, *Make Me a Map of the Valley: The Civil War Journal of Stonewall Jackson's Topographer,* ed. Archie P. McDonald (Dallas, Tex.: Southern Methodist Univ. Press, 1973), iii–viii; Robert Seager II, *And Tyler Too: A Biography of John & Julia Gardiner Tyler* (New York: McGraw-Hill Book Company, 1963), 300–1; Tryphena Blanche Holder Fox to her grandmother, June 25, 1853, Tryphena Holder Fox Papers 1826–1885, SM; Berkeley, *A Yankee Botanist,* 166–67.

46. Trulock quoted in Malloy, "The Health of Our Family," 17–18; Amanda Trulock to her family, March 21, 1838, quoted in ibid., 28.

47. Blanks, "Caroline Lee Hentz: Antebellum Author, Antebellum Woman," 72.

48. O. T. Hammond to Charles Henry Ray, October 12, 1838, quoted in Cuthbert, "Yankee Preacher-Teacher in Florida, 1838," *Huntington Library Quarterly,* 100–1.

49. Masur, *1831: Year of Eclipse.*

50. One adoptive southern slave-owner, Stephen Duncan, used to allow his slaves to travel back and forth among nearby plantations freely, but after Turner's revolt he enforced much stricter controls and inflicted punishments against slaves who stepped out of line. Brazy, *An American Planter,* 14–15, 54–56.

51. Quitman quoted in James, *Antebellum Natchez,* 176.

52. Clapp quoted in Ashton Phelps, Jr., *Theodore Clapp: The Ante-bellum South's Only Unitarian Minister,* Yale Univ., May 18, 1966, 19–20, Manuscripts Department, Special Collections Division, Tulane University Library, Tulane University, New Orleans (repository hereafter cited as Tulane). Still, by the 1850s, Clapp tried to find a middle ground by calling on those who opposed slavery in principle to still obey the law. See Clapp, *Autobiographical Sketches,* 1–30, 43, 83–114, 417–19; Phelps, *Theodore Clapp,* 3–12, Tulane.

53. George D. Armstrong, D.D., *"The Good Hand of Our God Upon Us:" A Thanksgiving Sermon, Preached on Occasion of the Victory of Manassas, July 21st, 1861 in the Presbyterian Church, Norfolk, VA* (Norfolk, Va.: J. D. Ghiselin, 1861), 6–7, 10–11, UVA; *A Discussion on Slaveholding. Three Letters to a Conservative by George D. Armstrong, D.D. of Virginia,* 88–89, UVA.

54. *A Discussion on Slaveholding. Three Letters to a Conservative by George D. Armstrong, D.D.,* 86, UVA. It should be noted, however, that unlike Clapp, Armstrong received his theological training at a Virginia academy.

55. F. G. De Fontaine, *American Abolitionism, From 1787 to 1861: A Compendium of Historical Facts Embracing Legislation in Congress and Agitation Without* (New York: D. Appleton & Company, 1861), 8–33, 55–56, Library of Virginia, Richmond (repository hereafter cited as LV).

56. Ibid., 5–7.

57. Ibid., 55–56.

58. Theodore Clapp to Rev. Thomas Whittemore, September 1853, quoted in Clapp, *Autobiographical Sketches,* 211–13. In the same letter, Clapp did refer to Boston as "the metropolis of my native state" but only to demonstrate how many Bostonians ended up residing in New Orleans by the 1850s.

59. Sanchez-Saavedra, "Beau Ideal of a Soldier," 26. Sanchez-Saavedra dismisses the episode as mere opportunism, since Dimmock wanted an appointment to the state militia and feared his past ties to Massachusetts would hurt his chances. What he neglects to consider, however, was that Dimmock had left Massachusetts before the rise of abolitionists and so never shared the same type of anti-slavery opinions.

60. Harriet Beecher Stowe, *Uncle Tom's Cabin, 150th Anniversary Edition* (New York: Penguin Books, 1998).

61. McPherson, *Battle Cry of Freedom,* 88–90.

62. Seager, *And Tyler Too,* 402–5. The author also argued that southerners praised her defense of their institutions and even some northern newspapers lauded its power and elegance.

63. Caroline Lee Hentz, *The Planter's Northern Bride* (Philadelphia, Pa.: T. B. Peterson and Brothers, 1870), iii–viii. Author Robert LeRoy Hilldrup points out that other female writers in the South praised Hentz's fair judgment because of her personal knowledge of slavery versus Stowe's reliance on second-hand accounts. Hilldrup, "Cold War Against the Yankees," *The North Carolina Historical Review,* 38.

64. For more on Hentz's background in relation to her writing, see Blanks, "Caroline Lee Hentz," 51–54, 69–70.

65. Hentz, *The Planter's Northern Bride,* 406–7, 445. Further evidence of the novel as a pseudo-autobiography appeared when Hentz wrote about Mooreland's wife, who was also a native northerner, claiming she had not only gotten used to the South but became strongly attached to it. Mr. Brainard then said in astonishment how quickly one could adapt to new surroundings, "to the point that One would suppose . . . that my fair countrymen here had been born and bred at the South, instead of a simple New England village." Ibid., 404–5.

66. Ibid., 578–9.

67. Tryphena Fox to Anna Holder, August 31, 1857, quoted in Fox, *A Northern Woman*, 61.

68. O. T. Hammond to Charles Henry Ray, October 12, 1838, quoted in Cuthbert, "Yankee Preacher-Teacher," *Huntington Library Quarterly*, 100–1.

69. Franzetti, "Elisha Marshall Pease," 7–8.

70. Sally Baxter to George Baxter, April 15, 1855, in Hampton, *A Divided Heart*, 22.

71. Amelia Lines Diary, November 27, 1860, quoted in Amelia Akehurst Lines, *To Raise Myself a Little: The Diaries and Letters of Jennie, A Georgia Teacher, 1851–1886*, ed. Thomas Dyer (Athens: Univ. of Georgia Press, 1982), 170. See also Amelia Lines Diary, February 25–March 25, 1861, quoted in ibid., 178–80.

72. Timothy Flint, *Recollections of the Last Ten Years in the Valley of the Mississippi*, ed. George Brooks (Carbondale: Southern Illinois Univ. Press, 1968), 246–50.

73. Ingraham, *Southwest By a Yankee*, 2: 264–70.

74. William Pierce to Ellen Pierce, December 10, 1852, Ellen E. Pierce Papers, Duke.

75. Berkeley, *A Yankee Botanist*, 166–67.

76. The majority of adoptive southerners largely came to the same conclusion. In one instance, an adoptive southerner in New Orleans boasted that abolitionists would soon destroy their own influence as both white northerners and southerners turned against them. He cited a letter written to him by a Democrat in Massachusetts wanting to relocate to Texas because "He says he is obliged to hear at least one abolition sermon every Sunday, and two prayers for the 'niggers,' and can't stand it any longer—the infliction is too great." George Kendall to Henry Randall, January 18, 1860, quoted in Kendall, *Letters From a Texas Sheep Ranch*, 44.

77. Out of the others, one hundred and fifty-six did not own slaves in 1860 and thirty-eight did not leave behind sufficient records to determine one way or the other.

78. Warner, *Generals In Gray*, 347–48; Brazy, *An American Planter*, 14–15, 54–56.

79. Allardice, *More Generals in Gray*, 15–16; Wakelyn, *Biographical Dictionary of the Confederacy*, 246–47; Warner, *Biographical Register of the Confederate Congress*, 128–29; Trimpi, *Crimson Confederates*, 372; B. F. Perry and Hext M. Perry, *Reminiscences of Public Men* (Philadelphia, Pa.: J. D. Avill and Company, 1883), 208–14; William McFeely, "Amos T. Akerman: The Lawyer and Racial Justice," in Kousser, *Region, Race and Reconstruction*, 395–412; Tarrant, *Hon. Daniel Pratt*, 20–22, 41–43, 56–57, 94, 111; John Michael Burton, *Gracie's Alabama Volunteers: The History of the Fifty-Ninth Alabama Volunteer Regiment* (Gretna, La.: Pelican Publishing Company, 2003), 22; Evans, "Daniel Pratt," 8–23, 47–52, 64, 72–75.

80. Warner, *Generals in Gray,* 62–63, 93–94, 97; Allardice, *More Generals in Gray,* 148–49.

81. Fox, *A Northern Woman in the Plantation South,* xi, 1–21; Hampton, *A Divided Heart,* xi–xv; Malloy, "The Health of Our Family," 1–10; Seager, *And Tyler Too,* 1–47; Sinkler, *Between North and South,* 1–11.

82. The remaining nine came from Ohio and Europe.

83. Ingraham, *Southwest By a Yankee,* 2: 92–93; Peabody quoted in Grant, *North Over South,* 52–53.

84. Keiley, *Prisoner of War,* 103, 105; Mary Boykin Chestnut Diary, March 13, 1862, quoted in Mary Boykin Chesnut, *A Diary From Dixie,* ed. Isabella Martin and Myrta Avary (New York: D. Appleton & Co., 1905), 142–43; Kate Cumming Diary, November 29, 1863, quoted in Kate Cumming, *Kate: The Journal of a Confederate Nurse,* ed. Richard Harwell (Baton Rouge: Louisiana State Univ. Press, 1998), 175–76. Europeans also occasionally commented on this phenomenon. See Arthur Fremantle Diary, April 24, 1863, quoted in Arthur J. L. Fremantle, *Three Months in the Southern States: April–June, 1863* (Edinburgh: William Blackwood and Son, 1863), 48, footnote.

85. Kate Cumming Diary, November 29, 1863, quoted in Cumming, *Kate: The Journal of a Confederate Nurse,* 175–76.

86. French, *Two Wars,* 180, 181–85. See also Charles Quintard Diary, November 30, December 1, 12, 15–20, 1864, Charles Quintard Diaries 1864–1884, UT; Charles T. Quintard, *Doctor Quintard Chaplain C.S.A. and Second Bishop of Tennessee: The Memoir and Civil War Diary of Charles Todd Quintard,* ed. Sam Davis Elliott (Baton Rouge: Louisiana State Univ. Press, 2003), xv; Samuel Pasco Diary, October 14, 1862, quoted in Pasco, *Private Pasco,* 8.

87. Handerson, *Yankee in Gray,* 73; Henry Handerson, "Capture in the Wilderness," in Thomas Streissguth, ed., *The Civil War: The South* (San Diego, Calif.: Greenhaven Press Inc., 2001), 206–7; Edward Drummond Journal, March 18–19, April 6, 1862, quoted in Drummond, *Confederate Yankee,* 22–23; Silas Grisamore, *Reminiscences of Uncle Silas: A History of the Eighteenth Louisiana Infantry Regiment,* ed. Arthur W. Bergeron, Jr. (Baton Rouge, La.: Les Comite des Archives de la Louisiane, 1981), 109. One exception was General Franklin Gardner, who reportedly ordered his men to adopt a "take-no-prisoners" policy when it came to black soldiers during the battle at Port Hudson. "TELEGRAPHIC NEWS. VICTORY AT PORT HUDSON," *Charleston Mercury,* June 6, 1863.

88. Edmund DeWitt Patterson Journal, August 4, 1863, quoted in Patterson, *Yankee Rebel,* 128.

89. Brian K. Robertson, ed., *Things Grew Beautifully Worse: The Wartime Experiences of Captain John O'Brien, 30th Arkansas Infantry, C.S.A.* (Little Rock, Ark.: Butler Center for Arkansas Studies, Central Arkansas Library System, 2001),

25–26. Admittedly, only a couple of northern-born Confederate soldiers ever brought up the link between blacks and prisoner exchanges.

90. On a few occasions adoptive southerners even expressed willingness for the Confederacy to use black soldiers as long as they helped to win the war. See Josiah Gorgas to George Rains, October 30, 1864?, George Rains Papers, #1510, SHC; James W. Raab and John McGlone, eds., *A Dual Biography: Lloyd Tilghman and Francis Asbury Shoup, Two Forgotten Confederate Generals* (Murfreesboro, Tenn.: Southern Heritage Press, 2001), 202–9.

91. Edward Drummond Journal, May 4, 1862, quoted in Drummond, *Confederate Yankee*, 48.

92. Grisamore, *Reminiscences of Uncle Silas,* 131. For similar comments among adoptive southerners about the conditions of slaves in slavery versus emancipation, see Amelia Lines Diary, December 22–25, 1865, quoted in Lines, *To Raise Myself a Little,* 219–20; French, *Two Wars,* 321, 394–96; Handerson, *Yankee in Gray,* 21–23; Joseph Garey Diary, February 8, 1862, quoted in Joseph Garey, *A Keystone Rebel: The Civil War Diary of Joseph Garey, Hudson's Battery, Mississippi Volunteers,* ed. David Welker (Gettysburg, Pa.: Thomas Publications, 1996), 71; Quintard, *Doctor Quintard,* xv.

93. Amelia Lines to Maria Akehurst, Summer 1862, quoted in Lines, *To Raise Myself a Little,* 192–93. See also Amelia Lines diary, February 7, July 1, 1863, quoted in ibid., 197, 203.

94. Edmund DeWitt Patterson Journal, June 10, 1864, quoted in Patterson, *Yankee Rebel,* 171.

95. French, *Two Wars,* 313–15. For exceptions to this pattern, see William McFeely, "Amos T. Akerman: The Lawyer and Racial Justice," in *Region, Race, and Reconstruction*, ed. Kousser and McPherson, 399; Amos Akerman to his sister, July 17, 1870, quoted in ibid., 400; Dolly Lunt Burge Diary, November 8, 1864, quoted in Burge, *Diary of Dolly Lunt Burge,* 156.

96. Malloy, "The Health of Our Family," 28, 32–33.

4. Adoptive Southerners Choose Sides

1. For a sample of detailed studies on the secession crisis, see McPherson, *Battle Cry of Freedom;* Freehling, *The Road to Disunion: Secessionist Triumphant;* Ayers, *In the Presence of Mine Enemies;* Maury Klein, *Days of Defiance: Sumter, Secession, and the Coming of the Civil War* (New York: Knopf, 1997); Eaton, *Freedom-of-Thought Struggle,* 383–404; Bonner, *Mastering America;* Varon, *Disunion;* McCardell, *Idea of a Southern Nation,* 277–338; Russell McClintock, *Lincoln and the Decision for War: The Northern Response to Secession* (Chapel Hill: Univ. of North Carolina Press, 2008).

2. For examples of the literature on southern unionists, see Freehling, *The South vs. the South;* Hutchinson, *Divided Loyalties;* Current, *Lincoln's Loyalists;* David C. Downing, *A South Divided: Portraits of Dissent in the Confederacy* (Nashville, Tenn.: Cumberland House, 2007); R. B. McDowell, *Crisis and Decline: The Fate of Southern Unionists* (Dublin: Lilliput Press, 1997); Smith, *The Courage of a Southern Unionist*.

3. Weston Rhea quoted in Smith, *Courage of a Southern Unionist*, 31.

4. Eaton, *Freedom-of-Thought Struggle*, 390–404. He cites the case of New Orleans, where six of the seven state officers who opposed secession were either foreigners or northerners, as well as professors like Frederick Barnard and George Junkin, Sr., who both returned to the North after their adopted states seceded, and Isaac Murphy, a native New Englander who cast the only nay vote in the final vote in the Arkansas secession convention.

5. Out of the remaining individuals, five ended up supporting both sides during the war (either by first joining the Union and later supporting the Confederacy or vice versa), while another three avoided the war entirely by seeking refuge abroad.

6. McPherson, *Battle Cry of Freedom*, 282. To back up this argument, McPherson cites Pennsylvanian Josiah Gorgas, the head of the Confederate Ordnance Bureau, who married the daughter of an Alabama governor, as well as New Jersey native General Samuel Cooper and Pennsylvanian General John C. Pemberton, who both married Virginians.

7. Keller, "Keystone Confederates," in Blair, *Making and Remaking Pennsylvania's Civil War*, 16. See also Drummond, *Confederate Yankee*, xxxi–xxxiv.

8. For a further review of this line of reasoning by biographers of native northerners who joined the Confederacy and others, see Ballard, *Pemberton*, 85–86; "Pemberton, Yankee", *Sunday News*, August 30, 1942, Folder 11, John Clifford Pemberton Papers 1814–1942, SHC; Gary Skubal, "Loyalty and the Army: A Study of Why the Civil War Generals Robert E. Lee, John Pemberton, Thomas Jackson, and Edwin Alexander Joined the Confederacy," (master's thesis, U.S. Army Command and General Staff College, 1995); Keller, "Keystone Confederates," in Blair, *Making and Remaking Pennsylvania's Civil War*, 20–21; Strong, *Keystone Confederate*, 54; Wiggins, "The Marriage of Amelia Gayle and Josiah Gorgas," in Bleser, *Intimate Strategies of the Civil War*, 119.

9. "Lieutenant Colonel Ripley," *Charleston Mercury*, July 20, 1861.

10. Stephen D. Lee to Charles Wright, October 22, 1904, Folder 5, John Clifford Pemberton Papers 1814–1892, #586, SHC. Jedediah Hotchkiss, himself an adoptive southerner, ascribed such motivations to Irish immigrants who fought for the Union. Jedediah Hotchkiss to Sarah A. Hotchkiss, November 16, 1862,

http://valley.lib.virginia.edu/papers/A2563, from the Letters of the Hotchkiss Family, 1861–1865, Augusta County Letters and Diaries, The War Years, The Valley of the Shadow: Two Communities in the Civil War, University of Virginia, Charlottesville. Accessed via the library's web page.

11. Patterson, *Yankee Rebel*, vii–ix; "Williams College Class Report 1865," typescript, H. B. McClellan Papers 1857–1904, VHS; Johnson, "Yankees in Gray," *America's Civil War*, 64.

12. Duncan, *Reluctant General*, 134–35, 156–59.

13. Keller, "Keystone Confederates", in Blair, *Making and Remaking Pennsylvania's Civil War*, 17–18.

14. His biographer, Frank Vandiver, agrees that Gorgas made his decision with no urging from his wife. Vandiver personally believes Gorgas joined the Confederacy because of a feud with his superior officer, the urging of his southern friends, his hatred of Republicans, and because the Confederacy offered him a place to go. Vandiver quoted in Gorgas, *The Journals of Josiah Gorgas*, 37; Vandiver, *Ploughshares into Swords*, 50–53.

15. A similar argument can be made for Samuel Cooper and Johnson Kelly Duncan, who likewise had southern wives but also close ties to the South through Virginia and Louisiana respectively. Cooper himself did not leave behind his thoughts on the matter, but in all likelihood a variety of factors led him into the Confederacy. As a sign of his early dedication, Cooper resigned from the U.S. Army a full month before Virginia seceded and offered his services in the Virginia state army. Duncan's biographer, Michael J. Strong, speculates that marriage provided some motivation for Duncan but does not provide any proof. William Davis, "General Samuel Cooper," in Gary W. Gallagher and Joseph Glatthaar, eds., *Leaders of the Lost Cause: New Perspectives on the Confederate High Command* (Mechanicsburg, Penn.: Stackpole Books, 2004), 102–3; Jefferson Davis to Fitzhugh Lee, April 5, 1877, Papers of Samuel Cooper, #8610, UVA; George Mason to Samuel Cooper, March 10, 1861, 11–12, Section 2, Samuel Cooper Letters, VHS; Strong, *Keystone Confederate*, 1–30, 54.

16. Allan Nevins quoted in Gould B. Hagler, Jr., "Yankees in Grey: John C. Pemberton, C.S.A. A Series Concurring Northern Born Men Who Fought for the Southern Confederacy," *Confederate Veteran* 5 (2001): 12. For other arguments in favor of this interpretation, see Keller, "Keystone Confederates," in Blair, *Making and Remaking Pennsylvania's Civil War*, 20–21; Ballard, *Pemberton*, 84–86.

17. Pemberton quoted in Ballard, *Pemberton*, 32.

18. Ibid., 84; Mrs. Pemberton to Martha Thompson, April 23, 1861, in John Pemberton, *Pemberton, Defender of Vicksburg* (Chapel Hill: Univ. of North Carolina Press, 1942), 23–24.

19. A few authors argue that the reason places like New York City had scores of pro-secessionist voices, especially among Democrats, was because of economic ties to the South. Write, *The Secession Movement*, 154–56; Keller, "Keystone Confederates," in Blair, *Making and Remaking Pennsylvania's Civil War*, 3.

20. Gower, *Charles Dahlgren*, 36–37, 42–43, 76–77.

21. Warner, *Generals in Gray*, 347.

22. French, *Two Wars*, 132–33; Davis, *The Confederate General*, 1: 192–93; Brazy, *An American Planter*, 128, 150–53; Robert MacClay mentioned in Cummings, *Yankee Quaker*, 70. Admittedly, Duncan did move back to the North but only after hanging on in Mississippi for two years and seeing his plantation devastated by both armies.

23. Duncan, *Entrepreneur for Equality*, 11.

24. Cummings, *Yankee Quaker*, 168–69.

25. In Bushrod Johnson's case, Cummings writes that along with gaining property, living in Tennessee gave Johnson acceptance in a community and a feeling of achievement after the disgraces he suffered in the army. This sense of purpose likely weighed on Johnson's mind as much as his financial stake. Also, Bullock's biographer admitted that as soon as Georgia seceded, Bullock immediately joined a militia company as a private and helped storm the federal arsenal at Augusta months before the war began. Duncan, *Entrepreneur for Equality*, 11; Cummings, *Yankee Quaker*, 1–20, 146–49.

26. Ayers, *In the Presence of Mine Enemies*. 126.

27. For another example of an author claiming that a native northerner joined the Confederacy for financial reasons, see Duncan, *Entrepreneur for Equality*, 11. Duncan insists that Rufus Bullock originally joined because he was motivated by money and the desire to prove himself as a committed Confederate. Duncan seems to indicate Bullock did this reluctantly, since he originally opposed secession. However, Bullock was in the forefront of volunteers after Georgia seceded, even participating in the takeover of the U.S. arsenal in Augusta as a private.

28. Quintard, *Doctor Quintard*, 10–16; Henry Handerson to his father, July 1, 1861, quoted in Handerson, *Yankee in Gray*, 88.

29. Editors and biographers make this argument on several occasions. See Drummond, *Confederate Yankee*, xxxi–xxxiv; Bell, *Confederate Seadog*, 20–21; Bryan, *More Zeal Than Discretion*, 5, 102–4; Keller, "Keystone Confederates," in Blair, *Making and Remaking Pennsylvania's Civil War*, 13. For a native southerner's take on northerners' ties to a southern community, see Susan Eppes Diary, October 1863, in Susan Bradford Eppes, *Through Some Eventful Years* (Macon, Ga.: Press of the J. W. Burke Company, 1926), 208–9.

30. Gorgas quoted in Vandiver, *Ploughshares Into Swords*, 47.

31. Handerson, *Yankee in Gray*, 28–29.
32. Vandiver, *Ploughshares Into Swords*, 50–51.
33. Memphis *Daily Appeal*, November 17, 1865.
34. Handerson, *Yankee in Gray*, 29. Admittedly, Handerson did write a letter to his uncle in July 1861 indicating he had joined a Louisiana regiment to be with his friends. Henry Handerson to Lewis Handerson, July 1, 1861, quoted in ibid., 88.
35. Some historians even believe that bonds formed in the prewar army, and the prospect of obtaining higher rank, helped propel some native northerners into the Confederacy, especially those in the officer corps. Samuel Cooper, Josiah Gorgas, John Pemberton, Richard Griffith, and Charles Clark did have close ties to southern officers and were offered commissions by President Davis. Out of all possible motivations for adoptive southerners, however, this one likely ranks as the least convincing. First of all, no adoptive southerner who served in the army ever explicitly stated that he abandoned his oath simply for the sake of higher rank. In addition, if association with southern men was enough to steer a native northern officer toward the Confederate cause, the Confederate army should have seen a huge swell of northerners in its officer ranks. The defectors would have included the likes of Ulysses S. Grant and William Tecumseh Sherman, since the former had southern in-laws while the latter taught at a Louisiana college right up until secession. For further analysis on this theory, see Johnson, "Yankees in Gray," *American Civil War*, 38; Gallagher, *Leaders of the Lost Cause*, 105–7; Vandiver, *Ploughshare Into Swords*, 52–54; Bryan, *More Zeal Than Discretion*, 5, 102–4; Keller, "Keystone Confederates," in Blair, *Making and Remaking Pennsylvania's Civil War*, 13.
36. Grant, *North Over South*, 19–20. Nina Silber argues similar points in her study on minstrels and how northerners wanted to see an "authentic" South during Reconstruction. See Nina Silber, *The Romance of Reunion: Northerners and the South 1865–1900* (Chapel Hill: Univ. of North Carolina Press, 1993), 132–33, 140.
37. Weathersby, *J. H. Ingraham*, 128.
38. Even those newly arrived in the South attempted to dispel sectional myths. See Juliet Bestor to her mother and sister, January 5, 1834, quoted in Glass, *Connecticut Yankee in Early Alabama*, 32; Sarah Williams to her parents, December 10, 1853, Folder 1, Sarah Williams Letters, #3210, SHC.
39. Pike, *Letters to the People of the Northern States*, Letter I, p. 1, Microfiche 11759, UT. In another letter, Pike reinforced his credentials as a southern slaveholder by arguing that he never felt apprehensive about working with slaves or sleeping in a house filled with slaves. He also criticized free labor ideology by claiming he saw more misery in New York in a week than during years of slavery in the South. Pike, *Letters to the People of the Northern States*, Letter IV, p. 29, ibid.

40. Pike, *Letters to the People of the Northern States,* Letters II and III, pp. 16–28, UT.

41. Pike, *Letters to the People of the Northern States,* Letter IV, p. 35, UT.

42. Sally Hampton to George Baxter, December 22, 1860, and January 7, 1861, quoted in Hampton, *A Divided Heart,* 82, 93–95; Sally Hampton to Samuel Ruggles, January 1, 5, and 12, 1861, quoted in ibid., 86, 92; Sally Hampton to Anna Baxter, January 11, 1861, quoted in ibid., 97–98.

43. Sally Baxter to George Baxter, April 15, 1855, quoted in Hampton, *Divided Heart,* 22. Even the weather itself symbolized the seemingly unbridgeable differences between the sections. Few native northerners failed to comment on the influence of weather in forming sectional character. For more information, see Lucadia Pease to Augusta Niles, December 28, 1853, February 27, 1854, quoted in Pease, *Lucadia Pease,* 175–76, 184; Caroline Lee Hentz diary, February 18, 1836, Folder 16, Hentz Family Papers, #332, SHC; Thomas Wharton Diary, August 17, 1859, quoted in Wharton, *Queen of the South,* 207; William Pierce to Ellen Pierce, January 28, 1853, Ellen Pierce Papers, Duke; Tryphena Fox to Anna Holder, June 8, 1857, quoted in Fox, *A Northern Woman,* 51; Henry Watson to Julius Reed, January 8, 1831, Box 1, Folder 1831, Henry Watson Papers, Duke; Edwin Hall to Cyrus Woodman, March 24, June 13, August 30, 1837, quoted in Gara, "A New Englander's View of Plantation Life," *Journal of Southern History,* 344–51; Ashbel Smith to Cousin Lydia, January 31, 1850, Ashbel Smith Journal, 1832–1857, Box 2G234, Ashbel Smith Papers, UT; Caroline Lee Hentz Diary, February 12, 1836, Folder 16, Hentz Family Papers, #332, SHC.

44. Sally Hampton to George Baxter, December 22, 1860, quoted in Hampton, *Divided Heart,* 79–80.

45. Sally Hampton to Samuel Ruggles, January 5 and 12, 1861, quoted in ibid., 92.

46. Sally Hampton to Samuel Ruggles, January 1, 1861, quoted in ibid., 87–88.

47. Sally Hampton to George Baxter, December 22, 1860, quoted in ibid., 82; Sally Hampton to Samuel Ruggles, January 1, 1861, quoted in ibid., 86.

48. Sally Hampton to Samuel Ruggles, January 5 and 12, 1861, quoted in ibid., 92; Sally Hampton to George Baxter, January 7, 1861, quoted in ibid., 93–95; Sally Hampton to Anna Baxter, January 11, 1861, quoted in ibid., 97–98. The types of warnings given by the likes of Pike, Hampton, and others did not arise out of paranoia. Northern and southern ultras viewed each other with contempt and predicted that the other side would either back down or get crushed in a short war. Secessionists firmly believed in the idea that one southerner could defeat ten Yankees. Senator James Chesnut of South Carolina offered to drink all the blood spilled in a civil war, while others claimed that a woman's handkerchief or a

ladies thimble would be sufficient to hold the blood spilled in such a war. In contrast, northerners predicted that after one good battle, the Union armies would storm Richmond, capture the rebel traitors, and end the war within a month. McPherson, *Battle Cry of Freedom*, 238, 333–35; Elisha Pease to Lucadia Pease, July 21, 1856, quoted in Pease, *Lucadia Pease*, 280–81; Tarrant, *Hon. Daniel Pratt*, 78–81; Tryphena Fox to Anna Holder, November 18, 1856, quoted in Fox, *A Northern Woman*, 43–44; Seager, *And Tyler Too*, 430–33.

49. Arthur McArthur to his sister, November 8, 1853, Box 15, Folder 61 1853, McArthur Family Papers 1790–1890, Bowdoin.

50. William Pierce to Ellen Pierce, December 10, 1852, Ellen Pierce Papers, Duke; Clapp, *Autobiographical Sketches*, 62–63. See also Henry Watson to Julius Reed, January 8, 1831, Box 1, Folder 1831, Henry Watson Papers, Duke; Edward Wells to his mother, March 4, 1861, Folder 1, Papers of Smith and Wells Families 1856–1907, Manuscripts Plb, USC; Cash, *Mind of the South*, 28–29.

51. Prentiss quoted in ibid., 27.

52. *Addresses of Doctor Ashbel Smith*, 3, UT.

53. *Addresses Delivered in the Chapel at West Point, Before the Officers and Cadets of the United States Military Academy, by The Hon. Ashbel Smith, of Texas, and Col. A. W. Doniphan, of Missouri. June 16, 1848. Published by Order of the First Class of the United States Corps of Cadets* (New York: W. L. Burroughs, Printer, 1848), 8–9, UT.

54. Henry Watson to a Dear Friend, December 23, 1860, Folder 1860, Box 6, Henry Watson Papers, Duke; Henry Watson to his cousin, January 28, 1861, Folder Jan–July 1861, Box 6, ibid.

55. Henry Watson to Mr. Baker, March 8, 1861, Folder Jan–July 1861, Box 6, ibid.

56. Henry Richardson to his parents, January 6, 1861, Henry B. Richardson Materials, Richardson and Farrar Family Papers 1860–1876, SHC; John S. Ryan to A. F. Girard, January 15, 1861, John S. Ryan Papers, USC.

57. Julia Tyler to Juliana Gardner, January 21, 1861, quoted in Seager, *And Tyler Too*, 451; Amelia Lines Diary, November 3, 1860, quoted in Lines, *To Raise Myself a Little*, 166. See also Horace Maynard, "Still More Truth: No Compromise With Traitors, Speech of Hon. Horace Maynard of Tennessee in the House of Representatives, January 31, 1863," 2–3, UT.

58. Frederick Barnard, *Letter to the President of the United States by a Refugee* (Philadelphia, Pa.: J. P. Lippincott, 1863), 14–17, UVA.

59. Pike, *Letters to the People of the Northern States*, Letter II, p. 16, UT.

60. For similar statements of northerners as the main aggressors in the secession crisis, see Henry Watson to a Dear Friend, December 23, 1860, Folder 1860, Box 6,

Henry Watson Papers, Duke; Sally Hampton to George Baxter, December 22, 1860, quoted in Hampton, *Divided Heart,* 79; Robert Hatton to Sophie Hatton, January 30, 1860, quoted in Drake, *Life of General Robert Hatton,* 227; Julia Tyler to Juliana Gardner, January 21, 1861, quoted in Seager, *And Tyler Too,* 451; John S. Ryan to A. F. Girard, January 15, 1861, John S. Ryan Papers, USC; Amelia Lines Diary, November 3, 1860, quoted in Lines, *To Raise Myself a Little,* 166.

61. James McPherson, *For Cause and Comrades: Why Men Fought in the Civil War* (New York: Oxford Univ. Press, 1997), 104. For similar arguments, see Aaron Sheehan-Dean, *Why Confederates Fought: Family and Nation in Civil War Virginia* (Chapel Hill: Univ. of North Carolina Press, 2007), 1–10; Bernath, *Confederate Minds,* 1–9; Bonner, *Mastering America,* 286–89.

62. Quoted in Faust, *The Creation of Confederate Nationalism,* 14.

63. Frances Henderson to Ashbel Smith, May 13 and August 19, 1861, Box 2G224, Folder 8, Ashbel Smith Papers, UT.

64. Wright, *The Secession Movement,* 104; Keller, "Keystone Confederates," in Blair, *Making and Remaking Pennsylvania's Civil War,* 6–7.

65. Ashbel Smith to his nephew, February 24, 1861, Folder 8, Box 2G224, Ashbel Smith Papers, UT.

66. Arthur McArthur to his father, December 31, 1860, McArthur Family Papers, Bowdoin.

67. Arthur McArthur to his father, April 14, 1861, ibid. In this letter, McArthur also talked about how the Confederacy would eventually become a mighty Caribbean empire rivaling that of Ancient Rome.

68. Edward Wells to Thomas Wells, December 6, 1860, Folder 1, Papers of Smith and Wells Family, USC.

69. Edward Wells to Thomas Wells, April 20, 1861, Folder 2, ibid.

70. Edward Wells to Thomas Wells, April 28, 1861, Folder 2, ibid. Wells never regretted his stance and espoused the same views fifty years after the end of the war. Edward Wells to unknown, March 3, 1904, and June 1909, Fiche 5, Edward Laight Wells Papers, Manuscripts Fiche M.73, USC.

71. F. G. De Fontaine, *American Abolitionism,* 39–40, LV.

72. Joseph Garey Diary, May 10, 1862, quoted in Garey, *A Keystone Rebel,* 95.

73. Though he did not elaborate on what those rights entailed, he likely meant freedom from coercion and the right to own property, including slaves. Garey made several references in his journal about his pro-slavery and anti-black views and the need to repel Union forces from southern soil. Garey, *A Keystone Rebel,* 45, 71.

74. Krick, *Staff Officers in Gray,* 191; Langhorne quoted in W. G. Bean, "The Unusual War Experience of Lieutenant George G. Junkin, C.S.A.," *Virginia Magazine of History and Biography* 76 (May 1968): 184.

75. For further examples of the role ideology played in decisions about secession, see Charles Dahlgren to Jefferson Davis, December 23, 1861, quoted in Gower, *Charles Dahlgren,* 60; Ashbel Smith to his nephew, February 24, 1861, Box 2G224, Folder 8, Ashbel Smith Papers, UT; Blevins, *Albert Pike,* 88–89; Richard Taylor, *Destruction and Reconstruction: Personal Experiences of the Last War* (New York: D. Appleton and Company, 1864), 116–17.

76. "Loving Mother" to "My Dear Children," December 16, 1860, quoted in Caroline Howard Gilman, "Letters of a Confederate Mother, Charleston in the Sixties," *The Atlantic Monthly* 137 (April 1926), 504–5, USC.

77. Moses Curtis to Asa Gray, December 5, 1860, quoted in Berkeley, *A Yankee Botanist,* 190–91.

78. John Slidell to S. L. M. Barlow, November 20, 1860, quoted in Green, *The Role of the Yankee,* 23.

79. Thomas Wharton Diary, April 14, 1861, quoted in Wharton, *Queen of the South,* 248. Nor did adoptive southerners retreat from their convictions once the end of the war put the secession question to rest. If anything, they still believed in preserving the rights of the South and would not have hesitated to make the same decision if they had to do it over again. Quintard, *Dr. Quintard,* 15; Amos T. Akerman to his sister, July 17, 1870, quoted in McFeely, "Amos T. Akerman," in *Region, Race, and Reconstruction,* ed. Kousser and McPherson, 399–400; Charles Dahlgren to John Adolph Dahlgren, June 10, 1868, quoted in Gower, *Charles Dahlgren,* 169.

80. Robert Hatton to Lawrence Lindsley, January 13, 1861, quoted in Drake, *Life of General Robert Hatton,* 319–20. For further examples of native northerners using these types of arguments, see Edward Wells to his mother, January 1, 1861, Folder 1, Papers of Smith and Wells Families, USC; "Mother" to "Dear Daughter", August 7, 1861, in Gilman, "Letters of a Confederate Mother," *The Atlantic Monthly* 137 (April 1926): 505, USC; Charles Dahlgren to John Adolph Dahlgren, June 10, 1868, quoted in Gower, *Charles Dahlgren,* 169.

81. Silverthorne, *Ashbel Smith,* 146–47; Pratt quoted in Tarrant, *Hon. Daniel Pratt,* 75–76, 111; George Kendall to Henry Randall, December 4, 1860, quoted in Kendall, *Letters From a Texas Sheep Ranch,* 129–30. Several historians argue that adoptive southerners who ended up supporting the Union nevertheless often did so because they felt it was the best way to protect their adopted section. They believed secession would unleash civil war and tear apart their adopted homes. Griffin, "Connecticut Yankee in Texas,", 173; Smith, *Courage of a Southern Unionist,* 21–33; Brazy, *An American Planter,* 150–53; Bowman, *Abiel Leonard,* 220–21.

82. Keller, "Keystone Confederates," in Blair, *Making and Remaking Pennsylvania's Civil War,* 21–22. Biographers of adoptive southerners admit to the

influence of location in drawing native northerners into the Confederate armies. Peter Carmichael claims that, after Fort Sumter, Maine native Edward Drummond joined the Confederacy because of his deeper attachments to Georgia. Ernest Dibble cites Massachusetts-born William Chase's residency in Pensacola as critical for his embrace of the Confederacy. Nina Baker shows that Native New Yorker Gail Borden's family was torn apart by the secession crisis, with one son living in New York who joined the Union and another living in Texas who joined the Confederacy. Nevertheless, links to a southern state did not automatically cause an individual to abandon his native state and section. Borden himself stayed in New York, former President of the University of Mississippi Frederick Barnard moved back to New York, and William Tecumseh Sherman left his position at the University of Louisiana to join the Union ranks as a general. For more information, see Drummond, *A Confederate Yankee*, xii; Dibble, *Ante-bellum Pensacola*, III: 41; Nina Brown Baker, *Texas Yankee: The Story of Gail Borden* (New York: Harcourt, Brace and Company, 1955), 121; Wharton, *Gail Borden;* Marvin Lazerson, "F. A. P. Barnard and Columbia College: 1864–1888" (PhD diss., Columbia Univ., 1964).

83. William Freehling argues that secessionists in South Carolina utilized the idea of state sovereignty to give the veneer of legality and legitimacy to secession without having the whole movement fall to "mobocracy." Other Lower South secessionists then followed suit. Freehling, *Road to Disunion: Secessionists Triumphant*, 332–36.

84. Patterson Diary, September 19, 1863, quoted in Patterson, *Yankee Rebel*, 136–37. Upon further reflection after the war, Patterson admitted that he thought about returning to Ohio but wanted to counter accusations that he was working as a northern spy. He also recalled how he achieved success in his first jobs as a teacher and clerk in Alabama and how, if he had returned to Ohio, his family might have considered him a failure. These statements indicate Patterson saw himself as much more of a Confederate than a southerner when he first entered the army. Patterson, *Yankee Rebel*, xviii–xix.

85. Jed Hotchkiss to Sarah Hotchkiss, August 16, 1861, http://valley.lib.virginia.edu/papers/A2563, from the Letters of the Hotchkiss Family, 1861–1865, Augusta County Letters and Diaries, The War Years, The Valley of the Shadow: Two Communities in the Civil War, University of Virginia, Charlottesville.

86. *Governor Joseph Johnson,* 15. For further professions of pride for adopted states, see Gorgas, *Journals of Josiah Gorgas,* xv–xvi; George Kendall to Henry Randall, July 7 and August 7, 1860, quoted in Kendall, *Letters from a Texas Sheep Ranch,* 83, 92; French, *Two Wars,* 181–82; Eggleston, *A Rebel's Recollections,* 3–4.

87. Pemberton quoted in "The Siege of Vicksburg," *Vicksburg Daily Herald,* April 19, 1874, Folder 3, John Clifford Pemberton Papers 1814–1942, #586, SHC.

88. Rebecca Pemberton to Caroline Pemberton, April 23, 1861, Folder 2, John Clifford Pemberton Papers, SHC.

89. Robert Hatton to Sophie Hatton, January 22, 1860, quoted in Drake, *Life of General Robert Hatton*, 222.

90. Robert Hatton, "State of the Union, Speech of Hon. Robert Hatton, of Tennessee, in the House of Representatives, February 8, 1861," *Speeches, Second Session, 36th Congress, 1860–1861, Vol. 1*, p. 1, H. Garnet, Rare Pamphlets, Vol. 94, UVA.

91. Albert Pike, "State or Province? Bond or Free? The Vital Principle of Equality which cements the Union of the States. Addressed Particularly to the People of Arkansas. 1861," UT; French, *Two Wars*, 134–35; Henry Handerson to Lewis Handerson, April 27, 1865, quoted in Handerson, *Yankee in Gray*, 112–13. Even biographers of adoptive southerners acknowledge the power of adopted states in formulating their identities. See Roper, *Rebel Mapmaker*, 23–24; Tarrant, *Hon. Daniel Pratt*, 56–57; and Prince, "Edward Aylsworth Perry," preface.

92. Hatton, "State of the Union, Speech of Hon. Robert Hatton," 4–7, Rare Pamphlets, Vol. 94, UVA.

93. Pike, *Letters to the People of the Northern States*, Letter I, pp. 2–4, Microfiche 11759, UT; Pike, *Letters to the People of the Northern States*, Letter II, pp. 16–17, 21, ibid.; Albert Pike, "State or Province? Bond or Free?" 31–37, UT. In a more colorful description, another native of Massachusetts, Samuel Gilman, likened the North and South to France and Turkey, with each hating yet respecting the other. He even said his northern friends might look upon him "as a respectable Imam or Turkish priest, at too awful a distance for them to approach or meddle with." Samuel Gilman to Eliza Gilman, August, 1856, Folder 2, Samuel Gilman Papers 1828–1961, USC.

94. John S. Ryan to A. F. Girard, December 4, 1860, John S. Ryan Papers, USC.

95. John S. Ryan to A. F. Girard, January 30, 1861, ibid.

96. Moses Curtis to Asa Gray, December 5, 1860, quoted in Berkeley, *A Yankee Botanist*, 190–91.

97. *Daily Morning News,* January 12, 1861, quoted in Shippey, *William Tappan Thompson*, 153.

98. Barnard quoted in Chute, "The Life of Frederick A. P. Barnard," 321.

99. Robert Hatton to Mary Hatton, January 17, 1857, quoted in Drake, *Life of General Robert Hatton*, 103; Robert Hatton to Sophie Hatton, March 24, 1860, quoted in ibid., 254–55.

100. John S. Ryan to A. F. Girard, December 20, 1860, John S. Ryan Papers, USC.

101. Seager, *And Tyler Too,* 460–66.

102. John H. B. Latrobe, "What Next?", printed in the *Baltimore American,* January 14, 1861, Pamphlet Collection 3444, Duke. Though far-fetched, this idea gained a few adherents in northern states like New Jersey and Pennsylvania. Write, *The Secession Movement,* 104; Keller, "Keystone Confederates," in Blair, *Making and Remaking Pennsylvania's Civil War,* 6–7.

103. Willington quoted in Way, *History of the New England Society of Charleston,* 18.

104. Edward Wells to Thomas Wells, April 20, 1861, pp. 1–4, Folder 2, Papers of Smith and Wells Families, USC.

105. Edward Wells to Thomas Wells, April 20, 1861, pp. 10–12, ibid.

106. Edward Wells to Thomas Wells, April 28, 1861, ibid.

107. Edward Wells to Thomas Wells, April 20, 1861, pp. 1–4, Folder 2, ibid.

108. John S. Ryan to A. F. Girard, December 20, 1860, John S. Ryan Papers, USC.

109. Ashbel Smith to Cousin Lydia, January 31, 1850, Ashbel Smith Journal, 1832–1857, Box 2G234, Ashbel Smith Papers, UT.

110. Gilman quoted in Peter Gilman Pinckney, *Samuel Gilman,* Senior Term Paper, April 20, 1977, 10, Caroline Gilman Papers, CC.

111. Patterson Journal, September 19, 1863, quoted in Patterson, *Yankee Rebel,* 136–37. A few authors acknowledge that adoptive southerners either slowly or quickly adapted to an emerging southern nationalism. Virgil Baker, *Albert Pike: Citizen Speechmaker of Arkansas* (Reprinted from Southern Speech Journal, Jacksonville, Fla., 1951, Vol. 16), 194; Sears, *John Slidell,* 8; "Letter from the Late Maj. Henry B. Richardson to his Parents, in Maine, in his Defense as a Soldier of the Confederacy," *Tensas Gazette,* October 25, 1935, Henry B. Richardson Materials, Richardson and Farrar Family Papers 1860–1876, SHC.

112. Perry and Perry, *Reminiscences of Public Men,* 208–14; Warner, *Biographical Register of the Confederate Congress,* 213–14, 230; Diary of Susan Eppes, January 8, 1861, quoted in Eppes, *Through Some Eventful Years,* 143; Green, *Role of the Yankee,* 31; Wakelyn, *Biographical Dictionary of the Confederacy,* 187; The other delegates who voted for secession included Samuel Moore in Virginia and Aaron Conrow in Missouri. In addition, Ohio native Charles Clark ran as a secessionist delegate in Mississippi but failed to win the election. The remaining delegates, Lee Roy Kramer and Spicer Patrick in Virginia, Isaac Murphy in Arkansas, and Levi Marvin of Missouri, voted against secession and supported the Union. Wakelyn, *Biographical Dictionary,* 147; Tyler, *Encyclopedia of Virginia Biography,* II: 120; Smith, *Courage of a Southern Unionist,* 64–76, 92–93.

113. Quintard, *Doctor Quintard,* 10–12; Tazewell, *Major Edmund Bradford,* 18; Lane, *The Adventures and Recollections of General Walter P. Lane,* 83, 122; J. K. Duncan to William Duncan, December 27, 1860, William Duncan Papers 1847–1868, Manuscript A, Duke; Strong, *Keystone Confederate,* 29–30; *New York Herald,* February 11, 1861; Raab, *A Dual Biography,* 155–56. See also Wharton, *Queen of the South,* xviii–xix; Silverthorne, *Ashbel Smith,* 147; Commission to John C. Pemberton from the Governor of Virginia, April 28, 1861, Folder 2, John Clifford Pemberton Papers, SHC; Samuel B. Myers, "Memoir of Samuel B. Myers," in *The*

Memoirs of General Turner Ashby and His Compeers, ed. James B. Avirett (Baltimore, Md.: Selby & Dulany, 1867), 361; Daniel Ruggles to General Cocke, May 8, 1861, Box 1, Folder 1, Daniel Ruggles Correspondence, 2nd 83B, Duke; *New York Herald,* November 12, 1861.

5. Adoptive Southern Unionists

1. Tim Kent's Civil War Tales, http://trrcobb.blogspot.com/2011/07/southern-born-federal-generals-in-civil.html.

2. Gerald M. Capers, Jr., "Confederates and Yankees in Occupied New Orleans, 1862–1865," *Journal of Southern History* 30 (November 1964): 411–12.

3. Farmer, *The Times and Journal of Alice Farmer,* 24–25. Franklin Farmer ended up voting for John Bell of the Constitutional Unionist Party as the best alternative to Lincoln.

4. Phoebe Farmer to L. B. Wright, August 27, 1860, quoted in ibid., 21–22.

5. Farmer, *The Times and Journal of Alice Farmer,* 31–43.

6. Robinson, *A Yankee in a Confederate Town,* 12–16, 41.

7. Ibid., 17–18.

8. Ibid., 9–10, 37, 44–45.

9. Sally Hampton to Baxter family, December 1860, quoted in Hampton, *A Divided Heart,* 76; Sally Hampton to Samuel Ruggles, December 14, 1860, quoted in ibid., 74–75.

10. Sally Hampton to William Thackeray, April 5, 1862, quoted in Hampton, *A Divided Heart,* 118; Sally Hampton to Alfred Huger, January 5, 1862, quoted in ibid., 111.

11. Frank Hampton to Anna Baxter, January 1861, quoted in ibid., 95–96; Sally Hampton to George Baxter, March 19, 1861, quoted in ibid., 108.; Sally Hampton to Sarah Weeks Carnes, March 23, 1861, quoted in ibid., 110.

12. Sherman, *Memoirs of General William T. Sherman,* 148.

13. Ibid., 155–56.

14. Ibid., 157–58.

15. Junkin quoted in Robertson, *Stonewall Jackson,* 213.

16. Ibid., 213.

17. John H. B. Latrobe, "What Next?," *Baltimore American,* January 14, 1861, 1–2, Pamphlet Collection 3444, Duke. Such arguments echoed those of native southern unionist slaveholders, who also feared the consequences war might bring in terms of their slave property.

18. Abiel Leonard to James O. Broadhead, December 25, 1860, quoted in Boman, *Abiel Leonard,* 218.

19. Murphy quoted in Smith, *Courage of a Southern Unionist,* 21–38.

20. Ibid., 21–38, 52–56. Ironically, at the same time Murphy served as provisional governor, the acknowledged Confederate governor was Harris Flanagin, a native of New Jersey. Wartime Arkansas thus had separate leaders representing the Union and the Confederacy who were both adoptive southerners.

21. Roger Allen Griffin, *Connecticut Yankee in Texas: A Biography of Elisha Marshall Pease* (PhD diss., University of Texas at Austin, 1973), 167–73.

22. Ibid.

23. Griffin, "Connecticut Yankee in Texas," 173. Another adopted Texan, George Kendall, also spoke out in favor of southern rights and based his unionism on the protection of those rights. George Kendall to Henry Randall, December 4, 1860, quoted in Kendall, *Letters from a Texas Sheep Ranch,* 129–30.

24. William Plumer to "Reverend," December 1, 1860, William Swan Plumer Papers 1858–1865, Manuscript A, Duke.

25. Green, *The Role of the Yankee,* 126. Residing in a northern state certainly did not automatically cause a person to side with the Union. Josiah Gorgas served in an army post in Pennsylvania before he offered his services to Jeff Davis. Mansfield Lovell stayed in New York City as a street commissioner for months before resigning and going South. Frank Armstrong even fought in the Union army at the First Battle of Bull Run before joining the Confederacy. Warner, *Generals in Gray;* Krick, *Staff Officers in Gray.*

26. For more on Borden, see Frantz, *Gail Borden: Dairyman to a Nation,* 256–57; Joseph J. Mansfield, *Life and Achievements of Gail Borden, Speech in the House of Representatives, January 11, 1930* (Washington, D.C.: Government Printing Office, 1930), 6.

27. Wharton, *Gail Borden,* 198. Another northern emigrant, William Botswick, also returned to the North in the 1850s and had no thoughts of joining the Confederacy. In fact, Botswick's biographer argued that he only saw the South as a place to make money and never held an emotional or identifiable attachment to the region. Lavin, *William Bostwick,* 364–65.

28. Mason, "Henry Watson," 55–61; Henry Watson to unknown, January 24, 1861, Box 6, Folder Jan–July 1861, Watson Papers, Duke; Henry Watson to Rev. Charles Barnard, January 21, 1861, Box 6, Folder Jan–July 1861, Watson Papers, Duke.

29. Henry Watson to Captain Allen Jones, April 22, 1861, Box 6, Folder Jan–July 1861, Watson Papers, Duke.

30. Mason, "Henry Watson," 65–69; Henry Watson to his mother, December 28, 1860, Box 6, Folder 1860, Watson Papers, Duke. For more on Watson's views of secession, see Henry Watson to Sereno Watson, October 2, 1860, Box 6, Folder 1860, Watson Papers, Duke; Henry Watson to a Dear Friend, December 23, 1860, ibid.

31. Mason, "Henry Watson," 65–69.

32. Henry Watson to his mother, December 28, 1860, Box 6, Folder 1860, Watson Papers, Duke.

33. Henry Watson to Mr. Baker, March 8, 1861, Box 6, Folder Jan–July 1861, ibid.

34. Henry Watson to Sarah Coughton Colebrook, April 3, 1861, ibid.

35. Thomas Wharton Diary, January 2, 7, 8, 9, 28, and 30, 1861, quoted in Wharton, *Queen of the South*, 240–44; Edward Wells to Thomas Wells, December 4, 1860, Folder 1, Papers of Smith and Wells Families, USC.

36. Caroline Seabury Diary, October 20, 1860, quoted in Seabury, *Diary of Caroline Seabury*, 59.

37. Caroline Seabury Diary, June 18, 1861, quoted in ibid., 61–62. For information on other adoptive southern women in a similar situation, see Tryphena Fox to Anna Holder, December 16, 1860, quoted in Fox, *A Northern Woman*, 106–7.

38. Chute, "The Life of Frederick A. P. Barnard," 249–53, 285–88, 328–31; Charles Davenport, "Frederick Augustus Porter Barnard," in National Academy of Sciences of the United States of America, *Biographical Memoirs, Vol. XX* (Washington D.C.: National Academy of Sciences, 1939), 261; Barnard, *Letter to the President of the United States by a Refugee*, 20, UVA.

39. Davenport, "Frederick Augustus Porter Barnard," in National Academy of Sciences, *Biographical Memoirs*, 261.

40. Ibid., 5–13, 20.

41. *Record of the Testimony and Proceedings*, 2–3.

42. Fulton, *Memoirs of Frederick A. P. Barnard*, 285–88; Chute, "The Life of Frederick A.P. Barnard," 328–29.

43. In the United States Court of Claims. *Stephen Duncan, Jr., Samuel P. Duncan, and Samuel M. Davis, Executors of Stephen Duncan, Deceased, v. the United States*, 5, UT.

44. In the lawsuit filed by Duncan's children after the war, Stephen Duncan, Jr., alleged that Union soldiers burned over one hundred and twenty bales of cotton from his father's plantation. See Ibid., 1–2, UT.

45. Brazy, *An American Planter*, 154–57; Martha Jane Lee Brazy, *The World a Slaveholder Made: Stephen Duncan and Plantation Society* (master's thesis, University of Wisconsin-Milwaukee, 1987), 128; A. S. Tanan to Stephen Duncan, October 7, 1863, Folder 1, Duncan Family Papers 1826–1888, UT.

46. Robinson, *A Yankee in a Confederate Town*, 56–72, 87–99.

47. Horace Maynard, *Still More Truth: No Compromise With Traitors. Speech of Hon. Horace Maynard of Tennessee In the House of Representatives, January 31, 1863*, 2–5, UT.

48. Ibid., 3, UT.

49. George Denison to Salmon Chase, April 25 and December 4, 1863, quoted in George Denison and Samuel Dodson, *Diary and Correspondence of Salmon P. Chase* (Washington, D.C.: American Historical Association, 1903), 381, 425–26.

50. George Denison to Salmon Chase, February 5, 1864, quoted in ibid., 430.

51. George Denison to Salmon Chase, March 5, May 1, and October 8, 1864, quoted in ibid., 433–34, 437, 447–48.

52. George Denison to Salmon Chase, March 5, 1864, quoted in ibid., 433–34.

53. Gideon Welles Diary, September 17, 1864, quoted in Edgar Welles, ed., *Diary of Gideon Welles, Secretary of the Navy Under Lincoln and Johnson, Vol. 2* (Boston: Houghton, Mifflin and Co., 1911), 148–50.

54. Salmon Chase to Benjamin Flanders, January 13, 1864, Letters by Salmon Chase, Rauner Manuscripts, Dartmouth College, Hanover.

55. "Facts for the People," and "The Issue Explained", Free State Nominations, JK 4795 1878, UT.

6. Northern Confederates in War

1. In all likelihood, the vast majority of native northerners in the Confederacy fought as privates or non-commissioned officers, but since enlistment records do not indicate a soldier's native state, they are difficult to track. Officers, on the other hand, were more likely to leave behind commission records or discuss their exploits in their own recollections or correspondence. As a result, the individuals in this study skew more toward the officer ranks. For the sources used to determine the ranks of known Northern Confederate officers, see Krick, *Staff Officers in Gray*; Krick, *Lee's Colonels*; Warner, *Generals in Gray*; Allardice, *More Generals in Gray*; Davis, *The Confederate General*; Hughes, *Yale's Confederates*; Trimpi, *Crimson Confederates*.

2. William Owen, *In Camp and Battle With the Washington Artillery of New Orleans. A Narrative of Events of the Late Civil War From Bull Run to Appomattox and Spanish Fort* (Boston: Ticknor & Co., 1885), 5; *Charleston Mercury*, September 27, 1862; Quintard, *Doctor Quintard*, 10–12; Tazewell, *Major Edmund Bradford*, 19; Captain C. A. Alexander, Point Post, Atlanta Military Pass, May 12, 1862, Folder 1, Charles Quintard Papers 1857–1899, Duke; John W. Hinsdale, *History of the Seventy-Second Regiment of the North Carolina Troops, in the War Between the States, 1861-'65* (Goldsboro, N.C.: Nash Brother Book and Job Printers), 15–29.

3. Osterhout, *Stonewall Jackson's Map-Maker*, 45–48. For other examples of native northerners appointed as Confederate officers, see Grisamore, *Reminiscences of Uncle Silas*, 4–7; Edmund Kirby-Smith Order, 1863, George A. Magruder Papers, 1862, 1863, 1870, Mss 27169 a-e, LV; A. N. Jordan to Ashbel Smith, June 11, 1861, Box 2G224, Folder 8, Ashbel Smith Papers, UT; William Byrd to Ashbel Smith, July 12, 1861, ibid.; H. B. DeBray, Special Orders No. 19, July 31, 1861, ibid.

4. Frank A. Montgomery, *Reminiscences in Peace and War* (Cincinnati: Robert Clarke Company Press, 1901), 39.

5. Samuel French to Henry Storm, January 27, 1874, Henry Storm Papers 1872–1894, Manuscript A, Duke; J. M. Cayloe to General Ruggles, August 25, 1861, Box 1, Folder 1, Daniel Ruggles Correspondence, Daniel Ruggles Papers, Duke; Daniel Ruggles to Major G. G. Garnes, May 16, 1862, ibid.; Burton, *Gracie's Alabama Volunteers.*

6. Even Northern Confederates who met resistance from native southerners suspicious of their intentions continued to receive commissions. For instance, Indiana native Francis Shoup, after assisting in mounting cannon in Saint Augustine, applied to Secretary of War Leroy Walker to join an artillery regiment, but Walker refused because he believed Shoup was a Yankee spy. Shoup then took his appeal directly to President Davis, who assigned him to Fort Morgan in Alabama. Sadly for Shoup, when he was nominated for promotion in 1862, congressmen from Arkansas blocked the nomination out of fear that he was an abolitionist. Raab, *A Dual Biography*, 156–57, 168.

7. *New York Herald*, April 10, 1861; George Randolph to John Pemberton, August 28, 1862, Folder 2, John Clifford Pemberton Papers 1814–1942, #586, SHC.

8. Mansfield Lovell to Judah P. Benjamin, December 29, 1861, quoted in "Correspondence Between the War Department and General Lovell, Relating to the Defences of New Orleans. Submitted in Response to a Resolution of the House of Representatives Passed Third February, 1863" (Richmond, Va.: R. M. Smith, Public Printer, 1863), 28, Duke; Strong, *Keystone Confederate*, 31–33; Powell A. Casey, *The Story of Camp Moore and Life at Camp Moore Among the Volunteers* (s.l.: FPHC Inc., 1985), 24–25, 29; *New York Herald*, August 19, 1862.

9. Major General Breckinridge, General Order No. 20, August 4, 1862, Box 1, Folder 1, Daniel Ruggles Correspondence, Daniel Ruggles Papers, Duke.

10. Warner, *Generals in Gray*, 232–33, 282–83.

11. Arthur Fremantle Diary, July 1, 1863, quoted in Fremantle, *Three Months in the Southern States*, 257; *Charleston Mercury*, August 19, 1861; Hinsdale, *History of the Seventy-Second Regiment*, 5; Osterhout, *Stonewall Jackson's Mapmaker*, 45–48; Unknown, "Lee: Sermon by Bishop Quintard, of the Protestant Episcopal Church," newspaper clipping, unknown date, Folder 3, Charles Quintard Papers 1857–1899, Duke.

12. Handerson, *Yankee in Gray*, 29, 32–35, 41–59, 62–71.

13. Patterson, *Yankee Rebel*, ix–xv. Henry Richardson had a nearly identical career and was even sent to the same prison. Henry Richardson to his parents, March 8, 1865, Henry B. Richardson Materials, Richardson and Farrar Family Papers 1860–1876, SHC.

14. Myers, "Memoir of Major Samuel B. Myers," in Avirett, *The Memoirs of General Turner Ashby*, 361–71.

15. Prince, "Edward Aylsworth Perry," 35, 38–40, 45–49.

16. Arthur Green, *Gracie's Pride: The 43rd Alabama Infantry Volunteers* (Shippensburg, Pa.: Burd Street Press, 2001), 4–28; Burton, *Gracie's Alabama Volunteers*, 15, 27, 32–33, 41–51, 65–75, 89–91, 97, 109–13.

17. Drummond, *Confederate Yankee*, xvi, 110–15.

18. "Memoir of John Milton Hubbard," in James Longstreet, *From Manassas to Appomattox: Memoirs of the Civil War in America* (Philadelphia, Pa.: J. B. Lippincott & Co., 1896), 23; "Memoir of James Longstreet," in ibid., 482; "Memoir of Loreta Juanita Velazquez," in Loreta Velazquez, *The Woman in Battle: A Narrative of the Exploits, Adventures, and Travels of Madame Loreta Janeta Velazquez, Otherwise Known As Lieut. Harry T. Buford, Confederate States Army*, ed. C. J. Worthington (Hartford, Conn.: T. Belknap, 1876), 292–93; *New York Herald*, April 29, 1865.

19. Raab, *A Dual Biography*, 175–200; *Charleston Mercury*, September 21, 1864. For more information on Northern Confederates serving in the Western Theater, see *Charleston Mercury*, June 16, December 30, 1864; *New York Herald*, July 19, 1863, November 28, 1864; Thomas House to Charles Quintard, July 4, 1895, Folder 3, Charles Quintard Papers, Duke; George P. Swift to Louis Hamburger, April 11, 1865, Louis Hamburger Papers 1857–1900, Manuscript A, Duke; French, *Two Wars*, 180, 190–95, 223; Silverthorne, *Ashbel Smith*, 161–67.

20. Wakelyn, *Biographical Dictionary of the Confederacy*, 78; Warner, *Generals in Gray*, 12–13, 321.

21. Ed Gleeson, *Illinois Rebels: A Civil War Unit History of G Company 15th Tennessee Regiment Volunteer Infantry* (Carmel: Guild Press of Indiana, 1996), 1–22.

22. "Memoir of John Daniel Imboden," in *The Century War Series*, vol. 1: *Battles and Leaders of the Civil War* (New York: Century Co., 1887), 112–23. Charles Dimmock later died in 1863 in Richmond because of ill health. A state legislator delivered his eulogy, claiming that, though Dimmock was a northerner by birth, he loved Virginia like a son and would be sorely missed. Holograph copy of Letcher's eulogy to the Legislature, October 28, 1863, quoted in Sanchez-Saavedra, "The Beau Ideal of a Soldier," 75–76.

23. Frances Casteevens, *George W. Alexander and Castle Thunder: A Confederate Prison and Its Commandant* (Jefferson, N.C.: McFarland & Company, 2004), 17–25; *Charleston Mercury*, July 4, 1861. The story took a strange twist when the *Mercury* revealed that the leader of the first squad actually dressed as a French lady, and Alexander, who also spoke French, was able to communicate with the "lady" in French to plot the takeover of the ship without anyone else knowing.

24. Casteevens, *George W. Alexander,* 17–25. When Alexander returned to Maryland on a similar mission, Union troops captured him and sent him to Fort McHenry to face charges of treason and piracy.

25. Though not as spectacular, Albert Pike accepted a commission from President Davis to recruit soldiers from Native American tribes in Indian Territory. Pike successfully signed several treaties with the Cherokee and even organized several regiments of Cherokee Confederate troops that served in Arkansas, most famously at the battle of Pea Ridge. Duncan, *Reluctant General,* 168.

26. Edward Wells to unknown, March 3, 1904, and June 1909, 22–28, Fiche 6, Edward Laight Wells Papers, Manuscripts Fiche M.73, USC; Edward Wells to Unknown, March 3, 1904, and June 1909, 12–13, Fiche 5, ibid.

27. John Harleston to his cousin, July 2, 1864, Folder 5, Papers of Smith and Wells Families, USC; Edward Wells to his mother, May 1, 1865, Folder 9, ibid. Wells saw action in Virginia, was severely wounded in July, recovered and rejoined his regiment by early 1865. At that point, his regiment transferred to South Carolina, where they helped in the evacuation of Columbia and fought skirmishes with General Sherman's army until the very end of the war. In one notable instance, he and seven of his comrades charged over sixty Union soldiers and routed them at Fayetteville.

28. Diary of John Beauchamp Jones, January 25, March 10, April 10, 27, October 25, 1864, quoted in John B. Jones. *A Rebel War Clerk's Diary at the Confederate State Capitol,* 2 vols. (Philadelphia: J. B. Lippincott & Co., 1866), 2: 134, 169, 185, 193, 315; Casteevens, *George W. Alexander,* 148.

29. McPherson, *Battle Cry of Freedom,* 319–20; Vandiver, *Ploughshares into Swords;* Josiah Gorgas to George Rains, September 30, 1861, February 27, 1862, George Rains Papers, #1510, SHC. In addition, William Wadley served as superintendant of railroads on behalf of the Confederate government while President Davis appointed several Northern Confederates to his own staff. Catherwood, *The Life and Labors of William W. Wadley,* 8–9; Mary Boykin Chesnut Diary, April 11, 1864, quoted in Chesnut, *A Diary From Dixie,* 302; *Charleston Mercury,* May 3, 1862.

30. *New York Herald,* March 16, 1861, January 13, February 13, 1862.

31. Sears, *John Slidell,* 1–13; McLure, *Louisiana Leaders,* 35–43.

32. John Slidell to Count Wolneski, October 26, 1861, Ignatius Brock Correspondence 1861–1864, Duke; *New York Herald,* March 28, 1865.

33. Caleb Huse, "The Supplies for the Confederate Army: How They Were Obtained in Europe and How Paid For, Personal Reminiscences and Unpublished History," in Thomas W. Green, *Major Caleb Huse C.S.A.: A Memoir and Appreciation Being a Reprint of the Huse Pamphlet of 1904 Together with an Appreciation and*

Two Appendices (London: Studies in Confederate History No. 1, Confederate Historical Society, 1966), 8–9.

34. John B. Jones Diary, September 12–26, quoted in Jones, *Rebel War Clerk's Diary,* 2: 42–53; *New York Herald,* November 17, 1863; Huse, "The Supplies for the Confederate Army," in Green, *Major Caleb Huse,* 8–9.

35. E. Merton Coulter, *William Montague Browne, Versatile Anglo-Irish American, 1823–1883* (Athens: Univ. of Georgia Press, 1967), 2–11, 54–59, 121–25; Wakelyn, *Biographical Dictionary,* 114; Warner, *Generals in Gray,* 36–37.

36. Another native northerner, Lewis Parsons, may have served in the Confederate Congress at some point, but this cannot be verified.

37. Warner, *Biographical Register of the Confederate Congress,* 230; Edward Sparrow Deed, 1866, UT; Wakelyn, *Biographical Dictionary,* 397.

38. Alexander Downing Diary, February 10, 1863, quoted in Alexander Downing, *Downing's Civil War Diary,* ed. Olynthus Clark (Des Moines: Iowa State Department of History and Archives, 1916), 99–100; Jones Diary, November 11, 1864, quoted in Jones, *Rebel War Clerk's Diary,* 2: 329; Warner, *Biographical Register of the Confederate Congress,* 128–29, 213–14; Wakelyn, *Biographical Dictionary,* 246–47, 378–79.

39. Wakelyn, *Biographical Dictionary,* 147; Warner, *Biographical Register,* 61–62.

40. Massachusetts native John Leonard Riddell may also have served as a governor for Louisiana in 1863, but no clear records exist. Green, *Role of the Yankee,* 64–65.

41. Montgomery, *Reminiscences in Peace and War,* 40–41.

42. Wakelyn, *Biographical Dictionary,* 187; Timothy Donovan and Willard Gatewood, *The Governors of Arkansas: Essays in Political Biography* (Fayetteville: Univ. of Arkansas Press, 1981). Ironically, the unionist wartime governor of Arkansas, Isaac Murphy, was also a native northerner.

43. Peter Gilman Pinckney, *Samuel Gilman,* Senior Term Paper, April 20, 1977, 11, Caroline Gilman Papers, CC; Confederate States of America Bond certificate to Caroline Gilman, March 15, 1864, Caroline Gilman Papers, CC.

44. Burge Diary, February 10, May 1, 1862, September–October 1864, quoted in Burge, *Diary of Dolly Burge,* 123, 126, 152–53.

45. Burge Diary, December 31, 1861, quoted in ibid., 122.

46. Malloy, "The Health of Our Family," 112–15. In desperation, Trulock actually sent one of her sons back to Connecticut to keep him out of the army.

47. Malloy, "The Health of Our Family," 112–15; Seabury, *The Diary of Caroline Seabury,* 10–14.

48. Gower, *Charles Dahlgren,* 69–73, 75.

49. Ibid., 88–91; French, *Two Wars,* 304–5; Blevins, *Albert Pike,* 107.

50. Kate Cumming Journal, July 18, 1863, quoted in Cumming, *Kate: The Journal of a Confederate Nurse,* 116.

51. Kate Cumming Journal, August 16, 1863, quoted in ibid., 129. For further references Cumming made to Quintard, see Kate Cumming Journal, July 5, 1863, quoted in ibid., 113–14.

52. Kate Cumming Journal, May 4, 1864, quoted in ibid., 197; A. F. Freeman to Charles Quintard, January 10, 1864, Folder 2, Charles Quintard Papers, Duke; W. W. Lincoln to Charles Quintard, April 25, 1864, Folder 2, ibid.

53. Berkeley, *A Yankee Botanist,* 193–95; Kendall, "George Wilkins Kendall," *The Louisiana Historical Quarterly,* 284.

54. George D. Armstrong, "'What Hath God Wrought': A Historical Discourse Preached June 25th, 1876, On the Completion of a Twenty-Five Years Ministry in the First Presbyterian Church, Norfolk, VA," (Norfolk, Va.: The Congregation, 1876), 11–12, UVA.

55. Slate, *Biographical Memoir of Eugene Woldemar Hilgard,* 118–19; Smith, "Memorial of Eugene Woldemar Hilgard," *Bulletin of the Geological Society of America,* 41. The Governor of Mississippi also appointed him to look after the buildings and library of the University of Mississippi.

56. Jonathan Worth to Ebenezer Emmons, April 5, 1862, quoted in *The Correspondence of Jonathan Worth,* 2 vols., ed. Joseph Hamilton (Raleigh: Edwards & Broughton, 1909), 1: 166–67. For information on another Northern Confederate engaged in scientific surveys, see Lander, *Calhoun Family,* 210–12, 227.

57. Ibid., 210–12, 227.

58. Duncan, *Entrepreneur for Equality,* 11–14.

7. Emergence of a Confederate Identity and Nationalism

1. For a more detailed look at the debate on Confederate nationalism, see Gallagher, *Confederate War;* Jacqueline Glass Campbell, *When Sherman Marched North From the Sea: Resistance on the Confederate Home Front* (Chapel Hill: Univ. of North Carolina Press, 2003); Freehling, *South Versus the South;* Sheehan-Dean, *Why Confederates Fought;* Escott, *After Secession;* Bernath, *Confederate Minds;* Ayers, *In the Presence of Mine Enemies;* Emory M. Thomas, *The Confederate Nation: 1861–1865* (New York: Harper & Row, 1979).

2. Jedediah Hotchkiss to Nelly Hotchkiss, December 17, 1862, Box 1, Folder 1, Jedediah Hotchkiss Papers, UVA; Jedediah Hotchkiss to his daughter, March 27, 1863, ibid.

3. Slidell quoted in Louis Martin Sears, "A Confederate Diplomat at the Court of Napoleon III," *American Historical Review* 26 (January 1921): 257–59.

4. Edward Drummond Journal, January 28–February 28, March 24, 1862, quoted in Drummond, *Confederate Yankee*, 4–14, 25.

5. Drummond Journal, February 21, 1862, quoted in ibid., 10.

6. Drummond Journal, May 29, June 2–5, 1862, quoted in ibid., 59–64.

7. Henry Handerson to Lewis Handerson, September 11, 1861, quoted in Handerson, *Yankee in Gray*, 90–91; Edmund DeWitt Patterson Journal, July 30–31, August 8, 17, 1861, June 28, 1862, quoted in Patterson, *Yankee Rebel*, 8–9, 28; Jedediah Hotchkiss Journal, May 9, 1862, quoted in Hotchkiss, *Make Me a Map of the Valley*, 42; Robert Hatton to Sophie Hatton, August 23, 30, November 2, 1861, quoted in Drake, *Life of General Robert Hatton*, 375–78, 382; Edward Wells to his sister, January 21, 1864, Folder 4, Papers of Smith and Wells Families, USC; Edward Wells to his mother, January 12, 1865, Folder 8, ibid.; *Speech of the Hon. T. Butler King, Delivered in the Hall of the House of Representatives, At Milledgeville, GA., November 10th, 1863* (Milledgeville, Ga.: Doughton, Nisbet, Barnes & Moore, State Printers, 1863), 4–6, #2779, SHC.

8. For further reiteration of this use of language by Northern Confederates, see Handerson, *Yankee in Gray*, 45–47, 53, 78; French, *Two Wars*, 167–68, 183; Samuel Pasco Diary, September 16–17, 1862, quoted in Pasco, *Private Pasco*, 4; Drummond Journal, March 24, 1862, quoted in Drummond, *Confederate Yankee*, 25.

9. Joseph Garey Diary, November 26, 1861, February 3, 1862, quoted in Garey, *A Keystone Rebel*, 45, 68.

10. Thomas Wharton Diary, November 30, 1861, quoted in Wharton, *Queen of the South*, 262.

11. George D. Armstrong, D.D., "The Good Hand of Our God Upon Us," 6–7, UVA.

12. John B. Jones Diary, May 14, 1863, quoted in Jones, *Rebel War Clerk's Diary*, 1: 324.

13. Grisamore, *Reminiscences of Uncle Silas*, 122–23.

14. De Fontaine, *Marginalia*, 59, LV.

15. Historian Edward Ayers hinted at this phenomenon in his own study of two communities in Virginia and Pennsylvania. Both communities shared many characteristics and worked hard to maintain the Union, but once President Lincoln issued his call for troops in the wake of Fort Sumter, a near instant transition occurred among the Virginians from unionism to firm support for the Confederacy. One of the people in his study, Kenton Harper, happened to have ties to both communities, but because he had developed an adopted southern identity in Staunton, he sided with the Confederacy. Ayers, *In the Presence of Mine Enemies*, 93–187.

16. Patterson, *Yankee Rebel*, xxiii.

17. Patterson Journal, July 23, 1861, quoted in Patterson, *Yankee Rebel*, 8.

18. Patterson Journal, December 31, 1861, quoted in ibid., 11–12.

19. Patterson Journal, March 20, 1862, quoted in ibid., 14.
20. Patterson Journal, August 31, 1862, quoted in ibid., 55.
21. Patterson Journal, August 16, 21, 28, 1862, July 2, 1863, quoted in ibid., 37–42, 116.
22. Henry Handerson to Lewis Handerson, July 18, 1861, quoted in Handerson, *Yankee in Gray*, 89.
23. *New York Herald*, May 21, 1861.
24. John Slidell to Edward Butler, May 30, 1861, Folder 3, Edward Butler Papers 1858–1874, Duke.
25. Thomas K. Wharton Diary, July 28, 1861, quoted in Wharton, *Queen of the South*, 256. For further evidence of this theme, see *Speech of the Hon. T. Butler King*, 3–12, #2779, SHC; "Your Loving Mother" to Annie, October 20, 1861, quoted in Caroline Howard Gilman, "Letters of a Confederate Mother, Charleston in the Sixties," *The Atlantic Monthly*, 507–8; French, *Two Wars*, 137–39.
26. *Charleston Mercury*, April 24, 1862; Duncan quoted in Strong, *Keystone Confederate*, 46.
27. *Charleston Mercury*, June 4, 1863.
28. Daniel Ruggles to Benjamin Butler, July 15, 1862, quoted in Benjamin F. Butler, *Private and Official Correspondence of Gen. Benjamin F. Butler, During the Period of the Civil War*, 2 vols. (Springfield, Mass.: Plimpton Press, 1917), 2: 67–69.
29. Armstrong, "*The Good Hand of Our God Upon Us*," 6–7, UVA; Samuel Pasco Diary, July 4, 1863, quoted in Pasco, *Private Pasco*, 44; Patterson Journal, July 4, 1863, quoted in Patterson, *Yankee Rebel*, 119; Henry Richardson to his parents, March 8, 1865, Henry B. Richardson Collection, Richardson and Farrar Family Papers, SHC. See also Dolly Hunt Burge Diary, June 29, July 4, 1862, quoted in Burge, *Diary of Dolly Lunt Burge*, 129–30.
30. Southern correspondents and northern observers alike seconded the eagerness of such soldiers' acts of defiance. See George Perkins to unknown, April 27, 1862, quoted in Carroll Alden and George Perkins, *George Hamilton Perkins, Commodore, U.S.N.: His Life and Letters* (Boston: Houghton, Mifflin, & Co., 1914), 121–22; Sarah Edmonds, *Nurse and Spy in the Union Army* (Hartford, Conn.: W. S. Williams and Co., 1865), 342; "THE SURRENDER OF VICKSBURG. The Official Correspondence Between Generals Grant and Pemberton," *New York Herald*, July 13, 1863.
31. Davis, a close friend of Pemberton's from their West Point days, later promoted Pemberton to lieutenant colonel of artillery, a rank he held for the rest of the war.
32. *Charleston Mercury*, September 4, 1863. In Petersburg, General Samuel French declined a transfer back to his adopted state of Mississippi so he could continue to serve in Virginia. French, *Two Wars*, 159, 169.

33. Josiah Gorgas Journal, June 28, 1863, quoted in Gorgas, *Journals of Josiah Gorgas*, 71.

34. Handerson, *Yankee in Gray*, 32. Edmund Dewitt Patterson uttered similar denunciations of unionists, especially those who followed the Union army's hardwar policies. Patterson Journal, November 2, 1862, quoted in Patterson, *Yankee Rebel*, 75.

35. Ashbel Smith to the Governor of Texas, February 1, 1862, Box 2G224, Folder 9, Ashbel Smith Papers, UT.

36. Charles T. Quintard Diary, "A Prayer for Our Country," November 17, 1864, Charles Quintard Diaries 1864–1884, UT.

37. Henry Richardson to his parents, March 8, 1865, Henry B. Richardson Materials, Richardson and Farrar Family Papers, SHC.

38. Ibid.

39. Ibid.

40. Ashbel Smith to the Governor of Texas, February 1, 1862, Box 2G224, Folder 9, Ashbel Smith Papers, UT.

41. Wharton Diary, March 15, 1862, quoted in Wharton, *Queen of the South*, 266.

42. Ashbel Smith to the Governor of Texas, February 1, 1862, Box 2G224, Folder 9, Ashbel Smith Papers, UT.

43. Drummond Journal, May 16, 1862, quoted in Drummond, *Confederate Yankee*, 54.

44. Henry Handerson to Lewis Handerson, March 5, 1862, quoted in Handerson, *Yankee in Gray*, 94.

45. Strong, *Keystone Confederate*, 49–50.

46. Burge Diary, June 29, July 4, 1862, quoted in Burge, *Diary of Dolly Lunt Burge*, 129–30.

47. For more analysis on the theme of Confederates renewing their determination and nationalism in the face of military disaster, see Gallagher, *The Confederate War;* Campbell, *When Sherman Marched North*.

48. Pasco Diary, July 4, 23, 1863, quoted in Pasco, *Private Pasco*, 44, 51.

49. Josiah Gorgas certainly thought so when he heard of the double defeat. He openly wondered if the Confederacy could ever go on. Gorgas Diary, July 28, 1863, quoted in Gorgas, *Journals of Josiah Gorgas*, 71.

50. Patterson Journal, July 4, 1863, quoted in Patterson, *Yankee Rebel*, 119.

51. "Your Loving Mother" to "Dear Children," August 21, 1863, quoted in Gilman, "Letters of a Confederate Mother," *Atlantic Monthly*, 509.

52. Caroline Gilman to Eliza Dodge, June 2, 1865, quoted in Takahashi, "Home of Their Choice," 3.

53. McPherson, *Battle Cry of Freedom,* 771–81, 803–19.

54. Josiah Gorgas to George Rains, September 3, October 30, 1864, George Rains Papers, #1510, SHC.

55. Samuel Cooper to Maria Cooper, October 3, 1864, Samuel Cooper Papers 1775–1893, #2482, SHC.

56. Quintard Diary, December 12, 1864, quoted in Quintard, *Doctor Quintard,* 195.

57. Quintard Diary, November 30, December 1, 12, 15–20, 1864, Charles Quintard Diaries 1864–1884, UT.

58. "Your Loving Mother" to "Eliza," December 25, 1864, quoted in Gilman, "Letters of a Confederate Mother," *Atlantic Monthly,* 509–10.

59. Josiah Gorgas to George Rains, March 4, 14, 1865, George Rains Papers, SHC.

60. Quintard Diary, January 9, 1865, quoted in Quintard, *Doctor Quintard,* 214.

61. John Slidell to James Mason, April 26, 1865, quoted in Sears, "A Confederate Diplomat," *American Historical Review,* 277–78.

62. Quintard Diary, January 9, April 7, 1865, Charles Quintard Diaries 1864–1884, UT.

63. Henry Richardson to his parents, March 8, 1865, Henry B. Richardson Materials, Richardson and Farrar Family Papers, SHC.

64. John Slidell to James Mason, April 26, 1865, quoted in Sears, "A Confederate Diplomat," *American Historical Review,* 277–78.

65. Edward Wells to his aunt, March 20, 1865, Folder 9, Papers of Smith and Wells Families, USC.

66. De Fontaine quoted in Mary Boykin Chesnut Diary, April 7, 1865, quoted in Chestnut, *A Diary From Dixie,* 377; Davis quoted in McPherson, *Battle Cry of Freedom,* 847.

67. Silverthorne, *Ashbel Smith,* 166–69; William McCarver to Ashbel Smith, May 2, 24, 1865, Box 2G225, Folder 1, Ashbel Smith Papers, UT; Ashbel Smith to General Canby, May 30, 1865, ibid.; Henry Handerson to Lewis Handerson, May 3, 5, 1865, quoted in Handerson, *Yankee in Gray,* 113–14.

68. Quintard, *Doctor Quintard,* 19, 25–36; Jed Hotchkiss to Sarah Hotchkiss, September 17, 1861, http://valley.lib.virginia.edu/papers/A2563, from the Letters of the Hotchkiss Family, 1861–1865, Augusta County Letters and Diaries, The War Years, Valley of the Shadow; Jedediah Hotchkiss Diary, May 9, 1862, quoted in Hotchkiss, *Make Me a Map of the Valley,* 42; De Fontaine, *Marginalia,* 1–20, 70–75, LV. For further evidence of Northern Confederates using derogatory language against Union soldiers, see Burge Diary, July 23–24, 1864, quoted in Burge, *Diary*

of Dolly Burge, 147–48; Gorgas Diary, June 12, 1862, quoted in Gorgas, *Journals of Josiah Gorgas,* 41–45; Drummond Journal, March 24, 1862, quoted in Drummond, *Confederate Yankee,* 25; Handerson, *Yankee in Gray,* 45–47, 53, 78; French, *Two Wars,* 167–68, 183; Garey Diary, January 10, 1862, quoted in Garey, *Keystone Rebel,* 60; *Speech of the Hon. T. Butler King,* 4–6, #2779, SHC.

69. Drummond Journal, February 23, 1862, quoted in Drummond, *Confederate Yankee,* 11–12; Henry Handerson to Lewis Handerson, July 13, November 6, 1862, May 13, 1863, quoted in Handerson, *Yankee in Gray,* 95–101. Handerson also wrote to his uncle explaining the many differences between the Union and Confederate armies, along with policies passed by "our southern Congress" versus "your draft on New York." Henry Handerson to Lewis Handerson, September 11, 1861, quoted in ibid., 90–91.

70. Cummings, *Yankee Quaker,* 221; Robert Hatton to Sophie Hatton, August 23, 1861, April 30, 1862, quoted in Drake, *Life of General Robert Hatton,* 375–76, 414. For further examples, see Patterson Journal, April 4, 1862, quoted in Patterson, *Yankee Rebel,* 17; Pasco Diary, September 16–17, October 20, 1862, quoted in Pasco, *Private Pasco,* 4, 10.

71. Wharton Diary, April 6, 1862, quoted in Wharton, *Queen of the South,* 268; Patterson Journal, November 8, 1862, quoted in Patterson, *Yankee Rebel,* 77; French, *Two Wars,* 8–10.

72. Wharton Diary, April 18–20, May 30, July 19, 1861, quoted in Wharton, *Queen of the South,* 248–49, 251, 256.

73. Samuel French Diary, July 17, 1864, quoted in French, *Two Wars,* 216. For a more detailed explanation of "hard war" policies, see Charles Royster and Mark Grimsley, *The Hard Hand of War: Union Military Policy Toward Southern Civilians* (New York: Cambridge Univ. Press, 1997).

74. Samuel Cooper to George Mason, September 12, 1862, Samuel Cooper Letters, VHS.

75. Drummond Journal, April 6, July 15, 1862, quoted in Drummond, *Confederate Yankee,* 30, 87.

76. Josiah Gorgas to George Rains, October 30, 1864, George Rains Papers, SHC.

77. Jedediah Hotchkiss to Sarah Hotchkiss, August 28, 1864, http://valley.lib.virginia.edu/papers/A2563, from the Letters of the Hotchkiss Family, 1861–1865, Augusta County Letters and Diaries, The War Years, Valley of the Shadow; Jedediah Hotchkiss to Nelly Hotchkiss, October 25, 1863, Box 1, Folder 1, Jed Hotchkiss Papers, UVA.

78. Pasco Diary, June 17, 1863, quoted in Pasco, *Private Pasco,* 41.

79. Duncan, *Reluctant General,* 259.

80. French, *Two Wars,* 184.

81. Burge Diary, July 29–August 1, 1864, quoted in Burge, *Diary of Dolly Burge,* 149–50.

82. Armstrong, "The Good Hand of Our God Upon Us," 11, UVA.

83. Wharton Diary, November 6, 26, 1861, quoted in Wharton, *Queen of the South,* 260, 262.

84. De Fontaine, *Marginalia,* 18, LV.

85. Ibid., 42, LV.

86. In a continuation of the theme regarding irreconcilable differences between northerners and southerners, a Union army captain stationed at Vicksburg encountered a Mississippi woman living on Pine's Bluff above the city and asked for advice. She told him that northerners did not know how to live in the South, citing their stupidity in sleeping outdoors without any protection from mosquitoes. The result was a spread of fever. The captain implied the woman did not believe northerners would ever understand the southern environment and custom. L. A. Furney, ed., *Reminisces of the War of the Rebellion, 1861–1865* (N.Y.: Estate of Jacob Roemer, 1897), 118.

87. Jedediah Hotchkiss to Nelson Hotchkiss, August 15, 1863, http://valley.lib.virginia.edu/papers/A2563, From the Letters of the Hotchkiss Family, 1861–1865, Augusta County Letters and Diaries, The War Years, Valley of the Shadow.

88. For a more detailed analysis of the common lives of Civil War soldiers, see Bell Wiley, *The Life of Johnny Reb, the Common Soldier of the Confederacy* (Indianapolis, Ind.: Bobbs-Merrill, 1943); Bell Wiley, *The Life of Billy Yank, the Common Solider of the Union* (Indianapolis, Ind.: Bobbs-Merrill, 1952).

89. Pasco Diary, January 4–7, 23, 1864, quoted in Pasco, *Private Pasco,* 90, 93.; Pasco Diary, November 27–28, 1863, quoted in ibid., 83. Similar expressions of distant respect for northern soldiers can be seen in Patterson Journal, June 28, 1862, quoted in Patterson, *Yankee Rebel,* 31–33; Jedediah Hotchkiss to his wife, January 21, 1863, quoted in Osterhout, *Stonewall Jackson's Map-Maker,* 52–53.

90. Burge Diary, July 22, August 2, November 19, 1864, quoted in Burge, *Diary of Dolly Burge,* 147, 150–51, 159–62. Having close relationships with a few Union soldiers still did not mean Burge felt a reawakening of her northern identity. She, like many others, viewed both "Yankees" and "northerners" as outsiders with whom she did not have a kindred spirit. Burge Diary, August 2, November 19, 1864, January 29, 1865, quoted in ibid., 150–51, 159–62, 170.

91. Jedediah Hotchkiss to Nelson Hotchkiss, January 24, 1864, http://valley.lib.virginia.edu/papers/A2563, From the Letters of the Hotchkiss Family, 1861–1865, Augusta County Letters and Diaries, The War Years, Valley of the Shadow.

92. Malloy, "The Health of Our Family," 110–11.

93. Burge Diary, November 19, 1864, quoted in Burge, *Diary of Dolly Burge,* 159–62.

94. Ashbel Smith to his nephew, February 24, 1861, Box 2G224, Folder 8, Ashbel Smith Papers, UT. Smith did manage to keep some contact with northern friends, specifically James Cox of Pennsylvania. James Cox to Ashbel Smith, May 10, 1862, Box 2G224, Folder 9, ibid.

95. Quintard Diary, December 30, 1864, quoted in Quintard, *Doctor Quintard,* 209.

96. Burge Diary, February 10, 1864, quoted in Burge, *Diary of Dolly Burge,* 143.

97. Burge Diary, December 31, 1864, quoted in ibid., 167.

98. Patterson Journal, August 31, 1862, quoted in Patterson, *Yankee Rebel,* 52.

99. Patterson Journal, March 20, 1863, quoted in Patterson, *Yankee Rebel,* 96.

100. Sally Hampton to William Thackeray, April 5, 1862, quoted in Hampton, *Divided Heart,* 118.

101. Henry Richardson to his parents, March 5, 8, 1865, Henry Richardson Collection, Richardson and Farrar Family Papers, SHC. Richardson's aunt showed her love by sending him money and letters while he was in prison. Aunt Mary to Henry Richardson, November 28, 1864, ibid.

102. Edward Wells to his mother, November 18, 1863, Folder 4, Papers of Smith and Wells Families, USC; Edward Wells to Thomas Wells, April 21, 1864, Folder 5, ibid.; Edward Wells to his mother, July 25, 1864, Folder 6, ibid.

103. Edward Wells to his mother, January 12, 21, 1864, Folder 4, ibid.; Edward Wells to his sister, January 21, 1864, Folder 4, ibid.

104. Pasco Diary, August 14, December 29–31, 1863, quoted in Pasco, *Private Pasco,* 55, 89–94; Samuel Pasco to his family, October 3, 1864, quoted in ibid., 177–78. Occasionally, to their relief, Northern Confederates found kindred spirits among their northern relatives. See Sabina Wells to Julia Wells, April 4, 10, 1865, Folder 9, Papers of Smith and Wells Families, USC; Aunt Mary to Henry Richardson, November 28, 1864, Henry Richardson Collection, Richardson and Farrar Family Papers, SHC.

8. Northern Confederate Prisoners of War

1. Some historians even speculate that General Grant, after taking over as General-in-Chief of all Union armies, used the entire issue as an excuse to hurt the Confederacy's manpower in his quest to bleed its population to death. Grant himself believed the Confederacy violated the parole system by putting paroled prisoners back into the ranks without properly exchanging them. He cited

prisoners he captured after the siege of Chattanooga, some of whom still had their original parole slips in their pockets. McPherson, *Battle Cry of Freedom,* 791–800.

2. For more analysis on Civil War prisons, see McPherson, *Battle Cry of Freedom,* 791–800; Roger Pickenpaugh, *Captives in Gray: The Civil War Prisons of the Union* (Tuscaloosa: Univ. of Alabama Press, 2009); Roger Pickenpaugh, *Camp Chase and the Evolution of Union Prison Policy* (Tuscaloosa: Univ. of Alabama Press, 2007); Sandra V. Parker, *Richmond's Civil War Prisons* (Lynchburg, Va.: H. E. Howard, 1990); Michael P. Gray, *The Business of Captivity: Elmira and Its Civil War Prison* (Kent, Ohio: Kent State Univ. Press, 2001); Benton McAdams, *Rebels at Rock Island: The Story of a Civil War Prison* (DeKalb: Northern Illinois Univ. Press, 2000); Frances Harding Casteevens, *"Out of the Mouth of Hell": Civil War Prisons and Escapes* (Jefferson, N.C.: McFarland & Co., Inc., Publishers, 2005); Casteevens, *George W. Alexander;* William Marvel, *Andersonville: The Last Depot* (Chapel Hill: Univ. of North Carolina Press, 1994).

3. Hughes, *Yale's Confederates;* Trimpi, *Crimson Confederates,* 314–15; Bean, "The Unusual War Experience of Lieutenant George G. Junkin," *Virginia Magazine of History and Biography,* 181–83, 189. Tucker went even further when he joined the Union army and fought at Nashville in 1864.

4. Northern Confederates did not have to serve in the ranks or even be taken prisoner for such defections to occur. New England natives Charles Johnson and Daniel Shearer took the oaths after the capture of New Orleans in order to remain in the city under Union occupation. Connecticut native Amos Darrow and New York native Daniel Frost abandoned their regiments in 1863 and went to New York and Canada, respectively, Darrow to be with his brothers and Frost to take care of his wife, who was banished from St. Louis. Hughes, *Yale's Confederates;* Warner, *Generals in Gray,* 94–95; Davis, *The Confederate General,* 2: 150; Garey, *Keystone Rebel,* 102–3.

5. Diary of Lawrence Sangston, December 6, 1861, quoted in Lawrence Sangston, *Bastilles of the North* (Baltimore, Md.: Kelly, Hedian, and Piet, 1863), 106–8.

6. Casteevens, *George W. Alexander,* 26–29.

7. Krick, *Staff Officers in Gray,* 191; Keller, "Keystone Confederates," in Blair, *Making and Remaking Pennsylvania's Civil War,* 11.

8. Lieutenant George Junkin to General T. J. Jackson, Boonsboro, n.d., September 10, 1862, Junkin personal file, National Archives, quoted in Bean, "The Unusual War Experience of Lieutenant George G. Junkin, C.S.A.," *Virginia Magazine of History and Biography,* 186–88.

9. Drummond, *Confederate Yankee,* xiv–xxviii.

10. Edward Drummond Journal, April 23, 30, 1862, quoted in Drummond, *Confederate Yankee*, 44–46. Drummond also mentioned that he had "New York friends" in the area, though he did not elaborate.

11. Drummond Journal, April 27, 1862, quoted in Drummond, *Confederate Yankee*, 45.

12. Drummond Journal, May 6–7, 11, 1862, quoted in Drummond, *Confederate Yankee*, 50–52.

13. Upon hearing about his siblings' efforts to secure his parole, Drummond remarked that he was grateful but did not say what he would do if the parole came through. He gave no indication he would actually abide by the terms of the parole; like Junkin, he might have even violated it after his release. Drummond appeared willing to deceive his family if it enabled him to return to the South. Drummond Journal, May 6–7, 11, 1862, quoted in ibid.

14. Drummond Journal, August 10, 1862, quoted in Drummond, *Confederate Yankee*, 94–95.

15. Drummond Journal, April 25–May 25, 1862, quoted in ibid., 44–60.

16. Drummond Journal, June 28, 1862, quoted in ibid., 78.

17. Drummond Journal, July 1, 1862, quoted in ibid., 79.

18. Drummond Journal, July 6, 1862, quoted in ibid., 81.

19. Drummond Journal, July 4, 1862, quoted in ibid., 80.

20. Drummond Journal, June 29, July 4–5, 1862, quoted in ibid., 78–81.

21. Drummond Journal, September 8, 1862, quoted in ibid., 102.

22. Pasco, *Private Pasco*, ii–v; Trimpi, *Crimson Confederates*, 231–33.

23. Samuel Pasco Diary, June 2, August 12, 28, 1864, quoted in Pasco, *Private Pasco*, 120, 147, 155.

24. Pasco Diary, January 11, 21, February 8, 1864, quoted in Pasco, *Private Pasco*, 91–92, 97.

25. Pasco Diary, February 1, 1864, quoted in ibid., 95.

26. Pasco Diary, July 18, 1864, quoted in ibid., 134.

27. Pasco Diary, August 24, 1864, quoted in ibid., 153.

28. Pasco Diary, March 15–31, 1864, quoted in ibid., 103–6. Interestingly, when Pasco read Andrew Jackson's response to the nullification crisis, he praised Jackson's arguments in favor of Union as the most superior of all documents in that episode. Nevertheless, despite that praise, he still believed in the justice of the Confederate cause. Pasco Diary, April 6, 1864, quoted in Pasco, *Private Pasco*, 107–8.

29. Pasco Diary, August 29, 1864, quoted in Pasco, *Private Pasco*, 156.

30. Pasco Diary, September 6, 1864, quoted in ibid., 160. For further discussion on the ebb and flow of morale and its links between the battlefield and home front, see Gallagher, *Confederate War*; Campbell, *When Sherman Marched North*.

31. Pasco Diary, May 13, 1864, quoted in Pasco, *Private Pasco,* 116.
32. Pasco Diary, April 10, 1864, quoted in ibid., 109.
33. Keiley, *Prisoner of War,* 26, 99–100. See also Pasco Diary, February 6, April 3, July 3, 1864, quoted in Pasco, *Private Pasco,* 96, 107, 127.
34. Pasco Diary, August 14, 1864, quoted in Pasco, *Private Pasco,* 148.
35. Ibid.
36. Pasco Diary, August 11, 1864, quoted in Pasco, *Private Pasco,* 152.
37. Patterson, *Yankee Rebel,* viii–xxiv.
38. Edmund Dewitt Patterson Journal, May 15, September 30, 1864, quoted in Patterson, *Yankee Rebel,* 166, 191. Patterson also received letter and packages from southern friends in Maryland, Virginia, and Alabama.
39. Patterson Journal, July 30, 1863, quoted in Patterson, *Yankee Rebel,* 125.
40. Patterson Journal, August 16–18, 1863, quoted in ibid., 129–30.
41. Patterson Journal, October 10, 1863, quoted in ibid., 140.
42. Patterson Journal, August 18, 1863, quoted in ibid., 130.
43. Patterson Journal, August 16–18, 1863, quoted in ibid., 129–30.
44. Patterson Journal, December 31, 1863, quoted in ibid., 153–55.
45. Ibid.
46. Patterson Journal, August 26, September 20, 1863, quoted in Patterson, *Yankee Rebel,* 133, 137–38.
47. Patterson Journal, December 23, 1863, quoted in ibid., 151.
48. Patterson Journal, March 2, 1864, quoted in ibid., 158–59.
49. Patterson Journal, March 20, 1864, quoted in ibid., 160–61.
50. Patterson Journal, September 20, December 17, 1863, quoted in ibid., 137–38, 150.
51. Patterson Journal, December 1, 5, 1863, August 25, September 14, 1864, quoted in ibid., 147, 189–90, 194.
52. Patterson Journal, September 20, 1863, quoted in ibid., 137–38.
53. Patterson Journal, December 17, 1863, quoted in ibid., 150.
54. Patterson Journal, September 14, 1864, quoted in ibid., 194. Patterson made several other references in his journal to the closeness he felt with his southern friends versus those of his family. Patterson Journal, September 9, 11, 1863, quoted in Patterson, *Yankee Rebel,* 135–36.
55. Patterson Journal, August 26, September 20, 1863, January 11, 1864, quoted in Patterson, *Yankee Rebel,* 133, 137–38, 157.
56. Krick, *Staff Officers in Gray,* 253.
57. Henry Richardson to his parents, June 8, September 1, 1864, Henry Richardson Materials, Richardson and Farrar Family Papers 1860–1876, SHC. Ironically, Richardson actually complained that he had to be careful not to say

anything negative about the Union lest the guards confiscate or destroy his mail as contraband. He did not seem to appreciate that his fellow prisoners suffered far more handicaps in maintaining contact with their own families.

58. Henry Richardson to his parents, March 8, 1865, Henry Richardson Materials, Richardson and Farrar Family Papers, SHC.

59. Ibid.

60. Ibid.

61. Ibid.

62. Henry Richardson to his parents, March 8, 1865, Henry Richardson Materials, Richardson and Farrar Family Papers, SHC.

63. Richardson was not the only one to reference the Founding Fathers in defense of his actions. Patterson did so as well, and several historians cite the struggle for control of the founder's legacy as a major catalyst for the outbreak of war itself. Grant, *North Over South;* Parish, *The North and the Nation;* Patterson Journal, January 22, 1864, quoted in Patterson, *Yankee Rebel,* 158.

64. Krick, *Staff Officers in Gray,* 148; Handerson, *Yankee in Gray,* 4–12.

65. Henry Handerson, "Capture in the Wilderness," in Streissguth, *The Civil War: The South,* 208; Henry Handerson to Lewis Handerson, August 18, 1864, quoted in Handerson, *Yankee in Gray,* 105.

66. Handerson, *Yankee in Gray,* 83.

67. Henry Handerson to Lewis Handerson, April 27, 1865, quoted in Handerson, *Yankee in Gray,* 112–13.

68. Ibid.

69. Henry Handerson to Lewis Handerson, May 3, 5, 1865, quoted in Handerson, *Yankee in Gray,* 113–14.

70. Patterson Journal, July 31, 1863, quoted in Patterson, *Yankee Rebel,* 126.

9. Native Southern Reactions toward Northern Confederates

1. Gower, *Charles Dahlgren,* 15; *Portsmouth Old Dominion,* July 4, 1840.

2. Biographers and historians of northern emigrants tend to agree that their subjects received a warm welcome when they decided to take up residence in the South, as long as they did not cause trouble. See Chute, "The Life of Frederick A. P. Barnard," 213–17, 274–75; Fox, *A Northern Woman,* 5–7; Chenault and Reinders, "The Northern-born Community of New Orleans in the 1850s," *Journal of American History,* 242–43; Green, *The Role of the Yankee,* 4–5, 39–57; Takahashi, "Home of Their Choice," 43–44; Dangerfield, *The Awakening of American Nationalism,* 285–87; Pryor, "An Anomalous Person," *Journal of Southern History,* 373–74, 376;

Rainer, "The Honorable Fraternity," 241; Howe, "A Massachusetts Yankee," *New England Quarterly,* 199–200; Hilldrup, "Cold War Against the Yankees," *The North Carolina Historical Review,* 381.

3. Clapp, *Autobiographical Sketches,* 26–30, 409; Ashton Phelps, Jr., *Theodore Clapp: The Ante-bellum South's Only Unitarian Minister,* Yale University, May 18, 1966, 3–4, Tulane. For more examples of southern churches inviting northern clergymen, see John Sumner Wood, *The Virginia Bishop: A Yankee Hero of the Confederacy* (Richmond, Va.: Garrett & Massie Inc., 1961), 5; Henry Watson to his mother, May 18, 1834, Box 2, Folder April–May 1834, Henry Watson Papers, Duke.

4. J. W. Stuart to M. D. William, November 6, 1837, quoted in *Record of the Testimony and Proceedings,* 26.

5. O. E. Carmichael to M. D. Williams, November 6, 1837, quoted in ibid., 26. Nearly two decades later, Barnard's reputation as an educator and adoptive southerner caused the president of the University of Mississippi to ask for his services as well. Chute, "The Life of Frederick A. P. Barnard," 270–73.

6. For more evidence on northern teachers and tutors finding a welcoming environment and request for their services by southerners in the antebellum era, see O. T. Hammond to Charles Henry Ray, June 20, October 12, 1838, reprinted in Cuthbert, "Yankee Preacher-Teacher in Florida, 1838," *Huntington Library Quarterly,* 97–99, 103; Ingraham, *The Southwest By a Yankee,* 2: 210–13; Cummings, *Yankee Quaker,* 142–43.

7. George Poll to Stephen Duncan, December 26, 1833, Folder 1, Duncan Family Papers 1826–1888, UT; Trinity College Historical Society, *An Annual Publication of Historical Papers,* 2: 36; Amanda Trulock to Nicholas, Polly, Bronson, and Marcia Beardsley, October 24, 1837, quoted in Malloy, "The Health of Our Family," 15; Emily Sinkler to her mother, November 1842, quoted in Sinkler, *Between North and South,* 7–8.

8. Not all northern emigrants remained above suspicion, but a hostile reception generally only occurred with northern visitors who tried to disrupt the status quo or from southerners who did not know native northerners personally. For examples of this phenomenon, see Sydnor, *The Development of Southern Sectionalism,* 240–41; Rainer, "The Honorable Fraternity," 236–37, 280–81; Dibble, *Antebellum Pensacola,* 3: 115–16.

9. O. T. Hammond to Charles Henry Ray, October 12, 1838, reprinted in Cuthbert, "Yankee Preacher-Teacher," *Huntington Library Quarterly,* 103; Samuel Gilman to Eliza Gilman, April 2, 1856, Folder 2, Samuel Gilman Papers, USC; David Burnet to E. M. Pease, March 7, 1854, Box 3G483, Folder 32, Paul C. Crusemann Collection, UT.

10. Ingraham, *The Sunny South,* 267–70; Dangerfield, *Awakening of American Nationalism,* 15; Flint, *Recollections of the Last Ten Years,* 52–53; Caroline Seabury Diary, July 15–16, 1857, quoted in Seabury, *Diary of Caroline Seabury,* 50–51; Amelia Lines Diary, February 19, 1857, quoted in Lines, *To Raise Myself a Little,* 45; Way, *History of the New England Society of Charleston,* 53; Tryphena Fox to Anna Holder, June 24, September 14, 1860, quoted in Fox, *A Northern Woman,* 103–4; Rea Bryant Aldous, "The First Bazaar of the Unitarian Church of Charleston, S.C. 1836", 2–3, Caroline Gilman Papers, CC.

11. Mason, "Henry Watson," 65.

12. Lebanon *Herald,* 1859, quoted in Drake, *Life of General Robert Hatton,* 159.

13. William Sheen to "My Dear Friend," January 8, 1857, Hugh Buchannan Papers 1835–1861, Duke.

14. Thomas Burman to Stephen Duncan, January 18, 1841, Folder 1, Duncan Family Papers, UT.

15. Bryan, *More Zeal Than Discretion,* 59; Griffin, "Connecticut Yankee in Texas," 35.

16. *Texas State Gazette,* July 16, 1853.

17. *Obituary Addresses on the Announcement of the Death of Hon. John A. Quitman of Mississippi: in the House of Representatives, January 5, 1859,* 8, 12, SHC.

18. "Biographical Sketch and Letters of Caroline Howard Gilman," 13–14, Folder 4, Caroline Howard Gilman Papers, USC.

19. Charleston *Daily Courier,* February 10, 1858, quoted in Takahashi, "Home of Their Choice," 1.

20. "Death of Rev. Dr. Samuel Gilman," newspaper clipping, February 11, 1858, photocopied, Folder 5, Caroline Howard Gilman Papers, USC.

21. Several historians agree that this pattern existed throughout the antebellum South. Fletcher Green argued that the term "Yankee" generally only applied to New Englanders or resident northerners; not to those who physically moved to the South. Chenault and Reinders likewise wrote in their article, "As might be expected, newspaper accounts that disparaged 'Yankees' did so almost entirely in the context of northern abolitionism, never with reference to local northerners." Green, *Role of the Yankee,* ix-x, 3–4; Chenault and Reinders, "The Northern-born Community of New Orleans in the 1850s," *Journal of American History,* 242–43.

22. Rainer, "The Honorable Fraternity," 2–14, 236–40, 280–81.

23. Rousey, "Friends and Foes of Slavery," *Journal of Social History,* 373–74. Rousey also pointed out that such suspicions only increased as time passed. He cited Henry Connor of South Carolina writing to his colleague John C. Calhoun about the increasing unreliability of southern cities thanks to the large influx of northern emigrants. Ibid., 386–87.

24. McPherson, "Was Blood Thicker than Water?" *Proceedings of the American Philosophical Society*, 102. Another author claims that sectional hostility ran so deep that Northern Confederate soldiers never obtained the full confidence of their comrades and were looked upon as potential traitors. Cummings, *Yankee Quaker*, 9–10.

25. Tryphena Fox to Anna Holder, November 18, 1856, quoted in Fox, *A Northern Woman*, 45; Ingraham, *The Sunny South*, 271; Robinson, *A Yankee in a Confederate Town*, 7. For further examples, see Frederick Barnard to Eugene Hilgard, August 14, 1857, quoted in Chute, "Life of Frederick Barnard," 313; *Record of the Testimony and Proceedings*, 7–9; Eaton, *Freedom-of-Thought Struggle*, 100–3, 110, 125–26, 143, 259–60.

26. Griffin, "Connecticut Yankee in Texas," 141–42. Two years later Pease ran into similar trouble when he supported Sam Houston for governor and came out in opposition to the African slave trade. Even though most other southerners opposed the trade as well, at least one Texas newspaper attacked Pease as a closet northern abolitionist. Ibid., 159.

27. Sylvanus Lines to Amelia Lines, October 24, 1858, quoted in Lines, *To Raise Myself a Little*, 114. Several other northern emigrants voiced such treatment in earlier decades as well. See Julius Reed to Henry Watson, Jr., April 14, 1832, quoted in James, *Antebellum Natchez*, 141; Samuel Crocker journal, n.d., quoted in Davies, "A Yankee in the South," *New England Quarterly*, 281–82; Holbrook Diary, August 5, 1852, quoted in Hall, "A Yankee Tutor in the Old South," *New England Quarterly*, 88; Flint, *Recollections of the Last Ten Years*, 27–28, 233; Hilldrup, "Cold War Against the Yankees," *North Carolina Historical Review*, 374–75.

28. Caroline Seabury Diary, July 15–16, 1857, quoted in Seabury, *Diary of Caroline Seabury*, 50–51; Handerson, *Yankee in Gray*, 20; Arthur McArthur to his father, December 31, 1860, McArthur Family Papers, Bowdoin.

29. Tryphena Fox to her grandmother, June 25, 1853, Tryphena Holder Fox Papers, SM; Robinson, *Yankee in a Confederate Town*, 7; Amelia Lines Diary, February 19, 1857, quoted in Lines, *To Raise Myself a Little*, 45. In another sign of such positive feedback, Emily Sinkler told her father that while attending a Tournament of Champions in South Carolina, she found it amusing that the band played the song "Yankee Doodle." Emily Sinkler to Thomas Wharton, April 25, 1851, quoted in Sinkler, *Between North and South*, 151.

30. For more instances of southern acceptance of native northern residents in the 1850s, see *Texas State Gazette*, May 14, 1853; Sally Baxter Hampton to Lucy Baxter, December 23, 1855, Folder 2, Sally Baxter Hampton Papers, USC; Amelia Lines to Maria Akehurst, February 16, 1858, quoted in Lines, *To Raise Myself a Little*, 78; Amelia Lines Diary, June 6, 1858, quoted in ibid., 81; "Hon. T. Butler

King," *Savannah Republican,* September 21, 1855, quoted in *Address of Hon. T. Butler King,* 20, SHC; Seager, *And Tyler Too,* 402–5.

31. *Richmond Enquirer,* February 8, 1861.

32. *Arkansas Gazette,* May 11, 1861, quoted in Smith, *Courage of a Southern Unionist,* 34.

33. Chute, "Life of Frederick Barnard," 262–63, 298, 309–17. In addition to outlining the argument above, Chute also wrote that the entire affair simply represented an attempt by Barnard's enemies to destroy him professionally, using the secession crisis as an excuse. A similar smear campaign occurred with adopted Texan Elisha Pease when he ran for the Senate in 1857. Pease's biographer shows that, despite everything Pease had done for the state, some Texans, fueled by southern rights rhetoric, saw any connection with northerners or even moderate policies as treasonous. Griffin, "Connecticut Yankee in Texas," 143–44.

34. Pamphlet dated July 8, 1857, quoted in Chute, "Life of Frederick Barnard," 294–95; *Record of the Testimony and Proceedings,* 20; J. J. Ormond and E. G. Garland to Professor Sterns, February 13, 1860, quoted in ibid., 17.

35. *Record of the Testimony and Proceedings,* 28–29. Though these attacks likely centered more on personal quarrels, the fact that the charges resonated at all potentially spelled trouble for adoptive southerners if war broke out.

36. Green, *Major Caleb Huse,* 2. The whole affair seemed out of place because Huse had married a Florida woman ten years earlier.

37. Ibid., 2; Green, *Role of the Yankee,* 44–45.

38. "Our Richmond Correspondence," *Charleston Mercury,* June 26, 1861.

39. *New York Herald,* April 30, 1861.

40. Georgiana Walker Journal, November 1864, quoted in Georgiana G. Walker, *Private Journal of Georgiana Gholson Walker, 1862–1865, with Selections from the Post War Years, 1865–1876,* ed. Dwight Henderson (Tuscaloosa, Ala.: Confederate Publishing, 1963), 112–14.

41. Julia Tyler to Juliana Gardiner, January 8, 1863, quoted in Seager, *And Tyler Too,* 478. See also *Charleston Mercury,* February 13, 1861; De Fontaine, *Marginalia,* 20, LV.

42. Sallie Brock Putnam, *Richmond During the War: Four Years of Personal Observation* (New York: G. W. Carleton & Co., 1867), 102–3.

43. Robinson, *Yankee in a Confederate Town,* 19–21; Elizabeth Robinson to her sister, March 17, 1862, quoted in ibid., 128.

44. Alice Farmer quoted in Farmer, *Times and Journal of Alice Farmer,* 30–31.

45. Richmond *Enquirer,* May 14, 1861.

46. *Charleston Mercury,* April 4, 1862. Author Dennis Rousey agrees that, during the war, many Confederate congressman and senators blamed foreigners for

undermining the Confederacy and insisted that only "birthright southerners" could be trusted. Rousey, "Friends and Foes of Slavery," *Journal of Social History,* 388.

47. John Clark quoted in Rousey, "Friends and Foes of Slavery," *Journal of Social History,* 388.

48. Mary Boykin Chesnut Diary, March 23, 1862, quoted in Chesnut, *Diary From Dixie,* 149–50. Chesnut made a similar error a few months later when she told the story to a group of friends and one of them happened to have a New York–born husband serving as a colonel in the Confederate army. Chesnut Diary, August 7, 1862, quoted in ibid., 211.

49. In order to combat these allegations, several Northern Confederates resorted to measures no native southerner had to contemplate. In 1863, Josiah Gorgas, despite loyal service for two years, asked that the Confederate government file an oath of allegiance, signed by him, renouncing any previous ties to the United States and to Pennsylvania. Similarly, Edmund Dewitt Patterson reflected on his early days in the Confederacy and how northerners came under suspicion. He even considered returning to Ohio but, after facing accusations of working as a spy, decided to stay to prove his critics wrong. John Beauchamp Jones Diary, March 7, 1863, quoted in Jones. *A Rebel War Clerk's Diary,* 1: 270; Patterson, *Yankee Rebel,* xix.

50. "Letter From Richmond (Correspondence of the Mercury)," *Charleston Mercury,* July 22, 1863; Gower, *Charles Dahlgren,* 52–53; Duncan, *Entrepreneur For Equality,* 13. For more examples of these types of accusations, see Kate Cumming Journal, May 22, 1863,quoted in Cumming, *Journal of a Confederate Nurse,* 106; *New York Herald,* November 19, 1861; Green, *Major Caleb Huse,* 28.

51. Jones Diary, May 26, 1861, January 27, December 23, 1862, April 3, 1863, quoted in Jones, *Rebel War Clerk's Diary,* 1: 43, 107, 221–22, 286. Incredibly, Jones' invective against non-native southerners extended to Border State men as well, since those states still aligned with the Union. Soldiers from Maryland, Kentucky, and Missouri thus joined native northerners as potential internal enemies of the Confederacy. Jones Diary, August 7, November 1, 1861, April 25, May 17, October 9, December 31, 1862, quoted in Jones, *Rebel War Clerk's Diary,* 1: 70, 89–90, 121, 125, 165–66, 227.

52. Jones Diary, May 26, 1861, quoted in ibid., 43.

53. Jones Diary, October 31, 1862, quoted in ibid., 178. Similar criticisms appeared in Jones' diary a few months later when he reflected on Pemberton's performance in Mississippi. Jones predicted Davis himself would have to go to Mississippi to take command because the army there had "no confidence in Pemberton, because he is a Yankee." Jones Diary, December 23, 1862, quoted in ibid., 221.

54. Jones Diary, January 23, 1863, quoted in ibid., 245. Jones also chastised Northern Confederates in the Western Theater. Notably, he mocked General

Albert Pike for blaming the disasters in Arkansas on Generals Holmes and Hindman. He also claimed Pike wanted everything done his way and blamed southern generals to cover his own mistakes. Jones Diary, December 23, 1862, April 14, 1863, quoted in ibid., 221, 292.

55. Jones Diary, July 13, 1863, quoted in ibid., 378. For similar opinions, see Arthur Fremantle Diary, May 20, 1863, quoted in Fremantle, *Three Months in the Southern States,* 116; Kate Cumming Journal, May 22, 1863, quoted in Cumming, *Journal of a Confederate Nurse,* 106; Joseph Brown to James Seddon, August 10, 1863, quoted in Joseph E. Brown, *Official Correspondence of Joseph E. Brown, 1860–1865, Inclusive* (Atlanta, Ga.: C. P. Byrd State Printer, 1910), 390–91.

56. Jones Diary, March 2, 1865, quoted in Jones, *A Rebel War Clerk's Diary,* 2: 437.

57. William Russell Diary, May 25, 1861, quoted in William Russell, *My Diary North and South* (T. O. H. P: Burnham, 1863), 237.

58. Thomas Moore to Judah P. Benjamin, September 22, 1861, quoted in *Correspondence Between the War Department and General Lovell,* 94, Duke.

59. Davis demonstrated this trait many times during the war. He appointed Lucius Northrop as commissary general and refused to replace him after Northrop failed to keep the armies adequately supplied. In another instance, Davis appointed Judah Benjamin as secretary of state, though much of the Confederacy distrusted Benjamin because he was Jewish and from his perceived failures as secretary of war. For more information about Davis keeping controversial figures in power, see McPherson, *Battle Cry of Freedom,* 319, 373; Steven E. Woodworth, *Jefferson Davis and his Generals: The Failure of Confederate Command in the West* (Lawrence: Univ. of Kansas Press, 1990), 305–16; Herman Hattaway and Richard E. Beringer, *Jefferson Davis, Confederate President* (Lawrence: Univ. of Kansas Press, 2002), 110–11, 121–24, 139–40, 220–40.

60. Letter from Jefferson Davis, December 12, 1861, February 21, 1863, quoted in James D. Richardson, compiler, *A Compilation of the Messages and Papers of the Confederacy, Including the Diplomatic Correspondence, 1861–1865* (Nashville, Tenn.: United States Publishing Company, 1905), 149–51; Jefferson Davis to Samuel Cooper, 1864, John Hunter Harrison Papers, UVA.

61. Davis quoted in French, *Two Wars,* 180–82. Davis expressed similar confidence for New York native Martin L. Smith, whom Davis described as one of the best officers in the engineer corps. Jefferson Davis to Thomas Moore, September 26, 1861, quoted in *Correspondence Between the War Department and General Lovell,* 96, Duke.

62. Jefferson Davis to John Pemberton, August 9, 1863, Folder 4, John Clifford Pemberton Papers 1814–1942, SHC.

63. Longstreet, *From Manassas to Appomattox,* 469–70; "LETTER FROM RICHMOND," *Charleston Mercury,* October 22, 1863.

64. Jefferson Davis to John Pemberton, March 11, 1864, Folder 4, John Clifford Pemberton Papers, SHC. Even after the war, Davis never wavered in defending Pemberton's conduct. See Jefferson Davis to Fitzhugh Lee, April 5, 1877, Samuel Cooper Papers, UVA.

65. Even John B. Jones sometimes expressed his admiration for the exploits of Confederate officials he apparently did not know originated in the North, including Caleb Huse and John Slidell. Since he cited a person's native state whenever possible, he inadvertently undercut his own criticisms. Jones Diary, May 26, 1861, quoted in Jones, *Rebel War Clerk's Diary,* 1: 43–44; Jones Diary, November, 1863, quoted in ibid., 2: 93–103.

66. *Charleston Mercury,* June–July, 1863. The editors of the *Mercury* wrote articles of a similar nature for several other Northern Confederates, including William Gilham, Frank Armstrong, Julius de Lagnel, Charles Clark, and Daniel Ruggles. *Charleston Mercury,* January 1, 1861, August 18, 1862, May 6, August 25, 1863.

67. S. G. Pryor to Penelope Pryor, August 3, 1861, quoted in S. G. Pryor, *A Post of Honor: The Pryor Letters, 1861–63, Letters from Capt. S.G. Pryor, Twelfth Georgia Regiment and his wife, Penelope Tyson Pryor,* ed. Charles R. Adams, Jr. (Fort Valley, Ga.: Garret Publications Inc., 1989), 33.

68. "THE CAPTURE OF NEW ORLEANS," Richmond *Dispatch,* quoted in *New York Tribune,* May 3, 1862.

69. "We the Undersigned Members of Company G 1st Tenn Regt," Camp Near Tupelo, June 27, 1862, Folder 1, Charles Quintard Papers, Duke; "We the Undersigned Members of Co H," June 27, 1862, ibid.; "We the Undersigned Members of Company 'I,'" June 27, 1862, ibid.; "We the Undersigned Members of Co B," June 27, 1862, ibid.

70. Unknown chaplain to Charles Quintard, April 8, 1863, Folder 1, Charles Quintard Papers, Duke; J. Fostesly to Col. R. B. Snowden, March 23, 1864, Folder 2, ibid.; Dinsman Divine to Charles Quintard, March 23, 1864, ibid.; W. W. Anderson to Charles Quintard, December 7, 1863, Folder 1, ibid.; J. B. Cayfield to Charles Quintard, September 19, 1861, ibid.; Unknown to Charles Quintard, November 6–7, 1861, ibid.; "Dr. Quintard," *Columbia Times,* February 7, 1865, found in Charles Quintard Diary, February 7, 1865, Charles Quintard Diaries, UT.

71. *The War and Its Heroes* (Richmond, Va.: Ayres & Wade, 1864), 88, in *Confederate Imprints, 1861–1865,* Reel 84, Microfilm B, 1664, Cushing Memorial Library and Archives, Texas A&M University, College Station (repository hereafter cited as Texas A&M).

72. *The War and Its Heroes,* 86, in *Confederate Imprints, 1861–1865,* Texas A&M.

73. Francis W. Dawson, *Reminiscences of Confederate Service 1861–1865,* ed. Bell Wiley (Baton Rouge: Louisiana State Univ. Press, 1980), 63; *Charleston Mercury,* October 3, 12, 1861. See also Ralph J. Smith, *Reminiscences of the Civil War, and Other Sketches* (Waco, Tex.: W. M. Morrison, 1911), 8; C. Cruger to Thomas Wells, August 1, 1864, Folder 6, Papers of Smith and Wells Families, USC; Sally Hampton to Baxter family, April 1, 1862, quoted in Hampton, *Divided Heart,* 113–14.

74. Longstreet, *From Manassas to Appomattox,* 501–5.

75. Joseph E. Johnston, *Narrative of Military Operations, Directed, During the Late War Between the States* (New York: D. Appleton and Co., 1874), 332; Joseph Johnston to James Seddon, June 5, 1863, quoted in ibid., 508.

76. Sarah Morgan Dawson Diary, May 14, 1862, quoted in Sarah Morgan Dawson, *A Confederate Girl's Diary: Sarah Morgan Dawson* (Boston: Houghton, Mifflin, & Co., 1913), 31–33.

77. Osterweis, *Romanticism and Nationalism,* 78–79; *Charleston Mercury,* December 30, 1861.

78. Even southern unionists used such arguments for their own benefit. Paul Ambrose, a unionist in Louisiana, wondered how secessionists felt threatened when the Union guaranteed equal rights among all the states. He cited John Slidell as a perfect example because the latter came from New York, remade his life in Louisiana, and enjoyed all the prosperity he earned. The fact that Slidell then backed the Confederacy offended Ambrose because Slidell not only betrayed his own heritage but wanted to deny the same rights others might use to obtain their own riches and prestige. Paul Ambrose to William Seaton, January, 1865, quoted in John Pendleton Kennedy, *Mr. Ambrose's Letters on the Rebellion* (New York: Hurd & Houghton, 1865), 187–90.

79. W. B. Richmond to Charles Quintard, May 15, 1861, Folder 1, Charles Quintard Papers, Duke.

80. Mary Jones Mallard quoted in Gower, *Charles Dahlgren,* 89.

81. Eliza Andrews quoted in ibid., 99–100.

82. George Mason to Samuel Cooper, March 10, 1861, MSS 1C7887 a 58, VHS.

83. Krick, *Staff Officers,* 191; Langhorne quoted in Bean, "The Unusual War Experience of Lieutenant George G. Junkin," *Virginia Magazine of History and Biography,* 184.

84. For more examples of this pattern, see William Russell Diary, May 25, 1861, quoted in Russell, *My Diary North and South,* 237; Pemberton, *Pemberton: Defender of Vicksburg,* 22; Gower, *Charles Dahlgren,* 76–77; *Charleston Mercury,*

April 1, 1861; Mary Boykin Chesnut Diary, March 10, 1861, quoted in Chesnut, *Diary From Dixie*, 16.

85. *Charleston Mercury*, July 20, 1861. In one case, even an editor for the *New York Herald* recognized the dedication of a native New Yorker, Franklin Gardner, in his stand against the Union army at Port Hudson. *New York Herald*, June 12, 1863.

86. Constance Cary Harrison, *Recollections Grave and Gay* (New York: Charles Scribner's Sons, 1911), 154–55.

87. Arthur Fremantle Diary, June 8, 1863, quoted in Fremantle, *Three Months*, 179.

88. General Orders No. 18, Henry Heth, December 19, 1862, William Duncan Papers, Duke; General Orders No. 157, General Bragg, written by AAG George Garner, December 20, 1862, printed in "The Late General Duncan, C.S.A.," William Duncan Papers, Duke.

89. William Byrd to Ashbel Smith, July 12, 1861, Box 2G224, Folder 8, Ashbel Smith Papers, UT; E. H. Winfield to Ashbel Smith, March 2, 1865, Box 2G225, Folder 1, ibid.; William McCraver to Ashbel Smith, December 1863, Box 2G224, Folder 10, ibid.; Colonel Bradford to Major West, January 19, 1865, Box 2G225, Folder 1, ibid.

90. Osterhous, *Stonewall Jackson's Mapmaker*, 47. After the war one of Hotchkiss's friends in New York still tried to claim Hotchkiss as a part of New York but acknowledged that the Confederacy had the most legitimate claim to his identity, because of his past service. Ibid., 88.

91. *Charleston Mercury*, January 29, 1861.

92. "The Late General Robert Hatton," quoted in Drake, *Life of General Robert Hatton*, 423–25.

93. Rolfe S. Saunders, "The Late General Robert Hatton," *Memphis Daily Commercial*, November 19, 1865, quoted in ibid., 439–46. A Nashville paper also claimed Hatton as a native Tennessean. R. L. C. White, "Funeral Obsequies of Robert Hatton—An Affecting Incident—The Eulogy—The Grave—The concourse of Citizens, etc., etc.," *Nashville Republican Banner*, March 27, 1866, quoted in ibid., 448–50.

94. McPherson, *Battle Cry of Freedom*, 665.

95. *Charleston Mercury*, April 1, 15, 1861. At the end of the year, the editor also praised Ripley's efforts to save Charleston from a devastating fire. "THE ENERGY AND FIRMNESS displayed by Gen. RIPLEY," *Charleston Mercury*, December 16, 1861.

96. *Charleston Mercury*, April 30, 1862; "General Roswell S. Ripley," *Charleston Mercury*, May 31, 1862; "GEN. RIPLEY ARRIVED," *Charleston Mercury*, October 15, 1862.

97. Fremantle Diary, June 8, 1863, quoted in Fremantle, *Three Months*, 179; *Columbia Carolinian* article quoted in *Charleston Mercury*, May 6, 1864; Jones Diary, December 3, 1864, quoted in Jones, *Rebel War Clerk's Diary*, 2: 346. Incredibly, Ripley received such laudatory comments despite the fact that his origins were well known. His past in the North meant nothing next to his military contributions. "Colonel Ripley–And Our Forts," *Charleston Mercury*, July 9, 1861.

98. Warner, *Generals in Gray*, 77–78, 194–95; Wakelyn, *Biographical Dictionary*, 290; Davis, *Confederate General*, 4: 101–2; Strong, *Keystone Confederate*, 35.

99. George Washington Cable, "Memoir of George Washington Cable," in *Battles and Leaders of the Civil War*, 4 vols. (New York: Century Co., 1887), 2: 17–18.

100. Julia LeGrand Diary, May 1862, quoted in Julia LeGrand, *The Journal of Julia LeGrand, New Orleans, 1862–1863*, eds. Kate Rowland and Agnes Croxall (Richmond, Va.: Everett Waddey Co., 1911), 39–40.

101. Kate Cumming Diary, April 30, 1862, quoted in Cumming, *Journal of a Confederate Nurse*, 29; Jones Diary, June 25, 1862, quoted in Jones, *A Rebel War Clerk's Diary*, 1: 135–36.

102. Julia LeGrand Diary, May, 1862, quoted in LeGrand, *Journal of Julia LeGrand*, 39–40; *Charleston Mercury*, May 5, 1862; Jones Diary, June 25, 1862, quoted in Jones, *Rebel War Clerk's Diary*, 1: 135–36. LeGrand even praised Duncan in the same entry and accused Lovell of not providing the necessary equipment to maintain the forts.

103. Warner, *Generals in Gray*, 194–95; Wakelyn, *Biographical Dictionary*, 290; Davis, *Confederate General*, 4: 101–2.

104. "MAJOR GENERAL LOVELL AND THE FALL OF NEW ORLEANS," *Charleston Mercury*, May 28, 1862. Admittedly, the *Mercury* had a reputation of blaming Jefferson Davis for every Confederate defeat and so may have just wanted to find a scapegoat other than Lovell. The editor insisted that not enough guns and supplies reached New Orleans for a proper defense and blamed the government for its negligence.

105. *New Orleans Delta*, April 26, 1862.

106. As further evidence of Lovell's dedication to the Confederate cause, he continued to serve in the army after losing his commission as a general. When he failed to receive another command because of his reputation as a failed commander, he resigned and rejoined the army as a volunteer staff officer in the Army of Tennessee. *Charleston Mercury*, August 11, 1863; Jones Diary, February 1, 1864, quoted in Jones, *A Rebel War Clerk's Diary*, 2: 140; Johnston, *Narrative of Military Operations*, 332.

107. "MAJOR GENERAL LOVELL AND THE FALL OF NEW ORLEANS," *Charleston Mercury*, May 28, 1862.

108. Porter quoted in Strong, *Keystone Confederate,* 49–50.

109. New Orleans City Council Resolutions, New Orleans, April 29, 1862, printed in "The Late General Duncan, C.S.A," William Duncan Papers, Duke.

110. *New Orleans Picayune,* May 1, 1862, printed in "The Late General Duncan, C.S.A," ibid.

111. "General J. K. Duncan," Richmond *Enquirer,* 1862, printed in "The Late General Duncan, C.S.A.", ibid. In addition, officers of the Louisiana Regular Artillery issued a series of resolutions after Duncan's death lauding his conduct as a Confederate soldier and deflecting any blame for the disaster. W. C. Capers, W. B. Robertson, and J. B. Grayson, "Tribute of Respect," December 30, 1862, printed in "The Late General Duncan, C.S.A.," ibid.

112. In contrast, General Gardner did not come under the same scrutiny. He held his post at Port Hudson longer than Pemberton did at Vicksburg and gave the impression he did everything possible to prevent defeat. After receiving his parole, President Davis appointed him as commander of the Department of the Gulf with no objections from the Confederate Congress or population at large. *Charleston Mercury,* July 22, 1863, August 18, September 2, 1864.

113. The *Charleston Mercury* ran a brief biography of Pemberton in one of its issues, mentioning his birth in Pennsylvania and West Point career, but otherwise did not make a big deal out of the appointment. "TWO MORE NEW GENERALS FOR THE SOUTH CAROLINA COAST," *Charleston Mercury,* December 3, 1861.

114. Mary Chesnut wrote that, during his time in Charleston, Pemberton arrested Generals Mercer, Smith, and Ripley. If nothing else, he showed that Northern Confederates did not show favoritism toward each other. Mary Chestnut Diary, June 10, 1862, quoted in Chesnut, *Diary From Dixie,* 181.

115. George Randolph to John Pemberton, August 28, 1862, Folder 2, John Clifford Pemberton Papers, SHC.

116. "Major General John C. Pemberton.," *Charleston Mercury,* September 29, 1862.

117. Taylor, *Destruction and Reconstruction,* 116–17.

118. Newspaper clipping, Folder 3, John Clifford Pemberton Papers, SHC. The editor of the *Charleston Mercury* gave a similar account through its own correspondent in the area. *Charleston Mercury,* December 31, 1862.

119. "Lieutenant-General Pemberton," late 1862 or early 1863, newspaper clipping, Folder 3, John Clifford Pemberton Papers, SHC; J. Cutler Andrews, *The South Reports the Civil War* (Princeton: Princeton Univ. Press, 1970), 56, 269–84; T. J. Wharton, "The Late General Pemberton," *New York Herald,* August 17, 1881. Wharton claimed that a majority of citizens distrusted Pemberton because of his background, but Wharton expressed that opinion over fifteen years after the end

of the war. Plus, Wharton himself was convinced of Pemberton's dedication to the cause and claimed the entire Confederate command structure felt the same way.

120. "Our Dangers," Mississippi newspaper clipping, May, 1863, Folder 3, John Clifford Pemberton Papers, SHC.

121. *Charleston Mercury,* May 20, 27, 1863; Mary Ann Webster Loughborough, *My Cave Life in Vicksburg, With Letters of Trial and Travel* (New York: D. Appleton & Co., 1864), 44–45.

122. George Forney to his mother, May 27, 1863, George Forney Papers 1862–1864, Duke; Robert Bevier, *A Soldier's Story of the Siege of Vicksburg: From the Diary of Osborn H. Oldroyd* (H. W. Rokker, 1885), 169–70.

123. *Charleston Mercury,* June 6, 1863.

124. "Noble Words," newspaper clipping, May or June, 1863, Folder 3, John Clifford Pemberton Papers, SHC; "Gen. J.C. Pemberton—Cruel Ingratitude Towards Our Generals," taken from the *Knoxville Register,* June 18, 1863, newspaper clipping, Folder 3, ibid.

125. For further examples of civilian reactions of Pemberton, see Jones Diary, June 23, 1863, quoted in Jones, *Rebel War Clerk's Diary,* 1: 359; Kate Cumming Journal, July 3, 27, 1863, quoted in Cumming, *Journal of a Confederate Nurse,* 113, 121.

126. Pemberton later explained that he chose July Fourth as the day for surrender in order to get the best possible terms from Grant. He believed that Grant would want to utilize the propaganda value among the northern populace and so would be more willing to negotiate better terms if Pemberton threatened to hold out beyond the fourth. Pemberton's strategy did seem to work, because Grant offered to parole all the prisoners rather than send them to prison camps. "The Fall of Vicksburg," *Charleston Mercury,* March 22, 1864.

127. Jones Diary, July 26, 1863, quoted in Jones, *Rebel War Clerk's Diary,* 1: 388.

128. Montgomery, *Reminiscences in Peace and War,* 127; Captain W., quoted in Putnam, *Richmond During the War,* 229–31; Taylor, *Destruction and Reconstruction,* 116–17.

129. Joseph Brown to James Seddon, August 10, 1863, quoted in Brown, *Official Correspondence of Joseph E. Brown,* 390–91.

130. Longstreet, *From Manassas to Appomattox,* 469–70; John C. Pemberton, *Compelled to Appear in Print: The Vicksburg Manuscript of General John C. Pemberton,* ed. David Smith (Cincinnati, Ohio: Ironclad Publishing, 1999), 69. Davis, as per his character, remained deeply loyal toward his friend Pemberton for the rest of the war and never blamed him for the disaster at Vicksburg. Jefferson Davis to John Pemberton, August 9, 1863, March 11, 1864, Folder 4, John Clifford Pemberton Papers, SHC.

131. *Charleston Mercury*, July 23, 1863.

132. E. Leapens to Joseph Palmer, August 7, 1863, Joseph Palmer Letters & Papers, 1863–1865, Manuscript A, Duke.

133. Jones Diary, August 20, 1863 quoted in Jones, *Rebel War Clerk's Diary*, 2: 16.

134. *Charleston Mercury*, May 24, 1864. John B. Jones expressed a similar opinion in his diary entries in 1864. Jones Diary, May 14, October 9, 1864, quoted in Jones, *Rebel War Clerk's Diary*, 2: 210, 302.

135. Colonel A. J. Gonzalez to John Pemberton, September 17, 1863, Folder 4, John Clifford Pemberton Papers, SHC; P. H. Colquitt to John Pemberton, August 20, 1863, Folder 4, ibid; Montgomery, *Reminiscences in Peace and War*, 129.

136. "General Pemberton," newspaper clipping, Folder 3, John Clifford Pemberton Papers, SHC.

10. The End of an Era

1. For further discussion of this argument, see Lawrence Powell, "Carpetbaggers in the Deep South," in Kousser, *Region, Race, and Reconstruction*, 315–37.

2. McPherson, *Battle Cry of Freedom*, 853–62.

3. For detailed analyses of the Reconstruction Era, see Eric Foner, *Reconstruction: America's Unfinished Revolution 1863–1877* (New York: Harper and Row, 1988); Kenneth Stampp, *The Era of Reconstruction 1865–1877* (New York: Knopf, 1965); Dan Carter, *When the War Was Over: The Failure of Self-Reconstruction in the South 1865–1867* (Baton Rouge: Louisiana State Univ. Press, 1985); Michael Les Benedict, *The Fruits of Victory: Alternatives in Restoring the Union* (Philadelphia, Pa.: Lippincott, 1975); Michael Perman, *Reunion Without Compromise: The South and Reconstruction 1865–1868* (Cambridge, Eng.: Cambridge University Press, 1973); Michael Perman, *Emancipation and Reconstruction* (Wheeling, Ill.: Harlan Davidson, 2003); David Herbert Donald, Jean Baker, and Michael Holt, *The Civil War and Reconstruction* (New York: Norton, 2001); Barney, *Battleground for the Union*.

4. David Blight argues that the agreement between northern and southern whites to celebrate the valor of Civil War soldiers, instead of addressing the thornier issues of slavery and race relations, allowed a smoother path for Reconstruction at the expense of blacks. David W. Blight, *Race and Reunion: The Civil War in American Memory* (Cambridge, Mass.: Belknap Press of Harvard Univ. Press, 2001), 1–5, 381–97.

5. For detailed analyses on Civil War memory and the Lost Cause, see Alice Fahs & Joan Waugh, eds., *The Memory of the Civil War in American Culture* (Chapel Hill: Univ. of North Carolina Press, 2004); Blight, *Race and Reunion*; Gary W. Gallagher, *Lee and His Generals in War and Memory* (Baton Rouge: Louisiana State

Univ. Press, 1998); Gary W. Gallagher and Alan Nolan, eds., *The Myth of the Lost Cause and Civil War History* (Bloomington: Indiana Univ. Press, 2000); W. Fitzhugh Brundage, *The Southern Past: A Clash of Race and Memory* (Cambridge, Mass.: Belknap Press of Harvard Univ. Press, 2005); William Blair, *Cities of the Dead: Contesting the Memory of the Civil War in the South 1865–1914* (Chapel Hill: Univ. of North Carolina, 2004); Edward Pollard, *The Lost Cause* (New York: Gramercy Books, 1994); James M. McPherson and William Cooper, eds., *Writing the Civil War: The Quest to Understand* (Columbia: Univ. of South Carolina Press, 1998); Michael Martinez, William Richardson, and Ron McNinch-Su, eds., *Confederate Symbols in the Contemporary South* (Tallahassee: Univ. of Florida Press, 2000); John R. Neff, *Honoring the Civil War Dead: Commemoration and the Problem of Reconciliation* (Lawrence: Univ. Press of Kansas, 2005).

6. Sheehan-Dean, *Why Confederates Fought,* 189–95; Barbara J. Fields, "Ideology and Race in American History," in Kousser, *Region, Race, and Reconstruction,* 164–67; Bernath, *Confederate Minds,* 283–99. Sheehan-Dean even describes efforts at reconciliation as an uneasy alliance with an embittered southern nation, while Bernath adds that defeated Confederates attempted to keep alive Confederate nationalism as a cultural struggle against northern domination. Bernath admits, however, that the experiment died down over the years because it could not survive without the southern nation. In this case, he echoes arguments made by Anne Sarah Rubin. Anne Sarah Rubin, *A Shattered Nation: The Rise & Fall of the Confederacy 1861–1868* (Chapel Hill: Univ. of North Carolina Press, 2005).

7. James W. Loewen, *Lies My Teacher Told Me: Everything Your American History Textbook Got Wrong* (New York: Simon & Schuster, 1995), 192; James W. Loewen, *Lies Across America: What Our Historic Sites Get Wrong* (New York: Simon & Schuster, 1999), 102–6.

8. Hutchinson, *Divided Loyalties,* 261.

9. A story circulated for years that the entire city refused to celebrate the holiday for that reason. Historian Christopher Waldrep argues that the National Park Service superintendant at Vicksburg generated the story in 1945 to garner publicity. He also points out that both whites and blacks celebrated the holiday constantly between 1863 and 1945. Christopher Waldrep, *Vicksburg's Long Shadow: The Civil War Legacy of Race and Remembrance* (Lanham, Md.: Rowman and Littlefield, 2005).

10. For further details, see Appendix Ten.

11. Drummond, *Confederate Yankee,* 120–28. Drummond and most of his family ended up dying of yellow fever in 1876 in Georgia.

12. Warner, *Generals in Gray,* 240–41; Albert Pike to Laura, June 11, 1874, Albert Pike Letters 1855–1891, Manuscripts A, Duke.

13. George P. Swift to Louis Hamburger, January 21, October 17, 1867, Louis Hamburger Papers, Duke; Louis Hamburger to George Swift, April 18, 1867, Louis Hamburger Papers, Duke.

14. Kendall, "George Wilkins Kendall," *The Louisiana Historical Quarterly,* 284–85; George Kendall to Henry Randall, May 6, 1867, quoted in Kendall, *Letters From a Texas Sheep Ranch,* 136–39. Kendall actually had high hopes for the future of his adopted section because he predicted that Texas would soon become the largest wool producer in the Union.

15. Edward Wells to his mother, March 13, 1866, Folder 10, Papers of Smith and Wells Families, USC; Alfred Huger to Thomas Wells, September 1, 1867, Folder 10, ibid.

16. Edward Sparrow Deed, 1866, UT.

17. For further examples, see Osterhout, *Stonewall Jackson's Map-Maker,* 67–68; Shippey, "William Tappan Thompson," 180–86; Albert Pike to Professor Hermann Humbull, March 31, 1880, Albert Pike Letters, Duke; Slate, *Biographical Memoir of Eugene Hilgard,* 120–42; Handerson, *Yankee in Gray,* 10; *Memorial Services in Honor of James Kennedy Patterson President of the University of Kentucky 1869–1910 at the Unveiling of the Memorial Tablet, Placed on the Front Wall of the Former Residence of President Patterson, on the Campus of the University of Kentucky, Sunday, June the First, 1924* (Lexington, Ky.: publisher unknown, 1924), 14–15, 24, LV; Bryan, *More Zeal Than Discretion,* 155–66; Allardice, *More Generals in Gray,* 15–16; Krick, *Staff Officers in Gray,* 68.

18. Krick, *Staff Officers in Gray,* 206; *Lexington Morning Herald,* October 2, 1904; Osterhout, *Stonewall Jackson's Mapmaker,* 101–3; Hughes, *Yale's Confederates.*

19. Wiggins, "The Marriage of Amelia Gayle and Josiah Gorgas," in Bleser, *Intimate Strategies of the Civil War,* 109–17; Jefferson Davis to Varina Davis, December 25, 1869, quoted in Hudson Strode, ed., *Jefferson Davis: Private Letters 1823–1889* (New York: Harcourt Brace Jovanovich, 1966), 330; Jefferson Davis to Josiah Gorgas, January 6, 1870, quoted in ibid., 333–34; Braxton Bragg to G. M. Green, June 7, 1868, Episcopal Church Diocese of Tennessee Papers 1868–1923, Manuscript A, Duke; "Bishop Quintard's Mission," and "The Progress of the University," in Charles Quintard Diary, December 1872, Charles Quintard Diaries 1864–1884, UT; Josiah Gorgas to Charles Quintard, January 12, 1873, quoted in Charles Quintard Diaries, UT; Josiah Gorgas to Jefferson Davis, June 12, 1878, Folder 2, Confederate States of America Records, UT.

20. Despite their shared status as Northern Confederate veterans, Gorgas and Quintard did not like each other very much and argued constantly about the proper administration of the school. By the late 1870s, Gorgas left the university to take up a new post at the University of Alabama.

21. Silverthorne, *Ashbel Smith,* 170–81, 192.

22. Warner, *Generals in Gray,* 27.

23. Prince, "Edward Aylsworth Perry," 85; Charles F. Ritter and John Wakelyn, *American Legislative Leaders, 1850–1910* (New York: Greenwood Press, 1989). Phillips also served as attorney general of North Carolina in the 1880s.

24. Krick, *Staff Officers in Gray,* 291; www.infoplease.com/biography/us/congress/upson-christopher-columbus.html.

25. Oliver Perry Temple and Mary Temple, *Notable Men of Tennessee, From 1833–1875, Their Times and Their Contemporaries* (New York: The Cosmopolitan Press, 1912), 137–38; William McFeely, "Amos T. Akerman: The Lawyer and Racial Justice," in Kousser, *Region, Race and Reconstruction,* 395–412.

26. Other Northern Confederates who held public office included Hugh Buchannan, a congressman from Georgia; Harris Flanagin, former wartime governor of Arkansas and a member of the Arkansas constitutional convention; Daniel Reynolds, an Arkansas state senator; William Steele, the adjutant general of Texas; and Killian Whaley, congressman from West Virginia. Jedediah Hotchkiss tried but failed to run for Congress as an independent. Wakelyn, *Biographical Dictionary,* 187; Warner, *Generals in Gray,* 255–56, 289–90; F. W. James, *Brigadier-General Commanding, Annual Report of First Brigade Texas Volunteers, for the Year Ending August 31st, 1877, Respectfully Submitted to General William Steele, Adjutant-General State of Texas* (Austin: 1877), UT; Tyler, *Encyclopedia of Virginia Biography,* 3: 133; "Independent Candidate for Congress," Box 1, Folder 9 (n.d. Correspondence), Jedediah Hotchkiss Papers, UVA; Jedediah Hotchkiss to Nellie Hotchkiss, November 18, 1877, Box 1, Folder 2, ibid.

27. For more detailed discussions on symbols and Civil War memory, see Blight, *Race and Reunion;* Edward Ayers, *The Promise of the New South: Life After Reconstruction* (New York: Oxford Univ. Press, 1992); Martinez, *Confederate Symbols in the Contemporary South;* Fahs, *The Memory of the Civil War;* Gary W. Gallagher, *Causes Won, Lost and Forgotten: How Hollywood and Popular Art Shape What We Know About the Civil War* (Chapel Hill: Univ. of North Carolina, 2008).

28. J. H. Williams to Ashbel Smith, September 21, 1874, Box 2G225, Folder 10, Ashbel Smith Papers, UT.

29. Several historians agree that northerners felt separated from the South for generations. Nina Silber argues that, in the latter half of the nineteenth century, northerners consistently wanted to see a more "authentic" version of the South and so looked to an exotic past rather than the promise of the future when thinking about the region. Carl Degler also remarks that many northerners in the twentieth century still viewed the South as an exotic place. For more information, see Silber, *The Romance of Reunion,* 89–91, 132–33, 140; Degler, "Thesis, Antithesis, Syn-

thesis: The South, the North, and the Nation," *Journal of Southern History,* 3–4; Davidson, *Regionalism and Nationalism,* 112–13, 224–25.

30. Hunter McGuire to Jedediah Hotchkiss, January 22, 1897, Box 1, Folder 10 (Correspondence Dr. Hunter McGuire), Jedediah Hotchkiss Papers, UVA.

31. Hunter McGuire to Jedediah Hotchkiss, July 15, 1897, Box 1, Folder 10, ibid. McGuire did not seem to notice that Hotchkiss, as a native northerner, did not have the upbringing or background apparently required for the invincible southern soldier.

32. Taylor, *Destruction and Reconstruction,* 20.

33. *Charleston Mercury,* July 31, 1861; Sydney Andrews, *The South Since the War, as Shown by Fourteen Weeks of Travel and Observation in Georgia and the Carolinas* (Boston: Ticknor & Co., 1866), 1–10; H. L. Gilbert to a Dear Friend, December 8, 1864, Manuscript A, Duke; Horace Allis to Colonel Charles H. Smith, April 1867, Rauner Manuscripts, Rauner Special Collections Library, Dartmouth College, Hanover. For further discussion on this theme, see Sutherland, "Southern Fraternal Organizations in the North," *Journal of Southern History,* 596–607; Sutherland, "Former Confederates in the Post–Civil War North," *Journal of Southern History,* 402; Charles Joyner, "Forget, Hell! The Civil War in Southern Memory," in Grant, *Legacy of Disunion,* 20–21; Snay, *Fenians, Freedmen, and Southern Whites,* 140–50; Silber, *The Romance of Reunion,* 122, 142, 164–65; Burton, *Gracie's Alabama Volunteers,* 11–12; Hutchinson, *Divided Loyalties,* 261; Charles Ritter, "The Press in Florida, Louisiana, and South Carolina and the End of Reconstruction, 1865–1877: Southern Men With Northern Interests," (PhD diss., Catholic University of America, 1976), 1–23, 61–64, 70–80, 136, 165; Richard Nelson Current, *Arguing With Historians: Essays on the Historical and the Unhistorical* (Middletown, Conn.: Wesleyan University Press, 1987), 124–27; Cash, *Mind of the South,* 105–23, 186–89.

34. Edward Wells to Judge Charles Simonton, August 27, 1898, Fiche 2, Edward Laight Wells Papers, USC. General Jubal Early expressed similar reservations while attempting to publish his own book. Jubal Early to Henry Richardson, September 7, 1872, Henry B. Richardson Materials, Richardson and Farrar Family Papers 1860–1876, SHC.

35. Josiah Gorgas to Jefferson Davis, February 22, June 12, 1878, Folder 2, Confederate States of America Records, UT.

36. For more examples of such phrasing, see "Your Loving Mother" to unknown, August 5, 1865, quoted in Gilman, "Letters of a Confederate Mother, Charleston in the Sixties," *The Atlantic Monthly,* 510–11, USC; "Your Own Mother" to "Eliza," December 12, 1865, quoted in ibid., 514, USC; Edward Wells to his sister, May 1, 1865, Folder 9, Papers of Smith and Wells Families, USC; Green, *Major Caleb Huse,* 16–17.

37. Ashbel Smith to General John Brown, August 16, 1876, Box 2G225, Folder 12, Ashbel Smith Papers, UT.

38. Address on the Laying of the Corner Stone of the University of Texas, November 17, 1882. By the Late Ashbel Smith, First President of the Board of Regents, 91, UT.

39. John Hammond Moore, ed., South Carolina and the Southern Claims Commission, 1871–1880, 1982, 12, Manuscripts P, USC. Out of the four that did admit non-southern backgrounds, one came from Ireland, two from New England, and one from Pennsylvania. Ibid., 86, 107–8, 120–21, 140–41.

40. French, *Two Wars,* Preface.

41. Ibid., 8–10.

42. Ibid., 297–99.

43. Ibid., 316–17, 345–49.

44. Ibid., 310–12, 328–35.

45. Ibid., 349–50.

46. Dawson, *Reminiscences of Confederate Service*, 152.

47. Charles Dahlgren to John Adolph Dahlgren, June 10, 1868, quoted in Gower, *Charles Dahlgren,* 169.

48. Edward Wells to unknown, March 3 1904 and June 1909, pp. 12–13, Fiche 5, Edward Laight Wells Papers, USC.

49. Edward Wells to unknown, March 3, 1904, and June 1909, pp. 14–21, Fiche 5–6, Edward Laight Wells Papers, USC.

50. Some Northern Confederates did emphasize their renewed loyalty to the Union and urged others to do the same to avoid further bloodshed. This did not mean, however, that they were prepared to give up their connections with the South in the process. They merely acted like every other paroled Confederate soldier. Montgomery, *Reminiscences in Peace and War,* 261–62; *Memphis Daily Appeal,* November 17, 1865; Form No. 3—Oath to be taken by those who have aided Reconstruction UNITED STATES OF AMERICA. STATE OF LOUISIANA—PARISH OF TENSAS, Henry B. Richardson Materials, Richardson and Farrar Family Papers, SHC; Dolly Burge Diary, April 29, 1865, quoted in Burge, *Diary of Dolly Lunt Burge,* 171–72; Jonathan Worth to Andrew Johnson, July 10, 1866, quoted in Worth, *The Correspondence of Jonathan Worth,* 1: 677; Jonathan Worth to William Seward, July 1866, quoted in ibid., 1: 661–62.

51. Amelia Lines to Maria Akehurst, September 1865, quoted in Lines, *To Raise Myself a Little,* 217–18.

52. Amelia Lines Diary, October 24, 1871, quoted in ibid., 252. For similar references, see Amelia Lines Diary, September 1–20, October 18, 1871, quoted in ibid., 245–49.

53. Susan Eppes Diary, February 1866, quoted in Eppes, *Through Some Eventful Years*, 312. Novelist Caroline Lee Hentz, herself a northern emigrant, touched on this theme in her novels, especially *The Planter's Northern Bride*. In the prose, the protagonist's northern-born wife, when asked if she has gotten used to the South, replies, "Far more than reconciled—strongly attached." Another character, Mr. Brainard, says of her, "It is astonishing . . . how soon one gets weaned from old habits and associations. One would suppose . . . that my fair countrymen here had been born and bred at the South, instead of a simple New England village." Though fiction, Hentz's own feelings as an adoptive southerner clearly came through in her writings. Hentz, *The Planter's Northern Bride*, 404–5, 578–79.

54. Patterson, *Yankee Rebel*, xx.

55. Osterhout, *Stonewall Jackson's Map-Maker*, 55–56, 74, 86; Jedediah Hotchkiss to Hunter McGuire, February 17, 1897, Box 1, Folder 10 (Correspondence Dr. Hunter McGuire), Jedediah Hotchkiss Papers, UVA.

56. Jedediah Hotchkiss to Nellie Hotchkiss, November 18, 1877, Box 1, Folder 2, ibid.; Jedediah Hotchkiss to his daughter, November 27, 1872, ibid. Samuel French made a similar claim in his own memoirs, when he considered the South superior because of its homogeneity of native-born people and implicitly included himself in that category. French, *Two Wars*, 353–57.

57. George Kendall to Henry Randall, January 30, 1867, quoted in Kendall, *Letters From a Texas Sheep Ranch*, 18.

58. Ashbel Smith to Francis Allan, September 25, 1875, Box 2G225, Folder 11, Ashbel Smith Papers, UT; Ashbel Smith to unknown, September 8, 1868, Box 2G225, Folder 4, Ashbel Smith Papers, UT.

59. Joseph Garey Diary, April 24, 1866, quoted in Garey, *A Keystone Rebel*, 102–3.

60. "Your Own Mother" to "Eliza," December 12, 1865, quoted in Gilman, "Letters from a Confederate Mother," *Atlantic Monthly*, 514, USC. Edmund Bradford also talked about wanting to return home with his family, in his case Norfolk, when the war ended. A. E. T. Bradford to Sally Tazewell, May 11, 1865 (with an add on by Edmund Bradford dated May 12, 1865), quoted in Tazewell, *Major Edmund Bradford*, 29.

61. Clemson quoted in Lander, *Calhoun Family*, 231–32.

62. Washington Diary of Charles G. Dahlgren, November 13, December 10, 1865, quoted in Gower, *Charles Dahlgren*, 147, 156.

63. John Slidell to James Mason, October 7, 1866, quoted in Sears, "A Confederate Diplomat," *American Historical Review*, 279–80.

64. John Slidell to Edward Butler, December 20, 1867, Folder 3, Edward Butler Papers 1858–1874, Duke.

65. Gideon Welles Diary, August 24, 1866, quoted in Welles, *Diary of Gideon Welles*, 585.

66. For more examples of Northern Confederates fleeing abroad after the war, see Krick, *Staff Officers in Gray*, 59; Warner, *Generals in Gray*, 71, 94–95, 257.

67. Casteevens, *George W. Alexander*, 156–59.

68. Warner, *Biographical Register of the Confederate Congress*, 61–62; Warner, *Generals in Gray*, 176–77.

69. Warner, *Generals in Gray*, 292.

70. Bell, *Confederate Seadog*, 56–66; Koke, "John Taylor Wood," 91–93. Wood did have some contact with the North as an agent for the Boston Insurance Company in the 1880s. President Grover Cleveland even issued Wood a pardon in 1897, making Wood the second to last Confederate soldier to receive a pardon from the federal government. The lateness reflected Wood's determination to live out his life in Canada, where he eventually died in 1904.

71. John Slidell to Edward Butler, December 20, 1867, Folder 3, Edward Butler Papers, Duke.

72. Krick, *Staff Officers in Gray*, 59; Warner, *Generals in Gray*, 94–95, 257.

73. Gower, *Charles Dahlgren*, 180–86, 198.

74. Brazy, *An American Planter*, 157; Wade Hampton to Stephen Duncan, May 24, 1866, Folder 1, Duncan Family Papers, UT; W. Olson to Stephen Duncan, November 27, 1866, Folder 1, ibid.

75. Krick, *Staff Officers in Gray*, 83.

76. Wakelyn, *Biographical Dictionary*, 168.

77. Slate, *Biographical Memoir of Eugene Woldemar Hilgard*, 129–31; Smith, "Memorial of Eugene Woldemar Hilgard," *Bulletin of the Geological Society of America*, 42.

78. Warner, *Generals in Gray*, 194–95, 382 (note 286).

79. See also Krick, *Staff Officers in Gray*, 206.

80. Henry Handerson to Lewis Handerson, April 24, May 3, 14, 21, 1865, quoted in Handerson, *Yankee in Gray*, 112–16.

81. Mason, "Henry Watson," 73–76.

82. Malloy, "The Health of Our Family," 116–20; Josiah Gorgas to Jefferson Davis, February 8, 1878, Folder 2, Confederate States of America Records, UT; Mansfield, *Life and Achievements of Gail Borden*, 7; Moore, South Carolina and the Southern Claims Commission, 120–21, USC. For a reiteration of the theme of Northern Confederates expressing continued affiliation with the North, see Osterhout, *Stonewall Jackson's Map-Maker*, 74, 86; Moore, South Carolina and the Southern Claims Commission, 86, 107–8, 140–41, USC; Jedediah Hotchkiss to Hunter McGuire, February 17, 1897, Box 1, Folder 10 (Correspondence Dr. Hunter McGuire), Jedediah Hotchkiss Papers, UVA.

83. Duncan, *Entrepreneur for Equality*, 122–37.

84. Warner, *Generals in Gray,* 157–58.

85. "Biographical Sketch and Letters of Caroline Howard Gilman," 15–16, Folder 4, Caroline Howard Gilman Papers 1810–1880, USC.

86. Warner, *Generals in Gray,* 232–33.

87. In fact, one Union veteran who lived near Pemberton during his final years claimed that Pemberton endured some good natured teasing but more than held his own when it came to arguing questions involving the war. The veteran also said his friends found it fascinating to have a "real live Rebel" in their midst. Testimony quoted in Sutherland, "Former Confederates in the Post–Civil War North," *Journal of Southern History,* 407.

88. For more information and other examples, see Silber, *Romance of Reunion,* 55–65; Robinson, *A Yankee in a Confederate Town,* 112–24; Mansfield, *Life and Achievements of Gail Borden.*

89. In contrast, historian Daniel Sutherland implies that native southerners still considered Northern Confederates as outsiders because they were lumped together with Copperheads. He shows that the New York Southern Society, an organization formed for ex-Confederates living in New York City, was created "to 'cherish and perpetuate the memories and traditions of the Southern people' . . . In 1891, perhaps recalling northern-born Confederates and Copperheads who had stood by the South a quarter century earlier, the society also welcomed as members men who had "'rendered signal service to the South.'" In reality, these veterans represented something more because, unlike Copperheads, they actually fought in the Confederate ranks. Sutherland also does not mention that nearly all Northern Confederates qualified under the original conditions, since they lived in the South long before 1864. Sutherland, "Southern Fraternal Organizations," *Journal of Southern History,* 594.

90. Johnston, *Narrative of Military Operations,* 169–70. In a further sign of camaraderie, native southerners and Northern Confederate veterans sometimes exchanged friendly correspondence and joined the same veterans' organizations. See Charles Quintard Correspondence, Folder 3, Charles Quintard Papers 1857–1899, Duke; Edward Well Correspondence, Edward Laight Wells Papers, USC; Josiah Gorgas to Jefferson Davis, September 5, November 28, 1877, Folder 2, Confederate States of America Records, UT; Josiah Gorgas to Jefferson Davis, January 23, February 8, 22, June 12, 1878, Folder 2, ibid.; Osterhout, *Stonewall Jackson's Map-Maker,* 103; Bryan, *More Zeal,* 167–78; E. M. Pease, Tx. Veteran's Assoc. Certificate, April 17, 1882, Box 3G484, Folder 104, Paul C. Crusemann Collection, UT.

91. Samuel Watkins, *Company Aytch* (Chattanooga, Tenn.: Time Printing Company, 1900), 49, 112–13.

92. "The First Regiment of Tennessee Volunteers," Folder 3, Charles Quintard Papers 1857–1899, Duke; Captain Polk Johnson, "Brig.-General William A. Quarles," Clarksville, Tn., Tobacco Leaf, Folder 3, ibid.

93. *Baltimore Sun,* 1904. For further examples of praise for Northern Confederates by native southerners, see Sydney Andrews Diary, November 17, 1865, quoted in Andrews, *The South Since the War,* 327–28; R. E. Lee Letter, September 9, 1870, George A. Magruder Papers 1862, 1863, 1870, LV.

94. T. J. Wharton, "The Late General Pemberton," *New York Herald,* August 17, 1881.

95. William Preston Johnston to John Pemberton, June 15, 1874, Folder 4, John Clifford Pemberton Papers, SHC.

96. Jubal Early, "General Dick Taylor's Utterances in Regard to General Pemberton," *Daily Register,* May 6, 1879, Folder 3, John Pemberton Papers, SHC.

97. Stephen D. Lee to Charles Wright, October 22, 1904, Folder 5, ibid.

98. Even Northern Confederate generals who resided in the North before the war, such as Mansfield Lovell and Josiah Gorgas, had their defenders as well. See Braxton Bragg to G. M. Green, June 7, 1868, Episcopal Church Diocese of Tennessee Papers, Duke.

99. Eulogy quoted in Tarrant, *Hon. Daniel Pratt,* 134.

100. Montgomery, *Reminiscences in Peace and War,* 40–41; John Cussons to Jedediah Hotchkiss, September 29, 1897, Box 1, Folder 8 (1895–1913), Jedediah Hotchkiss Papers, UVA; "Major Jed Hotchkiss," *National Geographic Society,* 1898, Box 4, Folder 4 (Newspaper Clippings), ibid.; Clarence Wm. Smith, "Private Pasco," quoted in Pasco, *Private Pasco,* 184–85; General B. W. Partridge eulogy quoted in ibid., 187–88; quoted in Gower, *Charles Dahlgren,* 144–45.

101. Chute, "The Life of Frederick A. P. Barnard," 274–75; Mansfield, *Life and Achievements of Gail Borden.*

102. Clopton, *A Eulogy on the Life and Character of Dr. Ashbel Smith,* 5, Duke.

103. Taylor quoted in Jubal Early, "General Dick Taylor's Utterances in Regard to General Pemberton," *Daily Register,* May 6, 1879, Folder 3, John Clifford Pemberton Papers, SHC.

104. Stephen D. Lee to Charles Wright, October 22, 1904, Folder 5, ibid. T. J. Wharton also vouched for Pemberton's independent political views in favor of the Confederacy. T. J. Wharton, "The Late General Pemberton," *New York Herald,* August 17, 1881.

105. Memoir of Major Samuel B. Myers," in Avirett, *The Memoirs of General Turner Ashby,* 360; General B. W. Partridge eulogy quoted in Pasco, *Private Pasco,* 186–87.

106. Jos. T. Derry, "Northern Men Who Held Positions Under the Confederacy," *The Atlanta Constitution,* February 4, 1900; "Army Letters," *The State,* October 7, 1896, Felix G. De Fontaine Papers, 1869–1911, Manuscripts P and mfm R 163, USC.

107. Several biographers, however, argue that these men remained northerners throughout their lives and that native southerners believed this, as well. For further discussion on this argument, and some contemporary evidence for it, see Tarrant, *Hon. Daniel Pratt,* 94, 139, 142, 145–46; Griffin, "Connecticut Yankee in Texas," 270–71; "Funeral of Major Edmund Bradford," *The Public Ledger,* April 29, 1889, quoted in Tazewell, *Major Edmund Bradford,* 36; Montgomery, *Reminiscences in Peace and War,* 223–24; Jos. T. Derry, "Northern Men Who Held Positions Under the Confederacy," *The Atlanta Constitution,* February 4, 1900.

108. The seventh state was West Virginia, which elected Pennsylvania native William Erskine Stevenson as a Republican governor in 1868 for one term.

109. Ritter, "The Press in Florida," 140–47.

110. Prince, "Edward Aylsworth Perry," 65–67, 75, 80–82, 89–90, 101, 114, 120; Warner, *Generals in Gray,* 235–36.

111. A sixth, Benjamin Conley, ascended to the governorship of Georgia after the resignation of the previous governor in 1871.

112. Sobel, *Biographical Directory of the Governors of the United States,* 1: 254–55; Smith, *Courage of a Southern Unionist,* 92–93, 144; Benjamin Flanders to Winfield Hancock, July 1, 1870, quoted in Winfield Scott Hancock, *Correspondence Between General W. T. Sherman, U.S. Army and Major General W. S. Hancock, U.S. Army* (St. Paul, Minn.: Privately Published, 1871), 24–25; Philip Sheridan, *Personal Memoirs of P. H. Sheridan, General United States Army* (New York: C. L. Webster, 1888), 267–69.

113. "Proclamation of Governor Lewis E. Parsons, July 20, 1865," Alabama Broadside Collection, Broadside Case AL, Duke. Ironically, Louis Parsons came under attack from unionists who felt he did not represent their interests very well. Both unionists and secessionists in the state thus hated him for different reasons, but neither specifically for his northern roots. "The Alabama Delegation," *Jackson County News,* June 10, 1865, Alabama Broadside Collection, Broadside Case AL, Duke; D. H. Bingham and J. H. Larcomb, "To the President and Members of the Cabinet of the United States," June 27, 1865, ibid.

114. Griffin, "Connecticut Yankee in Texas," 187–202; Franzetti, "Elisha Marshall Pease," 18–20; Gideon Welles Diary, August 1, 1866, quoted in Welles, *Diary of Gideon Welles,* 568–69.

115. Griffin, "Connecticut Yankee in Texas," 217–21, 226–27, 238–41; Franzetti, "Elisha Marshall Pease," 11–20; E. M. Pease to Schuyler Colfax, January 15, 1868, quoted in *Affairs in Texas. Letters from Governor Pease and Hon. C. Caldwell in Regard to Affairs in the State of Texas. January 31, 1868—Referred to the Committee on Reconstruction and Ordered to Be Printed. House of Representatives, 40th Congress, 2nd Session,* UT.

116. Franzetti, "Elisha Marshall Pease," 29.

117. *Austin Southern Intelligencer,* April 20, 1866, quoted in Griffin, "Connecticut Yankee in Texas," 194. See also "The Alabama Delegation," *Jackson County News,* June 10, 1865, Alabama Broadside Collection, Broadside Case AL, Duke.

118. Speech Delivered by Hon. E. M. Pease at Turner Hall, Galveston, Texas, July 12th, 1880 (Galveston, Tex.: McKenna & C., 1880), 4, UT.

119. Ibid., 21–22, UT.

120. *Speech Delivered by Hon. E. M. Pease at Turner Hall, Galveston, Texas, July 12th, 1880,* 19–20, UT. Pease also warned that northerners would not support a northern candidate if he was secretly controlled by southerners, like former presidents Franklin Pierce and James Buchannan. Those events were long remembered and still influenced late nineteenth century politics. For more on the internal political civil war in Reconstruction Texas, see C. C. Caldwell to Major Longley, January 2, 1868, quoted in *Affairs in Texas. Letters from Governor Pease and Hon. C. Caldwell in regard to Affairs in the State of Texas. January 31, 1868—Referred to the Committee on Reconstruction and Ordered to Be Printed. House of Representatives, 40th Congress, 2nd Session,* UT.

121. E. W. Cullen quoted in Griffin, "Connecticut Yankee in Texas," 261.

122. Duncan, *Entrepreneur For Equality,* 18–19, 25–38, 42–49.

123. Ibid., 52–55, 70–80, 98–101, 122–37; *State of Georgia, Message of His Excellency Benjamin Conley, Governor. Atlanta, GA., January 11, 1872* (Atlanta, Ga.: New Era Steam Printing Establishment,1872), 5–6, UVA.

124. Duncan, *Entrepreneur For Equality,* 45–46; "Pen Photograph of an Extraordinary Bullock," newspaper clipping, February 9, 1871, Thomas Norwood Papers, #559-z, SHC. Margaret Mitchell even criticized Bullock directly in her famous novel, *Gone With the Wind.*

125. Duncan, *Entrepreneur For Equality,* 45–46, 83–84.

126. "Pen Photograph of an Extraordinary Bullock," newspaper clipping, February 9, 1871, Thomas Norwood Papers, SHC.

127. Duncan, *Entrepreneur For Equality,* 141–45.

128. Address of Rufus B. Bullock, Ex-Governor of Georgia, Delivered August 22, 1891, Before the Alumni Association of the Albion Academy. Albion, Orleans County, New York, 5–6, UVA.

129. "An Open Letter to Horace Greeley by Rufus Bullock, August, 1872," quoted in *Address of Rufus B. Bullock To the People of Georgia. A Review of the Revolutionary Proceedings of the Late Repudiating Legislature. The Slanders and Misrepresentations of the Committees Exposed. A Republican Administration Contrasted With the Corrupt and Reckless Action of the Present Usurping Minority Under the Lead of General Toombs.* October, 1872, 53, UVA.

130. Duncan, *Entrepreneur For Equality,* 149–58, 168–69.

Conclusion

1. The remaining thirty-one left behind insufficient records to determine their last whereabouts.

2. Communication From R. W. Simpson, Executor of Will of T. G. Clemson, Deceased, Accompanied by Copy of Said Will and Other Papers Relating Thereto, December 4, 1888, Pamphlet Collection 48355, Duke; Gower, *Charles Dahlgren,* 204–6, 241.

3. *Lexington Morning Herald,* October 2, 1904.

4. Prince, "Edward Aylsworth Perry," 126–31.

5. Trinity College Historical Society, *An Annual Publication of Historical Papers,* 2: 42–43.

6. Way, *History of the New England Society of Charleston,* 18–21, 49–53. Even northern newspapers occasionally praised the exploits of their wayward sons. See "Death of Gen. Pike," *Ledger and Transcript,* April 3, 1891; Philadelphia *Public Ledger,* July 15, 1881.

7. Perry and Perry, *Reminiscences of Public Men,* 208. Perry did qualify these remarks by asserting that Dunkin never forgot his roots in the North.

8. General B. W. Partridge eulogy quoted in Pasco, *Private Pasco,* 187–88.

9. L. H. L, "To the Memory of Edward L. Wells—Soldier of the Confederacy," Fiche 6, Edward Laight Wells Papers, USC.

10. "Monument to Gen. F. A. Shoup", *Confederate Veteran* XI (July, 1903): 311, Sarah Elliott Letters, #1004, SHC.

11. Ibid.

12. Dr. A. G. Clopton, *An Eulogy on the Life and Character of Dr. Ashbel Smith, Delivered At the Texas States University Commencement, Before the Regents Faculty and Students By Invitation of Board of Regents, In the City of Austin, Texas, June 15, 1886* (Jefferson, Tex.: Iron News Print, 1886), 6, Duke. For other references to Smith's connection to Texas, see Joe Byne to Ashbel Smith, April 17, 1865, Box 2G225, Folder 1, Ashbel Smith Papers, UT; William Webb to Ashbel Smith, May 9, 1865, ibid.; H. P. Bee to Ashbel Smith, June 13, 1873, Box 2G225, Folder 9, ibid.; Joseph Demhl to Ashbel Smith, April 8, 1874, Box 2G225, Folder 10, ibid.

13. Bryan, *More Zeal Than Discretion,* 148–54, 180–81; Moore's Rural New Yorker, November 2, 1867, quoted in Kendall, *Letters From a Texas Sheep Ranch,* 19.

14. Catherwood, *Life and Labors of William W. Wadley,* 3–13; Black, *The Railroads of the Confederacy,* 108–11.

15. Catherwood, *The Life and Labors of William W. Wadley,* 13–19, 31–32.

16. A. O. Bacon quoted in Catherwood, *The Life and Labors of William W. Wadley,* 57–59.

17. Joseph Cumming quoted in ibid., 40. Cumming was not the only one to cite the theme of bridge-building among northern emigrants. Samuel and Caroline Gilman had the same effect upon their community in South Carolina. See "In Memory of Dr. Gilman," *News and Courier,* March 30, 1934, Folder 5, Caroline Howard Gilman Papers, 1810–1880, USC.

18. At least one historian challenges this argument. Richard Current cites several postwar northern emigrants who found acceptance in the South despite their status as carpetbaggers. In fact, Current argues that northern settlers who stayed out of politics or toed the line on southern racial policy did not even acquire that label. Current, *Arguing With Historians,* 117–20.

19. Sutherland, "Southern Fraternal Organizations," *Journal of Southern History,* 609.

Bibliography

PRIMARY SOURCES

Manuscripts

Bowdoin College, George J. Mitchell Department of Special Collections & Archives, Bowdoin College Library, Brunswick, Maine
- McArthur Family Papers

College of Charleston, Special Collections, Marlene and Nathan Addlestone Library, Charleston, South Carolina
- Gilman, Caroline, Papers

Dartmouth College, Rauner Manuscript Collection, Rauner Special Collections Library, Hanover, New Hampshire
- Allis, Horace, Letter

Duke University, Manuscript Department, William R. Perkins Library, Durham, North Carolina
- Alabama Broadside Collection
- Brock, Ignatius, Correspondence
- Buchannan, Hugh, Papers
- Butler, Edward, Papers
- Duncan, William, Papers
- Episcopal Church Diocese of Tennessee Papers
- Forney, George, Papers
- Gilbert, H. L., Letter
- Hamburger, Louis, Papers
- Latrobe, John H. B. "What Next?" Printed in the *Baltimore American*, January 14, 1861.
- Palmer, Joseph, Letters and Papers
- Pamphlet Collection
- Pierce, Ellen E., Papers

Pike, Albert, Letters
Quintard, Charles, Papers
Ruggles, Daniel, Papers
Speech of Hon H. M. Shaw, of North Carolina, in the House of Representatives, May 29,1854. *North Carolina Pamphlets,* 1841–59, Volume 3, Number 1.
Speech of Hon. H. M. Shaw of North Carolina, in the House of Representatives, April 20, 1858. North Carolina Pamphlets, 1841–59, Volume 3, Number 2.
Storm, Henry, Papers
Watson, Henry, Papers

Johns Hopkins University, Manuscript Department, Sheridan Libraries, Baltimore, Maryland
Greenway, Edward, Papers

Library of Virginia, Richmond, Virginia
De Fontaine, F. G. *American Abolitionism, From 1787 to 1861: A Compendium of Historical Facts Embracing Legislation in Congress and Agitation Without.* New York: D. Appleton & Company, 1861.
Magruder, George A., Papers
Memorial Services in Honor of James Kennedy Patterson President of the University of Kentucky 1869–1910 at the Unveiling of the Memorial Tablet, Placed on the Front Wall of the Former Residence of President Patterson, on the Campus of the University of Kentucky, Sunday, June the First, 1924. Lexington, Kentucky, 1924.

State of Mississippi, Department of Archives and History, Division of Records Management, Jackson, Mississippi.
Fox, Tryphena Holder, Papers

Texas A&M University, Cushing Memorial Library and Archives, College Station, Texas.
The War and its Heroes. Richmond: Ayres & Wade, 1864. *Confederate Imprints, 1861–1865,* Reel 84, Microfilm B, 1664.

Tulane University, Manuscripts Department, Special Collections Division, Tulane University Library, New Orleans, Louisiana.
Phelps, Ashton, Jr. *Theodore Clapp: The Ante-bellum South's Only Unitarian Minister.* Yale University, May 18, 1966.

University of North Carolina, Southern Historical Collection, Chapel Hill, North Carolina.
Cooper, Samuel, Papers
Elliot, Sarah, Letters
Hentz Family Papers

Norwood, Thomas, Papers
Obituary Addresses on the Announcement of the Death of Hon. John A. Quitman of Mississippi: in the House of Representatives, January 5, 1859. Rare Book Collection Southern Pamphlet Folio-2
Pemberton, John Clifford, Papers
Rains, George, Papers
Richardson and Farrar Family Papers
Williams, Sarah Francis Hicks, Papers

University of South Carolina, Manuscripts Department, South Caroliniana Library, Columbia, South Carolina.
De Fontaine, Felix G., Papers
Gilman, Caroline Howard, Papers
Gilman, Samuel, Papers
Hampton, Sally Baxter, Papers
Hora, William Henry, Letter
Ryan, John S., Papers
Smith and Wells Family Papers
South Carolina Claims Commission
Wells, Edward Laight, Papers

University of Texas at Austin, Dolph Briscoe Center for American History, Austin, Texas.
Address on the Laying of the Corner Stone of the University of Texas, November 17, 1882. By the Late Ashbel Smith, First President of the Board of Regents.
Confederate States of America Records
Crusemann, Paul C., Collection
Dana, Charles Backus, Papers
Duncan Family Papers
Maynard, Horace. "Still More Truth: No Compromise With Traitors, Speech of Hon. Horace Maynard of Tennessee in the House of Representatives, January 31, 1863."
Pike, Albert. *Letters to the People of the Northern States on the Nebraska and Kansas Act, and Southern Slavery.* Washington, D.C.: Dieon Printer, 1856. Microfiche 11759.
Pike, Albert. "State or Province? Bond or Free? The Vital Principle of Equality which cements the Union of the States. Addressed Particularly to the People of Arkansas. 1861."
Quintard, Charles, Diaries 1864–1884
Smith, Ashbel, Papers
Sparrow, Edward, Deed

University of Virginia, Albert and Shirley Small Special Collections Library, Charlottesville, Virginia.
> *Address of Rufus B. Bullock, Ex-Governor of Georgia, Delivered August 22, 1891, Before the Alumni Association of the Albion Academy.* Albion, Orleans County, New York.
>
> *Address of Rufus B. Bullock To the People of Georgia. A Review of the Revolutionary Proceedings of the late Repudiating Legislature. The Slanders and Misrepresentations of the Committees Exposed. A Republican Administration Contrasted With the Corrupt and Reckless Action of the Present Usurping Minority Under the Lead of General Toombs.* October, 1872.
>
> Cooper, Samuel, Papers
>
> Harrison, John Hunter, Papers
>
> Hatton, Robert. "State of the Union, Speech of Hon. Robert Hatton, of Tennessee, in the House of Representatives, February 8, 1861," *Speeches, Second Session, 36th Congress, 1860–1861, Vol. 1*, Vol. 94.
>
> Hearne, Madge Williams, Collection
>
> Hotchkiss, Jedediah, Papers
>
> *In Memoriam.* General Lewis Baldwin Parsons
>
> Quitman, John Anthony, Papers
>
> Rare Pamphlets

Virginia Historical Society, Richmond, Virginia.
> Cooper, Samuel, Letters
>
> Mason, George, Letter
>
> McClellan, H. B., Papers

Periodicals

Adams Sentinel
Charleston Mercury
Lexington Morning Herald
Memphis Daily Appeal
New Orleans Delta
New York Herald
New York Times
Richmond Daily Register
Richmond Enquirer
Tensas (La.) Gazette
Texas State Gazette
Vicksburg Daily Herald

Published Primary Sources

A Discussion on Slaveholding. Three Letters to a Conservative by George D. Armstrong, D.D. of Virginia and Three Conservative Replies by C. Van Rensselaer, D.D. of New Jersey. Together with Two Rejoinders, On Slaveholding, Schemes of Emancipation, Colonization, Etc. Philadelphia, Pa.: Joseph M. Wilson, 111 South Tenth Street, 1858.

Addresses Delivered in the Chapel at West Point, Before the Officers and Cadets of the United States Military Academy, by The Hon. Ashbel Smith, of Texas, and Col. A.W. Doniphan, of Missouri. June 16, 1848. Published by Order of the First Class of the United States Corps of Cadets. New York: W. L. Burroughs, Printer, 1848.

Addresses of Doctor Ashbel Smith(An Oration Pronounced Before the Connecticut Alpha of the Phi Beta Kappa at Yale College, New Haven, August 15, 1849, by Hon. Ashbel Smith, of Texas. New Haven, Conn.: B. L. Hamlen Printer to Yale College, 1849.

Address of Hon. T. Butler King to the People of the First Congressional District. Savannah, Ga.: Steam Press John M. Cooper & Co., 1859.

Andrews, Sydney. *The South Since the War, as Shown by Fourteen Weeks of Travel and Observation in Georgia and the Carolinas.* Boston: Ticknor & Co., 1866.

Armstrong, George D. *"What Hath God Wrought": A Historical Discourse Preached June 25th, 1876 On the Completion of a Twenty-Five Years Ministry in the First Presbyterian Church, Norfolk, VA.* Norfolk, Va.: The Congregation, 1876.

———.*"The Good Hand of Our God Upon Us": A Thanksgiving Sermon, Preached on Occasion of the Victory of Manassas, July 21st, 1861, in the Presbyterian Church, Norfolk, VA.* Norfolk, Va.: J. D. Ghiselin, 1861.

Barnard, Frederick A. P., LL. D. *Letter to the Honorable The Board of Trustees of the University of Mississippi.* Oxford: University of Mississippi, 1858.

———. *Letter to the President of the United States by a Refugee.* Philadelphia: J. P. Lippincott, 1863.

Brown, Joseph E. *Official Correspondence of Joseph E. Brown, 1860–1865, Inclusive.* Atlanta, Ga.: C. P. Byrd State Printer, 1910.

Burge, Dolly Lunt. *The Diary of Dolly Lunt Burge 1848–1879.* Edited by Christine Jacobson Carter. Athens: University of Georgia Press, 1997.

Butler, Benjamin F. *Private and Official Correspondence of Gen. Benjamin F. Butler, During the Period of the Civil War.* 2 vols. Springfield, Mass.: Plimpton Press, 1917.

Catlin, George. *Letters and Notes on the Manners, Customs, and Condition of the North American Indians.* 2 vols. London: Published by the Author, 1841.

Chestnut, Mary Boykin. *A Diary From Dixie.* Edited by Isabella Martin and Myrta Avary. New York: D. Appleton & Co., 1905.

Claiborne, J. F. H. *Life and Correspondence of John A. Quitman: Major General, U.S.A., and Governor of the State of Mississippi.* 2 vols. New York: Harper & Brothers Pub., 1860.

Clapp, Theodore. *Autobiographical Sketches and Recollections During a Thirty-Five Year Residence in New Orleans.* Boston: Phillips, Sampson & Co., 1857.

Clopton, A. G. *An Eulogy on the Life and Character of Dr. Ashbel Smith, Delivered At the Texas States University Commencement, Before the Regents Faculty and Students By Invitation of Board of Regents, In the City of Austin, Texas, June 15, 1886.* Jefferson, Tex.: Iron News Print, 1886.

Correspondence Between the War Department and General Lovell, Relating to the Defences of New Orleans. Submitted in Response to a Resolution of the House of Representatives Passed Third February, 1863. Richmond: R. M. Smith, Public Printer, 1863.

Cumming, Kate. *Kate: The Journal of a Confederate Nurse.* Edited by Richard Harwell. Baton Rouge: Louisiana State University Press, 1998.

Dawson, Francis W. *Reminiscences of Confederate Service 1861–1865.* Edited by Bell Wiley. Baton Rouge: Louisiana State University Press, 1980.

Dawson, Sarah Morgan. *A Confederate Girl's Diary: Sarah Morgan Dawson.* Boston: Houghton, Mifflin, & Co., 1913.

De Fontaine, Felix G. *Marginalia, or Gleanings From an Army Notebook.* Columbia: Steam Power Press of F. G. De Fontaine & Co., 1864.

Downing, Alexander. *Downing's Civil War Diary.* Edited by Olynthus Clark. Des Moines: Iowa State Department of History and Archives, 1916.

Drake, James Vaulx. *Life of General Robert Hatton, Including His Most Important Public Speeches, Together With Much of His Washington & Army Correspondence.* Nashville: Marshall & Bruce, 1867.

Drummond, Edward. *Confederate Yankee: the Journal of Edward William Drummond, a Confederate Soldier From Maine.* Edited by Roger S. Durham. Knoxville: University of Tennessee Press, 2004.

Edmonds, Sarah. *Nurse and Spy in the Union Army.* Hartford, Conn.: W. S. Williams and Co., 1865.

Eggleston, George Cary. *A Rebel's Recollections.* New York: The Knickerbocker Press, 1905.

———. *Recollections of a Varied Life.* New York: Henry Holt and Co., 1910.

Eppes, Susan Bradford. *Through Some Eventful Years.* Macon, Ga.: Press of the J. W. Burke Company, 1926.

Farmer, Alice. *The Times and Journal of Alice Farmer: Yankee Visitor to Acadiana-New Orleans.* Edited by Christopher G. Pena. Thibodaux, La.: C.G.P. Press, 2001.

Flint, Timothy. *Recollections of the Last Ten Years in the Valley of the Mississippi.* Edited by George Brooks. Carbondale: Southern Illinois University Press, 1968.

Fox, Tryphena Blanche Holder. *A Northern Woman in the Plantation South: Letters of Tryphena Blanche Holder Fox 1856–1876.* Edited by Wilma King. Columbia: University of South Carolina Press, 1993.

Fremantle, Arthur. *Three Months in the Southern States: April-June, 1863.* Edinburgh: William Blackwood and Son, 1863.

Garey, Joseph. *A Keystone Rebel: The Civil War Diary of Joseph Garey, Hudson's Battery, Mississippi Volunteers.* Edited by David Welker. Gettysburg: Thomas Publications, 1996.

Gorgas, Josiah. *The Journals of Josiah Gorgas, 1857–1878.* Edited by Sarah Woolfolk Wiggins. Tuscaloosa: University of Alabama Press, 1995.

Green, Thomas W. *Major Caleb Huse C.S.A.: A Memoir and Appreciation Being a Reprint of the Huse Pamphlet of 1904 Together with an Appreciation and Two Appendices.* London: Studies in Confederate History No. 1, Confederate Historical Society, 1966.

Grisamore, Silas. *Reminiscences of Uncle Silas: A History of the Eighteenth Louisiana Infantry Regiment.* Edited by Arthur W. Bergeron, Jr. Baton Rouge: Comité des Archives de la Louisiane, 1981.

Hampton, Sally Baxter. *A Divided Heart: Letters of Sally Baxter Hampton 1853–1862.* Edited by Ann Frip Hampton. Spartanburg, S.C.: Reprint Co., 1980.

Hancock, Winfield Scott. *Correspondence Between General W. T. Sherman, U.S. Army, and Major General W.S. Hancock, U.S. Army.* St. Paul, Minn.: Privately Published, 1871.

Handerson, Henry E. *Yankee in Gray: The Civil War Memoirs of Henry E. Handerson with a Selection of His Wartime Letters.* Edited by Clyde Lottridge Cummer. Cleveland: Western Reserve University Press, 1962.

Harrison, Constance Cary. *Recollections Grave and Gay.* New York: Charles Scribner's Sons, 1911.

Hotchkiss, Jedediah. *Make Me a Map of the Valley: The Civil War Journal of Stonewall Jackson's Topographer.* Edited by Archie P. McDonald. Dallas, Tex.: Southern Methodist University Press, 1973.

Ingraham, Joseph H. *The Southwest By a Yankee.* 2 vols. New York: Harper & Brothers, 1835.

Johnston, Joseph E. *Narrative of Military Operations, Directed, During the Late War Between the States.* New York: D. Appleton and Co., 1874.

Jones, Anson. *Memoranda and Official Correspondence Relating to the Republic of Texas, Its History and Annexation, Including a Brief Autobiography of the Author.* New York: D. Appleton and Company, 1859.

Jones, John B. *A Rebel War Clerk's Diary at the Confederate State Capitol.* 2 vols. Philadelphia, Pa.: J. B. Lippincott & Co., 1866.

Keiley, Antony M. *Prisoner of War, or Five Months Among the Yankees. Being a Narrative of the Crosses, Calamities, and Consolations of a Petersburg Militiaman During an Enforced Summer Residence North.* Richmond, Va.: West & Johnson, 1865.

Kendall, George Wilkins. *Letters From a Texas Sheep Ranch: Written in the Years 1860 and 1867 by George Wilkins Kendall to Henry Stephens Randall.* Edited by Harry James Brown. Urbana: University of Illinois Press, 1959.

Kennedy, John Pendleton. *Mr. Ambrose's Letters on the Rebellion.* New York: Hurd & Houghton, 1865.

Lane, Walter. *The Adventures and Recollections of General Walter P. Lane, a San Jacinto Veteran; Containing Sketches of the Texan, Mexican, and Late Wars, with Several Indian Fights Thrown In.* Edited by Mary Jane Lane. Marshall, Tex.: News Messenger Publication Company, 1928.

LeGrand, Julia. *The Journal of Julia LeGrand, New Orleans, 1862–1863.* Edited by Kate Rowland and Agnes Croxall. Richmond, Va.: Everett Waddey Co., 1911.

Lines, Amelia Akehurst. *To Raise Myself a Little: The Diaries and Letters of Jennie, A Georgia Teacher, 1851–1886.* Edited by Thomas Dyer. Athens: University of Georgia Press, 1982.

Longstreet, James. *From Manassas to Appomattox: Memoirs of the Civil War in America.* Philadelphia, Pa.: J. B. Lippincott & Co., 1896.

Loughborough, Mary Ann Webster. *My Cave Life in Vicksburg, With Letters of Trial and Travel.* New York: D. Appleton & Co., 1864

Montgomery, Frank A. *Reminiscences in Peace and War.* Cincinnati: Robert Clarke Company Press, 1901.

Osterhout, Charles Hotchkiss. *Stonewall Jackson's Map-Maker(Jed Hotchkiss): Excerpts From His Letters and Papers.* s.l.: s.n., 1977.

Owen, William. *In Camp and Battle with the Washington Artillery of New Orleans. A Narrative of Events of the Late Civil War from Bull Run to Appomattox and Spanish Fort.* Boston: Ticknor & Co., 1885.

Pasco, Samuel. *Private Pasco: A Civil War Diary.* Edited by William Pasco. Oak Brook, Ill.: McAdams Multigraphies, 1990.

Patterson, Edmund DeWitt. *Yankee Rebel: The Civil War Journal of Edmund DeWitt Patterson.* Edited by John G. Barrett. Knoxville: University of Tennessee Press, 2004.

Pease, Lucadia. *Lucadia Pease & the Governor: Letters 1850–1857.* Edited by Katherine Hart and Elizabeth Kemp. Austin, Tex.: The Encino Press, 1974.

Perry, B. F. and Hext M. Perry. *Reminiscences of Public Men.* Philadelphia, Pa.: J. D. Avill and Company, 1883.

Pryor, S. G. *A Post of Honor: The Pryor Letters, 1861–63, Letters from Capt. S. G. Pryor, Twelfth Georgia Regiment and his wife, Penelope Tyson Pryor.* Edited by Charles R. Adams, Jr. Fort Valley, Ga.: Garret Publications Inc., 1989.

Putnam, Sally Brock. *Richmond During the War: Four Years of Personal Observation.* New York: G. W. Carleton & Co., 1867.

Quintard, Charles T. *Doctor Quintard Chaplain C.S.A. and Second Bishop of Tennessee: The Memoir and Civil War Diary of Charles Todd Quintard.* Edited by Sam Davis Elliott. Baton Rouge: Louisiana State University Press, 2003.

Record of the Testimony and Proceedings, in the Matter of the Investigation by the Trustees of the University of Mississippi, on the 1st and 2nd of March, 1860, of the Charges Made by H. R. Branham, Against the Chancellor of the University. Jackson, Miss.: The Mississippian Office, 1860.

Richardson, James D., compiler. *A Compilation of the Messages and Papers of the Confederacy, Including the Diplomatic Correspondence, 1861–1865.* Nashville, Tenn.: United States Publishing Company, 1905.

Robinson, Calvin L. *A Yankee in a Confederate Town: The Journal of Calvin L. Robinson.* Edited by Anne Robinson Clancy. Sarasota, Fla.: Pineapple Press Inc., 2002.

Russell, William. *My Diary North and South.* T.O.H.P: Burnham, 1863.

Sangston, Lawrence. *Bastilles of the North.* Baltimore, Md.: Kelly, Hedian, and Piet, 1863.

Seabury, Caroline. *The Diary of Caroline Seabury, 1854–1863.* Edited by Suzanne Bunkers. Madison: University of Wisconsin Press, 1991.

Sheridan, Philip. *Personal Memoirs of P. H. Sheridan, General United States Army.* New York: C. L. Webster, 1888.

Sherman, William T. *Memoirs of General William T. Sherman by Himself.* Bloomington: Indiana University Press, 1957.

Sinkler, Emily Wharton. *Between North and South: The Letters of Emily Wharton Sinkler 1842–1865.* Edited by Anne Sinkler Whaley LeClercq. Columbia: University of South Carolina Press, 2001.

Smith, Ralph J. *Reminiscences of the Civil War, and Other Sketches.* Waco, Tex.: W. M. Morrison, 1911.

Speech of the Hon. T. Butler King, Delivered in the Hall of the House of Representatives, at Milledgeville, GA., November 10th, 1863. Milledgeville, Ga.: Doughton, Nisbet, Barnes & Moore, State Printers, 1863.

Speech of Mr. Ashbel Smith, on the Public Debt Bill. Delivered in the House of Representatives of the State of Texas, December 11th, 1855. Austin, Tex.: State Times Job Office, 1856.

State of Georgia, Message of His Excellency Benjamin Conley, Governor. Atlanta, GA., January 11, 1872. Atlanta, Ga.: New Era Steam Printing Establishment, 1872.

Strode, Hudson, ed. *Jefferson Davis: Private Letters 1823–1889*. New York: Harcourt Brace Jovanovich, 1966.

Taylor, Richard. *Destruction and Reconstruction: Personal Experiences of the Last War*. New York: D. Appleton and Company, 1864.

U.S. Census Office. *Statistics of the United States (Including Mortality, Property, &c.,) in 1860; Compiled from the Original Returns and Being the Final Exhibit of the Eighth Census, Under the Direction of the Secretary of the Interior*. Washington, D.C.: Government Printing Office, 1866.

Velazquez, Loreta. *The Woman in Battle: A Narrative of the Exploits, Adventures, and Travels of Madame Loreta Janeta Velazquez, Otherwise Known As Lieut. Harry T. Buford, Confederate States Army*. Edited by C. J. Worthington. Hartford, Conn.: T. Belknap, 1876.

Walker, Georgiana G. *Private Journal of Georgiana Gholson Walker, 1862–1865, with Selections from the Post War Years, 1865–1876*. Edited by Dwight Henderson. Tuscaloosa, Ala.: Confederate Publishing, 1963.

Watkins, Samuel. *Company Aytch*. Chattanooga, Tenn.: Time Printing Company, 1900.

Welles, Gideon. *Diary of Gideon Welles, Secretary of the Navy Under Lincoln and Johnson*. Edited by Edgar Welles. Boston: Houghton, Mifflin and Co., 1911.

Wharton, Thomas K. *Queen of the South: New Orleans, 1853–1862, The Journal of Thomas K. Wharton*. Edited by Samuel Wilson, Jr. New Orleans: Historic New Orleans Collection and New York Public Library, 1999.

Worth, Jonathan, *The Correspondence of Jonathan Worth*. 2 vols. Edited by Joseph Hamilton. Raleigh: Edwards & Broughton, 1909.

Secondary Sources

Books and Articles

Allardice, Bruce. *More Generals in Gray*. Baton Rouge: Louisiana State University Press, 1995.

Alden, Carroll, and George Perkins. *George Hamilton Perkins, Commodore, U.S.N.: His Life and Letters*. Boston: Houghton, Mifflin, & Co., 1914.

Anderson, Benedict. *Imagined Communities: Reflections on the Origin and Spread of Nationalism*. New York: Verso, c. 1983, 1991.

Andrews, J. Cutler. *The South Reports the Civil War*. Princeton: Princeton University Press, 1970.

Avirett, James B., ed. *The Memoirs of General Turner Ashby and His Compeers*. Baltimore: Selby & Dulany, 1867.

Ayers, Edward. *In the Presence of Mine Enemies: War in the Heart of America, 1859–1863.* New York: W. W. Norton, 2003.

———. *The Promise of the New South: Life After Reconstruction.* New York: Oxford University Press, 1992.

Baggett, James Alex. *The Scalawags: Southern Dissenters in the Civil War and Reconstruction.* Baton Rouge: Louisiana State University Press, 2003.

Baker, Nina Brown. *Texas Yankee: The Story of Gail Borden.* New York: Harcourt, Brace and Company, 1955.

Baker, Virgil L. "Albert Pike: Citizen Speechmaker of Arkansas." *Arkansas Historical Quarterly* 10 (Summer 1951): 138–56.

Ballard, Michael B. *Pemberton: The General Who Lost Vicksburg.* Jackson: University of Mississippi Press, 1999.

Barney, William L. *Battleground for the Union: The Era of the Civil War and Reconstruction 1848–1877.* Englewood Cliffs, N.J.: Prentice-Hall, 1990.

Bean, W. G. "The Unusual War Experience of Lieutenant George G. Junkin, C.S.A." *Virginia Magazine of History and Biography* 76 (May 1968): 181-190.

Bell, John. *Confederate Seadog: John Taylor Wood in War and Exile.* Jefferson, N.C.: McFarland & Company, Inc., 2002.

Benedict, Michael Les. *The Fruits of Victory: Alternatives in Restoring the Union.* Philadelphia, Pa.: Lippincott, 1975.

Berkeley, Edmund, and Dorothy Smith Berkeley. *A Yankee Botanist in the Carolinas: The Reverend Moses Ashley Curtis, D.D. (1808–1872).* Berlin, Pa.: J. Cramer, 1986.

Berlin, Ira. *Generations of Captivity: A History of African-American Slaves.* Cambridge, Mass.: Belknap Press of Harvard University Press, 2003.

Bernath, Michael T. *Confederate Minds: The Struggle for Intellectual Independence in the Civil War South.* Chapel Hill: University of North Carolina Press, 2010.

Binkley, William C. "The South and the West." *Journal of Southern History* 17 (February 1951): 5-22.

Black, Robert C., and Gary W. Gallagher. *The Railroads of the Confederacy.* Chapel Hill: University of North Carolina Press, 1998.

Blair, William. *Cities of the Dead: Contesting the Memory of the Civil War in the South, 1865–1914.* Chapel Hill: University of North Carolina, 2004.

Blair, William, and William Pencack, eds. *Making and Remaking Pennsylvania's Civil War.* University Park: Pennsylvania State University Press, 2001.

Bleser, Carol, and Lesley Gordon, eds. *Intimate Strategies of the Civil War: Military Commanders and Their Wives.* New York: Oxford University Press, 2001.

Blevins, Bill. *Albert Pike, 1809–1891.* Pangburn, Ark.: Tumbling Shoals Publishing Company, 2005.

Blight, David W. *Race and Reunion: The Civil War in American Memory.* Cambridge, Mass.: Belknap Press of Harvard University Press, 2001.

Blumin, Stuart M. *The Emergence of the Middle Class: Social Experience in the American City, 1760–1900.* New York: Cambridge University Press, 1989.

Boman, Dennis. *Abiel Leonard, Yankee Slaveholder, Eminent Jurist, and Passionate Unionist.* New York: Edwin Mellen Press, 2002.

Bonner, Robert E. *Mastering America: Southern Slaveholders and the Crisis of American Nationhood.* New York: Cambridge University Press, 2009.

Brazy, Martha Jane. *An American Planter: Stephen Duncan of Antebellum Natchez and New York.* Baton Rouge: Louisiana State University Press, 2006.

Brundage, W. Fitzhugh. *The Southern Past: A Clash of Race and Memory.* Cambridge, Mass.: Belknap Press of Harvard University Press, 2005.

Bryan, Jimmy, Jr. *More Zeal Than Discretion: The Westward Adventures of Walter P. Lane.* College Station: Texas A&M University Press, 2008.

Burnett, Arthur C. *Yankees in the Republic of Texas, Some Notes on their Origin and Impact.* Houston, Tex.: Anson Jones Press, 1952.

Burton, John Michael. *Gracie's Alabama Volunteers: The History of the Fifty-Ninth Alabama Volunteer Regiment.* Gretna, La.: Pelican Publishing Company, 2003.

Butler, Mildred Allen. *Actress in Spite of Herself: The Life of Anna Cora Mowatt.* New York: Funk & Wagnalls Company, Inc., 1966.

Campbell, Jacqueline Glass. *When Sherman Marched North From the Sea: Resistance on the Confederate Home Front.* Chapel Hill: University of North Carolina Press, 2003.

Carter, Dan. *When the War Was Over: The Failure of Self-Reconstruction in the South 1865–1867.* Baton Rouge: Louisiana State University Press, 1985.

Casey, Powell A. *The Story of Camp Moore and Life at Camp Moore Among the Volunteers.* FPHC, Inc., 1985.

Cash, W. J. *The Mind of the South.* New York: Vintage Books, 1941.

Casteevens, Frances. *George W. Alexander and Castle Thunder: A Confederate Prison and Its Commandant.* Jefferson, N.C.: McFarland & Company, 2004.

Catherwood, T. B. *The Life and Labors of William W. Wadley, with an Account of the Wadley Memorial Association, and the Ceremony of Unveiling the Statue.* Savannah, Ga.: Morning News Steam Printing House, 1885.

Chenault, William W., and Robert C. Reinders. "The Northern-born Community of New Orleans in the 1850s." *Journal of American History* 51 (September 1964): 232-247.

Cobb, Jacob. *The Most Southern Place on Earth: The Mississippi Delta and the Roots of Regional Identity.* New York: Oxford University Press, 1992.

Coulter, E. Merton. *William Montague Browne, Versatile Anglo-Irish American, 1823–1883.* Athens: University of Georgia Press, 1967.

Crofts, Daniel. *Reluctant Confederates: Upper South Unionists in the Secession Crisis.* Chapel Hill: University of North Carolina Press, 1989.

Cummings, Charles M. *Yankee Quaker, Confederate General: the Curious Career of Bushrod Rust Johnson.* Rutherford, N.J.: Fairleigh Dickinson University Press, 1971.

Current, Richard Nelson. *Arguing With Historians: Essays on the Historical and the Unhistorical.* Middletown, Conn.: Wesleyan University Press, 1987.

———. *Lincoln's Loyalists: Union Soldiers from the Confederacy.* Boston: Northeastern University Press, 1992.

Cuthbert, Norma B., and O. T. Hammond. "Yankee Preacher-Teacher in Florida, 1838." *Huntington Library Quarterly* 8 (November 1944): 95-104.

Cyclopedia of Eminent and Representative Men of the Carolinas of the Nineteenth Century, Volume II. c.1892; Spartanburg, S.C.: Reprint Company, 1972.

Dalzell, Robert F., Jr. *Daniel Webster and the Trial of American Nationalism, 1843–1852.* Boston: Houghton Mifflin Company, 1973.

Dangerfield, George. *The Awakening of American Nationalism, 1815–1828.* New York: Harper and Row, 1965.

Davidson, Donald. *Regionalism and Nationalism in the United States: The Attack on the Leviathan.* New Brunswick, Maine: Transaction Publishers, 1991.

Davies, Caroline S. "A Yankee in the South in 1833." *New England Quarterly* 10 (March and June 1937): 63-83, 270-289.

Davis, William C., and Julie Hoffman. *The Confederate General.* 6 vols. Harrisburg, Pa.: National Historical Society, 1991.

Dawson, Jan C. "The Puritan and the Cavalier: The South's Perception of Contrasting Traditions." *Journal of Southern History* 44 (November 1978): 597–660.

Degler, Carl N. *Place Over Time: The Continuity of Southern Distinctiveness.* Baton Rouge: Louisiana State University Press, 1977.

———. "Thesis, Antithesis, Synthesis: The South, the North, and the Nation." *Journal of Southern History* 53 (February 1987): 3-18.

Desjardin, Thomas A. *These Honored Dead: How the Story of Gettysburg Shaped American Memory.* Cambridge, Mass.: Da Capo Press, 2003.

Diamond, Jared. *Guns, Germs, and Steel: The Fates of Human Societies.* New York: W. W. Norton & Company, 1999.

Dibble, Ernest F. *Ante-bellum Pensacola and the Military Presence, The Pensacola Series Commemorating the American Revolution Bicentennial.* 3 vols. Pensacola, Fla.: Mayes Printing Company, 1974.

Dirck, Brian R. *Lincoln & Davis: Imagining America, 1809–1865.* Lawrence: University Press of Kansas, 2001.

Donald, David Herbert, Jean Baker, and Michael F. Holt. *The Civil War and Reconstruction.* New York: Norton, 2001.

Donovan, Timothy, and Willard Gatewood. *The Governors of Arkansas: Essays in Political Biography*. Fayetteville: University of Arkansas Press, 1981.

Duncan, Robert Lipscomb. *Reluctant General: Life and Times of Albert Pike*. New York: Dutton, 1961.

Duncan, Russell. *Entrepreneur for Equality: Governor Rufus Bullock, Commerce, and Race in Post–Civil War Georgia*. Athens: University of Georgia Press, 1994.

Dunn, Durwood. *An Abolitionist in the Appalachian South: Ezekiel Birdseye in Slavery, Capitalism, and Separate Statehood in East Tennessee, 1841–1846*. Knoxville: University of Tennessee Press, 1997.

Eaton, Clement. *The Freedom-of-Thought Struggle in the Old South*. New York: Harper Torchbooks, 1964.

Eggleston, George Cary. *Life in Early Indiana*. Fort Wayne, Ind.: Public Library of Fort Wayne and Allen County, 1953.

Escott, Paul D. *After Secession: Jefferson Davis and the Failure of Confederate Nationalism*. Baton Rouge: Louisiana State University Press, 1978.

Fahs, Alice, and Joan Waugh, eds. *The Memory of the Civil War in American Culture*. Chapel Hill: University of North Carolina Press, 2004.

Faust, Drew. *The Creation of Confederate Nationalism: Ideology and Identity in the Civil War South*. Baton Rouge: Louisiana State University Press, 1988.

Fehrenbacher, Don E., ed. *History and American Society: Essays of David M. Potter*. New York: Oxford University Press, 1973.

Foner, Eric. *Free Soil, Free Labor, Free Men: The Ideology of the Republican Party Before the Civil War*. New York: Oxford University Press, 1970.

———. *Reconstruction: America's Unfinished Revolution, 1863–1877*. New York: Harper and Row, 1988.

Fox-Genovese, Elizabeth, and Eugene Genovese. *The Mind of the Master Class: History and Faith in the Southern Slaveholder's Worldview*. New York: Cambridge University Press, 2005.

Frantz, Joe. *Gail Borden: Dairyman to a Nation*. Norman: University of Oklahoma Press, 1951.

Freehling, William. *The Road to Disunion: Secessionists at Bay ,1776–1854*. New York: Oxford University Press, 1990.

———. *Road to Disunion: Secessionists Triumphant, 1854–1861*. New York: Oxford University Press, 2007.

———. *The South vs. the South: How Anti-Confederate Southerners Shaped the Course of the Civil War*. New York: Oxford University Press, 2001.

French, Samuel G. *Two Wars: An Autobiography of Gen. Samuel G. French, An Officer in the Armies of the United States and the Confederate States, A Graduate from the U.S. Military Academy, West Point 1843. Mexican War; War Between* the States, A Diary; Reconstruction Period, His Experience; Incidents, Reminiscences, Etc. Nashville, Tenn.: Confederate Veteran, 1901.

Fulton, John, and Margaret Barnard, eds. *Memoirs of Frederick A. P. Barnard, Tenth President of Columbia College in the City of New York.* New York: MacMillan and Co., 1896.

Gallagher, Gary W. *The Confederate War.* Cambridge, Mass.: Harvard University Press, 1997.

———. *Causes Won, Lost, and Forgotten: How Hollywood and Popular Art Shape What We Know About the Civil War.* Chapel Hill: University of North Carolina Press, 2008.

———. *Lee and His Generals in War and Memory.* Baton Rouge: Louisiana State University Press, 1998.

Gallagher, Gary W., and Alan Nolan, eds. *The Myth of the Lost Cause and Civil War History.* Bloomington: Indiana University Press, 2000.

Gallagher, Gary W., and Joseph Glatthaar, eds. *Leaders of the Lost Cause: New Perspectives on the Confederate High Command.* Mechanicsburg, Penn.: Stackpole Books, 2004.

Gambrell, Herbert. *Anson Jones: The Last President of Texas.* Austin: University of Texas Press, 1964.

Gara, Larry. "A New Englander's View of Plantation Life: Letters of Edwin Hall to Cyrus Woodman, 1837." *Journal of Southern History* 18 (August 1952): 343-354.

Genovese, Eugene. *Roll Jordan Roll: The World the Slaves Made.* New York: Vintage Books, 1976.

Gerster, Patrick, and Nicholas Cords. "The Northern Origins of Southern Mythology." *Journal of Southern History* 43 (November 1977): 567-582.

Glass, Mary Morgan Ward, ed. *Connecticut Yankee in Early Alabama: Juliet Bestor Coleman, 1833–1850.* Alabama: National Society of Colonial Dames of America in the State of Alabama, 1980.

Gleeson, Ed. *Illinois Rebels: A Civil War Unit History of G Company 15th Tennessee Regiment Volunteer Infantry.* Carmel, Ind.: Guild Press of Indiana, 1996.

Governor Joseph Johnson of Virginia: A Brief Sketch of His Life and Character. Baltimore, Md.: John H. Foster's Steam Printing and Publishing House, 1877.

Gower, Herschel. *Charles Dahlgren of Natchez: The Civil War and Dynastic Decline.* Washington, D.C.: Brassey's Inc., 2002.

Grant, Susan-Mary. *North Over South: Northern Nationalism and American Identity in the Antebellum Era.* Lawrence: University Press of Kansas, 2000.

Grant, Susan-Mary, and Peter Parish, eds. *Legacy of Disunion: The Enduring Significance of the American Civil War.* Baton Rouge: Louisiana State University Press, 2003.

Green, Arthur. *Gracie's Pride: The 43rd Alabama Infantry Volunteers.* Shippensburg, Pa.: Burd Street Press, 2001.

Green, Fletcher. *The Role of the Yankee in the Old South.* Athens: University of Georgia Press, 1972.

Hagler, Gould B., Jr. "Yankees in Grey: John C. Pemberton, C.S.A. A Series Concurring Northern Born Men Who Fought for the Southern Confederacy." *Confederate Veteran* 5 (2001): 12-13.

Hall, D. D. "A Yankee Tutor in the Old South." *New England Quarterly* 33 (March 1960): 82-91.

Hattaway, Herman, and Richard E. Beringer. *Jefferson Davis, Confederate President.* Lawrence: University of Kansas Press, 2002.

Heartsill, William. *Fourteen Hundred and Ninety-One Days in the Confederate Army: A Journal Kept by W.W. Heartsill, For Four Years, One Month, and One Day, or Camp-Life: Day-by Day, of the W. P. Lane Rangers, from April 19th, 1861, to May 20th, 1865.* Edited by Bell Wiley. Wilmington, N.C.: Broadfoot Publishing, c. 1992.

Hentz, Caroline Lee. *The Planter's Northern Bride.* Philadelphia, Pa.: T. B. Peterson and Brothers, 1870.

Hilldrup, Robert LeRoy. "Cold War Against the Yankees in the Antebellum Literature of Southern Women." *The North Carolina Historical Review* 31 (July 1954): 370-384.

Hinsdale, John W. *History of the Seventy-Second Regiment of the North Carolina Troops, in the War Between the States, 1861–'65.* Goldsboro, N.C.: Nash Brothers Book and Job Printers.

Holt, Michael F. *The Rise and Fall of the American Whig Party: Jacksonian Politics and the Onset of the Civil War.* New York: Oxford University Press, 1999.

Howe, Daniel Walker. *What Hath God Wrought: The Transformation of America, 1815–1848.* New York: Oxford University Press, 2007.

———. "A Massachusetts Yankee in Senator Calhoun's Court: Samuel Gilman in South Carolina." *New England Quarterly* 44 (June 1971): 197-220.

Hughes, Nathaniel Cheairs. *Yale's Confederates: A Biographical Dictionary.* Knoxville: University of Tennessee Press, 2008.

Hutchinson, Jack T. *Divided Loyalties: The Border States of the Upper South, Delaware-Maryland-West Virginia-Kentucky and Missouri, Their Cultural Heritage and Divided Civil War Loyalties.* Loganville, Ga.: Jack Hutchinson and Signature Printing, 2005.

Ingraham, J. H., ed. *The Sunny South: or, the Southerner at Home, Embracing Five Year's Experience of a Northern Governess in the Land of the Sugar and the Cotton.* 1860; reprint New York: Negro University Presses, 1968.

James, D. Clayton. *Antebellum Natchez.* Baton Rouge: Louisiana State University Press, 1968.

Johnson, Norman K. "Yankees in Gray: A Myriad of Reasons—Some Professional, others Personal—Impelled 30 Northern-Born Soldiers to Become Generals for the South. With Few Exceptions, They Served Valorously and Unselfishly for the Southern Cause." *American Civil War* 5 (September 1992): 38-44, 64.

Joslyn, Mauriel Phillips, ed. *Confederate Women.* Gretna, La.: Pelican Publishing Company, 2004.

Kendall, John S. "George Wilkins Kendall and the Founding of the New Orleans 'Picayune.'" *The Louisiana Historical Quarterly* (April 1928): 261-285.

Kersh, Rogan. *Dreams of a More Perfect Union.* Ithaca: Cornell University Press, 2001.

Kousser, J. Morgan, and James M. McPherson, eds. *Region, Race and Reconstruction.* New York: Oxford University Press, 1982.

Krick, Robert E. L. *Staff Officers in Gray: A Biographical Register of the Staff Officers in the Army of Northern Virginia.* Chapel Hill: University of North Carolina Press, 2003.

———. *Lee's Colonels: A Biographical Register of the Field Officers of the Army of Northern Virginia.* Dayton, Ohio: Press of Morningside Bookshop, 1979.

Lander, Ernest McPherson, Jr. *The Calhoun Family and Thomas Green Clemson: The Decline of a Southern Patriarchy.* Columbia: University of South Carolina Press, 1983.

Lavin, Marilyn. *William Bostwick: Connecticut Yankee in Antebellum Georgia.* New York: Arno Press, 1978.

Loewen, James W. *Lies Across America: What Our Historic Sites Get Wrong.* New York: Simon & Schuster, 1999.

———. *Lies My Teacher Told Me: Everything Your American History Textbook Got Wrong.* New York: Simon & Schuster, 1995.

Mansfield, Joseph J. *Life and Achievements of Gail Borden. Speech in the House of Representatives January 11, 1930.* Washington, D.C.: Government Printing Office, 1930.

Martinez, Michael, William Richardson, and Ron McNinch-Su, eds. *Confederate Symbols in the Contemporary South.* Tallahassee: University of Florida Press, 2000.

Masur, Louis P. *1831: Year of Eclipse.* New York: Hill and Wang, 2001.

McCardell, John. *The Idea of a Southern Nation: Southern Nationalists and Southern Nationalism, 1830–1860.* New York: W. W. Norton & Company, 1979.

McClintock, Russell. *Lincoln and the Decision for War: The Northern Response to Secession.* Chapel Hill: University of North Carolina Press, 2008.

McLure, Mary Lilla. *Louisiana Leaders, 1830–1860.* Shreveport, La.: Journal Printing Co., 1935.

McDonald, Archie P., ed. *"To Live and Die in Dixie": How the South Formed a Nation.* Murfreesboro, Tenn.: Southern Heritage Press, 1999.

McPherson, James M. *Battle Cry of Freedom: The Civil War Era.* New York: Oxford University Press, 1988.

———. *For Cause and Comrades: Why Men Fought in the Civil War.* New York: Oxford University Press, 1997.

———. "Was Blood Thicker than Water? Ethnic and Civic Nationalism in the American Civil War." *Proceedings of the American Philosophical Society* 143 (March 1999): 102-108.

McPherson, James M., and William Cooper, eds. *Writing the Civil War: The Quest to Understand.* Columbia: University of South Carolina Press, 1998.

Miller, James D. *South by Southwest: Planter Emigration and Identity in the Slave South* Charlottesville: University of Virginia Press, 2002.

Nash, Charles Edward. *Biographical Sketches of Gen. Pat Cleburne and Gen. T. C. Hindman, Together with Humorous Anecdotes and Reminiscences of the Late Civil War.* Dayton, Ohio: Morningside Bookshop, 1977.

National Academy of Sciences of the United States of America. *Biographical Memoirs, Vol. XX.* Washington, D.C.: National Academy of Sciences, 1939.

Neff, John R. *Honoring the Civil War Dead: Commemoration and the Problem of Reconciliation.* Lawrence: University Press of Kansas, 2005.

Oakes, James. *The Ruling Race: A History of American Slaveholders.* New York: W. W. Norton & Company, 1998.

Osterweis, Rollin G. *Romanticism and Nationalism in the Old South.* New Haven: Yale University Press, 1949.

Parish, Peter, Adam I. Smith, and Susan-Mary Grant, eds. *The North and the Nation in the Era of the Civil War.* New York: Fordham University Press, 2003.

Pemberton, John. *Pemberton, Defender of Vicksburg.* Chapel Hill: University of North Carolina Press, 1942.

Perman, Michael. *Reunion Without Compromise: The South and Reconstruction, 1865–1868.* Cambridge: Cambridge University Press, 1973.

———. *Emancipation and Reconstruction.* Wheeling, Ill.: Harlan Davidson, 2003.

Pessen, Edward. "How Different From Each Other Were the Antebellum North and South?" *American Historical Review* 85 (December 1980): 1119-1149.

Phillips, Christopher. *Missouri's Confederate: Claiborne Fox Jackson and the Creation of Southern Identity in the Border West.* Columbia, Mo.: University of Missouri Press, 2000.

Pollard, Edward. *The Lost Cause.* New York: Gramercy Books, 1994.

Poole, Robert. *Thomas G. Clemson: His Influence in Developing Land-Grant Colleges.* Princeton, N.J.: Newcomen Pub., 1957.

Potter, David M. *The Impending Crisis, 1848–1861: Completed and Edited by Don E. Fehrenbacher.* New York: Harper & Row, 1976.

Power, Richard Lyle. "A Crusade to Extend Yankee Culture 1820–1865." *New England Quarterly* 13 (December 1940): 638-653.

Prentiss, George Lewis, ed. *A Memoir of S. S. Prentiss.* 2 vols. New York: Charles Scribner's Sons, 1891.

Pryor, Elizabeth Brown. "An Anomalous Person: The Northern Tutor in Plantation Society, 1773–1860." *Journal of Southern History* 47 (August 1981): 363-392.

Raab, James W., and John McGlone, eds. *A Dual Biography: Lloyd Tilghman and Francis Asbury Shoup, Two Forgotten Confederate Generals.* Murfreesboro, Tenn.: Southern Heritage Press, 2001.

Ritter, Charles F., and John Wakelyn. *American Legislative Leaders, 1850–1910.* New York: Greenwood Press, 1989.

Robertson, James I., Jr. *Stonewall Jackson: The Man, The Soldier, The Legend.* New York: Macmillan Publishing USA, 1997.

Roper, Peter. *Jedediah Hotchkiss: Rebel Mapmaker and Virginia Businessman.* Shippensburg, Pa.: White Mane Publishing Co., 1992.

Roshwald, Aviel. *The Endurance of Nationalism: Ancient Roots and Modern Dilemmas.* New York: Cambridge University Press, 2006.

Rousey, Dennis C. "Friends and Foes of Slavery: Foreigners and Northerners in the Old South." *Journal of Social History* 35 (Winter 2001): 373–96.

Rubin, Anne Sarah. *A Shattered Nation: The Rise & Fall of the Confederacy, 1861–1868.* Chapel Hill: University of North Carolina Press, 2005.

Ryan, Mary P. *Cradle of the Middle Class: The Family in Oneida County, New York, 1790–1865.* New York: Cambridge University Press, 1981.

Seager, Robert, II. *And Tyler Too: A Biography of John & Julia Gardiner Tyler.* New York: McGraw-Hill Book Company, 1963.

Sears, Louis Martin. *John Slidell.* Durham, N.C.: Duke University Press, 1925.

———. "A Confederate Diplomat at the Court of Napoleon III." *American Historical Review* 26 (January 1921): 255-281.

Sheehan-Dean, Aaron. *Why Confederates Fought: Family and Nation in Civil War Virginia.* Chapel Hill: University of North Carolina Press, 2007.

Sheriff, Carol. *The Artificial River: The Erie Canal and the Paradox of Progress 1817–1862.* New York: Hill and Wang, 1996.

Shields, Joseph D. *The Life and Times of Seargent Smith Prentiss.* Philadelphia, Pa.: J. B. Lippincott, 1884.

Silber, Nina. *The Romance of Reunion: Northerners and the South, 1865–1900.* Chapel Hill: University of North Carolina Press, 1993.

Silverthorne, Elizabeth. *Ashbel Smith of Texas: Pioneer, Patriot, Statesman, 1805–1886.* College Station: Texas A&M University Press, 1982.

Slate, Frederick. *Biographical Memoir of Eugene Woldemar Hilgard, 1833–1916.* City of Washington: National Academy of Sciences, 1919.

Smith, Anthony D. *The Ethnic Origins of Nations.* Oxford: Basil Blackwell Ltd., 1986.

Smith, Eugene A. "Memorial of Eugene Woldemar Hilgard." Reprinted from the *Bulletin of the Geological Society of America* 28 (March 1917): 40-67.

Smith, John I. *The Courage of a Southern Unionist: A Biography of Isaac Murphy, Governor of Arkansas, 1864–68.* Little Rock: Rose Publishing Co., 1979.

Snay, Mitchell. *Fenians, Freedmen, and Southern Whites: Race and Nationality in the Era of Reconstruction.* Baton Rouge: Louisiana State University Press, 2007.

Sobel, Robert, and John Raimo, eds. *Biographical Directory of the Governors of the United States, 1789–1978.* 4 vols. Westport, Conn.: Meckler Books, 1978.

Speer, William S. *Sketches of Prominent Tennesseans, Containing Biographies and Records of Many of the Families Who Have Attained Prominence in Tennessee.* Easily, S.C.: Southern Historical Press, 1978.

Stampp, Kenneth. *The Era of Reconstruction, 1865–1877.* New York: Knopf, 1965.

Streissguth, Thomas, ed. *The Civil War: The South.* San Diego, Calif.: Greenhaven Press, Inc., 2001.

Strong, Michael. *Keystone Confederate: The Life and Times of General Johnson Kelly Duncan, C.S.A.* York, Pa.: The Historical Society of York County, 1994.

Sumners, Cecil. *The Governors of Mississippi.* Gretna, La.: Pelican Publishing Company, 1980.

Sutherland, Daniel. "Former Confederates in the Post–Civil War North: An Unexplored Aspect of Reconstruction History." *Journal of Southern History* 47 (August 1981): 393-410.

———. "Southern Fraternal Organizations in the North." *Journal of Southern History* 53 (November 1987): 587-612.

Sutherland, Daniel, ed. *Guerrillas, Unionists and Violence on the Confederate Home Front.* Fayetteville: University of Arkansas Press, 1999.

Sydnor, Charles S. *The Development of Southern Sectionalism, 1819–1848.* Baton Rouge: Louisiana State University Press, 1948.

Tarrant, S. F. H. *Hon. Daniel Pratt, a Biography, with Eulogies on his Life and Character.* Richmond: Whittet & Shepperson, 1904.

Taylor, William. *Cavalier and Yankee: The Old South and American National Character.* Cambridge: Harvard University Press, 1979.

Tazewell, C. W., ed. *Major Edmund Bradford, U. S. Army and Confederate States Army.* Virginia Beach: W. S. Dawson Co., 1994.

Temple, Oliver Perry, and Mary Temple. *Notable Men of Tennessee, From 1833–1875, Their Times and Their Contemporaries.* New York: The Cosmopolitan Press, 1912.

Thomas, Emory M. *The Confederate Nation: 1861–1865*. New York: Harper & Row, 1979.

Trimpi, Helen. *Crimson Confederates: Harvard Men Who Fought for the South*. Knoxville: University of Tennessee Press, 2010.

Trinity College Historical Society. *An Annual Publication of Historical Papers, Reconstruction, and State Biography*. 8 vols. Durham, N.C.: Trinity College Historical Society, 1897.

Turner, Frederick Jackson. *The United States, 1830–1850: The Nation and Its Sections*. New York: W. W. Norton & Company, 1935.

———. "New England, 1830–1850." *Huntington Library Bulletin* 1 (May 1931): 153–98.

Tyler, Lyon Gardiner, LL. D. *Encyclopedia of Virginia Biography*. 3 vols. New York: Lewis Historical Publishing Company, 1915.

Vandiver, Frank Everson. *Ploughshares Into Swords: Josiah Gorgas and Confederate Ordnance*. Austin: University of Texas Press, 1952.

Varon, Elizabeth R. *Disunion: The Coming of the American Civil War, 1789–1859*. Chapel Hill: University of North Carolina Press, 2008.

Wakelyn, Jon, with Frank Vandiver. *Biographical Dictionary of the Confederacy*. Westport, Conn.: Greenwood Press, 1977.

Waldstreicher, David. *In the Midst of Perpetual Fetes: The Making of American Nationalism, 1776–1820*. Chapel Hill: University of North Carolina Press, 1997.

Warner, Ezra, and W. Buck Yearns. *Biographical Register of the Confederate Congress*. Baton Rouge: Louisiana State University Press, 1975.

———. *Generals In Gray: Lives of the Confederate Commanders*. Baton Rouge: Louisiana State University, 1959.

Watson, Harry L. *Liberty and Power: The Politics of Jacksonian America*. New York: Hill and Wang, 1990.

Way, William. *History of the New England Society of Charleston, South Carolina, for One Hundred Years, 1819–1919*. Charleston: The Society, 1920.

Weathersby, Robert W. *J. H. Ingraham*. Boston: Twayne Publishers, 1980.

Wharton, Clarence R. *Gail Borden, Pioneer*. San Antonio: The Naylor Company, 1941.

Woodworth, Steven E. *Jefferson Davis and His Generals: The Failure of Confederate Command in the West*. Lawrence: University of Kansas Press, 1990.

Wright, William. *The Secession Movement in the Middle Atlantic States*. Rutherford, N.J.: Fairleigh Dickinson University Press, 1973.

Wood, John Sumner. *The Virginia Bishop: A Yankee Hero of the Confederacy*. Richmond, Va.: Garrett & Massie, Inc., 1961.

Zelinsky, Wilbur. *Nation Into State: The Shifting Symbolic Foundations of American Nationalism*. Chapel Hill: University of North Carolina Press, 1988.

Dissertations and Theses

Blanks, Viki Leigh. "Caroline Lee Hentz: Antebellum Author, Antebellum Woman." Master's thesis, University of West Florida, 1999.

Chute, William Joseph. "The Life of Frederick A. P. Barnard to His Election as President of Columbia College in 1864." PhD diss., Columbia University, 1951.

Evans, Curt John. "Daniel Pratt: Yankee Industrialist in the Antebellum South." Master's thesis, Louisiana State University, 1993.

Franzetti, Robert. "Elisha Marshall Pease and Reconstruction." Master's thesis, Southwest Texas State University, 1970.

Griffin, Roger Allen. "Connecticut Yankee in Texas: A Biography of Elisha Marshall Pease." PhD diss., University of Texas at Austin, 1973.

Koke, Harold J. "John Taylor Wood, Confederate States Navy." Master's thesis, Humboldt State College, 1963.

Lazerson, Marvin. "F. A. P. Barnard and Columbia College: 1864–1888." PhD diss., Columbia University, 1964.

Malloy, Sarah Brooke. "The Health of Our Family: The Correspondence of Amanda Beardsley Trulock, 1837–1868." Master's thesis, University of Arkansas, 2005.

Mason, J. Parker. "Henry Watson: Assimilation of a Yankee in the Land of Cotton." PhD diss., Duke University, 1983.

Miller, Benjamin Hillon. "Elisha Marshall Pease: A Biography." Master's thesis, University of Texas at Austin, 1927.

Prince, Sigsbee C., Jr. "Edward Aylsworth Perry Florida's Thirteen Governor." Master's thesis, University of Florida, 1949.

Rainer, Joseph. "The Honorable Fraternity of Moving Merchants: Yankee Peddlers in the Old South, 1800–1860." PhD diss., College of William and Mary, 2000.

Ritter, Charles. "The Press in Florida, Louisiana, and South Carolina and the End of Reconstruction, 1865–1877: Southern Men With Northern Interests." PhD diss., Catholic University of America, 1976.

Sanchez-Saavedra, Eugene M. "'The Beau Ideal of a Soldier': Brigadier General Charles Dimmock." Master's thesis, University of Richmond, 1971.

Shippey, Herbert Phinehas. "William Tappan Thompson, A Biography and Uncollected Fictional Writings." PhD diss., University of South Carolina, 1991.

Skubal, Gary. "Loyalty and the Army: A Study of Why the Civil War Generals Robert E. Lee, John Pemberton, Thomas Jackson, and Edwin Alexander Joined the Confederacy." Master's thesis, U.S. Army Command and General Staff College, 1995.

Takahashi, Setsuko. "Home of Their Choice: Samuel and Caroline Gilman in Antebellum Charleston, South Carolina." Master's thesis, University of North Carolina, 1981.

Tongate, Vicki Adams. "Transcendent Ties: A Northern Girl's Sojourn in Confederate Texas The Lucy Pier Stevens Diary." Master's thesis, Southern Methodist University, 2002.

Internet Sources

The American Civil War: Letters and Diaries. http://solomon.cwld.alexanderstreet.com.

http://trrcobb.blogspot.com/2011/07/southern-born-federal-generals-in-civil.html.

From the Letters of the Hotchkiss Family, 1861–1865, Augusta County Letters and Diaries, The War Years, The Valley of the Shadow: Two Communities in the Civil War, University of Virginia, Charlottesville. http://valley.lib.virginia.edu/papers/A2563.

http://www.encyclopediavirginia.org/Culp_s_Hill_and_Wesley_Culp_1839–1863.

http://www.infoplease.com/biography/us/congress/upson-christopher-columbus.html.

Index

abolitionists, 67, 80, 91, 125; adoptive southern attitudes toward, 82–83, 86–88, 95, 115–18, 197–99; native southern attitudes toward, 229, 233–34, 237, 239

adopted states, 2, 28, 45, 54, 60–65, 83, 126, 131–32, 186, 232, 246, 281–83, 295, 305–6; assimilation into, 39–42, 49–51, 64, 70, 96, 228–32, 244, 294; connections with, 10, 28, 39–41, 51, 57, 145–46, 153, 184, 205, 220, 300; protection of, 80, 119, 151, 162, 167, 172, 176–79, 183, 200, 205, 213, 237, 242, 306; ties through marriage, 33, 40–42, 61–63, 90, 101, 104–7, 168, 264

adoptive southerners: allegiance to adopted states, 29–32, 35–38, 41–42, 50–55, 58–63, 106–7, 126–29, 132–33, 163–65, 183, 205–7, 223, 242–43, 250, 279–83, 295–97, 305–9; allegiance to the Confederacy, 4–5, 101, 109–11, 119, 125–26, 129–33, 162–63, 170–74, 184, 187, 192, 200–201, 205, 208–10, 217, 221, 224–25; assimilation into southern society, 4, 39–42, 58–60, 65, 70, 77, 94–96, 191, 230, 237, 271–72, 276, 294–95; attachments to the South, 3, 39, 43, 48–56, 64, 118, 127, 136, 144, 147–48, 175, 224, 231, 282–83, 292–93; background, 17–18, 55–56, 83–85, 102–3, 135–37, 144–45, 149–50, 175, 180, 183, 212–15, 218–23, 251–53, 274–77; contrast to Copperheads, 12–13; definition of, 13; and identity formation of, 14–15, 45, 49–53, 56–57, 61–63, 80, 97, 102, 111, 114–16, 125, 128–29, 132, 171, 177, 200; initial impressions of the South, 22–32, 35–38, 58–61, 74–76, 112, 116; and the middle class, 20–21; motivations for moving to the South, 16–21, 24–42, 51, 57–62, 65–66, 89–90, 107–11, 122–24, 162–64, 175–77, 271–72; as northern emigrants to the South, 3, 6–7, 10, 15–21, 24–42, 45–51, 57–64, 107, 171, 229, 268; opposition to Republicans, 12, 120, 127, 276, 284; and secession crisis, 101–3, 106–12, 115–20, 125–33, 141–143, 146, 149; slave-owners, 27–29, 39–40, 59, 63, 70, 78, 89–92, 107–8, 113–115, 140, 147–49, 163–68, 272, 286, 288; views of free blacks and slaves, 6–8,

adoptive southerners (cont.)
11, 29, 39–40, 47, 63, 68–96, 99,
107–8, 141, 146–49, 163, 166–67,
189, 196; views of slavery, 65, 67–97,
107, 113, 118, 140, 144, 147

Adoptive Southern Unionists, 101, 119,
123–25, 135–44, 147–51, 238, 271–
73, 288, 297–98, 305; as conditional
unionists in the secession crisis, 114,
117, 123, 133, 182, 223

Alexander, George W., 159–60, 205–6,
285–86

Armstrong, Frank C., 158–59

Armstrong, George D., 80–81, 168–69,
174, 180

Atlanta, 158, 187, 213

Barnard, Frederick, 22, 32, 39–41,
117–18, 293; experiences at University of Mississippi, 52, 56, 62, 129,
147–48, 235

blacks, free and slave: *See* adoptive
southerners, views of free blacks and
slaves

Borden, Gail, 17, 22, 25, 41, 144, 288,
293

Border States: as compared to adoptive
southerners, 116, 140–41

Bullock, Rufus, 108, 170, 239, 288,
300–3

Burge, Dolly, 167, 185, 196–98

Canada: postwar residence, 284–86

Charleston, 103, 153–55, 181, 239, 249,
252–55, 258–59

Clapp, Theodore, 57, 81, 116, 229–30

Clemson, Thomas, 61, 169–70, 283

Confederacy, 101–3, 111, 128, 132–36,
155–56, 159–62, 170–76, 184–86,
200–201, 208, 215–19, 224–26,
241, 248–50, 257–59, 278–79,
294–95, 306–7. *See also* adoptive
southerner; Confederate identity;
Confederate nationalism; Northern
Confederate

Confederate identity: expressions of,
130–31, 165–66, 170–77, 184–91,
204, 208–10, 215–25, 228, 249,
256, 278–83; Northern Confederate
transition to, 5, 103–105, 132, 153,
171–77, 182–83, 200, 220, 225,
248; reflected in service in Confederate armies, 4, 172–75, 191–193,
218, 225, 242, 256, 279, 307; reflected in support of the Confederate government, 94, 110, 128, 176,
180, 213, 224, 241

Confederate nationalism: reflection
of solidified sectional identity,
5–6, 265, 268–69, 279, 289, 293;
strength and viability of, 5, 9–10,
100–2, 153–59, 162–63, 172, 175–
76, 179–80, 187–89, 203–5, 215–17,
227–28, 247–49, 264–65

Cooper, Samuel, 20, 90, 160, 188,
240–42, 248–49

Culp, Wesley, 1–4

Dahlgren, Charles, 27, 40, 51, 107, 167,
239, 247–48, 280, 283–88, 293,
305

Davis, Jefferson, 124, 147, 177, 190,
225, 239, 276, 285, 291; appointment of Northern Confederate
officers, 154–58, 163, 242–44, 254,

258–59; support of Northern Confederates, 242–44, 259–60
de Fontaine, Felix, 82–83, 121, 190–91, 195, 287, 295
Dimmock, Charles, 38–41, 61, 83, 159, 235
Drummond, Edward, 27, 272; expressions of Confederate identity, 173, 185, 191–93, 208–10; as a prisoner of war, 202, 207–10, 214; views on slaves, 93–95
Duncan, Stephen, 23, 38, 69–71, 75, 89, 149, 178, 231, 254, 257, 265, 286, 288

families of adoptive southerners, northern, 17–19, 54, 59, 63–65, 105–6, 119–22, 132–33, 138–40, 176–77, 182–83, 197–99, 202–204, 207–8, 215–25, 287–89; viewed as traitors by, 2, 101, 105, 121, 131, 143, 180, 227, 235, 251, 262–63, 284, 302–3
families of adoptive southerners, southern, 17, 54, 61–66, 103–6, 121–22, 126–32, 138–39, 167–68, 176–79, 191, 196–200, 204–8, 215–22, 281–83, 288–89; and divided families, 140, 144, 246
Flanders, Benjamin, 150–51, 297
Fox, Tryphena Blanche Holder, 59–61, 64–65, 72, 87, 164, 234
French, Samuel, 93, 168, 192, 242–43, 278–79

Gardner, Franklin, 20, 91, 253
Garey, Joseph, 122–23, 174, 283

Gettysburg, 2, 157, 160, 177, 186, 216–17, 220, 225
Gilman, Caroline, 57, 166, 186, 283, 289
Gilman, Samuel, 231–32
Gorgas, Josiah, 20, 61, 276; expressions of Confederate identity, 181, 187–89, 193; and Confederate Ordnance Bureau, 161, 249, 273; and secession crisis, 105, 109–10
governors: adoptive southerners who served as, 65, 231, 296–97; adoptive southern unionists who served as, 142, 150–51, 297–303
Grant, General Ulysses S., 167, 187–89, 224, 260–61, 271–73, 297

Hampton, Sally Baxter, 58–60, 72, 87, 90, 114–115, 118, 137–138, 199
Handerson, Henry, 17, 34, 93–94, 234; expressions of Confederate identity, 173, 177, 181–82, 185, 190–91, 224–25, 287; as a prisoner of war, 190, 202, 223–25; and secession crisis, 109–10, 127
Hatton, Robert, 124, 127–29, 173, 191, 231, 250–51
Hentz, Caroline Lee, 78–79, 84–86
home-front, 14, 153, 166–67, 171, 185–86, 194, 245
Hotchkiss, Jedediah, 17, 22–23, 34, 154, 196–97, 250, 272–74; expressions of Confederate identity, 126, 173, 191–95; expressions of southern identity, 62, 250, 281–82, 292
Huse, Caleb, 162, 235–36, 285

identity: adoptive southern, 12, 15, 46, 49–51, 56–57, 60–62, 119, 129, 135–40, 200–203, 206–10, 274–75, 279–83, 287–89, 298–99; American, 10, 14, 46–47, 125, 172, 228; land as a symbol of, 26, 38, 58–60, 66, 106, 116–17, 132, 189, 203, 230, 249, 281, 286, 304–6; malleability of, 45–46, 60, 175; northern, 4–5, 10–11, 20, 45–46, 56–58, 64–65, 79, 86, 92, 109–15, 132, 136–40, 143–44, 147–48, 171–72, 237–38, 274–75, 294; uncertainty of, 48, 62–63. *See also* Confederate identity; sectional identity

identity formation, 6, 45, 56, 80; factors involved in, 3–4, 7, 13–16, 22, 29, 50, 53, 83, 112, 172, 176, 220, 228–29, 232, 309; flexibility of, 4–5, 9, 47

identity transformation: difficulty after the Civil War, 5, 265, 269; into Northern Confederates, 133, 171–73, 177, 183, 189, 200, 22–27, 281; from northern to southern, 6, 15–16, 21–22, 38, 41–43, 47–51, 54–57, 66, 148; options for, 46–47, 57, 60–62, 66

Ingraham, Joseph, 35, 51, 57–59, 73, 88, 91, 112, 234

Johnson's Island, 94, 204, 209, 216, 220
Jones, Anson, 28, 36, 42
Jones, John B., 174, 239–41, 254–55, 258, 262–63
Junkin, George G., 122–23, 139, 204–7, 248
Junkin, George Sr., 122, 139–40

Kendall, George, 22, 25–26, 124, 168, 282–83
King, T. Butler, 53, 161–62

Lee, General Robert E., and Northern Confederate opinions of, 161, 185, 189–90, 209, 224
Leonard, Abiel, 51, 69, 72, 140–41
Lovell, Mansfield, 155, 240, 243, 246, 254–59, 265
Loyalty Oaths: acceptance by Northern Confederate prisoners, 204, 273; rejection by Northern Confederate prisoners, 204–12, 215–25, 287

Maynard, Horace, 149–50, 273
McArthur, Arthur, 29, 76, 116, 120–21, 234
Murphy, Isaac, 141–42, 235, 297

nationalism, 4, 10, 100–102, 125, 129–33, 157–58, 171–72, 175–78, 182–84, 187–92, 200, 209–10, 223–25; American, 5–9, 276; effect of the Civil War on, 5, 246, 268, 270
native northerners: antislavery views, 67–68, 71, 80, 83–84, 87; Northern Confederate opposition to, 56, 119, 191–96, 209, 218, 229–32, 247, 268, 275, 278–79; sympathies for the Confederacy, 119–20, 136
native southerners: denunciation of Northern Confederates, 175, 180, 212, 227, 235–41, 251, 255, 258–63, 284, 291, 302–3; denunciation of northern emigrants, 59, 63, 83, 92, 138, 233–37, 268, 274–75, 279,

289; proslavery views of, 68, 74, 77, 80–81, 92, 96; support for Northern Confederates, 228, 235–37, 241–53, 264–65, 289, 292–96, 305–7; support for northern emigrants, 31–32, 35, 229–33; unionist views of, 100–101, 140

native states, 10, 15–18, 45–47, 54–55, 99–102, 105–7, 124–26, 130, 154, 16–62, 179–83, 239–41, 280–83

New Orleans: adoptive southerners impact on, 21–23, 38; Northern Confederate defense of, 21–23, 38, 136–37, 150–51, 155–56, 178, 184–85, 240, 243–46, 249, 253, 257; unionists in, 136–37, 150–51

Northern Confederates: ambassadors to Europe, 161–62; Confederate commanders, 154–56, 180, 253, 256, 290; and Confederate homefront, 166–68, 172, 185–86, 194, 245; and Confederate nationalism, 166, 171–72, 175–78, 187; definition of, 13; graduates of West Point, 20–23, 32–33, 37–38, 91, 105–7, 159, 235–36, 243, 252, 278; identification with the Confederacy, 5, 111, 129–33, 153, 163, 170–71, 175–78, 181–92, 200–203, 208–10, 217, 223–24, 262; morale, 185–88, 208–10, 213; motivations for supporting the Confederacy, 101–11, 119, 125–28, 132–33, 145, 159, 176–77, 183, 192, 195, 200, 205, 220–22, 226, 280–81, 294, 303, 307; office holders, 163–66; participation in secession conventions, 132, 164–65; postwar exile, 268, 284–86; postwar governors, 295–97, 300–303; postwar identity, 271–76, 278–82, 288–90, 292–93, 304–5, 308; service in Confederate armies, 4, 153–54, 157–60, 172–76, 191–93, 218, 225, 228, 242, 256, 279, 307; states' rights views of, 121–25, 129, 176–77, 194, 213, 287, 291, 294

northern identity. *See* identity

northerners. *See* native northerners

Oaths. *See* Loyalty Oaths

Parsons, Lewis, 31, 297

Pasco, Samuel, 186, 193–95, 199–201; interactions with Union soldiers, 196; native southern opinions of, 292–96, 306–7; as a prisoner of war, 202, 210–15

Patterson, Edmund DeWitt, 94, 157, 176–77, 198, 216–20; connections with family, 198, 216–17, 219; expressions of Confederate identity, 173–77, 180, 186, 217–20, 225, 281; as a prisoner of war, 202, 216–18; secession decision, 126, 131–32; and sectional identity, 176, 219

Pease, Elisha, 87, 297–300; as governor of Texas, 42, 50, 231, 234, 297–99; identification with Texas, 25, 54, 143, 300; unionist views, 87, 142–43, 298

Pease, Lucadia, 62–66, 75

Pemberton, John C., 104, 167, 258–65; and adoptive southern identity, 38, 41, 106; Civil War commands of, 156, 179–81, 240, 258–61, 264; comparison to General Lee, 244, 258–62; defense of by native southerners, 264–65, 291–94; military

Pemberton, John C. (cont.)
  failures, 180, 240, 243–46, 260–63, 291; secession decision, 104–6, 126
Perry, Edward, 22, 296–97, 306
Pierce, William, 25, 29–31, 62
Pike, Albert, 24–25, 40–41, 50–51, 55, 73, 105, 112–14, 118, 127–28, 194, 242
Pratt, Daniel, 28–29, 59, 78, 89
Prentiss, Seargent, 28, 31–32, 35–36, 116
Prisoners of war, 94, 158, 186, 190, 201–25, 293, 306; escape attempts, 204–6; exchanges, 158, 204–6, 210, 221

Quintard, Charles, 154, 198, 273; and Confederate home-front, 168, 182, 188–89; and Confederate identity, 188–91, 247; secession decision, 109; work as a pastor, 168, 245, 290
Quitman, John, 29, 35, 41, 56, 71, 77, 80, 165, 231

race: relation to sectional identity, 48, 117, 233, 246
reconciliation: Confederate resistance to, 269–70, 274–75, 279, 289
Reconstruction, 6, 270, 274–76, 279–83, 286–89, 296–97, 301–5
Richardson, Henry, 117, 183, 189, 199; justification for joining the Confederacy, 180, 182–84; as a prisoner of war, 202, 220–23
Richmond, 40, 106, 158, 163–65, 169, 174, 185–90, 208–9, 220, 224, 239–41, 249, 258

Ripley, Roswell, 20, 103, 155, 181, 249, 252–55, 258–59, 265
Robinson, Calvin, 72, 76, 137, 140, 149, 234, 238
Ruggles, Daniel, 154–55, 178–79, 245
Ryan, John S., 64, 117, 128–31

Seabury, Caroline, 35, 58–60, 72–75, 146–47, 167, 234
secession: adoptive southern rejection of, 101, 123–24, 135–44, 148; Northern Confederate support of, 101–3, 110, 113, 119–28, 131–48, 164–65, 177, 182, 213, 220, 243, 247–48, 254, 285
secession crisis, 97, 99–100, 110–13, 129, 192, 205, 233–35, 241
sectional identity, 3–5, 18–23, 27, 38–39, 48, 68, 102, 119, 153, 175, 299; connection with nationalism, 4, 6–10, 46–48, 54, 115, 132; effect of the Civil War on, 5, 171, 278; and government, 48, 94, 110, 128, 176, 180–82, 213, 223–24, 241; hardening of, 5, 48, 233, 246, 265, 268–70, 274–76, 299, 309; malleability of, 4–5, 10–11, 14, 46–47, 54, 57, 60, 66, 96, 100, 103, 116, 125, 172, 229–32, 275; and secession, 97, 102–3, 147, 247; transformation of, 16, 46–51, 61, 65, 132, 294; uncertainty of, 61–62
Sherman, William T., 32–33, 143, 187–92, 253; military campaigns, 166, 168, 170, 187–90, 196, 224, 259; rejection of southern identity, 138–39
Sinkler, Emily, 76, 90, 230

Slidell, John, 42, 124, 162, 178, 189–90, 241, 284, 286
Smith, Ashbel, 29, 32, 36, 64, 120, 197, 273–77; and Confederate identity, 182, 184, 190; postwar, 273–74, 276–77, 282, 293; secession decision, 124; and Texas identity, 42, 50, 54, 131, 250, 282–83; thoughts on sectionalism, 116
Smith, Martin Luther, 241, 245–46
southerners. *See* native southerners
Sparrow, Edward, 133, 163–64, 272

Texas: adoptive southerners fighting for independence of, 25, 28, 50, 250, 294, 299–300, 307–8; adoptive southern governors of, 42, 234, 295, 298–300
Trulock, Amanda, 31, 54–56, 63, 78, 90, 96, 167, 197, 230, 288
Tyler, Julia, 84–85, 117–18, 130, 237

Union, 4–5, 8, 45–46, 53–56, 95–96, 103, 114–16, 123–24, 127, 131, 139, 144, 184, 190, 212–17, 228; as enemies of Northern Confederates, 128, 167, 172–73, 176–77, 182, 191–94, 224–26; as a symbol of oppression for Northern Confederates, 81, 85, 176–77, 214, 218
Union armies and soldiers: Northern Confederate hatred of, 95, 182, 191–97, 246, 281, 286

Vicksburg, 153, 156, 179–80, 185, 240, 243–46, 253, 258–64

Watson, Henry, 25–27, 117–18; expressions of southern identity, 53, 60, 146; uncertainties about identity, 58–60, 144–46, 288
Wells, Edward, 199, 272, 276, 306; expressions of Confederate identity, 130–31, 173, 190, 280–81, 306–7; secession supporter, 121, 130–31, 280; spy mission to the North, 160, 280
Wharton, Thomas, 22, 146, 174, 178, 184, 192–94, 291
Wood, John Taylor, 285–86, 290

Yankees. *See* native northerners
York, Zebulon, 89, 107